Handbook of Spirituality
for Ministers, Volume 2

Also edited by Robert J. Wicks (available from Paulist Press)

HANDBOOK OF SPIRITUALITY FOR MINISTERS, VOLUME 1 (1994)

Handbook of Spirituality for Ministers, Volume 2

Perspectives for the 21st Century

Edited by
Robert J. Wicks

paulist press/new york and mahwah, n.j.

The Publisher gratefully acknowledges use of the following: "Midwives and Mothers of Grace," by E. Glenn Hinson, published originally in *The Theological Educator*, 43 (Spring 1991), 65–79. "The Stance of Christians Toward Enemies" (found in "Savoring the Psalter" by Maribeth Howell), reprinted by permission from *THE PSALMS THROUGH THREE THOUSAND YEARS* by William Holladay, copyright © 1993 by Augsburg Fortress. "Chaos and Creation," a slightly different form of which appears in *This Blessed Mess*, A SORIN BOOKS Publication, published in fall 2000.

Cover design by Nicholas T. Markell

Library of Congress Cataloging-in-Publication Data

Handbook of spirituality for ministers, vol. 2 / by Robert J. Wicks, editor.
    p.   cm.
    Includes bibliographical references and index.
    ISBN 0-8091-3971-5
    1. Clergy—Religious life—Handbooks, manuals, etc. 2. Pastoral theology—Handbooks, manuals, etc. 3. Spirituality. I. Wicks, Robert J.
BV4011.6.H36 1994
248.8'92—dc20
                                                                94-23022
                                                                CIP

Published by Paulist Press
997 Macarthur Boulevard
Mahwah, New Jersey 07430

www.paulistpress.com

Printed and bound in the United States of America

Contents

Contents

III. SPIRITUALITY AND WHOLENESS

IV. SPIRITUAL DIRECTION AND MENTORING

V. PRAYER

VI. GROUP, COMMUNITY, AND MARITAL WORK

VII. HOMILETICS, SOCIAL THOUGHT, AND LITURGY

VIII. MINISTRY

Dedication

For my friends who remain faithful to a life of ministry and compassion, especially—

Chet Artysiewicz, John Ball, Jim Barker, Mel Blanchette, Dan Boyd, Helen Maureen Campbell, Muriel Curran, Jeffrey Dauses, Charlene Diorka, Fran Dorff, Mary Dunne, Susan Engel, Mary Filan, Constance FitzGerald, Sue France, Kevin Gillespie, Marie Gipprich, Loreto Hogge, Agnes Hughes, Jody Kearney, William Keeler, Timothy Kelly, Ed Killackey, Barbara Jean LaRochester, Joe Luca, Kevin Lynch, Cathy Maguire, Bob Morneau, Rita J. Murphy, Charlie Pereira, Maria Rieckelman, Joyce Rupp, John Joseph (Hilde) Schuyler, Bill Sneck, Loughlan Sofield, Mike Steele, Kevin Strong, Alice Talone, Julie Thompson, Ed Thomson, Virginia Unsworth, Ann Raymond Welte, and in memory of Ken Wicks.

For those who are not included, it is not for a lack of gratitude but rather because of an increasingly faulty memory. Now that I am past fifty, I lament with Mark Twain that when I was younger I could remember everything... whether it happened or not.

Robert J. Wicks

Introduction

Volume 2 of the *Handbook of Spirituality for Ministers* follows the tradition that was set by the first volume, published in 1995: Namely, as was the first volume, this book

> is first and foremost meant to be a practical book for persons involved in or considering entering the field of ministry. Under one cover are the contributions of experienced professionals who are particularly versed in the areas they address. But more than this, they are persons who **model** what they are writing about here.
>
> Most of the contributors I know personally and chose not only because of their respective areas of expertise but also because I believe in what they espouse and can see it in the way they live their lives and practice ministry. This is important since adults like children always favor actions seen over words uttered. And, in the case of the contributors to this volume, we are fortunate to have both their words and a history of their actions which ring true.

Also, as in the first volume, the entries are meant to be practical aids for the modern, caring, religiously committed adult. It brings together topics and well-known authors under one cover to educate, challenge, support, encourage, and stimulate new thinking. In line with these goals, this book is meant both for the individual nourishment of one's spiritual life and as a sourcebook for faith sharing groups (for example, parish/school/diocesan staffs, local religious communities, spirituality/ministry courses...).

If there is a departure from the first volume, other than the different composition of contributors, it is that the author was given greater latitude. Given entry into the new millennium, I wanted some of my favorite authors and pastoral leaders to present what they felt was important for the changing demands of society and the People of God today.

1

They responded with creative pieces on prayer, standing in the darkness, women's liturgy, our need to minister to Catholics left behind after Vatican II, and how to feed our soul through good reading. Also, you will find very comprehensive chapters on Jung, *lectio divina,* issues in contemplation, Moses and the Christian Minister, and Catholicism and theology in the new millennium. Group spirituality, gender issues in ministry to couples, a number of fine works on scripture and ministry, and speaking the just word are also included.

Varied views from people known for their ministry and/or writings will provide you with an "intellectual place" to study, pray, reflect, and enliven your own spirituality and life of compassion. I wish you well with this book, and I share it with a sense of gratitude for what the writers have already done for me. This work is a gift.... *They* are a gift.

SECTION I.

SCRIPTURE

"Moses and the Christian Minister" by Leslie J. Hoppe invites us to seek guidance and inspiration from the paradigmatic servant of God in the Old Testament. In this opening paper he suggests we "look to the Torah," and especially to Moses, whose personality dominates the Torah, for such inspiration. Who more than Moses stood with the people of God? Who, like us today, was chosen by God for ministry but was a *person* "with all the potential and limitation that this implies"? As a mediator, lawgiver, priest, prophet, intercessor, and more, Moses' "loyalty to God and gentleness toward the people [is in fact] an excellent summary for the Christian minister."

In Wilfrid J. Harrington's "The Paradox of Mercy," he reminds us that God is in love with all creation. "He is Parent who will not give up on his children, in spite of their ungraciousness." In the prophetic books, Harrington notes God's abrupt change of mood. "There is warning and threat, often usually extensive, to a stubborn and unfaithful people. Then, out of the blue, comes the word of salvation." He points out that in offering such mercy, God is "exuberantly illogical." No matter what happens, "God's word always is forgiveness." But more important than the focus of this paper is the process of it. Following the meandering mind of a wonderful exegete who is steeped in the pastoral dimension of life, as Harrington is, we are given greater thirst for reading both scripture and commentary as a way to refresh our souls and ministry.

"Savoring the Psalter" by Maribeth Howell encourages greater familiarity with the psalms by noting the relevance of the ICEL translation and citing a sample of contributions on psalms study by Gunkel, Brueggemann, and Holladay (from whom she quotes ten points to aid us in praying the psalms of lament with an "appropriate Christ-like disposition"). She then closes the paper with very helpful suggestions as to "how the psalms might become more familiar to the pastoral minister and thus be better utilized...within the context of both counseling and spiritual direction."

"From Being Loved into Loving" is presented by Jude Winkler to encourage us to appreciate some of the profound ways in which the Gospel of John has implications for ministry. Beginning with a brief summary of the

3

gospel view of the meaning of the statement, "Jesus has redeemed (or saved) us," he presents John's emphasis on God's constant love for us. Following this he examines several pericopes (Woman at the well; Man born blind; the Last Supper; Resurrection) to show the various ways this dynamic is at work. The implications for the minister as loved and loving are then briefly explored.

Leslie J. Hoppe

1. Moses and the Christian Minister

For his loyalty and gentleness God sanctified him....(Sir 45:4)

What are the sources of a spirituality of Christian ministry? From where do Christian ministers derive their self-image? What is the inspiration in their ministry? For many, a primary source is an individual they look up to as a living model of what ministry ought to be: a mentor, a spiritual director, a pastor. These charismatic individuals have the power to ignite a fire within us. They do not tell us what ministry is; they show us. They do not lecture about the spirituality of ministry; the testimony of their lives makes it evident how close they are to God. Other Christian ministers find a time of spiritual formation to be the cornerstone of their ministerial spirituality. Most programs that prepare people for ministry have spiritual formation as a central piece of that preparation. Such programs offer the prospective minister training in prayer, opportunities for theological reflection, and help with integrating one's spiritual quest with one's ministerial responsibilities. Still another source for the spirituality of ministry is socialization. One learns to be a minister by working with other ministers, praying with them, learning from them, growing with them. The ministry of the gospel is not for "Lone Rangers." Collaboration is a key element in any successful ministry.

Our ancestors in the faith also can be helpful in developing a spirituality for the Christian ministry. Some saints, like Francis of Assisi, had to learn how to integrate their calling to preach repentance with their preference for the contemplative life. Others, like St. Ignatius of Loyola and Francis DeSales, became masters of the spiritual life. The founders of religious communities, like St. Elizabeth Seton and St. Frances Xavier Cabrini, remain sources of practical guidance not only for the members of their communities but for others looking for patterns of integrated spirituality and ministry. How far back in the tradition ought we to go? Certainly we need to examine the biblical tradition.

The Word of God, as found in the scriptures, ought to be at the center of our theological and spiritual traditions. Indeed, our call to ministry derives from the commission Jesus gave to the Eleven: "Go, therefore, make disciples of all nations..." (Mt 28:19). Like the Eleven, we have been called by God to discipleship and empowered by his Spirit to proclaim the good news. Certainly, then, Christian ministers look to the gospel for the ideals that must animate. They look to Jesus Christ as the model for their ministry—the One who "came not to be served but to serve..." (Mt 20:28). Christian ministers hear the words of Jesus addressed to the Twelve, who were about to embark on their mission, as addressed to them as well (Mt 10). Grateful for what God has done in their lives, they wish to share this experience with others, as Jesus has counseled them: "You have received freely, give freely" (Mt 10:8).

The New Testament also describes the preaching ministry of Peter (Acts 2:14–41), Stephen (Act 7:1–54, and Philip (8:26–40). Of course, the Book of Acts devotes more than half of its content to describing the ministry of Paul (Acts 13–28). Also, Paul's letters testify to the pastoral concern he had for the people he evangelized. The pastoral and Catholic epistles also show the pastoral sensitivity, the theological insightfulness, and the practical advice that were characteristic of the church's first ministers. Though the New Testament underplays the role of women in early church ministry, women in ministry today look to Phoebe (Rom 16:1) and Priscilla (1 Cor 16:9; Rom 16:9) as biblical support for their ministerial role in the church today. Even the Book of Revelation, though some modern readers have problems with its rhetorical style, was clearly the work of both a visionary and a pastor. The New Testament offers pastoral ministers the ideals that should undergird their ministry and provides examples of the commitment and caring that ought to shape it.

Still, there is more to the Christian Bible than the New Testament. Do Christian ministers look to the Old Testament for guidance in giving shape to their ministry, and especially the religious ideals that support it? Certainly those involved in social justice ministry find the prophets such as Amos, Hosea, and Micah helpful in providing a biblical foundation for their work. Similarly, those whose ministry involves helping people deal with losses can find certain of the psalms and the Book of Job an inspiration as they stand with people who are grieving. The ritual of ordination speaks of ancient Israel's priests and Levites, but they offer only a one-dimensional model for ministry—the liturgical. Beyond this, most Christian ministers have not fully exploited the possibilities that the Old Testament has to help them formulate a spirituality for their service to the People of God. In this essay, I suggest that we look to the Torah and specifically to Moses, the personality who dominates the Torah.

When most Christians think of Moses, they think of him as the "lawgiver"—hardly the most appealing image for a minister of the gospel. But the image of Moses that the Torah paints is certainly more polychromatic. It would have to be, just to sustain interest in the principal character of four of the five books that make up the Torah. In fact, the books from Exodus to Deuteronomy appear to have been edited as a biography of Moses, reporting his birth at the beginning (Ex 2:1–10) and his death at the end (Dt 34:1–9). Between these two events, the Torah's story of Moses reveals a character of great complexity. But does the story of Moses speak to the Christian minister today? It should, since the most common title given to Moses in the Old Testament is "the servant of the Lord" or "the Lord's minister." More than forty times, books of the Hebrew Bible give Moses that title. What can this "servant of the Lord" of so long ago tell those who would be servants of the Lord today?

Moses as "General Practitioner"

For a long time, scholarship tried to give a title to Moses and to the role the Torah gives him in early Israel's life with God. Who was Moses and what did he do? One historian claimed that Moses was the founder of ancient Israelite religion. The text asserts that he was a Levite, a member of the tribe that gave Israel its priests (Ex 2:1–2). It also claims that there "has never been such a prophet in Israel as Moses…(Dt 34:10a). The story of the plagues (Ex 6:6–10:29, 12:28–34) makes Moses out to be a worker of wonders—far more skilled than the magicians of Pharaoh. He was Israel's leader as it escaped from Egyptian bondage and God's spokesperson in giving the law to the people. He made possible Israel's military victory over the Amalekites (Ex 17:8–13). Still, Moses is not a king nor a commander of any army. He is not a tribal sheik nor a priest. He is not a prophet nor a seer. Moses was these and more. To some extent, Moses belongs to all these categories, but none of them adequately explains his position. Moses was God's servant "whom the Lord knew face to face" (Dt 34:10b). What Moses is in the Torah cannot be summed up in the generally accepted notions of ancient Israelite leadership. Moses is something beyond all this—he is set apart to speak with God and for God. In the end, there is near-consensus that Moses is beyond categories.

Inevitably, when several people speak about their experiences of the same pastoral minister, one finds it amazing that one person could affect so many people in so many different ways. A stranger may wonder if they can all really be speaking about the same person. Some people will remember the pastoral minister's preaching. Another will remember words of comfort and support during a time of loss. Others will remember the efforts he or she made to learn their language and lead them in prayers whose words were familiar and comforting. Someone else will speak of the minister's well-considered advice and supporting presence in a perplexing situation. A member of the financial council or board of directors will remark about the minister's attention to the budget. A succession of testimonials will speak of the minister's ability to relate to seniors and young people, to both married and single people, to people of means and to the poor, to people of influence and ordinary folks. People will be amazed at how the minister was equally at ease in the sanctuary leading the congregation in prayer, on the athletic field cheering the parish team, in the classroom teaching little children, in the hospital visiting the sick. The expectations people have of their ministers are amazing, and it is even more amazing to hear how well these expectations are met by those whom some would call "ordinary" pastoral ministers. The work of those in ministry today is anything but ordinary. Like Moses, they may bear a lot of titles, though none tells the whole story.

What is the whole story of pastoral ministry today? It is precisely the same as Moses' calling. Moses was set apart to speak with God and for God. Today someone must speak for God. Someone must speak about sin and judgment, grace and redemption. Someone must call people to discipleship, challenge them with the ideal of the gospel, urge them to pick up their cross and follow Jesus daily. Someone must proclaim the gospel—though they may not understand it completely and though they may not be able to articulate it adequately. The key to their success in ministry will be the extent to which that ministry flows from an authentic and continuing experience of the divine. Moses was ushered into the presence of the divine to hear God's word and transmit it to the people. The Book of Exodus emphasizes the intensity of Moses' encounter with God by asserting that Moses had to place a veil over his face after leaving God's presence, so radiant did it become with God's reflected glory (Ex 34:29–35). People can see the reflected glory of God when those who minister to them give themselves to prayer and the study of God's word. This encounter with the divine makes it possible for pastoral ministers to fulfill the steadily increasing demands on their time and talent. Without it, ministers are left to their own resources, which quickly dissipate.

Moses as Called by God

Even before God called him for his special task, Exodus portrays Moses as a person of ideals who cannot abide the blatant abuse of a slave (Ex 2:11–12). Though he showed great courage in standing up to the perpetrator of this evil, he did not display the self-discipline needed in a true leader. Uncontrolled sporadic violence was not the way to liberate the Hebrew slaves.

While in Midian, Moses marries, works for his father-in-law as a shepherd, and begins a family (Ex 2:16–22), seemingly oblivious to the fate of the Hebrew slaves. God, of course, remembered Israel (Ex 2:23–25).

Eventually God did call Moses as the instrument through which he would free the Hebrew slaves. Exodus 3:1–4:31 and 6:2–7:7 describe Moses' call to a vocation that defined his life's work. The story begins with the familiar story of the "burning bush." It is the "hook" that gets the readers' attention. The centerpiece of the story is, of course, God's words to Moses:

I have witnessed the affliction of my people in Egypt and have heard their cry of complaint against their slave drivers, so I know well what they are suffering. Therefore I have come down to rescue them from the hands of the Egyptians and lead them out of that land into a good and spacious land, a land flowing with milk and honey.... So indeed the cry of the Israelites has reached me, and I have truly noted that the Egyptians are oppressing them. Come, now! I will send you to Pharaoh to lead my people, the Israelites, out of Egypt. (Ex 3:7–10)

A particularly significant statement occurs at the beginning of God's speech: "I know well what they are suffering...." In Hebrew, this verb *(know)* carries with it connotations of intimacy not found in English (see Gn 4:1; Jos 23:14). This phrase implies that God, too, experiences the pain of Israel's suffering. The oppression of the Hebrew slaves becomes God's own. Out of the relationship implied by the use of this verb, God is committed to Israel's liberation. For God to know Israel's pain means that God will act to effect its end. God begins Israel's liberation by promising to end its suffering. Notice the repetition of the word *I*: "*I* witnessed...*I* heard...*I* know well...*I* have come down...*I* will lead them out...*I* have truly noted...*I* will send you...." The word *you* (= Moses) does not appear until the very end of God's speech. The primary parties concerned here are God and Israel.

God's liberation of the Hebrew slaves was not to take the form of some direct, supernatural intervention at first. It begins with the commission God gave to Moses that he go to Pharaoh and speak with him about the condition of the Hebrew slaves, whom God called "my people" (Ex 5:1). Israel is and always remains God's people. Moses' vocation, then, has to be seen in relationship to that people. The calling he receives from God is quite specific. Whatever Moses does will be done for the sake of God's people; there is no way to understand Moses' vocation apart from the people that God calls him to serve. This is underscored when God gives Moses instructions about what is to follow the liberation of the Israelites: "After you have led the people out of Egypt, you will worship God on this mountain" (Ex 3:12b). The first *you* in this sentence is singular. It refers to Moses. The second is plural; it includes both Moses and the people. Moses and the children of Israel will worship *together.* Moses does not worship God alone; he is to lead the Israelites in worship. But it is not that Moses leads them to share an experience he alone had. Moses and the people stand together before God. It is God who will liberate Israel; Moses stands with the people as a beneficiary of God's goodness, leading them in praising God's fidelity.

Though Christian ministers may experience their call in a very personal way, the call to ministry is not a call to personal sanctification, though we expect that those who minister to us will grow in holiness. The call to ministry is a call to service. There would be no "Moses" apart from the people who needed to hear of God's promise of liberation, so there would be no Christian minister apart from the people who hear the good news of Jesus Christ. What the minister proclaims is what God has done for all people in Jesus Christ. The minister announces the salvation that *God* offers and that is *God's* gift. Those who proclaim the good news need to receive that salvation as a gift just as those to whom they minister. Like Moses, Christian ministers stand with the people as beneficiaries of God's goodness. It is their calling to lead the people in praising God's mercy given through Jesus Christ.

It is important, then, for pastoral ministers to stand *with* the people of God—no matter what rank they may hold in any hierarchical or administrative structure. Whether those ministers are called elders, deacons, priests, bishops, superintendents, pastoral assistants, or popes, the simplest believer is their equal before the Lord, who is the One who gives all the grace of salvation. This has been demonstrated most clearly in the Catholic Church with the revised liturgy for Christian burial. Gone are the elaborate rites and absolutions that set apart funerals of bishops from those of the rest of the Christian faithful. Ecclesiastical rank makes no difference in death. Moses reminds us that it should make no difference in life.

The rest of the account of Moses' call does speak about his authority. God assures a skeptical Moses, "(The people) will listen to your words..." (Ex 3:18). This text implies that the relationship between Moses and the Israelites will be a supportive one. They will embrace Moses as one of their own. Moses is still skeptical, so he asks, "But suppose they will not believe me or listen to my words...?" (Ex 4:1). Of course, Moses' fears accurately anticipate the difficulties he will have in his ministry. The people will murmur and rebel against his leadership. Despite their witnessing the wonders that Moses works in bringing to fulfillment the promise God made to lead the Israelites to freedom, it is not enough for the people to believe that Moses heard God's promise of freedom. They had to act on their belief. It was the people's responsibility to believe in God and Moses. Just as God "knew" the people's pain; the people had to "know," that is, commit themselves to God and to Moses, the Lord's servant.

Christian ministers have to prepare themselves for a similar response from some people. Despite the ministers' best efforts, absolute sincerity, and complete commitment, there will always be people who find it difficult to discern the presence of God's liberating power in their pastoral ministers. Moses' hesitancy was well founded. Like him, pastoral ministers need to go into their service with their eyes wide open. They need to be aware that they will not succeed with every single person they encounter. This does not mean that their ministry is deficient in some way, nor does it mean that the people who do not accept them are obtuse or insincere. It may be nothing more than a matter of personal incompatibility. The murmuring that Moses experienced troubled him, of course. Still, it did not lead him to abandon the commission he received from God. In the end, he remembered that it was God who freed the Israelites from bondage, who gave them the commandments, who guided them in the wilderness and led them to the land of Canaan. As long as Christian ministers remember that they are simply making people aware of God's action in their lives, they can live with an occasional experience of rejection.

Moses as Mediator

The most popular image of Moses is that of *the* lawgiver. Indeed, Deuteronomy 33:4 says plainly, "Moses gave us a law." Still, the biblical story of Israel at Sinai (Ex 19–34) is a bit more complex, and this complexity serves to make a subtle but significant theological point. Deuteronomy's introduction to the Decalogue (5:4–5) provides a neat summary of the tension that exists in the Sinai narratives in the Book of Exodus:

> v. 4: The Lord spoke with you face to face on the mountain from the midst of the fire.
> v. 5 Since you were afraid of the fire and would not go up the mountain, I stood between the Lord and you at that time, to announce to you these words of the Lord....

Verse 4 states that God spoke the Ten Commandments directly to the people. The phrase *face to face* does not envision any mediation. Verse 5, on the other hand, suggests just the opposite. The latter verse states that Moses was a mediator. It even rehearses the reason for Moses' role: The people were simply afraid of the thunder and lightning that accompanied God's revelation of the Decalogue. Deuteronomy alludes to the traditions surrounding Israel's stay at the foot of Mt. Sinai—traditions that are now found in the Book of Exodus.

Exodus 19:9 has God determining to legitimatize Moses before the people so that "when the people hear me speaking with you, they may always have faith in you also." God takes the initiative in assuring that the Israelites will trust and obey Moses, who exercises authority bestowed on him by God. Exodus 20:18–20 reflects an entirely different perspective. After God had revealed the Ten Commandments to the people directly, they become terribly frightened by the thunder and lightning in the sky and smoke coming from the top of the mountain. The Israelites flee some distance from the mountain. They ask God that Moses' serve as a mediator, relaying the rest of what God intends to say to them while they will remain at a safe distance from the mountain that appears ready to explode. God agrees to their request. The effect of Moses' mediation, however, is not to secure people's belief in his leadership but to ensure that the people live in obedience to God: "Moses answered the people, 'Do not be afraid, for God has come to you only to test you and put his fear upon you, lest you should sin'" (20:20). The primary issue here is not whether the people believe and trust in Moses but whether they will believe and trust in God. What these two traditions underscore is the goal of Moses' mediation: He is to lead people to respond to God with faith and obedience.

Yes, Moses is the lawgiver. Giving the law to the Israelites is an external mode of Moses exercising the authority given him by God. Still, the law is God's word—God's law; it commands the people's obedience because it is God's. Moses communicates that law to the people. But Moses does more than simply transmit the Torah to Israel. The Book of Deuteronomy presents him as trying to motivate the people to obey. Before Moses begins with the specific laws found in Deuteronomy 12–26, he tries to set the law within the framework of Israel's relationship with God. The principal commandment, then, is "You shall love the Lord, your God, with all your heart, and with all your soul, and with all your strength" (Dt 6:5). This Jesus would affirm during his ministry (see Mt 22:38). After Moses completes his task of transmitting the law, he again seeks to persuade the people that obedience means life: "For this is no trivial matter for you; rather, it means your very life, since it is by this means that you are to enjoy a long life on the land which you will cross the Jordan to occupy" (Dt 32:47).

The subtlety of the Bible's portrait of Moses as the lawgiver prevents two equally faulty conclusions. The first mythologizes Moses, exaggerating his contributions to Israel, as important as they were. The law, Israel's path to life, is God's gift to Israel—not Moses'. The biblical tradition never permits Moses to be anything else but God's instrument. On the other hand, Moses is not a passive instrument. Coming into play as he mediates the law to Israel are his freedom, his generosity, his commitment, his persuasiveness. The scriptures, then, give Moses his due without making him something that he was not. Moses was a man, chosen by God to be sure, but he was a man with all the potential and limitations that this implies. The Bible never forgets this.

Like Moses, Christian ministers stand between the people and God—at their request. In calling individuals to minister in the church, the People of God recognize the gifts that God has given these individuals. These gifts, however, are given for the sake of service. They are not the "property" of the ones endowed with them. They are given, yet they remain God's, just as the law always remained God's law—God's gift to Israel. The sole purpose of the charisms that God has given to those called to ministry is to build up the body of Christ. But ministers never become automatons as they fulfill their mission. They are not merely tools in the hands of God. Their freedom, creativity, generosity, and commitment come into play. While we cannot exaggerate the role of the minister in people's encounters with the divine, we cannot ignore it either.

When we think of making ourselves fit for the ministry of the gospel, too often we limit our thoughts to prayer and other spiritual disciplines. Of course, the continuing spiritual formation of the minister is indispensable. If we don't grow in our life with God, ministry becomes a function, a job, a duty—and people will recognize when this happens. One spiritual discipline that needs more attention by most ministers is study. Again, we do not usually think of study as a spiritual discipline, but of course it is. For believers, study is an act of worship. It takes a different form than the liturgy—but it is still worship. We need to think of our desk as an altar, our books as the instruments of worship, the library as our cathedral. Through our continuing study of the scriptures and the church's theological and moral reflections on the Word of God, we submit our intellect to God's revelation and we devote our energy to encountering God in the word God has given the church. This encounter equips us for ministry.

Yes, Moses was a mediator, but his mediation was always directed at leading people to greater faith and obedience to God. His own position was always subordinate to that goal. The success of any pastoral ministry can be measured only by whether it leads people to Christ, whether it strengthens the bonds between believers and the Lord, and whether it challenges people to hear the gospel call to conversion. Often preachers will stand in the vestibule or outside the church as people are leaving the service. Some people will take the time to offer a comment to the preacher, and usually these comments are positive. How many preachers listen actively to these comments? Why do some people appreciate our preaching? Were they entertained? Were the illustrations interesting and the jokes funny? Did people leave feeling good about themselves? Was the homily short? Sometimes people can appreciate what is actually very bad preaching. The goal of the preacher is not necessarily to please the congregation but to lead people to repentance and faith.

A desire to please the congregation will sometimes lead ministers to avoid the controversial because it will "upset the people." Dealing with personal issues such as guilt, identity, relationships are less threatening to some congregations than the "political" issues such as racism, economic and social justice, or the integrity of creation. Of course, ministry is not about the minister's position or popularity. It is about proclaiming the Word of God, showing how that word sheds light on the shape of the Christian life today. As we will see, Moses' position as a mediator did not increase his popularity among the people: an important motif in the Exodus tradition is that of the people murmuring and revolting against Moses. Any biblically based spirituality for ministry must consider very carefully how Christian ministers can serve as mediator, for that is their calling.

Moses as Priest

Moses was a member of the tribe of Levi, but the Torah does not call him a priest. It was his brother Aaron who served as the priest of the newly constituted Israelite community, though Exodus 24:6–8 describes Moses sprinkling the blood of communion sacrifices on the altar and on the people—a priestly prerogative. Moses is intimately connected with Israel's worship. It was Moses who revealed the name of God, which the Israelites were to invoke in prayer (Ex 3:13–15). Much of the legislation in the Torah deals with liturgical forms: feasts, sacrifices, altars, priestly attire, the sanctuary, and the Ark. Moses' role became so identified with Israel's worship that in 2 Chronicles 30:16; 35:12 and Nehemiah 10:30–39 there are rites ascribed to Moses that are not found in the Pentateuch at all. Finally, Psalm 99:6 calls Moses a priest.

Israel's identity expressed itself in its worship. Throughout the biblical period, the one constant in Israel's self-consciousness was its belief that it was a religious community—people bound together by a common link to God: the covenant. Common worship, first at shrines throughout the land and later in Jerusalem alone, was to celebrate that covenant and strengthen the bonds uniting the people to God and to each other. The prophets severely criticized Israel's liturgical life when it served to mask the growing socioeconomic gulf separating the rich and the poor. Still, the ideal was that all Israel should join in the pilgrimages to Jerusalem to bring their offerings as a thanksgiving to God, who gave their land its bounty (Dt 16:1–18). It was at God's sanctuary that people were to make reparation for their sins (Lv 6:17–7:6). And it was Moses who instructed the people in how they were to offer worship that was worthy of the God who brought them out of the house of slavery and led them to a good and bountiful land.

The New Testament speaks about three types of priesthood. First, of course, is the unique priesthood of Jesus Christ. In introducing its presentation of Jesus' priesthood, the Letter to the Hebrews begins by affirming that Jesus ranks higher than Moses. Jesus is "trustworthy as a son is," while Moses was trustworthy "as a servant is" (Heb 3:1–6). Hebrews goes on to describe the authentic and eternal priesthood of Jesus Christ with images and vocabulary taken from the Torah that Moses gave to ancient Israel. The second priesthood is that of all the faithful. In what was likely a baptismal homily, Peter speaks to the newly baptized of their calling:

> You are "a chosen race, a royal priesthood, a holy nation, a people
> of his own, so that you may announce the praises" of him who
> called you out of darkness into his wonderful light. (1 Pt 2:9)

Again, the source of the imagery used here is taken from the Torah (Ex 19:6). Moses was the first to call the People of God "a kingdom of priests." The people's priestly service was their fidelity to the covenant. Finally, the pastoral letters speak about a pattern of church leadership consisting of bishops, elders, and deacons (see 1 Tm 3:1–13; 5:17–22). Though the liturgical leadership is not mentioned as a responsibility of the "elders," the church has identified them with its priests. The New Testament, however, never associates liturgical leadership with any persons designated as priests except Jesus and the entire body of the Christian faithful. We owe this association of liturgical leadership with the church's ordained ministers to the Torah of Moses. The Roman Catholic ordination rituals make this clear.

The privilege of leading the Christian community at prayer is central to the identity of all pastoral ministers, whether or not they are ordained. The Christian faithful have the right to expect their ministers to be competent, creative, and authentic as they stand with them in offering praise to God. More than this, pastoral ministers have to empower the Christian faithful to fulfill their baptismal responsibilities as members of "a royal priesthood." It is not enough that the faithful be encouraged in their personal prayer life, they too ought to have the opportunity to lead the community in prayer. They have a place in the liturgical life of the community that goes beyond passive witnessing of rituals performed entirely by ordained clergy. The church's ordained ministers maintain control over the most powerful symbols of the Christian faith—those associated with its worship. But ministry is not about control—it concerns service and empowerment.

The flowering of a variety of ministries in the Roman Catholic Church that do not require ordination has started a process through which the Christian faithful are fulfilling their destiny as "a chosen race, a royal priesthood, a holy nation." While some may see this phenomenon as a threat to the identity of the ordained ministry, it is not. The Torah (Nm 11:10–30) tells of Moses' complaining to God about having to bear the burdens of leadership alone. God instructs Moses to choose seventy elders to share these burdens with him, so Moses invites these elders to join him. God, then, took some of the spirit that was on Moses and "put it on the seventy elders." Two of the elders were not present for the ceremony, yet they were "prophesying," that is, speaking for God nonetheless. When this was called to Moses' attention, he recognized the operation of the spirit in the two and exclaimed, "If only all God's people were prophets" (v. 29). Moses recognized that the gift of the spirit manifests itself in ways that can be unexpected but genuine.

The spirituality of all Christian ministers, ordained and non-ordained, must be "priestly" because there is no clearer expression of the church's identity than when it is at worship. The prayer that the People of God come together to offer marks them as "a chosen race, a kingdom of priests, a holy nation." A principal duty of ministers is to lead the Christian faithful in prayer. Their leadership ought to help people find the Christian worship community to be the joyous, life-giving, and spiritual experience it should be. Their leadership should empower all believers to take an active part in the church's worship. No one should be a spectator as the community praises God. Christian ministers ought to help all believers be fully engaged in the liturgy when the church is most fully being the church.

Moses as Prophet

Just as the Torah never calls Moses a priest, it never calls him a prophet. The most it does is compare Moses to the prophets (see Dt 18:18; 34:10). Of course, these texts consider Moses the paradigm of prophets, the standard that can never be matched. There is some justification for considering Moses a prophet. First, the story of his call in Exodus 3 is similar to the call narratives of prophets like Isaiah (ch. 6) and Jeremiah (ch. 1). Deuteronomy 33:1 calls Moses "the man of God," a title that is frequently given to prophetic figures. If we understand prophets to be those who speak a message given them by God, of course Moses would be *the* prophet. He acts like a prophet when he confronts Pharaoh, condemning the injustice done to the Hebrew slaves and calling for their freedom. Though Moses does not bear the title *prophet* in the Torah later generations of believers honored him as such (see Hos 12:14).

If Christian ministry needs to be priestly in character, it needs to be prophetic as well. If the Christian ministry needs to serve as a link with the church's tradition, it also needs to be a source of inspiration to the Christian faith. Indeed, the church's ministry is where the tension between charism and order is usually played out. On the side of order are tradition, the institution, the conventional, and the reflective. On the side of charism are innovation, direct action, the creative, and the spontaneous. Charism and order need to be kept carefully balanced. If tradition manages to stifle all inspiration, the result will be a lifeless and paralyzed church, unable to respond to changing needs. If tradition is abandoned in favor of inspiration, the church can expect nothing but instability as people latch on to every fad that comes along.

Christian ministers cannot afford to devote all their energy to maintaining the institution—as valuable and necessary as that may be. They need to make themselves open to the movement of the spirit in their lives, carefully and prayerfully discerning the authentic call of God. This call can come at any time in the lives of believers, urging them to a greater generosity and creativity in proclaiming the good news of Jesus Christ. Dom Halder Camara, the late bishop of Recife in Brazil, went to the Second Vatican Council as a bishop concerned about his administrative responsibilities. He came back a champion of the poor and homeless. The Council was, for him, an experience of conversion. He came to see his vocation as a bishop in an entirely new light. It is not that he rejected the institution and its maintenance; he experienced the call of the spirit leading him in a new direction in the final years of his episcopal ministry. Similar stories are told by many American clerics, Protestant and Catholic, who describe a change in their approach to ministry because of their participation in the civil rights and antiwar movements of the 1960s.

The Second Vatican Council's *Constitution on the Church in the Modern World (Gaudium et spes)* is an essential spiritual document for the church's pastoral ministers today. When it was first proposed at the council, there was some objection because some bishops thought it was allowing the world to set the agenda for the church. What this document tells Christian ministers is that their ministry ought to meet the people where they are. The proclamation of the gospel does not take place in a social, political, or economic vacuum. The gospel is addressed to real people, living at a real time, facing real challenges. Christian ministers need to deal with these realities in order to make the gospel credible. This may require new forms of ministry that do not follow familiar patterns: ministry to those living with AIDS, ministry to abused and abandoned children, ministry to women involved in prostitution, ministry to people on death row, ministry to those involved in gangs. These are just a few examples of ministries that are anything but conventional. There are no "rules" for these ministries. There is little experience to build on. Ministers can fall back on the grace of God, the genuineness of their commitment to the gospel, and support from their sisters and brothers. Even those involved in more institutional ministries will find the spirit calling them to go beyond the ordinary in the way they fulfill their responsibilities. It may mean convincing the school board to allow the gym to be used as a shelter for the homeless after school hours, learning a new language and culture to make recent immigrants feel at home in their new land, setting up a General Educational Development program to help adults earn a high school diploma.

Moses was both priest and prophet. Christian ministers have to examine the shape of their ministry to see if they are able to maintain a healthy tension between tradition and inspiration in their lives. Are all their energies directed at maintaining an institution, or have they neglected good order in their ministry? Does their understanding of the gospel not allow the church the flexibility it needs in responding to the world today? Is their ministry a flight into the fanciful and faddish? Unfortunately, there is no quantitative way to balance tradition and inspiration. Christian ministry does not consist of 50 percent creativity and 50 percent conventionality. Here is where the Christian maturity of the minister comes into play. Careful discernment, theological reflection, self-criticism, peer and supervisor evaluation—these are some of the keys to balancing the priestly and prophetic components of the Christian ministry. Moses' words, "If only all the Lord's people were prophets..." (Nm 11:29), are still true.

Moses as Intercessor

The Books of Exodus and Numbers tell a series of stories about the crises faced by the people of Israel as they were making their way through the wilderness to the land promised them by God. They faced hunger (Ex 16; Nm 11), thirst (Ex 15; 17; Nm 20), and armed attacks (Ex 14; 17; Nm 21). One feature common to all these stories is that the people blame Moses for the difficulties they encounter and challenge his position as leader. Certainly the most serious rebellion against Moses' leadership is the golden calf incident, which is usually understood as the Israelites' rejection of the God who brought them out of Egypt. But that is not how the text reads. The rebels' intention was not to replace God, but Moses. The golden calf that Aaron made was a response to Moses' prolonged absence on the mountain of God. This image was to replace Moses in order to continue the trek to the land of promise:

> When the people became aware of Moses' delay in coming down from the mountain, they gathered around Aaron and said to him, "Come, make us a god who will be our leader; as for the man Moses who brought us out of the land of Egypt, we do not know what has happened to him." (Ex 32:1)

God's reaction to the rebellion is to announce to Moses that God will do away with the Israelites and start over with Moses and his descendants:

> "I see how stiff-necked this people is," continued the LORD to Moses."Let me alone, then, that my wrath may blaze up against them to consume them. Then I will make of you a great nation." (Ex 32:9–10)

As soon as God pronounced this terrible judgment against the Israelites, God implies that Moses must accept it: "Let me alone...that my wrath may blaze up against them...." Moses takes this statement as an open door for intercession. He initiates a process of persuading God not to follow this threat to annihilate the rebellious Israelites. Moses takes a hint from God's promise to make of him "a great nation"—the identical words used in God's promise to Abraham (see Gn 12:2). This gives Moses the idea of how he will plead for mercy. In his prayer, Moses does not try to excuse Israel's folly. He reminds God of the promise made to patriarchs:

> Remember your servants Abraham, Isaac and Israel, and how you swore to them by your own self, saying, "I will make your descendants as numerous as the stars in the sky; and all this land that I

promised, I will give your descendants as their perpetual heritage." (Ex 32:13)

Still, his intercession for Israel was not simply a matter of a persuasive rhetoric. In retelling the story of the golden calf, Deuteronomy says that Moses prostrated himself, praying for God's mercy through forty days and nights (9:25). The result of Moses' intercession is that God decides not to destroy Israel. This forbearance at Moses' behest shows God to be "a God of tenderness and compassion, slow to anger and rich in faithful love and constancy" (Ex 34:7).

A similar pattern of rebellion, a threat of divine punishment, Moses' intercession and God's relenting repeats itself several times in the stories of Israel's wilderness trek. These stories of Moses' intercession assume a singular intimacy between Moses and God. Moses has the temerity to negotiate for his people. He is even willing to risk his life in pleading for the people:

> If you would only forgive their sin! If you will not, then strike me
> out of the book that you have written. (Ex 32:32)

Moses stands for and with his people before God, since he even offers to share their fate. His intercession is successful not only because of the power of God's promises to Israel's ancestors but because of Moses' standing before God. Moses has absolute trust in the power of God's mercy. This faith makes it possible for Moses to complain before God without becoming a rebel himself. What Moses asks is that God act in accordance with who God is.

Besides leading the Christian faithful in prayer, their ministers ought to lift them up in prayer. Like Moses, the Christian minister intercedes for God's people, praying that they experience God's mercy and fidelity so that they can join the minister in praising God's goodness. The circumstances of some people's lives make it difficult to believe in God's love for them. The sickness or death of a child, a serious financial crisis, the problems in caring for aged parents—these types of problems can leave people asking, "Why is this happening to me? What did I do to deserve this?" Pastoral ministers wishing to respond to these questions can only do so out of the type of intimacy with God that characterize Moses' experience of the divine. They need to display in their lives faith and trust in God that make it possible for the Christian faithful to find peace in a situation where there is no peace. People will find their ministers' words meaningful if they experience their ministers as those who stand with them and for them before God.

Still, the intercession of the minister is not limited to people's spiritual needs. Ministers will have to stand with the people they serve in a variety of situations. They will stand with the refugee before the Immigration and Naturalization Service. They will stand with a troubled young person before the courts. They will stand with the poor before the welfare system. They will stand with the physically challenged before the barriers to access. They will stand with the substance abusers as they fight their addictions. They will stand with the pregnant teen who needs support to choose life for her unborn child. These are some of the crises that believers are facing today. Like Moses, pastoral ministers will do all that they can to prevent these crises from destroying the believers' relationship with God.

Moses as Transparent

There is one other story of a rebellion against Moses' leadership that calls for our attention. Numbers 12:1–15 describes opposition to Moses from people that one would never suspect of mounting such opposition: Moses' own family. Aaron and Miriam, Moses' brother and sister, complain about his exclusive role as the one who delivers God's word to Israel. In describing Moses' reaction to this opposition, the writer says that "Moses himself was by far the meekest man on the face of the earth" (v. 3). The Hebrew word that is rendered by *meek* is *'ānāw*. The problem with translating an ancient Hebrew text into modern English is the very wide semantic field that most Hebrew words have. This is especially true of adjectives, since Hebrew uses very few of them. While *'ānāw* does mean "humble" or "meek" in certain contexts, it is unlikely that Numbers 12 is speaking either of any self-effacing humility that kept Moses from being terribly hurt by his siblings' complaints or some reticence that prevented him from lashing out at them. Here *'ānāw* describes Moses' style of leadership. It was one of integrity. He fulfilled his responsibilities despite the uncalled-for actions of Aaron and Miriam.

As the story continues, God confirms Moses' status as the one to whom God's entire household has been entrusted (v. 7). Then, in anger, God strikes Miriam with a skin disease that leads to her isolation from the community (v. 11). What does Moses do? He intercedes for Miriam as he did in every other instance when people rebelled against his leadership. His responsibility overcomes any ill feelings prompted by Miriam and Aaron. Because of Moses' intercession, God brings the entire unfortunate affair to a happy conclusion. Miriam is healed so she can rejoin the community on its way to Canaan.

Pastoral ministers have to be prepared for conflicts with their colleagues and with the people they serve. Sometimes serious differences arise between people who have collaborated on any number of projects but suddenly find themselves on opposite sides of some issue. Moses helps ministers see these inevitable differences for what they are. They will not take them personally but will go on trying to overcome or at least work around differences that emerge in any relationship. Pastoral ministers need to adopt Moses' style of leadership, which does not allow personal issues to interfere with the fulfillment of their responsibilities. Francis of Assisi had serious differences with some of his brothers regarding the direction the order was taking after it grew to embrace thousands in just a short time. Still, despite these differences he always considered those he differed with to be his brothers. He handed on the leadership of the order to another and became subject to a superior like every other friar.

Ministers have to be very vigilant about developing a personality cult around themselves. What should always remain the only priority is the ministry. The minister is God's instrument and should never become the focus. So many of the misunderstandings that develop among people who work together in ministry happen because of the development of a personality cult. Though Moses was the exclusive channel of communication between God and Israel, he remained focused on his service to the Israelites. He did not allow himself to be concerned about himself. The biblical tradition captures this by not mythologizing Moses. He remained just a man. He had his moments of failure. Because of one of these, God did not permit him to enter Canaan with the people he led through the wilderness (Dt 32:48–52). To use a modern idiom, Moses did not take himself too seriously. What were important for him were his responsibilities to God and to God's people. These he took quite seriously.

The story of Moses makes it clear that God was solely responsible for the liberation of Hebrew slaves from Egypt. It is only as God's agent that Moses had any significance, and then it is only the reflected glory of God (see Ex 34:29–35). Moses is an important character in the story of the Exodus, but he is not the central character—God is. The biblical tradition makes that very clear. Moses' first attempt at helping a fellow Hebrew leads to murder and a flight to escape punishment (Ex 2:11–15). When God does call Moses to be an instrument of the divine liberation of the Hebrew slaves, Moses expresses his reluctance four different times (Ex 3:11–4:17). God overcomes that reluctance by endowing him with undreamed-of capabilities to fulfill his mission. The focal point of the Torah is God's self-revelation to Israel at Sinai, the centerpiece of which is the giving of the Ten Commandments. Moses plays no role in that giving of the Decalogue since God gave the commandments directly to Israel (Dt 4:36; 5:22; 9:10). Throughout the Pentateuch Moses remains subordinate to God. He is, after all, the "servant of God." Even in death, this subordination continues. God buries Moses in an unknown place (Dt 34). This prevented the Israelites making his tomb a place of pilgrimage.

When later generations remembered what God had done for their ancestors, they were to bring gifts to the Temple and recite this confession of faith:

> My father was a wandering Aramean who went down to Egypt
> with a small household and lived there as an alien. But there he
> became a nation great, strong and numerous. When the Egyptians
> maltreated and oppressed us, imposing hard labor upon us, we

cried to the LORD, the God of our fathers, and he heard our cry and saw our affliction, our toil and our oppression. He brought us out of Egypt with his strong hand and outstretched arm, with terrifying power, with signs and wonders; and bringing us into this country, he gave us this land flowing with milk and honey. Therefore, I have now brought you the first fruits of the products of the soil which you, O LORD, have given me. (Dt 26:5–10)

Moses merits no mention in this act of remembrance. This pattern has been continued by Jews for millennia as they recite the Passover *Haggadah* during the Seder meal. In this dramatic retelling of the ancient biblical story of their ancestors' liberation from slavery in Egypt, Moses is never mentioned. Moses, then, is a transparent figure for Israel. People see through him to the God who continues to free them from bondage.

To find their truest self and greatest happiness, Christian ministers need to become as transparent. Any attempts at self-aggrandizement will fail ultimately. Pastoral ministers are to lead people to Christ—not to themselves. They are to make disciples for Christ—not for themselves. They are to promote the glory of God—not their own. People need to meet the living Christ who is at work in and through the minister. People need to see beyond the minister to the Lord who is calling them personally to repentance and faith. Unfortunately, the sins of Christian ministers make them opaque, preventing people from having an authentic encounter with Christ. That is why growth in holiness is an essential component of pastoral ministry. We need to remove that which renders us opaque. The light of Christ needs to shine through us.

Centuries after Moses, another son of Abraham, whom some of his contemporaries believed to be another Moses, gave a bit of advice that also subordinates the minister to the ministry:

> When you have done all you have been commanded, say, "We are unprofitable servants; we have done what we were obliged to do."
> (Lk 17:10)

The paradox is that by becoming transparent, Christian ministers will become the persons God wants them to be. They will not be forgotten. Moses was not. Less than two hundred years before the birth of Jesus, Sirach wrote a poem celebrating the achievements of Jewish people's ancestors (Sir 44–50). Of course, he mentions Moses, though Aaron rates four times as many lines. Still, Sirach says something about Moses that Christian ministers should be glad to have said about themselves: "For his loyalty and gentleness God sanctified him..." (Sir 45:4). Loyalty to God and gentleness toward the people—an excellent summary of spirituality for the Christian minister.

Wilfrid J. Harrington

2. The Paradox of Mercy

One finds in the Old Testament prophetical writings a remarkably consistent pattern. It is a pattern of abrupt contrast between the divine word of threat and condemnation and the word of forgiveness and salvation. Not infrequently—and this is especially so in 2 Isaiah—the message of consolation stands by itself, without immediate negative contrast. I argue that, in either case, we have a firm pointer: God's last word is forgiveness and salvation. This is no more than Paul, in his Christian context, had declared, "God was in Christ reconciling the world to himself" (2 Cor 5:19). Always, salvation is of God alone. And God is loving and faithful. He is Creator, in love with his creation. He is Parent who will not give up on his children, in spite of their ungraciousness.

God

We cannot know God through and through. Our *theo*logical speculation may deceive us into imagining that, somehow, we do. It could be argued that our theological portrait of God veils rather than reveals the true God. We do issue warnings on the hazards of God-language—on the need for realizing that it is always analogical, that anything we can say of God falls very short of the mark. It seems that we regularly ignore the warnings. We end up with a scientifically neat God who does not recognize himself in our portrait of him. If human language is an inadequate medium for conveying the reality of God, it may be that our only hope of reflecting anything of him is in the language of poetry. We might hearken to the genial poet-author of Job. He had sketched the might and wonder of the Creator (Jb 26:5–13) and then ruefully observed:

> Lo, these are but the outskirts of his ways;
> and how small a whisper do we hear of him! (26:14)

When one looks closely at the text of the prophetical books one observes a striking and consistent factor. Not only in the juxtaposition of oracles but regularly, within an oracle, we find an abrupt change of mood. There is warning and threat, often extensive, to a stubborn and unfaithful people. Then, out of the blue, comes word of salvation. There is no logic to it. That is the beauty of it, and the comfort. There can be no logic, because salvation is sheerly grace. God is exuberantly illogical. God's word always is forgiveness; it has to be. He freely took the risk of creating humans as free beings. He must consequently take responsibility and pay the price. His divine generosity in creation must be matched by the divine generosity of his mercy. A prophetic Paul had glimpsed that. When, at the close of Romans 9–11 he had said good-bye to logic, he could declare not only that "all Israel will be saved," but also "For God has imprisoned all in disobedience so that he may be merciful to all" (Rom 11:26, 32). The prophet Paul is here in the line of the prophets of Israel. And of course, in line with the prophet Jesus.

God and Sin

God's attitude toward sin is in question here. In this respect, the story of the Flood (Gn 6–9) is of major theological significance. It dramatizes the destructive nature of sin and the reaction of God to sin. The episode of the "sons of God and daughters of humans" (Gn 56:1–4) is meant to mark a stage, far beyond that of the man and woman in Genesis 3, in the futile human striving "to be like God." What is in question is wholesale corruption—to such a degree as to threaten human existence. God *has* to do something about the situation. Though his reaction is grief and sorrow, he unleashed the floodwaters.

The center of the story is "God remembered Noah" (8:1)—when God *remembers*, things happen (see 19:29; 30:32). That is the turning point: from a path of destruction there is a turn to salvation. The story ends in hope and promise: "I establish my covenant with you, that never again shall all flesh be cut off by the waters of flood, and never again shall there be a flood to destroy the earth" (9:11). Even more noteworthy is the statement repeated in the introduction and conclusion of the story. At the beginning, "every inclination of the thoughts of their hearts was only evil continually" (6:5). At the close, after the promise that there will never be another Flood, the repeated observation is, "For the inclination of the human heart is evil from youth" (8:21). God has decided to live with humankind's tendency to evil.

Throughout Genesis we are in the presence of myth, an expression of universal truth. The Flood story is paradigmatic of an ongoing biblical concern. God represents infinite love and mercy and forgiveness. He wills the salvation of all. God would never launch a flood to destroy humankind; he is not in the business of destruction. The Book of Wisdom puts it aptly: "All existing things are dear to you and you hate nothing that you have created—why else would you have made it?" (12:24). But…does that mean God is unconcerned with evil and sin? Obviously not. Here our limited understanding faces a daunting problem. How is one to portray the divinely loving forgiveness of God without conveying the false impression that he shrugs off sin as incidental? The beginning of an answer emerges when we understand that sin is not, and cannot be, direct affront to God. Sin does not affect God in himself. Sin hurts God through his creation. Human sin, whatever shape it takes, is betrayal of our humanness. Sin is an affront to God's purpose for his creation. And God, Creator, grieves over sin. As Creator, God will have the last word, as he spoke the first.

The Prophets

It is not by chance that the prophets, all of them, were poets. Why is it that the prophets have achieved and sustained such influence? It is in large measure, surely, because of the power of their language. The God imaged by them is presented in words that match their poetic insight. In painting divine emotion, they play on the gamut of human emotions. And, with poetic abandon, they can present contradictory pictures of God: a God who will not hesitate to punish sinners; a God who has a preferential option for sinners. The biblical God is anything but the immutable, impassible God of our theological tradition. He, along the line of prophetic understanding, is a fullblooded, indeed an earthy God. And never for a moment is he any other than *God.*

People of their day, the prophets took divine causality very seriously. Theirs was the common assessment voiced in Job: "Shall we receive the good at the hand of God, and not receive the bad?" (2:10). Again, they went along with the doctrine of retribution: God rewards virtue and punishes sin. Since, by and large, the prophets had to contend with national disasters—or the threat of them—it was natural for them to view such disasters not only as arising from the sinfulness of the people but also as divine punishment of sin. It is not surprising that oracles of woe predominate. It is an aspect of their keen pastoral concern.

Like anthropomorphism (the attribution of human features and behavior to God), anthropopathism (the attribution of human feelings to God) is common in biblical language. The Old Testament never speaks of Yahweh without attributing human traits to him. Anthropo*pathism* must point to the *pathos* of God. The Greek word refers to what one has experienced; it surely includes experience of suffering. If we are to be true to the whole biblical picture we shall need to pay far more attention than we have to the metaphors that point to the *suffering* of God.[1] Neglect of them has contributed, in its measure, to the dominant image of God as a dominating Being. Neglect of them has caused many to turn away in disgust from a God who seems to display disdainful unconcern for human suffering. Most important, these metaphors of pathos are essential ingredients of a balanced portrait of God. They add immeasurably to his attractiveness and effectively counter many false gods of our religious heritage.

There is, surely, something compelling about a God who grieves for humankind gone astray. A God who suffers because of his people's rejection of him, who suffers with his suffering people, who suffers on behalf of the people, is indeed a challenging God. He is surely the foolish God discerned by Paul. He is the God who has shown that he is a God not aloof from pain and sorrow and death. He *is* the God of humankind. He is the *kind* of God we need. He is *our* God.[2]

Our traditional ideas of God may cause us to be somewhat upset by biblical language. It is all very well to hear about the "love" of God. What of God's "anger"? We need to observe again that human language is incapable of enunciating the ineffable reality of God. However, it remains our only tool. Biblical language reminds us that God is not some vague "force"; God is *personal.* The language reflects a vitally important perception. The prophets and biblical writers were conscious of the transcendence of Yahweh. They were intensely aware that he was a God close at hand, a God with whom they could and did have dialogue. In speaking of him, and to him, they were prepared to take what we might term "risk."

A striking case in point is Hosea. He was the first to represent the covenant relationship of Yahweh with his people as a marriage. It would have seemed natural enough that the covenant between God and Israel might have been likened to the marriage contract. In practice, it is not the contract aspect that is exploited, but instead the love aspect, and especially the love of a husband for his wife. Hosea harked back to the wilderness and the entry into the land. He looked to the graciousness of Yahweh and the rank ingratitude of Israel (Hos 9:10; 11:1–12; 13:4–6). Doubtless, Hosea idealized the wilderness years and painted them as the honeymoon period of God and his people. What matters is that he did not hesitate to cast Yahweh as spouse of Israel. Bold imagery indeed when the Canaanite religion of Baal was the great challenge— the fertility cult of Baal and his consort Astarte. The prophet knew that, despite the risk of confusion, what he needed to do was to proclaim the love of God. Theological prudence would not deter him from flaunting his profound conviction. Some might misunderstand—too bad. But those who, like himself, had known the joy and pain of love would recognize in his long-suffering spouse their one, true God.

It is plain that the prophets who had, pastorally, to face intransigence from political and religious leaders and from their own people retained an insight into divine mercy. Beyond their warnings there is ever a prophetical perception of the profligacy of God. He just will not be confined. His last word simply has to be word of forgiveness.

Amos is the exception that proves the rule. He is a prophet of unrelieved gloom. On the other hand, the present shape of the Book of Amos firmly sustains our argument. The final editor felt compelled to provide a thoroughly optimistic conclusion. Nothing up to Amos 9:10 would lead us to expect 9:11–15.

On that day I will raise up the booth of David that is fallen....
I will restore the fortunes of my people Israel....
I will plant them upon their land,
and they shall never again be plucked up
out of the land that I have given them,
says the Lord your God. (9:11, 14, 15)

There is no human logic: the oracle is wholly out of tune. Instead there is divine logic. It is dramatic expression of God's final word—the word of salvation. The prophets bear abundant witness to divine illogicality.

Hosea

The prophet Hosea bears startling witness. Nothing makes any sense—except the crazy sense of an illogical God.

Hosea 2:1–23 (2:3–25, Hebrew)

Therefore...
Plead with your mother, plead—
for she is not my wife, and I am not her husband—...
Therefore I will hedge up her way with thorns;
and I will build a wall against her,
so that she cannot find her paths...
Therefore I will take back my grain in its time...
I will punish her for the festival days of the Baals,
when she offered incense to them...
and went after her lovers,
and forgot me, says the Lord. (2:2, 6, 9, 13)

In verses 6 and 9 the *therefore (laken)* introduces, as generally in prophetic texts, a threat (see Am 3:2; Mi 3:12; Hos 4:3). The next *therefore* (v. 14) strikes a startlingly different note.

Therefore, I will now allure her,
and bring her into the wilderness,
and speak tenderly to her...
There she shall respond as in the days of her youth,
as at the time when she came out of the land of Egypt....
And I will take you for my wife forever; I will take you
for my wife in righteousness and in justice, in steadfast
love and in mercy. I will take you for my wife in
faithfulness; and you shall know the Lord. (2:14–15, 19–20)

In verse 14, "the 'therefore' of intense judgment has been transposed into an act of protection and solidarity.... The voice of *harsh threat* has inexplicably become the sound of *assurance*."[3]

In sorrow, Yahweh had divorced his spouse: "She is not my wife, and I am not her husband." Here, as at Babel, where his will to scatter humankind out of his sight (Gn 11:1–9) faltered on his call of Abraham to a new beginning (12:1–3), and as with the Flood, when his grim decision—"I will blot out from the earth the human beings I have created...for I am sorry that I have made them"—flows directly into the declaration, "But Noah found favor in the sight of the Lord" (6:7–8), God is inconsistent. Ever, God's weak side is his love. Divorced Israel may be: it is the price of unfaithfulness. In God's eyes Israel is still his spouse, and he will not give her up.

Hosea 11:1–9 How Can I Give You Up?

> When Israel was a child, I loved him,
> and out of Egypt I called my son.
> The more I called them, the more they went from me....
> Yet it was I who taught Ephraim to walk,
> I took them up in my arms;
> but they did not know that I healed them.
> I led them with cords of human kindness, with bands of love.
> I was to them like those who lift infants to their cheeks.
> I bent down to them and fed them.
> They shall return to the land of Egypt,
> and Assyria will be their king,
> because they have refused to return to me....
> How can I give you up, Ephriam?
> How can I hand you over, O Israel?...
> My heart recoils within me;
> my compassion grows warm and tender.
> I will not execute my fierce anger;
> I will not again destroy Ephraim;
> for I am God and no mortal,
> the Holy One in your midst,
> and I will not come in wrath. (11:1–5, 8–9)

As in chapter 2, Hosea did not hesitate to present God as spouse of his people, so now he daringly pictures him as doting father (arguably, as mother) of a firstborn son. As with marital love (ch. 2), parental love, too, meets with ingratitude (11:3–4). The poem had begun on a sad note: "The more I called them, the more they went from me" (v. 2). They deserve to be sent back to

Egypt again (v. 5). God would leave them where he had found them. And he would—but for his vulnerable love (vv. 8–9).

For I am God and no mortal. Taken out of context (as it often is), it might be an assertion of God's transcendence. For Hosea, it is a declaration of God's love. Where human love would say, "Enough," God will never set limits. Paradoxically, "I am God and no mortal" expresses the "humanness" of God. It asserts that God is more "human" than humankind—the *Deus humanissimus.* It is not by chance that the Son of God, come at last to show humankind what being human means, will set nothing else than love as the mark of true humanness.

There is a further point. I have followed the generally accepted exegetical course of interpreting the image of Hosea 11 to reflect the father-love of God. In fact, a case can be made, and has been made, for an understanding of the passage as imaging God's mother-love.[4] One may observe that the picking up of an infant and a bending down to feed (vv. 3–4) is a vivid description of a mother breastfeeding an infant—all the more indeed when the phrase "lifting to the cheeks" may be rendered "lifting to the breasts." More thought-provoking is verse 9: "I am God and no mortal." "Mortal" (literally, "man") is not *adam* ("humanity"), but *ish*—specifically male. Yahweh is rejecting male behavior. She is not going to act with stern anger and destroy her people; strong maternal emotions resist such conduct on her part. In chapter 11, then, Yahweh as mother is a warm image of God for Hosea. The mother-love of God shines through the father-love of a prophet. What is undoubted, in either interpretation, is the prophet's stress on God's measureless love.

Jeremiah

"The Book of Jeremiah as it now stands makes statement about the juxtaposition of judgment and deliverance."[5] The truth of this observation can be readily documented. In the former it emphatically asserted his conviction of the inevitable invasion and conquest of Nebuchadnezzar (28:13–14). Then, directly, follows Jeremiah's letter to the exiles of the first deportation to Babylon in 597 B.C. (Jer 29:4–14). They were urged to settle down in Babylon and were warned against prophets (like Hananiah) who did not speak in the name of the Lord (29:8–9). Jeremiah offered steadfast hope, but called for patience:

> Thus says the Lord: Only when Babylon's seventy years are completed will I visit you, and I will fulfil to you my promise and bring you back to this place. For surely I know the plans I have for you, says the Lord, plans for your welfare and not for harm, to give you a future with hope. (29:10–11)

National disaster was unavoidable. Yet, Jeremiah can assure these early exiles that their God had promised a restoration.

A regular assessment of Jeremiah, reflected in the term *jeremiad,* is not really true to the prophet. Certainly, the Jeremiah of the book emerges, in the last analysis, as a prophet of hope. The vocational passage (1:4–10) had specified that the message of the prophet would involve not only plucking up and destruction but also building and planting (1:10). The texts of "building and planting" are concentrated in chapters 29–33. These chapters all concern hope. The poetic center is chapters 30–31. And here we find the contrast:

> For thus says the Lord: your hurt is incurable, your wound is grievous. There is no medicine for your wound, no healing for you…. Because your guilt is great, because your sins are so numerous, I have done these things to you. (30:12–13, 15)

The ring of finality seems to exclude all hope. Then abruptly is the assurance:

> Therefore all who devour you shall be devoured…. I will restore health to you, and your wounds I will heal, says the Lord. (v. 17)

It is noteworthy that the transitional verse 16 opens with *therefore.* We have previously noted the significance of the word.

Jeremiah 32:26–44 The Fate of Jerusalem

In 32:26–35 the word of the Lord to Jeremiah tells of his decision to surrender Jerusalem to Nebuchadnezzar because of the appalling sinfulness of the people. This is wholly consonant with the burden of the prophet's message. Suddenly, in verses 36–44, is a promise of restoration: "They shall be my people, and I will be their God…. I will make an everlasting covenant with them" (vv. 38, 40). No reason is offered for the radical turnabout; it is, solely, God's sovereign decision. "For thus says the Lord: Just as I have brought all this disaster upon this people, so I will bring upon them all the good fortune that I now promise them" (v. 42). Perhaps, after all, the reason *is* given: "I will rejoice in doing good to them" (v. 41). The reason is God himself: his last word is always forgiveness.

Ezekiel

Walter Brueggemann speaks of Ezekiel's "two-stage theology." The first stage is the work of judgment; the second stage is the work of life.[6] Here again is that contrast we have been stressing. We look to the more striking passages.

Ezekiel 11:5–20 Oracle against Jerusalem

The prophet, now exiled to Babylon, has a vision of leaders of the people at the temple: "These are the men who devise iniquity and who give wicked counsel in this city.... Therefore prophesy against them" (11:2, 34). The prophet pronounced his oracle against the leaders (11:5–12): "I will bring the sword upon you.... I will judge you at the border of Israel. Then you shall know that I am the Lord" (1:8, 11–12). In verse 13 there is his pained protestation: "Ah, Lord God! will you make a full end of the remnant of Israel?" Then, the Lord's immediate response (11:14–20) is a word of firm promise:

> Thus says the Lord God: I will gather you from the peoples, and assemble you out of the countries where you have been scattered, and I will give you the land of Israel....I will give them one heart, and put a new spirit within them; I will remove the heart of stone from their flesh and give them a heart of flesh....Then they shall be my people, and I will be their God. (11:17–20)

Ezekiel 16:1–63 Jerusalem the Unfaithful

Ezekiel 16:1–52 is the lengthy, and consciously crude, allegory of the "brazen whore" Jerusalem. One must candidly acknowledge that the imagery and language are offensive to women. This is a salutary reminder not only that the Bible is an androcentric text, but that, until very recently, the whole of theology was firmly male-centered. Granted this, the Ezekiel text is important. Jerusalem had acted more abominably than her sisters Samaria and Sodom: "So be ashamed and bear your disgrace, for you have made your sisters appear righteous" (v. 52). Then, with startling abruptness, comes verse 53: "I will restore their fortunes, the fortunes of Sodom and her daughters, and I will restore your own fortunes along with theirs." The passage 16:53–63 is an oracle of restoration:

> I will remember my covenant with you in the days of your youth and I will establish with you an everlasting covenant.... I will establish my covenant with you, and you shall know that I am the Lord...when I forgive you all that you have done, says the Lord God. (vv. 60, 62–63)

Ezekiel 33:10–11 Restoration

Ezekiel 33–39 is, in the main, a collection of oracles of restoration. The two verses 33:10–11 sound the keynote:

> Now you, mortal, say to the house of Israel, Thus you have said: "Our transgressions and our sins weigh upon us, and we waste away because of them; how then can we live?" Say to them, As I live says the Lord God, I have no pleasure in the death of the wicked, but that the wicked turn from their ways and live; turn back, turn back, from your evil ways; for why will you die, O house of Israel?

The sinfulness of Israel is manifest and acknowledged. Against it is the generous invitation to return to life. Death (separation from God) is not the desire of God. He seeks not death but life—loving union with him.

In the three historical reviews (chs. 16; 20; 23), Ezekiel seemed to wish to say all that could be said about Israel's unfaithfulness, its indifference to the love of God, and its utter failure to obey. The picture he painted could scarcely be blacker than it is. But we need to keep in mind that he, in keeping with his theology, was justifying the divine chastisement that must fall in the near future: even divine patience had at last run out. We need also to observe that the prophet pointed to God's saving will—now more than ever seen to be free and unmerited (see 16:60–63; 20:40–44). In this sense, the three somber chapters are the prelude to the glory of Yahweh's deed, for it is evident that his salvation cannot be based on any worth in Israel itself. Paul will follow much the same technique when, on a broader canvas, he will paint in black the sinful helplessness of humankind, as a backdrop to God's incredibly gracious saving deed in Christ (Rom 1–8).

Isaiah

The first matter to be cleared up is the complex structure of the Book of Isaiah and its broad chronological sweep. The acknowledged scholarly view is that Isaiah falls into three parts: Isaiah 1–39, which contains oracles of the eighth-century prophet, Isaiah ben-Amoz; Isaiah 40–55, known as 2 Isaiah; and Isaiah 56–66, often referred to as 3 Isaiah. The background of 2 Isaiah is the close of the Babylonian captivity, while 3 Isaiah is set in Judah in the early days of the return. So far so good. But there is the complicating factor that, in chapters 1–39, only chapters 1–12 and 28–33 give, in the main, the words of Isaiah ben-Amoz—the rest is largely post-exilic. Our interest here is the present form of the Book of Isaiah—which may be called its canonical shape. And our concern is to discern the juxtaposition of threat and promise.

Isaiah 30:1–26 Waiting for Yahweh

In Isaiah 30:1–17 there is a severe indictment:

> Oh, rebellious children, says the Lord,
> who carry out a plan, but not mine...
> For they are a rebellious people, faithless children,
> children who will not hear the instruction of the Lord...
> For thus said the Lord God, the Holy One of Israel:
> in returning and rest you shall be saved;
> in quietness and in trust shall be your strength.
> But you refused and said, "No!" (vv. 1, 9, 15–16)

Then, at verse 18, an abrupt change of tone:

> Therefore the Lord waits to be gracious to you;
> therefore he will rise up to show mercy to you.

And verses 19–26 spell out the blessedness to come. Notable are the truly beautiful verses:

> Though the Lord may give you the bread of adversity and the water of affliction, yet your Teacher will not hide himself any more, but your eyes shall see your Teacher. And when you turn to the right or when you turn to the left, your ears shall hear a word behind you, saying, "This is the way; walk in it." (vv. 20–21)

Isaiah 40:1–11 Call to Return

The opening passage (Is 40:1–11) strikes the note of the Book of Consolation (Is 40–55). The exuberant language serves a purpose. It is evident that, among the exiles, there was little yearning for a return. This was predominantly a second generation, doing quite nicely in Babylon. A devastated and impoverished homeland of their fathers did not beckon, so the prophet has to drum up some enthusiasm. While, humanly speaking, there were no grounds for optimism, he can assure his people that God is ready once again to bring them out of captivity and into the promised land. This time Yahweh will lead them in solemn procession along a Via Sacra, a processional way hewn through mountain, valley, and desert, all the long way from Babylon to Jerusalem. This time there will be no years of wandering. God will manifest his glory (40:3) through his saving deeds on behalf of his people. He is the constant God, unlike the ephemeral grasslike nature of humanity (vv. 6–8). His "word" stands forever: "For the mountains may depart and hills be removed, but my steadfast love shall not depart from you, and my covenant of peace shall not be removed, says the Lord, who has compassion on you" (54:10).

Isaiah 49:14–18 Consolation

> But Zion said, "The Lord has forsaken me,
> My Lord has forgotten me."
> Can a woman forget her nursing child,
> or show no compassion for the child of her womb?
> See, I have inscribed you on the palms of my hands. (vv. 14–16)

The human cry of godforsakenness is answered by words of most tender assurance. One is reminded of another cry of godforsakenness—answered by the new life of resurrection (see Mk 15:34–39).

Isaiah 51:17–23 I Will Comfort You

> Stand up, O Jerusalem,
> you have drunk at the hand of the Lord
> the cup of his wrath....
> These two things have befallen you
> — who will grieve with you—
> devastation and destruction, famine and sword
> —who will comfort you?...
> Thus says your Sovereign, the Lord,
> your God who pleads the cause of his people:
> see, I have taken from your hand the cup of staggering;
> you shall drink no more from the bowl of my wrath. (vv. 17, 19, 22)

On the one hand, God's people had been given to drink of the bowl of his wrath. This same Sovereign Lord is he who pleads the cause of his people; there will be no more "wrath." This is remarkably like the Genesis flood story (see Gn 6:5–7; 8:21–22). Perhaps, even more, is it like Romans 8:31–39.

54:4–10 The Faithful Spouse

This stirringly beautiful passage goes to the heart of the matter. Here we see, with clarity, *why* God's final word is mercy: It is because it cannot be other. He is this kind of God.

Do not fear, for you will not be ashamed....
For your Maker is your husband,
the Lord of hosts is his name;
the Holy One of Israel is your Redeemer,
the God of the whole earth he is called.
For the Lord has called you
like a wife forsaken and grieved in spirit,
like the wife of a man's youth when she is cast off,
says your God.
For a brief moment I abandoned you,
but with great compassion I will gather you.
In overflowing wrath for a moment I hid my face from you,
but with everlasting love I will have compassion on you,
says the Lord, your Redeemer.
This is like the days of Noah to me:
Just as I swore that the waters of Noah
would never again go over the earth,
so I have sworn that I will not be angry with you
and I will not rebuke you.
For the mountains may depart and the hills be removed,
but my steadfast love shall not depart from you,
and my covenant of love shall not be removed,
says the Lord, who has compassion on you. (54:4–10)

Hosea 1–3 and the Flood story (Gn 6–9) stand behind this passage. Israel, unfaithful wife, had been divorced; now her faithful spouse welcomes her back. He can do no other. His "wrath" is momentary; his compassion is as firm as his everlasting love. God recalls his promise to Noah and rephrases it, in stronger terms, in favor of Israel. An unshakable covenant of peace is based on his steadfast love. He is Lord of *com*-passion: a God who suffers *with* his suffering children. God does suffer *because* of his people's rejection of him. God suffers *for* the people.

Isaiah 1:2–3; 66:10–13 Beginning and End

The opening and the close of canonical Isaiah aptly illustrate the contrast of threat and salvation.

Hear, O heavens, and listen, O earth;
for the Lord has spoken:
I reared children and brought them up,
but they have rebelled against me.

The ox knows its master's crib;
but Israel does not know,
my people do not understand. (1:2–3)

The book opens on this note of bewilderment. God is a parent, cut to the quick by the ingratitude of children. That sad ingratitude is documented in chapter after chapter of Isaiah. Nevertheless we have, in the meantime, been so well prepared that we have come to take for granted the tone of the closing chapter:

Rejoice with Jerusalem, and be glad for her,
all you who love her;
rejoice with her in joy,
all you who mourn over her—
that you may nurse and be satisfied
from her consoling breasts;
that you may drink deeply with delight
from her glorious bosom.
For thus says the Lord:
I will extend prosperity to her like a river,
and the wealth of the nations like an overflowing stream;
and you shall nurse and be carried on her arm,
and dandled on her knees.
As a mother comforts her child,
so I will comfort you;
you shall be comforted in Jerusalem. (66:10–13)

Here, God's children nurse at the breast of Jerusalem—a lovely image of peace and contentment. Striking is the switch in verse 13 to the motherhood of God. In Ezekiel 34, God had had enough of alleged shepherds; he decided to take personal charge. We get a similar picture here, with God becoming a nursing mother. And we are back, again, to Hosea, chapter 11.

Conclusion

What has been offered here is a very confined cross-section, no more than that. The remarkable fluctuation we have noted in the prophets can be documented over and over again. It is not rarity; it is the norm. This must surely tell us something of our God. And this feature is to be found not only in the prophets. The God of the Bible, the Father of our Lord Jesus Christ, is the foolish God (see 1 Cor 1:18–21). His gamble was in making us free. He stands, stolidly, by that gamble. God is, happily, not an Unmoved Mover. He is not even Creator. He is *Parent*. And there is his divine vulnerability. What loving parent can ever, ever, reject the child? Our human grace is not that we are creatures of God, not even that we are image of God. The ultimate divine foolishness, made public in Christian revelation, is that we are *children* of God. That is Christian truth—but it must reach into all of humankind.

Notes

1. T. E. Fretheim, *The Suffering God* (Philadelphia: Fortress, 1984); W. Harrington, *The Tears of God* (Collegeville, Minn.: Liturgical Press, 1992).

2. See Harrington, *Tears of God,* 26–37.

3. W. Brueggemann, *Hopeful Imagination: Prophetic Voices in Exile* (Philadelphia: Fortress, 1986), 38.

4. See Helen Schüngel-Straumann, "Gott als Mutter in Hosea 11," *Theologische Quartalschrift* 1656,2 (1986): 119–34.

5. Brueggemann, *Hopeful Imagination,* 11.

6. Ibid., 72.

Maribeth Howell

3. Savoring the Psalter

In recent years, publications on the psalms, both spiritual and academic, have filled countless pages of books and journals. The popularity of the psalms is also evidenced by the number of well-known liturgical hymns that are based upon these texts: "Only in God Is My Soul at Rest," "My Soul Is Longing for Your Peace," "Shepherd Me Oh God," "Taste and See," to name but a few. Many people are surprised to learn that their favorite hymns are inspired by the psalms, prayers of the heart that have spoken both to Jews and Christians for countless generations, prayers that express every imaginable emotion before God.

Our intention here is to assist pastoral ministers, particularly those who are engaged in the ministry of spiritual direction or pastoral counseling, to become more familiar with the psalter. It is our hope that by introducing a recent psalm translation, by highlighting the work of several significant and insightful authors, and by making some suggestions for becoming better acquainted with these texts, ministers and those with whom and for whom they minister might become more at home with these ageless prayers.

We will begin with an introduction to a recent English translation of the psalter—a translation that is the product of countless contributors, women and men who have labored for a contemporary, meaningful, and gender-inclusive rendering of these sacred poems. This new psalter, commonly referred to as the ICEL Psalms, has become best known through its two editions published by Liturgical Training Publications: one is *The Psalter,* with the 150 psalms appearing in sequence; the other is entitled *Psalms for Morning and Evening Prayer,* and presents these psalms in the traditional four-week cycle of the Liturgy of the Hours.[1]

What Is ICEL and What Is Unique about the ICEL Psalter?

The International Commission on English in the Liturgy, better known as ICEL, was conceived in Rome during the fall of 1963,[2] during the second period of the Second Vatican Council. Having already determined that the vernacular was to be used in the liturgy, a meeting of appointed bishops representing the ten bishops' conferences in whose countries English was spoken officially established the commission. In 1967, membership was increased to include eleven conferences. While the initial task of ICEL was to oversee the production of a commonly accepted English translation of soon-to-be revised Latin liturgical texts, in time it became clear that the creation of new texts was an even more important task.[3]

Aware of the magnitude of their undertaking, the bishops established an advisory committee comprised of specialists from various and related fields, whose responsibility was to produce the desired texts. The advisors, who first numbered eight, grew to include over a dozen members representing "liturgical studies, English language and literature, biblical studies, original languages (chiefly Latin of course), church music, pastoral and sacramental theology, church law, etc."[4] After having completed a significant portion of their task, a subcommittee on the liturgical psalter was formed in 1978.

This subcommittee had inherited guidelines for the new psalter; it developed these into "a *Brief on the Liturgical Psalter,* the internal working document that guided the translation process and was itself revised and expanded more than once on the basis of the work in progress."[5] The aim of the subcommittee was to produce a translation: "1) that would faithfully render into English the best critical Hebrew and Greek texts available; 2) that would be guided by the liturgical use of the psalms and canticles, and be fitting for musical setting; 3) that would be received by the reader or auditor as idiomatic English in contemporary poetic style; and 4) that would be sensitive to evolving gender usage in English."[6]

While each of these aims could be elaborated upon, and while such an exploration into the workings of the subcommittee might provide us with a greater appreciation of the membership's labor and dedication, this is detailed elsewhere.[7] Furthermore, for our purposes, it seems sufficient for us to recognize the primary goals of the ICEL psalter subcommittee and to be aware of the unique composition of its members.

Not only does the ICEL Psalter attempt to be faithful to the "meaning" found within the best manuscripts, it also attempts to respect the poetic features of these texts (for example, sounds and rhythm) in order that the English renderings be appropriate and attractive to musicians and composers. Perhaps the feature that many readers would find especially significant is the sensitive manner with which gender-inclusive language is used.

In recent years, a variety of gender-inclusive psalters have been published. Some of these editions are either (1) a simple "reediting" of existing psalm translations, consisting of a more inclusive word choice (for example, replacing *man* or *men* with *person* or *people,* and extracting multiple *he's* that refer to God and reworking a line so that no masculine pronouns are used); and/or (2) removing much of the masculine imagery that some would find offensive (for example, deleting references to the king, the kingdom, and God's reign). The quality of these gender-inclusive psalters varies considerably. To the author's knowledge, only the psalter found in the *New Revised Standard Version* of the Bible and that of ICEL are the products of rigorous scholarly labor that has attempted to use gender-inclusive language on a *consistent* basis.[8]

While the translations of both the *New American Bible* and the *New Revised Standard Version* are of excellent quality, a perusal of the ICEL Psalter reveals a much more contemporary mode of expression than either of the other two. To demonstrate how these translations differ, we present the same verses as they appear in these three translations—the NAB, NRSV, and ICEL. For an adequate sampling, we provide selections from three different types of psalms: a hymn of praise, a lament, and a thanksgiving. These three psalm types reflect the kinds of prayer that traditionally have been referred to as praise, petition, and thanksgiving. The first example is taken from Psalm 19:8–9 (NRSV verse numbering is 7–8), a hymn of praise.

> NAB　　The law of the Lord is perfect, refreshing the soul;
> 　　　　The decree of the Lord is trustworthy, giving wisdom to
> 　　　　　　the simple.
> 　　　　The precepts of the Lord are right, rejoicing the heart;
> 　　　　The command of the Lord is clear, enlightening the eye.

> NRSV　The law of the Lord is perfect, reviving the soul;
> 　　　　the decrees of the Lord are sure, making the wise simple;
> 　　　　the precepts of the Lord are right, rejoicing the heart;
> 　　　　the commandment of the Lord is clear, enlightening the
> 　　　　　　eyes.

> ICEL　　God's perfect law revives the soul.
> 　　　　God's stable rule guides the simple.
> 　　　　God's just demands delight the heart.
> 　　　　God's clear commands sharpen vision.

The second sampling of texts is taken from the first four verses of Psalm 77, a lament.

> NAB　　Aloud to God I cry; aloud to God, to hear me;
> 　　　　on the day of my distress I seek the Lord.
> 　　　　By night my hands are stretched out without flagging;
> 　　　　my soul refuses comfort.
> 　　　　When I remember God, I moan;
> 　　　　when I ponder, my spirit grows faint.

NRSV   I cry aloud to God, aloud to God, that he may hear me.
       In the day of my trouble I seek the Lord;
       in the night my hand is stretched out without wearying;
       my soul refuses to be comforted.
       I think of God, and I moan;
       I meditate, and my spirit faints.

ICEL   I cry to you, God! I plead with you!
       If only you would hear me!
       By day I seek you in my distress,
       by night I raise my hands in prayer,
       but my spirit refuses comfort.
       I groan when I remember you;
       when I think of you, I grow faint.

The final sample is from a psalm of thanksgiving, Psalm 116: 5–7.

NAB   Gracious is the Lord and just; yes, our God is merciful.
       The Lord keeps the little ones; I was brought low, and he
          saved me.
       Return, O my soul, to your tranquillity, for the Lord has
          been good to you.

NRSV   Gracious is the Lord, and righteous; our God is merciful.
       The Lord protects the simple; when I was brought low,
          he saved me.
       Return, O my soul, to your rest, for the Lord has dealt
          bountifully with you.

ICEL   Kind and faithful is the Lord, gentle is our God.
       The Lord shelters the poor, raises me from the dust.
       Rest once more, my heart, for you know the Lord's love.

These few samples provide the reader with a taste for how the translations differ one from another. Perhaps what is most immediately evident is the relative similarity between the NAB and the NRSV translations, while what seems to set the ICEL texts apart is the terseness of line, simplicity of expression, and inclusive manner in which God is identified—characteristics that are in keeping with the subcommittee's guidelines.

As stated earlier, our intention is to assist pastoral ministers, particularly those who are engaged in the ministry of spiritual direction or pastoral counseling, to become more familiar with the psalter. Having completed the first part of our threefold task, to introduce the reader to the ICEL translation, we now turn to our second aim, to highlight the work of several significant and insightful authors whose contributions to psalm study, we believe, can be of great assistance to pastoral ministers.

Selected Contributors to Psalm Research

Since the time of the renowned German scholar, Hermann Gunkel (1862–1932), whose work shaped twentieth-century psalm study, it has become customary to identify the psalms according to their literary form, genre, or type. Gunkel's research resulted in the identification of five main psalm types as well as several minor types. The five main types are known as the hymn of praise, the communal lament, the individual lament, the individual thanksgiving, and the royal psalm. While the referents *praise, lament,* and *thanksgiving* provide us with a clear idea of a psalm's disposition, "royal" psalm does not. Although this type of psalm is related to an event in the life of Israel's earthly king, this referent does not tell us of the text's disposition. A royal psalm may refer to a poem that was used at the king's coronation, the king's wedding, or some other situation. Gunkel's "minor" classifications are even less helpful to individuals interested in understanding the prayerful disposition expressed within these psalms.[9] Even with these shortcomings, his contribution to psalm study cannot be exaggerated.

In recent decades, scholarly focus on the psalms has flourished, and has moved beyond the work of Gunkel. Many very fine introductory works and commentaries that have greatly enhanced our understanding of and appreciation for these texts have appeared. Among the many writers who have advanced our understanding of the psalms in recent years, one of the most prolific is Walter Brueggemann, Professor of Old Testament at Columbia Theological Seminary in Atlanta, Georgia. As he has done with many other biblical texts, Brueggemann has written on the psalms with profound insight and passion, identifying relevant technical contributions of other scholars while always probing texts for their religious meaning.

In his 1982 work, *Praying the Psalms,* Brueggemann introduces readers to a most creative way of approaching these texts.[10] Recognizing the psalms as the *prayers* of a faith-filled people and believing that these prayers come from real-life experiences, Brueggemann builds and expands upon previous psalm research, then provides a new vocabulary for speaking about, examining, understanding, and praying these texts. In essence, Brueggemann puts new names, experiential referents, upon terminology that had been used by form critics for decades. While his "names" or classifications do not perfectly match the more traditional classifications of praise, lament, and thanksgiving, they do for the most part closely identify the tenor or mood of these psalm types.

Acknowledging that our faith life goes through various periods or seasons, Brueggemann writes "that our life of faith consists in moving with God in terms of (a) being securely *oriented,* (b) being painfully *disoriented,* and (c) being surprisingly *reoriented.*"[11] Speaking in this way, Brueggemann helps us to recognize that the life of faith is a process; it changes and it is affected by life experiences. He then associates the psalms with our life of faith and identifies psalms as relating to these various seasons. While the terminology of orientation, disorientation, and reorientation does not perfectly match what form criticism has called psalms of praise, lament, and thanksgiving, there are many close connections. What we believe to be especially significant is that Brueggemann has taken his knowledge of the psalms and clearly identified how these texts relate to and speak of the life of faith.

Yes, the psalms are prayers that grew out of Israel's relationship with God. They are poems that have been used by countless generations of women and men who have called upon God in response to wondrous events and out of desperate situations. They are prayers that can speak for us as well, both when we desire to join our prayer with those who have gone before us in faith and when we are unable to find words that can articulate our deepest joys, desires, and pains. The scheme proposed by Brueggemann can be of great assistance to those who are intimately engaged in the lives of God's people. Pastoral ministers, familiar with these classifications and with the richness of the psalms themselves, can direct individuals to psalms that might be helpful in expressing to God deep joy, hope, sorrow, or gratitude.

Since Brueggemann's scheme does not perfectly match the traditional terminology, we will attempt to clarify how he identifies psalms as representing the seasons of *orientation, disorientation,* or *new orientation,* and we will identify by number those texts that he has named specifically as belonging to each of these categories.[12] We begin with the psalms of orientation.

Most persons of faith would acknowledge that they have had the experience of feeling in harmony with God, of knowing the joy of being at home with God, of delighting in the goodness of God's creation and God's ways. The psalms that praise God for this reality are often associated with hymns of praise. In his work, *The Message of the Psalms: A Theological Commentary,* Brueggemann elaborates upon these prayers of *orientation,* stating that they "express a confident, serene settlement of faith issues…. They are statements that describe a happy, blessed state in which the speakers are grateful for and confident in the abiding, reliable gifts of life that are long-standing from time past and will endure for time to come. Life, as reflected in these psalms, is not troubled or threatened, but is seen as the well-ordered world intended by God."[13] These poems speak of life when all is well, when the psalmist or prayer of these texts cannot help but take pleasure in God's blessings. Among the psalms that Brueggemann has identified as poems of orientation are Psalms 1, 8, 14, 15, 24, 33, 37, 104, 111, 112, 119, 127, 128, 131, 133, and 145.

We all know that life changes, and that is precisely what Brueggemann's schema emphasizes. While it is not possible to explain or account for the multiple ways in which our lives can take a slow or a sudden turn, we can acknowledge that that happens, and when it does we are often taken off guard. This is what Brueggemann describes as the state of *disorientation.* It is a season vastly different from that time when "all was well." The texts that speak of harmony, peace, and praise do not express the reality of the heart that is torn or devastated. Such words can seem foreign, even repulsive to one whose torment is overwhelming. The texts that do speak powerfully and truthfully to and for the wounded heart are the psalms that Brueggemann refers to as the *psalms of disorientation,* more commonly known as the laments.

Often people are surprised to learn that approximately one-third of the 150 texts that comprise the psalter are identified as laments or psalms of disorientation. This fact itself can be a source of comfort to those whose hearts are heavy and who may feel that it is "inappropriate" to speak strong words of pain and complaint to God. A perusal of these texts reveals language that is far from polite. The words found within the laments or psalms of disorientation are tremendous testimony to the profound relationship between the pray-er and God. Since it is extremely rare that Brueggemann identifies a lament psalm as belonging to either of the other classifications, the reader may find a listing of the psalms of disorientation in Table 1, where they are identified as *Laments.*[14]

The final classification in Brueggemann's scheme are the psalms of *new orientation,* poems that "speak boldly about a new gift from God, a fresh intrusion that makes all things new. These psalms affirm a sovereign God who puts humankind in a new situation."[15] Reflected in these prayers is the experience of God's unpredictable, yet unfailing love. These texts do not explain away the mystery of *how* God acts, but they do testify to the fact *that* God acts. Many of the psalms in this classification seem to narrate a story, telling what God has done and proclaiming God's wondrous actions.

Psalms that Brueggemann places within this collection tend to fall into several of the more "traditional" categories, including hymns of praise, thanksgiving, and confidence, as well as the royal psalms. Since Table 1 presents the psalms according to the more traditional classification, we will note here the texts that the author specifically identifies as psalms of new orientation. They are Psalms 2, 9, 11, 18, 20, 21, 23, 27, 29, 30, 34, 40, 41, 45, 47, 62, 63, 65, 66, 67, 72, 89, 91, 92, 93, 96, 97, 98, 99, 100, 101, 107, 113, 114, 115, 116, 117, 118, 121, 124, 125, 129, 132, 135, 138, 144, 146, 147, 148, and 150. *New orientation psalms* can be rather difficult to distinguish from those of orientation. Brueggemann himself acknowledges this and holds that on occasion "it is a matter of interpretation as to whether a psalm articulates the surprise of

Table 1
Types of Psalms

1. *Hymns*
   A. Hymns Proper: 8, 19, 29, 33, 66a, 95, 100, 103, 104, 111, 113, 114, 117, 135, 136, 145, 146, 147, 148, 149, 150
   B. In Praise of God's Reign: 47, 93, 96–99
   C. Songs in Praise of Zion: 46, 48, 76, 84, 87, 122

2. *Laments*
   5, 6, 7, 12, 13, 14, 17, 22, 25, 26, 28, 31, 35, 36, 38, 39, 42, 43, 44, 51, 52, 54, 55, 56, 57, 58, 59, 60, 61, 63, 64, 69, 70, 71, 74, 77, 79, 80, 82, 83, 85, 86, 88, 90, 94, 102, 106, 108, 109, 120, 123, 126, 130, 137, 140, 141, 142, 143

3. *Thanksgivings*
   9, 10, 30, 34, 40, 41, 65, 66b, 68, 75, 92, 107, 116, 118, 124, 138

4. *Psalms of Confidence or Trust*
   3, 4, 11, 16, 23, 27, 62, 91, 115, 121, 125, 129, 131

5. *Psalms Related to Israel's King*
   2, 18, 20, 21, 45, 72, 89, 101, 110, 144

6. *Psalms of Instruction*
   A. Wisdom: 1, 37, 49, 73, 112, 119, 127, 128, 133, 139
   B. Historical: 78, 105
   C. Liturgical: 15, 24, 50, 67, 81, 132, 134

new grace or whether it speaks of the *enduring graciousness* of God, which always sustains and so is rather taken for granted."[16]

Brueggemann's contribution to psalm study is far more comprehensive than what we have identified here. His attempt to articulate how the psalms reflect the rhythms of the life of faith is invaluable. As in so much of his work, Brueggemann has demonstrated that biblical scholarship has much to offer the pastoral minister.

With the 1993 publication of William L. Holladay's *The Psalms through Three Thousand Years,* we have been gifted with a marvelous work indeed. Although very different from Brueggemann's style and approach, Holladay's text is bursting with the wonderful story of the psalter's growth, its use by Jews and Christians for centuries upon centuries, and current theological issues related to these texts.[17]

In a chapter entitled "Censored Texts," Holladay addresses what can be identified as problematic psalms or problematic verses within psalms, many of which have been excluded from the revised Divine Office of 1970. He observes that three psalms—Psalms 58, 83, and 109—are omitted in their entirety, while an additional nineteen psalms have had one or more verses deleted.[18] Within the pages of this chapter, Holladay patiently addresses each of the "censored" verses, then makes the observation that "the Liturgy of the Hours has thus omitted some, if not all, of the harsh language regarding enemies." While the *context* of Holladay's focus may not be of special interest to all pastoral ministers, we believe that his *purpose* in examining these texts is extremely relevant.

Each of the selected texts or verses that Holladay examines is identified with the laments. Since these prayers of lament speak openly of struggle and pain, they also plead with God for deliverance from affliction. Closely associated with this plea for deliverance, one often finds the additional request that those responsible for the psalmist's plight be "repaid in full." In other words, enemies are openly cursed, using language that is difficult to accept as Christian prayer.

In his text, after having carefully examined each of the difficult verses, some of which are terribly blatant in their wish for either some form of evil or utter destruction of the enemy, Holladay then confronts us head on with a harsh truth and challenge. He writes, "There really are people of malice in the world. So the question before us is this: What attitude are Christians to have toward their enemies?"[19] Holladay then offers a provisional answer in the form of ten propositions. We find them so insightful and challenging that they appear following.

1. Jesus taught Christians to love their enemies (Mt. 5:44 [Lk 6:27]). Therefore such an expression as Psalm 139:21–22 is excluded from Christian use without a thorough reconception of "hate" and the identity of the enemies (on which, see chapter 19). Such love of enemies can hardly be a matter primarily of the emotions but is more a matter of the will: it would be fair to say that if one does not like one's enemies, one's calling is still to will the best for them. This is certainly implied by the correlative of "love your enemies," namely, "Pray for those who persecute you." Even some of the psalmists sensed what this might mean: "In return for my love they accuse me, even while I make prayer for them. So they reward me evil for good, and hatred for my love" (Ps 109:4–5; compare 35:12).

2. The call to love one's enemies must be exercised within the context of the claims of justice: if an injustice has been done, then it needs to be made right. Here the matter becomes complicated,

for one must deal with one's own stance, the stance of one's enemies, and the stance of God.

3. The psalmist claims he is "righteous" (or "innocent"); that is, the psalmist claims he is on the side of God, for otherwise he would not be singing a psalm at all. Even a psalm such as Psalm 51 hardly contradicts this statement. By contrast, Christians are warned in many ways against self-righteousness (Mt. 7:11; Rom. 12:3). Christians must never assume that the wrong is all on the side of their enemies. In this regard, passages in the psalms that encourage self-righteousness are misleading to Christians.

4. However, it is a fact that sometimes Christians are abused, oppressed, persecuted, and in such situations they need the help of protectors and, above all, of God; this is what I stressed in chapter 15. The same psalms that might be harmful to Christians who tend to self-righteousness might be empowering for Christians who lack power or self-esteem. How many Christians blame themselves for a bad relationship at home or at work when the fault is really more in their adversaries?

5. Christians who are oppressed by enemies seek not only an end to their oppression but vindication, both among their peers and before their enemies. Here the psalms may be truly helpful (Pss 54 and *passim*).

6. The crucial question then is: With regard to their enemies, what are Christians to wish for and pray for? Ideally, one would wish for their change of heart (Lk 17:3-4) and for reconciliation with them (Mt 5:24). Lacking that, one would wish for their recognition that they are in the wrong; that is the burden of the psalmists' prayers that the enemy be shamed (Pss 6:11 [10]; 31:18 [17]; and *passim*). One would further wish that they might cease their oppression (Ps 7:10 [9]), or that God would take away their power to oppress (Ps 59:12 [11]). But any attitude of gloating over one's enemies' fall is excluded; expressions such as that in Psalm 52:8–9 (6–7) can be dangerous: "The righteous will see, and fear and will laugh at the evildoer, saying, 'See the one who would not take refuge in God.'"

7. It is difficult to say whether it is legitimate for Christians to wish for commensurate hurt on their enemies, whether that hurt be exercised by the psalmist empowered by God (Ps 41:11 [10]) or

by God alone (Pss 28:4; 109:20; 137:8). Jesus' words in Mt. 5:38–39 would seem to exclude the possibility. By contrast, I discussed Psalm 41:11 (10) in Chapter 15, and there I suggested how necessary it is that there come to be parity between the one who is oppressed and the oppressor. Commensurate hurt on one's enemy is certainly one kind of parity, but it may not be the best kind; the removal of power from one's enemies may be preferable.

8. It follows from what has been said that it is not legitimate for Christians to wish death on their enemies. Expressions such as are found in Psalms 55:16 (15); 58:11 (10); or 137:9 are excluded for Christians, unless one's notion of the identification of one's "enemies" is drastically transformed (on which, see chapter 19).

9. Passages in which God is cited as showing contempt toward the national enemies of Israel are likewise questionable. In Psalm 60:10 (8), duplicated in Psalm 108:10 (9), God speaks, "Moab is my washbasin; on Edom I hurl my shoe; over Philistia I shout in triumph." This is a passage, as it happens that is retained in the Liturgy of the Hours; whether it is retained because of the peoples of Moab, Edom, and Philistia are gone from history by those names, so that the expressions are not perceived to be concretely relevant; or whether the listing in the previous verse of peoples of which God is understood to approve (Gilead, Manasseh, Ephraim, Judah) makes it difficult to exclude the disapproved territories; or whether those who prepared the Liturgy of the Hours simply hesitated to censor God's quoted words, would be hard to say. But the mood of contempt put in the mouth of God ("with exultation": Ps 60:8 [6]) is difficult to harmonize with the Christian understanding of God.

10. Most difficult is the question of the stance of Christians in a nation at war, when the civil authorities have declared another nation or group of nations to be enemies. One might defend as a legitimate goal for Christians the destruction of enemy military or political institutions, but Christians must always seek to minimize the destruction of human life.[20]

We have selected the work of Holladay because we believe that, while it is very important that God's faithful become familiar with the psalter, perhaps particularly with the psalms of lament, we also believe that it is extremely important that Christians pray these texts with the appropriate "Christlike" disposition. Holladay's propositions, we contend, put those difficult texts into proper perspective. Furthermore, it would seem that many of his observations are applicable to other biblical texts that seem to be in conflict or tension with how we believe Christians are called to live.[21]

We have taken a brief look at some of the contributions of only three biblical scholars whose work has focused on the psalms. Gunkel's identification of various types of psalms set the tone for psalm studies of the twentieth century. Brueggemann's use of the terms *orientation, disorientation,* and *new orientation,* along with his insight into the life of faith, provides us with some clear ways of connecting these biblical prayers with our own faith life. And finally, Holladay's attentive examination of those psalm texts that speak so strongly of revenge and destruction, and his profoundly sensitive attempt to address these in the light of Christian faith, invite each of us to reflect upon how our prayer, our beliefs, and our daily life are intricately intertwined. We now turn to the final portion of our threefold task, to offer some suggestions for how the pastoral minister might become better acquainted with the psalms.

Practical Information and Suggestions

It is important that the pastoral minister who intends to use the psalter with either individuals or groups have a fairly good understanding of the diversity of its contents. As the references to both Gunkel and Brueggemann have indicated, within the psalter one can find expressions of every imaginable prayer: the utter delight of one overwhelmed with God's creation; the sobs of one whose torment seems unbearable; the desperation of a people who have been devastated; the agonizing "whys" of those who deeply desire to understand the confusing world that surrounds them; the soft sigh of one who knows God's sustaining love, as well as resounding shouts of a jubilant congregation. These as well as so many other outpourings of the human heart are freely expressed in the psalter.

Following are a few simple suggestions as to how the psalms might become more familiar to the pastoral minister and thus be better utilized within the contexts of both counseling and spiritual direction.

1. Select a Bible translation. If you are not familiar with the major differences between various translations or do not have a favorite translation, you may wish to examine several of the more popular versions. The sampling of texts in part one of this article should provide you with a taste of what you will find within the *New American Bible, The New Revised Standard Version,* and the psalter produced by ICEL. Another translation that many people seem to favor is the *New Jerusalem Bible.* We recommend that you become acquainted with one translation before moving back and forth between several different Bibles. Then, once familiar with one of these versions, you may wish to turn your attention to another translation.

2. Before proceeding further, consider keeping a journal in which you jot down a few notes on individual psalms and the various classifications. This can be invaluable both for you and for those to whom you minister.

3. Select one major type of psalm from Table 1, for example, "Hymns." Reflectively read several of these psalms, being attentive to the tone or prayerful disposition expressed in each. When you come across lines that are especially appealing to you, sit with them, savor them, allow them to speak to your heart or for your heart. You will find that many of the lines within these texts will resonate within you. Return to them often. Gradually, over time, make your way through the entire selection of prayers of this type. In your journal, try to capture for yourself the general "characteristics" of these psalms. As you make your way through these texts, consider various circumstances when these psalms might be especially relevant or helpful to those with whom and for whom you minister.

4. Continue to explore each of the various categories of psalms, becoming familiar with the unique disposition of each.

5. Once acquainted with a variety of texts, it may be helpful to compare how your favorite psalms are rendered in several different translations. Here, you may begin to develop strong preferences for one translation over another. Since turning to a different Bible translation can be very helpful to individuals who already have a fondness or appreciation for the psalms but have run into a dry period and may benefit from hearing the texts anew, it is important that the pastoral minister to be acquainted with several of the many translations that are currently available.

6. If the practice of praying morning and evening prayer is not part of your prayer life, consider making it part of your prayer experience. It may be helpful to do this during the liturgical season of Advent or Lent, special times when we are often drawn to be more reflective and/or to adopt some additional religious practices. It may be helpful to keep in mind that morning and evening prayer is, in fact, the prayer of all Christians; it should not be identified exclusively with clerics or monastics.

7. Consider opening or closing sessions, either in counseling or spiritual direction, with a portion of a psalm that is appropriate for the situation.

These few suggestions are intended to encourage the pastoral minister to become familiar with the psalms, to grow in love with them, to savor them, and to make them a part of his or her prayer life. Having done so, the individual minister will know how best to incorporate these rich prayers into his or her ministry. We offer Table 1 as a "guide" to meeting and savoring the psalms. They are listed according to the traditional categories that can be found in most introductory works on the psalms. Though some variation exists, the differences are minor. Table 1 is the product of the author.

Notes

1. While this essay was in progress, announcement was made on August 6, 1998, that the United States Bishops, following the instructions of Cardinal Joseph Ratzinger, were withdrawing the *imprimatur* that they had granted the psalter in 1995. In an article by John L. Allen, Jr. in the *National Catholic Reporter* (August 28, 1998: 5), the following statement is attributed to Bishop Anthony Pilla of Cleveland, who, at the time, was president of the NCCB: "The revocation of the imprimatur should in no way be perceived as a revocation of the judgment of the censors' opinions concerning the fidelity or accuracy of the text," he said, nor should it be seen as reflecting negatively on "the judgment of our bishops."

2. See Frederick R. McManus, "ICEL, The Early Years," in *Shaping English Liturgy*, Peter C. Finn and James M. Schellmann, eds. (Washington, D.C.: Pastoral Press, 1990), for a wonderful and detailed accounting of the early history of this commission. This is a revised and expanded version of a document of the same title that was first published in 1981.

3. Frederick R. McManus, "Texts and Translations," in *The Living Light* 31 (1995): 49–51.

4. Ibid., 50.

5. Mary Collins, "Glorious Praise: The ICEL Liturgical Psalter," in *Worship* (1990): 292.

6. "Afterword," xxv.

7. Collins, "Glorious Praise," 292–95.

8. A revised psalter of the *New American Bible* was published in 1991. This edition, while more gender-inclusive than the previous psalter of the *NAB*, has undergone further editing, and the most recent publications of the *New American Bible* are not as inclusive as the 1991 publication. For "christo-logical" reasons, certain psalms have retained masculine terminology.

9. Our brief overview of Gunkel's contribution to psalm study is presented to demonstrate how psalm classifications might be beneficial to persons interested in using the psalms for personal or communal prayer. The reader should be aware that Gunkel's work is far more involved than what is summarized in this paragraph. A recent translation of the fourth edition of Gunkel's *Einleitung in die Psalmen: die Gattungen der religiösen Lyrik Israels* has appeared under the title *Introduction to the Psalms: The Genres of the Religious*

Lyric of Israel, trans. James D. Nogalski (Macon: Macon University Press, 1998).

10. Walter Brueggemann, *Praying the Psalms* (Winona: St. Mary's, 1982). This book first appeared as a series of articles in *Professional Approaches for Christian Educators (PACE).* In an excellent, more technical article, "Psalms and the Life of Faith: A Suggested Typology of Function," *JSOT* 17 (1980): 3–32, Brueggemann relates the language of the psalms to the work of Paul Ricoeur. The text cited from 1982 is a much more simplified presentation of some of this material. See also *The Message of the Psalms: A Theological Commentary* (Minneapolis: Augsburg, 1984).

11. Brueggemann, *Praying the Psalms,* 16.

12. Since the author does not identify each of the 150 psalms within the three classifications that we are examining, and because he acknowledges that the poems of orientation and new orientation are not always clearly identified one from the other, we have chosen to place within our text those psalms that Brueggemann does cite under one or the other of these two classifications. For an elaboration of his disposition, see *Message of the Psalms,* 158.

13. Brueggemann, *Message of the Psalms,* 25.

14. Exceptions among the "laments" that Brueggemann identifies as either of the other two categories are Psalm 14, which he identifies as a poem of orientation, and Psalm 63, which he cites as a psalm of new orientation.

15. Brueggemann, *Message of the Psalms,* 19.

16. Ibid., 125.

17. William L. Holladay, *The Psalms through Three Thousand Years: Prayerbook of a Cloud of Witnesses* (Minneapolis: Fortress, 1993).

18. Ibid., 304.

19. Ibid., 311.

20. Ibid., 311–13.

21. While newer works have examined some of the psalter's "difficult texts," a work of C. S. Lewis continues to be insightful. See "The Curses," in *Reflections on the Psalms* (London: Collins, 1958), 223–33.

Jude Winkler

4. From Being Loved into Loving: The Gospel of John as a Paradigm of Ministry

The Gospel of John is often considered to be the most spiritual of gospels, more concerned with heavenly issues than earthly. The Gospel, in fact, often condemns those who are worldly.[1] It speaks of Jesus as the revelation of God's love for us. The stated goal of the Gospel is to invite us to place our faith in Jesus as the only begotten Son of God and to abide in him and in the Father. There is relatively little emphasis on how to live one's life (for example, observing the commandments). All that is essential is that one make Jesus the center of one's life (that is, observing the one commandment of this Gospel: believing that Jesus is the Son of God).

Yet, as one decodes the symbolism of this Gospel, one observes that it is not only about allowing oneself to be loved by Jesus and abiding in that love. It is also about sharing that love with others. If Jesus encounters us at the well and teaches us that we are loved, then we must go into our home village and share that love with our sisters and brothers. If he washes our feet, then we must be ready to wash other people's feet. If he grants us a miraculous catch of fish, then we must learn to be fishers of all people throughout the world.

What Is Salvation?

In order to understand the significance of this message, we must start with the question of what Jesus did for us when he came into this world. How did his presence, his life, and his death affect our reality? In other words, what does it mean to say that he redeemed (or saved) us?[2]

The four Gospels treat this question in different ways. The Gospels of Matthew and Mark speak of expiation. We created a debt for ourselves through our sin. We brought death into our lives (for sin is a subtle form of death). Jesus paid this debt through his death on the cross; he allowed his

53

blood to be poured out (remember that blood is symbolic of life) to destroy the power of death (spiritual and physical).

The Gospel of Luke is less juridical in its treatment of the concept of salvation. It speaks of salvation both in terms of Jesus coming into our lives to show us that we are loved and also his teaching us how to be obedient to the will of the Father. By our sins, we had made ourselves lonely, for one of the most insidious effects of sin is alienation. We had cut ourselves off from the love of God and of our brothers and sisters. Jesus shows great compassion and love. He responds to the deepest needs of our heart.

Furthermore, Luke shows Stoic tendencies. In Stoicism, one finds peace and true joy only by discerning the plan of one's life and responding to it with obedience. Jesus, unlike Adam, who led us astray into disobedience, teaches us how to be obedient to the will of the Father. He does this by word and by example.[3] God is presented as being both our king and our father. As king, he exercises control over everything that occurs. He has established a plan for our lives. We will find joy only in discerning and observing that plan. But he is also father, for his is not an impersonal plan or the whim of a tyrant, but rather one established by a loving parent. God's will is that we grow fully in love.

The Gospel of John concentrates on the idea of salvation as a revelation of God's love for us. God has always loved us; we have cut ourselves off from that love through our sins. God has not stopped loving us; we have turned our backs on that love. God sent the law and the prophets, but these could never reveal the profundity of God's love for us. They tried to express God's word in human words, and God's message is always distorted when it is expressed in human speech. For this reason, God sent his word, his only begotten son, into the world to reveal to us how much we are loved.[4] Jesus is the incarnation of that love. "From his fullness we have received grace upon grace"[5] (Jn 1:16).[6]

In this soteriology, we have hurt ourselves through sin. When God created us, God breathed the spirit into us. We were called to participate in the life of God. Something of the divine was inside of us. We were not simply animals. God has called us to a far greater dignity. Through sin, we have denied the presence of God within us. We have chosen to act in an animalistic manner. Effectively, we proclaimed that we were no better than trash, and that we might as well act like trash.

Sin reinformed that image. Sin was a choice for selfishness and self-hatred. It was a choice against what God intended us to be. When we sin, we proclaim that we believe the lie of the evil one, that we are worthless. We come to believe that we are unlovable and unloved. Furthermore, when people try to break that cycle of self-deception by loving us, we push them away. We simply cannot believe that they truly want to love us, because we feel that we do not deserve their love. Therefore, we reason, they must be trying to use us. We feel that their love must be a lie, for how could they possibly love us when we do not even love ourselves?

Jesus came into the world to prove the lie of this logic. Jesus reveals that we are always loved. He reveals that there is nothing that we could ever do that would make God love us less.[7] He teaches us that we are truly lovable and loved.

The cross is the fullest manifestation of this fact. It is the revelation that Jesus loves us so much that he would be willing to die for us. It is not God changing his mind about us, but rather what God has always felt toward us.[8]

But, as stated earlier, if God has loved us this much, then we must share that love with others. "In this is love, not that we have loved God, but that he has loved us and sent his Son as an expiation for our sins. Beloved, if God so loves us, we must also love one another"[9] (1 Jn 4:10–11).

It would be useful now to examine several pericope that show this dynamic.

The Samaritan Woman at the Well

John 4 contains a story concerning an encounter between Jesus and a Samaritan woman who had gone to a well to obtain water. Jesus asks her for a drink, and she responds in a somewhat defensive manner. Jesus then offers her living water. He reveals that he knows everything about her. The woman suggests that he must be a prophet and asks him where they should worship God (Mt. Gerazim where the Samaritans worshiped, or Mt. Zion where the Jews worshiped). Jesus reveals who he is to her, and the woman leaves Jesus and informs the people of her village about him. They come out of the village and meet Jesus and ultimately proclaim him as the savior of the world.

The story is written in a leitmotif pattern.[10] The pattern is drawn from the Hebrew Bible and is called "the well story." It usually involves a man who goes to a well, where he meets a woman who offers him water. He takes the water, takes the woman, and they live happily ever after. One finds this pattern in Genesis 24 (Isaac and Rebekah), Genesis 29 (Jacob and Rachel), Exodus 2 (Moses and Zipporah), and Ruth 2 (Ruth and Boaz).

When Jesus goes to the well, he is going to meet his wife. This is a spiritual marriage. The people of Israel had, in a sense, married God in the First Covenant. The people of Samaria and the pagans were excluded from that marriage. They were now being invited into a new covenant. They would espouse the true God.[11] In this scene, Jesus is the groom, while the Samaritan woman is the bride. Notice that the Samaritan woman is not given a name. In the Gospel of John, whenever a character is named by a title and not by name (for example, the beloved disciple, the man born blind, the mother of Jesus), that character is playing a symbolic role. The Samaritan woman represents all of the Samaritans and pagans who were now being invited into a relationship with God that was to be so profound and intimate it could only be described in matrimonial terms.

This interpretation of the scene explains why there is such an odd progression of themes throughout the pericope. It begins with a question of receiving water at a well, passes on to the question of husbands and wives, and finishes with the question of where one should worship God. This only makes sense if the Samaritan people were being invited to marry God. They had been espoused to many false gods. The woman's husbands represent those gods. She had been married five times, and she was living now with a sixth. Seven is the perfect number in the Bible. Her six husbands (gods) had not been perfect. They had left her feeling unloved and unlovable. Jesus would be the seventh. He would respond to her deepest need.

Some of the elements of the story are unusual. We hear that the woman went to draw water at the well at noon. One would normally go the well very early in the morning, before it grew too hot. The woman was most probably at the well at this strange hour because she wanted to avoid contact with others because of her reputation; she wanted to avoid gossip and derision. She is not really pictured as evil in this account. If anything, she is seen as a person who had allowed herself to be used by others. The six men (gods) in her life have not truly loved her. She was used by them. This would explain why she was so hesitant to enter into dialogue with Jesus. The last thing that she wanted was for another man to use her.

Jesus breaks through her isolation and self-hatred by treating her with great dignity, more dignity than she would think that she deserved. He offered her living water.[12] He told her that if she were to accept that water, which symbolizes the life and love of God, it would become a font within her. In the well story leitmotif, the well represents either the woman or the womb. In this case, it represents the womb, for she would become fertile with the love of God and produce children who would bear the name of the Christ: Christian. Jesus then fulfills that promise, for when the woman departs from the well, she leaves the water jar there. She no longer needs it. She is overflowing with the love of God.

Her first action upon entering her village was to tell the people there, "Come see a man who told me everything I have done. Could he possibly be the Messiah?" (Jn 4:29). This was an incredible risk, for the response could easily have been a raucous catalog of her past misdeeds. She had avoided her countrymen for this very reason. Now she was making herself vulnerable and sharing her discovery with them. They came out to Jesus and experienced his saving love themselves.[13]

From this overview of some of the symbolism in the account, we can see that Jesus first healed the woman with his unconditional love. He encountered someone who felt that she was hated by everyone and who even hated herself. Worse, she believed that she deserved everything that she had received. Jesus refused to view her that way. He treated her with great respect and gentleness. He accepted her and invited her into an intimate relationship. She was healed by that love. She came to understand that she was lovable and loved. She was so overwhelmed with joy and gratitude that her first action was to share that love with others (ironically, those who had often rejected her and treated her like an object). She was the one who planted the fields that were white for the harvest. She went from being one who was horribly broken to being an instrument of healing, from being an outcast to becoming a missionary.[14]

The Man Born Blind

A second example of the passage from being healed to giving witness is found in John 9: the story of the man born blind. This is a story told at two levels. At the surface level, it is the story of a person who was physically blind. Jesus healed him by rubbing mud on his eyes and sending him off to wash in the pool of Siloam. Jesus did this on the Sabbath, and he therefore provoked the wrath of the Jewish leaders who considered what he did to be sinful.

Even at this surface level of the story, there is a profound message concerning the healing of the man. He is not only blind, he is also oppressed by his situation. The disciples of Jesus debate whether he is blind because of his sin or the sins of his parents (9:2). This was incredibly rude, for these arguments seem to have been made within his hearing. He found himself used as an object lesson for their philosophical ramblings. Even his so-called friends did not treat him with respect. They do not seem to have known him by name; they knew him only by his disability. When he is healed, they do not even recognize him. Jesus, on the other hand, immediately treats him with great dignity. He explains to his disciples that the man is blind "so that the works of God might be made visible through him" (9:3). Before Jesus healed him physically, he had already begun to treat him with dignity. One can almost see the spreading smile on the man's face. He could be proud of the fact that he was to be instrumental in the revelation of God's love.

Below this surface level, however, there is another level of symbolism. There are certain elements of the story that are incongruous and that give us an indication that there is more to the story than meets the eye. Once the man is healed, he is brought before the Pharisees for interrogation. Normally, if one were to be questioned in Jerusalem at the time of Jesus, one would be brought before the Sanhedrin, which was composed of Pharisees and Sadducees. Why was he brought only before the Pharisees?

A second and third difficulty are found in the interrogation of the parents of the man born blind. Although they knew that Jesus had healed their son, they would not admit it for fear that they would be expelled from the synagogue. This is odd, for if they were living in Jerusalem they would have been afraid of being expelled from the temple, not from the synagogue. Furthermore, we know that the leaders of the Jews did not definitively expel Christians from the synagogue until around A.D. 80. Before the destruction of the temple in A.D. 70, Christians continued to consider themselves Jews and continued to worship in the temple (even if there were occasional local persecutions). After the destruction of the temple, the Jewish leaders met at Jamnia and reached the decision to exclude Christians from the community.

These difficulties give us an indication that there is a second level to the story. It concerns a Christian community that was spiritually blind, but which came to the light (Jesus, who is the light of the world). When the Jewish leaders (the Pharisees after the destruction of the temple, for the Sadducees no longer existed) decided to expel Christians, they had the courage to give witness to their faith. For this, they were punished by being shunned. This meant not only being expelled from the community, but also physical danger. Because there were only two legitimate religions in the Roman Empire, Judaism and the emperor cult, expulsion from the synagogue was a question of life and death. Jewish Christians could no longer claim that they were Jews when they were brought before the Roman judges, and they were therefore convicted of the capital crime of atheism.

The courage of the Johannine community is contrasted with the temerity of those Jewish Christians who would not proclaim their faith when the decision had been made that "if anyone acknowledged him (Jesus) as the Messiah, he would be expelled from the synagogue" (Jn 9:22). These fearful Christians are commonly called crypto-Christians. They are represented in this story by the parents of the man born blind.[15]

One should notice that their story occurs in the central section of the pericope, the third section of five.[16] This five-part structure is known as a *chiasm*.[17] The author is thus implying that the question of giving witness to one's faith in Jesus was of central importance. It was not enough to believe in Jesus in one's heart (to have been healed of one's spiritual blindness), one had to live a life of witness to that love.[18]

The Last Supper

Possibly the most explicit passage that deals with the process of allowing oneself to be loved and then loving one's brothers and sisters is the Last Supper (Jn 13). In that chapter, Jesus performs an act of humble service to the disciples—he washes their feet—and invites them to do the same to each other. This action is understood by most scholars to be a demonstration of the spiritual significance of the sacrament of the eucharist.[19]

The beginning of chapter 13 strongly emphasizes these connections. We hear that the feast of the Passover was near. There are three Passovers in this Gospel, and each is connected with important events (the cleansing of the temple, the multiplication of loaves and fish, and the Last Supper and death of

Jesus). Furthermore, Jesus would be presented as being the new Passover lamb in his death (for he dies at the very hour that the Passover lambs were being slaughtered in the temple,[20] and his death fulfills the prescription that none of the lamb's bones were to be broken).

Jesus knows that he is from the Father and is going to the Father. This fact is important, for the washing of the disciples' feet must not be seen as an action that Jesus performed because he did not really know who he was. On the contrary, this Gospel considers that action to be a manifestation of the dignity of Jesus. God is love, and to serve others is a godly act.[21]

This is also an action of profound love: "He loved his own in the world and he loved them to the end" (13:1b). Again, the action of washing feet is not described as one of duty or social responsibility. It is an act of love, a love that extends "to the end."[22]

Jesus begins to wash his disciples' feet, but Peter objects to this action. We must ask why Peter would object. Unlike the other Gospels, John presents Peter as being impetuous[23] and a bit obtuse. While he is called Peter ("rock") in the Gospel of Matthew because he was the rock on which the Church was being built, it seems as if he received the name *rock* in this Gospel because he is thick as rock and slow to understand.[24]

Thus, it is no surprise that Peter would not understand the significance of Jesus' action.[25] Jesus wants to serve Peter, and Peter does not want to be served. This could refer to the difficulty of making oneself vulnerable enough to allow oneself to be served and loved. True love both gives of itself and is willing to receive.

This is even more significant when one considers how Jesus explains his action. Peter did not want to be washed at all, but Jesus told him that he could not share in his inheritance if he did not allow himself to be washed. Peter then asked to be bathed all over. Jesus responded that one who has been bathed (probably a reference to the bathing sacrament, baptism) did not need to be washed all over, he only needed a partial bathing (probably a reference to the forgiveness of sins committed after baptism).[26]

Unless one allows oneself to be forgiven, one cannot live in God's love.[27] One must admit one's need and accept the healing love being offered in order to be made whole.

But once one accepts that love and is healed, that person must share that love with others. Jesus tells his disciples, "I have given you a model to follow, so that as I have done for you, you should also do" (13:15). Although the followers of Jesus are consistently called disciples and not apostles in this Gospel,[28] they must nevertheless wash other's feet (they must be instruments of healing and the forgiveness of sins).

This idea is stated in different words later in the chapter when Jesus says, "If I have loved you, so you should love one another. This is how all will know you are my disciples, if you have love for one another" (13:34–35).

Chapter 21

The last chapter of the Gospel[29] repeats the lesson of allowing oneself to receive God's love and then sharing that love in two different connected episodes.

The first is found at the beginning of the chapter. The risen Jesus appears to the disciples and invites them to fish from the right side of their boat. They receive a miraculous catch of fish, 153 of them.[30]

When the disciples arrive on shore, Jesus offers them a breakfast of fish and bread (the same meal described in chapter 6, the miraculous multiplication of bread and fish). Here, though, unlike in chapter 6 where the bread is emphasized, the fish is emphasized. There are two reasons for this. First, the risen Jesus, the bread of life, is standing in their midst. Second, the scene is stressing the mission dimension of the eucharist. After one has been fed by the Lord (seen both in the miraculous catch and in the breakfast being served), one must go out and fish. The disciples are being called to be fishers of all people. Their catch would extend from throughout the entire earth (remember the 153 fish).[31]

Later in the chapter, Peter is asked three times by Jesus whether he loves him. Peter responds that he does three times. This triple affirmation of his love is a symbolic healing of the triple denial of Jesus while he was being tried (18:15–18, 25–27).

This is not simply a moment of healing; it is also a call to service. Peter is invited to feed and tend for the flock. Jesus is the good shepherd, and he has now invited Peter to continue that work and to watch over and protect the sheep.

The cost of that mission is seen in 21:18, when Peter is told that he would be called to the ultimate sacrifice of giving his life for the flock. This Gospel calls disciples to give witness, and the Greek word for "witness" is *martureo,* the root of the English word *martyr.* Peter would give witness even to his death.

The Risen Jesus

Finally, we consider one of the resurrection narratives of this Gospel (20:19–23). Jesus appears to the disciples and proclaims, "Peace be with you" (20:19b). This most unexpected proclamation begins the process of healing the frightened and confused hearts of the disciples.

Jesus then breathes on them. This is his act of conferring the Holy Spirit upon them.[32] The Gospel of John has a different sense of history than the writings of Luke. While Luke emphasizes time and history being fulfilled (for example, forty days until the Ascension, fifty days until Pentecost), John speaks of time as if, with the death and resurrection of Jesus, it has come to an end. We have now entered into eternity, so the passage of time is unimportant. Thus, he can present the conferring of the Holy Spirit as an event that happened on the same day as the resurrection.

The action of breathing on the disciples is also an allusion to the creation account of Adam found in Genesis 2. God breathes on a lump of mud and makes the first human being. Jesus breathes on the disciples, breathing the Holy Spirit into them, and makes them a new creation in his life and his love.[33] The disciples are now fully alive, fully what God always intended them to be.

Typical of this dynamic, Jesus then orders them to go forth and to forgive sins. They must now share the new life that they have received from him.

Other Passages

All of these pericope are fairly overt in their message: The disciple learns what love means and experiences it from Jesus, but the disciple must then share that love with others.

There are other passages in this Gospel that, while not being as complete in their presentation of this theme, imply the same dynamic.

One, for example, could consider Nicodemus. He appears three times in the Gospel. In the first appearance (Jn 3), he comes to Jesus by night, for he is frightened and does not yet know Jesus, the light of the world. In the second appearance, in chapter 7, he half-defends Jesus. The Pharisees wanted to put Jesus in prison, but Nicodemus quoted the law as saying that one cannot condemn a person who has not been tried. Then, in chapter 19, Nicodemus and Joseph of Arimathea risk their lives to bury Jesus with great love and dignity, burying him with 100 pounds of myrrh and aloes.[34] As he has come to know and love Jesus, he recognizes the need to give witness to his faith through action.

In chapter 15, Jesus speaks of the vine and the branches. Disciples are told that they cannot bear fruit unless they remain in Jesus. While this pericope is speaking of the first half of this dynamic (the abiding in Jesus), it nevertheless follows that if one abides in Jesus, then one would want to bear fruit.

Throughout the Last Supper discourse, Jesus speaks both of the fact that he and the Father love the disciples and that they would have to give witness to that love. They cannot possibly do that on their own, so the Father and Jesus would send another Paraclete[35] to guide them (14:15– 20, 25–31; 15:26–27; 16:5–15). The disciples would be hated by the world, for the world could not accept God's love, but the disciples would continue to fulfill their mission of giving witness to that love. They will have received the loving presence of God's Holy Spirit, and they would share that love, even at the price of their lives.

Conclusion

The implications of all of this to ministry are profound. The minister is first the disciple, the follower. She must allow herself to be healed by God's love. He must be vulnerable and accept the forgiveness and mercy that God always offers and that God has communicated in a most incarnate manner in the person of Jesus.

One must abide in Jesus. It is a continuing relationship that is the source of one's strength and love. To choose to abide apart from Jesus is to choose that which cannot give life.

But abiding is not a passive experience. One must go beyond the therapeutic model (to want to be healed) to the prophetic model (to be willing to give witness). One must be nourished at the table of the Lord, and then one must go fishing. One must be willing to share the water and the word, even at the cost of one's life.

This, ultimately, is what it means to share in Jesus' glory. This word, *glory,* is usually interpreted as power or magnificence or prestige. In this Gospel, the word is redefined as "the outpouring of love." Jesus' hour of glory is thus not the transfiguration or the resurrection; it is the cross. That is the moment when Jesus most clearly manifested his love and the Father's love for us.

We are called into Jesus' glory. We are given the dignity of being friends and children of God. As friends and children, we abide in God's intimate love, but we also do that which Jesus our brother did: we love the world into healing. God treats us with such great dignity that we not only realize that we share in God's own life, but we even participate in God's mission.

Notes

1. This does not mean that the Gospel opposes the physical world, as some Gnostic commentators would propose. Rather, "the world" refers to those who do not accept the message of Jesus into their lives.

2. In certain New Testament writings (e.g., the letters of Paul), the words *redemption* and *salvation* are two different realities. Redemption occurred when Jesus died on the cross, but salvation is a future event. We will be saved from the wrath of God on the Last Day. In other New Testament writings, these words are used interchangeably.

3. We can especially see his obedience in the fact that he is constantly praying to the Father. In the other Gospels, Jesus is only occasionally pictured as praying to the Father. Here he prays often, for it is in prayer that he discerns the will of the Father and finds the courage to respond with full obedience.

4. This is the point that the author of the Letter to the Hebrews makes in the first verses of his presentation. He speaks of how God spoke in many and

varied ways in times past, but now was speaking through the Word of God, his only son. The multiplicity of the previous revelations should not be interpreted as something positive. The author was saying that multiple revelations were needed because none fully expressed God's message.

5. *Grace* means an experience of God's love in our lives. The Greek phrase that is translated as "grace upon grace" is actually a bit ambiguous. It could mean that we first received one grace, then we received another that built upon it. Or it could mean that we received one grace, and then another grace was substituted for it. Finally, it could mean that we had received "tons" of grace. Given the statement that is made in the next verse, that the law came through Moses and grace came through Jesus, the second possibility seems the most probable.

6. All quotations from sacred scripture are taken from the *New American Bible*, copyright 1970, revised New Testament 1986, revised Psalms 1991.

7. The problem when we sin is not with God, it is with us. Using an image from the Hebrew Bible, when we sin, we turn our back on God's love. God still loves us, but we are ignoring that love.

8. The God of the Hebrew Bible is often stereotyped as an angry God. This is inaccurate, for there are many passages that speak of God's compassion (e.g., Hosea). But what if the anger of the Hebrew Bible was not *at* us, but rather *for* us. God was angry at the poison (sin) that was destroying the lives of his beloved children. Unfortunately, we misinterpreted the object of his anger as being us and not our sin.

9. The First Letter of John speaks of salvation in terms of expiation (similar to the ideas found in Matthew and Mark). This is not the case with the Gospel of John, where the word *expiation* is never found. In the Gospel salvation occurs through revelation. While the Letters of John were probably produced by the same community that produced the Gospel, they were probably not written by the same author.

10. A leitmotif is a pattern found in music or literature that recurs either in an individual production or throughout the works of a school. One must pay close attention both to the usual elements to be expected in a leitmotif and the ways in which those elements are changed.

11. For more information on this theme, see "Marriage and the Samaritan Woman," *New Testament Studies* 26 (1980): 332–46.

12. *Living water* could mean either water that flows or water that gives life. She understands the former, while Jesus intends the latter. Only gradually does she come to understand what Jesus really means.

13. Jesus speaks of the Samaritans as the harvest. He tells the disciples to look out and see that the grain was white for the harvest (in English this is often mistranslated as "ripe" or "gleaming"). He was not pointing at the wheat fields;

he was pointing at the Samaritans who were coming to meet him. Samaritans wear white robes.

14. This overview in no way exhausts the intricate symbolism of this passage. One could speak of the Samaritan/Jewish issue, of the role of Jesus as *Ta'eb* (the Samaritan word for "Messiah"), of worshiping God in spirit (Holy Spirit) and truth (Jesus), etc.

15. Note their symbolic role, for their names are not given and they therefore stand for an element in the community.

16. The man is first healed by Jesus (9:1–12), he is interrogated by the Pharisees (9:13–17), the parents are interrogated (9:14–23), the man is interrogated a second time by the Pharisees (9:24–34), and Jesus speaks with the man a second time (9:35–41).

17. A chiasm is a literary structure with an odd number of sections in which the first and last, second and second last, etc., sections have similarities. The central section is always the most important section and the focal point of the pericope.

18. For a more extensive treatment of the man born blind pericope, consult J. Louis Martyn, *History and Theology in the Fourth Gospel* (Nashville: Abingdon, 1979), or Raymond Brown, *The Community of the Beloved Disciple* (New York: Paulist Press, 1979).

19. Some scholars (e.g., Bultmann) have argued that the community that produced this Gospel was anti-sacramental. It is difficult to defend this position when there are three chapters that address the eucharist in one form or another: chapter 6, which speaks of the eucharist as the flesh and blood of Jesus; chapter 13, which speaks of it in symbolic terms as an example of Jesus' service (in sacrament here and in deed when he dies on the cross); and finally the beginning of chapter 21, which speaks of eucharist as an invitation to mission.

20. The Gospel of John presents the Last Supper as occurring on Thursday night, the night before the beginning of the Passover. The Synoptics propose that Thursday night was the beginning of the Passover.

21. The rabbis were asked what God's name, Yahweh, meant. Some responded that it meant, "I am who I am, and it is none of your business who I am." Others stated that it meant, "I am who I am for you, who I have always been for you, who I will always be for you." God defines who he is in terms of service to us.

22. "To the end" could mean until the last moment or up to the ultimate degree (death).

23. When the beloved recognizes Jesus on the shore in John 21:7, Peter throws on his clothes and jumps in the water, the exact opposite of what one would normally do when jumping in the water.

24. When Peter enters the tomb after the resurrection, he only sees (20:6). The beloved disciple, who is often contrasted with Peter, sees and believes (20:8).

25. This is a typical literary device in this Gospel: the characters involved in the plot are terribly confused. This allows the author to explain to the greater audience, the reader, what is happening and why.

26. This scene thus demonstrates the penitential aspect of the sacrament of the eucharist, for it is the sacrament of the pouring of Jesus' blood for the forgiveness of sins.

27. To hold on to low self-esteem is actually a subtle form of control, for the person is rejecting what God made the person to be and is opting for another image, which the person cannot possibly become. This does not imply that one should not seek conversion, but since conversion is based on love, it must be an act of transformation and not rejection of what one is.

28. *Apostle* means one who is sent, implying a commission with a certain authority. *Disciple* means a follower. If the Gospel calls them disciples, one would not expect them to have an active mission.

29. It is probable that chapter 21 was not added to the Gospel until after chapters 1–20 were already issued. Chapter 20 has what appears to be a concluding statement (20:30–31) for the Gospel. Yet, the vocabulary and the theology of chapter 21 are consistent with the rest of the Gospel, which would mean that it was probably added by the same author who was responsible for the final version of the rest of the Gospel. Furthermore, all of the most ancient manuscripts of this Gospel contain this chapter, so it must have been added relatively early, before many copies of the Gospel were made.

30. Many scholars, modern and ancient, have speculated on the meaning of the number 153. One proposal that would seem to offer some promise is that certain ancient philosophers believed that there were 153 different species of fish in the world. The number 153 would thus signify the universality of the catch.

31. This same idea of the universality of the catch is presented in Acts of the Apostles in chapter 2, when Peter is pictured as speaking on Pentecost Sunday to people who have come from all of the nations on the earth.

32. The word for *breath* is the same as that for *wind* and *spirit* in both Hebrew and Greek.

33. This idea that there is a new creation in Christ is also found in Acts 2, where the Holy Spirit is pictured in the form of wind, reminding one of the spirit (wind) over the waters in Genesis 1, and also with the clarification of languages that were confused through the sin of arrogance at the Tower of Babel.

34. This fulfills the prediction in Psalm 45 that the bridegroom's raiment would be fragrant with myrrh and aloes.

35. The word *Paracletos* is ambiguous. It could mean advocate or advisor or consoler. Jesus portrays himself as the first Paraclete and the Holy Spirit as the "other" Paraclete.

SECTION II.
DARKNESS AND HOPE

In "What Really Matters: Suffering and Spirituality," Lucien Richard writes about loving in darkness and emptiness. He also recognizes suffering as a natural cost of the spiritual journey toward the fullness and fulfillment of personhood. The amazing impact of this essay is that it is simultaneously well-footnoted and poignant; it is one of the finest papers on suffering that I have ever read. I not only studied it so that my pastoral work would become more intelligent, I prayed over it so the heart of my ministry would be deeper.

Dermot Lane, in "Death, the Self, Memory, and Hope" raises ultimate issues and offers some ways of responding to them. Underlying his work is the belief that experiencing darkness (in this case death) allows us to see our lives and the world before us in a new way. In a short amount of space, he covers a remarkable amount of ground. The concept of "soul pain," the illusion of the self-sufficient subject, and memory and its role in hope are just part of the material with which he stirs up our feelings and beliefs about death.

The loss of identity and link to God because of sexual abuse are poignantly and carefully presented in "An Experience of Darkness and the Search for a Compassionate God." In this essay by Marie Gipprich and Michaele Barry Wicks, the stark reality of being personally touched by deep suffering and the reality of both near desperation and new possibility are clearly presented. Given the statistics that one in every three girls and one in every seven boys under the age of eighteen have been sexually abused, this essay will be of great help in providing knowledgeable ministry to many people. Moreover, the reality that "innocent and unjust suffering doesn't necessarily build character; it very often destroys it" makes us realize the importance such pastoral guidance has for people who have been abused.

In Gerald Archbuckle's article, "Letting Go in Hope," he makes the point that "people desperately need, in the midst of an ever-changing and secularizing world, a spirituality of letting go and appropriate rituals to express that spirituality." He focuses especially on the role of ministers as ritual leaders in the process of grieving. How persons in ministerial roles can help people who are experiencing personal and cultural chaos to let go in order to be given to the new is a particularly germane topic at the beginning of this new millennium. His use of sacred scripture and the four simple lessons that "Moses gives to all community leaders within the church" make this essay especially rich.

The final essay of this section, "Prayer from Calvary: A Passion Spirituality," is a classic John Mossi reflection: practical, scripturally rooted, and inspirational. This essay contains wonderful healing messages to share with those whom we serve and to use for our own meditation. His "suggestions for action" make it a beautiful piece to adopt for use in faith-sharing groups and for one's own periods of recollection.

5. What Really Matters: Suffering and Spirituality

Introduction

Genuine communion with God is never removed from the seasons, turns, and crises of life. So the modes of God's presence and absence and the quality of our relationship are very different in times of joy and of suffering. One's conversation with God is deeply shaped by one's circumstances, not only personal but also cultural. A relationship with God is not immune to the surprises and costs of daily life. The focus of this essay is on the experience of God within the experience of suffering. It is about spirituality *and* suffering; it is not about the spirituality *of* suffering, although the two aspects cannot be fully separated. Suffering is not peripheral to Christian spirituality. This essay is not an attempt to write about a particular spirituality within the Christian tradition; it is an attempt to get to the heart of Christian spirituality. It is not an attempt to construe a new spirituality "for our times," although cultural contexts are significant.

I begin by defining what I understand spirituality to be. This is followed by an exposition on the nature of suffering. I then attempt to demonstrate how spirituality and suffering relate to one another, and apply my notion of suffering to two issues in the history of spirituality: the perceived dualism of action and contemplation and that of body and soul. Last, I consider the transformative nature of suffering in spirituality.

Spirituality

To proceed logically, I must define what I understand by *spirituality* and by *suffering*. Spirituality has to do primarily with spirit, with the spirit of God, with the spirit of Christ.[1] From the beginning of the Judeo-Christian tradition, the spirit of God has been understood as God in the midst of men and women, God as the energy of this world, God as dwelling with us.[2]

Spirit names a kind of being that is somehow shared by man and woman with God. Spirit expresses most deeply the radically self-giving nature of God,

69

the "going out" of God, the self-transcending of God, the ecstatic nature of the Godhead, the surging forth of God. The spirit is the deepest dimension of God; this spirit is shared with us, a spirit through which we have access to God.

> "What no eye has seen, nor ear heard, nor the heart of man conceived, what God has prepared for those who love him." God has revealed to us through the Spirit. For the Spirit searches everything, even depths of God. For what person knows a man's thoughts except the spirit of the man that is in him? So also no one comprehends the thoughts of God except the Spirit of God. But we have not received the spirit of the world but rather the Spirit that comes from God, that we might know what God has given us in grace. (1 Cor 2:9ff.)

From the Christian perspective, to be spiritual means to be filled with the spirit of God, as revealed and as given through Christ. For Paul, it was the Spirit who stood at the heart of spirituality; it was having the spirit that made someone spiritual (1 Cor 2:11–14). To have the spirit means to have life.[3] Spirituality is a pilgrimage of transformation in and through the Holy Spirit. The pilgrimage model of the spiritual life contrasts with the classical model of the "finished man." On the American scene, the "finished man" is the one who "has made it." Spirit, however, points to the mysterious affinity that binds man and woman to God. The dynamic mode of being that we call "spirit" may be described as a capacity for going out of oneself and beyond oneself, as the capacity for transcending oneself.

Spirit and Personhood

Spirituality is about that deepest dimension of personhood—where a person encounters ultimate reality. Spirituality can be understood as a pilgrimage, a journey, and way that leads to self-transcendence, and transcendence is what personhood is all about.[4] While *spirit* and *person* are not synonymous, the two are intimately connected. Person, as Aquinas wrote, is "that which is most perfect in all of nature." And the formal reason for this is that personal being is self-transcending.

There is a for-otherness that is constitutive of the person as person. The essence of human personhood is a being-there-for-others. It is the self turned toward others that finds fulfillment. We are authentic selves only in direct proportion to our ability to be affected by and related to other selves. The substance-self of classical tradition is at best an abstraction. In reality I am the person I am, precisely because of my relationship to this history, this family, these friends. I am a profoundly relative, not substantial, being. Whether I know it of not, I am the person I am because this friend, person, idea has literally entered my life.

While for-otherness is constitutive of personhood, so is from-otherness. The fact that we derive from others, that we live from others is fundamental. It is through being loved that we learn to love; we have to be given to in order to be able to give. The fact of derivation from others is fundamental to personhood, and a breakdown in this basic from-otherness may lead to a radical breakdown of self. Since we are not autonomous or self-sufficient, we have to be given to in order simply to be. Interdependence is the basic structure and dynamic of personal existence. The independent life is made up of mutuality, exchange, and reciprocity.

This is why at the core of personhood lies the ability and the necessity to love. The capacity to love is the capacity to place the other within the reality of self-existence in such a way that real modification occurs for each. In light of this, one can say that the essence of the person is to love. Hegel had already affirmed this: "It is in the nature or character of what we mean by personality or subject to abolish its isolation or separateness. In friendship and love, I give up my abstract personality and in this way win it back as concrete personality."[5] Hegel considers the person to become concrete by entering into the community with the other or by surrendering to the other. In the process of loving, the self is enriched and embodied in a genuine presence to others.

Self-transcendence demands a recentering of the self and a centering on the other. This self-transcending is nothing else but love. Only in love can I and do I open up to the breadth of the infinite and God-given horizon. Only in love can I touch the innermost core of my personhood.[6] Self-transcendence is not simply horizontal; it is also vertical—a radical recentering of consciousness from self to God: to love as God loves; to take on God's eye view of all things, seeing them as he sees them in the ordered unity of being as a whole.

Spirituality can be defined as the radical drive of the person toward self-transcending authenticity in knowing, naming, and loving the Other. Spirituality is the lived quality of a person *qua* person. Spirituality as such is not formally concerned with "perfection" but with growth, and consequently it is not the concern of a select few but of everyone who experiences himself or herself drawn toward the fullness of personhood. Spirituality is not concerned solely with the "interior life" as distinguished from or in opposition to bodily, social, political, or secular life. On the contrary, spirituality relates to the integration of all aspects of human life and experience. Again, here the nature of personhood helps us grasp more fully what spirituality is. In a Christian context, Paul spells out the process in the following way: "According to the riches of God's glory, may you have the power for your hidden self to grow strong, so that Christ may dwell in your hearts through faith and you may be filled with the utter fullness of God" (Eph 3:16–19).

Suffering and Personhood

Suffering is a universal characteristic of human existence. Suffering, personhood, and love have much in common, for personal transcendence is realized in loving. To love is to act: love requires a movement toward the other. While the freedom to act is a condition of love, it follows that the capacity to be acted upon, to be moved by another is also implied. There is always a process of transformation that occurs in the act of loving. To love is to be shaped by the other. And while union or communion is an important aspect of love, the essence of love is a letting-be, an allowing, an enabling of the other into the full realization of his or her potentialities. Such "kenotic" love is costly.

The cost of love is suffering. Suffering is not accidental to love; it is an essential element of love. And it is because of our status as persons that we can and do suffer. Personhood demands mutuality, and because love lies at the core of personhood, suffering occurs. We are condemned to suffer in the same way that we are condemned to love. The nature of personhood determines the nature of suffering. It is not simply bodies that suffer nor minds: suffering is experienced by persons. Suffering is most acute when the person perceives its impending destruction. In fact, our daily language reflects this situation: "I'm going to pieces," "She's breaking apart at the seams." From the perspective of the person, suffering can be defined as a state of severe distress.

To suffer connotes an impingement upon a person. It points to the passive-receptive and dependent quality of life. In a deeper but also consistent meaning, to suffer can also mean to be threatened by an alien reality. It is this meaning that H. Richard Niebuhr points out when he writes, "Suffering occurs when we are threatened by the presence in our existence of that which is not under our control, that which operates under a law other than our own."[7] Suffering is the potential result of the malfunctioning of the interdependence of love; love abused is traumatic. There can be no interdependence, there can be no love without suffering. Suffering means to be affected by the action of the other, to be acted upon; as such it follows that the nature of personhood, of interdependence; our fulfillment as persons is dependent upon the other.

Suffering in its many forms is a transgression against the person; suffering reveals the vulnerability of our personhood and the precariousness of our personal existence. Vulnerability is the capacity to undergo the frustration of needs and desires. Vulnerability in the personal sphere has to do with interdependence, with love. Some of the most severe forms of suffering occur through separation from loved ones or from what happens to a loved one. Suffering can occur in two primary forms: from commiseration with the other and from the breakdown of interpersonal relations themselves. The most serious form of suffering consists in relations violated, in intimacy destroyed, in various forms of alienation, in betrayal and abandonment.

The suffering that comes about because of the interpersonal nature of our existence takes two basic forms: that of affliction and that of tragedy. Affliction has to do with the social nature of our personhood.[8] As social beings dependent for much of our identity on others, on society and its cultures, we are vulnerable to the fragility of social worlds. The need for social solidarity makes us vulnerable.[9] Affliction involves isolation, abandonment. The infant's most despairing cry is not the one that he utters when he feels pain, but rather when she feels herself abandoned, when she no longer sees familiar faces around her, and when all contact with the universe seems suddenly to be broken off. Affliction involves abandonment and degradation or the fear of them in some form or another. The degradation is felt in the isolation that accompanies affliction. The loss of solidarity experienced by the afflicted is a common phenomenon. This dimension of affliction is more fully understood when one realizes the significance of the ongoing quest for the esteem of others. Affliction is the kind of suffering that alienates. Affliction is suffering that has at the same time physical, psychological, and social elements.

Suffering can also be tragic.[10] The ancient Greek tragedians described the dynamic of tragic suffering against a background of conflict, of forces beyond control. All love is exposed to terrible danger. Love exists in a tragic world where love and lovers are constantly threatened. There is an intimate connection among freedom, love, and suffering. Nicolai Berdyaev felt profoundly the tension between the personal reality of love in human life and the demands of finite historical existence. He saw this aspect as the tragedy of spirit.[11] Daniel Day Williams, in his study of the nature of love,[12] affirms that self-love, an essential element of love, is itself nothing else than a desire to belong. At the core of selfhood lies the desire to "feel at home in the world," to be accepted and in community. In the very assertion of self there is a need to reach out, to participate in the lives of others. And so we are condemned to love and therefore to suffer. And so suffering is tragic, inescapable, a dimension of our human reality. We are destined to a distinctive vulnerability because of our being as persons. Our interpersonal holding environment renders us vulnerable to the breakdown of relationships, to losses of devastating consequences.

All vulnerabilities, all losses, all specific sufferings are for the personal being indications and symbolizations of the ultimate loss, which is death. This inevitable destiny is the most tragic form of suffering. No life can be managed so as to render it invulnerable to the anxiety engendered by the anticipation of death—our beloved's and our own. The anticipation of death is often the source of our deepest suffering.

To grasp the implications of suffering for spirituality within the Christian tradition, one must consider some specific characteristics of Christian spirituality, and also some of its particular difficulties. In the history of Christianity many spiritualities have developed over the centuries. Most of them have emphasized one of two traits: the ascetic or the mystic. All Christian spiritualities also contend with the historical dualism of body and soul. It is my contention that a spirituality that appropriates the experience of suffering can avoid the either/or of asceticism and mysticism and the dualism of body and soul.

Suffering and Modes of Knowing

Christian spiritualities have been characterized by an active mode, often perceived as ascetical, and a more receptive mode, often considered as contemplative. In the active mode there is an intrusion of the individual as an agent in the making of his or her existence and surroundings. The role of the individual—his or her choices, actions, ethical stances—is emphasized. Agency describes an ordering, a manipulating; it is concerned with accomplishment, progress, and self-development. It is strongly individual, autonomous, isolated, and controllingly single-minded. There is a tendency to repress, even deny, feeling and impulse.

In the receptive, mystical, contemplative mode, there is a yielding, a responding, a surrendering of self to God's action. Emphasis is on communion and contemplation. In contemplation one finds an otherness that compels and allows one to a becoming without the ascetical, conquering, and objectifying mode. Communion is relationship-making; it establishes and cements bonds. In the active mode, the ascetical intends to transform the world; the mystical accepts the world. The ascetical seeks to be an instrument of God; the mystic, to become a vessel of God. The former seeks control; the latter favors acceptance.

Both of these modes have pitfalls as well as advantages. The mode of acceptance may foster an unreasonable and unrealistic degree of perceived self-knowledge; it may bring about a tendency to shrink from the demands of the active making of oneself. The active mode tends toward opposite faults: pride, irritability, despair. Both self-congratulation and self-denigration are real possibilities of the active mode. Asceticism may come to be enjoyed for its own sake. A certain harshness toward the human fallibility of self and others may develop. Depression is never far removed. Again the active mode can lead to the illusion that one's salvation is of one's own making. Accepting human finitude becomes difficult; powerlessness becomes unacceptable.

Traditional binary division of the spiritual life into action and contemplation or work and prayer adumbrate a more fundamental polarity between activity and passivity. In suffering, we meet a third dimension wherein passivity meets and merges with its active opposite. Suffering affords a dialectical approach to activity and passivity: not one or the other but both. Suffering involves an epistemology that has the potential to eliminate the either/or of activity and passivity.[13] Suffering offers us an epistemology aimed to help us focus our attention on what should govern our knowing and doing.

According to Schillebeeckx, "Human suffering has a particular critical and productive epistemological force."[14] Human knowledge and knowing, while complex, have been categorized as contemplative and practical. These two dimensions of knowing are related to the various facets of nature: nature as a given to be contemplated, enjoyed ("Consider the lilies of the field"); and nature to be changed and transformed ("Fill the earth and subdue it"). Yet there is an element of nature that is refractory both to contemplation and transformation. While nature has an increasing role to play in human history, "still, there is an impassable barrier between the two; nature retains a remnant of independence and therefore also of resistance; it refuses to be incorporated entirely into the plans of our human history."[15] Nature has two faces turned simultaneously toward humanity. This twofold aspect of nature results in two possible stances: contemplating and controlling.

The epistemological value of suffering is that it is critical of and yet links these two kinds of knowledge because it has characteristics of both. Like contemplation, suffering involves being acted upon. But we do not simply "suffer" in a purely passive way; we are also impelled to struggle with it actively. And yet by nature suffering is resistant both to contemplation and to transformation. Here Schillebeeckx speaks about contrast experience. "Contrast experience…especially in recollection of man's/woman's actual history of accumulated suffering, has a critical cognitive value of its own, which is not reducible to a purposive technology or to the diverse forms of contemplative, aesthetic and ludic 'goal-less' knowledge."[16] Suffering's peculiar cognitive value is critical of both. "It is critical vis-à-vis a purely contemplative total perception and every theoretical, unitary system because they have already accomplished universal reconciliation; but it is critical too vis-à-vis the world-manipulating knowledge of science and technology insofar as they postulate man/woman only as the controlling subject and pass over the ethical priority to which the suffering among us have a right."[17]

In its power to both criticize and bind the two forms of knowledge—contemplative and controlling—suffering is "a critical epistemological force which leads to new action, which anticipates a better future and seeks to put it into practice."[18] The contrast experience of suffering is possible only on the basis of an implicit longing for happiness, and unjust suffering at least presupposes a vague awareness of the possible significance of human integrity. "In that sense activity designed to overcome suffering is only possible by virtue of an at least implicit or confused anticipation of a possible universal meaning yet to come."[19]

For Schillebeeckx it is not possible to approach the question of salvation that lies at the core of the Christian message without attending to the experience of suffering. As he writes,

"Well-being" is a concept which…is brought to life and made intelligible only through contrasted negative experiences, conjoined with at least sporadic experiences of what "makes sense"— whence there arises in hope an anticipation of "total sense" or "haleness," being whole.[20]

Thus, humanity cannot know what it means to be saved without the experience of suffering and the memory of the history of all human suffering. For the desire to be saved

presupposes an implicit craving for happiness, a craving for well-being or "making whole"…a vague consciousness of what in a positive sense human integrity or wholeness should entail,…an awareness of a positive call of and to the *humanum*…a positive, if so far unarticulated, feeling for value, at the same time releasing it and compelling its expression in the conscience, which begins to protest.[21]

The refractory dimension of suffering and therefore of reality frustrates every attempt by human reason to control or manipulate it. Reality resists human reason, but as such—that is, in its resistance—it is also revelatory, since as such it "constantly directs our planning and reflection like a hidden magnet" moving us to "an ever-wider searching."[22] Thus suffering becomes the foundation of the revelation of "a transcendent power, something that comes from elsewhere."[23] Many of the deepest insights into human nature, revelatory insights, come in moments of suffering when the reality of the present contradicts the fundamental trust undergirding one's existence. Such experience of suffering reveals the fragility of our own humanness and our inability to bring about our own salvation. Such contrast experiences subvert any uncritical trust in the current state of things. They urge us forward to struggle for a world of greater justice. They inculcate within us a "critical negativity," a constant questioning toward everything that promised to be the fulfillment hoped for. In the overcoming of suffering our knowledge of God grows.

What God is must emerge from our unrestrained involvement with [one another], and through building up liberating structures without which human salvation proves impossible.[24]

Such involvement remains the test of our affirmations about God:

through and in the way in which persons live, they themselves really confirm the nature of God where (whether or not they have a religious motivation) they further good and fight evil and suffering.[25]

A genuine spirituality demands honesty about the real—no denial of the truth of reality. Such honesty demands an adequate knowledge of reality. Spirituality must begin with an act of profound honesty about the real, the recognition of things as they actually are. There is a manner of knowing that is shaped out of a concern to defend oneself against the real. Simone Weil saw with clarity that the sufferer often has a more accurate cognitive view of reality.[26] Apart from honesty with the real, things lose their revelatory, sacramental character, and our image of God becomes distorted, for God is no longer revealed in reality. Violence is done to reality. In the face of life, a Christian spirituality challenges one to live in the as-it-is, without illusions. A spiritual existence takes place in the midst of the questions and temptations, the doubt and near-despair that daily experiences bring about.

Since spirituality is in the process of becoming a person, the one reality that is most important is the reality of our own selves. Spirituality makes self-identity a central concern. Spirituality assumes that action flows from the specific identity of the person, the constellation of habits, commitments, and emotions that we call "character." Spiritual writers and psychologists have used the term "false self" to suggest how untruthful our self-image can be when aspects of the self are denied. When the self overidentifies with external goods like success, power, and pleasure, it is bound to be inauthentic.

What is most important about the experience of suffering is that it leads one to the acceptance of self as limited and the other as other. It leads to the fundamental acceptance of interdependence of the for-otherness and from-otherness of personal existence. We do not experience directly the radical dimension of our finitude. What we experience directly are particular expressions of our finitude, such as suffering, the death of someone else, the other's needs, and our needs of them. We only become more aware of the radical dimension of limitedness after reflection upon these particular events. There is a movement from the particular to the universal, from the concrete to the more abstract; from the immediate and specific experience, the individual person universalizes about his or her total situation. As Simone Weil writes, unless constrained by experiences, it is impossible to believe that everything in the soul, all its thoughts and feelings, its every attitude towards ideas, people, and the universe, and above all, the most intimate attitude of the being towards itself, that all this is entirely at the mercy of circumstances."[27]

Suffering and the Dualism of Body and Soul

The kind of understanding suffering brings about, one that encompasses both active and passive, mitigates the problems accompanying a one-sided active or passive spirituality. Suffering also helps Christian spirituality come to terms with a never-ending temptation to dualism, where body is contrasted to spirit. Whatever is spiritual and not of the flesh is higher than what is bodily and sensuous. The one is inward, the other external; the one profound, the other superficial; the one reflective, the other thoughtless. The spiritual Christian tradition is marked by a conflict between "spirit" and "flesh"; by a dualism of body and soul. Western spirituality has been characterized by a devaluation of the body and nature and a presence for inward self-experience as the way to God.[28] The self in need to be known is the interior self to the neglect of the social self, of the embodied self. Exclusive emphasis on the inner self can lead to the repression of the body and to nature's subjection to the dominance of man and woman; such emphasis has generated a form of individualism for which the values of the human spirit take precedence over the values of person, embodied soul.

A spirituality that involves the person, the making of the person, must include body and soul, individual and community, the inner and outer life. While it is in the ineffable regions of the soul's solitude that God is chiefly present, the external world and the internal world of the self are not separate. Whatever is spiritual or personal is also bodily. No dichotomy between the inward and the external, no antithesis that splits life into two. In the scriptures, God's spirit is the life-force of created beings and the living space in which they can grow and have their being. For as Paul proclaimed, "The body is meant for the Lord and the Lord for the body" (1 Cor 6:13). In reality there is no devaluation of the body and nature, in preference for inward direct self-experience as a way to God and to a neglect of sensuous experience of sociality and nature. Every such form of devaluation flies in the face of God's affirmation of his creation.

Suffering is a constant reminder that no dualism of body or soul is viable even in spirituality. While pain and suffering are not exactly the same—one emphasizing the physical, the other, the personal—the two cannot be separated. It is the whole person who suffers; it is the whole person who is in pain. Simone Weil writes about affliction as a suffering that is social, psychological and physical. Suffering reminds us forcefully that the external world and the interior world of the self are not separable. In suffering one can no longer perceive the person as subject and the human body as object. Walter Kasper writes,

> According to scripture the body is so vital to humanity, that a being without a body after death is unthinkable (1 Cor 15.35ff; 2 Cor 5.1ff). For the Hebrew the body is not the tomb of the soul as it is for the Greek and certainly not the principle of evil from which humanity's true self has to be set free, as it was for the Gnostics. The body is God's creation and it always describes the whole of the human and not just a part. But this whole person is not conceived as a figure enclosed in itself, as in classical Greece,

nor as a fleshy substance, as in materialism, nor as a person and personality, as in idealism. The body is the whole human in relationship to God and humanity. It is human's place of meeting with God and humanity. The body is the possibility and the reality of communication.[29]

Spirituality, Suffering, and Meaning

Suffering as we have presented it is not something incidental or external to the becoming of a person, to the spiritual journey. Suffering enters into the very texture of one's spiritual journey. As necessary as suffering is in a persona existence, it is always a negative that cannot so easily be transformed into a positive. No one can pretend to have ultimate answers to the *why* of suffering. There is a question of intractability about suffering. The real anguish of suffering is found in its perceived meaninglessness. More than 2,500 years ago, Job stood under the cause of meaninglessness. He could not find a reason or a purpose for his suffering. A particularly painful expression of the meaninglessness of suffering is the suffering of children. Humanity calls out for its elimination. There is so much innocent and meaningless suffering that no easy interpretation is possible. History presents itself to us as a mixture of meaning and meaninglessness, of sorrow and happiness. Such a mixture raises the question whether, in the last resort, we can trust life at all.

According to Clifford Geertz, meaning-making is the central function of a culture, because "culture can be viewed as the structure of meaning through which men give shape to their experience."[30] He also understands religion as a cultural system. Religion is a "system of symbols which acts to establish powerful, pervasive, and long-lasting moods, and motivations in men by formulating conceptions or a central order of existence and clothing these conceptions with such an aura of factuality that the moods and motivations seem uniquely realistic."[31] Inspired by Geertz's definition, George A. Lindbeck, in his suggestive book, *The Nature of Doctrine,* describes religion in the following way: "Religions are seen as comprehensive interpretive schemes, usually embodied in myths or narratives and heavily ritualized, which structure human experience and understanding of the self and the world."[32] Central to religion's function is the question of meaning, of ultimate meaning, and the greatest threat to religion is that of meaninglessness. It is therefore not surprising that the common address to suffering has been religious. All religious traditions have attempted to address the fact of suffering, and most religious traditions are rooted in the belief and fundamental trust that life is good and meaningful despite the suffering it entails. Religion must constantly ask: Does life have some central meaning despite the suffering and the succession of frustrations and tragedies it brings? For Geertz, the condition of suffering is "an experiential challenge in whose face the meaninglessness of a particular pattern of life threatens to dissolve into a chaos of thingless names and nameless things."[33] He then affirms,

> As a religious problem, the problem of suffering is, paradoxically, not how to avoid suffering but how to suffer, how to make physical pain, personal loss, worldly defeat, or the helpless contemplation of others' agony something bearable, unsupportable— something, as we say, sufferable.[34]

To ask the question about meaning in a situation of suffering and in the context of a religious tradition is to pose the theodicy issue. It is to ask a question about the character of God. Theology, to be adequate, must concern itself with the theodicy issue. Since spirituality has to do with the making of the person, its formal issue relative to suffering has to be that of meaning. To repress the question about meaning could easily lead to an apathetic or even fatalistic attitude toward life itself. Suffering has often been understood as a great teacher, as a source of wisdom and maturity. But there are limits to perceiving suffering as a fundamental cause for the promotion of human maturation. Yet all forms of spirituality need to be grounded in a refusal to ignore suffering. In the search for a spiritual style appropriate to the American cultural setting, a spirituality that does not ignore suffering will inevitably be countercultural.

The Christian spiritual tradition offers many examples of suffering that has been given meaning. For Christianity, Christ is the way, the model. This is affirmed with great emphasis in Paul's Letter to the Philippians and the Letter to the Hebrews.

Throughout Judeo-Christian history, theologians, mystics, and ascetics have been led and have led others to accept suffering as a positive reality. This acceptance is in itself a profound mystery, for such acceptance is believed to be transformative. To suffer with Christ, the claim is made, transforms mere suffering into renewed trust in God and openness to the life-giving spirit. Yet the willingness to accept suffering as a means to perfect one's total personality is a hard doctrine for technological man or woman to follow. That pain, suffering disposes for personal transformation goes against the optimism of a technological culture. Americans consciously regard the technological culture. Americans consciously regard the technological problem-solving culture as liberating and life-enhancing.

Despite important distinction in meanings, *pain* and *suffering* are often treated as synonyms. Similarly, *suffering* and *evil* are often used interchangeably. Such synonyms and use imply that suffering is always negative in value, an experience that inescapably diminishes human existence. But is suffering all bad? Is it always a net loss, or can it sometimes be the occasion for real growth? Can suffering actually enhance human life, the spiritual life? Consider the classics of world literature. Many of them are inconceivable apart from the saga of human suffering. We even say that a work of art lacking in tragic dimension is shallow. Yet something in us recoils from affirming that "suffering is good for us." There is much too much suffering in the world that can in no way be of any value for anyone. Our issue here is the role that suffering can have in spiritual growth, development, and transformation. Can suffering be the occasion for real growth? The word occasion here is important.

Spiritual writers and psychologists have used the term "false self" to suggest how illusory our self-image can be when aspects of the self are denied and repressed. This journey in self-knowing requires going deeper into ourselves, images of journey rather than ascent seem more descriptive of this aspect of the spiritual journey. Thus terms such as "going deeper!" "soul-searching," and "uncovering" more closely capture what the spirit involves. No self-image can at any time express fully the reality of the self; one can always be more. A limited self-image can easily stifle growth. A spiritual existence cannot be content with superficial consciousness, with the illusion of control. The experience of suffering motivates us to serious self-searching. Suffering can serve as a gateway to further growth by nudging us into places we would otherwise not go. Suffering forces the self to pay attention and be the source of a revelatory experience.

In suffering, I am most totally alone. My suffering is exclusively mine: it bears my name as no other experience does, because it seems to insulate me from others. This painful isolation gives access to the bottom depth of selfhood—the locus of transcendence—that can remain unsuspectingly hidden to the untroubled mind. Suffering makes us aware of the self's hidden depth and of its insufficiency. Suffering can bring about a desert experience.

The Desert Period was the time of Israel's encounter with Yahweh. This theme runs through many writings that exist quite independently of one another. This was something deeply rooted in the settled and basic tradition about the origins of Israel's relation to God. The desert experience is of fundamental importance in understanding Israel's perception of God: It was in the desert that God revealed himself to Moses. It was in the desert that the people of Israel experienced the care and guidance of God. "God sustained him in a desert land in a howling wilderness waste; God shielded him as the apple of God's eye" (O.T. 32.10).

Israel sought help in the wilderness, for it was the dwelling place of demons, of poisonous serpents, of the hostile forces of darkness. It is in the midst of trial and temptation that God is made known as Healer. The Desert Period was a time of struggle; for Israel it is represented as one of hardship and suffering. In the Passion narratives, especially in the narratives of Gethsemane,

Jesus' own solitude is emphasized. On the cross, Jesus is alone. Suffering attendant upon total isolation of the self was known to much earlier ascetical writers.

In mystical writings the night is normally a time of reduced sensory input, of sensory deprivation, leaving the self more or less to itself, isolated. Solitude does not mean solipsism, a turning upon oneself, a flight inward for refuge. The solitude and isolation brought about by suffering leads to acceptance, to a transformative acceptance: "Not my will but yours."

Unlike his pious friends who try to divert him through dogmatic compensation and consolation, Job fixes his attention on the reality of his affliction and refuses to divert his eyes until he discovers God there. Because of this attentiveness, an attentiveness only possible because Job continues to love God in the midst of his affliction, God reveals to Job his own "true reality" and "the beauty of the world."

To reject one's suffering marks the beginning of the loss of selfhood. The making of the self depends upon the self's courage to face fully the negativity of suffering. When fully faced and accepted, suffering can be incorporated into the creativity of the self. Acceptance can be the most difficult, and at the same time most important element of one's spiritual existence. Acceptance is in no way an issue of "rejoicing" in one's suffering nor one of "offering up" one's suffering. Nor does acceptance resolve the problem of theodicy. Acceptance does not eliminate the negativity of suffering and/or transform it into a positive reality. Acceptance cannot simply be defined as endurance. The willingness to accept suffering does not diminish its harsh reality. "Every acceptance of suffering," writes Dorothy Soelle, "is an acceptance of that which exists. The denial of every form of suffering can result in a flight from reality."[35]

Jesus' prayer in the Garden of Gethsemane shows us a way to move from the realm of meaningless suffering to creative suffering. Acceptance of suffering is acceptance of mystery; acceptance of mystery is crucial to any spiritual existence.[36] In the same way there is no logical answer to suffering, there is no logical answer to mystery. Mystery must be accepted in faith. It is in this acceptance that we are set on the road to meaning. In the following psalm, note the acceptance of suffering and the acceptance of mystery:

> Hasten to answer me, O Lord,
> For my spirit fails me.
> Hide not your face from me
> Lest I become like those who go
> Down to the pit.
> At dawn let me hear of your kindness,
> For in you I trust.
> Show me the way in which I should walk,
> For to you I lift up my soul.

Rescue me from my enemies, O Lord,
For in you I hope. (Ps 143:7–9)

When Job listened to God in abandonment and solitude, Job saw his place in the mystery of things.

I know that you can do all things,
And that no purpose of yours can be hindered.

I have dealt with things that I do not understand;
Things too wonderful for me, which I cannot know.

I had heard of you by word of mouth,
But now my eye has seen you.
Therefore I disown what I have said,
And repent in dust and ashes. (Jb 42:2–6)

Conclusion

Acceptance is an attunement of tonality of our spiritual consciousness. In its journey of transcending, the person must finally arrive at the fundamental conclusion that God alone is God and that what counts ultimately is love of God. When everything goes, God alone remains: nothing is God but God. From early on, Christians have been made aware that there can be no suffering that separates us from the love of God (Rom 8:38–39).

Simone Weil was familiar with the consequences of affliction: God appears to be absent. Here is her advice:

The soul has to go on loving in the emptiness, or at least to go on wanting to love, though it may only be with an infinitesimal part of itself. Then one day God will come to show himself to this soul and to reveal the beauty of the world to it, as in the case of Job.[37]

In this passage Simone is describing what is the main task of a spiritual journey: to go on loving in darkness and emptiness. Loving is the fulfillment of personhood. Spirituality is the fullness of personhood, and suffering the cost of both.

Notes

1. On the meaning of spirituality, the following article are useful: Sandra Schneiders, "A Hermeneutical Approach to the Study of Christian Spirituality," *Christian Spirituality Bulletin* 2, 1 (1994): 9–14; Walter H. Principe, "Toward Defining Spirituality," *Studies in Religion/Sciences Religieuses* 12

(1983): 139ff.; Jon Sobrino, *Spirituality of Liberation: Toward Political Holiness* (Maryknoll, N.Y.: Orbis, 1988), 13–45.

2. Cf. Jurgen Moltmann, *The Source of Life: The Holy Spirit and the Theology of Life* (Philadelphia: Fortress, 1997).

3. Ibid., 19–22.

4. For a concept of person adequate to spirituality, cf. John MacMurray, *The Form of the Personal,* vol. 1: *The Self as Agent* (London: Faber, 1957); *The Form of the Personal,* vol. 2: *Persons in Relation* (London: Faber, 1961).

5. G. W. F. Hegel, *Lectures on the Philosophy of Religion*, vol. 3 (London: Routledge and Kegan Paul, 1962), 24–25.

6. Cf. Karl Rahner, *The Love of Jesus and the Love of Neighbor* (New York: Crossroad, 1983).

7. H. Richard Niebuhr, *The Responsible Self* (New York: Harper and Row, 1963), 32.

8. On suffering as affliction, cf. Simone Weil, "The Love of God and Affliction," in *The Simone Weil Reader* (New York: David McKay, 1977), 439–68.

9. On society and suffering, cf. "Social Suffering," *Daedalus* (Winter 1996).

10. On tragic suffering, cf. M. DeUnanumo, *Tragic Sense of Life,* trans. T. E. Crawford Flitch (New York: Dover, 1954), 207.

11. N. Berdaev, *Freedom and Spirit* (New York: Charles Scribner's Sons, 1933) 31–33.

12. Daniel Day Williams, *The Spirit and Form of Love* (New York: Harper and Row, 1968).

13. Cf. Mary M. Solberg, *Compelling Knowledge: A Feminist Proposal for an Epistemology of the Cross* (New York: State University of New York Press, 1997).

14. Edward Schillebeeckx, *Christ: The Experience of Jesus as Lord* (New York: Crossroad, 1980), 81.

15. Ibid., 530.

16. Edward Schillebeeckx, *Jesus: An Experiment in Christology* (New York: Crossroad, 1978), 621.

17. Ibid.

18. Ibid.

19. Ibid.

20. Ibid., 24.

21. Ibid.

22. Schillebeeckx, *Christ*, 35–36.

23. Ibid., 60.

24. Ibid.

25. Ibid.

26. Cf. Weil, "God and Affliction."

27. Ibid., 187.

28. Cf. Peter Brown, *The Body and Society* (New York: Columbia University Press, 1988).

29. Walter Kasper, *Jesus the Christ* (New York: Paulist Press, 1976), 150.

30. Clifford Geertz, *The Interpretation of Cultures* (New York: Basic Books, 1973), 312.

31. Ibid., 90.

32. George A. Lindbeck, *The Nature of Doctrine* (Philadelphia: Westminster Press, 1984), 32.

33. Geertz, *Interpretation of Cultures,* 12.

34. Ibid., 13.

35. Dorothy Soelle, *Suffering* (Philadelphia: Fortress, 1975), 88.

36. Ibid.

37. Weil, "God and Affliction," 442.

Dermot A. Lane

6. Death, the Self, Memory, and Hope

The purpose of this essay is to address the much-neglected question of death, a subject suppressed in much contemporary cultural and theological debate in spite of its omnipresence and inevitability for everyone. The question of death provokes immediate questions: Who am I? Where am I going? What is my destiny? Such questions are anthropological in character. The nature of the human self is increasingly to the fore, with a wide acknowledgment within philosophy, psychology, and theology that the modern self is in a state of crisis. Questions about human identity of necessity involve some reference to memory. Memory is a central category in understanding the human self and the historical constitution of the self. In approaching the question of death via anthropology and the invocation of memory, one finds oneself coming very close to some of the basic ingredients of a theology of hope.

The thesis of this essay is that important and profound links exist between death, the self, memory, and hope. The only appropriate response to the experience of death is hope, and the way beyond death to the act of hope is via a renewed anthropology and a rehabilitation of the power of memory.

Of course there are equally other valid approaches to death, such as an examination of near-death experiences or an exploration of the links that exist between death and environmental destruction or an analysis of the ever-increasing fascination in the West with the doctrine of reincarnation from the East. I believe, however, that these other approaches will of necessity raise issues related to anthropology, memory, and hope.

The essay has four parts. In the first part, we deal with the contemporary experience of death and the questions that it raises. The second part addresses our changing understanding of the human self. The third looks at the role of memory in understanding who we are, and the fourth concludes with some reflections on the possibility of hope in the face of death and what kind of content might be attached to Christian hope.

Death

The latter half of the twentieth century saw dramatic changes in the way we experience and understand the phenomenon of death. Some of these changes have been positive and have brought many benefits to the way we die. The advances of modern science and technology, especially in their application to medicine, have increased the longevity of life and given humanity greater control over death. What was once regarded as "an act of God" coming from the outside is now more often than not seen as "an act of man" coming from the inside.

On the other hand, this changing sociology of death has brought with it a series of new questions about the meaning of both life and death. Not all of these changes can be described as life enhancing. For example, the removal of death from the home to the hospital has brought its own pastoral difficulties, and the relocation of the dying from the community into institutions has often deprived people of the privilege of participating in the death of loved ones.

It is difficult to balance the pros and cons of these shifts in our modern experience of death. Perhaps we are still too close to the changes, caught as it were between the moving moods of modernity and postmodernity, to evaluate them objectively. Nevertheless there are growing concerns that must be expressed in relation to the question of death at the beginning of the third millennium. Do we know more or less about the phenomenon of death? Does this knowledge enable us to deal more humanely with the death of others and to face with some confidence our own death? Is death a matter of conscious concern in the public domain? Is our understanding of death something that affects our understanding of living?

It is fairly evident within these changes that death was one of the great taboo subjects at the end of the twentieth century. In contrast to the nineteenth century, there is very little public discussion about death and when death is addressed it is usually done so in rather hushed tones. Further, the changes introduced in the past fifty years have resulted in a privatization of death. In many instances there has been what might be called a "depersonalization" of death. For instance, the scientific advances of modern medicine have increasingly encroached upon the last days and hours before death, when a personal and familial engagement with death would be more in keeping with the dignity of the individual. A conspiracy of silence seems to surround the subject of death. Modern culture, with its emphasis on self-fulfillment, self-realization, and self-reliance, contrives to deny the reality of death as omnipresent. A culture that denies death is out of touch with reality, and this loss of contact with death has implications for the way we see life. A death-denying culture has life-denying consequences.

Many would hold today that the spirit of Epicurus, in spite of himself, has come back to haunt the new twenty-first century with his icy claim: "If I am alive, I am not dead. If I am dead, I am not alive. Why should I think about death while I am still alive. It only spoils my pleasure in living and gets in the way of my work."

Any discussion of death must make reference to two important authors of the early 1970s who addressed the question of death head on. Elizabeth Kübler-Ross published a best-selling book titled *On Death and Dying,* in which she outlined five stages that people go through when faced with death: the denial of death, anger at the prospect of death, bargaining about death with one's family, doctor, and God, the onset of depression about death, and finally the acceptance of death.[1]

Perhaps even more significant in the early 1970s was a publication by Ernest Becker entitled *The Denial of Death* (1973), which received the 1974 Pulitzer Prize for general nonfiction. Becker's book on death and his other publications are complex and not easily summarized. He holds that anxiety about death occupies a central place in the human heart and influences more than we realize the way we organize life. He suggests that "fear of death must be present behind all our normal functioning in order for the organism to be armed towards self-preservation. But the fear of death cannot be present constantly in one's mental functioning, else the organism could not function."[2] In spite of the fact that anxiety about death is repressed, it does nonetheless unconsciously drive many human activities, including the frenzied will to gain power and to accumulate material possessions as coping mechanisms. The response to Becker's work was mixed. Some argued that the untestable is untenable. However, recent interdisciplinary studies show that "there now is strong, sophisticated, empirical scientific evidence that substantiates Becker's basic insight."[3] These two texts continue to be important in any discussion about death, especially Kübler-Ross's elaboration of the five stages that people go through in the face of death and Becker's thesis about the existence of an underlying anxiety about death that influences so much human activity.

Against the background of these two books it is instructive to note the emergence in the 1990s, on the eve of the millennium, of a new body of reflective literature on death. This literature has considerable authority behind it because of its origins. Some of it comes from those who are dealing directly with death on a daily basis within the hospice movement. Other parts of it come from those who have the courage and generosity to write about their own death in the face of terminal illness.

Coming from the hospice movement is the book *Mortally Wounded: Stories of Soul Pain, Death and Healing* by Michael Kearney, a consultant in palliative medicine at Our Lady's Hospice and St. Vincent's Hospital, Dublin, Ireland. Kearney is concerned to enable people who are terminally ill to address not just body pain but the far more troubling reality of soul pain. He presents a series of case histories in which he tries to bring his patients on a journey. This personal journey is from the outer surface of life to the inner depths of the human psyche, to move from the purely medical to the psychological, from the physical to the spiritual, from the personal to the mythological. The purpose of this journey is "to enable the person to find his or her own way through the prison of soul to a place of greater wholeness, a new depth of living and a falling away from fear."[4] Kearney recognizes the "danger of getting lost in this place (of soul pain), of being devoured by its monsters, being possessed by its energies, in short of entering the depths all right, but then failing to make the return part of the journey."[5] To make this journey he employs different techniques for different case histories: body work, image work, music therapy, massage, and dream work. Toward the end of his book he notes that many who are terminally ill find it difficult to make this journey and that often it can be too late in life when faced immediately with the prospect of death. For those who work with the terminally ill and indeed those who are interested in the question of death, it is desirable to have made this journey before the onset of terminal illness. The best way to understand death is to make this personal journey before illness takes over.

A similar work has been written by Marie de Hennezel, who gives an account of her work in a palliative care unit in Paris extending over a period of seven years in a book entitled *Intimate Death: How the Dying Teach Us to Live*. The opening lines of this book are instructional: "We hide death as if it were shameful and dirty. We see in it the horror, meaningless, useless struggle and suffering, an intolerable scandal, whereas it is our life's culmination, its crowning moment, and what gives it both sense and worth."[6] Her intent, amply illustrated throughout the book with case histories, is to show that "when death comes so close, and sadness and suffering rule, there is still room for life, and joy, and surges of feeling deeper and more intense than anything known before."[7] The stories that de Hennezel represents illustrate most poignantly the underlying truth that time spent with people before their death can be enriching and transforming for both the ill and the living. In brief, for de Hennezel, death is "a splinter lodged in the heart of our humanity."[8] Attention to that splinter in the lives of those we love exposes us to our own vulnerable humanity in a way that has potential for all concerned to live life more fully.

The overall impact of these books is that there can be life after the announcement of terminal illness, that the discovery of this new kind of life requires an inner journey, somewhat akin to a "rite of passage," and that once the journey is made, usually life and death become united in a way that is liberating and enriching for both. For this to happen, however, it is imperative to go beyond the contemporary denial of death and to begin to reunite our understanding of living and dying. The making of this journey, the painful experience of passing over and coming back, awakens new levels of human awareness, personal freedom, and self-transcendence. The experience of the nearness of death can cause a human being to arrive at new levels of self-discovery.[9]

The number of people who reflect self-consciously on death in the face of its immediacy is increasing, and here we can only select two samples for comment.[10] One of the many visitors to the hospital in which Marie de Hennezel worked was François Mitterrand, the former president of France, who wrote what can only be described as an extraordinary foreword to her book just months before his own death. In that short foreword, Mitterrand comments, "Never perhaps have our relations with death been so barren as they are in this modern spiritual desert."[11] Mitterrand asks, Are there not some fragments of eternity in humankind, something that death brings to the world, gives birth to?[12] Almost by way of protest Mitterrand concludes that he does not "believe that we can just be reduced to some bundle of atoms. Whatever tells us that there is something beyond matter—call it soul, or spirit, or consciousness, whatever you prefer—I believe in the immortality of *that.*"[13]

An equally striking account of the meaning of life in the immediacy of death is given by Gillian Ross, former professor of philosophy at the University of Warwick, England. Ross, diagnosed as having ovarian cancer, kept a diary right up to her death; it was subsequently published as *Love's Work* (1995). This diary covers a wide range of subjects including sickness, mortality, and death. In her diary she confronts explicitly her advanced ovarian cancer and in doing says, "I seek to convey the impasses, the limitations and cruelties, equally, of alternative healing and of conventional medicine."[14] Concerning conventional medicine, she points out that "surgeons are not qualified for the one thing with which they deal: life. For they do not understand, as part of their profession, 'death' in the non medical sense, nor therefore 'life' in a meaningful sense, inclusive of death."[15] She is equally critical of "the screwtape spirituality of alternative healing"[16] that is made up of "poor psychology, worse theology and no notion of justice at all."[17] This strange spirituality requires that you "dissolve the difficulty of living, of love, of self and of other, of the other in the self."[18] Whereas the issue to be faced is "that to live, to love, is to be failed, to forgive, to have failed, to be forgiven for ever and ever."[19] And so she concludes in the face of death, "If I am to stay alive, I am bound to continue to get love wrong, all the time, but not to cease wooing, for that is my life affair, *love's work.*"[20]

One final example of a very honest and public attempt to address the question of death can be found in John Updike's multilayered novel, *Towards the End of Time.* This is a novel that allows of different readings, but ultimately it is about "an unfocused dread of time."[21] The story is about a man, Ben Turnbull, suffering from prostate cancer at the age of sixty-five and now moving toward death. The location is Boston, Massachusetts, the year is A.D.

2020 in the wake of a nuclear war between China and the United States, and the subtext is the irreversibility of time.

All the big existential questions about meaning, purpose, and destiny are present: What gives edge to this novel is that Updike situates the angst of existence within the larger context of the "big bang" and "big crunch" cosmologies: "But why did nothingness ever leave home, as it were? What placed the stars in the galaxies, the quasars and black holes and oceans of neutrinos out there? Whence this inordinate amount of sparkling dust?"[22] The issues, however, are not just cosmic or metaphysical; they are also deeply personal: "What doesn't fade into the void?...Some day I will be as forgotten, as dissolved back into compacted silt, as your typical grunting, lusting, hungry Neanderthal man. I cannot simply believe it. And that is simply stupid of me."[23] And yet, even after the diagnosis of cancer he muses, "What bliss life is, imagined from the standpoint of a stone or a cubic yard of black water in icy ocean depths? Even there, apparently, conglomerated molecules manage to light a tiny candle of consciousness. The universe hates death, can it be?...Alive. A pitiable but delicious reprieve from timelessness."[24]

This new body of literature on death is prophetic in its critique of the way death is dealt with in modern culture. It shatters the silence surrounding death and brings the issues out into the open. This new literature speaks on behalf of all, articulating unspoken fears and questions that will not go away or lie down, questions about the darkness and disintegration that accompanies every human death.

But there is another question lurking around in all five examples, and that is the question of the human self. Who am I in the face of death, and what is my destiny? These are deeply human questions, questions about the nature, character, and identity of the human, which every discussion about death must sooner or later address.

The Self

The foundational issue underlying most discussions about death is about the meaning of the *humanum:* the question of death is ultimately a question about how we understand the human person. What does it mean to be a human being at the beginning of the third millennium? What is the nature of human identity? Does the self survive death, and if so what is it that does survive—human consciousness, the soul, the spirit, the self, an embodied person? The way we answer these questions will influence enormously the way we address issues relating to death and destiny.

When we examine these complex questions about the human self we discover a wide range of discussion taking place in philosophy, psychology, cosmology, and theology. Much of this discussion suggests that our contemporary

understanding of the self is in crisis and therefore under review. Many commentators are of the view that we need to recast, reposition, and redescribe our
understanding of the self today.[25] This review of the self should be done in the
light of critiques coming from feminism, ecology, and cosmology. Most of these
critiques arise out of a dissatisfaction with the specifically modern understanding of the human self. Within this discussion it is possible to charter a movement
from the modern self through the postmodern self to a narrative account of self.[26]

The modern self is perceived as too individualistic, too independent, and
too autonomous. This understanding of the modern self is seen in large part as
the legacy of Descartes. Such a self is painted as self-sufficient, self-grounded,
and therefore self-enclosed. The Irish philosopher, Joe Dunne, sums up quite
accurately this understanding of the modern self in the following way: "No
one else can be in a relationship with me of a kind that would enable her or him
to interpret for me where my interests or 'good' might lie; nor can any prior
relationship in which I stand have any constitutive role in shaping what my
preferences will be."[27] The modern self is so independent it has no need of
others and so decides for itself and by itself whether it will interact and relate
with other human selves.

In contrast to this modern self and by way of reaction to it, there has
emerged what may be loosely designated the postmodern self. This term
"the postmodern self" is itself rather slippery and of its nature is intended to
be free-floating and lacking in content. In its extreme form the postmodern
self has abandoned all meta-narratives and become engulfed by particular
surrounding contexts. Human subjectivity is to a large extent abolished.
This new self is decentered from the modern throne of sovereignty and displaced from the position of independence that it held in the modern era; it is
now tossed about by the play of language, different social practices, ever-
expanding information technologies, and the reigning culture of uncontrolled capitalism. There is no longer any center of human experience or
human agency.

These two extremes, however, do contain grains of truth that cannot be
altogether dismissed. On the one hand there is a deep drive within every
human self to affirm and assert some form of personal individuality. It is difficult, indeed undesirable, to eliminate all sense of self-identity. On the other
hand it is equally important to acknowledge that there is a strong need within
every self to be in relationship with others and to be connected. In seeking to
reconstruct the human self it is essential to keep these two primal needs
together in a creative tension. To this end it seems possible to begin to talk
about "the self-as-social" or "the self-in-community" or the self as individual
and relational. The best way of achieving this balance seems to be available in
what Paul Ricoeur has called a "narrative form of the human identity" or Joe
Dunne refers to as the "storied self."

The human self is historical from beginning to end; the self exists as a story; the self requires a narrative to account for its experience, activities, and relationships. The value of a narrative account of the self is that it is able to integrate continuity within changes while maintaining an awareness of some form of personal individuation alongside relationality. A sense of "I" is not pre-given but rather something that develops out of a web of human relationship with significant others, the environment and God. This development of the "self-in-community" or the "person-in-relation" is something that occurs in time and is only available in narrative form. Important elements within the narrative include the range of human experiences the self has and actions undertaken by the self.

Relationality is at the center of every narrative account of self-identity. The self is constituted by a series of relationships with other selves, the earth, and ultimately God. The self is relational, and this emphasis stands out in contrast to the ironclad individualism of the modern self. All the evidence coming from the postmodern natural sciences, and in particular from the new cosmic stories about origins, indicates that we live in a world that is interconnected, interrelated, and interdependent. Awareness of this interdependence is increasingly apparent in the mutuality of relationships that exist between higher forms of life and lower forms of life. This relationality that we find throughout the universe is intensified in the relationality of the individual self. The relational self is matter personified in an exquisite state of self-conscious freedom and reflection.

The question must be asked at this stage: What is the source of the relationality of the human self? Where does this extraordinary capacity of the self to be in relationship come from? Is it the accidental outcome of a particular configuration of "cosmic soup" and chemical compounds? There is a view that suggests that the individual is simply a spark in the spiral of evolution, an accidental twig on a tree as it were, a source merely for replenishing the pool of genes in the world. It is this kind of possibility that haunts the troubled spirit of Ben Turnbull in John Updike's novel *Towards the End of Time*. And yet it is difficult to see how experiences of enduring self-consciousness and human agency, of personal freedom and the exercise of responsibility, of selfless love in the face of the needs of the other, and the vitality that comes out of trusting relationships can all be reduced to a particular chemical or genetic configuration. To be sure these experiences exist only as embodied in the materiality of the central nervous system and the brain. To move in this direction is not to answer the question posed; but it is to point the question in a particular direction, and that direction is ultimately religious and theological.

It is in part the experiences of self-conscious freedom, human agency, personal trust, and love that enables the presence of another dimension in life to impinge upon the human self. This presence is the overpowering and fascinating mystery of life *(mysterium tremendum et fascinans)* revealed historically in the Hebrew religion and personally in the life of Jesus, the Christ. The God of Judaism is revealed as a creator God, a God who creates out of love the human, or as the Book of Genesis puts it, "The human made in the image and likeness of God." This doctrine of being created in the image of God *(imago Dei)* is central to the reconstruction of an adequate anthropology. The theological doctrine of creation is the ground and foundation of understanding the person as a relational being. This Hebrew view of the human person is further grounded in the Christian revelation of God as a trinity of relationships. The being of God is relational, and this relational character of God is communicated to every human being in the act of creation.

A number of points begin to emerge in this transition toward a theological anthropology. It is the doctrine of God as creator that establishes the individual as person. Personhood is conferred jointly, in creation and procreation, out of love by God. The human person is the outcome of the coming together of the creative love of God and the procreative love of parents. Further, the nature of personhood is radically relational because it is sourced in the triune God, who is relational, and in the procreating parents, who are in relationship.

This grounding of the person as a relational being in God is important for at least two reasons. It means that the individual cannot be reduced simply to the level of the most recent set of contingent relationships, even though these relationships do play a part in the development of the human person. Furthermore, it establishes in the light of the Christian doctrines of God as creator and triune that the human person is relational from conception onward. In brief, the person is primordially relational.

This move toward the establishment of the human person as relational is an important corrective to the self-sufficiency of the modern self. In emphasizing this relationship of the self, care must be taken not to obscure the invisible existence of personhood as present at the very beginning of life and at the end of life. The individual person is always more than his or her historical and contingent relationships. To see the self simply as a series of relations is to run the risk of forgetting what is unique and distinctive about the human self, namely personhood. It is the underlying existence of personhood that is the source of key values, such as the equality of all human beings, the dignity of every individual, and the irrepeatability of each self. Individual personhood is the gift of God's creative love, which transcends the contingency of all human relationships.

There is a double truth about personhood that the classical Christian tradition has sought to affirm in the light of christology and trinitarian theology. There is, first of all, "the relational character of personhood over and against the reduction of the person to self-consciousness" and equally there is "the integrity of the person over and against the reduction of personhood to the product of social relations."[28] The classical Christian tradition has always sought to safeguard the primacy of personhood in its understanding of the human self. The concept of person as worked out by the Cappodocian theologians of the fourth and fifth centuries "is not the product of nature: it is that in which nature exists, the very principle of its existence."[29] A similar point is made by Boethius (d. 524) in his definition of the person as "the individual substance of a relational nature." The trouble with this definition of the person within the classical tradition is that it gave rise to a static view of the person as fixed and rational. Today we perceive the person as dynamic because of its relational character from the beginning of its human existence. There is no reason why the underlying insight of the classical tradition concerning the primacy of person as rational cannot be wedded to a contemporary emphasis on the person as relational, provided the person is not reduced only to the sum of his or her relationship. The intention of the classical Christian tradition was to secure personhood as something that exists over and above the changing circumstances of existence.

A number of important consequences flow from this theological anthropology for the way we approach death. Once the person is described as relational and recognition is given to the creative love of God as a source of relationality, questions about life "after" death are transposed into questions about life "before" death. What survives in death is the love of God for the human person initiated in history and now transformed in death into eternal communion with God. The God who historically creates the person out of love and redeems the person in Christ is the same God who welcomes the person into eternal communion in death. In addition, the quality of relationships lived out in history with other human beings, relationships that transcend death such as love, compassion, and forgiveness, in brief what is often referred to as "love's labor," are also gathered up and transformed in death. St. Paul reminds us it is love that endures: the unfailing love of God initiated in the gift of personhood and the fragile love of humans for God and others.

Given this relational view of the person, it is at least reasonable to suggest that one can face death with hope, a hope that is inspired by the love of God expressed in the gift of human existence. On the other hand it is equally reasonable to understand how an anthropology based on the illusion of the self-sufficient subject would want to deny death or equally have a continual dread of death. The illusion of the independent, self-sufficient subject collapses in the face of death, whereas the relational self can face death with a hope that the God who created the self out of love and redeemed the self in Christ will continue to sustain and transform the relational self, even in death itself. However, if that response of hope is to take place, then it will have to be prompted and informed by the power of memory.

Memory

Memory is the bridge between the outline of a relational anthropology and the possibility of a theology of hope. Having opted for a narrative account of human identity as a way forward beyond the modern and postmodern self-understanding, it is now necessary to give some content to the narrative by invoking memory. Narrative arises out of the human capacity to remember. Memory is the springboard to the construction of a sustained narrative about the self because memory plays an important part in the constitution of the self. Memory is the source of human identity, and we know that when we lose our memory we lose a key ingredient in the makeup of human identity. For example, it would be difficult to understand Jewish identity without the help of memory. On the other hand it is the human capacity to remember that enables the self to have hope in the present and the future. To this extent it must be stated that memory, as well as playing an important role in the constitution of the human self, is also the ground of hope.

Memory has been neglected, ironically forgotten, in many modern and postmodern discussions about the self. Part of the reason for this is that memory is often confused with nostalgia or dismissed as sentimentality. However, the memory we are talking about here is the human capacity to re-present and make alive the past in the present. This kind of memory is far from nostalgia or sentimentality; it is the kind of memory that calls into question the present, the memory that actively interrupts the prison of the present and challenges the givenness of the status quo. Memory reminds us that the way things are is not necessarily the way things have to be in the present or the future. To this extent the memory we are talking about is often described as disturbing and "dangerous," liberating and healing.[30]

In spite of, or perhaps because of this neglect of memory, it is possible to discern a rehabilitation of memory in contemporary thought. This rehabilitation can be found in locations as diverse as Jewish studies, the contemporary retrieval of Augustine, the ecumenical movement, the philosophy of critical theory, and eucharistic theology. We will confine ourselves here to a summary of the impulses coming from Augustine and the philosophy of critical theory.

Augustine gives explicit treatment to memory in Book 10 of the *Confessions.* He invokes the role of memory in the quest for knowledge and understanding of who the self is. In searching for the self he also discovers simultaneously the mystery of God.[31]

In Book 9 of the *Confessions* Augustine asks the question, "Who am I and what manner of man *(quis ego et qualis ego)."*[32] In responding to this question he sets out on a journey through what he calls "those innumerable fields and dens and caves of my memory."[33] He extols "this power of memory" and goes on to describe it as "a thing...to be amazed at, a profound and infinite multiplicity, and this thing is the mind, and this thing am I *(et hoc animus est, et hoc ego ipse sum)*."[34] The human memory is no less and no more than the human self. In effect Augustine is identifying memory with the self because it is through the journey into memory that self becomes present to itself and finds itself. Through the power of the many-mansioned memory, the self not only discovers itself but also finds itself in the presence of God. In the journey through the lengthy layers of memory, layers "of images…things present to themselves,…and of affections of the mind," Augustine finds himself in the presence of God who was co-present from the beginning within this journey inward.[35] "And behold you were within me, and I outside and there I sought for you and in my deformity I rushed headlong into the well formed things you have made. You were with me and I was not with you."[36] It would be incorrect to interpret Augustine's interior journey through memory in the search of self and God as exclusively an interior journey. There are links between the inner and outer self in the journey through memory and its discovery of God as co-present. What is revealing here is that it is through memory that the self becomes present to itself and in that moment of self-presence the individual discovers God as co-present.

Clearly, for Augustine, memory enables the human self to have a sense of continuity within the experience of history. This sense of continuity is important because it ensures that the self does not become trapped in the present moment in the way that the postmodern self does. Equally the sense of continuity enables the modern self to overcome its isolation and independence. Close links exist for Augustine between memory, self-presence, and the co-presence of God to the self.

Moving from Augustine to the Frankfurt School of Critical Theory, we find a different appreciation of the power of memory. In a famous debate in 1937 between Walter Benjamin and Max Horkheimer, the question arose as to whether history, past history, is open or closed. For Benjamin the power of memory enables us to keep history open in the present. The suffering and injustices inflicted on the dead in the past must be remembered in the present so that they are not repeated again. In this way the past can influence the present and history can remain open. For this to happen, Benjamin invokes what he calls "empathetic memory," that is, a memory which out of solidarity with the dead victims of past history is able to influence the shape of present history. In reaction to this view, Max Horkheimer objects that the past is past and history remains closed for all time. Benjamin, it should be kept in mind, was Jewish, and even though he abandoned his religious faith, there can be little doubt that the Jewish understanding of memory remained imbedded in his thinking.[37] Benjamin's views on memory are important because they show how memory, when expressed out of empathetic solidarity with the past, can transform the present. Memory, empathetic memory, can break the vicious cycle of history in the grip of the given in the present. When this happens memory generates hope in the present for the future. What is even more significant in Benjamin's vision is that the power of memory enables the dead, especially the dead victims of history, to rise up and influence the present. Here there is no denial of death or forgetfulness about the dead, but rather a turning upside down of such forgetfulness in a way that keeps the dead alive in the present. In this way memory is the bearer of hope for the future. For Benjamin, hope is given to some on behalf of those who have no hope.

This subversive role of memory stands out as an important critique of both the modern and postmodern approaches to the human self. The modern self can be freed from its lonely isolation through the power of memory, a power that links the living with the dead in a way that frees the living from repeating past injustices and oppressions. A new unity is established between the dead and the living, between the past and the present, through the power of memory so that the modern self is no longer alone but rather part of a living past. In a similar way the memory of the dead in the present can overcome the rootlessness of the postmodern self in its exclusive entrapment in contemporary social and cultural practices.

In the words of one Jewish commentator, "Forgetfulness leads to exile, while remembrance is the secret of redemption."[38] Both the modern and postmodern self suffer from forgetfulness, cutting themselves off from the creative force of memory within history. In contrast a narrative account of human identity that invokes memory can face the future with the possibility of hope.

A further ingredient within memory is the significant link that exists between human history and cosmic history. While it is important for theology not to attach too much significance to scientific theories about Big Bang cosmologies, it must be acknowledged that contemporary cosmologies concerning human origins do establish an important unity among the cosmos, human history, and the self. The memory of this unity overcomes the disenchantment of the universe that took place in the post-Enlightenment period. Scientists remind us that human beings are cosmic dust in a state of conscious freedom, and that every human being contains within himself or herself a story that goes back some fifteen thousand million years ago. The discovery of this cosmic history highlights how we live in a universe that is weighted in the support and service of life over millions and millions of years. The cosmos, with its extraordinary order and beauty, stretching forward from the galaxies into the earth is "seeded with promise."[39] This promise has come to decisive fruition in the relatively recent advent of the human and as such seems to imply the potential for further life. Within this complex scheme of things, it must be noted that there are significant breaks and discontinuities within the lines of evolution and that this seems to suggest that whatever potential there is for the new will involve more breaks and discontinuities. Death is in some sense the fullest expression of such discontinuity within the evolutionary process. What is striking is that when death does arise it seems to come in order to make room for new life. If nothing ever died, then nothing new would ever come into being. Personal death, therefore, makes way for the life of others and contributes, however slightly, to the larger project of the human species of which we have been privileged to be part. This memory of the disruptive modulations within cosmic and human history is important and must be kept to the fore when we come to discuss the possibility of hope in the face of death.

Hope

When faced with death, the only adequate response is hope. However, when we look around at contemporary culture, we find that there is a crisis of hope in life after death and an eclipse of hope itself. This is the import of François Mitterrand's moving foreword to Marie de Hennezel's book *Intimate Death*. To be sure, there is plenty of optimism but very little hope. This crisis in hope is caused by a variety of factors. Foremost is the cult of individualism that refuses to recognize the interdependent and derivative dimensions of human existence. Likewise, the denial of death that characterizes contemporary culture is a factor in the eclipse of hope, because without death there is very little need for hope. Similarly, the presence of so much *amnesia* concerning the unity and history of the human species makes hope more difficult to attain.

In spite of this crisis in hope, we must recognize that the dynamism of human reason cannot bloom without hope and that hope cannot speak without the support of reason. Hope, therefore, must not be construed as an escape from the world *(a fuga mundi)* or a neglect of human responsibility for the world (an opium of the people). A credible theology of hope must be grounded in human experience, the life of the world, and the vagaries of history.

The significance of our discussions of anthropology and memory is that hope is only possible on the basis of an integrated understanding of what it means to be human alongside the creative power of memory. Certain styles of anthropology do not lend themselves to hope or indeed do not even require hope. For example, the modern subject that sees itself as self-sufficient will have little need of hope. Likewise, the free floating postmodern self who lives out of the particularity of discontinuous moments with no roots in history will find it difficult to have hope in the future. To this extent anthropology and memory are the building blocks in the construction of hope.

In discussing anthropology and memory, the theme of creation becomes important because it is one of the pillars of hope. Hope as a response to death must be informed by some sense of God as creator of heaven and earth. Without an awareness of the world of God's creation and some sense of the sacramentality of the universe, hope in the face of death is difficult to maintain. Likewise an appreciation of God's action in history, especially in Judaism and the life of Jesus, is essential to the creation of hope. What we know of God's action in creation and in history is the basis of hope in the future. The presence of God in creation, in the work of redemption in Christ, and in the ongoing spirit of God in the world today is what enables human beings to hope that God will continue to be present and active, not only in life, but also in death. Hope in the God of the future must be consistent and coherent with an appreciation of the action of God in the past and in the present. We cannot hope in the future without reference to our faith in God who has been active in the past and in the present. Hope and the possibility of eternal life, therefore, is not some kind of idle speculation or personal projection without reference to the experience of God in the present. Instead, hope is a particular interpretation of the promise present or absent in human experiences. As such, hope is a trusting interpretation that the glimpses of life and beauty and glory in the present are not empty but full of promise. Equally important is the claim that hope is also a response, a type of resistance and protest, against the presence of so much suffering, death, and tragedy in the world. Hope must be able to face the whole of life in its ambiguous mixture of joy and grief, loss and creativity, suspicion and trust.

If God has been creatively present at the beginning of life, is it not plausible that the same God can be similarly active at the end of life? Is not this part of the claim made about what happened in the historical life, death, and destiny of Jesus? The God who is active in the ministry of Jesus is the God who is equally active in the death of Jesus, bringing new life out of the collapse of Jesus on the cross and unexpected glory out of the darkness of Calvary. For the Christian, therefore, the complete narrative of the human self embraces a process of creation and recreation. Whereas the first creation is a creation out of nothing *(creatio ex nihilo),* the second creation is a recreation out of the raw material of personal freedom in history *(creatio ex vetera).* It is important to affirm here that within the journey from creation to the new creation there are both continuity and discontinuity, change and transformation, underlying identity coupled with newness. The element of continuity must contain reference to the personal self and not appear simply as slipping away into some amorphous matrix of the divine. In discussing anthropology we saw the importance of affirming ontological personhood as that which endures the changes of history and the contingency of human relationships. To use the language of process philosophy, it is necessary to affirm that hope embraces objective and subjective immortality. Objective immortality refers to the entry of the individual's life into the transcendence of God, whereas subjective immortality implies a continuation of the human "I" in a process of active participation in the trinitarian life of eternal communion.

In response to the question, "What happens in death?" or more specifically, "What can I hope for in death?" care must be taken to stress that all answers are symbolic and analogical, and that as such are merely intimations in the language of this world of something that belongs to a totally other-worldly reality. At the same time some faltering statements must be issued. By far the most popular model is that of "the fruition scenario" outlined by Elizabeth A. Johnson and inspired by Karl Rahner's transcendental anthropology.[40] According to the fruition model, eternal life is about the fulfillment of the exercise of human freedom in history, the self-realization of the personal interiority and the full flowering of the dynamism of the human spirit.[41] Such hope in the possibility of human flourishing in eternity is based in the first instance on the relationality between God and the human self set in motion in the gift and grace of creation.

It should be clear at this stage that the doctrine of creation must be preeminent in any theology of hope. But the doctrine of creation is itself a carefully worked-out response to the most existential question of all questions: "Why is there being rather than non-being?" or, "Why do I exist rather than not exist?" The theological doctrine of creation recognizes that life is ultimately a gift. It is on the basis of this fundamental intuition and experience that I can dare to hope in the future. If I have no sense that my life and my historical existence and my personal identity are derivative, being constituted by others and ultimately God, then when I am faced with death and have only my own fading self-sufficiency to rely upon, I will find it difficult to see with hope beyond death. The challenge articulated by Michael Kearney in his book *Mortally Wounded: Stories of Soul Pain, Death and Healing* is that of enabling people to make a journey beyond the lonely confines of the self-enclosed subject. This journey can only be made in the company of others and with the realization that life is gift and every single moment of existence is pure grace. The hardest lesson for modern people to learn is that they cannot save themselves, that salvation is not a human achievement but ultimately a gift from God that comes from outside the self.

In conclusion, we must give some general content to Christian hope in spite of the proper agnosticism that must attach to all statements about the future and eternal life. This concluding outline can only be depicted as threads in a tapestry.

The shape of Christian hope is cruciform. The future, both individually and collectively, is stamped with the sign of the cross. There is no way around the vulnerable, finite, and mortal character of human existence. Christian hope does not ignore the broken dimension of human existence; instead it confronts the flawed character of the human condition and sees light in the brokenness of Jesus on the cross. Gillian Ross in *Love's Work* correctly critiques New Age spirituality and alternative medicine for failing to face life and death with realism. There is no escaping the reality of the cross in our lives, whether through sickness, tragedy, or death itself; it is this stark reality of the cross that is the most potent symbol of hope for Christian faith.

The rhythm of Christian hope is one of daily dying and rising, of decentering and recentering the self, of passing over and returning renewed. This is the rhythm of life intimated by Michael Kearney in *Mortally Wounded* when he invites his patients to journey from the physical to the physiological and from the medical to the mythological. Something of this paschal rhythm is captured by Emily Dickinson in her striking observation:

> A death blow is a Life blow to some
> who 'till they died, did not alive become,
> who had they lived, had died but when
> they died, vitality begun.

This creative unity of living and dying, the integration of death into life, is the underlying meaning and message arising out of the historical death and resurrection of Jesus for Christian living.

The color of Christian hope is that of a "bright darkness." There is darkness in life and in death, and this darkness can become a special kind of light. Often it is the experience of darkness that enables us to see the world in a new way: "In a dark time, the eye begins to see" (Theodore Roethke). There is disintegration in life, especially in death, but for the Christian the historical disintegration of death is the basis of reintegration into eternity. Take the image of the flawed statue. The statue with a hairline fracture can only be fully mended by being broken down so that it can be reconstructed. This image represents something of what happens in death: The disintegration of life gives rise to the reintegration of life in God. The realism of Christian hope demands that we embrace light in darkness and glory in death.

And finally, *the outcome of Christian hope is some form of embodied existence.* Christianity is "a material" religion, and therefore it claims that future existence, both individual and cosmic, embraces bodiliness transformed. If scientists can talk about the self as stardust come alive, why cannot Christians affirm that the dust of the dead becomes new creation? The Christian doctrines of the incarnation, the word made flesh, and the resurrection of the body each in their own way point toward God's adoption of the material universe as part not only of history but of eternity. Aquinas points out in his argument for the resurrection of the body that the disembodied soul is not a complete person. In short, Christian hope assures us that in the darkness of death we fall not into emptiness but the fullness of new life, not into the black holes of outer space but the glory of eternity, not into the abyss of nothingness but the depth of everlasting communion in the triune God.

Notes

1. E. Kübler-Ross, *On Death and Dying* (1970). This book was followed by another entitled *Death: The Final Stage of Growth* (1975), in which Kübler-Ross argues persuasively for the integration of living and dying. In 1991 she published *On Life after Death* (Berkeley, Calif.: University of California Press).

2. Ernest Becker, *The Denial of Death* (New York: Free Press, 1973), 16.

3. "Guest Editor's Introduction," *Zygon* 33, 1 (March 1998): 5. This issue of *Zygon,* devoted to the work of Ernest Becker, contains some of the results of these interdisciplinary studies.

4. Michael Kearney, *Mortally Wounded: Stories of Soul Pain, Death and Healing* (Dublin: Marino Books, 1996).

5. Ibid., 144.

6. Marie de Hennezel, *Intimate Death: How the Dying Teach Us to Live* (New York: Little, Brown & Co., 1995), xi.

7. Ibid., xiii.

8. Ibid.

9. A similar account of the hospice movement in the United States is outlined by Paul Wilkes in "Dying Well Is the Best Revenge," *New York Times Magazine,* July 6, 1997, 323–40 and 48.

10. See the Editorial Comment in *New Blackfriars* (June 1988) entitled "Death and Some Philosophers."

11. François Mitterand, Foreword, in Marie de Hennezel, *Intimate Death,* vii.

12. Ibid., ix.

13. Ibid., ix–x.

14. Gillian Ross, *Love's Work* (London: Vintage, 1995), 71.

15. Ibid., 73.

16. Ibid., 96.

17. Ibid., 97.

18. Ibid.

19. Ibid., 98.

20. Ibid., 99.

21. John Updike, *Towards the End of Time* (New York: Alfred Knopf, 1997), 3.

22. Ibid., 327.

23. Ibid.

24. Ibid., 299.

25. See Dermot A. Lane, "The Self in Crisis: The Demise of Eschatology," *Keeping Hope Alive: Stirrings in Christian Theology* (New York: Paulist Press, 1996), 25–41.

26. This movement is helpfully outlined by Joseph Dunne, "Beyond Sovereignty and Deconstruction: The Storied Self," *Philosophy and Social Criticism* 21, 5/6: 137–57.

27. Ibid., 139.

28. See Catherine LaCugna, *God for Us: The Trinity and Christian Life* (San Francisco: HarperCollins, 1991), 292.

29. John Meyendorft, *Christ in Eastern Social Thought* (New York: St. Vladimir's Seminary Press, 1987), 77.

30. See J. B. Metz, *Faith in History and Society: Towards a Practical Fundamental Theology* (London: Burns & Oates, 1980), chs. 6, 7, 11.

31. I am indebted for some of the material that follows to the helpful article by Pamela Bright, "Singing the Psalms: Augustine and Athanasius on the Integration of the Self," in *The Whole and Divided Self: A Bible and Theological Anthropology* (New York: Crossroad, 1997), 115–29.

32. *Confessions* 9/1 in *Augustine of Hippo: Selected Writings,* trans. and intro. Mary T. Clarke (New York: Doubleday Image Books, 1984).

33. *Confessions* 10/17.

34. Ibid.

35. Ibid.

36. *Confessions* 10/27.

37. A more elaborate account of this debate between Benjamin and Horkheimer can be found in Lane, *Keeping Hope Alive,* 119–21, 201–5.

38. Baal Sham Tow.

39. John Haught, *The Promise of Nature* (New York: Paulist Press, 1993), 109.

40. See Elizabeth A. Johnson, *Friends of God and Prophets: A Feminist Theological Reading of the Communion of Saints* (New York: Continuum, 1998), where she distinguishes between the recycling scenario, the fruition scenario, and the dissolution scenario (195–201).

41. See Karl Rahner, "Ideas for a Theology of Death," *Theological Investigations,* Vol. 13 (London: D.L.T., 1975), 169–86.

Marie D. Gipprich and Michaele Barry Wicks

7. An Experience of Darkness and the Search for a Compassionate God

A Prologue

In a world where professional and financial prowess are the paradigm for successful living, and instant gratification is the norm, religious consciousness, when it is considered at all, is at best a "back burner" issue. God's presence is little recognized in the good things of life. How much more difficult is it then to find God in the "darkness"? And yet to reflect on and to explore the interweaving of spiritual and psychological darkness can be a life-giving affirmation of one's journey toward holiness and wholeness. Nevertheless, to live and to pray in the dark is to assume the experience of the psalmist who cries out in near despair, "How long, O Lord...how long...?" (Ps 13:2). Two analogies can be made concerning our patient or impatient waiting in the dark. The first is the experience of walking into a room that's devoid of both artificial and natural light. If we are patient, our eyes will usually accommodate to the darkness, allowing us to make out our surroundings at least in outline form. The second and more difficult situation is when we are "blinded" by the sun. In this case, an excess of light forces us to shade our eyes or even close them because we cannot tolerate the intense illumination.

There are many ways to experience and journey through darkness. In this essay we will be reflecting on an experience of one of the authors, an experience that incorporates both analogies just related. The darkened room is analogous to psychological depression in which the victim loses a sense of self and the ability to function in her environment. Psychological counseling is the remedy that eventually moves one toward a new accommodation to life. Spiritual darkness is more closely related to the concept of excessive light, in which God is illuminating the God-human relationship with a great intensity that at least for a time conceals God's presence in prayer, in liturgy, in work, in friends, in all ways that once God was so central. In this case, the focus is on God. It is the faithfulness of the one who suffers through the darkness and the fire of God's transforming love that motivates the believer to traverse the long dark tunnel of desolation and moves one toward self-knowledge and healing.

In times of such "illuminating" darkness, the person deeply rooted in relationship with Christ can look to Karl Rahner's meditation on Christ's passion for encouragement and consolation. He writes,

> You are with us, You who endured the agony in the Garden.... Your heart is the heart that it is because of what it experienced and suffered then, and all this experience and suffering remain in it. It is with this heart that You are present with us.[1]

It is the Christ who suffered alone, in body and soul, who is indispensable to the believer held prisoner by darkness and despair. Certainly the Jesus who asked to be relieved of his suffering, who was betrayed and abandoned by his followers, and who in the hour of his greatest need felt abandoned by his Father in heaven, certainly this Jesus is the one who can understand the deep and oftentimes unutterable anguish of human pain. It is this very human, suffering Jesus who offers us his hand, stretched out in hope and consolation and who rescues us from the depths of darkness and despair.

What follows is a retrospective reflection on Marie's six-year experience of suffering and healing in Christ Jesus, our incarnate God. We offer this reflection now for one reason: to offer hope, insight, and some measure of comfort and validation to those who find themselves experiencing or traveling with another on a similar journey of faith. And now the story...

While attending a workshop on religious life, I experienced a sudden and inexplicable memory of childhood sexual abuse. The initial memory was like looking at a slide flashing on and off a screen in a matter of seconds. Though I didn't understand this experience, it was extremely disturbing to me, and over the course of the next few weeks and months, more memories flooded my mind and gripped my body. Each memory was like a piece of a puzzle that my mind refused to assemble until very gradually the pieces began to fit together to form a picture of abuse that I had repressed for thirty-three years.

In the initial phase of this experience of darkness, my immediate reactions to the discovery of the abuse were denial ("This didn't *really* happen!"), minimization ("It wasn't that bad!"), and rationalization ("He didn't mean to hurt me!"). Each time another memory surfaced, each time I read something about abuse that I could relate to, it was like admitting again for the first time that I was a victim of sexual abuse. The pain would not quit; it expressed itself in panic attacks, nightmares, and depression. Only much later and very reluctantly, I came to recognize my pain in its psychological description as PTSD (Post-Traumatic Stress Disorder), a long-delayed response to trauma experienced in my youth.

As I moved into the second phase of darkness, I became overwhelmed by sorrow, anger, guilt, depression, and fear. I began to realize that my low self-esteem, lack of self-confidence, problems with relationships, and fear of loving and being loved were the consequences of the long-reaching arm of abuse. It had caused me to suffer the humiliation of so many deficiencies in my life, and to grow up much too quickly. The recognition that abuse was at the root of all this pain became more clear to me each day. As the cause became more clear, the sorrow over what I had lost as a consequence became overwhelming!

During this time of painful revelation and recognition, I cried out to God in utter terror. The third phase of darkness filled me with anger at God for not protecting me from such violence as a child and for not protecting me from my present pain. God was so absent! And in the midst of this agony my efforts to locate God through prayer were seemingly fruitless.

While trying to find God, to feel God's presence, and to experience some consolation, the old images of God that I carried with me from my youth were useless and meaningless. I felt truly alone and lonely, abandoned by a God whom I had trusted. This movement from anger to abandonment was the fourth phase of darkness. In order to survive spiritually, emotionally, and psychologically, I knew I had to search for a God who understood the suffering of the innocent and whose compassionate love could heal the wounds of such suffering. For me, this meant shattering all the old images of God and starting from scratch.

Phases three and four of my experience of darkness proved to be the most difficult and painful. On a very basic level, I had lost my identity, one that for so many years of my life had been directly connected and intimately linked with God's identity as I understood it.

My God had always been a comfortable God. My primary understanding of this God was that of a loving Father and all that that image implies. I believed that God was and always would be "there" for me, that God acted in my life and in my world, supported me in my life decisions, and was the object of my prayers of praise, love, and thanks. I also believed that, along with death, suffering and pain were a part of life. My nonchalance regarding suffering rested on a belief that this comfortable God would see me through whatever was in store for me or whatever pain I would experience as a result of my humanity. I admitted that there was unjust suffering in the world; I saw it in cancer victims, in starving children in Somalia, in pictures of the death camps at Auschwitz, in the poverty of the homeless, in the many tragedies of war, and in the devastation following earthquakes and tornadoes. But all of this suffering was outside myself. Although it touched my heart, it didn't touch my life directly. So God continued to reside in heaven, and all was right with the world.

Then one day my tidy, comfortable world collapsed. The devastation of sexual abuse and its effects turned my beliefs about God upside down. It seemed as though all the unjust suffering in the world that I had successfully kept at a distance came crashing in on me as stark reality. Now, in the midst of my personal suffering, I knew that the God I was once so sure of would be inadequate to the task of answering my whys. Like C. S. Lewis,[2] it wasn't that I didn't believe in God; I questioned what kind of God it was that I proclaimed! It was out of the depths of my own personal suffering that the questions about God arose. What kind of God would allow this to happen to me when I was a child? What kind of God continued to allow me to experience the effects of such abuse? Where was and is the God of mercy and justice, the almighty and kind God? Why had God abandoned me in my darkest hour? Even as I screamed these questions, I knew that I had lost the God of my childhood and immaturity, the God of my complacency. "For God who lets the innocent suffer and who permits senseless death is not worthy to be called God at all."[3]

My questions about God were intertwined with questions about my suffering: Did God cause or will my suffering? Does God need my suffering in order to be the omnipotent God? Is God trying to break my spirit? Is my suffering necessary to atone for some past sins? The questions continued and became more frightening: Was I somehow responsible for the abuse and the subsequent suffering? Am I being punished for some sin, for the perpetrator's sin? Do I deserve these feelings of guilt and shame? I gradually began to realize that while I was asking the questions, something inside me believed the answer to each question was *yes!* The fearsomeness of that reality was yet another pain. I suffered the abuse as a child; I continued to suffer through its effects and even more so through the realization that the God I once knew and trusted had abandoned me.

And so another phase of the suffering began: the journey to healing. With the help of a good friend and a competent therapist, I began the search for God and for myself.

In my desolation and isolation I knew I needed a God who would hear and understand my suffering and pain, a God with whom I could relate. It became an obsession with me. I turned to the incarnate God in the hope that Christ would be this person for me. Though guilt, shame, and oftentimes paralyzing doubts obscured the way, eventually and with great effort and encouragement, I was able to see my suffering as innocent suffering. Liberation and feminist theologians spoke most profoundly to my heart. Through their explication of christology, they call us to recognize the unjust suffering of an oppressed group, listen to their cries, and seek action to alleviate or change the situation. As Moltmann says, "Only the person who has suffered can help other sufferers."[4] This was of great importance to me because I needed to know that Christ recognized my pain; that he was, indeed, suffering with me and that he had not abandoned me; that there was hope for healing; and that my suffering could be transformed into positive action.

Like the Greeks who approached Philip saying, "Sir, we would like to see Jesus" (Jn 12:21), I too needed to see Jesus and through him rediscover and reclaim a God whose presence could be made known in compassion and whose love could withstand the fires of pain. The God of my complacency had become little more than a crumbling idol in my hour of darkness. My heart yearned for the real God, the faithful God, the God who "once set up walls and ramparts to protect us" (Is 26:1–4). It was Jesus, Emmanuel, God-with-us who transformed my desperation into hope and offered me a faith much more mature than that which I had left behind. It was the Jesus who preached the kingdom, ministered to the marginalized, suffered and died out of love, and whose faithfulness reached even beyond death that restored my hope and belief in a compassionate God.

Jesus' Ministry: God Is Present in Compassion

Jesus Christ identified with the poor and suffering. He walked with them, ate with them, and taught them. To discover Jesus, I looked to those with whom he walked and continues to walk in solidarity.

Victims of sexual abuse can be counted among the poor, the oppressed, the suffering, the exploited, and the powerless. Like the poor, they are stripped of dignity, self-esteem, and trust. Like the oppressed, they are betrayed and victimized by the very people who should have offered them support. The sexually abused person suffers physical, psychological, and spiritual wounds in childhood that they then must carry throughout their adult lives. Oftentimes their bodies are exploited to satisfy the needs of others and they are victimized by strength and power greater than their own. They are left emotionally crippled and powerless by authority figures who abuse their trust.

Jesus' ministry of preaching led him to proclaim the good news. At the heart of his teaching was the symbol of the kingdom of God. When we "listen" carefully to that teaching, we recognize that the kingdom comes when God's will is done, and God's will is our well-being. "I have come that you may have life and have it to the full" (Jn 10:10). In short, God's will for all of us is our wholeness, our salvation. When people are poor, oppressed, suffering, exploited, and powerless, the kingdom of God is an elusive concept and it is difficult to accept it as a possibility.

And yet it was to these very people that Christ proclaimed that the kingdom of God was not only a future possibility but a present reality experienced in his compassion and love for God's people. Jesus' message fell on the deaf ears of the rich, the powerful, and the complacent. It didn't take long for people to discover that "the good news was only good if you were the last, the least, or the lowest."[5] Through his ministry of healing the sick, forgiving sinners, accepting outcasts, and welcoming women and children, Jesus proved himself to be the wrong kind of Messiah for the powerful and the power-hungry. After Peter's response to Jesus' questions, "Who do you say that I am?" (Mk 8:29), the two clashed over Jesus' prediction that he must suffer and die. These were not the words of a kingly messiah who would destroy all pain and suffering in his kingdom.

I, like Peter, had to learn that worshiping a God of glory meant emphasizing the "rightness" in our world, a world that stresses only the positive in terms of power and being in control. But I felt powerless and out of control. This suffering of mine, the abuse and its effects, kept me from living life "to the full" as Jesus promised. If Jesus promised this fullness of life, he would have to stand with me against such unjust suffering. He would have to reveal God to me as a compassionate God. Jesus would have to minister to me and the countless innocent victims who have been and are abused every day.

Jesus' Crucifixion: God Suffers with Us

The crucified Christ is at the center of all our questions about God, the meaning of life, our relationship with others, and our own existence. The awareness of our fragility leads us to search for answers that will help us embrace suffering as a means of discovering who God is for us. How we interpret the suffering and death of Christ *in our own life experiences* is the point of departure for finding answers to these questions.

The statistics of sexual abuse are staggering: one in every three girls and one in every seven boys are sexually abused before the age of eighteen![6] The struggle to understand such widespread suffering challenges one's image of God. The experience of a loving God turns into an experience of God as a male oppressor who abandons the innocent victims of violent and unjust acts. "For incest victims, the image of God as an all-powerful male, as father, is problematic."[7] The maleness of Jesus poses like problems. How can a male redeemer understand this pain? Therefore, added to the physical, emotional, and psychological pain of sexual abuse is the spiritual pain of experiencing God's absence, or at the very least, a God who cannot or does not understand.

Realizing that I wasn't alone in suffering the painful effects of sexual abuse didn't comfort me. It helped validate my feelings, but it started a slow, silent rage of protest within me. I started questioning the suffering of *all* innocent victims. This *cannot* be God's will. There is no justification in such senseless violation. God is not justified in Auschwitz or in Somalia or in the lives of abused children. God can only be justified if in fact God shares in this suffering.

I continued my search for a "new" God by turning to Christ as the embodiment of a God who does indeed suffer with us. Solidarity with the poor, the suffering, the oppressed, the exploited, and the powerless became the center of my quest for a christology that reveals how God relates to our situation. It involved a rejection of my worship of a solely transcendent God as long as it invoked images of a God who cannot be controlled and who, therefore, cannot suffer. My traditional thought led me to the conclusion that a suffering God would be less God, but now I believed that this transcendent God would be no more than a mere spectator in the arena of worldwide suffering. As Brueggemann states, "Those who offer truth without experiencing the pain are likely not to be trusted." [8]

My image of an immanent God, however, is one whose presence in all creation is so intimate that God is also necessarily involved in the sufferings and pain of creation. It is this pathos of God that I began to explore.

The images of Jesus in Gethsemane and on Calvary were lifelines for me during my painful struggle to discover a God who could identify with my suffering. The painful cry of Jesus to his Father—"Let this cup pass…" (Mk 14:36)—helped me to give up my idea of God as all-powerful and to see in Christ one who is the "affirmation of the non-violent impatience of love in which God himself is no longer one who imposes suffering but a fellow sufferer."[9] This is a God who is accessible to me in my suffering. I found consolation in the words of the psalmist who had the courage to demand that God be a keeper of promises, "My comfort in my affliction is that your promise gives me life" (Ps 119:50).

The Calvary image also shattered my expectations of a just and merciful God. Jesus knew my agony because he experienced his own suffering as "hellish abandonment" by the God he proclaimed as one with him. Personally I was filled with conflicting emotions: I *felt* abandoned, but I didn't want to believe that I *was* abandoned. At this stage there was a ray of hope cracking through the despair. The image I clung to was that of a flickering candle burning at the far end of a long, dark, and still frightening tunnel.

This ray of hope first appeared as a reversal of my questioning, which previously had been aimed at God. Now I questioned my own insistence on believing in a God who would support my "self-interest in trying to hold and defend a specific form of deity."[10] It seemed to me that I had experienced the death of the God I once knew!

When I began to understand that I wasn't to blame for my abuse, I knew that I didn't deserve to be punished through the ongoing suffering caused by its effects and my own private agony. God is *not* in heaven and all is *not* right with the world! God, in Jesus, is hanging on the cross. As suggested by Soelle,[11] I let go of the belief that God who is Love asserts power in our lives and that this assertion—in whatever form it takes—is God's will for us. The cross is not a symbol for the mysticism of the dead Christ that legitimizes suffering as the will of God. The cross is not a glorification of a God-image that makes Christ no more than an obedient sheep being led to slaughter. Christ on the cross doesn't make restitution or serve as a warning to others. Innocent and unjust suffering doesn't necessarily build character; it very often destroys it. These images do nothing more than support and encourage acts of injustice in our world. Christ's desire that I be wholly human, that I "live life to the full," reinforced my emerging understanding that the only explanation for Jesus' agony on the cross lay in the connection between his life and his death. He died in solidarity with God and with others. He chose to die freely because he lived that way. It was his self-identity that led to his crucifixion.

But now, what about me? What about all the innocent people who suffer from the result of war, poverty, oppression, injustice? Do we suffer as a result of how we lived? Many of us barely had the chance to live when we became victims. The personal dimension of death means that Jesus was free to choose to die or to reject death. Because of his love for and solidarity with God and others (as evidenced by the way he lived), he surrendered to it. My suffering has no meaning of itself; Jesus died to give my suffering its meaning. His suffering was in solidarity with my suffering. No, God isn't in heaven; God is here in my pain, offering comfort and compassion as a fellow sufferer. God-in-Jesus knows my grief, my fear, my shame. The knowledge that God sided with me, that God stood against the destructive forces in my life, brought a glimmer of hope and peace I hadn't known for a long time.

There never can be a justification for innocent suffering—either that of Jesus or that of his followers. Knowing that, I began to search for meaning in my suffering. In a world where suffering is a stark reality, can there be meaning to life? Can I experience God as suffering in and with God's people? Is there hope on Calvary? The cross cannot be the end for me. I cannot separate Jesus' crucifixion from his resurrection any more that I can separate how he lived from how he died. In the resurrection, Jesus' last act of obedience—his crucifixion—accomplishes God's will for us all. "The relationship between Jesus and the Father…is extended to all."[12] The community of life that Jesus worked so hard to accomplish through his own life, preaching, and ministry is now possible.

Jesus' Resurrection: God Is Faithful

The power of the Paschal Mystery does not lie in the suffering experienced on the cross; it lies in the unconditional love of God revealed in the resurrection. Because of the resurrection, all the meaninglessness, hopelessness, and negativity of the cross are transformed into hope. The two key elements of the Paschal Mystery—the cross and the resurrection—are, therefore, a "single saving unity."

The healing of sexual abuse requires a courage that is remarkable. Each survivor makes a determined decision to look back at a frightening past, sift through long-repressed memories, deal with the pain, confusion, and frustration of their meaning, and accept it all as true in order to get on with her or his life. The desire to learn how to deal with the effects of sexual abuse on a day-to-day basis is the hope *that will one day produce new strength and an experience of wholeness.*

The cross forces me to change how I think about God, how I live with the effects of abuse, and what I hope for. Once I acknowledge God as totally engrossed in my world, as "fellow sufferer," wherein will lie my hope for recovery and healing? Does it all end with my knowledge of and belief in an immanent God who makes himself authentic through Jesus Christ? Will there be life after this "death" for me?

I have to reject any emphasis on the future where God will ultimately triumph as our only hope for release from suffering. This kind of thinking causes me more pain and leaves me grasping for some sign of hope for the present. I refuse to believe that my "reward" for suffering on this earth will be no more than the promise of eternal life in the world to come. I am committed to believing that Jesus lived, died, and rose so that I may know the possibility of fullness of life, of wholeness and holiness *here and now.*

On the cross Jesus did not know of his resurrection. Abandonment was his experience. He was separated from his Father. His death carried with it a finality. Resurrection reestablishes our right relationship with God and puts an end to this kind of death. In spite of our feelings of abandonment and rejection by God, we have the knowledge of the resurrection, of hope. Jesus' resurrection, then, is not a promise that we will not suffer pain and death; it is a promise that ultimately we will not be abandoned.

The very fact that I cry out to a God who seems so absent is an expression of my hope that God is very present. According to Brueggemann, "Hope is the virtue of those who see the imperfection of the present, who recognize the fear, insecurity, and inequalities that exist, and who work for a new order of things."[13] I experience this hope in the little successes of every day: believing in myself enough to accomplish a task, loving and accepting love, trusting someone, caring for myself, expressing the pain. I experience this hope in the strength, courage, and support I receive from wonderful friends and a caring family and community. I experience this hope in knowing that little children and adults no longer have to fear the scars of sexual abuse or hide behind masks because there are people who care and who want to help them experience freedom and wholeness again. I experience this hope in the act of opening "to the potential for love and support when feeling the most unlovable...."[14] *This* is resurrection hope.

The cross, for me, represents unjust suffering. The resurrection of Christ demonstrates the "righteousness of God which creates right for all."[15] It *transformed* (emphasis mine) but never justified the suffering and death experience."[16] The resurrection (Christ's and mine) is an annihilation of the power of death and dying through new life. It makes the future hope of the forgiveness of sins, reconciliation, and discipleship possible. The resurrection brings the future into the present!

Post-Resurrection Discipleship: God Transforms Creation

"A person's resurrection is no personal privilege for himself alone—even if he is called Jesus of Nazareth. It contains within itself hope for all, for everything."[17]

The peace and wholeness experienced by sexual abuse victims inspires others to seek help and to heal. Their determination to stop this ungodly victimization has resulted in greater public awareness of the seriousness of this crime, and the organization of individuals and groups who respond to the plight of victims and work—through the legal and political systems or agencies of healing—to mend this terrible wound in our society. Each individual's healing "will make an enormous difference to all those who come after (her), for (she) is helping to create a blueprint for the healing of the world."[18]

The grace of the resurrection lies in its transformative power. With this grace a victim becomes a survivor, passivity is converted to activity, hope replaces despair, and passion for justice reverses the pain of experienced injustices. Jesus' resurrection helps us to proclaim that all sufferings and injustices "need not be controlling factors in our lives, but that they can and must be challenged and overcome."[19]

In short, the resurrection is an invitation to all of us to believe and to trust. It demands a response. It implies discipleship. Praxis as the result of suffering leads to a new creation where compassion, healing, and liberation are the rule. The theology of glory that I claimed as my own led to my complacency; the theology of the cross and resurrection that I now claim will lead me to action. I had to suffer in order to understand the suffering of others and respond by working for an end to that suffering. It is *love* that teaches self-abandonment! And it is love of God and others that often results in suffering. If we don't love, we cannot feel; if we don't feel, we cannot see and empathize with the suffering people; if we don't empathize, we cannot work to bring about the kingdom of God. It seems, then, that as a disciple of Christ, I don't have a choice! I understand now what drives people like Elie Wiesel to work and spend their lives so that suffering like that which he experienced will not be allowed to continue. Compassion has *got* to be at the root of any viable reason for suffering, especially unjust, innocent suffering.

I know now that "the cross does not solve the problem of suffering, but meets it with voluntary solidarity which does not abolish suffering but overcomes what Moltmann calls the 'suffering in suffering': the lack of love, the abandonment in suffering."[20] It is in Jesus' solidarity with all who suffer that I am called to that same praxis. According to Johnson, "responsible action for resistance, correction, and healing are among the truest expressions of living faith."[21]

To change the plight of the innocent victim and to give suffering some meaning, it is necessary to work toward eliminating such suffering. This is the only response to innocent suffering. Jesus preached God as a compassionate God who does not want us to suffer. He talked to outcasts, ate with sinners, healed the sick, and proclaimed the poor "happy." By restoring our lost independence, Jesus' vicarious suffering takes on meaning in the light of the resurrection.

Those of us who have questioned the place and meaning of suffering in our lives and have recognized Christ's solidarity in our pain refuse to give that suffering power to destroy us. We know that it has no value in itself. It is not a "sign of a moral flaw in the one who suffers, but it may constitute a moral flaw for those who do not respond." [22] The only meaning to innocent suffering, then, must lie in a response to Christ's own suffering and resurrection. I must see myself as part of the effort to eliminate it and to see *my* suffering as part of the struggle for the sake of God's reign. It doesn't mean just working *for* others who suffer but *with* them, and never forgetting my own struggle, acknowledging that it is not over and that I too will need the compassionate support of "community." Wherever I find myself responding to the Lord's call to follow him, I must make my own needs the needs of the poor and suffering in that situation. At times, the only possible response will be my silent "being with." At other times, it will require an active participation in a plan to relieve the cause of the suffering. If I am not moved to work for the elimination of the effects of sexual abuse, then my christology is no more than a theory. The continuing cry of thousands of young children who are abused every day echoes in my heart—and I cry with them. I have no choice but to respond somehow, especially through my own efforts to heal. These victims need to know that God hears their cries, suffers with them, and ultimately will bring them to new life. They need to know who and where God is in this suffering, and this will be clear only in "our unrestrained involvement with one another."[23] Helping to remove people from oppressive situations is sharing in the redemptive work of Christ. It is "salvation already happening." It is discipleship. It is what makes a difference, all the difference in the world.

A Final Word

I continue to look for Jesus and to ask who God is for me. It is a very big part of the pain that survives the abuse to have continual doubts about God's presence in my life. I suspect that it is tied up with the search for who *I* am. So much of my life was lost, stolen, or manipulated that it may take a lifetime to integrate my past with my present and my future. And, like Job, I will continue to state my position of innocence only to learn again for the first time that God *has* never and *will* never abandon me. God will share in my suffering as well as my victory over that suffering, each day and one day at a time. When I look for God, I will see my God in Jesus, the crucified and risen one, the *compassionate God.*

An Epilogue

Whenever we struggle with the tragedy of undeserved suffering we find ourselves face to face with the age-old problem of theodicy. Reconciling the goodness and justice of a loving God with the unrelenting presence of evil in the world is not and has never been an easy task. For answers we often look to Job, the innocent sufferer of the Old Testament. Or perhaps we look to Jeremiah, the paradoxical prophet who at one moment is filled with extraordinary obedience and docility in relation to God and in other instances, filled with bitterness and outrage against God. Of course, neither Job nor Jeremiah can solve our problem, simply because there is no solution to the problem of evil (see Jer 15:18; 20:9; Jb 19:7,8).

Nevertheless, both Job and Jeremiah offer us validation for the very human and oftentimes fiercely emotional response to affliction. Despite their angry protests and accusations against God, they did not and perhaps could not give up on God completely. Their very anger was proof that God continued to provide a focus for their heart's desires. As such, Job and Jeremiah become symbols not only of Old Testament faith but also of hope in a God who seemingly does not care yet continues to draw us near.

As we move to Jesus, the God incarnate of the New Testament, we approach suffering from a different perspective. The Paschal Mystery tells us that God has indeed entered into our suffering and that God stands solidly on our side. Jesus did not have much to say about the reasons for suffering, though there is little reason to believe that he didn't share at least to some degree in the Old Testament presupposition of sin and guilt as justification for suffering. But whatever his opinion about suffering, Jesus did not seem as adamant about the relationship between sin and guilt as were the friends of Job or for that matter, any of his Old Testament counterparts. What we do know is that Jesus was a healing presence, and much of his ministry, in active protest against evil, was dedicated to relieving the pain of those who suffered in body, mind, or spirit. And like Job and Jeremiah, his ancestors in faith, Jesus suffered in his relationship with God. In the Garden of Gethsemane he was alone and afraid. In his passion and crucifixion he suffered not only physical torment but also the excruciatingly painful reality of feeling abandoned by his earthly friends as well as his heavenly Father. And yet, like Job and Jeremiah, Jesus remained faithful and hopeful to the end.

Likewise for the person traumatized by psychological or physical affliction. When that person is also a person of faith, deeply rooted in the Judeo-
Christian tradition, faith, hope, anger, and protest become intricately woven
together in a tapestry of suffering and healing. Feeling abandoned by the God
who once set up walls and ramparts to protect them (Is 26:1), they lash out in
angry protest only to become overwhelmed by shame and guilt at their lack of
faith and their very real desire to cast God from their hearts. They are deprived
of the ability to act on their own in terms of believing, hoping, and loving. And
yet their very anger is positive proof that their spirit still longs for the God who
once reigned at the center of their lives. To be angry with, to be repulsed by,
even to hate the very same reality toward whom one is overwhelmingly drawn
is to magnify the experience of suffering a hundredfold.

For the believer, at this point of helplessness and hopelessness, there are
only two alternatives. One is to run away, turning one's back completely on
God. The other is to abandon oneself, often unknowingly, into the arms of
grace, into the arms of the God who entered into our suffering in Christ, Jesus.
It is a time like no other, when the role of the theological virtues of faith, hope,
and love is as clearly delineated as the neon signs of Times Square. This is so
because for the person of deep faith, the reality that creates the tension
between abhorrence and adoration is nothing less than God—the God who
gifts us with inexplicable wellsprings of faith, hope, and love.

Experiences such as the one reflected upon in this paper offer the possibility of deep personal transformation and growth in compassion for all who
are intimately involved in the experience. The following story attests to the
fact that one of the most crucial aspects of relating in the "dark" is not necessarily providing answers but rather being with the other as a faithful presence,
a soothing voice, and a compassionate listener.

> A number of years ago, 1975 to be exact, my three-year-old
> daughter and I were negotiating our way through a dark stairwell
> during a power outage, when young Michaele asserted that there
> were probably ghosts lurking about. Wanting to allay her fears, I
> immediately responded that there were no ghosts present. Her
> reply set me straight: "How would you know? You can't see
> either." Not knowing how to respond to such an insightful com-
> ment, I simply held her hand more tightly until we had success-
> fully maneuvered our way back into the light of day.

It is important for the one who walks with the sufferer, whether that person be friend, minister, parent, spouse, therapist, or spiritual counselor, to be
cognizant of and even to cling to the dynamic of hope that lies concealed
within the angry protest of the one who suffers. Since the one who is afflicted

gives no recognition to hope herself, failure to recognize even its slightest glimmer on the part of her companion is all too likely to pull that companion into the whirlwind of pain, where she too will be drawn ever more deeply into the paroxysms of helplessness and hopelessness of the one who suffers.

On the other hand, by clinging steadfastly to the light, those who touch the heart and soul of another in the desire to love them back to life are themselves in some ways healed and forever changed. With spiritual discipline, competent psychological help, and most of all grace, those forced to wrestle with God and with one another in the course of suffering can maneuver together through the darkness often emerging with a clearer sense of God, self, and compassionate love than they ever could have achieved in the light.

Notes

1. Karl Rahner, *Prayers for a Lifetime* (New York: Crossroad, 1995), 65.

2. C. S. Lewis, *A Grief Observed* (New York: Bantam Books, 1976), 5.

3. Jurgen Moltmann, *The Trinity and the Kingdom* (New York: Harper and Row, 1981), 47.

4. Jurgen Moltmann, *Power and Powerlessness* (San Francisco: Harper and Row, 1982), 119.

5. Elizabeth A. Johnson, *Consider Jesus: Waves of Renewal in Christology* (New York: Crossroad, 1990), 53.

6. Sandra M. Flaherty, *Woman, Why Do You Weep?* (New York: Paulist Press, 1992), 5.

7. Ibid., 29.

8. Walter Brueggemann, *The Prophetic Imagination* (Philadelphia: Fortress Press, 1978), 14.

9. Dorothee Soelle, *Thinking about God: An Introduction to Theology* (Philadelphia: Trinity Press International, 1990), 187–88.

10. Jon Sobrino, S.J., *Christology at the Crossroads* (Maryknoll: Orbis Books, 1978), 222.

11. Dorothee Soelle, "A Critique of Christian Masochism" in *Suffering* (Philadelphia: Fortress Press, 1975), 9–32.

12. Herbert McCabe, O.P., *God Matters* (Springfield: Templegate Publishers, 1987), 100.

13. Walter Brueggemann, *Hope Within History* (Atlanta: John Knox Press, 1987), 84.

14. James Leehan, *Defiant Hope: Spirituality for Survivors of Family Abuse* (Westminster: John Knox Press, 1993), 21.

15. Rebecca Chopp, *The Praxis of Suffering: An Interpretation of Liberation and Political Theologies* (Maryknoll: Orbis Books, 1986), 109.

16. Joanne Carlson Brown and Carole R. Bohn, eds., *Christianity, Patriarchy, and Abuse: A Feminist Critique* (Cleveland: Pilgrim Press, 1989), 145.

17. Soelle, *Suffering*, 150.

18. Wayne Kritsberg, *The Invisible Wound: A New Approach to Healing Childhood Sexual Trauma* (New York: Bantam Books, 1993), 237.

19. Leehan, *Defiant Hope*, 97.

20. Lucien Richard, *What Are They Saying about the Theology of Suffering?* (New York: Paulist Press, 1992), 45–46.

21. Johnson, *Consider Jesus,* 268.

22. Leehan, *Defiant Hope,* 96.

23. Edward Schillebeeckx, *Christ* (New York: Crossroad, 1981), 60.

Gerald A. Arbuckle

8. Letting Go in Hope: A Spirituality for a Chaotic World

> Carefree, I used to think, "Nothing can ever shake me!" Your favor, Yahweh, set me on unassailable heights, but you turned away your face and I was terrified. To you, Yahweh, I call....What point is there in my death, my going down to the abyss? (Ps 30:6–9)

The first few words of the psalmist in the above passage aptly describe the self-confidence of the church and its constituent bodies (for example, dioceses, seminaries, parishes, missionary organizations, religious communities) in the years leading up to Vatican II. Especially in the Western world, the church had been a mighty, self-contained fortress, resting on unassailable heights of power, self-confidence, and prestige, secure in the never-ending supply of recruits to the priesthood and religious life, the number and size of its churches, universities, colleges, hospitals, and schools. It never dawned on us that anything could ever shake this edifice of the God.[1]

Now, for many in the church, the euphoria of the reforming council has dissipated. Now we are the poor church of sinners, shaken by massive defections from the ranks of the priesthood, religious life, and laity, by financial and sexual scandals, by internal polarizations. We feel burdened by the escapist uselessness of restorationist and fundamentalist forces in the church, as well as by the brashness of secularists in our midst who would destroy the richness of ascetical and civilizing traditions. We have been cast down from our seemingly unassailable heights of religious power and grandeur—all in the space of a few short years. We feel that God's face has been turned away from us, and we are terrified of the darkness, of our powerlessness. We cry, "How long, Yahweh, will you forget me? Forever? How long will you turn away your face from me? How long must I nurse sorrow in my heart day and night?" (Ps 13:1–2).

So often we ministers within the church feel the full brunt of this sadness. We feel shamed by, even guilty about the chaos around us. The journey is dark, frightening. What more calamities will hit the church, to be recorded in all their details in the mass media? The psalmist's cry is ours: "You have plunged me to the bottom of the grave, in the darkness, in the depths....You have deprived me of friends and companions, and all that I know is the dark" (Ps 88: 6,18). Since the council, the church has fallen into massive grief. This was an inevitable consequence of the reforms, which were essential. Reforms demand we let go of familiar moorings, and grief is the logical result. Yet paradoxically this grief can be an enormous blessing, the catalyst for spiritual and pastoral newness beyond imagination. And we ministers can be at the heart of this evangelical renaissance for the people we serve. But we must first understand the nature of grief and the grieving process before we can see the rich potential for radical newness that the church is now challenged to acknowledge within itself.

Understanding Grief and Grieving

Grief is the sorrow, anger, denial, guilt, and malaise that so often accompanies significant loss, for example, the death of a friend, the loss of a job, the closure of an institution. It is now well known that grief is experienced by individuals, and we are especially grateful to people like Elizabeth Kübler-Ross for alerting us to its dynamic.[2] But what is far less recognized is the fact that *cultures* of people—for example, cultures of nations, business organizations, parishes, dioceses—also experience grief because of loss. Unless cultures (or subcultures) acknowledge their losses in rituals of grieving in order to formally let them go, they—and the individuals that belong to them—remain haunted by or trapped in the past, unable to open themselves to new ways of thinking and acting. Grieving is a complex cultural (and psychological) process that involves the gradual acceptance and internalization of loss. The result of successful cultural grieving is the ability of groups of people to resume a full, rewarding life and relationships and to construct, and be initiated into, a new cultural integration. Rightly did Ovid claim that "suppressed grief suffocates" creativity or openness to newness.

In this essay we especially focus on the grief and grieving of cultures and the role of ministers as ritual leaders in this process. But *culture* is a very confusing term in popular literature, and it must be clarified. Commonly it is thought to mean just "what people do around here." However, this is a very superficial definition. A culture provides people with a set of explicit and informal guidelines that instructs them how to *view* the world, how to *behave* in it in relation to other people and environments, and particularly how to experience it *emotionally*.[3] The word *emotionally* is important because a culture penetrates into the deepest recesses of the human group and individuals, especially their feelings. For this reason, it is better to define a culture as the way people think *and* feel about things around here.[4] Anthropologist Clifford

Geertz highlights the deeper aspects of a culture in this way: A culture is a pervasive "pattern of meanings, embodied in symbols, a system of...conceptions expressed in symbolic forms by means of which (people) communicate, perpetuate, and develop attitudes towards life."[5]

These symbolic forms or patterns of interaction operate most powerfully at the level of the *unconscious,* giving us that all-important sense of *experienced* or felt meaning and order. For most of our lives we are rarely aware of the degree to which culture, through its constituent elements of symbols, myths, and rituals, influences our thoughts, emotions, and actions.[6] *Symbols* are any reality that by their very dynamism or power lead to (that is, make one think about, imagine, get into contact with, or reach out to) another deeper (and often mysterious) reality through the sharing in the dynamism that the symbol itself offers (and not by merely verbal or additional explanations).[7] A symbol has two particular qualities of meaning and emotion. The meaning dimension conveys a message about something; it causes me to react with negative or positive feelings. *Myths* are symbols in narrative form—for example, the creation stories in the Book of Genesis. They are narratives that claim to reveal imaginatively or symbolically a fundamental truth about the world, good and evil, human life. *Rituals* are the visible acting out of the myths, and they are as many and as various as human needs. Hence, to define a culture primarily in terms of what people do is to avoid what pertains to the feeling heart of all cultures—symbols and myths.

A final clarification: A culture provides people with a felt sense of order or predictability. It prevents people from falling into that which is most feared, namely, *chaos,* the radical breakdown of felt order. Just as individuals do in their journey through life and loss, cultures also develop defense mechanisms (for example, repression, regression, or denial) against anxiety—creating chaos. When significant loss occurs, cultures are thrown into the dreaded chaos. The art of cultural grieving, therefore, is to assist a particular culture (and its people) to face reality without denial or other escapist reactions, to let go of that which is lost in order to be open to the new.

In Western societies, in contrast to traditional cultures, we have commonly lost the art of grieving, especially of cultural mourning. In traditional societies, however, grieving rituals are frequent and are considered vital for the health and survival of tribal groups. Every grieving ritual has a dual function: the letting go of that which is lost and the initiation into new relationships. Three identifiable stages are found in these rituals: the *separation* stage, in which people are dramatically and ritually reminded that loss has occurred; the lengthy *liminal* stage, in which mourners are confronted with the chaos resulting from the breakdown of familiar relationships by being challenged to let go of attachments to that which is lost and to struggle to identify the newness they are now called to own; the *re-entry* phase, in which the people and their culture must struggle to move forward with their commitments to new relationships.

For example, commonly the initiation of young people into adulthood, the paradigm for all mourning rituals in traditional societies, begins with a ritually sanctioned sudden break with childhood culture; the young are dramatically separated from their mothers and then taken into seclusion under the direction of tribal elders who will instruct them experientially in the tribal myths. As anthropologist Victor Turner writes, "Accepted schemata and paradigms (of childhood) must be broken if initiates are to cope with novelty and danger."[8] Isolated from other tribal members, the initiates must learn the art of letting go of childhood cultural ways in order to be open to the new status of adulthood. Once this grieving is accomplished, the new adults move back into the tribal life; the actual return is the third stage, a phase not without its own dangers or risks. The Israelites belonged to a traditional culture, so the threefold stages of grieving are frequently evident in the books of the Old Testament. The words of Isaiah mirror this grieving dynamic: "Cease to dwell on days gone by and to brood over past history. Here and now I will do a new thing; this moment it will break from the bud. Can you not perceive it?" (Is 43:18f.).

Grief and Grieving in the Hebrew Scriptures

Throughout the Hebrew scriptures there are references to death, its symptoms, and its causes, either the death of a person or metaphorical death, such as the personal or national alienation from Yahweh through sin, sickness, plagues, famine, wars, exile. Indeed, misery, death, and chaos are never at rest in the Old Testament.[9]

However, from time to time, in vivid contrast to this frequent experience of personal and corporate distress and grief, there are eruptions of surprising, even dramatic, newness. The stages of grieving are readily identifiable, for example, in the Exodus story: the *separation* stage, when the people journey out of Egypt, the lengthy *liminal* or chaos stage, when they wander painfully in the desert struggling to let go their selfish attachments to allow the presence of Yahweh to enter their lives, the *re-entry* stage, the movement into the promised land. There is also the example of David's lament over Saul and Jonathan: "By your dying I too am stricken, I am desolate for you" (2 Sam 1:25). Then David in the depth of his mourning consults Yahweh, and the latter calls David to a startlingly new leadership, provided David allows his grief to retreat into the past: "Go up!...to Hebron.... The men of Judah came, and there they anointed David as king of the House of Judah" (2 Sam 2:1,4). David could experience the newness, however, only because he acknowledged the depth of his loss and through Yahweh's help let it go, thus leaving space for a newness beyond his dreams to enter his life.

The psalms themselves provide a pattern for grieving. Following Paul Ricoeur, Walter Brueggemann identifies three categories of psalms: hymns of *orientation,* which praise God's order in nature and society (for example, Psalm 104), psalms of *dislocation* or lamentation, which mark the liminal or chaos stage of mourning (for example, Psalms 74 and 88), and psalms of *re-orientation* or re-entry (for example, Psalm 23).[10]

About a third of the psalms fall into the category of lament. They are liminal prayers in which the psalmist grapples with the personal or community pain of loss, for example, the banishment of the people into exile following the destruction of the three pivotal symbols of Jewish culture, namely, the temple, Jerusalem, and the kingship. In the midst of the chaos the psalmist strains to name and let the haunting sadness go, admitting to their utter dependence on Yahweh as the preface to a new experience of hope. Thus two functions of the ritual pattern of the lament psalms are sharply evident: the articulation *and* legitimation of the individual's or community's feelings of grief. It is right, and essential, to express the sadness, even in violently angry or depressing terms: "My God, my God, why have you forsaken me?...My God, I call by day but you do not answer me" (Ps 22:1f.). The failure to articulate the anger over loss will continue to de-energize the people and hold them back from being open to God's newness in their lives. Psalm 74 is a lament: "By the rivers of Babylon we sat and wept at the memory of Zion" (Ps 74:1). The people feel deep in their hearts the loneliness and oppression that comes from being in a foreign and hostile land without God's ever-comforting presence. The psalm reminds the people that it is right to name the pain over and over again, reassuring them that it is quite fitting to do so publicly. Unless the pain of exile is openly identified, the people simply cannot move through the chaos in hope into a new relationship with one another and with Yahweh.

In each lament psalm there is finally a moment when the psalmist, having acknowledged the pain of loss and the darkness of the chaos, actually experiences a renewed surge of hope, a surprising newness or energy.

Psalm 74 aptly illustrates the tripartite pattern of grieving, including the psalmist's restored confidence in the future through the gift of hope. The pivotal symbols of Yahweh's presence to the people, the temple, has been destroyed and Yahweh gets the blame! With its devastation the fundamental identity of the Israelites as a people and their sense of power are shattered: "God, why have you finally rejected us, your anger blazing against the flock you used to pasture?...The enemy has sacked everything in the sanctuary" (vv. 1,3). And there is no indication that the situation will change: "We see no signs, no prophet any more, and none of us knows how long it will last" (v. 9). Desolation reigns supreme. But in the midst of this chaos the writer looks back to the founding myth of the Israelite people, the Exodus, when Yahweh saved them from destruction at the hands of the pursuing Egyptians: God's power "split the sea in two" (v. 13). And he returns to the moment of creation, the founding myth of the universe, when Yahweh molded the world into an orderly shape out of the primeval void: "You turned primordial rivers into dry land.... You caused sun and light to exist, you fixed all the boundaries of the earth, you created summer and winter" (vv. 15–17). With the temple's destruction, however, new chaos erupts. Yet Israel, encouraged by such previous dramatic interventions by God, hopefully anticipates that Yahweh will restore order and identity to the nation. Hope, new energy, replaces the sadness: "Do not let the downtrodden retreat in confusion, give the poor and needy cause to praise your name.... Arise, God, champion your own cause" (vv. 21f).

After angrily confronting God and acknowledging the depth of the chaos, the psalmist is surprised to feel an energy within his heart that has no human origin. God's power of recreation has triumphed again.

In brief, the Hebrew scriptures are filled with calls to sorrow over what has been destroyed or broken down as a condition for new life to come forth. Through the tripartite pattern of the psalms, and by following the stages within each lamentation psalm, we are taught not only the *imperative* of grieving, but also *how* to grieve. We are constantly reminded that no matter how chaotic our condition may be, God has the power to do the humanly impossible—to lift us out of "seething chasm, from the mud and mire." Yahweh can "set my feet on rock" and make "my footsteps firm... a fresh song in my mouth" (Ps 40:2,3). Lament psalms, writes Claus Westermann, transform the experience of chaos into a "way of approaching God with abandonment that permits daring and visioning and even ecstasy." [11] The call to grieve over loss, and not to be de-energized by the chaos, is directed to both the individual Israelite and the corporate person or the nation. Yahweh made a covenant with the people corporately so that when they experience chaos they must act in response as a whole. When they mourn with converting hearts in hope, then, God willing, the nation will relive the recreating power of their founding as a people, the time when God first freely formed them out of the nothingness of chaos.

Reflections from the Christian Scriptures

In the Hebrew scriptures several writers rather hesitantly express the hope that there will be life after death; in the Christian scriptures this hope that there will be a victory over forces of chaos in all its mortal forms is confirmed and affirmed in the death and rising of Christ. Biological death continues, but its meaning is profoundly changed, for now, after the death of Jesus, it is not the end of our life, but rather the beginning of our life in an unimagined fullness or newness: "This perishable nature of ours must put on imperishability, this mortal nature must put on immortality....Then will the words of scripture come true: Death is swallowed up in victory. Death, where is your victory?

Death, where is your sting?" (1 Cor 15:53–55). We become one in the death of Christ and one in the hope of his resurrection: "I am the resurrection. Anyone who believes in me, even though that person dies, will live, and whoever lives and believes in me will never die" (Jn 11:25f.).

This dynamic of acknowledging dying and death, letting go and resurrection, is evident in much of the personal life and teaching methods of Jesus. His followers must learn the art of ongoing grieving, with its tripartite stages, if they are to embrace the resurrection. Ponder just a few examples. The first stage of grieving in the transfiguration incident is when Jesus takes "with him Peter, John and James...up the mountain to pray" (Lk 9:28). This is followed by the liminal phase, the confrontation with chaos, which includes the dramatic change in Jesus' appearance and the presence of Moses and Elijah "appearing in glory" (v. 31). Peter and his companions wake up, and Peter's fear is evident in his attempt to control the thoroughly unpredictable through a flow of quite ridiculous speech and plans "to make three shelters" (v. 33). Peter just has to put order into the chaos that is overwhelming him, but the Father has other ideas for the three startled companions. They must be instructed to let go of Moses and Elijah, the pivotal symbols of the old covenant, if they are to embrace the newness of the new covenant in Christ. The two Old Testament people disappear from sight and "Jesus was found alone" (v. 36). They come down from the mountain, filled with the inspiring experience, but the message of letting go is very slow to be learned, so Jesus must continue to instruct his followers in the art of letting go into newness.

The incident of the blind man begging on the roadside as Jesus nears Jericho is itself a grieving ritual (Lk 18:35–43). To follow Jesus, one must let go the old or that which holds one back in order to be open to the newness beyond human imagination. The beggar calls in pain from the roadside, that is, the *separation* stage (v. 35). He enters into the chaos stage, because the bystanders scold him for disturbing the sense of order that surrounds Jesus, but he will not be silenced or paralyzed by their anger, and the loneliness he experiences: "He only shouted all the louder, 'Son of David, have pity on me'" (v. 39). Jesus hears him, draws him to himself, and the beggar experiences an unimaginable newness—his sight: "And instantly his sight returned and he followed (Jesus) praising God" (v. 43). The cost of the newness is his willingness in faith to risk letting go of his officially sanctioned role as a beggar in Jewish society.

In the suffering and death of Jesus Christ we have *the* model for all who mourn in hope the loss of security and predictability within the church today. He won the title of *Consoler* (Is 51:12) of those who grieve by his self-humiliation, self-forgetfulness, self-emptying, filial obedience to the Father: "The Father loves me, because I lay down my life in order to take it up again.... I lay it down of my own free will" (Jn 10:17f.).

The agony in the Garden of Gethsemane marks the first phase of the greatest of all social dramas and rituals of mourning: the agony, death, and resurrection of Christ. Jesus is both that which is mourned and the ritual leader at the same time. It is characterized by reactions of fear, anxiety, and numbness to actual or anticipated loss. After the example of the lament psalms, Jesus does not camouflage or deny the sufferings he is to experience. Thus the evangelist Mark records that as Jesus begins to pray he feels "terror and anguish" (14:32), but the English translation simply cannot convey the power of the Greek text; words like *horrified, shocked,* or *desolated* are still too weak to grasp what Mark is trying to say.

The evangelist Luke also highlights the intensity of the agony of Jesus, when he describes him praying with such earnestness that "his sweat fell to the ground like great drops of blood" (22:44). The dramatic nature of the emotional reaction is further accentuated by the fact that, when Jesus foretold his death previously, only the disciples had expressed anxiety and desolation. Peter rebuked Jesus for thinking of his coming death. The response of Jesus is filled with confidence, no hint of sadness: "Get behind me, Satan! You are thinking not as God thinks, but as human beings do" (Mk 8:33). But now in Gethsemane Jesus confronts the harsh reality of death, and this evokes in him the powerful emotions of horror, fear, and temptation to flee the pain. Jesus experiences the utter loneliness so poignantly described by the psalmist:

> I pour out my worry in his presence, in his presence I unfold my
>   troubles....
> On the road I have to travel they have hidden a trap for me.
> Look on my right and see—there is no one who recognizes me.
> All refuge is denied me,
> no one cares whether I live or die.
> I cry out to you, Yahweh....
> Listen to my calling, for I am miserably weak.... (Ps 142:2–4)

It is not only the anticipation of his sufferings and death that cause him distress. The loss of innocence of the world through sin and the way this alienates humankind from the loving concern of the Father weigh heavily upon him. He recognizes with more clarity than before the meaning of his mission of loving obedience to the Father and what this will cost him personally. An additional cause of his despondency is the failure of the disciples to remain empathetically alert and at prayer with him in his time of need. Three times he goes to them to revive the support of their friendship. But they fail him. They remain asleep, uninterested in the pain of his journey and grieving. Peter is admonished by Jesus, especially because a short time before he had proudly proclaimed that "Even if all fall away, I will not" (Mk 14:30). He who was so prepared to die for Jesus lacks the strength at the crucial moment to watch one hour with him. Jesus reminds Peter that the Father offers him the grace of detachment so that he can be of service to his master in his hour of need. Peter must decide between this gift and his attachments to the familiar world of order. He chooses the latter and once more fails to grieve or to risk letting go in hope his own securities (Mk 14:37-41).

Finally, in the midst of the loneliness and darkness, Jesus cries out to the Father with a vigorous trust and hope that he will intervene to help him. The spirit of detachment, integral to all authentic mourning, remains throughout the text: "Let your will be done, not mine" (Lk 22:43). Having prayed and allowed the old securities of companionship to go, Jesus is strengthened with new life to accept his death for the sins of the world in a fully conscious way. Now Jesus encounters a freshness and vitality in his actions that contrast markedly with his earlier fear. It is a surprising newness that can only have its source in the Father. He knows what the Father wishes of him and he now has the inner strength to do it, so he commands his sleeping followers to wake up and come with him to face the betrayal. Freshly energized, Jesus on his own initiative informs his captors-to-be that he is the one they want: "Jesus came forward and said, 'Who are you looking for?' They answered, 'Jesus the Nazarene.' Jesus replied, 'I am he.'" (Jn.18:4–5). This confident movement by Jesus out of the liminal turmoil of the garden forms the third stage of this ritual of letting go. Fear remains, but it is now controlled by hope.

The description by Luke of the ascension of Jesus follows the same tripartite pattern of a grieving ritual. There is the brief journey to the Mount of Olives, the first stage of the ritual in which Jesus again tells his disciples that he will now leave them. Then "they will receive the power of the Holy Spirit...and then you will be my witnesses not only in Jerusalem but throughout Judaea and Samaria, and indeed to earth's remotest end" (Acts 1:8). This formal statement of intended separation is followed by Jesus actually ascending into heaven. But the disciples become locked in the chaos of the liminal stage. They longingly wait for Jesus to return, forgetting in their grief everything Jesus had said about the necessity of his withdrawal as the condition for the spirit to come among them. The angels as ritual leaders of grieving jolt them back to reality, directing them to let Jesus go and move forward to wait in hope the coming of the spirit: "Why are you Galileans standing here looking into the sky? This Jesus who has been taken up from you into heaven will come back in the same way as you have seen him go to heaven" (Acts 1:11). They followed the angels' directive and moved in hope into the third phase of grieving to await the coming of the spirit: "So from the Mount of Olives...they went back to Jerusalem...went to the upper room...(and) joined constantly in prayer" (Acts 1:12,14).

Ministers as Ritual Leaders of Grieving

Walter Brueggemann writes that "prophetic ministry consists of offering an alternative perception of reality and in letting people see their own history in the light of God's freedom and his will for justice." Grieving, he says, "is a pre-condition....Only that kind of anguished disengagement permits fruitful yearning and only the public embrace of deathliness permits newness to come." [12] The basic theme of this essay is that healing involves readiness and the courage on the part of individuals, organizations, and cultures to allow the past to die. It also means arranging space for the new to emerge and be received. Ritual, based on the three stages explained previously and sanctioned by scripture, holds a critically important role in allowing the healing after loss to occur and the new to come forth. Hence, one of the fundamental obligations of a minister is to learn the art of leading people through grief into newness.

Ministers, in order to reflect on this challenge to be community grief leaders, may with profit reflect on the life of Moses, one of the greatest and most successful organizational administrators in history. He is an exemplary leader because he is able to pilot his community through an extremely difficult rite of passage; from a motley tribe they become through a wilderness experience of grieving a people with a known destiny. Moses is aware that there is a distinction between individuals and their community or culture; hence, if people are to be open to the new, there must be rites of passage not just for individuals but *especially* for the community or culture.

Ministers must be able to recognize the symptoms of grief and take appropriate ritual action, for Moses[13] did precisely that. He is aware that in the separation stage of the ritual of mourning, people feel the pain of leaving the old and familiar world behind; there is hurting, anger, the move to blame others for their misery: "To Moses they said: 'Was it for lack of graves in Egypt, that you had to lead us out to die in the desert? What was the point of bringing us out of Egypt....We prefer to work for the Egyptians than to die in the desert....'" (Ex 14:11f.). "Why did we not die at Yahweh's hand in Egypt, where we used to sit round the flesh pots and could eat to our heart's content!" (Ex 16:3).

Moses acts in four ways to turn the grief into a positive liminal experience to allow the new to emerge. *First,* he shrewdly understands the importance of permitting the people to experience the chaos. The new cannot develop without pain: "Remember the long road by which Yahweh your God led you for forty years in the desert, to humble you, to test you and know your inmost heart.... Learn from this that Yahweh your God was training you as a man trains his child...." (Dt 8:2,5). *Second,* he is thoroughly conscious of his own limitations as a person and a leader, so he constantly pleads from deep within his own inner chaos with Yahweh to help him. He cannot authentically lead if he is not himself struggling to let go his own attachments.[14] *Third,* Moses understands the need in the second or liminal stage of grieving, the wandering in the desert, to keep ties with the collective roots of his people back in Egypt. Hence, he collects the bones of Joseph and allows the people to carry them into the wilderness (Ex 13:19).

Fourth, at certain points in the journey through the wilderness chaos, Moses appreciates the need for rituals that encourage people to continue to let go of the past's negative aspects and to express hope in the vision of the future. Thus, there are the rituals of the sweet water (Ex 15:25), the manna and quails (Ex 16), the water from the rock (Ex 17:1–7). He believes that rituals must be well prepared and speak not just to the minds of the participants, but also to their feelings, so he becomes a master of the use of liturgical songs and visual aids.

Moses is aware throughout the exodus journey that the disintegration or the experience of chaos required for a new people to develop can lead to total destruction, if not guided prudently. Therefore, he wisely sought advice, and Jethro, his father-in-law, instructs Moses to group the people into manageable administrative units under the direction of "capable and God-fearing men, men who are trustworthy and incorruptible" (Ex 18:21). Moses is forthrightly reminded that he needs the space to think, pray, contemplate his own inner fragility and need of God. Without this space Moses cannot keep in touch with the vision Yahweh has for the people. The lesson is clear: Every grief leader must constantly rearticulate the vision, but for this to happen he or she requires periods of silence unburdened by the tiring pressures of daily administration.

The lessons that Moses gives to all community grief leaders within the church today are as relevant today as in his own time. They can be summarized as follows:

1. To be good ritual leaders of grieving, ministers must be good listeners. Moses is open to hear Yahweh and to be aware of the people's sufferings; he keeps contact with people by wandering around the camps and speaking informally to them outside their tents.

2. Recognize that communities or cultures, such as the church, parishes, and organizations within parishes, suffer grief, not just individuals. Their experience of grief can be creative, if rituals of mourning are encouraged and well led. As Brueggemann says, "The public sharing of pain is one way to let the reality sink in and let death go."[15]

3. Realize that chaos must not be allowed to lead to total disintegration; people throughout the liminal period need a clear and inspiring vision of what they should be aiming at, as well as structures and rituals that assist them to maintain unity; these facilitate the process whereby the past can be allowed to slip away and hope in the future fostered.

4. Be comfortable with the chaos in one's own journey. Unless one is able to mourn personally for one's own sins and losses, it will be impossible to be sensitive to the grieving needs of a community. This means the regular structuring of time and space to be with oneself and with God; feverish busyness is no atmosphere for contemplation, self-knowledge, creativity, and visioning.

Summary

Rites of passage are rituals that mark the progress of an individual and/or group between relatively stable and fixed, culturally or religiously recognized states of rank, status, office, calling, or profession. Each rite of passage means that there is an experience of death as the old status is put aside. The prophet Jeremiah was deeply pained by the fact that the Israelites failed to recognize that key symbols of their social structure were disappearing or about to be destroyed: the temple, Jerusalem, the kingship (Jer 4:19,20,22). In our terminology, the Israelites disdained to accept the stages of separation and liminality; they ignored the need to let go of a dying world and to enter into a revitalized relationship with Yahweh and with one another.

Jeremiah, however, did grieve. He expressed deep sorrow at the passing of the old symbols, and he agonized (the liminal stage) over what lay ahead. Finally, he trusts Yahweh, who will be his strength in his own journey of life.

Western society is no different from the world of Jeremiah. It is systematically removing significant loss and death from our consciousness—a form of planned obsolescence. Anthropologist Geoffrey Gorer speaks of the "pornography" of death, in that death is not to be mentioned publicly. It is to be dealt with as an object of fantasy only. Death is a puzzle to people who are uncertain about existence of an afterlife; the way to avoid being troubled by uncertainty is to deny death and whatever is related to it.[16]

An entire industry has developed to remove the reality of death from relatives and friends: the "loved one" is facially restored to "robust good health" by morticians and is laid out for viewing in the "slumber room." All public expression of feeling is discouraged. Yet this is the denial of one of the most basic needs of the human person and group: the need to acknowledge death through an appropriate ritual and spirituality, to grieve over the loss of the familiar, and to struggle to relate anew to a world without that which is lost.

Princess Diana's death reveals more about us than we may immediately think, as surging grief gives way to a developing mythology and the creation of a secular saint. At one level, many thousands grieved over the loss of a friend made present to them weekly or daily through the mass media. Yet, I sense, there is still a deeper meaning to this incredible outpouring of grief. The tragic death of this young lady provided the occasion for communal grieving in a culture where such ritual outlets are denied. It is reported that Diana's death led to a steep drop in the number of people in Britain seeking help for depression. This unprecedented public mourning allowed people to release, psychiatrists claim, deeply buried emotions about some of their own personal problems. And they did it together.[17] People desperately need, in the midst of an ever-changing and secularizing world, a spirituality of letting go and appropriate rituals to express this spirituality. In Diana's death, people found a focus for their free-floating grief.[18] We ministers must ourselves listen to this lesson.

Notes

1. The theme of this essay is more fully developed in my books *Grieving for Change: A Spirituality for Refounding Gospel Communities* (Westminster, Md.: Christian Classics, 1991); *Refounding the Church: Dissent for Leadership* (Maryknoll: Orbis Books, 1993); and article "Organizations Must Grieve Ritually," *Human Development* 12, 1 (1991): 22–27.

2. See E. Kübler-Ross, *On Death and Dying* (New York: Macmillan, 1969).

3. See C. G. Helman, *Culture, Health and Illness* (Oxford: Butterworth-Heinemann, 1990), 2–3.

4. See discussion by A. Williams *et al.*, *Changing Culture: New Organsational Approaches* (London: Institute of Personnel Management, 1993), 11–38.

5. C. Geertz, *The Interpretation of Cultures* (New York: Basic Books, 1973), 89.

6. See fuller explanation in my book *Earthing the Gospel: An Inculturation Handbook for the Pastoral Worker* (Maryknoll: Orbis Books, 1990), 26–44.

7. I am grateful to Adolfo Nicolas, S.J., for this definition.

8. V. Turner, *Dramas, Fields and Metaphors: Symbolic Action in Human Society* (New York: Cornell University Press, 1974), 256.

9. See relevant comments by W. Brueggemann, "Kingship and Chaos: A Study in Tenth-Century Theology," in *Catholic Biblical Quarterly* 33 (1971): 317–32, and "Weariness, Exile and Chaos: A Motif in Royal Theology," *CBQ* 34 (1972): 19–38.

10. See W. Brueggemann, "Psalms and the Life of Faith: A Suggested Typology of Function," in *Journal for the Study of the Old Testament* 17 (1980): 3–22; and P. Ricoeur, *The Conflict of Interpretations: Essays in Hermeneutics* (Evanston: Northwestern University Press, 1974), 369f. and *passim*.

11. C. Westermann, *Elements of Old Testament Theology* (Atlanta: John Knox Press, 1982), 103. See also B. Anderson, *Out of the Depths: The Psalms Speak to Us Today* (Philadelphia: Westminster Press, 1983), *passim*.

12. W. Brueggemann, *The Prophetic Imagination* (Philadelphia: Fortress Press, 1978), 110, 113.

13. See G. A. Arbuckle, *Change, Grief and Renewal in the Church* (Allen, Tex.: Christian Classics, 1991), 151–56.

14. See M. Martini, *Through Moses to Jesus: The Way of the Paschal Mystery* (Notre Dame, Ind.: Ave Maria Press, 1988), *passim*.

15. Brueggemann, *Prophetic Imagination*, 111.

16. See G. Gorer, *Death, Grief and Mourning* (London: Cresset Press, 1965), 42; Arbuckle, *Earthing the Gospel*, 103–4.

17. See *Sydney Morning Herald*, December 17, 1997, 12.

18. See N. Mitchell, *Worship*, 72, 1 (1998): 44–45.

John P. Mossi

---

9. Prayers from Calvary:
A Passion Spirituality

The lyrics of the African American spiritual, "Were You There When They Crucified My Lord?" evokes the graphic scene of Good Friday. Its melody causes us to ponder, to tremble interiorly, and to meditate on the redemptive event that occurred on Calvary. On that special Friday, which is described as "Good," Jesus was crucified for us so that the reconciliation of all humanity would be accomplished.

The Passion Accounts are the oldest sections of the Christian scriptures. Hence, they hold an important memory of the early church and are a valuable touchstone of the teachings of Jesus. The seven last sayings of Jesus from the cross are collectively found in Matthew, Luke, Mark, and John—no one Gospel contains all seven. They have been organized through a traditional preaching devotion referred to in Latin as *Tre Ore,* signifying the three hours Jesus hung on the cross. As contemporary ministers and disciples of the Word, these accounts help us to grapple with our own dark night experiences. Jesus assists us to address our own forms of suffering, abandonment, and crucifixion. Through these bitter moments, Jesus shows us how to pray, to forgive, to love, and to embrace life in the midst of trial and death.

It is critical to remember that these costly words of Jesus were spoken for our sake. The passion spirituality of the Seven Last Words[1] is a unique treasure for us to engage and imitate. Good Friday is in many ways the last temptation of Jesus. Jesus tempts us to be totally human, vulnerable, and surrender all to God. Jesus asks us, even in the confusion of darkness and the angst of dying, to pray.

The purpose of this essay is threefold: First, to provide the necessary texts so that the power of scripture may speak directly to our experience; second, to offer reflections on each Calvary saying of Jesus in order to unfold its wisdom; and third, to present suggestions for action so that the reader can adapt the gospel to everyday experience. This interactive design can be used for personal theological reflection, small group study sessions, or assembly preaching.

134

The First Word: Forgiveness

Father, forgive them, they know not what they do. (Lk 23:23)

Let us revisit some of the realities of this Calvary scene. Jesus now hangs as a condemned criminal on the cross. He is naked, alone, in extreme pain. The crown of thorns torments his head. Blood runs over his eyes. Rough iron nails pierce his hands and feet. The interior of Jesus is a sea of sorrow and anguish.

At the foot of the cross stand the skeptics and guards who listen for what Jesus might say. Some indifferently watch, others mock and jeer. The leaders taunt, "He saved others, let him save himself if he is the chosen one, the Messiah of God" (Lk 23:35). Some, no doubt, felt a divine favor had been done by eliminating a false prophet. The soldiers, after offering Jesus vinegar to drink, add their own scorn, "If you are the King of the Jews, save yourself" (Lk 23:37).

Questions assault our minds. We ask, "Is this the victory of darkness?" "What has Jesus done to merit such hostility, cruelty, and malice?" When we ourselves, or those dear to us, or the innocent, experience similar injustice and pain, we angrily question, "Why does God let this happen?"

What would have been our own first word if we were crushed under the weight of such despair? If we had the ability and the power, how would we have settled the score? Perhaps we would have clenched our fists in anger and exterminated those at our feet?

And Jesus? His response? He prays. He allies himself with life. He prays to the Father. He prays forgiveness. He invokes pardon. He prays from the heart.

Jesus does not deny the evil, the darkness, the injustice. He transforms it with compassion. In effect, Jesus models in three distinct movements a spirituality of forgiveness. First, focus on the Father who is the source of true forgiveness. Second, pray in conjunction with the Father to forgive all enemies. Third, pray for the divine insight that the aggression of evil is the result of not knowing the love of God. In the prayer of the first word, Jesus calls upon the tender mercy of the Father to pardon and forgive those who seek his death.

We petition to be living sacraments of God's mercy to others, aware that the Father is compassionate toward us every second of every day, no matter how poorly we respond. If God would ever fail to be so unconditionally compassionate and full of loving mercy toward us, even for a few moments, we and all creation would cease to exist. St. Paul, addressing the citizens of Athens in Acts 17:28, reflects on the totality of God's pervasive, continuous love for each one of us, "In him we live and move and have our being." God, the most merciful and compassionate one, cannot deny his very nature.

From the cross, Jesus invites us for the last time to love our enemies, to recommend them to the Father, to pray for them. To respond to the reality of darkness, not with darkness, but with the light of forgiveness and love.

However, we cannot omit Jesus' phrase, "They know not what they do." What is your reaction to these words? Does not Jesus pardon his persecutors lightly with an implausible excuse? Exactly what does this mean, "They know not what they do"? Is it tantamount to saying that Judas did not know his act of betrayal when he kissed Jesus? The crowd did not know they were shouting, "Crucify him! Crucify him!"? Are we exempt from the knowledge and conse-quences of what we do? When we sin, do we do so through ignorance? When someone robs a grocery store, shoots the manager, and runs over an innocent bystander, is this person without culpability?

Since childhood, we've known right from wrong. We know when we choose light and when we choose darkness. Is Jesus making a weak excuse for our inhumanity? Or is he saying something more profound? That is, there is one great reality that we don't know when we sin and choose evil: What we don't know is the overwhelming love of God for us.

In sin, we become trapped in our own addiction and gratification. In sin, we block the love of God. In sin, we postpone the knowledge and the love of God from living in us, and through us touching others. Jesus was in constant contact with this higher mercy and love of the Father. Hence, he could truly understand and pray, "Father, forgive them, they know not what they do."

Suggestions for Action

The living gospel continually invites us to make this first prayer of Jesus our own. To be a disciple means to pray as Jesus gives us example: "Father, forgive them." We do so in four steps. Apply the necessary time that each step requires.

1. Call to mind anyone who has hurt you, insulted you, or committed the offense that is impossible to erase from memory. This individual or group may be living or dead, a member of the family, a neighbor, a friend, a teacher, a minister, a coworker, someone who belongs to your club or association. Bring this person to mind.

2. As you see this person you despise, ask Jesus for the gift to forgive and to love that person as he does.

3. Center your attention completely on Jesus. Focus on his loving courage and the way he teaches us how to forgive. Look directly into the eyes of Jesus until you can join with him in saying to those who hurt you, "Father, forgive them."

4. As you continue to pray for forgiveness, place this person in the heal-ing love of Jesus. Hand over the memories of the painful experience

to Jesus, in whose hands such memories belong. Finally, pray from the heart asking the Father to bless that person.

Such a prayer of forgiveness is seldom easy to achieve the first time. To forgive one's enemies demands the purest love. Often we have to repeat the process again and again. When forgiveness is especially problematic to attain, do not attempt to pray alone. Call on the assistance of the Holy Spirit. It is important to keep focused on the unconditional way that Jesus instructs us to forgive.

The Second Word: To Give Away Heaven

Amen, I say to you, today you will be with me in Paradise. (Lk 23:43)

There is a classic legend[2] that when Mary and Joseph fled into Egypt with the child Jesus, they rested at a roadside inn. Mary asked the hostess for water to bathe Jesus. The hostess then requested if she could bathe her own child, who was suffering from leprosy, in the same water in which Jesus was immersed. The sick infant, upon touching the water, was instantly healed of the disease.

The legend continues that this cured child grew in strength and became a clever thief. He is the criminal, traditionally referred to as Dismas and called "the good thief," who hangs on his own cross to the right of Jesus.

Let us consider the good thief, and then, Jesus. What do they each have to teach about prayer and heaven? The lesson is uncomplicated: It is never too late. St. Paul reminds us in 2 Corinthians 6:2, "Behold, now is a very acceptable time; behold, now is the day of salvation."

As we hover over this Calvary scene, Jesus receives little sympathy or consolation. The people jeer, "Save yourself." The chief priests and scribes mock, "Come down from the cross that we may see and believe." The soldiers taunted as well and offered vinegar. The other thief joined in the abuse, "Save yourself and, of course, don't forget to include us too."

The only one to speak to Jesus with any compassion, with any note of concern is the thief on the right. He acknowledges that he is receiving what he deserves. The good thief speaks for us all. "We deserve the cross, not the Innocent One. We receive the consequences of what we have merited, but what action has Jesus done to merit crucifixion and to die as a criminal?" (Lk 23:41).

In dramatic contrast to all those present, the good thief addresses Jesus by name and in supplication. Dismas teaches us how to pray at the last minute, in the midst of difficulty, even in the face of death. The thief, ready for conversion, calls out in friendship to Jesus. Dismas is the only one on Calvary to speak to Jesus by name. He creates an inspiring, brief prayer: "Jesus, remember me when you come into your kingdom" (Lk 23:42). Dismas, during his quickly disappearing time on earth, expresses the desire to be associated with Jesus and his kingdom.

These final words of the thief are a gentle supplication, a last petition, and, perhaps, his very first plea as well. In Luke 11:9, Jesus invites us to ask, to seek, to knock. "And I tell you, ask and you will receive; seek and you will find; knock and the door will be opened to you." Maybe the thief appealed this one time only, sought this one time only, knocked this one time only? He risked everything and in return found the pearl of great price. The good thief provides us with needed courage, which affirms that it is never too late to reach out to Jesus. It is never too late to seek reconciliation with our Savior. That day, Jesus entered heaven with an exceptionally "good" thief. In a real sense, Dismas died a thief, having stolen heaven.

There is an insightful story[3] about Jesus appearing to a devout woman. The woman mentioned this favored vision to her bishop, who doubted the authenticity of this experience. He decided to test her story with a query. "When Jesus appears to you the next time, ask him to mention the specific sins of your bishop." A month later the devout woman returned and mentioned that she again had conversation with Jesus. "Did you ask Jesus my question?" "Yes, bishop, I did." "And what did he say?" Jesus said, "He doesn't remember your sins anymore."

In the first word, Jesus models for us how to forgive. In this second word, Jesus forgets instantaneously our track record in order to open the gates of heaven. The exchange between Jesus and the good thief is a reminder that Jesus is ever anxious to extend heaven to us no matter what we have done. Even at our last breath, it is never too late to pray with the good thief: "Jesus, remember me when you come into your kingdom."

The reassuring words of Luke 23:43 are for anyone who desires to be a follower of Jesus: "This day you shall be with me in Paradise." The over-whelming reality and insight of the second word is that Jesus is solicitous to give away heaven. He places no conditions whenever we turn to him. In fact, it is impossible for Jesus not to lavish us with heaven.

Suggestions for Action

As we reflect on this second word of Jesus, we can ask ourselves how we can give away heaven as well. The Seven Last Words of Jesus are like summary instructions, training manuals for his followers. They challenge us to be more Christlike.

Heaven is dispensed in diverse ways. To give away our love, compassion, time, talents, and skills are some different ways of making the kingdom of God genuine. To give away that heavenly gift that will lighten another person's cross makes paradise apparent today.

It is important to give heaven away not just to close friends but to the faceless, the homeless, the nameless, those whom society considers as outcast and nonimportant, those who are most in need of respect and dignity. In our petitions asking Jesus to remember us in our need, our response should always be to remember others, especially the marginal, in their plight.

1. Ask Jesus to show you those unique aspects of heaven you can give away. Your gift might be in the form of volunteer work, the donated help of a specific skill or knowledge, certain talents, or financial assistance. Spend time in conversation with Jesus, considering how you can best imitate his generosity on the cross.

2. Ask Jesus to present to you the faces of those in need of what you can give. Mother Teresa reminded us that we do not have to travel to distant lands to find and serve the poor. Often the needy are in our own neighborhoods and cities, not to mention in our families and social groups.

3. As you ponder the crucified one, ask Jesus for the courage, gospel imagination, and strength to take the first important step. To make that phone call, to establish that contact, to offer your services, to make a donation. The second step is similar: to develop the attitude to give away heaven spontaneously as a habitual way of life.

The Third Word: Community

"Woman, behold, your son."…"Behold, your mother." (Jn 19:26,27)

It is not surprising that at the foot of the cross we find Mary, the first believer and foremost disciple, the mother of Jesus. Mary is surrounded by a small community of believers: Mary Clopas, Mary Magdalene, and the beloved disciple. Matthew 27:56 also includes Salome, the mother of the sons of Zebedee. It is interesting to note that the women on Calvary outnumber the men four to one.

There is mentioned "the disciple whom he loved." Tradition tells us this is the Apostle John. However, scripture does not name the beloved disciple as John. This disciple is anonymous. In many ways, this disciple is every unnamed believer. Each one of us as a believer, as a person of faith, can insert our own name in the company of this group of disciples. For what disciple is there, no matter how weak, that Jesus does not consider as beloved?

Let us consider two special ways in which Mary is present on Calvary: first, as a disciple; second, as a person of faith.

Mary is the first disciple of Jesus. No one heard the Word of God better and responded to the Word more fully than Mary. She opened herself so completely to the Holy Spirit that through her the Word became flesh. St. Augustine in the fourth century speaks of Mary in this way: "She first conceived Jesus in her heart before conceiving him in her womb." It is in this role as the first and foremost disciple of Jesus that Mary is present on Calvary. Her following of Jesus is so total, so encompassing, even when this means standing at the foot of the cross, it is literally inconceivable for Mary not to be there.

Mary is also present as a person of faith. As a young person, she humbly said "Yes" to the invitation by the Holy Spirit to be the Mother of God. She literally surrendered her person and journey to the providential care of God. Like us, she had no idea of the future turns in her faith journey, those surprises and setbacks that are the consequences of being a follower of Christ. As a person of faith, she put her whole life at stake, acknowledging that God is present and active, not only in the joyful events of the Christian pilgrimage, but on Calvary as well.

To be a person of faith, associated with Jesus, demands total commitment. At the foot of the cross, Mary perhaps recalled the words that Simeon addressed to her when he blessed the child Jesus at the temple in Jerusalem: "And you yourself a sword will pierce" (Lk 2:35). From the beginning of her pilgrimage, Mary understood that she would intimately share in the sufferings of her son. The fulfillment of Simeon's words came when Mary held the limp body of the crucified Christ in her arms. She would know firsthand, and better than anyone else, the truth revealed in the Pietà.

One would think that the privilege of being the mother of Jesus would have somehow exempted Mary from Calvary. She was not dispensed, no more than Jesus was spared. Nor are we exempt. On Calvary, Jesus makes a profound statement. He enters into total solidarity with our human condition, even the ambiguous questioning that surrounds dying and the dark finality of death. Jesus, accepting the fullness of his humanity, chose to remain present on the cross. He reveals for us that the spirit of God was not absent from the mystery of Calvary. Daringly, Jesus helps us find God in the midst of suffering and darkness.

Let us try to plumb the intensity of this third prayer of Jesus. It is a selfless expression. Even to the very last, Jesus diverts attention from himself and invites those present to minister to one another. Jesus encourages us all to create community, to recognize one another, to enter into relationships. This art of building community is twofold: first, to behold others; second, to uphold and care for neighbor and stranger.

Jesus now asks Mary to behold her new son. To the beloved disciple, Jesus entrusts his mother as essential to his household. The wisdom from the cross that Jesus imparts is most obvious. Our task as God's chosen people, as parishioners, as neighbors, as family, is to pass beyond the barriers of isolation, to behold one another, to enter into deeper interpersonal relationships. Membership in community is not just an option for Jesus; it is a way of serving in his spirit.

Jesus in his act of dying is still creating community. He creates church, a new set of relationships where disciples are responsive to God and to one another. In Matthew 12:49–50, Jesus describes this new family of God, in which the only consideration in being related to Jesus as a brother, sister, or mother is to do God's will: "And stretching out his hand toward his disciples, he said, 'Here are my mother and my brothers. For whoever does the will of my heavenly Father is my brother, and sister, and mother.'"

This third instruction of Jesus asks us to embrace one another in reverence. Jesus does not desire that anyone on Calvary stand alone, as estranged, or passive. The challenge of Calvary demands that we use the cross to find and behold each another. In the demanding process of building church, we are called to overcome the darkness of Calvary that can blur creative vision. The outward response of Jesus is to behold and be attentive to others, thereby always making room for another sojourner.

Suggestions for Action

For our prayer meditation, let us learn from Mary, a mother of great faith and the first disciple of Jesus. Ask her for the grace and strength to face those personal Calvaries we shudder to endure. She stood at the cross; how can her wisdom and fortitude help us to address those realities we cannot change?

1. Focus upon one experience, event, relationship that is particularly difficult for you to face. Ask Mary to show the way. How was she, as a disciple, able to stand in solidarity with her son on Calvary? Is there a lesson here for us?

2. The next intercession we direct to Jesus. Ask him for the vision to go beyond our own suffering in order to see others in their need. In the face of opposition, how can you still create community and church, to behold the stranger as brother and sister of Jesus?

3. Call to mind the diverse community of people you belong to. In what specific way can you be a builder of relationships for these groups?

The Fourth Word: To Pray from the Depths

My God, my God, why have you forsaken me? (Mt 27:46)

Jesus addressed his first three prayers to three different groups. The first, to his persecutors: "Father, forgive them." The second, to sinners: "Today you will be with me in Paradise." The third, to his disciples: "Woman, behold, your son." ... "Behold, your mother."

The next two petitions, the fourth and the fifth, reveal the personal sufferings of Jesus on the cross. The fourth word illustrates the angst of one rejected by God: "My God, my God, why have you forsaken me?" The fifth word shows the interior suffering of the humanity of Jesus: "I thirst." With each of these words, Jesus continues to demonstrate to us how to live, how to die, and how to pray.

John of the Cross, the Spanish mystic of the sixteenth century, wrote about the "Dark Night of the Senses." It is that state of being and prayer when all consolation, interior peace and strength is absent, not felt. The spiritual senses seem dead.

John of the Cross then went on to describe what he referred to as the "Dark Night of the Soul." This is when even a sliver of God's presence is absent. The soul feels abandoned, rejected, orphaned. The isolation becomes crushing. Both emotionally and spiritually, the dark night experience rips apart and disintegrates any remaining, however minute, affinity with God.

In such a total dark night state we encounter this fourth prayer of Jesus. These are words of anger and rage. "My God, my God, why have you done this to me?" We have all expressed such sentiments at one time or another. It is that horrible, wrenching time when the forces of night seem to prevail, and the abyss separating us from God seems insurmountable.

And what does Jesus do? His response? He prays. He prays through the darkness. Jesus continues to cry out to God, whom he senses as not present. Jesus prays from the depths of his person, from his emotional core. There is no denial; he is very much in touch with his excruciating pain. In fact, Jesus actively uses his emptiness, anguish, and abandonment as the beginning point of prayer.

On Calvary, Jesus teaches us to pray. The prayer of this fourth word has four parts:

1. Be in touch with the wellsprings of your depths and the resources of your experience. The core of the emotions provide a directness and intensity for prayer.

2. Next, call on the Creator and make the prayer personal: "My God, my God."

3. Then, express the experience and the accompanying emotion as it is literally felt. Articulate this reality, uncensored, in its full strength. "Why have you forsaken me?" "I am in pain." "I don't know what to say or to believe anymore." "I feel lost at sea."

4. Ask Jesus for the courage to live through this time of trial, while at the same time, allowing your prayer to continue to rise from your depths.

This entreaty is referred to as the prayer of the passions, a prayer most visceral and real. Jesus is comfortable praying in this manner. He gives us permission to do the same. There is no despair, no raging question of why, no emotion, lamentation, or bitter agony that the Father is not able to hear.

"My God, my God, why have you forsaken me?" is the beginning verse of Psalm 22. Jesus, in crying out the first line, claims the entire psalm, which ends in a confidence of vindication. Let us reflect upon some of the graphic descriptions found in this psalm. It is the desperate cry of all the poor, powerless, and abandoned.

> My God, my God, why have you abandoned me?
>> Why so far from my call for help, from my cries of anguish?
> My God, I call by day, but you do not answer;
>> by night, but I have no relief.
> Yet you are enthroned as the Holy One;
>> you are the glory of Israel.
> In you our ancestors trusted;
>> they trusted and you rescued them.
> To you they cried out and they escaped;
>> in you they trusted and they were not disappointed.
> But I am a worm, hardly human,
>> scorned by everyone, despised by the people.
> All who see me mock me;
>> they curl their lips and jeer;
>>> they shake their heads at me:
> "You relied on the Lord—let him deliver you;
>> If he loves you, let him rescue you."
>
> Yet you drew me forth from the womb,
>> made me safe at my mother's breast.
> Upon you I was thrust from the womb;
>> since birth you are my God.
> Do not stay far from me,
>> for trouble is near,
>>> and there is no one to help.
>
> Like water my life drains away;
>> all my bones grow soft.
> My heart has become like wax,
>> it melts away within me.
> As dry as a potsherd is my throat;
>> my tongue sticks to my palate;
>>> you lay me in the dust of death.

Many dogs surround me;
    a pack of evildoers closes in on me.
So wasted are my hands and my feet
    that I can count all my bones.
They stare at me and gloat;
    they divide my garments among them;
        for my clothing they cast lots.

But you, Lord, do not stay far off;
    my strength, come quickly to help me.
Deliver me from the sword,
    my forlorn life from the teeth of the dog.
Save me from the lion's mouth,
    my poor life from the horns of wild bulls.
                (Ps 22:1–12,15–22)

Jesus, identifying with the sentiments of these verses, admits his vulnerability and releases his lament in order to claim a deeper strength in God. Jesus demonstrates how to use our distress as a beginning point of prayer. Only through appropriating the anguish and injustice can one move through the impasse of the dark night.

Suggestions for Action

In the meditation period that follows, ask Jesus for the courage to incorporate your own dark night experiences and emotions as important and necessary components in prayer. Reflectively consider the following three areas of examination.

1. When you are in crisis and God seems distant, how do you respond? What does your normal prayer, thought, and action pattern reveal? In what way does this fourth word of Jesus challenge and assist your spiritual growth?

2. How comfortable are you with others as they express their pain? Do you want to change the topic? Or do you attentively listen to their story and sorrow without trying to fix their feelings? The first step in healing is handing over the suffering to someone who is empathetic and compassionate.

3. How well do you share with others your own grief and disappointment? Do you protect yourself like a fortified city? How easily do you disclose to God in prayer your burdens and negative feelings? Who is your confidant, to whom you entrust the care of your person?

The Fifth Word: Thirsting For God

I thirst. (Jn 19:28)

The parched lips of Jesus disclose his fragile humanity. Seeking momentary relief, he cries out to anyone who can hear, "I thirst." The cumulative brutality of Good Friday, beginning with the scourging at the pillar, the crowning of thorns, the carrying of the cross and crucifixion, reveals its toll: dehydration of body and spirit. As the blood and sweat of Jesus seep into the earth, Jesus pleads for a drink to quench his fever and pain. Psalm 69:21–22 foreshadowed this fifth word of Jesus:

Insult has broken my heart, and I am weak,
    I looked for sympathy, but there was none;
    for comforters, and I found none.
Rather they put gall in my food,
    and in my thirst they gave me vinegar to drink.

On a spiritual level, the Gospel of John points to a deeper thirst of Jesus, a thirst to complete his mission, a thirst to fulfill scripture.

Again, Jesus teaches us how to pray. He uses his desert experience, his parched soul as a means to thirst for God. He is truly aware that his task is to fulfill scripture, to finish everything the Father has given him to complete. So, even in the human experience of thirsting, Jesus is actively demonstrating to us how to live and die, not as if passively assaulted with blind fate or as a helpless victim, but intentionally, yearning for God.

John 19:34 subsequently records, "But one soldier thrust his lance into his side, and immediately blood and water flowed out." One would imagine that Jesus in his last moments would have depleted his reservoirs of strength. What possibly more could be offered? Yet, even in his dying and death, his body continues to pour out whatever remains of the sacrament of his person; namely, his redemptive blood and water. St. Paul in the Letter to the Philippians 2:6–8 praises this total donation of Jesus.

Who, though he was in the form of God,
    did not regard equality with God something to be grasped.
Rather, he emptied himself,
taking the form of a slave,
coming in human likeness;
and found human in appearance
he humbled himself,
becoming obedient to death,
    even death on a cross.

Both the thirsting for God of Jesus and the emptying of his blood and water become images for our spiritual growth as well. As each of us experiences our own thirsting, the Gospel of John invites us to partake of the two redemptive sacraments that originate in Jesus, namely, baptism and eucharist.

Recall the words of Jesus as he teaches us how to satiate our thirst. At the Last Supper, Jesus took the cup of blessing and said, "Drink from it, all of you, for this is my blood of the covenant, which will be shed on behalf of many for the forgiveness of sins" (Mt 26:27–28). Elsewhere, on the last day of the feast of Tabernacles, Jesus exclaimed, "Let anyone who thirsts come to me and drink. Whoever believes in me, as scripture says: 'Rivers of living water will flow from within him'" (Jn 7:37–38).

This fifth word reveals the many thirsts of Jesus. On a physically human level, his body craves quenching relief. As one innocently condemned, he cries out for justice. In fulfilling his mission, he longs that we might partake of the waters and blood of salvation.

Litany

Placing the desires of Jesus in your heart, slowly pray this litany. The response to each petition is, "Jesus, help me to thirst."

For love and compassion...*Jesus, help me to thirst.*
For peace and justice...*Jesus, help me to thirst.*
For understanding and respect...*Jesus, help me to thirst.*
For your body and blood...*Jesus, help me to thirst.*
For your living waters...*Jesus, help me to thirst.*
For reconciliation among nations, families, and individuals...*Jesus, help me to thirst.*
For the church and its mission...*Jesus, help me to thirst.*
For those addicted to alcohol and drugs...*Jesus, help me to thirst.*
For those near death and those dying of cancer and AIDS...*Jesus, help me to thirst.*
For the elderly left abandoned...*Jesus, help me to thirst.*
For those who have no escape from the tyranny of poverty...*Jesus, help me to thirst.*
For jobs, health care, housing, decent education, and the distribution of food...*Jesus, help me to thirst.*
For the unborn who will die...*Jesus, help me to thirst.*
For those who have disappeared, refugees, those living under repression and martial law...*Jesus, help me to thirst.*
For exploited workers and those persecuted because of their beliefs.... *Jesus, help me to thirst.*

For the depressed...*Jesus, help me to thirst.*

For those who consume too much...*Jesus, help me to thirst.*

For those who suffer due to promiscuity, infidelity, spouse and child abuse...*Jesus, help me to thirst.*

For those who diminish the human dignity of another because of their color, sex, creed, race, religion, sexual orientation, or physical appearance...*Jesus, help me to thirst.*

For the physically impaired and the mentally and emotionally disabled...*Jesus, help me to thirst.*

For those who do not even know or care what it is to thirst...*Jesus, help me to thirst.*

Suggestions for Action

1. Reflect upon what you truly seek and desire. Be specific. How does the thirst of Jesus challenge these preferences and actions of your daily life, your work and leisure, your relationships?

2. In praying this litany, which petitions are the easiest to pray, which are the hardest? Realizing that Jesus thirsts for the entire human race, request from him the help to expand your thirsting, especially in those most difficult areas.

The Sixth Word: The Prayer of Surrender

Father, into your hands I commend my spirit. (Lk 23:46)

Whatever might be our gauge of importance and success, the equalizing, impartial act of dying invites us to surrender our measurements of fame and achievement. Death quickly erases our misplaced illusions.

From the cross, what does Jesus teach us about approaching death? Jesus reviews his life, his dreams and hopes, the miracles and healings, the friendships, those who walked away, and those now present who want him dead more than anything else. He examines the journey to which he has been faithful. And, most important, during these last moments, Jesus continues to pray to the Father.

No one aspires to crucifixion. Jesus did not. The cross suggests no victory, no first place, no Olympic gold; it is the sign of failure. We cannot spiritualize or anesthetize Jesus' dying on the cross. We only do an injustice to what he experienced and diminish the force of the words he uttered.

With death quickly approaching, Jesus has very few actions left. Finally, Jesus commends himself to God. He places everything, especially the hidden mystery of death, in the greater mercy and care of the Father.

This sixth word, "Father, into your hands I commend my spirit," is Jesus' prayer of surrender. There is nothing more for Jesus to say or do except to hand over his journey and person into the compassionate hands of the Father. Jesus admits the failure of the cross and becomes powerless. There is no bargaining, no asking for a miracle, no polemic against injustice, or outburst of rage. Jesus lets go of what little remains: the pain, the thirst, the darkness, doubts, even his last breath. Jesus commits everything into the higher wisdom and understanding of the Father.

The prayer of surrender is a profound gesture of trust and confidence in God. To concede at any time is difficult, but to surrender from the humiliating injustice and failure of the cross only increases the significance of the letting go. From a powerless position, Jesus prays, "Father, into your hands—not according to my control, my will, my plans—but into your hands I commend my spirit."

This prayer of surrender in the sixth word is tied to four other essential prayer words from the cross: the fourth word, the fifth, and the seventh. Together, these four words form a school of prayer.

The sixth word is the pivotal connection between the fourth and fifth words and the concluding seventh word. The prayer of surrender builds on the fourth word: "My God, my God, why have you forsaken me?" which is the prayer of the passions. The fifth word, "I thirst," further amplifies one's bodily and spiritual yearnings, and complements the content and emotional components necessary for the prayer of surrender.

Effective prayer needs to contain unfiltered human experience, whether this might be our diverse thirsts or our raw feelings. Jesus, in the fourth and fifth words, models for us how to begin our prayer from the depths of our immediate experience; that is, where I am, how I am, stating clearly what I am experiencing and precisely how I am feeling.

Then, the sixth word becomes the second step in this three-part prayer. Once we are in touch with our experience, Jesus invites us to surrender it, to hand it over to the Father. "Father, into your hands I commend my spirit." Lastly, the seventh word on the cross is the conclusion of the prayer of Jesus. This is the final amen: "It is finished."

Jesus' School of Prayer

Briefly, there are three movements to the prayer of surrender:

1. Begin with the prayer of the passions, your lived experience coming forth from one's depths (the fourth and fifth words).

2. Next, the prayer of surrender, hand over to the Father this experience (the sixth word).

3. Last, truly finish the prayer with the amen of Jesus (the seventh word).

It is necessary to spend time with the prayer of surrender. This is a difficult prayer for us to learn because to surrender is foreign to us as a Western people. Our culture encourages us to control, to be powerful, to be in charge. In contrast, on the cross we find a countercultural Jesus who teaches us to pray as powerless, crucified, dominating no one, handing everything over to the Father.

Luke 23:46 can easily be adapted as a mantra to fit your prayer needs. Use its structure as a base and just change the last word. The following are examples:

Father, into your hands I commend...

this day, this trial, this sorrow, this cross.

my resentments, prejudices, lack of generosity.

my helplessness, not knowing what to say or do.

my judging, worries, anger, and hatred.

my family and how I would like them to be, even though they are not.

my poor self-image, my lack of creativity and risk.

my blaming of others, my deceits and envy.

all the things I detest and cannot tolerate.

my out-of-control desires, acts of infidelity and inconsistency.

my darkness, pettiness, jealousies.

my addictions, dysfunctional habits, and fixations.

my obsessive-compulsive behavior and other toxic patterns that I crave.

my manipulations, perverseness, negativity.

my non-gospel, non-sacramental ways of living.

Jesus models for us to commit everything to the Father, the sorrowful and joyful mysteries of life, all that you are and have, to hand over the totality. Our ability to be powerless allows God to heal us on our journey and to embrace us as we truly are. The spirituality of surrendering to God requires a lifelong process. Of course, certain days we are able to let go better than other days. However, if we postpone learning the prayer of surrender, we will face it unprepared at death. Perhaps we can learn how to surrender to the providential care of God in advance, through our daily abandonment to the Father.

Suggestions for Action

To verbalize the prayer of surrender one does not have to spend long hours contemplating precisely what to hand over. A good clue is when you encounter an obstacle: that particular something, someone, circumstance, or some aspect of yourself you would like to change but cannot. Then, you are experiencing your minor Calvary.

1. Reflect over your past week. What were those experiences that you found difficult and that especially tested you to the limit? What is your normal response in these circumstances? How can the prayer of surrender assist you to channel these encounters?

2. In relationship to yourself, your shadow side and secret self, how do you process these areas? What do you do with negative emotions, dominating fears, and compulsions? These become rich areas to acknowledge and hand over to the Holy Spirit.

3. Is there a memory that saps your energy each time you recall it? Do you find yourself entertaining a certain event, conversation, or life experience that has become an emotional roadblock? Perhaps you have even sought help to deal with these experiences. Place these memories within the context of the prayer of surrender.

The Seventh Word: The Final Amen

It is finished. (Jn 19:30)

The moment of death finally arrives. After enduring three hours on the cross, Jesus expresses the inevitable: "It is finished." Even still, a profound transition is taking place. Jesus spoke of this mystery in John 12:24: "Amen, amen, I say to you, unless a wheat grain falls into the ground and dies, it remains just a grain of wheat; but if it dies, it produces much fruit." This verse expresses the mystery of the Christian passage from life to death, from death to eternal life. Jesus did not divert the total emptying of his person and journey in God. Prior to bowing his head, he said for all generations to hear, "It is finished, it is accomplished, it is fulfilled." By Jesus embracing death, life was changed, not ended.

At this pivotal moment of darkness, scripture became fulfilled and the mission of Jesus completed. Through the action of Jesus breathing his last, the glory of God fully took over his being. Death produces the greatest fruit of all, union with God.

The seventeenth chapter of John provides an insight into the significance of fulfilling the mission given to us by God. The entire chapter is referred to as the "Prayer of Jesus." Here Jesus speaks of the hour. This special "hour" has many levels of meaning. It is the gospel hour of scriptural completion, of finishing the work given to Jesus, of reunion with the Father, the hour of emptying self, the hour of glory. In Hebrew, one of the meanings of *glory* is "pregnant." The result of the emptying of self is becoming glorified, or, becoming pregnant in God.

Ponder the depth of this prayer of Jesus. He prays to enter fully into union with the Father, and just as important, that we, his followers, may also participate in this glory.

The Prayer of Jesus

> Father, the hour has come. Give glory to your son, so that your son may glorify you, just as you gave him authority over all people, so that he may give eternal life to all you gave him. Now this is eternal life, that they should know you, the only true God, and the one whom you sent, Jesus Christ. I glorified you on earth by accomplishing the work that you gave me to do. Now glorify me, Father, with you, with the glory that I had with you before the world began.
>
> And everything of mine is yours and everything of yours is mine, and I have been glorified in them. And I will no longer be in the world, but they are in the world, while I am coming to you. Holy Father, keep them in your name that you have given me, so that they may be one just as we are. (Jn 17:1–5,10–11)

Jesus is aware that nothing more remains to be said, nothing more to be done except that last of human acts, to die. There is no more blood left to be poured out, no more parables or beatitudes to convey. Everything is over and completed; the task finished. The gift of humanity's redemption and reconciliation accomplished. The death of Jesus reopens the pathway for all humanity to enter totally into God's presence and glory.

How can we apply this concluding statement of Jesus to our everyday experience? We can pray this seventh word in two ways: first, through daily discernment we can apply the final "Amen" of Jesus to those experiences that need to be embraced and to those that need to be completely finished and buried; second, we can make Jesus' last word our own concluding prayer at the hour of death.

First, the practice of daily discernment. As disciples of Jesus, the Father invites each of us in fidelity to complete the mission that is our privilege. The first way we can pray "It is fulfilled" is by staying true to our unique faith-journey. This discernment process entails a daily reflective awareness so that the gospel may become glorified in us.

Discernment also asks that we examine our behavior to ensure that the gospel seed is planted in good soil. To discern is that adult process by which we consciously choose to cater no longer to those destructive actions and thoughts that need to be discarded. In this manner, the seventh word of Jesus is the critical conclusion to the prayer of surrender.

The art of discernment means that we creatively take authority over negative, non-gospel life patterns. To the kingdom of darkness, addiction, and selfishness, we say with Jesus, "It is finished." We do not have the luxury, the energy, or the time to engage in such activity or even to entertain such memories or illusions. If the memory returns, address and inform it again with the words of Jesus, "It is finished." As disciples we are called to monitor the attitudes and spirits that we give access into our person.

There is a story of two monks on the way back to the monastery.[4] At the riverbank they met an exceedingly beautiful woman. She wished to cross the river, but the water was too high and swift. Upon her request, the older monk lifted the woman on his back and carried her across. Upon arriving on the other side, they exchanged pleasantries and each party resumed their journey.

Now the younger monk was thoroughly scandalized. For two full hours he berated his companion on the flagrant violation of the holy rule: Had he forgotten that he was a monk? How dare he touch a woman, and actually carry her across the river? What would people say?

The older monk listened patiently to the interminable harangue. Finally, he interrupted, "My friend, I left the woman on the river's edge. Are you still carrying her?"

There are certain events in life that need to be left at the river's edge. The seventh word helps us say to those experiences, "It is over, finished, done," and then go on with life.

Second, we can pray the seventh word when we come face to face with the moment of our own death. In imitation of Jesus we can express from the heart, "Father, it is finished. I have done my best to accomplish the mission you gave me." Then, in the example of Jesus, bow your head and surrender your spirit.

Suggestions for Action

Pray to the Holy Spirit for growth in two important virtues necessary for the journey: discerning wisdom and courage. Pray for wisdom to know your mission. Pray for courage to accomplish your mission, to fulfill it, to finish it.

- Review this past week, or, if needed, a longer period of time. Is there some unfinished business or postponed reconciliation that needs to be addressed? Why not tackle this issue today and bring it to completion? Pray to the Holy Spirit for the courage to finish those responsibilities that are yours to complete.

- To remain constant in one's mission demands a discerning awareness. As you examine your lifestyle, what are those patterns, thoughts, or desires that are non-lifegiving and destructive? How do you deal with these tensions? As in the story of the two monks, is there anything that needs to be left at the riverbank? Pray to the spirit for the discernment and creative authority to leave behind what needs to be finished once and for all.

- Jesus entered into the glory of the Father through the complete emptying of self. So that the glory of the Father may produce a rich harvest, what do you need to let go of so that God's spirit may blossom?

Epilogue: The Emmaus Pilgrimage

Jesus himself drew near and walked with them. (Lk 24:15)

In the various Easter accounts, the identity of the newly risen Jesus is initially mistaken. In John 20:16, Mary Magdalene thought Jesus was a gardener. In John 21:4, Jesus is seen as an ordinary person walking along the Galilee shore. In Luke 24:37, the disciples perceived Jesus as a spirit. They were startled, terrified. Under what conditions, by what power could anyone rise from the dead? Doubting Thomas refused to believe the apostles that they had truly seen the Lord. As a condition of faith, Thomas demanded to place his hands into the side of this allegedly risen Jesus.

While Jesus had spoken of his resurrection prior to his death, the disciples did not fully comprehend its meaning. They lacked the imagination and leap of faith to grasp the reality of Easter. So much so, that in the presence of the risen Jesus, they often did not recognize him. Perhaps we fail to recognize the diverse manifestations of Jesus as well: his presence in the Word, community, sacraments, the beauty of nature, or in the quiet resting of the spirit in one's being.

At the eucharist, following the consecration of the bread and wine, the assembly acclaims, "Christ has died, Christ is risen, Christ will come again." This concise formula is referred to as the mystery of faith. In credal fashion, it expresses the Christian transition from death to the rising of Easter, to the anticipation of Jesus coming again. While we pray and sing this acclamation, which provides a clear faith focus, we need to keep in mind that the early Christians were grappling with the reality of Jesus' resurrection, his appearances, and his Easter words to them. Many times, they lacked the capacity to see and understand completely. They did not have the benefit of a faith maturation that has taken centuries to develop.

The account of the two disciples on the road to Emmaus in Luke 24:13–35 offers many lessons for us as we face our own faith development challenges. Oftentimes, when we are so proximate to personal tragedy, loss, or crucifixion, we lose sight of the reassurance and meaning of the resurrection. We fumble as to how to reinterpret our crises in the light of Easter.

Our perception becomes clouded like the Emmaus-bound disciples who were dejected. There can be a tendency to walk away from the support of community. Here, the disciples discounted the story of the women who encountered the vision of angels at the tomb. This, in turn, affected what they were able to see and understand. They remained burned out and depressed.

In the midst of such spiritual confusion, there is noted a divine compassion. Jesus is present as a fellow pilgrim, a companion on the way. However, the disciples, who are so caught up with their grief, literally do not recognize Jesus, his voice, or sociability of relating. Throughout this scene, Jesus demonstrates great patience in accepting the disciples where they are on their journey. As Jesus teaches us from the cross how to pray, embrace life, and seek God; Jesus, as pilgrim, tolerantly assists us to reestablish our Easter faith once again.

Suggestions for Action

What are some of the lessons that Luke 24:13–25 helps us to remember when we experience our own dark nights? Luke reminds us that there are many ways to reconnect with Easter.

- As you encounter distress, know that the compassionate Jesus walks as a friend with you on your journey.

- In times of trial, notice if you have a tendency to walk away from the support of community toward separation and isolation. How can you take creative action to seek needed help?

- Jesus empathetically listened to the disciples, their crises and confusion. To whom do you pour out your doubts and grief? When people come to you, how does Jesus teach you to listen?

- Jesus used the scriptures to come to a deeper understanding of suffering and glory. How do you learn from the Emmaus journey to use the wisdom of the Word as a means of comfort and guidance? What are your favorite passages that reconnect you with Jesus risen?

- The disciples requested that the unrecognized Jesus stay and dine with them. They went out of their way to seek new company that was outgoing, healthy, and spiritual. What is the lesson here for you?

- At table, Jesus took the bread, blessed it, broke it, and gave it to the disciples. Along with an appreciation of the Word, the sacramental nourishment of the eucharist is an essential component of living an Easter life. In times of distress, how do you partake of the wellspring of sacramental life?

- Jesus spent an entire day on journey with the disciples. The images here are that of retreat and pilgrimage. In the midst of our confusion, Jesus spends quality time accepting us the way we are as we transition through stages of Easter healing. As you review the Emmaus story, what do you learn about your spiritual mending process?

- The effect of Jesus' visit was that the hearts of the disciples were burning. With a renewed faith and insight, they returned to the Jerusalem community. In what ways do you nourish your heart so that it receives the attention it needs to live and love? The disciples underwent a conversion experience. What are the opportunities for conversion in your life?

Prayer

Risen Jesus, pilgrim and friend,
as you did not turn away from Calvary,
you stand by us as we experience our cross.
You are not far, but always near, by our side.
Journey with us whether we walk toward Jerusalem or not.

You are the constant one,
always inviting us to rediscover Easter and Pentecost.
In the different seasons of our pilgrimage,
send your hovering spirit of wisdom and courage
so that when we enter our valleys of darkness
we may be refreshed by the brightness of the resurrection.

Together, let us roll back the Good Friday burial stone,
and walk with one another as companions
in the freedom and radiance of Easter.

Notes

1. Adapted contents of this chapter were previously published in *Prayers from the Cross: Solace for all Seasons*, by John P. Mossi, S.J., copyright 1994, Paulist Press. Used with permission.

2. Edited story from *The Seven Last Words*, by Fulton J. Sheen, copyright 1993 by the Century Co., Alba House (1982), 13.

3. Edited story from *Stories and Parables for Preachers and Teachers*, by Paul J. Wharton, copyright 1986, Paulist Press, 39.

4. Edited story from *Song of the Bird*, by Anthony de Mello, S.J., copyright 1982, Doubleday, 64.

SECTION III.

SPIRITUALITY AND WHOLENESS

In his essay, Robert Morneau makes a case for four ingredients in a paradigm for a "Spirituality for Book Lovers." They are "(1) courtesy, (2) benevolent interpretation, (3) ingestion, and (4) orthopraxis." He then offers several recommended readings for book lovers with a spiritual persuasion. In his description of these books, you can feel him modeling the four ingredients he has just described. This brief essay, like the process he describes, is a joy to read. His point about "ingestion" particularly struck a chord with my own bias that, if necessary, people should read less and absorb more, rather than broadening their skimming.

In John Welch's "St. Thérèse: Doctor of Hope?" he explores "the mixed messages" Thérèse offers in response to the questions: What kind of modeling is possible from a late nineteenth-century young woman with an extremely limited range of experience? What does it mean to hope? How did she express her hope? But he also moves beyond this to address "our images of hope," using an illustration from his own life and reflecting on the wrestling all of us must do when faced with the "last things" of life.

In "Trusting the Action of God in Ministry," William Barry seeks to raise—in simple ways—our consciousness of the need to trust the action of the spirit in the lives and experiences of those we meet. If we do believe God touches people in creative ways, we will be more sensitive to their presence and help people make sense of such experiences. In addition, such sensitivity will extend to helping people make discernment of spirits an everyday part of life. In doing our pastoral work, Barry reminds us, at a deep level, that "all of ministry has only one ultimate purpose, to make it easier for all of us to pay attention to God's action and to live in harmony with it, for that is our bliss."

William Sneck's "Carl Jung and the Quest for Wholeness" is filled with information on the journey toward greater integration and God. It is a veritable Jungian primer on the role and content of the unconscious, active imagination, the archetypes—the persona, shadow and animus/anima—and typology. Whether or not you are interested or experienced in Jung's approach, this essay is, as promised, a rich support in the quest for wholeness.

157

In "Self-Images of Oppression and Liberation in Ministry," Annice Callahan offers a very personal journey into theological reflection. In doing this she invites her readers to do the same by bringing their own self-images into conscious awareness. The implications—both good and destructive—of having certain images are shown through her offering of six illustrative images of her own. By increasing our awareness of the images that guide us, she moves us into a position both to understand and alter those views, so that we can better minister to ourselves and appreciate the motives that drive us.

In "I Want to Be Like God: A Birthright for Autonomy," George Aschenbrenner recommends that we reflect on the ideal of acceptance and actualization of the self. While he grants these are part of human maturity, there are cautions that must be kept in mind so we remain God-directed and not simply self-directed. This article is a wonderful reflection for these narcissistic times.

In "Time and Time Out of Time: Meeting God in the Ordinary and Extraordinary Moment," Suzanne Mayer offers a pause for thought and reflection on the wisdom provided by the rich religious tradition of kairos and its necessary grounding in the chronos.

Michael Blastic's "Attentive Compassion" brings to the fore Franciscan resources for ministry. Essentially these are present when "the incarnation of Jesus, which affirms the human condition as the lover for God's presence with creation" is at the heart of the dynamic of caring for others. As a way of capturing Franciscan ministry in light of this dynamic, Blastic addresses (1) poverty and the human condition; (2) the incarnation as God's gratuitous embrace of created goodness; and (3) sitting down at a table in the kingdom of God. This delightful essay provides a good flavor of Franciscan spirituality and how it can support and be a guide for all who do ministry.

In "Chaos and Creation," Patricia Livingston shares with us in a vivid story that "pain does not have the final say." By sharing with us—in the fascinating storytelling style for which she is known—the surprise of chaos in her own life, she helps us realize not only that chaos is a part of life but also that it is the stem of the flower of growth and depth. In effect, chaos is not desired, but it comes, it comes. What we do with it, though, is up to us.

"A Tradition of Spirits: Breathing New Life Into Ministry" by Elizabeth A. Dreyer looks to some of our medieval ancestors in the faith to "be on the watch" for images and narratives of the spirit that might shed new light on our own efforts at renewal. As Dreyer recognizes, "In the midst of a critical flock, it may be difficult for ministers to experience their own gifts." Being in touch with the spirit of God's generous love and the ability to model it for others is a source of the perspective and inner strength that persons such as Hildegard of Bingen, Bonaventure of Bagnoreggio, and Teresa of Avila have to offer us. A key point in this essay is that, just as the spirit transformed fear into courage in the medieval church, she is available to us now when we wish to share love and be of service in difficult times.

10. Spirituality for Book Lovers

Books are boats for some, carrying precious cargo,
or, for Emily, a frigate sailing us to new worlds.
Yet others see books as miracles, restoring life
and offering shelter against the forces of darkness.
Is there a spirituality for book lovers,
a nexus between the mystery of transcendence
and the wordy incarnations of human thought and feelings?
Four elements seem required:
an open heart imbued with *courtesy.*
Then an *interpretative* skill that is benevolent though critical.
Next comes *ingestion,* a holy conception of major or minor
     revelations.
Last but not least, *orthopraxis,* doing the truth conceived.
No greater treasure do we possess than our spiritual life.
We bring it to what we read and what we read to it.

Introduction

Books are many things to many people. For some, books are boats of precious cargo (Loren Eiseley) or repositories of insight (Ralph Waldo Emerson) or frigates that can carry us across the seas (Emily Dickinson). And books can do so many things: expand our world, provide shelter against life's storms, awaken our dormant spirit, set us thinking, guide our education, transform our lives. Books can also be trouble, as Mark Twain's Huckleberry Finn states:

> Here ain't nothing more to write about, and I am rotten glad of it, because if I'd knowed what a trouble it was to make a book I wouldn't a tackled it and ain't agoing to no more.

Books, whatever our perspective, make us pay attention, and this is the intersection between spirituality and reading. "Making eye contact with

159

reality" (Russell Baker) happens when we read well and when our consciousness embraces the spiritual realms of life. The reality is God, and any book that is substantial will point somehow in the direction of full reality, be it given the name truth, goodness, or beauty. But the question arises: What are the essential components of reading from a spiritual perspective? Is there such a thing as a spirituality for book lovers, or a spirituality for music lovers, for nature lovers, for lovers in general? I propose there is, and such a spirituality is one that is demanding and holistic. Four ingredients make up this paradigm. Book lovers grounded in a spirituality possess: (1) courtesy, (2) benevolent interpretation, (3) ingestion, and (4) orthopraxis.

Before developing each of these elements, let me add a further thought regarding spirituality. The Quaker writer, Douglas Steere, maintains that attention, adherence, and abandonment are the key factors of the spiritual life. Attention to God's love, adherence to this love, and abandonment to whatever that love asks of us is the spiritual life. There is a cognitive, affective, and behavioral component as well as a social dimension, in that we will be asked to share the gifts given to us. The whole person—head, heart, and hands—is engaged by the divine mystery, and a total response is required. Even book lovers, sometimes known for their ivory towerism, are mandated to share what they have received.

Four Ingredients in a Spirituality for Book Lovers

Courtesy

When opening a book, be it Shakespeare's *Hamlet,* Dante's *The Divine Comedy,* or Frank McCourt's *Angela's Ashes,* the reader must exhibit hospitality. If the doors of the heart and soul are closed, there will be no authentic contact with reality. If the mind is preoccupied and filled with excluding prejudices and biases, the book will remain a foreign substance. Only to the extent that there is intentional courtesy, a vulnerable receptivity, an openness filled with risk, will authentic encounter take place.

Courtesy is a virtue and should not be presumed. In an age of pervasive narcissism, that excessive self-preoccupation that sustains an individualistic way of life, one should not expect courtesy to be a common habit. There is considerable "self-sacrifice" in laying aside, however briefly, one's own conviction and perspective to entertain someone else's world and values. The newly opened book must be given a good listening if spiritual growth is to be realized. This means no interruptions until a point is made, a willingness to be taught or enlightened, a humility that acknowledges that we have much to learn. Courtesy is a demanding virtue, but one that contains great rewards: the joy of harboring new experiences and that sense of solidarity in being linked to a larger world.

In Tennyson's poem "Ulysses," we read, "I am part of all that I have met." Reading is a constant voyage that introduces us to new places, new people, new cultures, new dimensions of reality. When the reader's mind and heart are imbued with courtesy, entrance is given to these wide-ranging experiences, and one's very being expands and knows enlargement. If the courtesy is authentic and sincere, an inner transformation necessarily happens. We are, indeed, a part of all that we meet.

Benevolent Interpretation

In his essay on "Language," Ralph Waldo Emerson offers a basic hermeneutical principle that applies not only to scripture but to all written works: "Every scripture is to be interpreted by the same spirit which gave it forth." Obviously easier said than done. Yet unless we creep behind the text into the author's frame of mind (his metaphysics, epistemology, and temperament) the text will consistently be misunderstood. Reading involves that difficult art of interpretation.

By benevolent interpretation I mean giving the author the benefit of the doubt. One should assume that the author has something significant to say, that deception is not the intent, that there is a vision or an experience that can benefit the reader. Failure to bring a "genial eye" to this enterprise of reading puts the reader into a skeptical frame of mind that inhibits authentic conversation and dialogue, so much so that the critical faculties will kick in.

Spirituality does not prohibit a critical reading, but it does begin with an openness and receptivity to possible revelation, however major or minor. In a sacramental theology in which God is continually mediating grace and wisdom by means of concrete, sensuous objects, we never know exactly when and where such disclosure and epiphanies of the truth may happen. The spiritual life is grounded in truth, and one way of acquiring truth is through benevolent interpretation.

For many years Augustine was unable to penetrate the scriptures. Perhaps the difficulty lay in some philosophical preconception, ill-disposed psychological currents, or moral inconsistencies; we simply don't know. But the scriptures remained for Augustine a closed book, and he could not appreciate the worth and beauty of God's word. Eventually, after years of study and searching and profound conversion, things changed, and he became not only a devout reader of God's word but one of the giants in the scriptural exegesis. Such is the working of grace.

Ingestion

Book lovers are vulnerable to a major illness: overconsumption. In Robert D. Richardson's biography on Ralph Waldo Emerson (*Emerson: The Mind on Fire,* 173), a warning is issued about "the dangers of being overwhelmed and overinfluenced by one's reading." But it's more than just quantity and volume. Even when readers observe disciplined, intellectual temperance, there are still the pressing questions of assimilation, appropriation, ingestion. Reading well is more than a matter of courtesy and hermeneutical benevolence; it is essentially a matter of making what is read one's own. I label this process "ingestion."

Ducks have an innate quality that prohibits the waters in which they swim to penetrate their feathers. "Water off the duck's back" proverbially captures this experience. This blessing for ducks is a curse for readers. Many readers, upon completing Shakespeare's *Hamlet,* T. S. Eliot's "The Wasteland," or Augustine's *Confessions* can identify with ducks in that what has been read rolls across their minds and hearts without penetration, without being ingested, without being properly digested.

The causes are not hard to find: no note taking, no underlining and rereading, no discussion with friends of the story's context—no processing. No surprise that 80 to 85 percent of the text remains foreign to one's soul. Ingestion requires active reading and considerable effort. Unless the price is paid, one's reading, spiritual and otherwise, will be superficial and less than satisfactory.

This process of assimilation is part rational, part emotional, largely a question of affinity and connaturality. Many works remain alien because we are out of sorts, or we scan and hurry over that which demands undivided attention, or we fail to understand the context or motive of the author (or, of course, the material is simply beyond our capacity). By contrast, when our hearts are open, when we take our time and attempt to crawl inside the author's inspiration, we find communion in the communication.

Ingestion is fostered by doing a book review, discussing the text in a book club, extracting the main themes and images that permeate the work. Simply to read a book without any type of processing may help to pass the time but will fail to enrich the quality of our lives in any significant way. And, of course, if the book is truly worthwhile, a second, third, or even fourth reading is most helpful in appropriating its insights and wisdom.

Orthopraxis

Spirituality has a behavioral component. God's love is not merely to be known cognitively and experienced affectively; it should also find expression in our moral lives. Book lovers who live a complete spirituality necessarily transpose some of their contemplative ponderings into concrete actions. Right thinking (orthodoxy) with hope leads to right acting (orthopraxis).

This does not mean that pragmatism is at the heart of spirituality. Yet, without incarnating wisdom gained from serious dialogic reading, one has to wonder about the authenticity of the truth appropriated. It is here that we see the commingling of the transcendentals: truth flowing into love, which expresses itself in goodness, which is indeed a thing of beauty. Unity, not diversity, is the determinative quality of a spirituality for book lovers.

C. S. Lewis once warned that an atheist cannot be too careful what he reads. Without our knowing it, something divine may lie hidden in some unsuspected volume and bring about change (conversion) that reshapes the direction of our lives. When the confused and dissipated Augustine read about the asceticism and dedication of the hermit Anthony in the desert, something stirred in Augustine's heart, and a new lifestyle was initiated. When Gandhi read the works of Ruskin, Thoreau, and Tolstoy, ideas that led to the liberation of India were planted into the heart of this noble Hindu. Books have power to energize our actions and challenge us to become the person we are deep inside.

Recommended Readings for Book Lovers with a Spiritual Persuasion

Erich Fromm, *The Art of Loving* (New York: Harper and Row, 1956), 130 pp.
Spirituality is about love, its art and science. Erich Fromm views love as primarily an attitude and orientation of character involving five elements: giving, concern, responsibility, respect, and knowledge. When we have active concern for the growth and life of that which we love, we are practicing the art of loving. Our deepest need in life is to overcome our separateness. Only love, not material things nor power nor activity, can bring about the union we desire. Fromm talks about brotherly and motherly love, erotic love, self-love, and love of God. The closing section of this provocative work studies the possibility of love in contemporary Western society that is rooted in the principle of capitalism. When all is said and done, "the loving person responds" (25).

Melannie Svoboda, S.N.D., *Traits of a Healthy Spirituality* (Mystic, Conn.: Twenty-Third Publication, 1996), 131 pp.
An annual physical examination is a good idea. So too is an annual retreat or spiritual checkup to determine the quality of our health in relation to the spiritual life. S. Melannie Svoboda shares twenty traits which can be found in people or communities that have a vibrancy and vitality telling of the presence of the spirit. Here are ten of the twenty chapters that might whet your appetite:

- "Spirituality: Where Are You?"
- "Wonder: Sitting on God's Front Porch"
- "Friendship: The 'You Too' Experience"
- "Teachability: Prerequisite for Conversion"
- "Tolerance: Keeping Our Parachutes Open"
- "Joy: Does Your God Know How to Dance?"
- "Perseverance: Can You Wait to Eat the Marshmallows?"
- "Prayer: The Meeting of Two Loves"
- "Gratitude: Taking Nothing for Granted"
  "Restlessness: Is This All There Is?"

Dag Hammarskjöld, *Markings,* trans. Leif Sjoberg and W. H. Auden (New York: Alfred A. Knopf, 1981), 222 pp.

One means for making spiritual progress is to keep a journal, jotting down (without editing) the inner and outer movements of our lives that register upon our souls. Some define spirituality as the art of staying awake, the art of paying attention. Dag Hammarskjöld, former general secretary of the United Nations, knew how to pay attention, and he had the wisdom to write down what he thought and felt. We have his legacy in his journal *Markings.* He writes of forgiveness and loneliness, of work and love, of holiness and evil. One line: "To have humility is to experience reality, not in *relation to ourselves,* but in its sacred independence" (174).

Pierre Teilhard de Chardin, *The Divine Milieu* (New York: Harper Torchbook, 1960), 160 pp.

Teilhard (1881–1955) was a priest and scientist who searched for the truth and beauty of God. His desire was to teach people how to see God, a God present everywhere: "at the tip of my pen, my spade, my brush, my needle—of my heart and thought." He saw growth as a lovable duty and pleaded that we give eternal significance to our daily endeavors. His deep optimism and confidence were grounded in the mysteries of creation and incarnation. He writes, "The knitting together of God and the world has just taken place under our eyes in the domain of action" (64). In an era when people discount action and human effort, Teilhard is a voice calling us to growth and collaboration with God's initiative.

Mohandas K. Gandhi, *Autobiography: The Story of My Experiments with Truth,* trans. Mahadev Desai (New York: Dover, 1948), 468 pp.

Gandhi opens a window into Hindu spirituality, a spirituality of nonviolence, of gentleness, of truth. This great world leader who helped free India grounds his political activism in the silence of prayer and grace. His whole life was a search for truth that would find its expression in justice. His concern for the poor, his willingness to suffer for the sake of the common good, his witness to the world of a means toward peace other than violence made a deep impression on the twentieth century. And all this was done in the spirit of joy: "Service which is rendered without joy helps neither the servant nor the served" (153).

Evelyn Underhill, *The Way of the Spirit* (New York: Crossroad, 1993), 240 pp.

Evelyn Underhill is one of greatest spiritual writers of our time. In this volume we have a collection of her retreat conferences, which give us an insight into her understanding of our call to holiness. Her style is simple yet profound, direct while edging into the geography of poetry. She writes out of both a personal experience of God as well as scholarship. Here is a sprinkling of her sayings: "Joy, which is the very color of holiness" (65); "The mark of a saint is a burning interest in and love for other souls" (88); "Love cannot be lazy" (95); "The soul's basic law: 'We come from God. We belong to God. We tend toward God'" (136).

Peter Hebblethwaite, *Paul VI: The First Modern Pope* (New York: Paulist Press, 1993), 710 pp.

Biography is a good approach to spirituality. The lived life of someone seeking to respond to God's spirit helps to shape our own lives and education. Pope Paul VI strove to be a spiritual leader in one of the most turbulent times of history. His story is the story of the Vatican Council II as well as the story of the world's search for peace. Here is an insight that's worth much reflection: "The secret of the apostolate is to know how to love" (273).

Belden C. Lane, *Landscapes of the Sacred: Geography and Narrative in American Spirituality* (New York: Paulist Press, 1988), 237 pp.

What role do place and story have in spirituality? Professor Lane traces six traditions of spirituality in America (Native Americans, Hispanic, French, Puritans, Shakers, Dorothy Day and the Catholic Worker movement) and demonstrates how specific places mediate the holy. The clearer our understanding of "storied place," the greater is our capacity to appreciate the role of geography and narrative in our own spiritual journey. Here is Lane's thesis: "The experience of place and space profoundly structure our experience of self and other in relationship to God, that is, our spirituality" (xi).

Peter Brown, *Augustine of Hippo: A Biography* (Berkeley, Calif.: University of California Press, 1967).

One of the major influences of spirituality in the last 1600 years has been St. Augustine. This biography masterfully puts his theology and writings in context as well as gives us an appreciation of the forces that shaped and guided Augustine's life. His mother, Monica; his mentor, Ambrose; his teachers and friends are all given their due report. Brown writes of Augustine, "Despite his yearnings for contemplation, he had the busy man's fatal genius of generating more and more work" (273). "Augustine told them just what a demoralized group needs to hear. He gave them a sense of identity; he told them where they belonged, to what they must be loyal" (313). Another biography here to guide our feet upon the road of peace.

Abraham J. Heschel, *Man's Quest for God* (New York: Charles Scribner's Sons, 1954), 151 pp.

Heschel is one of the great Jewish writers of the twentieth century. Writing with sensitivity and insight, he challenges the modern person to be open to the mystery of God. He writes of prayer, silence, grace, compassion, obedience, and evil in profound and direct terms. Some words of wisdom: "To live without prayer is to live without God, to live without a soul" (59); "The voice of God is unambiguous; it is the confusion of man, of the best of us, that creates the ambiguity" (133); "What we need is honesty, stillness, humility. What we need is a new insight rather than new symbols" (144).

The Enlightened Heart: An Anthology of Sacred Poetry, ed. Stephen Mitchell (New York: Harper and Row, 1989), 171 pp.

One doorway into spirituality is through poetry. This special kind of language—intense, intimate, often intimidating—speaks directly to the heart by way of the imagination. Images and symbols help reveal (and conceal) the mysteries of our faith. In this excellent anthology we are given religious poetry from various traditions and diverse lands. There are selections from the psalms and the Bhagavad Gita, from Lao-tzu and Hildegard of Bingen, from Rumi and Kabir, from William Blake and Emily Dickinson, from Rilke and Yeats. One line from Blake captures much of the spiritual journey: "And we are put on earth a little space, / That we may learn to bear the beams of love."

John Welch

11. St. Thérèse of Lisieux: Doctor of Hope?

In his introduction to an excellent text on the life and teachings of St. Thérèse of Lisieux, Cardinal Godfried Danneels writes,

> All of our postmodern difficulties can be summed up in the single problem of hope. Can we still hope? On every street, behind every other door, lives someone who is troubled, if not actually desperate. In our time, hope is truly that "little girl" between her two big sisters [faith and charity] (of whom Peguy spoke), who is having problems growing. Everywhere existential anguish is in the air.
>
>   Who will teach us hope? Where can we find a model, someone who has gone before us through the darkness and the throes of death? Is there somewhere a "Doctor of Hope"?[1]

Cardinal Danneels points to Thérèse of Lisieux as that "Doctor of Hope." This essay examines the evidence for such a claim.

What kind of modeling is possible from a late nineteenth-century young woman with an extremely limited range of experience? What does it mean to hope? How did she express her hope?

For a few pages, I explore the mixed messages Thérèse gives to these questions. In particular, I look at the images that captured her desires and yearnings, the images that were expressive of her own hope.

That Never-Ending Sunday

The dominant image that captivated the young Thérèse's imagination was that of heaven. She yearned for all that heaven meant. She understood her life on earth as the story of an exile that would one day end in the everlasting land of the Father.

She tells us that "heaven" was the first word she could recognize and read. She pointed up to heaven and told her father that the stars in the evening sky were arranged in a large "T," for her name.

Her mother told her that after we die we go to heaven. And so Thérèse, with childlike logic, unsettled her mother by saying, "I wish you would die," believing she wanted the best for her mother.

Thérèse's Christian imagery may be charming, but it also may be tepid, unable to speak to our world.

Did Thérèse ever really inhabit our contemporary world? Did her images of hope help her engage the world, or did they take her dreamily out of it? Did she live in an alternate world of heaven, an eternal, endless Les Buissonnets, the family home? Does she offer any vision for us in our workaday world other than, "Wait it out!"?

The evidence is mixed. Encounters with this world leave her with a longing for the next world. Mornings and mid-day bring promise, but afternoons and evenings are often filled with melancholy.

Sundays are especially poignant. She recalls Sunday walks with the family, even early memories of her mother. Her experiences touched her deeply and still resonated within her as a young woman.

> I still feel the profound and *poetic* impressions that were born in my soul at the sight of fields enameled with *corn-flowers* and all types of wild flowers. Already I was in love with the *wide-open spaces*. Space and the gigantic fir trees, the branches sweeping down to the ground, left in my heart an impression similar to the one I experience still today at the sight of nature.[2]

Even after her mother's death, Sundays were always special. She lolled in bed longer. Her sisters gave her special attention. Pauline brought her chocolate in bed, and dressed her "like a queen." Marie curled her hair. Then it was off to church, holding her father's hand, even throughout the mass. But then, she writes,

> This *joyous* day, passing all too quickly, had its tinge of *melancholy*. I remember how my happiness was unmixed until Compline. During this prayer, I would begin thinking that the day of *rest* was coming to an end, that the morrow would bring with it the necessity of beginning life over again, we would have to go back to work, to learning lessons, etc. and my heart felt the *exile* of this earth. I longed for the everlasting repose of heaven, that neverending *Sunday of the Fatherland!*[3]

She loved it when her father took her fishing. She liked being out in the countryside with the flowers and birds. She attempted to fish, but preferred to go off somewhere by herself and think.

Without knowing what it was to meditate, my soul was absorbed in real prayer. I listened to distant sounds, the murmuring of the wind, etc. At times, the indistinct notes of some military music reached me where I was, filling my heart with a sweet melancholy. Earth then seemed to be a place of exile and I could dream only of heaven.[4]

Thérèse's attitude is, here on earth we are waiting in exile for the time we can live in our true home. In theological terms, Thérèse's images manifest a future eschatology in which the goal of our living is strictly ahead of us, some tomorrow of endless happiness. Compare this attitude with that of Elizabeth Barrett Browning:

> Earth's crammed with heaven,
> And every common bush afire with God;
> But only he who sees, takes off his shoes—
> The rest sit round it and pluck blackberries,
> And daub their natural faces unaware
> More and more from the first similitude.
>
> ...
>
> If a man could feel,
> Not one day, in the artist's ecstasy,
> But every day, feast, fast, or working-day,
> The spiritual significance burn through
> The hieroglyphic of material shows,
> Henceforward he would paint the globe with wings,
> And reverence fish and fowl, the bull, the tree,
> And even his very body as a man....[5]

Browning's imagery manifests more a realized eschatology that looks to the future as well, but also finds it, surprisingly, in the present, with less of a disjunction between present and future.

Remember Teilhard de Chardin's concern that "the seeking after, and expectation of, the Kingdom of Heaven might deflect human activity from its natural tasks, or at least entirely eclipse any interest in them." Thérèse identified with a vision given in the Book of Wisdom that says life is like a ship that ploughs the waves and leaves no trace in its wake. Chardin, on the contrary, argues,

> God, in all that is most living and incarnate in Him, is not withdrawn from us beyond the tangible sphere; He is waiting for us at every moment in our action, in our work of the moment. He is in some sort at the tip of my pen, my spade, my brush, my needle—of my heart and of my thought. By pressing the stroke, the line, or the stitch, on

which I am engaged, to its ultimate natural finish, I shall arrive at the ultimate aim towards which my innermost will tends.[6]

Yet, who has not experienced melancholy at the close of a Sunday or the end of a vacation? Who has not experienced a longing for more, even in the midst of wonderful fulfillment? Who has not, at times, agreed with the sentiments of the *Hail, Holy Queen* when life in this world is described as a "valley of tears"?

Our Images of Hope

Religious imagery does not speak to many in our world today; perhaps it does not speak to us either. Or if it did, it did not engage us deeply but remained a picturesque set of images that are "nice" but not gripping. Can we in our time and in our fashion respond to the apostle's challenge and give a reason for our hope?[7]

I remember my father, who had been suffering for years from emphysema, one night saying to me, "Jack, do you really think it is the way they say it is?" Dad was a lifelong Catholic who, each night, knelt beside the bed and ended the day in prayer. I never before heard him express any doubts. But obviously the "answers" he carried within were not meeting life's questions in his waning days.

We all question, from time to time, the foundations of our lives, the purpose of our existence. Every now and then someone actually comes out and says it, perhaps in a joking way. One old-timer in our community described us as "a bunch of good guys banded together for no good reason!"

Religious imagery is not necessarily founded on hope. And secular imagery (for want of a better phrase) is not necessarily devoid of hope. How can we tell which scene demonstrates more hope (and faith): a Thérèse who says to those around her in her dying moments, "I am falling into the arms of God," or my uncle Harry who said to my cousin at his bedside, "Jimmy, it looks like you better go home and get your suit cleaned."

When I was in the novitiate, daydreams often carried me through classes. The classes were a half-hour each, but at times seemed much longer. In particular, I remember daydreaming about diving, diving off a board into the pond on the property. I would imagine the experience of different dives. Classes were not energizing me, but that image did, and it remains with me in various adaptations. It was an image of freedom, of physical expression, of being natural in a natural setting.

Later, while studying theology in Washington, D.C., we had a basketball court behind Whitefriars Hall. I remember playing on the court, not the games themselves, but the times I was out there alone. On an overcast, drizzly afternoon,

I would go out on the court in the ubiquitous seminarian uniform, black wash pants, white T-shirt, and gym shoes, and shoot baskets in the rain. Shot after shot, from different spots on the court, splashing the water when I dribbled, chasing the ball down as it scooted off the backboard or rim, creating little games. It was an experience, again, of a mindlessness and yet total concentration of energies and expression of energies, a feeling of freedom and integration. The experience, and later the memory, energized and spoke to some part deep within me.

I remember reading an account of a dream by a professional football player. He was a lineman on the offense. In his dream, it was a beautiful, crisp, autumn afternoon; his team had the ball and they were driving down the field, play after play after play. In the dream he wanted it to go on forever.

These images from sports do not speak to everyone. But perhaps they remind us of times when we imagine, or remember, or dream about something that totally expresses us, who we are, speaks to dimensions of our soul unlike any other image or experience. It may be lovemaking; it may be caretaking; it may be adventurous; it may be serene. But we seem to have images of forever in our experience which, if truth be told, engage us often more powerfully than religious images.

When I was a young boy working at a scout camp, we had legends and ceremonies drawn from American Indian lore. During the academic year I was learning about the Christian tradition in a Catholic school; in the summers I was learning the lore of the first North Americans. The Ten Commandments were taught in a classroom with everyone sitting in rows and listening to the teacher. The values of Order of the Arrow, "a brotherhood of cheerful service," were passed on during a night-time ceremony: an arrowhead outlined with stones on the ground, candles on the stones, a huge bonfire at the base of the arrowhead, and at the point of the arrow a lectern from which was read, and danced, the story of heroic sacrifice for others.

I did not experience the two realms in conflict, or even in competition. They complemented and reinforced one another, but the Indian lore touched areas within me that were untouched by religious education. One tradition was coming to me from the heavens, as it were; the other was coming to me from the earth. I am reminded of Victor Turner's complaint that in our day we no longer have transforming rituals, but mere ceremonials.

Haunting Images

I have been reading the memoirs of several of the leaders of the Civil War. At times they evoke scenes which simply are awe-inspiring. Some are beautiful in a terrible way—the image of a long column of infantry marching at night through a thunderstorm, with the lightening glancing off the thousands of bayonets and turning the column into a river of fire.

Millions of people came to know the name, Joshua Lawrence Chamberlain, one of the real-life heroes of the Civil War. He was portrayed in the historical novel, *Killer Angels,* an account of the battle of Gettysburg.

In his reflection on the outcome of Gettysburg, Chamberlain writes,

> In great deeds something abides. On great fields something stays. Forms change and pass; bodies disappear; but spirits linger, to consecrate ground for the vision-place of souls. And reverent men and women from afar, and generations that know us not and that we know not of, heart-drawn to see where and by whom great things were suffered and done for them, shall come to this deathless field, to ponder and dream; and low! the shadow of a mighty presence shall wrap them in its bosom, and the power of the vision pass into their souls.[8]

In his memoirs Chamberlain presents scenes that linger in the memory. In the middle of a fierce battle during the final days, he challenges an officer to lead his men into the battle and promises him a promotion. The man, without a word, grabs the battle flag and leads his men into the woods aflame with firing guns. Moments later his men carry him out of the woods, mortally wounded. Chamberlain rides to him and the man says, "General, I have carried out your wishes," and dies. Chamberlain writes,

> Why choose out him for his death, and so take on myself the awful decision into what home irreparable loss and measureless desolation should cast their unlifted burden? The crowding thought choked utterance. I could only bend my face low to his and answer, "*Colonel,* I will remember my promise; I will remember *you!*" and press forward to my place, where the crash and crush and agony of struggle summoned me to more of the same. War!— nothing but the final, infinite good, for man and God, can accept and justify human work like that![9]

At the end of the war, at Appomattox, Chamberlain is chosen to be the officer in charge of the Union troops receiving the surrender of the Confederate soldiers. As the Confederates dejectedly march past the ranks of Union soldiers, Chamberlain orders a salute of respect for these gallant men. Confederate officers recognize the salute and order a similar salute back— honor answering honor. And Chamberlain writes,

> On our part not a sound of trumpet more, nor roll of drum; not a cheer, nor word nor whisper of vain-glorying, nor motion of man standing again the order, but an awed stillness rather, and breath-holding, as if it were the passing of the dead![10]

Is God in all this? Can God be apart from it all? Our theology today tells us that the world and God are inseparable. God is the depth level of all human experience. Theologian Karl Rahner talks about the mysticism of everyday life. Look deeply into any powerfully human experience and there find the flame of mystery. "Earth is crammed with heaven and only she who sees takes off her shoes." Perhaps the power in such experiences, in such memories, comes in part from the sense of touching a common humanity and realizing what we, together, really want deep down. A recent experience led to such a realization.

Each Memorial Day a concert is held on the grounds of the Capitol building in Washington, D.C. The event is in honor or those who gave their lives in the service of their country, in our service. On a recent occasion a letter was read from a mother writing to her firstborn, who had been killed while serving with special forces in Vietnam.

As her letter was read, pictures of the young man growing up were shown on the screen above the stage, and on television across the country. The experience of the sacrifice of this young life and the grief of the mother moved everyone in the audience. At that moment a common humanity was touched—fragile, noble, hopeful.

What was hopeful in such an image, such an experience of tragic dying? The fact that we all said through our thoughts, emotions, tears during the letter, that "this should not be." And the inarticulated sense that "something, someone, somehow should bring meaning and healing into this tragic scene."

What is the power of a scene? Why do certain scenes and their memory speak to us so powerfully? Why do some images pull us forward, give peace, joy, a sense of rightness? Why do some images pull us down into our common humanity and still us in reverence? Why do some images, somewhere deep within us, raise an unvoiced protest: "This should not be!"

Spirit and Psyche

Spirit and psyche inhabit the same country of the mind. Spirit is the dynamism in us to fullness of being, to knowing all, loving all, being one with all. Psyche expresses these desires with primordial words drawn from the body, from the earth. Psyche connects the organism of the body and its rootedness in the cosmos with the transcendence of spirit and its yearning for fullness. Our images of hope express both psyche and spirit.

Psyche's images are freighted with spirit's yearnings. They may stir up and express our longings for peace and justice, they may open us to profound repentance, they may throw light on our existence and illumine our path, they may provide hopeful scenarios of our future beyond this life, as Thérèse's did. But, none of them is adequate to finally and fully express the desires within us, the desire that we are. Our deepest yearning to know and to love, to be one with all there is, is never fulfilled. Our deepest hungers never find sufficient food in this life. Our wants are given voice, but what do we want?

Theologian Bernard Lonergan believed that if we follow the trail of our deepest desires, expressing them in truth, facing them, and responding to their call in our lives, we will undergo conversions. Our wants, our desires will be purified and transformed, until more and more we want what God wants in a consonance of desire.

The Last Things

Today we wrestle with the problem of the "last things," death, judgment, heaven, hell, purgatory having lost their power over the human imagination. Thérèse's imagery of heaven captivated her, at least in her youth, but leaves many of us unsatisfied; it does not engage us at any depth. As Chardin warned, the thought of heaven may lead us to disparage this world and our daily duties. It may also cause us to treat the earth as a vast waiting room, to be used without regard to future consequences. If it all passes away, what matter oceans, forests, mountains, animals? And if we envision attaining a heaven someday, finding ourselves with God, what about all our relationships? What happens to them? Is our destiny unaffected by them?

It is evident in reading Thérèse that she was a woman of tremendous affectivity. As a matter of fact, she said that with a heart like hers it is a good thing God preserved her from the usual friendships because she would have given herself so fully that there would have been no love left for God.

Her favorite Carmelite writer, John of the Cross, spoke to her affectivity and challenged her to see her desires as an invitation to enter into a loving union with God. John's language of love gave words to Thérèse's feelings. She quoted his *Dark Night* and *Spiritual Canticle*. And the Song of Songs in the Hebrew scriptures spoke to her about the love story taking place with Jesus. She wished she could write a commentary on this biblical story of desire.

The whole point of her life became to do God's will and to allow God's love to be expressed in her love. Even though her images of hope seemed quaint and even overly pious to us, at least on the surface, they did lead her into a great emotional and spiritual maturity.

Two factors entered into Thérèse's understanding of heaven. One was her lifelong conviction that those on earth, those in purgatory, and those in heaven are intimately related. The gulf between life here on earth and life in heaven is bridged by mutual relationships which death does not end.

And, second, heaven for her was not to be the final escape into everlasting security. The mature Thérèse was dissatisfied with a heaven disconnected from this world. She maintained that she would still care for those she left behind; she would not stop caring in heaven; she would continue the work she was doing in Carmel, namely, praying for the salvation of souls. Loving God would mean continually being concerned that all learn to love God. How she would live in heaven is the same way she lived on earth: loving God in all her activity. She once wrote that she would not pick up a pin to avoid purgatory. Whatever she does has to be done out of love, not to avoid something.

When Heaven Mocks

But no image satisfies. Time and again we are thrown back on the yearning, the ache, the muffled cry, the hunger itself, with no apparent relief or response. What happens when our images of hope, which pull us down into our humanity and forward into our destiny, begin to lose their power to touch us, are seen as inadequate, perhaps even false? What happens when our images of hope begin to mock us for believing in them? Have we truly touched something profoundly true and human within us, or were we deluded into putting faith into an illusion? Thérèse's last months dramatically raised such questions.

Thérèse's vision of heaven toward the end of her life was no longer a star to guide by, but a black hole that mocked her belief in heaven as naive, the product of wishful thinking. The darkness tormented her:

> Then suddenly the fog that surrounds me becomes more dense; it penetrates my soul and envelops it in such a way that it is impossible to discover within it the sweet image of my Fatherland; everything has disappeared!…The darkness…says mockingly to me: "…Advance, advance; rejoice in death which will give you not what you hope for but a night still more profound, the night of nothingness."[11]

She was sailing away from a known shore to an infinitely receding horizon. John of the Cross wrote that the greatest fear in the night is that God is receding, walking away, abandoning us.

When those words, beliefs, images that so consoled and nourished us on our pilgrimage no longer evoke our depths, when meaning evaporates from them, how do we go on? Here, perhaps, we see Thérèse earning the title, "Doctor of Hope."

Karl Rahner talks about one of the most common forms of mysticism being found in the lives of those who get up in the morning, who can give themselves no good reason for going into the day, but they do enter the day and fulfill their responsibilities. How are they able to do it? On what basis do they proceed? Where is the strength? The hope?

There is a lesson about love in all of this. To know something, especially to know someone, the ultimate knowledge is not to have mastery over all the details of that person's personality and life. Such knowledge brings us a certain distance. But to really know someone is to slowly be known by that one. Full knowledge has to eventually be love, a *surrender to the mystery of the Other.* Our thoughts, our images, even our inspiring images of forever, carry us only so far into the incomprehensible mystery. At a certain point, they promise too much and are in danger of being idols fooling us into their service.

One cannot shoot basketballs forever. Responsibilities call, infirmities limit, boredom sets in. One cannot play football forever and ever. Storms come, snow piles up, interest wanes, limits are revealed. One cannot make love forever, or watch tenderly innocent scenes for ever. Children grow up, energies find other channels. One cannot plumb the depths of the tragic forever. Even the tragic bottoms out, and something is met in the heart of the night that offers a barely audible "Yes" in the midst of all our "No's".

Can we feel the arms that have been embracing us? Is there any way of measuring the strength that is sustaining us? We can only go on in faith, putting one foot in front of the other, doing the next loving thing that presents itself, letting go of all the scenarios and scenes that emboldened us and led us on. We can only care for those whom God has put into our lives, and reverence the one earth we have. Our images have done their work, and then they too must fade into the mystery of God. All that is left is patience and perseverance and trust, the core of faith.

Thérèse of Lisieux was able to write about her night from a perspective of faith. She was not writing about faith crumbling, but of faith being purified. Earlier she had written, "And still *peace,* always *peace,* reigned at the bottom of the chalice."[12] She found a peace and a true joy, seen by her sisters, in the heart of her very human experience. She was at the heart of her little way, at the heart of the paschal mystery. "So it depends not upon a person's will or exertion but upon God, who shows mercy."[13]

I think my dad in his own way found the same answers. To know what it is all about, and to know one's future, and how it will all turn out, one has to love; that is, go on with an unspoken confidence and trust, surrendering into the incomprehensibility of God. It is the mystery of the cross, and, amazingly, the reason for our hope.

Mysticism in the new millennium, a transforming engagement with presence, will bring a challenge to our Christian faith, as it did during the two previous millennia. Our psyches will express our deepest desires in traditional Christian imagery, and the millennium will offer nontraditional images, images of a thoroughly secular world, or images from other ancient religions. We will be haunted, energized, stilled, delighted, aggrieved.

We will continue to tell of Thérèse's heaven and eternal Sundays, of athletes' dreams, of soldiers' haunting memories, of science's fantastic scenarios. The psyche will continue its flow of images and memories telling us about our hopes, our common humanity, the God who haunts the roots of our being. And spirit will continue to undermine these images and scenarios, saying "Yes, but...; yes this, but no not really, not finally, not fully...."

John of the Cross reminded us, "Every possession is against hope."[14] We hope in what is not possessed.[15] The psalmist knew this long ago: "The watchman counts on daybreak, while Israel waits for the Lord."[16]

Notes

1. Conrad DeMeester, O.C.D., ed., *Saint Thérèse of Lisieux: Her Life, Times, and Teaching* (Washington, D.C.: ICS Publications, 1977), 5.

2. Thérèse of Lisieux, *Story of a Soul*, trans. John Clarke, O.C.D. (Washington, D.C.: ICS Publications, 1976), 29, 30. Words in italics were underlined or written in larger script by Thérèse for emphasis.

3. Ibid., 42.

4. Ibid., 37.

5. Reference unknown. Quoted in Elizabeth A. Dreyer, *Earth Crammed with Heaven* (New York: Paulist Press, 1994), vi.

6. Teilhard De Chardin, *The Divine Milieu* (New York: Harper and Row, 1960), 33, 4.

7. 1 Peter 3:15.

8. Alice Rains Trulock, *In the Hands of Providence* (Chapel Hill: University of North Carolina Press, 1992), 157, 158.

9. Joshua Lawrence Chamberlain, *The Passing of the Armies* (New York: Bantam Books, 1993), 106.

10. Ibid., 196. Trained as a theologian and an academician, Chamberlain received the Congressional Medal of Honor for his efforts at Gettysburg. He was wounded six times during the war and received a battlefield promotion to general, the first such promotion by Ulysses S. Grant. After the war Chamberlain was elected governor of Maine four times and became president of Bowdoin College, where he had studied and taught before the war.

11. Thérèse of Lisieux, *Story of a Soul*, 213.

12. Ibid., 167.

13. Romans 9:16.

14. John of the Cross, *The Ascent of Mount Carmel*, in *The Collected Works of St. John of the Cross*, trans. Kieran Kavanaugh, O.C.D., and Otilio Rodriguez, O.C.D. (Washington, D.C.: ICS Publications, 1991), book 3, chap. 7, no. 2.

15. Hebrews 11:1.

16. Psalm 130.

---

12. Trusting the Action of God in Ministry

When I minister to people, do I expect that they will have experiences of a God who is active in their lives? When I preach, for example, do I count on the fact that the people in the congregation have experiences of deep joy and a desire for "they know not what" and can be reminded of them? When I make pastoral visits, do I ever engage in conversations that might elicit talk about such experiences? In my pastoral counseling, do I actually presume on God's healing presence to those whom I counsel? In other words, in my ministry do I put into practice the Christian (and Jewish) belief that God is actively pursuing God's dream, drawing people to want what God wants and actively helping them to live their lives authentically and fruitfully? Do we count on God's initiative when we engage in ministry? Can we count on God's initiative? In this essay, I engage us in critical reflection on the actual practice of our ministry in terms of these questions.

The Divine Initiative

In the fifteenth introductory explanation for directors of the *Spiritual Exercises* Ignatius of Loyola writes,

> The one giving the Exercises should not urge the one receiving them toward poverty or any other promise more than toward their opposites, or to one state or manner of living more than to another. Outside the Exercises it is lawful and meritorious for us to counsel those who are probably suitable for it to choose continence, virginity, religious life, and all forms of evangelical perfection. But during these Spiritual Exercises when a person is seeking God's will, it is more appropriate and far better that the Creator and Lord himself should communicate himself to the devout soul, embracing it in love and praise, and disposing it for the way which will enable the soul to serve him better in the future. Accordingly, the one giving the Exercises ought not to lean or incline in either

178

direction but rather, while standing by like the pointer of a scale in equilibrium, to allow the Creator to deal immediately with the creature and the creature with its Creator and Lord.[1]

Ignatius obviously believed that, at least while a person was making the exercises, God would deal directly with him or her. In other words, Ignatius believed that God was actively interested in the person who took the time to make the exercises. In addition, he seems to have believed that the director could get in the way of God's activity with the retreatant. Obviously Ignatius's professed belief that God takes an active interest in the lives of those who make the spiritual exercises affected not only how he did this ministry but also how he trained others to engage in the ministry. Indeed, if we were to presuppose that the kind of spiritual direction that an Ignatian director of the spiritual exercises does is a form of pastoral counseling (as I would maintain), then Ignatius developed a form of pastoral counseling that took seriously and acted on his belief that God communicates directly and effectively with those who make the exercises.

But, one of the hallmarks of Ignatian spirituality is that God can be found in all things. Ignatius came to believe that God is active not only during times of retreat or explicit prayer, but always. We Christians profess that God is the creator of the universe. As creator God has an intention or purpose in creation, a purpose that cannot ultimately be thwarted. If this is true, then God is always at work in this world, actively bringing about God's intention. At every moment of creation's existence, God is actively working to bring about the divine purpose. What is that intention or purpose? That we can only know if it has been revealed. And we Christians believe that God has finally revealed his intention in the life, actions, preaching, death, and resurrection of Jesus of Nazareth. Central to Jesus' teaching was the kingdom of God, the triumph of God's intention at the end of time, a triumph that is already inchoately present in Jesus himself and in his ministry.[2]

Because of the incarnation, our Christian faith holds, a part of this universe with ties to every other part is the second person of the Trinity. In addition, with the sending of the Holy Spirit every person is under the direct influence of God at every moment of existence. God is so ingredient to this universe that we can say that there is no place in the universe that is not holy ground. We are in contact with God at every moment and in every place. And the Triune God is actively working to bring about the kingdom of God.

But what does the kingdom of God mean? What does God want and continue to pursue actively through all of history? It would seem that God wants all men and women to live in intimate union with God and in harmony with one another and with the whole of creation. God creates the universe to invite all human beings into the intimate life of the Trinity. God brings each human being into existence for union with the Trinity, which includes unity with all other human beings and with all creation. In *Let This Mind Be in You,* Sebastian Moore makes the point that this creative desire of God not only brings us into being, but also creates in us a desire for "we know not what," for God and for what God wants. In other words, God's creative action, which is always present, can be experienced in us as a desire. Augustine expressed this desire in his famous aphorism: "The thought of you stirs him [a human being] so deeply that he cannot be content unless he praises you, because you made us for yourself and our hearts find no peace until they rest in you."[3] Moore indicates that this desire is what C. S. Lewis called "Joy," the joy by which he was surprised.[4] Do I demonstrate in my ministry that I believe that everyone experiences this desire?

Experiences of the Divine Initiative in Creation

It was certainly experienced by Jacque Braman, a thirty-five-year-old newlywed computer consultant, who writes of an experience she had as a youngster.

I was raised in the church, went to Sunday school every day, learned all the Bible stories, and pretty much accepted them as truth. After all, I had no reason not to believe. Then God, one night as I was riding in the car, gave me some tangible proof.

It was a peaceful evening. My mom and brother and sister and I were on our way to a high school basketball game that my dad was coaching. It was quiet in the car. The others may have been talking some, but not to me. I was just looking out the window at the still night, enjoying the stars, and the street lights, and happy to be on my way to the game. Then a strange thing started to happen. The happiness that I was feeling grew deeper and richer and fuller, and completely overwhelmed me, even though I still felt quiet and peaceful. Then I noticed that tears were rolling down my cheeks. This was really weird. I double checked: No, I wasn't sad. I had a huge grin plastered on my face, one that was beyond my ability to remove, try as I might....

Then I understood. This was how full joy could be. This was a joy that comes only from God. I relished the moment, immersed in joy, filled with thankfulness and contentment. I shared my thoughts with God in silent prayer, and knew he was right there with me.[5]

We find a similar experience in the autobiographical memoir *The Sacred Journey* by Frederick Buechner. He describes an experience he had in

Bermuda, where his mother had taken him and his brother after his father's suicide. At thirteen, near the end of his stay, he was sitting with a girl of thirteen on a wall watching ferries come and go. Quite innocently, he says,

> our bare knees happened to touch for a moment, and in that moment I was filled with such a sweet panic and anguish for I had no idea that I knew my life could never be complete until I found it.... It was the upward-reaching and fathomlessly hungering, heart-breaking love for the beauty of the world at its most beautiful, and, beyond that, for that beauty east of the sun and west of the moon which is past the reach of all but our most desperate desiring and is finally the beauty of Beauty itself, of Being itself and what lies at the heart of Being.[6]

Buechner acknowledges that there are a number of possible psychological explanations of this experience. However, he goes on to say that "looking back at those distant years I choose not to deny, either, the compelling sense of an unseen giver and series of hidden gifts as not only another part of their reality, but the deepest part of all."[7]

Another experience narrated by Buechner makes even clearer the creative touch of God at the heart of this desire. He and his wife and daughter were visiting Sea World in Orlando on a beautiful day. The bleachers were packed as six killer whales were released into the tank.

> What with the dazzle of the sky and sun, the beautiful young people on the platform, the soft southern air, and the crowds all around us watching the performance with a delight matched only by what seemed the delight of the performing whales, it was as if the whole creation—men and women and beasts and sun and water and earth and sky and, for all I know, God himself—was caught up in one great, jubilant dance of unimaginable beauty. And then, right in the midst of it, I was astonished to find that my eyes were filled with tears.

His wife and daughter had a similar experience, as did the Dean of Salisbury Cathedral on another occasion. Buechner goes on to write,

> My wife and I and our daughter Sharmy and the dean of Salisbury Cathedral—I believe there is no mystery about why we shed tears. We shed tears because we had a glimpse of the Peaceable Kingdom, and it had almost broken our hearts. For a few moments we had seen Eden and been part of the great dance that goes on at the heart of creation. We shed tears because we were given a glimpse

of the way life was created to be and is not. We had seen why it was the "morning stars sang together, and all the sons of God shouted for joy" when the world was first made, as the book of Job describes it, and of what it was that made Saint Paul write, even when he was in prison and on his way to execution, "Rejoice in the Lord always; again I will say, Rejoice." We had had a glimpse of part at least of what Jesus meant when he said, "Blessed are you that weep now, for you shall laugh."[8]

I have picked up in various novels echoes of the same experience, but the characters do not always make the connection to God. The novelists themselves, however, must be aware of the experience as having a religious dimension. For example, the mystery novelist P. D. James writes of one of Chief Inspector Dalgliesh's subordinates, Kate Mishkin:

> Standing now between the glitter of the water and the high, delicate blue of the sky, she felt an extraordinary impulse which had visited her before and which she thought must be as close as she could ever get to a religious experience. She was possessed by a need, almost physical in its intensity, to pray, to praise, to say thank you, without knowing to whom, to shout with a joy that was deeper than the joy she felt in her own physical well-being and achievements or even in the beauty of the physical world.[9]

If I were to meet Kate and she told me about this experience, would I tend to see the active hand of God in it? Would I ask her about it on the assumption that it was an experience of God's creative touch? Or would I be embarrassed to appear interested for fear that I might be seen as too "religious?" I wonder how often people are prevented from discovering that they have been touched by God by a certain reticence in believers to show interest in such experiences.

Perhaps these are enough citations to make the point that God's continuous creative activity is experienced by ordinary human beings. When I minister to people, do I expect that they will have such experiences? Experiences like Buechner's could be construed as experiences of God's creative dream for our world, the "peaceable kingdom" of prophecies such as that of Isaiah:

> The wolf shall live with the lamb, the leopard shall lie down with the kid, the calf and the lion and the fatling together, and a little child shall lead them. The cow and the bear shall graze, their young shall lie down together, and the lion shall eat straw like the ox. The nursing child shall play over the hole of the asp, and the

weaned child shall put its hand on the adder's den. They will not
hurt or destroy on all my holy mountain; for the earth will be full
of the knowledge of the LORD as the waters cover the sea. (Is
11:6–9)

If we believe that God does touch us with his creative intention, his dream,
then we will minister in such a way that people will be able to make sense of
such experiences.

God's Initiative and Conscience

Ho, everyone who thirsts, comes to the waters; and you that have
no money, come, buy and eat! Come, buy wine and milk without
money and without price. Why do you spend your money for that
which is not bread, and your labor for that which does not satisfy?
Listen carefully to me, and eat what is good, and delight yourselves in rich food. Incline your ear, and come to me; listen, so that
you may live. I will make with you an everlasting covenant, my
steadfast, sure love for David. (Is 55:1–3)

In addition to belief in God's creative activity, which is experienced as
the desire for "I know not what," we also profess to believe that God actively
tries to draw human being toward union with the Trinity and toward union
with the divine intention. Hence, we profess to believe, God draws people to
act in accordance with the divine purpose, to do good and to avoid evil, to
make the world more in accord with God's dream. Do I demonstrate such
belief in my ministry? Do I presume that in every person I meet God's spirit is
actively moving that person toward the good? In preaching and pastoral conversations do I try to help people pay attention to the voice of conscience,
trusting that this voice is present? Do I trust that because of the presence of the
spirit every adult can develop an informed conscience by which to guide his or
her life? If we believe in the action of the spirit, we might take a different
stance toward people who seem to be in serious sin. Perhaps before making
too quick a condemnation we would be more prone to probe their experience
in order to help them to realize that they are torn in conscience.

An example, not from real life, occurred during a role play in a training
program for spiritual directors.

A married man with three teen-aged children has been having
an affair with a younger woman. He feels energized and more
alive when he is with her. At home he feels under appreciated
both by his wife and his children. He seems to drag his way

through life. Since he has met the young woman, he has felt more alive, more able to be empathetic with his clients in his law office, more willing to take on cases for poorer clients. He asks to speak with his parish priest, and tells him about this new love. He wonders whether this new found love is God's answer for what has been ailing him. He feels so much more alive and helpful to others. The priest lets him talk about the new relationship, and then asks him about his feelings at home. At first he speaks of what a drag home life is, but then he says: "At times I feel really torn; I'm not at ease living a lie. I wonder whether I should tell my wife and get a separation." The priest continues to probe his experience asking him about his feeling torn. He begins to talk about his feelings of guilt, a sense that he is betraying his wife and failing his children.

Those of us who were present for the role play discovered that the man was experiencing the movements described by Ignatius of Loyola in his rules for the discernment of spirits.

In the case of persons who are going from one mortal sin to another, the enemy ordinarily proposes to them apparent pleasures. He makes them imagine delights and pleasures of the senses, in order to hold them fast and plunge them deeper into their sins and vices.

But with the persons of this type the good spirit uses a contrary procedure. Through their good judgment on problems of morality he stings their consciences with remorse.[10]

Ignatius presumes that God's spirit is active in people, moving them toward the morally good and away from what is morally bad. The priest in the role play acted with that presumption and found out that the man in question was troubled in mind and heart and that he faced a painful moral decision that would not easily be solved by the fact that his new love made him feel invigorated. If the priest had too quickly jumped in to give his own moral judgment on the man, he might not have found out that the man himself was deeply troubled. Now he could, with sympathy, help him to face the whole truth of his situation and come to a decision.

The Discernment of Spirits

In this last section we have been touching on the topic of the discernment of spirits. Ignatius of Loyola follows up the rule just cited with a second:

In the case of persons who are earnestly purging away their sins, and who are progressing from good to better in the service of God our Lord, the procedure used is the opposite of that described in the First Rule. For in this case it is characteristic of the evil spirit to cause gnawing anxiety, to sadden, and to set up obstacles. In this way he unsettles these persons by false reasons aimed at preventing their progress.

But with persons of this type it is characteristic of the good spirit to stir up courage and strength, consolations, tears, inspirations, and tranquility. He makes things easier and eliminates all obstacles, so that the persons may move forward in doing good.[11]

Many, if not most, of the people we meet in our ordinary ministry might well be persons of this type, people who are trying as best they can to live good Christian lives. Ignatius presumes that everyone will be under the influence of the good and bad spirits. Usually discussion of discernments of spirits has been confined to treatises on spirituality and spiritual direction. But our faith tells us that the discernment of spirits must be a part of every life. Our hearts and minds are a battleground. Jesus himself seems to have believed not only that God is always actively working out God's intention, but also that the archenemy of God is also active.

It is important to realize that, in the view of Jesus,...human beings were not basically neutral territories that might be influenced by divine or demonic forces now and then.... Human existence was seen as a battlefield dominated by one or the other supernatural force, God or Satan (alias Belial or the devil). A human being might have a part in choosing which "field of force" would dominate his or her life, i.e., which force he or she would choose to side with. But no human being was free to choose simply to be free of these supernatural forces. One was dominated by either one or the other, and to pass *from* one was necessarily to pass *into* the control of the other. At least over the long term, one could not maintain a neutral stance vis-à-vis God and Satan.[12]

When I engage in pastoral ministry, do I act as though I believe as Jesus believed, namely that God is actively engaged in bringing about his intention and that God's activity is actively opposed by the evil one? Do I, in other words, help people to discern the spirits?

In *Who Do You Say I Am?* I wrote:

Since the time of Jesus Christian religious geniuses (who have believed in Jesus as far more than just a religious genius, by the way) have also become aware of this epic battle. Ignatius of Loyola was one of them. In his own very turbulent time (the end of the medieval synthesis and the beginning of the modern world) he came to believe that the human heart was a battleground between God and the evil one, between good spirits and evil spirits, and that it was necessary to discern these different spirits and ask to be put under the influence of the good spirits. It is possible that the urgency of the coming of God's rule strikes religious geniuses in times of great turmoil such as in Jesus' time and the time of Ignatius. If that is so, then our time could certainly qualify, especially at the end of the second millennium, as a time of heightened awareness of how much the times are out of joint and far from what God intends and hence ripe for a new, and perhaps, final coming of God to rule.[13]

Many conceptualize the struggle for social justice as a struggle between the forces of good and those of evil. For example, it is easy to demonize those who engage in overtly racist activities, those who advocate abortion, or those who push for the death penalty, and to see those who oppose them as on the side of God. But the struggle between God and the evil one goes on in each human heart. In my ministry, do I take account of this epic struggle going on in me and in those to whom I minister, no matter what side of the social issues facing our society we espouse? If I do, then I will be better able to help people to reflect on the conflicting movements of their hearts and to begin to discern the way God is leading them. It may be that help to do such reflection will be more effective than exhortations or harangues in motivating people to engage in efforts to redress social ills.

The Divine Initiative in Difficult Pastoral Situations

Let me touch on some other situations that we often meet in our ministry, ones that may cause us to reflect on our real beliefs. Often enough we meet people who have suffered or are suffering grievously in life, parents whose child is dying of leukemia, people who have been physically and sexually abused by their parents, people suffering horribly painful and disfiguring diseases. They want to know how God could have let this happen. Many of them are angry at God for inflicting such sufferings on them. How we respond to such people may say a great deal about our alleged trust in God. We may feel helpless before such people. Such helplessness can lead to defensiveness. For example, we may feel the need to defend God. "You shouldn't be angry with God. God knows best." Do we believe that God can take care of himself? Or do we try to defend him when people who have suffered grievously express their anger at God? We might do well to meditate on the Book of Job, where Job's friends try to justify God to the innocently suffering Job. Job will not be satisfied until God speaks directly to him. After God has spoken, Job is satisfied. But God has not finished speaking.

> After the LORD had spoken these words to Job, the LORD said to Eliphaz the Temanite: "My wrath is kindled against you and against your two friends; for you have not spoken of me what is right, as my servant Job has. Now therefore take seven bulls and seven rams, and go to my servant Job, and offer up for yourselves a burnt offering; and my servant Job shall pray for you, for I will accept his prayer not to deal with you according to your folly; for you have not spoken of me what is right, as my servant Job has done."
>
> So Eliphaz the Temanite and Bildad the Shuhite and Zophar the Naamathite went and did what the LORD had told them; and the LORD accepted Job's prayer. (Jb 42:7–9)

We might learn from the Book of Job how to speak what is right about God.

The Divine Initiative: Miracles?

One of the surest things that we can say about the historical Jesus of Nazareth is that he was considered by others and considered himself a miracle worker.[14] Now it is true, as Meier in the second volume of *A Marginal Jew* notes, that no historian as such can say that an event was miraculous. Only a person of faith can attest that an out-of-ordinary event is a miracle, because, as he writes, "it is of the essence of a miracle that the event is seen to have as its only adequate cause and explanation a special act of God, who alone is able to bring about the miraculous effect."[15] A scientist might say that there is no known explanation for this phenomenon, but only as a person of faith could the scientist go on to say that this phenomenon is an act of God. How do we approach the miracles of the New Testament in our pastoral ministry? How do we approach the possibility of modern day miracles?

Are we, perhaps, imbued with the skepticism of many modern academics? Rudolph Bultmann spoke for many modern academics when he said, "It is impossible to use electric light and the 'wireless,' and to avail ourselves of modern medical and surgical discoveries, and at the same time to believe in the New Testament world of…miracles."[16] Bultmann's statement purports to be an empirical fact, but is it true? Meier refers to a Gallup poll of 1989 which found that 82 percent of Americans polled (all of whom, it is presumed, use electric light and the wireless and some of whom may even be scientists and professors) believe that "even today, miracles are performed by the power of God."[17]

We need not cede to the unbeliever or the agnostic the higher ground in the argument about either the existence of God or the possibility of miracles. An unbeliever denies the possibility of either on philosophical grounds, not on empirical proof. On these questions believers and unbelievers both plant their feet firmly in air and march on; i.e., both make leaps of "faith" that are not grounded on empirical evidence. As we approach the wonders attributed to the historical Jesus, it is well to remember that the presumption against the miraculous has no more solid footing than the presumption for the miraculous.[18]

What do I believe about the activity of God in our world? Does God still perform miracles?

Throngs of people who have made the pilgrimage to Lourdes have come away convinced that miracles have indeed occurred there through the intercession of Mary. Among the believers are doctors who have examined the scientific evidence and certified that there is no scientific explanation for many of the cures. But there are, perhaps, more ordinary instances of the power of God to heal. In an article in the *Boston Globe* a social scientist, John DiIulio, is quoted as saying, "Natural scientists have gone far in the last 10 to 12 years investigating the impact of faith-based approaches to various physical and mental outcomes...looking at patients who pray, or how being churched can inhibit various kinds of mental disorders. The findings are so strong that some 40 medical schools have incorporated it in their training."[19] Do we pastoral ministers trust in God's power to heal?

Here is an example from the writer Reynolds Price, who recounts his terrible struggle with cancer of the spinal cord. He had just had the first of many operations and was recuperating so that he could then undergo massive radiation therapy to try to kill the significant cancerous tumor that remained. He recounts this incidence:

So by daylight on July 3rd, morning thoughts of a stiff sobriety were plainly in order. But in the midst of such circular thinking, an actual happening intervened with no trace of warning. I was suddenly not propped in my brass bed or even contained in my familiar house. By the dim new, thoroughly credible light that rose around me, it was barely dawn; and I was lying fully dressed in modern street clothes on a slope by a lake I knew at once. It was the big lake of Kinnereth, the Sea of Galilee, in the north of Israel—green Galilee, the scene of Jesus' first teaching and healing. I'd paid the lake a second visit the previous October, a twelve-mile-long body of fish-stocked water in beautiful hills of grass, trees and small family farms.

Still sleeping around me on the misty ground were a number of men in the tunics and cloaks of first-century Palestine. I soon understood with no sense of surprise that the men were Jesus' twelve disciples and that he was nearby asleep among them. So I lay on a while in the early chill, looking west across the lake to Tiberias, a small low town, and north to the fishing villages of Capernaum and Bethsaida. I saw them as they were in the first century—stone huts with thatch-and-mud roofs, occasional low towers, the rising smoke of breakfast fires. The early light was a fine mix of tan and rose. It would be a fair day.

Then one of the sleeping men woke and stood.

I saw it was Jesus, bound toward me. He looked much like the lean Jesus of Flemish paintings—tall with dark hair, unblemished skin and a self-possession both natural and imposing.

Again I felt no shock or fear. All this was normal human event; it was utterly clear to my normal eyes and was happening as surely as any event of my previous life. I lay and watched him walk on nearer.

Jesus bent and silently beckoned me to follow.

I knew to shuck off my trousers and jacket, then my shirt and shorts. Bare, I followed him.

He was wearing a twisted white cloth round his loins; otherwise he was bare and the color of ivory.

We waded out into cool lake water twenty feet from shore till we stood waist-deep.

I was in my body but was also watching my body from slightly upward and behind. I could see the purple dye on my back, the long rectangle that boxed my thriving tumor.

Jesus silently took up handfuls of water and poured them over my head and back till water ran down my puckered scar. Then he spoke once—"Your sins are forgiven"—and turned to shore again, done with me.

I came on behind him, thinking in standard greedy fashion, *It's not my sins I'm worried about.* So to Jesus' receding back, I had the gall to say "Am I also cured?" He turned to face me, no sign of a smile, and finally said two words—"That too."

Then he climbed from the water, not looking around, really done with me. I followed him out and then, with no palpable seam in the texture of time or place, I was home again in my wide bed.[20]

Price recognizes the possibility that this was just a dream, even a wish fulfillment dream. But he avers, "From the moment my mind was back in my own room, no more than seconds after I'd left, I've believed that the event was an external gift, however brief, of an alternate time and space in which to live through a crucial act."[21] He was eventually cured of the cancer though only after much suffering, much radiation therapy and another operation, and he was left paralyzed from the waist down. The last lines of his memoir describe his present life, which includes long days of writing. Then he ends with these words: "Even my handwriting looks very little like the script of the man I was in June of '84. Cranky as it is, it's taller, more legible, with more air and stride. It comes down the arm of a grateful man."[22] How would I react if Price had come to me with this story of his experience? Would I be skeptical, more ready to give it a purely psychological explanation? What do I believe about God's activity in this world?

Of course, even in Jesus' time not every blind or deaf person was healed, not every grieving mother received her child back from the dead. Many people who pray for a miracle do not get one, at least not the one they want. Given this reality, how do we minister in situations where no miracle healing occurs? Do we believe that God can yet be a comforting presence to those who suffer? Do we expect that people can be comforted by God's presence, can even experience God's profound sympathy, and find this as much a miracle as a physical healing would be? People have found such a presence consoling. For example, after a talk on prayer as a personal relationship, a woman in the audience spoke of the aftermath of being sexually abused by her father. She had lost trust in her mother as well as her father. It was difficult for her to relate to God because he had allowed this to happen to her. She had expressed her anger directly to God. Eventually she felt that God communicated to her a profound sadness that she had been abused. She was greatly consoled that God suffered with her. The Dutch Jewess Etty Hillesum found profound consolation through her personal relationship with God as she saw her world gradually being destroyed by the Nazis. A short time before being shipped to Auschwitz and her death she wrote this "Sunday morning prayer" in her diary:

> Dear God, these are anxious times. Tonight for the first time I lay
> in the dark with burning eyes as scene after scene of human suffer-
> ing passed before me. I shall promise You one thing, God, just one
> thing: I shall never burden my today with cares about my tomor-
> row, although that takes some practice. Each day is sufficient unto
> itself. I shall try to help You, God to stop my strength ebbing away,
> though I cannot vouch for it in advance. But one thing is becoming
> increasingly clear to me: that You cannot help us, that we must
> help You to help ourselves. And that is all we can manage these

days and also all that really matters: that we safeguard that little piece of You, God, in ourselves. And perhaps in others as well. Alas, there doesn't seem much You Yourself can do about our circumstances, about our lives. Neither do I hold You responsible. You cannot help us but we must help You and defend Your dwelling place inside us to the last.... And there are those who want to put their bodies in safe keeping.... And they say, "I shan't let them get me into their clutches." But they forget that no one is in their clutches who is in Your arms. I am beginning to feel a little more peaceful, God, thanks to this conversation with You."[23]

Do I believe in this consoling intervention of God in people's lives even when there is no miraculous change in circumstances?

God's Initiative in Pastoral Counseling

In my pastoral counseling do I demonstrate a belief that by relating consciously to God in prayer a person can be transformed? In his autobiography, Ignatius of Loyola recounts his conversion from the life of a womanizing, ambitious, swashbuckling knight to a man dedicated to a life of service of God in the church. In the course of his conversion he went through an excruciating time of scruples. They were so bad that he contemplated suicide. He became aware that these scruples were destroying his enjoyment of God and of life and became convinced that they were temptations. In other words, he discovered in his own experience the truth he expressed in the second rule for the discernment of spirits cited earlier. He was thus freed of the power of these scruples to torture him. As he continued to engage in the relationship with God, he seems to have been transformed interiorly. He recounts, for example, three instances when he came close to death. The first time he seems to be terrified of meeting God. The second time he says that he examined his conscience but felt not fear on account of his sins and no fear of condemnation. The third time he experienced such joy and consolation at the thought of death that he burst into tears. One way to interpret what has happened is that through regular contact with God his image of self-in-relation-with-God has been transformed.[24] I have met people who have experienced similar shifts in their interior lives because of their perseverance in prayer. In one instance a person who had been plagued by obsessive thoughts for years without much relief through therapy became freed of them through regular spiritual direction and persistent dialogue with God in prayer. Do we trust in the efficacy of such prayer?

Throughout the history of Christianity, people have believed that they have encountered the risen Jesus in prayer. They have recounted experiences of engaging in dialogue with him. Many have also believed that in the dialogue with Jesus they could discover a call from Jesus to follow him, a call that might lead to a choice of a way of life. If a person comes to me and wants to discuss such experiences, what is my reaction? Am I more wary than expectant and hopeful? Or do I enter the dialogue with this person, expecting that together we can discern what is the wheat from the chaff in the experiences he or she will recount, that is, discern what is of God from what is not of God? My overriding attitude toward such an encounter will tell me a lot about my practical beliefs.

God's Action in Ritual Actions

In my various ministerial actions, do I believe that I am preparing the ground to make it easier for those to whom I minister to become conscious of encountering God? Imagine what it would be like if at a liturgy everyone who had a part in preparing and carrying out the rites was aware that they were participating in such an encounter. The ushers, the musicians, the deacons, the lectors, the communion ministers, the priest, all have a lively and conscious belief that God will be met by people during this liturgy. The lectors, for example, consciously believe that the word they read is powerful and a means for God to speak to his people; the communion ministers are conscious that they are facilitating communion with the Lord; the homilist consciously wants the congregation to hear the word as the Word of God; the presider prays to God the canon and other prayers consciously in the name of the people. There need be no overt soulful looks or shows of piety, no theatrics, but such a liturgy would have a powerful effect.

Are We Necessary for God's Action in This World?

What do we believe about our own necessity? It might be salutary for all of us who minister to reflect regularly on some words of J. D. Salinger's character Zooey. He and his mother are discussing Zooey's sister Franny and what might help her. Mrs. Glass has just asked about psychoanalysis. Zooey replies,

> For a psychoanalyst to be any good with Franny at all, he'd have to be a pretty peculiar type. I don't know. He'd have to believe that it was through the grace of God that he'd been inspired to study psychoanalysis in the first place. He'd have to believe that it was through the grace of God that he wasn't run over by a goddam truck before he ever even got his license to practice. He'd have to believe that it was through the grace of God that he has the native intelligence to be able to help his goddam patients at all. I don't know any *good* analysts who think along those lines. But that's the

only kind of psychoanalyst who might be able to do Franny any good at all.[25]

During a retreat a couple of years ago I spent a number of days pondering the servant song of Isaiah 42. In it Yahweh sings the praises of his servant. At the same time he makes it quite clear twice that he is the only God, that the servant for all his praiseworthy qualities is just a servant. What I realized was that God does not need the servant, but wants him. I also realized that the same is true of me and of all God's servants. We are not necessary to God, but God wants us as his servants. In a real sense the same is true of Jesus. God does not need the human Jesus, but God wants him. One evening as I was walking after dinner, these words suddenly came to me: "You could be dead now." I laughed aloud. It was true; I had had a bout of cancer of the vocal cord which could have killed me. My first cousin had lost his voice box to the same cancer and was dying at that very moment. The reason for the laughter was the thought: "That's right, and somebody else would be provincial, and the province would go on. You're not necessary." It was a freeing moment. It has not been easy to keep that freedom and that conviction that I was not necessary but wanted. When I have, however, I feel a freedom and a joy in my life and ministry that easily bubbles over into immense gratitude. When I have this gift, then I do minister with practical belief that God is indeed active in our world, and I work with a grateful heart.

Conclusion

Finally, how do I react to the breakdown of the religious culture in the United States and other developed countries? Do I get discouraged at the evidence that religion has so little impact on people? Do we who are Roman Catholics get depressed at the graying of the clergy and the diminishment of the number of seminarians and members of religious congregations? While I was provincial, I regularly challenged the members of my province to look the statistics in the eye as a test of our faith in God. When our numbers were on the increase, when we were building larger institutions to house our novices and seminarians, we could have been putting our faith in ourselves and in our manifest destiny rather than in God. But when our numbers are on the decline, when we no longer find ourselves being sought out by hordes of the brightest and the best, do we believe that God still wants us as servants, that God is still working to achieve the divine intention in this world? Ultimately Jesus had to surrender to the death of all his hopes for his mission and for his people and leave resurrection to his Father. Do we believe in God's activity in this world even in the face of what seems to be God's defeat?

Because God creates the universe with an intention, God is active in this world. God takes the initiative not only in creating the universe, but also in calling each human being to an intimate relationship of friendship. Moreover, God's intention will not ultimately be thwarted. All of ministry has only one ultimate purpose: to make it easier for all of us to pay attention to God's action and to live in harmony with it, for that is our bliss. I hope that the reflections of this essay will help us to carry out our ministry faithfully and trustfully. Of course, only God's grace will make this possible. Hence in all our ministry we might ask to be imbued with the spirit of Anselm of Canterbury who prayed in the first chapter of his *Proslogion:*

> Teach me to seek You, and reveal Yourself to me as I seek; for unless You instruct me I cannot seek You, and unless You reveal Yourself I cannot find You. Let me seek You in desiring You; let me desire You in seeking You. Let me find You in loving You; let me love You in finding You.[26]

Notes

1. *The Spiritual Exercises of Saint Ignatius*, trans. and commentary by George E. Ganss (St. Louis: Institute of Jesuit Sources, 1992), 25–26 [n. 15].

2. For a full discussion of Jesus' notion of the kingdom of God, cf. John P. Meier, *A Marginal Jew: Rethinking the Historical Jesus, Vol. II: Mentor, Message, and Miracles* (New York: Doubleday, 1994). For a more popular presentation of the same, see my own *Who Do You Say I Am?* (Notre Dame, Ind.: Ave Maria, 1996), ch. 3.

3. Augustine of Hippo, *Confessions*, trans. R. S. Pine-Coffin (Harmondsworth, England: Penguin, 1961), I, 1 (p. 21).

4. Sebastian Moore, *Let This Mind Be in You: The Quest for Identity through Oedipus to Christ* (San Francisco: Harper and Row, 1985). Cf. also C. S. Lewis, *Surprised by Joy: The Shape of My Early Life* (New York: Harcourt, Brace, 1955). For a fuller development of the insight in this section of the article cf. William A. Barry, *Allowing the Creator to Deal with the Creature: An Approach to the Spiritual Exercises of Ignatius of Loyola* (New York/Mahwah: Paulist, 1994), ch. 4.

5. In James Martin, ed., *How Can I Find God? The Famous and the Not-So-Famous Consider the Quintessential Question* (Liguori, Mo.: Triumph Books, 1997), 156.

6. Frederick Beuchner, *The Sacred Journey* (San Francisco: Harper and Row, 1965), 52.

7. Ibid., 56.

8. Frederick Buechner, *The Longing for Home: Recollections and Reflections* (San Francisco: Harper, 1996), 126–27.

9. P. D. James, *Original Sin* (New York: Time Warner, 1994), 148.

10. *Spiritual Exercises*, 121 [n. 314].

11. Ibid., [315].

12. Meier, *Marginal Jew*, 415.

13. William A. Barry, *What Do You Say I Am? Meeting the Historical Jesus in Prayer* (Notre Dame, Ind.: Ave Maria, 1996), 62–63.

14. Cf. Meier, *Marginal Jew*.

15. Ibid., 513.

16. Cited in Meier, *Marginal Jew*, 520.

17. Ibid.

18. Barry, *Who Do You Say I Am?*, 76–77. For a philosopher's interpretation of the struggle between science and faith, cf. Leszek Kolakowski, *Modernity on Endless Trial* (Chicago and London: University of Chicago Press, 1990), especially ch. 9, "The Illusion of Demythologization."

19. *Boston Sunday Globe*, "Focus," January 4, 1998, Section E, 2.

20. Reynolds Price, *A Whole New Life* (New York: Atheneum, 1994), 42–43, italics in original.

21. Ibid., 44.

22. Ibid., 193.

23. Etty Hillesum, *An Interrupted Life: The Diaries of Etty Hillesum 1941–1943* (New York: Washington Square Press, 1984), 186–187.

24. Cf. *A Pilgrim's Testament: The Memoirs of St. Ignatius of Loyola* as transcribed by Luis Conçalves da Camara and translated by Parmananda R. Divarkar (St. Louis: Institute of Jesuit Sources, 1995). Cf. also "The Changing Self-God Image of Ignatius of Loyola in Relation to Discernment," in Barry, *Creator*, ch. 8.

25. J. D. Salinger, *Franny and Zooey* (New York: Bantam, 1961), 109.

26. Anselm of Canterbury, Vol. I, "Proslogion," ed. and trans. by Jaspar Hopkins and Herbert Richardson (Toronto and New York: Edwin Mellen Press, 1974), 93.

William J. Sneck

13. Carl Jung and the Quest for Wholeness

Journeying into the Outer and Inner Worlds

Postmodern women and men of the twenty-first century are on the move. Tragically, hundreds of thousands find themselves displaced by bombs and guns, and forced to eke out a minimal existence as refugees. Even the well-to-do, those born to education, economic success, and political dominance, seem driven compulsively to change jobs, mates, commitments, living quarters, friends, family ties, club memberships, church affiliations in search of—what? Those of a Marxist mindset might reduce the explanation of these wandering migrations to economic determinism, that prepotent urge to acquire, possess, and hoard that's innate to individuals and societies, and ultimately affecting all political arrangements and ideologies.

Different branches of the psychological community also rush to understand our contemporary unrest and turmoil. Freudians invoke the sex drive; Adlerians point to the will to power, superiority, competence; existentialists locate the base of our strivings in an urgent search for meaning; cognitive behaviorists trace the source of our unhappiness to faulty belief systems.

Theologians would recall a line from the first page of St. Augustine's *Confessions:* "Thou hast made us for Thyself, O Lord, and our hearts can find no rest until they rest in Thee."

Diagnosis from both recognized and self-styled experts, however, cries out for a treatment plan. We could choose to describe the restless agitation and unsettledness of ourselves and those we know as a journey: a journey into the "outer" world of new places, novel experiences, and fantasized ideal relationships. Such a journey, nevertheless, expresses and actualizes an "inner" journey toward personal contentment. Whether we name such a state of contentment as the goal of happiness, the achievement of self-fulfillment, or the realization of integration, we cannot deny the reality of energetic journeyings, whether endured by refugees or embraced by the affluent.

Let us continue calling these outer world wanderings "journeys," and enlist the resources of the United Nations, for example, for the refugees; the advice of stockbrokers and market analysts for adventurous investors; the consultation of family therapists for new patterns of association and intimacy.

But I prefer to call our inner journeying a "quest." *Quest* suggests *question,* and we can give ourselves permission at this point in our process to question all that seems to fuel our inner striving, turmoil, and unsettledness.

Quest also implies some nobility of purpose in our undertaking, a goal that perhaps transcends the humdrum ordinariness of day-to-day existence. *Quest* undoubtedly brings with it romantic connotations of days of yore, of knights in armor rescuing damsels in distress, and subordinating all their passionate desires to a task inspired by a heroic champion. Such a hero would have promised fabulous wealth, everlasting honor, stirring adventures, but realistically also the possibility of suffering and torment. *Quest* hints at purposefulness, reflective stock-taking during the travels, and despite tenacious adherence to a vision, all manner of obstacles and difficulties.

In my own quest for inner wholeness, I have been guided and companioned by many gifted fellow questers, women and men on their own outer and inner journeys, who have generously shared their hard-won insights about particularly precipitous turns in the road, as well as their overall sense of the purpose of life's quest. My most helpful mentors and seers have in turn deferred to their teachers, two of whom have proven to be particularly practical visionaries: Ignatius of Loyola and Carl G. Jung. This series of reflections will focus especially on Jung, but my interpretations and comments will reveal an unmistakably Ignatian perspective.

My contention is simply this: Carl G. Jung, in his person and writings, proves himself a competent and compassionate fellow traveler on the road to integration and wholeness. Whether through suggesting an overview of the whole quest, or helping solve the puzzle of the very next step, Jung's good humor, mastery of world cultures, literatures, and philosophies, but most especially his psychiatrist's experience of healing tormented sisters and brothers invite trust and enthusiasm to learn from him. These pages record and share some of my own learnings reached through struggle, prayer, searching, psychotherapy, spiritual direction, sweating, and laboring sometimes in companionship and sometimes seemingly alone, but always accompanied by the unconscious.

Jung and the Unconscious

Materialism in our Western world has focused human effort on the "thumpable world," that which can be seen, tasted, grasped, smelled, and touched in all its concreteness, and still more pertinently, can be *acquired* so as to convince its owner and one's acquaintances that she or he is worthwhile, worldly wise, and wealthy. Yet the sense of hearing, perhaps more than the rest, opens us to other voices and whispers beyond the merely material, behind, beneath, above the measurable universe. An ancient Christian hymn to Christ in the eucharist chants:

> Visus, tactus, gustus in Te fallitur
> Sed auditu solo tuto creditur. (Adoro Te)

(Sight, touch, and taste are in Thee each deceived; hearing alone most safely is believed.) This couplet applies also to our unconscious.

While delighting in the applause of jealous onlookers, we may be fortunate enough to hear a "still small voice" (1 Kgs 19:12) within inviting us to reflect on questions of meaning, values, goals, reminding us that we are more than our money (whether a welfare check or a pile of paid-up credit cards). This voice will challenge us to take charge of our quest rather than suffer enslavement to others' estimations of us, or even to our ambitious ego's schemes.

Whether encountered in the guise of an inner voice, or in other ways both quietly subtle and highly dramatic, there exists a part of ourselves outside awareness that influences our behavior, day and night, but can be accessed through reverent curiosity and respectful attention. Jung, following Freud, named this aspect of our psyche the "unconscious," but as we shall see, described it in ways significantly different from his mentor.

Although the impact and even the existence of the unconscious is called into question by thinkers of different theoretical persuasions, I invite the reader on a personal experiential inventory. See whether some if not all of the following examples remind you of similar occurrences in life pointing to, if not proving, the reality of the unconscious:

- A dream, seemingly absurd at first, after reflection and discussion with a friend or therapist, yields a harvest of insight—perhaps not a five-year plan, but at least a next step. Jung paid special attention to dreams, and to other manifestations of the unconscious as well.

- I am the host of a pleasant dinner party, but one of the guests proves obnoxious. As he leaves at last, to my own relief and seemingly to that of several others, I try to see him off warmly. But I find myself expressing opposite sentiments: "Must you stay? Can't you go?" Such slips of the tongue speak aloud the inner voice's honest estimation of people and events often when we have consciously intended to convey quite a different impression.

- We have been stalled by a problem at work for days or weeks on end. Suddenly in the shower, or on a walk, or while channel-surfing on TV, a breakthrough step "clicks" into consciousness. The solution seems to pop out of nowhere, and is eagerly embraced by the team.

- Inner good sense suggests that I've been pushing myself for too many days with heavy, albeit enjoyable, work commitments. I refuse to listen, to slow down. Getting up from supper one evening, I trip, fall, damage my knee—not to the point of incapacitation, but enough to force a change of pace. The wisdom of the body, if ignored, sounds more shrill in the form of physical symptoms and even illness.

Despite the desperate suffering of the population whom he served in his younger days as he was developing his theories (hospitalized mental patients before the advent of psychotropic drugs), Jung taught an optimistic, hopeful perspective on the human person and the unconscious. Even within the psychotic ravings of his tortured clientele, Jung detected a deep-down striving for health and wholeness, and named the source of such inner yearnings the "Self." The Self guided the psyche (his term for conscious ego together with unconscious) toward integration and genuine self-realization, a higher goal than the often self*ish* strivings of the narrowly focused ego.

Although some critics have chided Jung for equating the Self with God, a more accurate reading of his text indicates that the Self is that within each human person through which God contacts us. (After all, God is infinite, we are finite; God is all-knowing, and we strain for insight; God is immaterial, we are enfleshed.) God's Holy Spirit, therefore, guides the Self in its own natural striving for true completeness.

Jung, in his therapeutic encounters, writings, and speeches, taught patients, disciples, and audiences the art of making the unconscious conscious. If indeed the Self is guiding us at all levels of the psyche, in our spiritual quest for fulfillment, we need to open up those hidden treasures buried in our unconscious depths. Unlike Freud who viewed the unconscious negatively as the realm of the "id," a storehouse of sexual and aggressive instincts and repressed (= "forgotten") memories, Jung experienced both darkness *and light* in these regions. Rather than fearing the unconscious, Jung would have us befriend it, woo it almost, so that as acquaintances, colleagues, and partners, we and our unconscious may stretch toward wisdom known and lived.

The clearest way I have found to describe for clients and spiritual directees a welcoming stance toward the unconscious is captured in the phrase, "reverent curiosity." Because the unconscious is one vehicle by which God can speak within our hearts and minds, it must always be respected and cherished. Yet because the unconscious functions more like the moon's light than with the ego's sunlike clarities, and because its offerings to us are often strange (refer back to the four previous examples), we need to renounce the temptation to ignore it as too bizarre, and instead approach our inner selves with curiosity.

A reverent curiosity, then, would incline us to pay attention to products of the unconscious like dreams, slips of the tongue, sudden "aha" moments, bodily symptoms. These are some of the means by which the Holy Spirit and our own spirit or psyche are trying to attract the ego's attention.

Active Imagination

But how, concretely, may we practice this recommended "reverent curiosity"? Ancient Egyptian desert wisdom advises, "The one who has oneself for a spiritual director has a fool for a director." So first we seek out a skilled spiritual companion, spiritual director, pastoral counselor, or psychotherapist to accompany us on our inner quest. Although market forces and managed care are causing many help-seekers to adopt short-term, problem-focused interventions from counselors and therapists, a determined spiritual quester will invite spiritual companioning or direction at least monthly throughout his or her life. At one level, such a regimen is most basically a matter of good health-preservation and prevention: we try for a physical exam every year or two, eye checkups, semiannual dental visits, and monthly spiritual direction. These practices may lack the romantic overtones of a quest, but even a wild-eyed youngster out to tour the country on his motorbike needs to begin at the gas station!

Between direction sessions our quester needs to...*pay attention.* Eastern and Western masters of the inner life stress awareness as key to growth. Jung pioneered two special methods of paying attention: the Word Association Test (used by trained analysts), and active imagination, a technique that can be employed by most reflective persons.

In the Word Association Test, the subject states as quickly as possible the word that comes to mind after each of a hundred stimulus words is presented. The test administrator uses a stopwatch to note hesitancies over certain words, then repeats the list and marks discrepancies between the first and second set of associations. Words causing delay or triggering a different response indicate the presence of a "complex," an emotionally tinged cluster of thoughts and feelings within the psyche that can behave like an autonomous personality within the unconscious. (Actually Jung first named his approach to the psyche "Complex Psychology.") An analyst and her client can then work on these complexes to achieve insight into their unconscious contents, and ultimately foster behavioral change along with spiritual growth.

Active imagination is an approach developed by Jung himself that he employed especially during the difficult days after his separation from Freud. In painting and stone sculpture, Jung drew and chiseled the emotion-drenched contents of his dreams. From Freud onward, analysts had advised recording dreams immediately upon awakening, but Jung paid intense attention to each dream symbol. Rather than merely using each dream item as the first in a chain of (Freudian) free associations leading away from the dream, Jung "circumambulated," that is, walked around each symbol with paint or stone so as to evoke its meaning, and thus stayed with the dream.

Modern Jungian analysts have developed this art further. For those afflicted with performance anxiety over drawing or painting, for example, a Jungian might recommend sketching with one's nondominant hand. After all, who would expect great art from one's "other" hand? Furthermore, great art is not the point of such an exercise.

Another technique is the sand tray: therapy clients choose tiny figures for arrangement on a sand surface, and then create a story about the people, animals, and objects placed on the tray. A photograph records the arrangement for comparison and contrast with earlier or later creations.

Easiest of all, however, to teach (if not necessarily to practice faithfully) is the method of writing out a dialogue with a dream figure, complex, or puzzling aspect of oneself.

A client with whom you've been working to get her free-floating anxiety under control is making good progress, but then mentions that "that same dream woke me again last night." When you inquire, she tries to make light of it, but then reports being chased by a "faceless, furry monster" in numerous dreams. Always she awakes in a sweat just as the monster almost catches her. Sometimes the conviction that it was "only a dream" fails to soothe her terror, and she has trouble returning to sleep. What would you do?

A male religious seeing you for spiritual direction seems happy in his life and productive in his ministry. He prays regularly and deeply, reports living a balanced life with supportive friends and moments for recreation scheduled in to offset his tendency to workaholism, and finds his community life "so-so." Yet there is one man in his community whose mere presence irrationally infuriates your directee. While your client has never acted out his fury, he struggles to understand why this colleague's topics of conversation, speech patterns, even style of laughter so successfully disturb him. He has prayed for light and clarity, but none has come. What would you do?

A Jungian might employ active imagination to assist these two counselees—and oneself as well—to gain clarity in the midst of a psychological tangle. In active imagination, one strengthens the observing ego by deliberately inviting contact with the unconscious by attempting to enter into conscious connection with such psychological phenomena. One does not strive to master the unconscious, but to become friends with it, as it were.

The technique is named "active" because it involves more than mere talk, either with oneself or even with one's therapist or counselor or spiritual director. Pretend that you are a playwright recording a conversation between yourself and a dream character (or other mysterious aspect of yourself). Relax with pen in hand (or at a computer terminal), see the scene with the dreamt companion (or fellow community member—see earlier), and write out what you hear. Do not censor the conversation with analysis or criticism—that can be done later. Let the words flow, but don't force them. Of course, such an active imagination exercise can be done in the context of one's daily prayer or examination of consciousness.

We can engage in dialogue with animals, plants, even inanimate objects from our dreams (or other realms of inner life) by personifying them, giving them a name with permission to share their story and message.

Similarly, body parts (an upset stomach, a bruised knee) can be addressed and allowed to use words instead of pain as their means of communication. One's feelings (anger, frustration, puzzlement, delight) can also enter into conversation, for example, by being addressed with one's middle name, or being given an appropriate made-up name, for example, Andy for *an*xiety-*de*pression.

Thus one engages the unconscious in dialogue by outwardly expressing the free-flowing contents of one's imagination in a focused meditation. Naming the technique "imagination" does not imply the possession of great creative gifts, but rather permission given for the unconscious spontaneously to express itself.

Accordingly, in the situations described above, the woman client chased by the horrible creature could be encouraged to draw the creature, to write a story describing what might happen when the monster catches her, or to pretend turning to face the creature and asking what it wanted, then writing down the ensuing dialogue. She chose the third alternative of writing a dialogue. The monster stopped as soon as the client turned to face it, reached into the folds of its black robe, and brought forth a gift for her. This gift pointed her in the direction of dealing with a whole dimension of her life that she had previously neglected.

In a similar way, the male religious chose to write a mini-drama with "inner Harry." (He easily grasped the distinction explained between "real Harry" and "inner Harry," the latter a creation of his projections. If he could create an "inner Harry," then he could employ his imagination again to recreate a different sort of inner character.) He imagined sitting down and informing Harry of all the things that annoyed him about "real Harry." "Inner Harry" behaved as novelists describe their own storied inventions by taking on a life of his own. Responding to my client's anger, he informed the client that the latter was afraid of becoming like Harry again since Harry's behaviors had been similar to the client's in years past, and had been changed only with great personal effort. Inner Harry asked if my client didn't really hate an older part of himself, now resurrected in the person of Real Harry. This written dialogue shifted the focus of our spiritual direction and my client's prayer away from rage at Harry and toward needed self-acceptance.

Some form of outward activity such as drawing or writing cannot be stressed enough. Merely rehearsing things in one's head is like getting lost in a forest: one goes around in a great circle, unknowingly retracing the same psychological ground over and over again. Activity "ob-ject-ifies" the intra-psychic reality, that is, projects it out in front of myself in a nonthreatening way for personal reflection, or for discussion with my counselor or spiritual director.

Paying attention to the unconscious seems to help it relax and present its important information in a nonintrusive, nonthreatening way. Employing this procedure has, without exception, brought a surprise to the client, an insight arrived at with less effort and greater conviction than many hours spent in other conversations, therapeutic or otherwise.

One word of caution: Defenses are in place for a reason. A director should not force this method on a client, just as a client should maintain an inviting stance throughout before the unconscious to yield up its secrets and treasures. The method should probably be used carefully with a person whose ego is fragile. (Notice that I did not veto its use even here because the method ultimately is aimed at strengthening the ego vis-à-vis inner psychic contents— "complexes" in Jung's terminology.)

I have found that this therapeutic technique can be worked into one's armamentarium of interventions for clients or directees almost regardless of one's theoretical stance. Other ways of accessing the unconscious upon which Jung would smile might include the following: *paying attention* to one's body, one's responses to the creative (artwork, poetry, drama, and film), daydreams (and not only night dreams!), handwriting, projections, transferences, *déja vu,* sudden insights, behavior patterns, hunches, yearnings, attractions, intrusive thoughts, moods, illnesses, things that make us angry or laugh, our prayer and meditation.

Unconscious Contents

Jung understood psychic life in terms of dynamic polarities in tension: conscious/unconscious, ego/Self, matter/spirit. Once again, from his own self-analysis and his patients' therapy sessions, Jung noticed the Self at work in its employing the unconscious to balance the strivings of ego-consciousness. Yet just as Jung went beyond Freud in discovering positive as well as negative aspects of the unconscious, so too did he find collective, species-wide, universally human dimensions of the unconscious, and not merely personally repressed materials. Thus he posited both a "personal" and a "collective" unconscious. The latter manifests itself, for example, in dream-symbols larger than life: a hero with features unlike those of the dreamer or anyone known to her; a villain evil beyond imagining; a mother/father who seems to sum up and exceed all that parent means. Often these "archetypes" (as Jung named them) resemble characters in great world art, literature, and folklore. Because the dreamer often has had no contact with these master-pieces, Jung deduced that they must enter the psyche through the doors of a collective unconscious that is shared with all people everywhere and throughout time.

Jung's hypothesis of a collective as well as a personal unconscious constitutes his most original contribution to psychology, and consequently is his most challenged construct. (Critics might ask themselves how they would themselves otherwise explain the appearance of similarly featured universal symbols, for example, a divine child, a sun god, appearing across time, continents, cultures, and individuals of varying degrees of education and sophistication.)

In interpreting one's own or one's client's or directee's dreams, a good principle to employ most often is the following: Assume generally that images, energies, conflicts arise from one's own "personal" unconscious. Manifestations of the collective unconscious seem weird and foreign both in terms of images and symbols, and the greater intensity of energies aroused.

Our unconscious functions with an observable purposiveness. Thus horror dreams may help us prepare for the worst, whereas seemingly frivolous dreams allow us a mini-vacation. Premonitory dreams may reflect our fears or may actually anticipate upcoming events. (Familiarity with one's own dream history can help interpret which function such dreams most often serve.) Dreams can present us with a warning, build up our sagging self-esteem, suggest a time for a change. Our unconscious can both issue a call to action or invite us into a time of refreshment and repose. The dream can assist in problem solving or grief resolution. Dreams reflect our inner states, and provide both a channel for creativity and a garbage dump for our woes and miseries. They have been characterized as informative, balancing, precognitive, even prophetic.

Dreams offer insight into relationships and mirror problematic behaviors. They reveal both our bright and dark sides. They can reduce guilt, provide clues for conflict resolution and a new perspective on life. Whether a source of entertainment, wish fulfillment, or guidance, dreams are a channel of communication with our inner Self.[1]

The Joseph stories in the first books of the Hebrew scriptures (Gn 37–50) and New Testament (Mt 1) also depict the dream as a means of communication from God. Hence spiritual questers prize such an avenue of revelation, and put into practice its wise suggestions and invitations to growth.

Many of Jung's essays trace dream images starting with a patient's production, and then following their manifestations cross-culturally in myths, poetry, religious icons.

Three key archetypes among many that will enlighten a spiritual quester are the persona, the shadow, and the animus/anima.

Persona

Persona is Latin for "actor's mask," and designated the tall faces work by ancient Roman actors so that people high in the outdoor amphitheaters could see each character. Every mask was equipped with a sort of megaphone through which the actor could *personare,* "sound through" his voice to the audience. Jung applied this dramatic metaphor to our conscious behavior in the world where each of us acts our part. We get up each morning and put on our mask-role of professional helper, student, steelworker, housewife. Our mask helps us cope in society, and allows other players to interact with us in comfortable and expectable patterns.

Children and teens can be observed trying different masks before they settle for their preferred persona in their early twenties—until midlife when they either adjust their persona to provide a better fit, or again try out a new role.

Jung points to this archetype to distinguish various levels of intimacy by which people communicate. Problems arise when the ego overidentifies with the persona, and people lead narrowly focused lives. They then restrict their interactions to societal role-expectations and stereotyped behaviors instead of revealing their real selves. The perpetually smiling pastor, the tough police officer, the maternal nurse, the helpful librarian—all live by rules in their public lives. But if their masks "grow into their faces," and they can never remove them (by behaving outside of role), their family members, acquaintances, and friends will never meet the person beneath the persona.

Sometimes the unconscious informs one that one is overly identified with one's persona: suppose that in dreams a surgeon always appears in her gown and mask. Such a dream series would suggest that the good doctor needs to "get a life" beyond her professional commitments and duties.

Incidentally, Jung states an important rule, that dreams are not to be interpreted in isolation but as what each is, a member of the complete series of dreams stretching backward and forward throughout one's life. Such an insight brings good news to the quester: if one doesn't get the point of a dream, he or she can return for clarification to an earlier dream, or expect another dream to repeat the message.

Thus the energies in the persona archetype can be helpful or harmful: positively, they help us navigate a complex world by structuring our impressions, conveyed and received. Negatively, these energies can distract the ego from its quest for growth, change, and development in favor of investment in the safe and the familiar.

Such a double polarity illustrates once again the dynamism inherent in Jung's way of thinking. He sees the human person always balancing his or her energies between conscious and unconscious, personal unconscious and collective unconscious, ego and Self, and now between positive and negative energies within the persona (and within other archetypes and psychic systems as well). One never "arrives" at perfection, but is continually challenged to grow toward greater consciousness and wholeness, toward fuller awareness of the forces at play within the psyche. Fortunately, the psyche seems to be blessed with an innate wisdom so that we are not immediately overwhelmed by all the complications of interacting subsystems, nor does it let us slip for long into lazy stasis and inertia. Prodding us with a dream, for example, it urges a next step, never a five-year plan, the latter an ego project.

To sum up: "The ego is who we think we are as opposed to the *persona* which is who we pretend to be" (Vivianne Crowley, 1998, 21).

Shadow

The shadow is that which we believe we are *not.* The shadow contains all those elements, negative *and positive,* personal and collective, that we consciously reject or unconsciously repress as not appropriate to our ego project, or as unfitting or unworthy of our persona. The word *shadow* evokes dark and sinister connotations, but Jung consistently taught that often the darkness was due to our lack of familiarity with the shadow and its contents, rather than to its inherent evil. Sample shadow elements include the following: unhappy "forgotten" memories of past pain, failures, and misfortunes; an undeveloped talent for which ego's choices and persona's role leaves no space or energy (for example, I enjoyed playing a French horn in a high school band, but chose to abandon music lessons for other pursuits); raw, untamed instinctual urges that "civilized" women and men decide to tame and focus rather than wantonly indulge; character traits that I or my fellow citizens idealize or despise.

As ever, we need to approach the shadow with "reverent curiosity" rather than revulsion. Jung believed that there is gold in the shadow, although searching for it can sometimes feel like digging for a jewel in our intrapsychic muck.

Returning to our earlier examples: the slip of the annoyed host's tongue at the moment of his bothersome guest's departure revealed the shadow's true feelings beneath the persona's politeness. Falling in the restaurant, and the injured knee's demand for a more humane schedule demonstrates the shadow's impact on our body as well as on our mind if its hints and warnings are ignored. In both these cases the ego was doing good: graciously hosting and working hard. Yet the shadow is wisely recommending balance: Do not overidentify with the "Mr. Nice Guy" persona in life; do not work oneself into a workaholic!

What good can revisiting unhappy painful memories accomplish? Unattended, such memories can manufacture the building blocks of complexes, those seemingly independent subpersonalities that push our buttons and pull our chains within the psyche. Working through old hurts, angers, guilts, shames, or fears concretely lives out the scriptural directive, "The truth shall make you free." Energy that had previously been expended repressing or denying a deep wound can be released for growth in the spiritual quest.

What about those talents and pursuits for which we didn't have time, or despite our attraction to them, didn't seem to fit our sense of ourselves in our teens and twenties? Focusing on midlife and beyond in many of his writings, Jung counseled wholeness and completeness (rather than an overly abstract "perfection"), and would advise developing those positive shadow gifts of which we're perhaps dimly aware, or which close friends sense lying latent in us. Everyone has the equivalent of an "inner" French horn player who is yearning to emerge in some way.

If everyone has an inner French horn player, do we also harbor an inner ax murderer? Jung would respond with a qualified "Yes." The brighter the light of one's persona, the darker the shadow. Sexuality, aggression, and other "animalistic" instincts are part of us, and need welcoming and honoring, not just sublimating. These can energize our decisions made in consultation with all our "parts," not merely our well-socialized intellect. If ignored, these instincts turn churlish, and we find ourselves striking out verbally and physically, sometimes in surprisingly horrifying and violent ways. Too familiar are headlines detailing murder of family members not by the "bad apples" of the brood, but by the boy scout, scholar-athlete, or neighborhood role model. If something small pushed him "over the edge," the edge had been erected over months and years by his squelching negative shadow energies.

Mention was made of characteristics idolized or hated by an individual or a culture. Again, these indicate manifestations of the individual or the collective shadow. Sports heroes and beauty queens provide American examples of positive shadow projections, while the demonization of the former Soviet Union as the "evil empire," or Saddam Hussein as "another Hitler" illustrate the negative shadow at work.

The term *projection* gives an important key for unlocking the shadow's treasure chest. (Although for Freud *the* defense mechanism was repression, Jung's attention was drawn to projection.) Projection is in gear whenever we feel driven to react in an intensely but irrationally positive or negative way to a person or situation. Some examples: a primary school youngster "worships the ground" on which his teenage brother walks despite the older youth's ignoring his sibling's attention. A woman unconsciously changes her hairstyle and dress in imitation of a popular and successful colleague at work. Inadvertently stepping on your toes in a crowded elevator and excusing himself, the stranger nevertheless provokes a barrage of rage from you. Only later does it strike you that the man resembles a cruel uncle. A woman goes on and on about an acquaintance's habit of gossiping while her knowing listeners stifle yawns as they wonder at her seemingly blind indulgence in exactly the same behavior.

Projection dynamics get into play when an admired or disliked trait of our own turns up in another, catches our attention, and "hooks" us. Then we need to "reel in" our projected enthusiasm or disgust as we name, claim, and tame the feature as also our own. This process takes just a brief sentence to write, but often years to accomplish! A good friend, counselor, spiritual director, or someone who knows us well can probably quickly confirm that the envied or loathed trait is ours as well. Such a response could assist the lad (above) to admit his own athletic ability, or the office coworker to endorse her own attractiveness. Yet we resist claiming the contents of the unconscious— that's in part *why* they're unconscious!

Even more difficult and challenging is the naming or claiming of our negatively evaluated traits. Americans used to rail at Soviet imperialism while conveniently "forgetting" our own oppressive policies toward native Americans and their lands, Hispanics in Central America, Third World economically dependent quasi-colonies. Gay bashing can be analyzed as an expression of some discomfort at one's own attraction to members of the same sex. "Who me? Never!" is often the first reaction to someone's teasing us about a foible that we find especially disgusting in someone we ourselves are criticizing.

Individuals, families, and communities engage in projection rather than face their own hard truths. It is so much easier to blame another for his or her failings than to work on our own, so much more satisfying to be dazzled by another's achievement than to submit to the discipline of honing our own talents.

Not surprisingly, Jung also looked to dreams for information about the shadow. A strange and unfamiliar same-sexed figure, either quite attractive or repulsive, can embody our shadow. Painting him or her, or letting it speak through an active imagination dialogue can tap into its insights. Then all that is required is to put the insights into practice!

Animus/anima

Yet a third pair of archetypes is discovered in the female contrasexual features of a male psyche (named *anima*), and the male contrasexual aspects of a female psyche (called *animus* by Jung). As with the shadow, animus and anima function at the level of the individual and of the collective psyche, and show up with positive and negative demeanor. Again as with the shadow, these archetypes can be accessed through noticing our projections, positive and negative, and paying attention to unfamiliar *opposite*-sexed dream characters.

The author routinely witnesses a charming display of animus/anima projections because he lives in a college dorm where young men and women routinely fall into and out of infatuations. "What does Ezechiel see in Hepsibah?" puzzle Zeke's buddies. The answer: a projection of the ideal feminine resident in his own psyche. "Hepsibah thinks Zeke is a 'hunk' (a.k.a. Greek god)," laugh her unbelieving roommates. Again, animus-projection explains the psychological dynamic involved.

Bearing another's idealized projections can be fun for awhile because one can flatter oneself into believing that the projection conveys the real truth about oneself. Yet this situation ultimately fails to satisfy because: (1) I am *not* a god, and believing that I am constitutes psychic inflation; (2) all too soon I realize that my beloved is not really loving me, but his or her imagined idealization of me provides the basis of infatuation, not genuine love; (3) trying to live up to projected godlikeness is exhausting; (4) the projector will soon notice the disparity between the behavior of the object of infatuation and his or her own fantasy. Consequently, the projector will either let go of the projection to allow genuine love to develop, or else rush off to find another god/dess.

This eternal tension between romantic infatuation and committed love impacts most relationships in Western culture. The myth of Tristan and Isolde (insightfully analyzed by Robert A. Johnson, 1983) describes the psychic roots of this struggle in the heart of every Western man and woman. The goal of this spiritual conflict? Anima/animus means soul/spirit, and thus each man/woman finds fulfillment of these contrasexual strivings within one's own heart through the spiritual quest. One can possess one's own soul, but never succeed in forcing another to embody it. Loving another's ordinariness (with both beauty *and* foibles) can begin in romance but never last there. The inner masculine/feminine must be named, claimed, and tamed just like the shadow.

Animus/anima projections influence not only the start of relationships, but their unfolding history as well. The office misogynist continually projects all that is negative about women (real and imagined) upon his feminine coworkers, and can describe them only in words ending in *-itch*. Although many feminists justifiably crusade against society's oppressive patriarchal arrangements, feminism can provide a convenient cover for the man-hater who "sees" all men as embodiments of her own negative animus.

As in the case of positively toned projections, one needs to make oneself aware and conscious of personal and cultural influences on one's anima/animus. What unhealed childhood wound is still festering, and leading me to generalize that *all* women are embodiments of the wicked fairy, that *all* men are trolls? Against what potential suffering am I defending myself by refusing an honest, intimate, vulnerable relationship with the real persons in my home or at work? What unconscious push is driving me to relive the ancient myth of the wicked stepmother, the violent war lord, the conniving witch or sorcerer?

Parenthetically, Jungians love mythology because they view myths not as untrue but as most true. They seek not historical truths in these ancient tales, but the psychological truth of our common human condition. Even the focus of this essay on the quest derives ultimately from the myth of the Holy Grail, perhaps *the* foundational myth of Western culture.

Another indication (besides the intensity of a positive or negative reaction to an other-sexed person or group) that anima/animus dynamics are governing interactions can be found in stereotyped behaviors and thoughts. (Notice again Jung's fondness for opposites: if intensity can indicate projective energies at work, so might boringly repetitive stereotypy.) Do you and your spouse seem to be having the same arguments over and over—same song, seventy-fourth verse? Perhaps anima/animus are speaking (probably shouting) through you. Do you often speak in universals, for example, "men/women always..."? You are in the grasp of the anima/animus, and are deluding yourself if you believe that you are speaking out your own personal opinions, especially if they feel like settled judgments or eternal truths. In general, whenever one talks or acts in culturally predictable patterns, one should try to bring into consciousness the motivating energies directing the behavior. Anima/animus, shadow, persona, or one of the many other archetypes may be running our lives like the strings of a puppet show. Here the spiritual quest will be furthered by becoming one's own Self instead of being recycled by archetypal forces ignored to our peril, and stopping our growth and development.

Anima/animus projected out onto others confuse and destroy relationships because their overly positive or negative coloring prevent the real person at both ends of a relationship from emerging. Instead, reclaim soul or spirit as one's own and acknowledge the *inner* reality of anima/animus as dimensions of my Self that need awareness and expanding. These contrasexual guides point me toward healthy androgyny and away from macho chest-thumping or cute feminine fluffiness.

Again we pose the "how" question: How do we contact the inner force of our soul, the inner power of our spirit? Because he saw this movement as ultimately religious, Jung would always begin by inviting his analysands to reconnect with their own spiritual traditions if they could: Catholics with Catholicism, Protestants with Protestantism, Jews with Judaism. But as in his day so in ours: institutional religions for many pose obstacles to genuine spiritual growth, and for those seekers, he recommended no less religious a quest through active imagination, dream analysis, prayer, and meditation. Though he did not employ this current distinction, he would understand and resonate with differentiating between the "religious" (understood as a collective experience) and the "spiritual" (meaning an individual's quest for genuine personal value and wholeness). Whether in a "religious" or "spiritual" framework, we are drawn consciously to take responsibility for discovering our own depths of psyche. We question old patterns of thinking, speaking, and doing. We decide consciously to change and to meet our soul or spirit.

Needless to note, such a process involves suffering a kind of death to the dominating ego that would rather live in the illusory world of projections, avoid self-questioning, escape having to change. The death and resurrection of

Christ inspires the Christian believer to look for new life—yet *not* only hereafter, but here as well. The nonreligious spiritual seeker sees in the Christian Paschal Mystery, the Egyptian Osiris myth, the Greek Dionysus myth a deep psychological and symbolic truth regarding the energies available in the psyche for genuine transformation.

If animus/anima dominates my interpersonal relationships, then this ancient force will render them illusory by clouding my interpretation of what is. Yet in its rightful place interposed between my ego and the unconscious, animus/anima leads me to God, guides me on the inner spiritual quest, and introduces me to other archetypal realities. (See Jung, *Collected Works 16,* para. 504.)

Typology

Lest this presentation makes Jung appear stuck in the inner world, we must make mention of Jung's contributions to a theory of behavior. In part seeking to explain the conflicts between Freud and himself, Jung developed the descriptions of the extraverted and introverted attitudes. The extravert's psychic energy pours into the world of events and relationships, whereas the introvert's energy is drawn within him or herself.

After ten years of weighing formulations that would add to the personality dimensions of attitudes, Jung settled on four "functions": two ways of taking in information (perceiving), that is, sensation and intuition, and two ways of coming to a conclusion (judging), that is, thinking and feeling. Jung observed, of course, that everyone is endowed with all four functions, but that each person would develop one of these four more than the rest. This "dominant" function would be found linked with one of the two attitudes (introversion or extraversion), and thus Jung came up with eight personality types, described in rich detail in his essay, *Psychological Types (Collected Works 6).*

Professionals as well as interested reflective persons have been introduced to typological thinking through the Myers-Briggs Type Indicator (MBTI) (Myers and McCauley, 1985), and the Singer-Loomis Inventory of Personality (SLIP) (Singer and Loomis, 1984). Reading Jung himself will deepen awareness of one's own behaviors and habits, and increase insight into the conscious and unconscious preferences of family members and friends.

Jung realized that the ego's task in the first half of life is to establish one's identity in the world of relationships and work through developing one's preferred attitude and dominant function. In the second half of life, when the quest leads one to seek meaning and wisdom, one incorporates the gifts of those undeveloped and underdeveloped aspects of the psyche.

Thus an extroverted feeling type may have become a school counselor, and as midlife approaches may sense an invitation to develop her introversion, and choose activities that call upon her "inferior" thinking function. Or an introverted intuitive type, someone at home in the world of poetry and artistic vision, will be drawn to venture more and more into the extrovert's world of concrete facts and activities.

As in his discussion of the unconscious and its various aspects, so too the teaching about types illustrates Jung's observation of the dynamic tension between opposing psychic polarities. As the quest for wholeness unfolds, more and more of the psyche's gifts become conscious, appreciated, and integrated in one's awareness and behavior.

On Reading Jung

The challenge of plunging into Jung's writings reminds me of what my father used to say about olives: "You have to cultivate a taste for them." For many beginners, encountering Jung presents all the difficulties of mastering a new foreign language. There is a strange vocabulary (archetypes, anima), an exotic cultural landscape where East and West, past and present fuse confusingly, a blend of religion, philosophy, observation, and mythology all somehow christened psychology by Jung. Yet just as fluency in more than one tongue enhances appreciation of human reality, so too does immersion into the thought-world of Jung repay one's struggle to grasp his particular perspective on the human psyche.

Nothing substitutes for encountering Jung himself, and to do this I recommend the following: his autobiography, *Memories, Dreams, Reflections* (1961) to encounter the man; *Man and His Symbols* (1964) to wade into the depths of his major thematic developments; *Modern Man in Search of a Soul* (1933), a still timely collection of some of his more readable essays. Frieda Fordham (1953) has penned a brief (150 pages) overview of his outlook and contribution called *An Introduction to Jung's Psychology*. (About Ms. Fordham's effort Jung himself declared in the foreword, "She has delivered a fair and simple account of the main aspects of my psychological work.") Robert Hopcke's *A Guided Tour of the Collected Works of C. G. Jung* (1992) devotes attention to forty Jungian themes and constructs. Each chapter provides a three- to five-page summary of the topic plus detailed citations of Jung's works (arranged at three levels of difficulty) with references to relevant secondary sources as well. Jung's *Collected Works* (1966) fill twenty volumes and have been published in paperback as well as hardcover.

On Entering the Quest

This discussion has deliberately centered on the practical—how to live out Jung's insights through reverent curiosity, active imagination. Many more of his vast interests have been hinted at (mythology, other archetypes), and some issues left to an interested reader to discover on her own (alchemical symbolism, synchronicity). Jung's writings and speculations provide endless delight for the quester, as well as ammunition for his critics. My hope is that this modest summary and analysis of some major Jungian constructs and themes will assist those on an inner quest for wholeness and their guides in reaching their goals.

Note

1. Materials in the last four paragraphs resulted in part from a discussion led by Arthur Funkhauser, Ph.D., on "Dreams and Healing" at the Jungian Summer Seminar, Zurich, August 5, 1996.

Selected References and Suggested Reading

Crowley, Vivianne. *Thorson's Principles of Jungian Spirituality*. London: Thorson's, 1998.

Fordham, Frieda. *An Introduction to Jung's Psychology*. New York: Penguin, 1953.

Hopcke, Robert H. *A Guided Tour of the Collected Works of C. G. Jung*. Boston: Shambhala, 1992.

Johnson, Robert A. *We: Understanding the Psychology of Romantic Love*. San Francisco: Harper San Francisco, 1983.

Jung, Carl G. *Modern Man in Search of a Soul*. New York: Harcourt/ Brace/Jovanovich, 1933.

————. *Memories, Dreams, Reflections*. Aniela Jaffé, ed. New York: Vintage, 1961.

————. *Man and His Symbols*. New York: Doubleday, 1964.

————. *Collected Works* (20 vols.) 2nd ed. R. F. C. Hull, trans. Princeton, N.J.: Princeton University Press, Bollingen Series XX, 1966.

Myers, J. B. and McCauley, M. H. *Manual: A Guide to the Development and Use of the Myers-Briggs Type Indicator*. Palo Alto, Calif.: Consulting Psychologists Press, 1985.

Singer, J. and Loomis, M. *The Singer-Loomis Inventory of Personality (SLIP)*. Palo Alto, Calif.: Consulting Psychologists Press, 1984.

Annice Callahan

14. Self-Images of Oppression and Liberation in Ministry

What are my experiences and images of myself in ministry? Which ones are oppressive? Which ones are liberating? How do I experience the burdens and blessings of my ministry? This question of self-images in ministry is, for me, a question that takes courage to articulate and probe. I can only explore it personally. Integration of one's being in ministry is the call and challenge of the life we have chosen. I want simply to indicate some areas that may need integration and raise some questions that may be pertinent to any search for wholeness. Theological reflection on ministry concerns itself with articulating and owning changing experiences and images of ourselves, God, others, ministry itself, and the church. I offer you my theological reflection on some of my own experiences and images of ministry and invite you to do the same. What are some of these self-images and how can we bring them into conscious awareness? In this essay I explore three self-images of oppression and then three self-images of liberation in ministry.

Giver of All Gifts

Giver of all gifts is one image I hold of myself in ministry. Some of us get mileage out of this one. After all, if I am the giver of all gifts, I can never say "No," I can crowd my day meeting others' needs, and I can feel totally responsible for what happens to everyone. Now if I cannot say "No," then I am compelled to say "Yes." I am not free to set limits, but I am free to resent those who are testing my limits. If I crowd my day with appointments all in the name of meeting others' needs, I never have to deal with leisure nor with the reality of my needs nor with the stark unwelcome fact that I may be using others to meet my need for attention, acceptance, affirmation, and intimacy. If I can feel totally responsible for what happens to everyone, then I can blame myself for everything that goes wrong and I can base my own self-esteem on others' approval. I am what I do.

214

If I see myself as the giver of all gifts, then how do I see God? Is there not some subtle competition that sets in? Do I really need God if I am the one doing all the giving? Do I end up feeling self-righteous before God: "Look at me. I pay my dues. I put in my forty-hour work week. I spend my days serving others." But underneath, doesn't there lurk the question, however faint: "What is the payoff? What is in this for me? Why is God such a harsh taskmaster always making me work, never letting me play, always directing me to respond to others' needs? What about my own?"

If I am the giver of all gifts, then how do I view others? Consciously, I may welcome their phone calls, their letters, their endless needs to see me and drink in my wisdom. But unconsciously, are they not a threat to my growth, since they may be what I am not? Consciously, I may respond to their requests night and day, during work hours and outside of work hours. But unconsciously, am I resentful if I overdo my response to them?

If I am the giver of all gifts, how do I view ministry? Is ministry viewed as giving to others in a condescending way, out of my riches to those less privileged than I? I do the giving; you do the receiving.

If I am the giver of all gifts, then how do I view the church? Is the church the church triumphant, the source of salvation? Yes, the church is the giver of all grace. Do I believe that "outside the church, there is no salvation"?

How can I get out of this trap? How can I change my image of myself, of God, and of others? Let us look at how Jesus models something for his disciples, described in Luke 4:42–44:

> And when it was day he departed and went into a lonely place. And the people sought him and came to him, and would have kept him from leaving them; but he said to them, "I must preach the good news of the kingdom of God to the other cities also; for I was sent for this purpose." And he was preaching in the synagogues of Judea.

He sought out the giver of all gifts in order to encounter the center of his life. He let formal times of prayer help him keep a perspective on his life of service. When those he served pressed him to stay, he kept his vision of what he was about: "I must preach the good news of the reign of God to the other cities also, for I was sent for this purpose" (Lk 4:43). He also let his sense of mission inform his ministry. He did not let himself get bogged down with any one person or group of people or cause. In all of these ways he took care of himself and his own needs.

I am reminded of a question raised in class one day: "What if you are to serve fifty afflicted people, and you can only serve thirty or forty of them?" I appreciated the responses made to this question. How we answer this question validates our ministry. We do not have to feel that we as the delegated ministers are the only ones who can serve others' needs. In fact, our time might be better spent delegating our authority, so that we can minister where we do best. If we don't ask and answer this question, we make ourselves vulnerable to burnout! If we have the courage to ask the question and to be at peace with a reasonable and faith-filled answer that acknowledges an acceptance of our limits, then we can engage the people we serve in a gradual process that weans them from us and us from them.

Rescuer

Another self-image that is very related to that of the giver of gifts is that of the rescuer. In this mode, I can consider myself not only God's providence but also God's salvation. I work with people in spiritual direction and pastoral counseling, and make myself available to them in their crisis moments. So far so good. But when the pastoral appointments exceed once a month or every two weeks, I need to examine my self-image. When the phone calls come and I am busy with other commitments, am I free to say that I am not available? Recently, I had a tangibly graced conversation here at Regis and wanted to celebrate it with God before getting back to work. Just then, the phone rang and I took the call. In that first instant of decision making, I robbed myself of my moment with God. The call was from a woman who worked with me in spiritual direction; she was in crisis. I had limited time to prepare for class, and she needed desperately to talk. As she began, I could feel my anger and resentment rising. Why did she have to call me just then? Why did I have to take her call just then? Only afterward, on reflection, did I realize that I could have listened to my instinct and said, "I can't talk with you right now but could I call you back later on, when you are free?" During the conversation, I could hear sharpness in my voice and a sting in my remarks. The anger I had not owned was coming out sideways. And all in the name of trying to rescue her, trying to save her from the pain and anguish of living with a decision she had made. There is the tendency to want to save people from pain, from loneliness, from an experience of their own fragile humanity. But is it the pure motive of being sent to serve? Or is that mixed with the need to be needed?

One of the subtlest ways I can practice rescuing is to keep raising challenging questions in such a way that the other person becomes increasingly dependent on my insight, rather than her own. This kind of exchange can be escalated by more and more frequent meetings and phone calls, all of which foster dependence. There is a point after which no matter how desperate and needy a person seems, I love that person more by letting go. In this episode, I could have let her be, let her make the mistake I want to save her from making. I could have let her abuse herself yet one more time, since she showed no sign of wanting to break her pattern. Or I could have made a declaration of independence that would have left her free to grow or not. Her dependence evoked in me a fostering of that very dependence.

When I am trying to be rescuer, what is my image of God? How can I rescue others without at some point being angry at God for not intervening to rescue? At some conscious level, I may imagine God to be my savior. But at another, perhaps unconscious level, I may be very disappointed in God's seeming apathy. I may, in fact, view God as incompetent and incapable of running the universe. Is this the loving God whose forgiving nearness heals and frees us?

When I minister as a rescuer, how do I view others? Do I relate to those my age as fellow adults? Or do I end up feeling like a doting parent with a needy child? Do I see them as gifts of God? Or am I angry that people do not claim their own inner authority and start helping themselves?

As a rescuer, what is my style in spiritual direction and pastoral counseling? Is it to feed back what the other is saying and to raise questions that help a person reflect, or is it to give advice?

How does a rescuer view ministry? Ministry can seem to be putting Band-Aids on situations. I rush around holding people's hands, feeling their dependency needs and my own.

What is the image of the church for the rescuer? The church, and religion in general, is the opiate of the people, is it not? The church is supposed to save people not only from their sins but also from their daily problems. The church is the refuge of the poor dishing out food and blankets, the illusion of protection, a mother's womb keeping us safe and warm.

If we find ourselves rescuing or trying to rescue, how can we disengage ourselves? Let us look at Jesus with the man by the pool in John 5. First of all, Jesus asked him a probing question that was asking for more than superficial information: "Do you want to be healed?" (Jn 5:6) The man makes excuses and talks about not being able to get into the water because no one will help him. He shifts responsibility and blame for his condition from himself to others. He needs and wants to be rescued desperately, but he does not even know how to express appropriately his need for help. Jesus does not fall into the trap. He does not walk away with no compassion for the afflicted, nor does he help the man into the pool. He challenges the man to claim his own inner authority and inner resources for healing: "Rise, take up your pallet, and walk" (Jn 5:8).

I find that while some needs get satisfied by rescuing, others do not. I can focus on the lost and the stray; I can focus on all I could or should do for them. Or I can focus on becoming independent in myself, dependent on God, and growingly interdependent with others. If I am rooted and grounded in my self, then others feel welcome, but I do not let them deny me what I need.

Victim

A third self-image that runs along concurrently with the others is that of victim. In this mode, I am used by others, exploited, manipulated, abused. In fact, I may end up discovering that I am using and abusing myself. Is there not a fine line between generosity and self-hate? I can keep pushing and pushing myself, only to discover that I am running from myself, from the critical voice inside of me that keeps trying to tell me I am not all right.

I can abuse myself sometimes by "biting off more than I can chew" and then wondering why I feel so cranky. My office gets to be a mess. I have no energy to prepare a class lecture or listen to a student. I do not look forward to seeing people.

I can abuse myself by taking on too many commitments at once. For example, several summers ago, I was inspired to edit a book and to edit an issue of the in-house *Journal of the U.S. Province* of my congregation.[1] At first, I was enthusiastic about collaborating with a dozen of my colleagues, each of whom agreed to contribute a chapter to my book. I was also excited to collaborate with a group of our nuns who were willing to write articles and book reviews for the journal issue. What I failed to calculate was the amount of time involved in communication about both of these projects, over and above a full-time teaching load. This correspondence involved writing and mailing letters to contributors, making phone calls to them, writing letters to the editors, making phone calls to them, writing letters to my editorial committees, relaying revision suggestions, nagging contributors to contribute, renegotiating deadlines. I might have found it possible to take on one of these editing projects at a time. Two was self-abuse.

Still another abusive behavior is to schedule too many appointments per day or per week. Several factors are involved here. Is quality more significant than quantity? Instead of my chiding myself for scheduling people back-to-back all afternoon, I could ask myself whether I feel energized or drained by these conversations. In other words, I can ask, "What am I giving? What are we sharing?" But I might better ask, "What am I getting out of this exchange?" That is not a selfish question in the pejorative sense. That is the question I may need to ask, rather than wonder why I resent having my afternoon eaten up.

It is easy to become ensnared as the victim. In the movie *Ironweed,* Jack Nicholson plays the part of Francis, a bum in Albany in 1938, who left his wife and two children twenty-two years earlier when their baby boy Gerald died after Francis dropped him. Francis could not forgive himself and became the victim of his past, of his ghosts, of memories that become so real in the movie that the character Francis no longer lives in the present moment. We, too, can play the victim, flagellating ourselves inside for the way things were instead of being open to the present and the future.

When I am playing the victim, how do I imagine God? When I am punishing myself and denying myself any chance to be and to relax, God can only be experienced as abusive. God is the "killjoy"! If I am my own victim, am I not at the same time somehow the victim of God's wrath? This may all be at an unconscious level, even as I preach and teach a merciful God. But underneath my external behavior, my distance from God gives me away.

When I am acting as victim, how do I perceive others? Do I not believe myself called to serve others because I believe I have been given much to share? Yet these very people to whom I minister may seem like persecutors because I have cast them in that role. Do I avoid their calls or not return phone messages? Do I take the time grudgingly to see them, yet am so churned up inside that I cannot be present to them?

How do I perceive my ministry from this position? Does my ministry seem like the prostitution of my finest gifts and the abuse of my needs? Do I end up in burnout, because I do not realize the levels of rage and resentment seething inside me, wearing down my energy, depriving me of hope?

How does the victim view the church? The church in this view is the suffering servant par excellence, the martyr that lets itself be persecuted through the ages, the "Super Mama" who has no limits and can meet all needs, totally oblivious to her own needs. This is the church still suffering, still straining to live up to an unrealistic self-image, victim of its own misplaced idealism.

Jesus did not allow himself to be victim of others' needs. He claimed his own inner authority and made choices that kept him free to minister: "I lay down my life, that I may take it up again. No one takes it from me, but I lay it down of my own accord. I have power to lay it down, and I have power to take it up again" (Jn 10:17–18).

How can we respond to others' needs in a way that does not allow us to become victim? For me one way is my use of time. Since I am an introvert, I may need to build in what I call "transition time" between appointments. Scheduling appointments right after lunch until right before faculty meetings might be too much for me. It may be that I need to schedule appointments with a breather in between. You need to learn and find your own rhythm. One of my friends, a social worker for several years, told me that she used to safeguard an hour and a half for each hourlong appointment just so that she would have cushioning time. In fact, she would take the long route driving from one appointment to the next just so that she had time to unwind from one session and prepare for the next one.

You take care of your needs by building in times during the day when you can listen to yourself. You might also do some stress management exercises, especially body relaxation, such as deep breathing. If I am tense, for example, I need to center myself and then I find I can accomplish twice as much from this centered place. Or I may need to let myself cry for a few minutes. To strut and fret behind the closed doors of an office is counterproductive. I like to bring to work favorite tapes. Before an appointment or at a break in the morning, I put one on and just sit and listen for a few moments.

I can also take care of my needs by socializing with my colleagues at work, in the halls, or over lunch. Just to share a joke or have an undemanding conversation is relaxing. Then I can appreciate and enjoy my class or next appointment.

Sharer of God's Gifts

A fourth self-image is that of sharer, where we are invited to share life, to share faith, to share God's gifts. We come "with open hands" to receive from our gracious lifegiver and then to share. Notice that the emphasis in this perspective is not on giving but on sharing. The ministry at l'Arche communities is not one of one-way giving. Some come only to give and so they may for a time. But if they choose to stay long-term, they need to come to see and live in mutuality of ministry. It is true that we receive more than we give. Take time to savor and celebrate God's gifts in daily life. An ordained spiritual director in this area told me once that he likes to take time after an important phone call with a friend to celebrate it by sipping a beer slowly and savoring the conversation! We are accountable for our own stewardship. We work with a spiritual director and/or a counselor, in order to stay in touch with our own journey in faith, our own spiritual growth. If we are working closely with other people, we get supervision. We build in the support system we need in order to be of mutual support to others.[2]

In this humble view of ourselves, we can let God be the giver of all gifts. Notice then, how gratitude opens us to this gifting, and generosity frees us to mediate this gifting. In the sharer's perspective, others are not only the recipients of our bounty but they reveal themselves to us in the richness of their giftedness. Those who work with poor people often say that they receive far more than they give.[3]

What is ministry for the sharer? Ministry is sharing. No longer do I condescend to let you have some of it. It is rather that I come to evoke in you the gift you are.[4]

The church in this stance is a community of equals, in which the hierarchical model gives way to a mutuality of ministry, a give and take. Such a church calls forth and celebrates the gifts of all its members. This church is especially alive in small communities of shared life and shared faith, basic Christian communities where leadership is shared and co-responsible.

Jesus models this self-image of the sharer in the accounts of the multiplication of the loaves and fishes, for example, in Mark 6:35–44. It is said that the multiplication was not some extraordinary miracle from outside the situation. Rather, the miracle was that once the disciples began to distribute the five loaves and two fish, then people began to share with each other whatever food they had brought, and there was enough for all.

As sharers of God's gifts, we appreciate and enjoy all God's gifts: of time and space, food and drink, flowers and animals, sports and novels, art, music, and solitude, conversation and friendship, science and the universe. In our ministry, we are open to receive as well as to give. And often we find that as we listen to people pour out their hearts to us, our own are changed. And the one in need of us turns out to be the angel unaware, the hostess, the host.[5]

Facilitator

A fifth self-image is that of facilitator. Instead of trying to rescue those I serve by protecting them from harm, I concentrate on empowering them to heal themselves. I facilitate their growth in self-ministry by being faithful to my own self-ministry. I take means to care for myself both on my own and through the facilitation of others. I do not delude myself into thinking I can save anyone; I am keenly aware of my own need for God's forgiving nearness. I facilitate others' growth in self-knowledge and self-awareness not by trying to hold their hands, but by being present to them in a caring and truthful way. Sometimes that may mean raising hard questions. At other times that may imply challenging them to look at patterns in their life and thought. Or it may lead me to tell them when I am feeling bored or I do not think what they are saying rings true. I facilitate their growth in self-acceptance not by approving of all their behavior, but by affirming their own unique giftedness. I facilitate their integration for ministry *by* being very attentive to my own personal growth process and by inviting others to become aware of neglected, undeveloped, or unconscious parts of themselves to which they may need to minister—their ways of relaxing, their ways of relating, their dream life, their prayer life.

Who is God for the facilitator? God facilitates our growth and empowers us to empower others. God mediates self-awareness and self-acceptance in an incarnate way through our questions, care, and concern. God integrates our lives by affirming us most deeply in who we are and how we are to be in relation to others. This God is not a projection of our needs or a punisher of our deeds. This God is the living God of our daily lives.

Who are others in this view? Others do not threaten our schedules or securities or insecurities. They welcome our mediations. They feel affirmed by our authenticity and by their own growing authenticity. I want to make two remarks about authenticity. One is that as ministers in our churches, we are called to be authentically "inauthentic." Let us not pretend that we do not feel hypocritical preaching and teaching one way and living another. Let us accept that this is all right, and that we are only "earthen vessels" (2 Cor 4:7). Second, authentic living has to do with being in touch with our feelings. That does not mean we act only on our feelings, but it does mean that we honor them by allowing them to come to consciousness and accepting them for what they are.

What is ministry for the facilitator? Ministry is mediating life and faith and hope and love.

What is the church in this approach? The church is the sacrament mediating grace and salvation to all who seek it. This church does not rely on the insights and expertise of its hierarchy. Rather it listens to the experience and struggle of its members, careful to give them a hearing and help them help themselves.

How did Jesus respond as a facilitator? I think of his encounter with the Samaritan woman. He did not feed her a script. He allowed her to work through her resistances slowly, gently. On the other hand, he challenged her to risk: "If you knew the gift of God, and who it is that is saying to you, 'give me a drink,' you would have asked him, and he would have given you living water" (Jn 4:10). Nor was he afraid to tell her the truth about herself: "You are right in saying, 'I have no husband; for you have had five husbands, and he whom you now have is not your husband. This you said truly" (Jn 4:18).

I experience ministry as facilitation in spiritual direction when the person is trying to get in touch with the presence and touch of God in her life, and I view my role as spiritual director to help facilitate her relationship with God. She initiates the topics for conversation. In fact, she does most of the talking, listening to herself as she begins to piece together the tapestry of the last month or two weeks. I feel privileged to overhear her dialogue with God and God's dialogue with her in which God speaks to her the word she is. She continues to read the book of her life. I can at times help her to translate the vocabulary or give a wider view in the context of church tradition, pointing out how others have been given similar experiences. But in a facilitating relationship of this sort, both people are independent and capable of becoming interdependent. She is not looking to me for answers or solutions. I am not looking to her for friendship or companionship. We are both focused not on our relationship, but on her relationship with God. She can raise questions. I can offer insights. But there is no urgency that the issue be resolved in this session and there is no demand on my part that she act on my suggestion. She shares what she wants, and I feed back to her what I hear, sometimes offering other ways of interpreting what has happened, at other times asking a question to help her get in touch with what she is feeling. We are both enriched by the exchange. I, in fact, can enter into a mutuality of self-revelation, sharing my own experience in faith as a way of helping her place what is going on.

Wounded Healer

A sixth image of self is that of "the wounded healer."[6] As a wounded healer, I do not play martyr or victim. I am familiar with suffering, especially heart-suffering, but I do not predetermine rejection or failure. I choose in faith to act justly, love tenderly, and walk humbly with my God (Mi 6:8). I do not become disheartened by my pain, but allow it to be transformed into compassion for others. I am keenly aware of my own brokenness and need of healing, but I do not let that stand in my way. I believe that the resurrection means not that my wounds are healed but that they no longer hurt.[7] I am deeply receptive to all of life's sufferings and joys, allowing each one to make a home in my heart quietly, comfortably, and contemplatively. I forgive myself, no longer holding on to past hurts.

Who is God from this standpoint? God in Christ is our wounded healer. God is our savior, not by rescuing us from life's struggles, but rather by being present to us.

Who are others? They, too, are wounded healers. Does not suffering have a way of relativizing us? It is hard to notice things like power, prestige, and fame when you are in a prison cell or concentration camp. You meet others on a wholly different level, the level of pain, the level of shared pain and shared weakness.

What is ministry? Ministry is the networking of wounded healers in the healing spirit of Jesus in order to transform the earth and the universe into God's maternal compassion.

What is the church? The church is a wounded healer, reaching out in hospitality to others like itself who do not have it all together. This church uncovers the vulnerable face of God to us in the face of Jesus crucified.

How did Jesus respond as a wounded healer? The most powerful symbol for me is his pierced heart on the cross, whereby he gave life out of death, hope in abandonment. It is there where he loved God in affliction.[8]

Knowing myself to be a wounded healer, I need to stay committed to myself and my own inner process of healing and wholeness. I need to strike a balance in my life between work and play and prayer, being alone, being with others, and being with God. I need to take good care of myself, broken and beautiful, so that I can take good care of those entrusted to me by God. Notice the people who seem capable of joy. They are not those who starve their needs for intimacy by hiding as workaholics behind their desks. Rather they are people who accept their wounds and limits, and those of others. They do not pretend they are not familiar with suffering. They allow it, however, to be transformed not into self-hate, but rather into compassion.[9]

Conclusion

I have described six images of people in ministry. I do not imply by this that one is exclusive of another. I imagine for most of us several of these images are operative at any one moment. Notice that I have described operative images rather than ideal images. By so doing, I chose to take praxis rather than theory as a point of departure. I want to ground my reflections on ministry in concrete experiences of ministry. I am convinced that spirituality itself *is* our experience of God in our daily lives, as well as our articulation of that experience.[10]

The underlying emphasis in this essay is on self-ministry. The way we minister to ourselves is the way we minister to others. The way we serve others is the way we serve God. If we never take time for ourselves and never listen to our real feelings, then the time we take to listen to others can often reflect our deficit need for attention. If we never appreciate ourselves and celebrate our growth, then the ways we affirm others can include a projection of our need for appreciation. If we are constantly putting ourselves down, discounting ourselves and the good we mediate, then the times we empower others may be the times we ourselves need affirmation the most. We love our neighbor and God as we love ourselves. Ministry is life-giving once we allow our images of ourselves to be both liberated and liberating.

Notes

1. See Annice Callahan, ed., *Spiritualities of the Heart: Approaches to Personal Wholeness in Christian Tradition* (New York: Paulist, 1990); and "A Spirituality of Christ's Heart," *RSCJ: A Journal of Reflection*, 9,1 (1988).

2. On the image of open hands, see Henri Nouwen, *With Open Hands* (Notre Dame, Ind.: Ave Maria, 1972). Cf. Callahan, "Henri Nouwen: The Heart as Home," *Spiritualities of the Heart*, 201–217; and "Henri Nouwen: Prophet of Conversion," *Spiritual Guides for Today* (New York: Crossroad, 1992), 117–35.

On l'Arche, see Jean Vanier, *The Broken Body* (Toronto: Anglican Book Centre, 1988); and Henri Nouwen, *The Road to Daybreak: A Spiritual Journey* (New York: Doubleday, 1988). Cf. Michael Downey, *A Blessed Weakness: The Spirit of Jean Vanier and l'Arche* (San Francisco: Harper and Row, 1986); and "Region of Wound and Wisdom: The Heart in the Spirituality of Jean Vanier and l'Arche," *Spiritualities of the Heart*, 186–200.

3. On receptivity in ministry, see Ann Belford Ulanov, *Receiving Woman: Studies in the Psychology and Theology of the Feminine* (Philadelphia: Westminster, 1981). Cf. A. Callahan, "Receptivity According to Ann Belford Ulanov and Henri Nouwen," *Spiritual Life* 38, 1 (1992): 33–44.

4. I believe this is Nouwen's insight in *Gracias*! See Henri Nouwen, *Gracias! A Latin American Journal* (San Francisco: Harper and Row, 1983).

5. See H. Nouven, "Hospitality and the Host," *Reaching Out: The Three Movements of the Spiritual Life* (Glasgow: William Collins, 1986), 95–101.

6. See Henri Nouwen, *The Wounded Healer: Ministry in Contemporary Society* (Garden City, N.Y.: Doubleday, 1972).

7. See Catherine de Hueck Doherty, "Showing the Wounds of Love," *The Gospel without Compromise* (Notre Dame, Ind.: Ave Maria Press, 1976), 88–90. See also Virginia Varley, "Culture and Current Practice," *The Way Supplement* 76 (1993), 32–43, esp. 42.

8. On love in affliction, see Simone Weil, *Waiting for God*, trans. Emma Craufurd (San Francisco: Harper and Row, 1951), 117–36; *Pensées sans ordre concernant l'amour de Dieu* (Paris: Editions Gallimard, 1962), 85–105; and *On Science. Necessity and the Love of God,* ed. Richard Rees (New York: Oxford University Press, 1968). Cf. Annice Callahan, "Simone Weil: Witness to Solidarity in Affliction," *Spiritual Guides for Today*, 79–96; Eric O. Springsted, *Simone Weil and the Suffering of Love* (Cambridge, Mass.: Cowley, 1986), 17–131.

On the symbol of the pierced heart, see K. Rahner, "'Behold This Heart: Preliminaries to a Theology of Devotion to the Sacred Heart," and "Some Theses for a Theology of Devotion to the Sacred Heart," *Theological Investigations, Vol. 3*, trans. Karl H. and Boniface Kruger (New York: Seabury, 1974), 321–52; and "The Theology of the Symbol," *Theological Investigations, Vol. 4,* trans. Kevin Smyth (New York: Seabury, 1974), 221–52. Cf. A. Callahan, *Karl Rahner's Spirituality of the Pierced Heart: A Reintergretation of Devotion to the Sacred Heart* (Lanham, Md.: University Press of America, 1985); and "Karl Rahner: Theologian of Everyday Christian Life," *Spiritual Guides for Today*, 61–78.

9. On balance and becoming a person of prayer as a minister, see Evelyn Underhill, "Concerning the Inner Life," in *The House of the Soul and Concerning the Inner Life* (New York: Seabury, 1984), 89–151. Cf. A. Callahan, "Evelyn Underhill: Pathfinder for Our Way to God," *Spiritual Guides for Today*, 25–42; and *Evelyn Underhill: Spirituality for Daily Living* (Lanham, Md.: University Press of America, 1997), esp. 81–155, 187–236.

10. See A. Callahan, "The Relationship between Spirituality and Theology," *Horizons* 16 (1989): 266–74.

Selected References and Suggested Reading

Callahan, Annice. *Karl Rahner's Spirituality of the Pierced Heart:A Reinterpretation of Devotion to the Sacred Heart*. Lanham, Md.: University Press of America, 1985.

———. "Receptivity According to Ann Belford Ulanov and Henri Nouwen." *The Spiritual Life* 38, 1 (1992): 33–44.

———. "The Relationship between Spirituality and Theology," *Horizons* 16 (1989): 266–74.

————. *Spiritual Guides for Today*. New York: Crossroad, 1992.

————. Ed. *Spiritualities of the Heart: Approaches to Personal Wholeness in Christian Tradition*. New York: Paulist, 1990.

————. "A Spirituality of Christ's Heart." *RSCJ: A Journal of Reflection* 9, 1 (1988).

————. *Evelyn Underhill: Spirituality for Daily Living*. Lanham, Md.: University Press of America, 1997.

de Hueck Doherty, Catherine. *The Gospel without Compromise*. Notre Dame, Ind.: Ave Maria Press, 1976.

Downey, Michael. *A Blessed Weakness: The Spirit of Jean Vanier and l'Arche*. San Francisco: Harper and Row, 1986.

Nouwen, Henri. *Gracias! A Latin American Journal*. San Francisco: Harper and Row, 1983.

————. *Reaching Out: The Three Movements of the Spiritual Life*. Glasgow: William Collins, 1986.

————. *The Road to Daybreak: A Spiritual Journey*. New York: Doubleday, 1988.

————. *With Open Hands*. Notre Dame, Ind.: Ave Maria, 1972.

————. *The Wounded Healer: Ministry in Contemporary Society*. Garden City, N.Y.: Doubleday, 1972.

Rahner, Karl. *Theological Investigations. Vol. 3*. Trans. Karl H. and Boniface Kruger. New York: Seabury, 1974.

————. *Theological Investigations. Vol. 4*. Trans. Kevin Smyth. New York: Seabury, 1974.

Springsted, Eric O. *Simone Weil and the Suffering of Love*. Cambridge, Mass.: Cowley, 1986.

Ulanov, Ann Belford. *Receiving Woman: Studies in the Psychology and Theology of the Feminine*. Philadelphia: Westminster, 1981.

Underhill, Evelyn. *The House of the Soul and Concerning the Inner Life*. New York: Seabury, 1984.

Vanier, Jean. *The Broken Body*. Toronto: Anglican Book Centre, 1988.

Varley, Virginia. "Culture and Current Practice," *The Way Supplement* 76 (1993): 32–43.

Weil, Simone. *On Science, Necessity, and the Love of God*. Ed. Richard Rees. New York: Oxford University Press, 1968.

————. *Pensées sans ordre concernant l'amour de Dieu*. Paris: Editions Gallimard, 1962.

————. *Waiting for God*. Trans. Emma Craufurd. San Francisco: Harper and Row, 1951.

George Aschenbrenner

15. I Want to Be Like God:
A Birthright for Autonomy

A yearning for God-likeness has been stirring human hearts for a long time. However quaint the story at the beginning of Genesis may seem, the issue of wanting to be like God confronts all our hearts, and will be a live issue until it is quieted in the complete fulfillment of eternity. Such a longing is like a raw nerve that can flare up in throbbing pain and yet, when properly treated and tempered, can stir great passion for life. This essay is precisely concerned with tempering this heartfelt desire, this live nerve, in a way that will avoid a raw destructive pain and galvanize a passionate energy for ministry.

To be like God! It is a desire that resonates in all our hearts, at times affirmed profoundly in prayerful peace while at other times echoed intensely in a shrill scream. A desire for divinity has misled many people to a frenzied search that has proven hurtful finally not only to themselves but to many others. At the same time, this desire has stretched many other people to a hero-ism way beyond the clutches of their own limitations. The desire for divin-ity—there is no ideal more attractive and stirring for a human heart. The challenge facing us all, however, is one of learning to see this desire for what it is: a gift of glorious hope inseminated in all our hearts by our loving Creator. Such learning is never automatic, nor easy. Perhaps no other human desire is more passionately capable of alluring deception and misleading destructive-ness. To understand and temper such a deep desire—it is hard to imagine a task more important.

In this essay I investigate two very different views of the human desire for divinity and how they take flesh in quite different types of autonomy. Gen-esis will help us to appreciate the glorious gift given and, then, its discourag-ing misuse. Jesus in his own humanity is God's word of forgiveness addressed to this misspent desire in a way that gives birth to autonomy. It is an autonomy, however, that invites a self-transcendence and communal bonding aimed, finally, at nothing less than the loving transformation of our whole universe. Harnessing this central human desire for good is not only an affair of individ-ual importance. Its most serious effect is in ministry, where its influence is

often subliminal though nonetheless real. I will point at some of this ministerial influence, but I will leave further insight to the reader. For a long time,
strangely enough, I personally viewed this desire to be like God as a misleading, even sinful, impulse throbbing in our bloodstream. Most of this essay is a
sharing of my own recent graced insight into the positive nature of this desire,
actually a gift from God, and its great potential for holiness in ministry.

Death or God-likeness?

Genesis speaks not only of forebears long ago but teaches about our
human condition in all ages. The greatest gift to human beings is as profound
and existential as our very being. Each of us is being created, moment by
moment, in the image of One who, right now, graciously breathes a spirited
breath of life into our nostrils and tabernacles a home deep in our heart. And
so, distinctively imaged in all creation, we human beings have a deep desire to
be like God. In the story of Genesis the Hebrew people, in their own way, are
expressing their experience of this desire, an experience that faces us all
sooner or later, however different its cultural expression may be and however
clearly we may confront it.

In the third chapter of Genesis an important encounter occurs that will
have long-lasting effects. The most subtle of the wild beasts corrects the
woman's and the man's apprehension that they will die if they eat the fruit of
the tree of knowledge of good and evil. The serpent lures them into a mistaken
remembering of God's promise. "No! You will not die! God knows in fact that
on the day you eat it your eyes will be opened and you will be like God, knowing good and evil" (3:4–5). These sly words activate a desire in the hearts of
the woman and man: to be like God in comprehending and controlling good
and evil. A deep longing has been touched in their hearts, and something
entrancingly attractive dances in their imaginations. They are glad to have
their memories corrected and lifted beyond a fear of death. More than they had
ever realized before, the cunning words of the serpent insinuate their way into
the rhythm of the strong desire of their hearts. They were never before quite so
aware of this. "We want to be like God" rings almost uncontrollably in their
hearts. And they ate the fruit.

What seemed so attractive and alluring, what was so "pleasing to the eye"
and "good to eat" (3:6) quickly turns sour with explosive social fallout. An original innocence suddenly evaporates and they look at one another differently.
They see one another sexually in a disordered, self-consciously tempting manner. They shirk personal responsibility for their own actions and place blame on
anybody but themselves. The joys of life together, especially the beauty of childbearing, take on a painful, toilsome prospect shrouded in suffering. Ashamed
and fearful, the woman and man went into hiding from all the original blessing

and beauty of life—and, worst of all, hiding from God. No more walking together with God in the cool of the day in the garden. As the man and woman left the garden they knew things had decisively changed. They knew they had misused a birthright incredibly precious. And yet, the throbbing continued: to be like God. It is the way they were still being created. In no way could they walk away from that desire, from that birthright. But to understand it, to temper it and to live it together properly would involve more than they originally imagined. The development of Genesis into chapter 11 with the tower of Babel and its failed communication and construction bears eloquent testimony to the continuing social fallout of failing to temper this core desire.

With the tang of good and evil still biting on their tongues, the woman and man are prevented by the flame of a flashing sword from eating from the tree of life and living forever. But *all* is not lost! Stirring in the heart of God is one like a "Son of Man" who will come "so that they may have life and have it to the full" (Jn 10:10). He is the one whose life, pruned unto death, will sheath the flaming sword and graft branches on to the vine of eternal life. Within the whole human family, this one alone will make possible our fullest identity at the end when seeing God in the face we shall finally know how fully we were always intended to be in the image of God (cf. 1 Jn 3:1–2).

Individual Autonomy: A Contemporary Test Case

The dynamics dramatized in Genesis are not limited to an ancient time and people. They are part of human experience in any age and culture. This desire for God-likeness is so deeply imbedded in the human heart that, whether recognized or not, it always figures prominently in a person's spirituality and thus also takes effect in ministry.

In contemporary American culture this desire to be like God is often entangled with the cultural ideal of individual autonomy. Our American culture in many ways canonizes such autonomy. Some explanations for this are obvious. Liberation movements of various sorts have spotlighted unjust oppression and called for and celebrated an autonomy of acknowledged self-identity and self-actualization. People freed from a denigrating discrimination will be enslaved no more. They have now assertively taken charge of their own lives and destinies. From another perspective, decades of reflection about the stages of development to human maturity have given a new and clearly articulated emphasis to the stage of individual autonomy. It is a stage of development intended for us all, and without which, so we are told, maturity just is not possible.

A basic confidence and autonomy have long been part of a mature person's presence in life. But now it is stated loud and clear and described with an attractive vigor. In the heady winds of liberation this ideal of individual autonomy spread like wild fire. We are trained assertively to desire it, to practice it, to become it. Breathed so bracingly into the bloodstream in recent decades, the contemporary ideal of human maturity stirs a whole lifestyle: Stand on your own feet, take charge of your own life, be autonomous.

Obviously this is not all bad. It is fundamentally true that without a basic acceptance and actualization of self, human maturity eludes us. However this ideal of self-autonomy must be carefully reflected upon. Though such an ideal seems to have an early salutary effect, it surely is not, in itself, the fullness of salvation. Rather than lead us deeper into the intimacy of God-likeness in Jesus, such autonomy can actually become a positive deterrent to the fulfillment of our deep-hearted desire to be like God.

1. An Important Part of Life

As mentioned above, autonomy has a healthy, even essential role to play in growth to human maturity. The science of human development, a fairly recent professional discipline, with its accompanying theories of personality development, provides a perspective that not only was not possible hundreds of years ago but that can now provide important help to floundering, confused people. Many people have a nagging feeling of dis-ease about themselves. If truth would be told, they feel bad about themselves; they are really down on themselves; they are their own worst enemy. And they would sure like to feel otherwise. In many cases, they are not very responsible for their state of affairs. They have been victimized chiefly at the cost of not being loved. In a saddening variety of ways, people from quite early in their development have been abused and trashed into a deadening attitude of profound dislike and discontent that becomes aimed at themselves. Of course, this is often not consciously realized, nor dealt with, but rather compensated for by a variety of defense mechanisms. Whether it has broken into explicit awareness or not, such an attitude sits in one's heart like a poison—and can sour the person's spirit in everything. Though we can become skilled at disguising our face and whole lifestyle, the rottenness in our heart is terribly real and sits like a dead weight.

But such a dingy dungeon does not have to be an eternal prison. Many can and do recover. Liberation comes in an experience of genuine love, however long it may take to trust and receive such love. This brings, slowly and gradually (no instant miracles here!), a whole new life and a new invigorating feeling good about oneself. A soul that felt a poisoning rottenness slowly begins to etch the lines of a smile. What a change! Often it is *felt* before it is *understood,* and these people must beware of the temptation to doubt the change that is actually happening. But it can become a change finally as monumental as the difference between a sickening wish for death and a throbbing desire for life. To love other people into such a change of feeling about themselves is a gift and service precious beyond words. The truth still stands: We receive ourselves as gift mirrored in the loving eyes of another.

2. *A Darksome Misunderstanding*

But there is another side to the human ideal of individual autonomy, a darksome underside. A *simpliste* unadulterated acceptance of this autonomy is dangerous today. A growing number of people are finding an unhappiness in the shallow emptiness and segregated insensitivity of such an autonomous life. But, by and large, this is still the ideal sought and often flaunted in our contemporary culture.

Feeling so much better about oneself after a long time of drudgery can have an intoxicating effect and fixate a person in an attitude of autonomous self-determination. The exhilaration of such confidence and self-actualizing autonomy can have the heady effect of beguiling one into a selfish stance in life. Now reality rotates about the self, a self that has become the measure and goal of life's success. At times, the person may even talk a God-centered, loving approach, but the walk of such a life is talking another center and goal. The focus has settled on, in fact is stuck on, self. Once again echoes are heard: No, you will not die; you will be like God. And those echoes can easily entrance a heart longing for God-likeness. But, obviously the perspective has narrowed and the gaze of heart is self-absorbed.

Concealed in the graced yearning to be like God is a frightfully destructive attraction: simply, to *be* God. Though the difference is gargantuan and the outcome costly to death, it seems only a short, quick stride from desiring to be like God to desiring actually to be God and to act as God. It is a stride known to us all. We have all done it, probably many times—even if we were not aware of it nor would have named it as such. We are back in Genesis again and a graced desire placed in human hearts by a loving Creator is being misdirected in a way that can lead to ultimate destruction.

When our inherent desire for God-likeness has been misguided and short-circuited into an individualist autonomy, personal worth is proven in the accomplishment and achievement of all sorts of successes. But such success and accomplishment always has the same ring to it: *my* development, *my* comfort, *my* gifts, *my* satisfaction. The ring is not always deafening but, however muted and soft, the ring is the same nonetheless. Sacrifice and sharing for love sound like unintelligible noise.

When transposed into a ministerial setting, this dynamic has disastrous results. Whose reign of love is being served? An unintended neediness and misguided sense of autonomy infests the ministry and collapses it into self-aggrandizement. Such ministers are hard to work with because they are not able to risk being overshadowed. The most serious effect of this deceptive autonomy is with the people who are misused and misguided. When an unconscious manipulation creeps into the ministry, they cannot help but wonder: Who is serving whom? And, worst of all, they are being given, often unwittingly, a very wrong model of Christian holiness and shared intimacy with Jesus. Somehow in all of this the desire to be like God has run amok and been insidiously misguided.

An Autonomy Born in Forgiveness

But, once again, in the goodness of God, all is not necessarily lost. It is precisely in the remorseful awareness of our attempted steal of Godly identity that a very different type of autonomy is born. Repentance and sorrow for such a monumental betrayal of God's loving hope for us brings a renewed and even more startling hope: forgiveness in Jesus. In the transformation such forgiveness works, we see clearly the enlightened discernment now needed to minister any autonomy before God.

The original blessing of a desire to be like God does not remain intact and unblemished in any of us. As mentioned earlier, for all of us a desire for God-likeness has corrupted into a desire and activity simply to *be* God. In fact, is this not the central arena of trial and test for us all? Except for Mary, the Mother of Jesus, and her special gift, we have all overplayed our original blessing through an aggressive misuse of autonomy.

No effort or merit of our own can recreate that pristine, unalloyed desire for God-likeness. Our only option is to take truthful cognizance of our sinful situation in shame and sorrow. This involves a vulnerability which for many cuts against the grain of the secular ideal of autonomy. Guilt, shame, and sorrow are not easy for us today though their unrecognized presence often nags us like an inner contagion. But it is precisely in recognizing and receiving these graces of shame and sorrow that we discover the beauty of Jesus, God's faithful son and forgiving Savior. The intimacy of such an encounter takes clearest expression on Calvary with its sure promise of resurrection. Such an encounter also enlivens for us a whole new image of God together with a renewed and more enlightened desire to be like God. And, in line with the point of this essay, precisely *there,* in the graced shame and sorrow, is also born another autonomy. More humble than the secular variety and yet energetically zealous beyond any weakliness, this different autonomy invites a renewed desire to be like God. But to fear and make light of our experience of shame and sorrow and a need to apologize, and then stubbornly to cling to the secular image of autonomy is actually to lose touch with the inherent desire for God-likeness. It is to forfeit a birthright that gives hope to all our future.

This autonomy born in forgiveness is not an individualistic experience. From the very beginning of Genesis, human existence is revealed as essentially communal. Walking together with God in the cool of the day is what life is all about. But this is seriously interrupted by the insidiously wily words of the serpent. A certain retrenchment occurs on the part of the woman and man into her and his own self. A shared responsibility and life has been shattered by a type of individualistic autonomy. This split can finally be healed only in welcoming God's forgiveness as expressed in Jesus, the one who uniquely comes from the heart of God and invites us all to a new table-fellowship. The autonomy born here is not self-focused. Concentrating within itself a confidence and self-acceptance, this autonomy is seen as precious gift renewed and restored by our loving Creator. It is always born of vulnerability, not arrogant self-assertiveness. It is focused on love of God and others, not predominantly on self. Such autonomy is rooted in the strong realization that we are all in the same boat, turbulently tossed on the waves, and yet strengthened by those words that ring above the din of the water and the wind: Do not be afraid! Get hold of yourselves! It is I AM! (Mt 14:22–23).

This autonomy born in forgiveness is in stark contrast to today's secular ideal. It is also meant to characterize much more than a momentary experience. It sets a direction for a whole way of living and ministering. Walter Brueggemann in his book *Hopeful Imagination* about the prophetic voices of Israel in exile presents a distinction that can be helpful at this point. While commenting on Jeremiah's experience of being called, he presents two very different views of life: a called and an uncalled life. A "called" life is one that "has a theonomous cast, is deeply referred to the purposes of God…is an ongoing dynamic of a growing and powerful claim."[1] A central point in this essay is that such a call and claim is heard in the experience of being forgiven. It is a call and claim that sets off the life and ministry of one who does not belong to self and is not fundamentally in charge but rather responds to that constant call and claim of God resonating in the human heart. This is a person who is not simply self-directed but, more appropriately, God-directed.

But Brueggemann is honest and strong about how "profoundly counter cultural" such a called life is in our contemporary world. "The ideology of our time is to propose that one can live 'an uncalled' life, one not referred to any purpose beyond one's self. It can be argued that the disease of autonomy besets us all, simply because we are modern people.… Autonomy is the predictable ground for resisting the truth of a call from outside self.[2] This is another description of what I call "secular autonomy." It can eat into our person so profoundly as to infect our whole life and ministry. After breathing this pollution into our bloodstream for many years we need a veritable blood transfusion as preparation for mature Christian ministry. The vulnerability and humiliation involved in acknowledging our need to be forgiven, and then undergoing the actual experience of accepting God's forgiveness[3] play a major role in this blood transfusion.

In the shared vulnerability and humiliation of being forgiven is found a drive to minister in love and service. The combustion of forgiveness sets loose a great energy for ministry, not now indulged in as proof of self-worth, but motivated by gratitude for all that has been so gratuitously given. This autonomy, never arrogantly flaunted but oriented to communal sharing, has its clearest effect in ministry. But to short circuit and trivialize the experience of being forgiven in Jesus will always corrupt the autonomy desired, will disguise those words with too much truth: "No, you will not die....You will be like God!" and, finally, will disappoint the Creator's hope for us all to be like God.

The whole development of this essay has made clear the careful enlightenment needed if we are to live an autonomous lifestyle that responds to and deepens our desire to be like God. The autonomy invited and made possible in Jesus is born in the experience of being forgiven and must daily be enlightened by a careful discernment. The missteps along the way are many and subtle. A naive trusting of all our heart's stirrings will quickly mislead us. The crucially important second look of reflection and respect for all God desires for us can take daily expression in our regular practice of Consciousness Examen.[4]

To be like God is the birthright graciously and intentionally given to us by our Creator. But it can easily be forfeited for any number of other identities, always of much less value—yes, even the mammoth attempt to take over God's own identity and being. This gift of God's true birthright promises the fulfillment of our deepest desire, sometimes in the quiet peace of union and always in exhilarated energy for ministry. The challenge, finally, for all ministers is not to squander such promise in overassertiveness but to recognize and cooperate with the unique role God is always giving each one of us in our world's great project of glory: Jesus.

Notes

1. Walter Brueggemann, *Hopeful Imagination* (Fortress Press, 1986), 18.
2. Ibid., 19.
3. Cf. George Aschenbrenner, S.J., "The Inner Journey of Forgiveness," *Human Development* (Fall 1989): 15–23.
4. Cf. George Aschenbrenner, S.J., "Consciousness Examen," *Review for Religious* (January 1972); "A Check on Our Availability: The Examen," *Review for Religious* (May 1980); "Consciousness Examen: Becoming God's Heart for the World," *Review for Religious* (December 1988).

===

16. Time and Time Out of Time: Meeting God in the Ordinary and Extraordinary Moment

Back in the early '70s, Jim Croce rose to musical heights as a kind of folk guru, a status secured by his sudden death in a plane crash. Among the songs Croce wrote and performed that earned him his cultic fame is his enigmatic "Time in a Bottle." In the title metaphor, Croce reflects, "If I could save time in a bottle, the first thing that I'd want to do / is to save every day 'til eternity passes away, just to spend them with you."

The image this singer ascribes to an enduring romantic relationship echoes a timeless and still urgent paradox that every person who attempts to live the "examined life" contends with—the living of days into the endless eternity of days. For a pastoral person—minister, counselor, therapist, or caregiver—who attempts to walk with others through the complexity of time toward the simplicity who is God, the paradox can become one of the most meaningful of all life's questions. The duality offered in living the present moment into that which will never end captures in its essence so many of the dynamics of self, others, and God that lie at the core of pastoral encounter.

Through many years now of sharing with others on issues related to time, change, and the pressures of both, in one-on-one counseling as well as in classes, retreats, and workshops, several motifs have emerged that sound at times almost contrapuntal. Often one or another stands out in particular and striking singularity; sometimes, the motifs overlap and complement each other as much with their contrasts as with their similarities.

While this echoing theme has been making itself heard for any number of years in the concerns of clients, students, and fellow spiritual searchers, a recent meeting with a sometimes supervisee seems to crystalize many of its elements. This woman, whom I shall call Joan, had been a student of mine in a pastoral counseling program several years ago. She comes on occasion to "bounce things off" when her ministry as a hospice worker and grief counselor becomes overwhelming. On her arrival this particular morning, Joan announced that what she had come to deal with that day had less to do with professional than with personal concerns, and yet, as she spoke, both ministerial and personal began to flow "all of a piece."

Her story that day opened with her telling of a recent plane trip from which she had returned just a few days before, a trip that took her to the west coast to visit a high school sorority sister. The trip, arranged by her friend's husband, formed a reunion of five women who through the thirty-plus years since graduation had remained close despite thousands of miles of distance and several decades of life intervening. The husband had negotiated the reunion because his wife, sick for a number of years, was in the final stages of MS, and the doctors' prognosis indicated that "her time was short." As Joan said, she went with trepidation, for while she wanted to support her friend and offer all she could at this special and sacred time, she worried that her background in dealing with death and dying would lead others—her friend, her friend's husband, and even her sorority sisters—to expect too much of her.

"It's a long plane ride across this country," Joan reflected as she began, "and on it I came to terms with my fears and the demands I was placing on myself. No one had asked me to come because of my work in hospice or with grieving. They had invited me as a longtime friend. I was the one redefining my position and I was the one who needed to let that go. I prayed I could enter into this visit moment by moment, and God heard me. From the minute I stepped into the airport lobby and saw Jim (my friend's husband) waiting for me, I felt something inside let go. Everything from Philadelphia lay behind me, just as if I shut it in a box and put it on a shelf. Everything with Evelyn (my friend) lay open before me. I could just be me."

Joan went on to speak of those five days with her friends and sisters as "time out of time." "We laughed and remembered the silliest stories. One recollection would lead into another. In a way we were those starry-eyed high school girls with poodle skirts and saddle shoes listening to *American Bandstand.* Frances Weaver (1996) has a book out that one of my daughters gave me, I think as a compliment. It's called *The Girls with Grandmother Faces* and in its closing she says that deep inside the grown woman 'warm and cherished, is the same person who has done the best she could through whatever came into her life' (198). In those five days that is what we celebrated: life lived to the full. I came expecting a wake and what I found was resurrection. When I went to Mass that Sunday with Jim and the 'girls' I knew in a different sense what the words of consecration really signify: 'Do this in memory of me.' Real doing in memory doesn't mean building some kind of edifice to the past, but bringing the past into today. It means breathing life and spirit into the now because of all that has been. That is what makes tomorrow possible, more than possible—hope-filled. Because I was able to seize the moment and not demand of myself a prepared response, I related to all of those very special people in that very holy time as a truly pastoral person: caring, compassionate, centered, and, most of all, connected."

Joan returned to the tarmac in Philadelphia, to her family, her daily routine, and her demanding ministry with a sense of entering from a time warp. Her days on the west coast had been draining yet uplifting: facing the reality of the death of someone whose presence had marked most of her life, yet whose imminent passing was not tragedy. What made the difference in Joan's coming and going? What motifs of time and timelessness wove their way through her five-day visit that capture the essence of this theme for the pastoral person? Four major ones stood out in her story as I listened that day: time as *chronos* with the impact that life today places upon us; time as *kairos* and how to allow ourselves to enter into its mystery; the challenge of integrating the two; and finally, Sabbath time and its call to live "out of time" in time.

Chronological time, or "Ordinary Time" as the church titles it, with its measure of minutes, hours, days into weeks, weeks into seasons, holds a poor connotation even in the liturgical cycle. We think of the dulling of the Alleluias of Paschaltide into the quiet chanting of daily antiphons; the fading of the bright gold of Christmas into everyday green; and even the downplay of prophetic announcements of Advent and Lent into the sequence of readings A, B, or C. In the secular city, a similar negativity can be heard even in the words that attach to time set to the world's clock. We think of structured, mundane, regular time and associate with it meeting deadlines, consulting calendars, and punching time clocks. Such words and phrases seem stultifying, imposing a rigid order on all— the poetic as well as the pedantic, the seraphic along with the servile. Yet, the right ordering of time can be as sacred as any eruption of exceptional grace, and in fact, as time unfolds in scripture, the truth that emerges is that without the measure of the chronos, the kairos cannot come to be.

We hear the first celebration of ordinary time in the opening lines of Genesis with the ordering of time in creation. The priestly author of Genesis 1 sets each of the focal creations into one day's passing: "God called the light day and the darkness night. Evening came and morning followed: the first day" (1:8). In a later chapter the floodwaters diminish over the length of 150 days with the marking of its passage like the log of some navigator: "The water kept going down and on the first day of the tenth month the tops of the mountains appeared" (8:5). But most especially and appropriately, the Book of Chronicles charts the schedules for the chosen people as they come to know their God: the Levites to keep their temple duty, the administrators to take the census, the guards to post the watch on the temple, and so on (1 Chr 26–27).

For the Hebrews, chronos, ordinary time, was not negative; in fact, as Genesis insists: "God looked on it and saw it very good" (1:22). For these ancient desert people, ordering of time allowed a saneness in a world where order and sanity were rare commodities. Against a horizon of shifting sand and within a culture that often exploded into chaos, the chronology of temple service, religious rituals, and sacred calendars allowed the people to carve out their place in the universe, to define their role as a nation, to name their tasks both menial and convenantal yet to be finished. As one philosopher notes, the Hebrews' seeing of time on a linear, chronological plane marks them as unique. Only such a people, a group who held a faith in a Supreme Being, could believe that time had a beginning, middle, and end, for such belief presupposes that someone must initiate the passage of time.

Perhaps one of the most beautiful and poetic paeans to the passage of ordinary time comes in the Book of Ecclesiastes, which opens, "To everything there is a season" and rejoices that "every action will happen at its own set time" (3: 1–8,17). As the modern pastoral person hears this litany, does he or she rejoice as did its author Qoheleth, son of David? Or does the minister feel the rub of "each season" and the pressure of "every action"? So many of those involved in the various service areas undertaken in ministry seem to be victims of either quick burnout or slow deterioration of zeal and buildup of chronic lethargy. Many in pastoral ministry find the reverse of Psalm 126 true for their lives as they go out full of joy "sowing the seed" but return sluggish, disheartened, or disillusioned "carrying the sheaves." What contributes to the loss of the initial zeal?

Certainly, the demands are many in any occupation that requires a committed extension of oneself to others, and any ministry that calls for constant availability can be both taxing and draining. Yet, why does it seem that some of the busiest people in ministry are also the happiest and most animated, while for others their plaintive chant is how tired, overworked, or short on time they always find themselves? One explanation for the difference might lie in a phenomenon that Dr. Carla Przybilla, a therapist at the New Life Center in Virginia, draws from physics and applies to psychological states: the process of *entrainment*. As Przybilla explains it, entrainment is a "dynamic of nature as pervasive as gravity that involves the process by which one system falls in synch with the other" as when a pair of pendulum clocks in near proximity originally swinging in different rhythms eventually match each other in pace and movement (1997, 8). Nature is full of such harmonies, as when water wheels or windmills in the same neighborhood turn in unison, or when the hooves of animals yoked together begin to clop in synchronized beat.

Our ancestors, for whom the backdrop of daily toil was the music of bird songs, the whir of harvester and plow, even the mechanical drone of sewing machine, bobbin and shuttle, or assembly line, entrained to sounds rhythmic and steady. What do we postmodern children entrain to as our ears open to the noise of the new millennium? The pace of our time sounds with computers that can't boot up fast enough, beepers whose signals can penetrate even our deepest privacy, fax machines that can spew out pages faster than a phone can ring, and the thunder of traffic, commerce, and machines. For many the din of modern society is a cacophony, and the distraction that pulls in several directions at once makes us an age of persons for whom attention deficit with hyperactivity seems normal. One of the most Christian of contemporary writers, the American Gothic Flannery O'Connor uses the symbol of the machine as her recurrent image of a world beset by the modern dragon of violence and sin. She addresses an audience, believer and non alike, who have become "almost deaf and near blind" and for whom she must shout loudly and "write large" of incarnational realities to penetrate the ether of ennui.

One of the casualties of modern entrainment comes with our misordering of priorities. Time analysts and repairer of schedules such as Stephen Covey and company warn modern CEOs and homemakers alike that the urgent and necessary will always get done, but the important has become too often neglected. If we number from most pressing to least our "to-do" list for any day, what is most likely to fall at the bottom or completely off the page? Even tedious chores and tasks we've taken on for others supersede those things that might make ourselves more human, those activities that can lift our heart and give us delight. As Przybilla notes, events filled with feeling are the ones most often omitted. This may be the product of overloading or an attempt at avoidance, but whatever its motive, the result is increased stress. "It takes time to experience a feeling.... We live in a hyperproductive society, and the moment we stop it's not okay" (1997, 8).

The answer for the pastoral minister, as for any creative person, is to learn to live in the now. Such a solution is not an easy one, for it means undoing sometimes decades of conditioning and contradicting all the world tells us is rational and key to success. However, to stand with both feet planted in the present moment is the only position for one who hopes to lean into the future and God. To lean into anything demands a sensitive sense of balance and enormous poise. Picture the trapeze artist perched high above the crowds who waits for the swing to reach just the right point to leap into mid-air. The acrobat stands reaching across emptiness watching for the precise moment, leaning literally into nothingness. The position is precarious, the need for balance extreme, but the outcome is connection.

Simone Weil, the French essayist, philosopher, and, some hold, mystic, calls such an attitudinal stance *attente*. For her "waiting on God" means to live in the present moment with hearts and spirits freed from both past fears and potential anxiety, "not seeking anything but ready to receive in its naked truth the object which is to penetrate it" (1950, 72). To live so mirrors the position that God takes toward us as the one who stands waiting. Weil writes,

> God waits like a beggar who stands motionless and silent before someone who will perhaps give him a piece of bread. Time is that

waiting. Time is God's waiting for our love…. By waiting humbly
we are made similar to God. (1950, 91)

To live in the present leaning into the future free of entanglement with the
past is to capture the essence of kairos, God's time unfolding in human history.
This kind of time has been called many names, including such descriptors as
sacred, sapiential, and *mythical* time. Mircea Eliade, the great commentator on
myths, speaks of *illo tempore,* time out of time. Kairos might also equate to Abraham Maslow's peak moment and T. S. Eliot's "still point." Perhaps one of the
fullest explanations comes with theologian Cornelius Ernst's "genetic moment":

> A mystery. It is dawn, discovery, spring, new birth, coming to
> light, bridal consent, gift, forgiveness, reconciliation, revolution,
> faith, hope, love. It could be said that Christianity is the consecra-
> tion of the genetic moment, the living centre from which it
> reviews the indefinitely various and shifting perspectives of
> human experience in history. That at least is or ought to be its
> claim: that is the power to transform and renew all things.
> "Behold! I make all things new." (Rev 21:5) (1974, 74–75)

Taking Ernst's definition to heart links kairotic time with the "hour" of
which the evangelist John speaks in the fourth Gospel and "the Day of the Lord"
that echoes throughout the Pauline epistles. The "hour" toward which Jesus
moves (Jn 7:30) and for which Jesus yearns (Jn 12:23) arrives in Johannine fullness as the *telos,* the realization of salvation history on Calvary (Jn 20:30). For
Paul, writing repeatedly to warn his converts to be alert for the Parousia, the present moment is a brief intermediary period (Rom 13:11); the "day of salvation," a
short earthy pilgrimage that allows for conversion of heart and right ordering of
lives (1 Cor 7: 26–31, Eph 5:16). Paul's "Day of the Lord," "right time," and
"fullness of time" come, not as with John in Calvary's final hour, but with the
"end of all ages" (Gal 4:4; 1 Cor 10:11; Eph 1:10), the eschaton that marks the
close of human history and victory over sin and death (Heb 1:2; 9:26).

Characteristics that mark kairotic time contrast it with chronos's linear
and historical time. With its onset at first signaled by a sense of disorientation,
uprooting, and loss, the qualities a person can identify in an experience of a
kairos include an amorphous or circular expanse of the moment, an absence of
movement or progress somewhat akin to being in a vacuum chamber, lack of
goal-orientation and closure, and a feeling that limits and boundaries are evap-
orating, that measured time is stretching into an unhurried, seemingly endless
period. Kathryn Rabuzzi (1982) notes that in comparing these two times we
are calling chronological and kairotic, the differences reflect those in the masculine and the feminine experience of time. She states that women's mode of
being is formed into a circularity, a kind of space-time experience "not hers to

fill as she pleases," but because of childbearing and -rearing, homemaking and the imposition of "standing and waiting" these entail, projected away from her and often out of her control. Apparent in archetypal literature, this ambivalent and circular pattern is a favorite of fairy tale heroines such as the ever-weaving Penelope, patient Griselda, and long-suffering Elaine. As their Odysseus, Walter, and Lancelot, living within the framework of masculine-ordered, goal-directed time, quest, fight and conquer, these valiant women endure.

Yet, even with its lack of definable goals and closure, the experience of feminine time is not all bad, for the very structures that "denied women entree to history" also provide potential for entrance into the transcendent. Such experience also contains

> the positive face of chaos, a letting go into the possibilities that freedom from externally fixed routine allows...(and) allows you to be one with the moment...both passive and totally free. It involves responding to the combination of your innermost self and the particular moment.... The passivity so induced is of a light object thrown into the water; it is not the object that determines its direction, but the movement of the water. (Rabuzzi, 1982, 151–53)

If this experience of kairos resounds with a lack of control, a need for spontaneous response, and a letting go of self, such is the waiting time of a Moses before the burning bush, a Jacob on Mt. Bethel, a Mary in her Fiat moment, a Joan stepping off a plane from Philadelphia and leaving her east coast life behind. Paul celebrates the witness of the openness required by the attentive waiter in his profile of the Hebrew patriarch: "For Abraham was waiting for the city which God has designed and built, the city with permanent foundations.... It was in faith that all our ancestors died. They did not receive the things God had promised, but from a long way off they saw and welcomed them" (Heb 11: 10, 13–16). The apostle's praise underscores a key component of the faith-filled waiter: attention to the ordinary "stuff of life" allows for the inbreaking kingdom of God. Only because these anawim were alive to the God potential within their world could they embrace theophany when and where it happened.

The raging fire of the burning bush springs into being before Moses not as he worships at the high altar of the temple but as he "tends the flocks of his father-in-law Jethro" on a miserable and out-of-the-way hillside (Ex 3:1). As this hesitant hero insists, God has come to the wrong person at the wrong time and in very much the wrong place. But because he believes that it truly is God who comes, Moses transforms from pedantic herder into prophetic leader and the great announcer that "I AM" has come among the people God has chosen. Jacob's dream of "the ladder into heaven...with Yahweh standing over him" and his subsequent call as father of the twelve tribes arrives not in some obviously religious institute but as he lies alien and alone with only a rock for a pillow and the dust of his own betrayal in his mouth (Gn 28:10–15). Again, the wrong person in the wrong place at the very worst time, yet God chooses this moment to touch this manipulator's heart and let him discover the sacredness of mountain and moment. "Surely, God is in this place though I never knew it before!" (Gn 28:16). Perhaps it is the very misery of the moment and the dregs of humanity touched by these ancestral persons that God uses for epiphany.

In the person of Mary we see the climatic merging of kairotic and chronological time. When Paul announces "the right time" to his friends at Galatia, it is her person who forms its crucible. "When the right time came, God sent his own Son. He came as the son of a human mother and lived under Jewish law to redeem those born under the law that we might become God's heirs" (4:4–5). Again to the Romans he announces that the "revelation of the mystery kept secret for endless ages (in the chronos)" is made clear now through "the inbreaking presence of Jesus Christ" in the advent of kairos (16:25-26). Mary is the woman par excellent who welcomes the word of such advent in her heart and the body of the Messiah into her womb. Because she has leaned into God's promise throughout her life and heard the prophetic word in its truth, she can now bow, *sub tuum,* open and receptive, to what God wants: "God has come to the help of servant Israel" (Lk 1:54). She can let go of her limits and celebrate the divine use of her lowliness: "The Almighty One has done great things for me; holy is God's name" (Lk 1:49). She can allow her questions of the right way and the right time to fade against God's invitation: "I am the Lord's servant; may it happen as God says" (Lk 1:38).

What does the rich religious tradition of kairos and its necessary grounding in the chronos have to say for the pastoral person ministering in the here and now? All of it connects to a very current topic, the contemporary concern with mindlessness and its opposite found in the spiritual practice of mindfulness. "Being mindless," says Harvard professor Ellen Langer, "means you're not there. You're not in the moment and aware of everything going on around you" (cited in Ryan, 1998, 8). Examples of it can range from the simple act of putting an unwashed mug back in the dish closet to missing your exit on a turnpike to a narcissistic preoccupation with self that social critics like Robert Bellah call an epidemic of our age. In contrast, mindfulness is a focused, accepting awareness anchored in the here and now that allows a person a clearer vision, a looking with new eyes into the heart of another person. Such an intense regard demands the ability on the edge of life.

One of the major proponents and practitioners of mindfulness is the Vietnamese Buddhist monk and teacher, Thich Nhat Hanh. A story is told of him when he was presenting his mindfulness practice at the National Cathedral in Washington, D.C. Having been led meditatively by him through the gardens early in the day, one of the participants met him in the evening at the hotel. Speaking to him and perhaps hoping for an invitation to continue her conversation with him over a meal, she asked what he was doing. Expecting a reply such as "going to dinner" or "heading to the dining room," she heard his reply, "I am walking in the corridor." Unlike most of us whose lives are always heading away from one event and toward another, Thich Nhat Hanh spends his life stopping in between, savoring the present moment (cited in *New Life Newsletter,* 1997, 9).

The promise for the pastoral person in such a stance is significant, especially whenever one has to sit with another in need. A pastoral counselor herself, Molly Layton says,

> The capacity for mindfulness, for sitting with others, is truly an exercise in slowing down and opening the heart. Being in the ebb and flow of a therapy session requires attention to nuances and shadings of another human being, nuances impossible to capture in texts and training manuals.... Wrestling with my own limits prepares me to sit with other people's struggles with loss and ambiguity.... A certain tolerance with not knowing can be a gateway to new learning, to ever-deepening connection with another human being. (1995, 29)

The paradox about living in the present moment that mindfulness invites is that what I await is not the change in someone else but the change within myself. A way to bring ourselves to the "capacity for here-and-now presence" is to open ourselves to opportunities that come in the midst of ordinary schedules to accept the gift that each minute chooses to offer. So as I end up on the tail end of a traffic jam, I can allow the enforced stillness to evolve within me into a quiet and still pause. Rather than drum on the steering wheel, honk my horn, or rage at the inefficiency of the Department of Streets, I let myself feel tension drain from me and tune into sounds other than the drum of tires, blare of radios, or racket of equipment. I listen for the gentle stir of a breeze, the silence of the inside of the car, the measured rise and fall of my own breathing. I can watch the faces of those around me and perhaps prayerfully ask God to intervene for their worried looks or angry eyes. I can settle into the peace that is my inner self and allow God to touch the deepest hidden parts of me.

Creating little rituals within our daily lives helps us to carve out moments of repose and open ourselves to the possibility for kairos to happen. To pause after work, for example, for ten or fifteen minutes, to sit with a cup of tea, and as Macrina Wiederkehr (1991, 172) suggests, to let the faces of those I love rise in the steam before me, in memory and prayer. To stop before beginning my class, my drive, my appointment to let a word or phrase from morning prayer or the day's liturgy rest in my heart and on my tongue. One of the young mothers who comes to our center for direction tells me that in the morning when she is chauffeuring her children to school, she stops at a Marian shrine that sits at the exit to the drive and prays by name for each of her children and their needs of the day. To signal a transition into mindfulness, some people use the lighting of a candle, the chiming of a small bell or gong, the sighting of some reminder like a cross or icon, or the fingering of a rosary ring. In the "old days" when my generation attended elementary school, each classroom had one student in charge of marking the hour with the ringing of a bell. At its peal all the students would stop, put pencils down, and pray a short ejaculation recalling God's presence in the here and now. This brief pause, like the monastic call of the bells to the seven "hours" of prayer throughout the day, helps the busy pedestrian "see the world sub specie aeternitatis: under the aspect of eternity," says Benedictine Brother David Steindl-Rast (quoted in O'Reilly, 1998, H7).

What the practice of mindfulness does to the rhythm of our ordinary days, Sabbath time does for our lives. Sabbath, coming from a root meaning to stop, desist work, is uniquely a Hebrew invention. The writer Cynthia Ozick notes that the Sabbath is not only

> not in nature, it is against nature. In nature all days are alike—the birds continue to fly, the fish to swim, the grass to grow, the beasts to forage, but the Sabbath enters human history as a creation, an invention, a transcendent idea: an idea imposed on, laid over, all of nature's evidences. The Greeks and Romans derided the Jews for observing the Sabbath, conduct so abnormal as to be absurd, and economically wasteful besides. From the pagan point of view, there was no profit in such idleness; Sabbath rest promoted both a household and communal laziness that extended from the cookstove to the cowshed, from employer to the most insignificant employee. For the Greeks and Romans, all days were weekdays. Both masters and slaves were slaves to a clock that never stopped.... The biblical Sabbath stands for liberation. (1997, 138)

The very contradictions to orderly citizenship and efficient production that the Sabbath represents are the heart of the creation of this sacred day by this monotheistic people. What the Sabbath does is to set a day apart, to consecrate it, make it holy, in Hebrew *kadosh,* like the temple inner sanctum and the vessels and vestments used within. The Sabbath anointed according to Yahweh's own decree (Ex 20:8–11) was meant to be free from labor and set apart from routine so that the delights of all that lay within creation could be savored without distraction. Only a life in danger can override the Sabbath's focus on spirituality, community, fellowship, study, remembrance, song, and intimacy.

Every festive Sabbath meal is a celebration of thanksgiving (in Greek, *eucharist*). Every Sabbath day is a freeing from petty concerns of power and powerlessness, profit and loss, win and lose, and, hence, is a mini-commemoration of Jubilee (Lev 25:81–7). And so they decreed: Remember keep holy the Sabbath, the Lord's own day.

But while Sabbath in the past literally meant a day off from daily duties, ordinary activities even, our culture does not invite us to keep Sabbath. Long gone are the blue laws that prohibited stores from opening before noon, that restricted buying of unnecessary items throughout the day. In my early youth I recall how when we vacationed in Ocean City, New Jersey, then a strong and devout Baptist stronghold, even cars had to be moved from the streets to back alleys, garages, and lawns to "keep holy the Sabbath." But these restrictions are mandates of the past.

Today, in order to support a family, in order to keep running the institutions of the community and service its citizens, a father or mother of a family has to work on the Lord's day. And if the parents have Sunday off from their weeklong occupations, other projects must get completed: wash done, errands run, rooms cleaned, food bought for the week ahead, meals prepared. As fewer and fewer social institutions govern their policies and that of their employees according to religious traditions, fewer and fewer people have the leisure to allow a Sabbath day to interrupt the pace of the other six days. So with postmodern industrialism we are more frequently thrown back to the pagan system of no difference among our days, no time off, no work away from work ethic mentality.

The less Sabbath is clearly defined by society's rules, the more Sabbath must become a discipline we mark for ourselves. This is the bottom line that pastor, preacher, wife, and mother Donna Schaper states in her book *Sabbath Sense* (1991). To make Sabbath sense is to carve out for ourselves time and place apart, perhaps on the seventh day of the week, perhaps by necessity at some other time, in between the acts of our life. The delineation of Sabbath as marked by a creative discovery of Sabbath sense has little to do with the name of the day and everything to do with finding the holy ground where we can meet our God. To make Sabbath sense is to claim for ourselves what the world in its profound efficiency and productivity cannot give. It is "anything that makes spacious what is cramped. That makes large out of small, generous out of stingy, simple out of complex, choice out of obligation" (Schaper, 1991, 27). She sees Sabbath sense much like a bridge between the person we must be and the person we strive to be, in the connection between drudgery and beauty, rest and labor.

One of the major elements that factors into the kadosh of Sabbath, its setting apart and making holy, is that of memory. Jesus told his disciples at the first Mass that this was his last supper, so "do this in memory of me" (Lk 22:19). We can carve out our holy time through the hallowing of memory.

One of my earliest recollections of Sundays is waking to the smell of baking bread and cinnamon buns. My family lived for most of my growing years across the street from one of the largest bread companies on the east coast. Throughout the week we could from the first hours of dawn catch the aroma of baking. However, Sunday did indeed mark a special day for on that morning the factory produced its famous cinnamon buns and raisin bread. The smells of syrup, spices, yeast, and warm dough interested me. That provides the nostalgic trigger for images of small girls in starched dresses and straw bonnets climbing into an old blue Plymouth and heading out, fasting and hungry, for early Mass with my Dad. Since this was the only day he had off, Sunday is always a day for memories of doing things with him—going to a park, watching the trains come in at a huge junction near us, having him help us carve soap sculptures for our Egyptian history project. For me then, Sabbath ritual has to do with bread and all its evocation, with connection to family—be that my own nuclear family or my religious community—with time out for doing special things, for wearing my "good clothes" and not doing the tasks that get them soiled.

So one of the suggestions for ministers for whom Sunday is often the busiest day of the week is to create Sabbath by setting aside a block of time when we can relax and renew. It could be an early morning when a walk in a local park around a pond or through woods allows just God and us to "walk in the garden" (Gn 3:8). It could be a Sunday morning before we have to get the doors open for services, or the choir tuned up for liturgy, or the roast in the oven, or whatever. Then we can just sit with a cup of coffee, look out a window on the pink of dawn, or light a candle and just inhale. It could be a few days away—at a beach refuge, a mountain campsite, along a hiking trail when I move away from phone and appointment book, from obligation and duty, to be with my God.

But more even than these special moments of Sabbath solitude, I need to set my Sabbath as the margin of the pages of my days. Then I need to allow the Sabbath moments to appear as so much white space between the paragraphs of my busy life. Even days spent in the punch of time clock and reset button can be transformed with Sabbath pauses. As the clock radio sends out its grating reminder of a new day, we can use the daily headlines to link to the world's starving need for God. Better yet, we can silence the radio and begin our day with a few minutes of quiet communion reserved just for God talk. Then through the day we can stop—for five minutes, ten, for twenty seconds—to catch our breath and inhale the creating spirit breathing over whatever chaos, darkness, void, lack of promise yawns before us. We can call upon Ruah to come and inspire us and all that surrounds and at times overwhelms us.

For the past several years, as I begin my college classes, I have moved from opening with some formal prayer and instead call the students to a few moments of quiet. At times I begin with a short phrases from scripture, poetry, the daily headlines. But most often I just ask that we spend the brief period in silence centering into the place within each of us where we find our God—now. My decision to undertake this centering form of prayer comes from a Sabbath sense of the need we have in our hectic, sound-barraged society for peace, pause, and refreshment. I had little idea if the silence spoke to anyone but me, or if the students appreciated or disliked the experience until one day several years into the effort. The class had a major test scheduled that day, and, since many arrived on time and others a few minutes after, I distributed the papers haphazardly and let each one begin as soon as he or she was seated. A short period into the session a young woman called me over. Thinking she had some question about wording on the test, I went over to her desk. She looked up and said, "Sister, aren't we going to begin with our quiet prayer? I really need that time today to settle in with God and I do it so much better when all of us join together."

Finally, in searching for Sabbath sense, this student's comment underscores an important aspect. As social beings part of our need for entering into the sacred is to do it as a part of community. It is in the connectedness we have one to the other that a sharing in the God who is trinity, unity, and community can be experienced. When the Lord commanded the commemoration of Jubilee, it was as a people that Yahweh called the Israelites. The blasts of silver trumpets announced the endurance of the covenant and recalled fidelity within relationships (Lev 25). As such, it was the community who enjoyed the healing, reconciliation, and thanksgiving that Jubilee brought. And as such, in the year of restoration all grudges were to be forgiven, slaves freed, debts canceled, and all that had been bought, traded, or stolen, restored.

For the minister who seeks a healing in time and who looks expectantly for the fulfilling of all time, a call to Sabbath is a call to social awareness, community presence, and strengthening of bonds of relationship. In a lovely poem called *Siostra* or *Sister,* written by Pope John Paul II long before his pontificate, under the pen name Stanislaw Andrzej Gruda, he lyrically celebrates so many of the themes of time, especially that of the call to community (1982, 170–71). In his second and third sections, the papal poet writes,

> We are always having to clear the paths, / they will be overgrown
>   again;
> they have to be cleared until they are simple / with the mature
>   simplicity of every moment:
> for each moment opens the wholeness of time, / as if it stood
>   whole above itself.
> You find in it the seeds of eternity.
> When I call you sister / I think that each meeting
> contains not only the communion of moments, / but the seed of the
>   same eternity.

Selected References and Suggested Reading

Ernst, Cornelius. (1974). *A Theology of Grace*. Notre Dame, Ind.: Fides Publishers.

Layton, Molly. (1995). "Mastering Mindfulness." *Networker*, November–December, 28–30+.

O'Reilly, David. (1998). "Making Each Hour Count." *Philadelphia Inquirer*, August 16, H7.

Ozick, Cynthia. (1997). "Remember the Sabbath Day, to Keep It Holy." *Self,* December, 138.

Pryzbilla, Carla. (1997). "Entrainment." *New Life Center Newsletter*. Middleburg, Va.: Fall, 9.

Rabuzzi, Kathryn Allen. (1982). *The Sacred and the Feminine*. New York, N.Y.: Seabury.

Ryan, Michael. (1998). "Are You Living Mindlessly?" *Parade*, March 1, 8–9.

Schaper, Donna. (1991). *Sabbath Sense: A Spiritual Antidote for the Overworked*. Philadelphia, Penn.: Innisfree Press.

Weaver, Frances. (1996). *The Girls with Grandmother Faces*. New York, N.Y.: Hyperion.

Weil, Simone. (1950). *Waiting on God*. London: Fontana Books.

Wiederkehr, Macrina. (1991). *Seasons of Your Heart: Prayers and Reflections*. San Francisco, Calif.: Harper.

Wojtyla, Pope John Paul II. (1982). *The Place Within*. Trans. Jerzy Peterkiewic. New York, N.Y.: Random House.

Michael W. Blastic

17. Attentive Compassion: Franciscan Resources for Ministry

The Franciscan tradition is communicated best in story. Narrative theologians point out that what is most personal can only be communicated by the person's own story, his or her own life. A definition or description of the identity of any person falls short of what a story can communicate about the identity of a person. The gospels are stories of Jesus, and communicate much more about the identity of Jesus than dogmatic formulations that define him as truly divine and truly human. Francis learned the meaning of Christ from the story of the gospels. He learned the meaning of Jesus so well that he was called "the gospel of the poor." Thus, to attempt to uncover Franciscan resources for a ministerial spirituality, it seems best to start with stories.

Many of the most engaging stories about Francis and Clare are handed down in the *Fioretti,* or *Little Flowers of St. Francis.* The text as we have it goes back to the fourteenth century, to the Italian province of the Marches, and the friars and sisters who cherished the memory of Francis and Clare together with the way things were at the beginning of the order. While the historical nucleus of the stories goes back to the actual lifetime of Francis and Clare, the process of retelling and remembering has transformed the historical nucleus into a mythic account of the story of the Franciscan movement. As a result of this process, though mythical, these stories do communicate fundamental insights and truths about the nature of Franciscan life and ministry. The following story of "How St. Francis converted three murderous robbers" is a story about attentive compassion, the heart of ministry in the Franciscan tradition.

The story takes place without a specific historical context or time. It begins with Francis traveling through the Marches, where he came upon a young nobleman, who at first sight seemed to Francis to be too delicate to live the life of rigorous poverty demanded by the order. But the young man pleaded for a chance, and Francis accepted him and gave him the name Brother Angelo. Not long after his reception, Brother Angelo was appointed the guardian of the hermitage, Monte Casale. The story depends on this background of Angelo as someone new to the Franciscan community, as his behavior would demonstrate:

> At this time there were in that area three famous robbers who
> committed many crimes thereabouts. One day those robbers came
> to the Place of the friars, and they asked Brother Angelo, the
> guardian, to give them something to eat. And the guardian
> answered, scolding them severely: "You robbers and cruel mur-
> derers—not only are you not ashamed of stealing from others the
> fruit of their labor, but in your audacity you even dare to eat up the
> offerings which have been given to the servants of God! You do
> not deserve that the earth should bear you up, for you respect no
> man and you scorn God who created you! So go about your busi-
> ness—and don't you ever come back here!"

Of course, the robbers didn't appreciate the treatment they received, while
Brother Angelo thought he handled the situation perfectly. In his enthusiasm
and conviction of having acted rightly, and thus demonstrating his worthiness
to be guardian of the friars, Angelo rushes into the account of his actions looking for affirmation from Francis:

> That same day St. Francis came back to the Place carrying a sack
> of bread and a little jug of wine which he had begged with his
> companions. And when the guardian told how he had driven the
> robbers away, St. Francis scolded him severely, saying: "You
> acted in a cruel way, because sinners are led back to God by holy
> meekness better than by cruel scolding. For our Master Jesus
> Christ, whose gospel we have promised to observe, says that the
> doctor is not needed by those who are well but by the sick, and 'I
> have come to call not the just but sinners to penance,' and there-
> fore He often ate with them. So, since you acted against charity
> and against the example of Jesus Christ, I order you under holy
> obedience to take right now this sack of bread and jug of wine
> which I begged. Go and look carefully for those robbers over the
> mountains and valleys until you find them. And offer them all this
> bread and this wine for me. And then kneel down before them and
> humbly accuse yourself of your sin of cruelty. And then ask them
> in my name not to do those evil things any more, but to fear God,
> and not to offend their neighbors. And if they do so, I promise
> them that I will supply them with provisions for their needs and I
> will give them food and drink all the time. And when you have
> humbly told them that, come back here.

Brother Angelo did as he was told. He found the robbers and offered them
the bread and wine and confessed his fault before them. He has learned an
important lesson about Franciscan identity and style of ministry. But more

than this, Angelo's confession of his fault effects a change on the part of the robbers:

> And it pleased God that while those robbers were eating the gifts which St. Francis had sent them, they began to say to one another: "What terrible tortures are waiting in hell for us who are such miserable and unhappy men! For we go around not merely robbing and beating and wounding our neighbors but also killing them! And yet we feel no fear of God or remorse of conscience over those horrible crimes and murders that we commit here. But here is this holy friar who just came to us because of a few words which he said to us quite rightly on account of our wickedness, and he very humbly accused himself of his fault before us. And besides, he brought us a very generous promise of the holy Father and charitably gave us the bread and wine. Those friars really are saints of God, and they deserve Paradise."

The initial experience of vindication gives way to recrimination—the robbers recognize their wretched condition with every bite of bread and drink of wine. The robbers have no hope to hold on to—it is their belief that their behavior has disqualified them as recipients of God's mercy. They do, however, decide to go back to Francis to see if there is any hope for them, determined to carry out anything that Francis might tell them:

> And so they went in haste to St. Francis and said to him: "Father, because of our many great sins we do not believe we can obtain mercy from God, but if you have confidence that God will have mercy on us, we are ready to do penance with you and to obey you in whatever you command us." St. Francis made them welcome with kindness and holy affection, and he consoled them by telling them many inspiring true stories, and he gave them back assurance that they would win God's mercy. He also taught them how the infinite greatness of divine mercy surpasses all our sins, even if they are boundless, and how, according to the Gospels and St. Paul the Apostle, Christ came into this world in order to redeem sinners.

The story concludes by relating that these robbers renounced the world and the devil and his works, and St. Francis received each of them into the order. Each lived a life of holiness, doing great penance.[1] The key to understanding Francis the minister is contained in a simple phrase: "St. Francis made them welcome with kindness and holy affection."

This story captures three foundational aspects of the Franciscan approach to ministry, which at the same time describe the spirituality of Franciscans—Franciscan spirituality is a ministerial spirituality! The three points concerning ministry which emerge from this story are (1) the poverty of the human condition; (2) the incarnation as God's gratuitous embrace of created goodness; and (3) sitting down at table in the kingdom of God. Each of these in turn describe the context for Franciscan life and ministry as modeled in the story.

Poverty and the Human Condition

The story revolves around a very basic, common, human experience—that of human need. The robbers normally satisfy their need by simply taking what they want without respect for person, place, or thing. In this case, contrary to their usual method, instead of simply taking what they need, they knock at the door of the friars and ask for something to eat. In his response to them, Brother Angelo does not seem able to move beyond the notorious reputation of the robbers. He scolds them for their audacity in coming to such a holy place, he points out their faults and sins, but he misses what brought the robbers to him, their basic human need. Francis was able to see beyond the reputation of the robbers, even to see beyond their sin. Francis was able to recognize the basic human need that occasioned the encounter, and Francis responds to that, and only to that. Further, for Francis, the human need of the robbers becomes the occasion for preaching the gospel by following the example of Jesus who ate and drank with sinners. Ultimately it is Francis's attention and response to their basic human need that brings about change in the robbers themselves.

Stories like that of the three robbers could be multiplied as one reads through the vast amount of hagiographical material surrounding the figure of Francis and the origins of the Franciscan movement in the thirteenth century. But common to most of these stories and memories of Francis and the early days of the order lies a very basic insight into the human condition that is shared by all regardless of gender, race, culture, status, or location. All humans share the same basic needs, and even more specifically, the basic human condition is one of poverty—the most difficult truth to accept about ourselves is that we are insufficient by ourselves. We have needs that we cannot satisfy for ourselves—each one of us is dependent ultimately on the Other, God, who alone can satisfy the desires of the human heart. For Francis, though, this is not something negative because the corollary to the human condition is the goodness of God—human need is met by the divine abundance. Francis becomes lyrical about this experience of the generous fullness of God:

And let us refer all good to the most high and supreme lord God,
   and acknowledge that every good is His,
   and thank him for everything, He from Whom all good things
      come.
And may He,
   the Highest and Supreme,
   Who alone is true God,
   have and be given and receive
      every honor and reverence,
      every praise and blessing
      every thanks and glory,
for every good is His,
He who alone is good. (Early Rule XVII:17–18)[2]

Francis refers here to God as good not in an abstract or ontological sense but in a very practical and concrete sense—God is the source of every concrete good that sustains humans in life—from him "all good things come." Every day at every moment humans are the beneficiaries of the generosity of God—they are at home in creation!

The bread and wine that Francis begged and gives to the robbers thus has God as the source. Francis becomes an instrument of God in sharing this goodness with the robbers in their need. But the crucial point here is that Francis stands with the robbers, on the same level, in their need. Francis does not place himself above the robbers as Brother Angelo did. Rather, Francis recognizes his own need in the need of the robbers. A need can only be met if it is expressed and recognized as such. To be ontologically poor is to say that the human person is fashioned to be receptive, to receive from outside oneself what one needs most for existence. The verb *receive* is one of the most frequent words used by Francis—it reflects Francis's own acceptance of the basic human condition. It also allows God to provide for the need of the robbers, through the instrumentality of Francis—the pieces of bread and the wine Francis begged was provided by God who is good and the source of all good. It is this awareness of the common human condition that is the starting point for both Franciscan ministry and Franciscan spirituality.

Another dimension of this fundamental insight into the human condition is expressed in Francis's description of the mission of the friars to the nonbelievers. The Franciscan Rule is the first religious rule that included mission beyond the Christian world in its basic project of life. There are a number of extant accounts of how Francis met the Sultan after the disastrous Fifth Crusade in August 1219, each of which underlines the positive impression Francis made on the Sultan. But the real significance of the event gets expressed in chapter 16 of the Early Rule, where Francis describes how the friars are to carry out this mission in response to divine inspiration:

> As for the brothers who go, they can live spiritually among [the Saracens and nonbelievers] in two ways. One way is not to engage in arguments or disputes, but to be subject *to every human creature for God's sake* (1 Peter 2:13) and to acknowledge that they are Christians. Another way is to proclaim the word of God when they see that it pleases the Lord.... And all the brothers, wherever they may be, should remember that they gave themselves and abandoned their bodies to the lord Jesus Christ. And for love of Him, they must make themselves vulnerable to their enemies, both visible and invisible.... (Early Rule, XVI:5–7, 10–11; pp. 121–22)

Francis distinguishes himself from the approach taken in the crusades by emphasizing that the first way to be a missionary is to "live among" nonbelievers without argument or dispute and to be subject to them, simply acknowledging that this manner of life is Christian. In other words, the theological insight that emerges here is that humanity is the common ground, is the primary and basic dimension of mission. "To be subject to every human creature" implies a stance of equality, of not claiming rights for oneself over and above the people one meets. It brings one back to the human condition that everyone shares—this, for Francis, is what it means to acknowledge that they are Christians, that they are human. Only when friars have accomplished this radical stance of being subject, of sharing the human condition, does it become possible to proclaim the Word of God, when it is pleasing to God. Here Francis implies that it is not proselytism that is the primary purpose of the missionary, but rather, the primary duty of the missionary is to establish common human bonds and relationships that qualify as Christian. The word that the friar would address to nonbelievers, when it pleases God, would further uncover the plan of God in Jesus who ate and drank with sinners. The preached word of example and sermon simply names the grace that is present in every truly human encounter.

Finally, in mission all friars are to make themselves vulnerable to their enemies—that is, they must not be hardened by resistance, but remain open, receptive, permeable, and sensitive. This chapter of the rule concludes with a collage of gospel texts that emphasize that the behavior of the friars must be modeled on that of Jesus, "for through your patience, you will possess your souls" (Early Rule, XVI:20; p. 122).[3] All of this directs the friar to what is most basic and essential in his approach to life and ministry, that is, the acceptance of the human condition in which everyone is equal before God.

The source for this stance toward ministry and life Francis reads in the gospel stories of Jesus, and Francis speaks about the implications of this stance toward life often. In an early Franciscan text, the *Legend of the Three Companions,* Francis speaks to the friars gathered in chapter in the following words:

> "The general behavior among the people must be such that all who see or hear them may be drawn to glorify our heavenly Father and to praise him devoutly." His great desire was that he and his brothers should abound in good works for which men give glory and praise to God. He also said to the brothers: "Since you speak of peace, all the more so must you have it in your hearts. Let none be provoked to anger or scandal by you, but rather may they be drawn to peace and good will, to benignity and concord through your gentleness. We have been called to heal wounds, to unite what has fallen apart, and to bring home those who have lost their way. Many who seem to us to be children of the Devil will still become Christ's disciples." (*Legend of the Three Companions,* par. 58; *Omnibus,* pp. 942–43)

One can read these words of Francis as a commentary on the story of the three robbers. Francis understood the mission of the friars to be about reconciliation and peacemaking. The life of the brothers should be enough to bring others to praise God before even a word is spoken. It is the behavior of the brothers, their way of being in the world, that is to preach the gospel. This is what Francis was trying to teach Angelo in ordering him to seek out the robbers and ask their forgiveness of his behavior toward them. Again, the focus on human behavior comes to the fore in the story. This is the matrix for living the gospel. What Francis comes to recognize is that the gospel, the example of Jesus is all about what it means to be human.

The Incarnation: God's Embrace of Creation

In the story of the three robbers, Francis characterized the initial reaction of Brother Angelo as going against charity and the example of Jesus Christ, who ate and drank with sinners. In fact, the whole of Franciscan life is understood by Francis to be nothing more than "following in the footsteps of Jesus Christ."[4] But the point here to note is that Francis does not reprimand Angelo for failing to convict the robbers of their sin. Francis does not congratulate Angelo for getting it right in telling the robbers that they don't deserve to have the earth support them because of their sin. What Francis does challenge Angelo on is his failure in basic, simple, Christian charity, and thus, his failure to follow the example of Christ.

The Franciscan theological and spiritual tradition is consistently described as a Christocentric tradition. The story of the three robbers points to this as the background for understanding the actions of Francis. The incarnate Christ is at the center of Francis's faith and life. But here it is important to underline how Francis understood the incarnation of Jesus, because his approach was new in his day.

For Francis, the incarnation is not about a distant God hiding himself in a kind of generic human form. For Francis, God becomes incarnate as the result of a deliberate choice of a very specific kind of human flesh that God chooses for God's embodiment. He writes in his Letter to the Faithful:

> Through his angel, Saint Gabriel, the most high Father in heaven announced this Word of the Father—so worthy, so holy and glorious—in the womb of the holy and glorious Virgin Mary, from which He received the flesh of humanity and our frailty. Though *He was rich* beyond all other things (2 Cor 8:9), in this world He, together with the most blessed Virgin, His mother, willed to choose poverty." (Second Version of the Letter to the Faithful 4–5; p. 67)

What is striking in these lines is the emphasis Francis gives to the concrete shape of the incarnation—it is not enough to say Christ took on the "flesh of humanity." Francis makes the description even more particular and real when he adds to the flesh of humanity the qualification of "our frailty." For Francis, Jesus was not ultimately different from us, but "willed to choose poverty" as the way to be human. In other words, the concrete circumstances surrounding the birth of Jesus as recorded by the evangelists are not merely accidental, but are essential to the reality of the humanity assumed by God in Jesus, and thus are constitutive of the meaning of the incarnation. The emphasis on the poverty of the incarnation is further highlighted by the contrast between the "worthy, holy and glorious" existence of the word with God who was "rich beyond all other things" and the frailty and poverty of the human condition embraced.

It is this focus on the human condition of the Word made flesh which captivated Francis and made the "form of gospel" the rule of life for Franciscans. In celebrating the feast of the nativity, the psalm Francis composed for that day includes the following verses:

> This is the day that the Lord has made, let us rejoice and be glad in it. For the most holy beloved child was given to us, and He was born for us along the way and placed in a manger since there was no room in the inn.… Take up your bodies and carry his holy cross and follow his most holy commands even to the end. (Office of the Passion, Psalm XV:6–7; 13; pp. 97–98)[5]

The celebration of the incarnation leads Francis to the embrace of his own human condition by taking up his own body, carrying the cross, and following

Jesus, because this is what Jesus chose and did. The incarnation is God giving God's self to humanity and creation. The incarnation is a positive affirmation of the goodness of creation—how better to affirm the dignity and goodness of something than by becoming one with it? Francis is in awe at what God did for humanity in the incarnation, and at what God continues to do for him today.

For Francis, the incarnation is redemptive—the embrace of the human condition is its completion and salvation even before any mention of sin. The companions of Francis recount that Francis's favorite feast was Christmas, and that he used to say, "Because he was born for us, we knew we would be saved."[6] The difference between the responses of Francis and Angelo to the three robbers finds their source in different perspectives on the incarnation. When Brother Angelo saw the three robbers, he saw sin, something that disqualified their need. When Francis saw the three robbers, he saw three men who had a need, and it would not be pushing the analogy too far to say that when Francis saw the three robbers he saw Jesus Christ, who took on our frailty and poverty. Clearly, Francis did not ignore the fact that they were sinners, but he begins at the human level of need, and by satisfying that need without condemnation or critique the robbers are moved to conversion. Here, the "Because he was born for us, we knew we would be saved," comes into play. The incarnation did not take place because of human sin. Rather, the incarnation was the affirmation of the goodness of the created world and God's wanting to bring that work to completion in Jesus. Jesus shows humanity and creation their true meaning. His pattern of life unlocks the meaning of creation and the meaning of ministry for the Franciscan.

It was the Franciscan John Duns Scotus (+1308) who would develop these intuitions of Francis into the theological position of the absolute predestination of Christ. Scotus affirmed that the incarnation was the highest and most noble work of God, and to make this conditional on human sin would be to trivialize its meaning. For Scotus, the incarnation was predestined from eternity to bring the work of creation to completion in Jesus Christ.[7] Even if humans had not sinned, there would be an incarnation to bring creation to completion through the divine embodiment of Jesus. There is a creation so that there can be an incarnation of love, and the incarnation is God's embrace of creation, of the human condition in particular.

The corollary to this approach to the incarnation is that creation exists for Christ. Thus, the primary revelation of God is creation—even after sin, scripture is given to humans to help them read creation, the first book of God, correctly, but scripture does not replace creation as the primary revelation of God.[8] Here, Francis's *Canticle of Brother Sun,* a hymn of praise and thanksgiving for the concrete reality of creation, celebrates a creation established in relationship as the reflection of the creator, a relationship of persons, Father, Son, and Spirit. Humans are invited by Francis to enter into the hymn of creation by becoming what they see, by simply being creation—"Praise and bless the Lord and give Him thanks and serve Him with great humility" (Canticle, 14; p. 39).

Reflecting back on the story of the three robbers one can see this incarnational perspective of Francis reflected in his behavior. For Francis, Angelo missed the point when he could only see the sin of the robbers. He missed the opportunity for salvation by focusing on their sin and therefore of their unworthiness. In satisfying their human need, by sending Angelo with the bread and wine, Francis was offering the opportunity for salvation. In fact, as the robbers ate the bread and wine, as their need was filled, they came to a clearer awareness of how they have missed the point and become guilty in their actions.

The perspective one takes on the meaning of the incarnation makes a significant impact on the understanding of ministry that flows from that meaning. To understand the incarnation as occasioned by human sin and having the primary purpose of atoning for that sin—the perspective of Anselm of Canterbury and the "Satisfaction Theory"—would suggest that the primary purpose of ministry is the overcoming and elimination of sin. To understand the incarnation as bringing creation to completion—the perspective of the Franciscan tradition—would suggest, on the contrary, that ministry is primarily about fostering genuine humanness in the pattern of Jesus Christ.[9] The implications of this perspective on the incarnation are vast and far-reaching when it comes to understanding Christian life and ministry. As the story suggests, Francis is simply present to the robbers in their human condition. His response to their condition occasions the grace of conversion, but the offer of salvation is made to the robbers in the gift of bread and wine, not in addition to it. The robbers are invited to accept the human condition as one of need by receiving from the source of all that is good. It is not so much what one does, but how one is attentively present to the other that becomes the primary expression of ministry.

It seems that the crucial experience that led Francis to this intuition about the meaning of the incarnation was the experience that occasioned his own conversion. Francis writes in his Testament,

> The Lord granted me, Brother Francis, to begin to do penance in this way: While I was in sin, it seemed very bitter to me to see lepers. And the Lord Himself led me among them and I had mercy upon them. And when I left them that which seemed bitter to me was changed into sweetness of soul and body; and afterward I lingered a little and left the world. (Testament 1–3; p. 154)

Until Francis met the leper, he was going about the construction of his life according to the values of his world, the merchant's world of the commune of Assisi. The life of the young Francis was comfortable and indulgent. Money, the right friends, the right clothes, the pleasure money could buy, glory and achievement—these were the values and characteristics of a person of worth and importance, which Francis was trying to become.

The leper was the antithesis to this myth of Assisi—for Assisi the leper did not really exist because the leper was not a real human being, and thus, the leper was to be avoided and excluded. This world of Assisi was destroyed with a simple embrace of a leper. And Francis understood this unplanned encounter as something that God did for Francis, not as something Francis did for himself. In the suffering leper Francis came to see the real human condition—if there was one leper, we could all be lepers. Even more than this, the leper was Christ, as Francis would come to recognize. The condition of the leper was the human condition that Jesus embraced in the incarnation—from Mary he received humanity and "our frailty." All that Assisi tried to do to disguise this fundamental truth became meaningless to Francis—what Assisi counted as sweet became bitter to Francis, and what was bitter to Assisi became sweet to Francis. Francis leaves the world of Assisi to live with the lepers and the beggars along the way, because that is where Jesus chose to live. The incarnation is God's ministry to creation. To be present to others is to offer salvation—that is the meaning of incarnation for Francis, and it is the motivation and method for ministry for Francis.[10]

Bread and Wine in the Kingdom of God

Attentive to the human need of the robbers, Francis offers them bread and wine. It is the taste of the bread and wine that moves the robbers to conversion. Bread and wine are universal symbols of the human need for nourishment. In the Christian tradition, and in the experience of Francis, bread and wine are eucharistic elements, and it would be difficult to ignore this connection in the story.

For Francis, the incarnation is continued in the celebration of the eucharist. He writes in the first of his admonitions:

> See, daily He humbles himself (cf. Phil 2:8) as when he came from *the royal throne* (Wis 18:15) into the womb of the Virgin; daily He comes to us in a humble form; daily he comes down from the bosom of the Father (cf. Jn 1:18) upon the altar in the hands of the priest.... And in this way the Lord is always with his faithful, as He Himself says: *Behold I am with you even to the end of the world* (cf. Mt 28:20). [Admonition I: 16–18, 22; pp. 26–27]

The mystery of the eucharist has as its primary meaning the continuation and the completion of the incarnation and God's desire to be with what God creates—the eucharist is the mystery of God's presence!

Francis emphasizes here the importance of seeing this mystery and recognizing its meaning. Medieval men and women seemed to focus on seeing
the consecrated host rather than on participating in eucharistic communion—it
was enough to see to be saved because in fact humans were not worthy enough
to approach the altar. The Fourth Lateran Council had to legislate that Christians receive communion at least once a year! But, Francis does not stay at this
external level with regard to the eucharist. In fact, he makes the eucharist the
center of his mission. He writes to the members of the Order in these words:

> Give praise to [God] *since He is good* (Ps 135:1) and *exalt* Him *by
> your deeds* (Tob 13:6), for He has sent you into the entire world
> for this reason: that in word and deed you may give witness to His
> voice and bring everyone to know that there is *no one who is all-
> powerful* except Him (Tob 13:4).... Therefore..., I implore all of
> you brothers to show all possible reverence and honor to the most
> holy Body and Blood of our Lord Jesus Christ in Whom that
> which is in the heavens and on the earth is brought to peace and is
> reconciled to the all-powerful God (cf. Col 1:20). [Letter to the
> Entire Order 8–9, 12–13; p. 56]

Francis's insight into the meaning of the eucharist leads him to the affirmation
that the mission of the brothers is eucharistic, that mission pertains to that peace
and reconciliation that are achieved in mystery of the eucharist. The bread and
wine of the eucharist symbolize what is happening in the world before our
eyes—everything is being transformed, even if not visibly or at first sight, into
the kingdom of God. The bread and the wine offered to the robbers become the
occasion for recognizing the gift of salvation, which is peace and reconciliation. Thus, far from a sentimental or simplistic devotional attitude, the eucharist
for Francis is the motive and means for mission and ministry. As he told the
brothers gathered, the Franciscan call is to unite what has fallen apart, to bring
home those who have lost their way, and to heal wounds. It all begins with a
piece of bread and some wine. In that simple, basic response to human need, the
kingdom is realized and made present and salvation is offered.

Implications for Ministry

In a recent book by C. H. Lawrence, *The Friars,*[11] the author vividly
describes the development of the Franciscan Order in the course of the thirteenth century from a small group of itinerant beggars to a major institutional
force and voice in the church. Lawrence concludes that it was the mendicants
that saved the cities for the church, for without the mendicant presence in the

cities, they would have been lost to heresy. Two fundamental points emerge from Lawrence's work that are appropriate to the issue of Franciscan ministry.

First, a reading of Lawrence's book suggests that the friars were successful ministers because they responded to the reality of the world as they found it. They did not arrive on the scene with a preconceived method of analysis or solution to theoretical problems that they would simply apply to the present situation. Rather, the success of the friars was due to their attentiveness to the needs of the people of their day.

Franciscan ministry is not limited by specific tasks or projects defined in a rule, but Franciscan ministry is defined by the quality of presence the friars and sisters bring to the situation. Further, the quality of Franciscan presence was characterized by what one might describe as ministerial virtues which include the following: *approachability*—they were not distant from the people they met; *adaptability*—they adapted to the situation rather than trying to change the situation; *creativity*—they did not fall back on only tried and true methods but created new responses to new situations; *responsibility*—they were responsible to the people they served, and were accountable for their presence; and *resiliency*—they did not give up easily. It was especially their resiliency that was noticed as they did not try to change or renew the ecclesiastical structures, "They simply by-passed it" to respond to the human need in the situation (Lawrence, 221).

These virtues should be added to the list of the Franciscan virtues of poverty, simplicity, and humility, which have traditionally characterized Franciscan life, and this leads to a second point that emerges from a reading of Lawrence. A large part of the success of the friars comes from the fact that the friars were not experienced to be different from the ordinary people of the towns. The friars did not define themselves against the faithful as "religious," but simply as "men of penance from Assisi." The friars spoke the same language as the people, conversed in the same idioms. The friars did not dress like clerics, but wore the garb of the ordinary peasant. In short, the friars presented themselves to the people as of the people—the "lay" quality of life was to the fore, and they fostered a lay spirituality. As Lawrence remarks,

> The new version of the religious life created by the Friars Minor and the Preachers deeply affected the way thirteenth century people thought about the Christian vocation. No subsequent religious organization could entirely escape their influence. The ideas they represented—that it was possible for the committed Christian to be in the world yet not of it, that in this world the appropriate condition of those who aspired to the Kingdom of God was one of simplicity and poverty, and that the imitation of Christ involved an

active mission of evangelization and service to the poor—proved
to be as dynamic as they were dangerous. (Lawrence, 89)

This connection with and to the lay Christian is essential to the meaning and
impact of the friars minor. It is another way of suggesting that Franciscan ministry is all about attention to human need. Attention to human need presumes
presence to the other. Authentic human need invites a response of compassion.
This, for Francis, was what the incarnation was all about—it was and is the
way God ministers to God's creation. All we have to do is follow the pattern
that can be discerned in the example of Jesus' life, who was born so that we
might be saved.

A final note about the relationship between spirituality and ministry in
the Franciscan tradition is in order here. The story of Francis and the three robbers demonstrates the close connection between an understanding of the incarnation and the stance one takes toward the other in ministry. But the
connection between the two is much deeper than merely at the level of understanding. Go back to the story of Francis's encounter with the leper. This
encounter, as described by Francis, resulted in a new understanding of what it
means to be human for Francis, and this was connected with Francis's recognition of Christ the leper, especially as presented in the passion narratives of the
gospels. But something much more profound than intellectual conversion took
place for Francis. The language Francis uses to describe his encounter and
embrace of the leper is language that the Western Christian tradition associates
with the mystical experience of God—sweetness/bitterness and transformation. What Francis tries to articulate in those lines from his Testament is that
when he embraced the leper, Francis was embracing God in a very intimate
and concrete way. To be sure, the leper was not simply a symbol, but a very
real suffering human person. When Francis was able to move out of himself
and open himself radically to the reality of the leper, the "other," Francis
encountered God there in that embrace.

What Francis describes here using his own experience is very different
from the tradition that dominated the West until that moment, which privileged the experience of finding God at the top of a mountain, or at the highest
rung of a ladder. These metaphors, emerging from a neo-Platonic worldview
that was adapted by Augustine in his *Confessions* as a pattern for Christian
conversion, suggest that somehow one cannot have both God and the world,
that it must be one or the other—both mountain peak and ladder suggest dis-
connection or separation from the earth.[12] In a sense, what Francis claims
about his own religious experience is that you can have both God and the
world; it is not an either/or proposition. Where do you find God? You find him
in the other, the one near you right now, the one inviting your attention at any
given moment. Francis replaces the metaphor of mountain and ladder with that

of the "footprint"—following footprints demands that one keep both feet and eyes on the ground. This demands, in turn, both attention and presence and describes the dynamic of Franciscan ministry.

The story of the three robbers teaches attentive compassion as the Franciscan method of ministry. Bread and wine offered in response to need are much more than simply bread and wine—they offer a taste of the kingdom of God if received with genuine openness to the goodness of God, who supplies everything that is good. The primary Franciscan resource for ministry is the incarnation of Jesus, which affirms the human condition as the locus for God's presence with creation.

Notes

1. This story can be found in the *Little Flowers of St. Francis,* in: *St. Francis of Assisi: Omnibus of Sources,* Marion Habig, ed. (Chicago: Franciscan Herald Press, 1973): 1360–67.

2. The English translation of the writings of Francis are taken from Regis Armstrong, Ignatius Brady, *Francis and Clare: The Complete Works* (New York: Paulist, 1982), here p. 123. References to the writings of Francis will be followed by page numbers from this edition of the writings.

3. Francis writes in another passage of the same rule, "Let us pay attention, all my brothers, to what the Lord says: *Love your enemies* and *do good to those who hate you* (Mt. 5:44), for our Lord Jesus Christ, Whose footprints we must follow (1 Peter 2:21), called His betrayer 'friend' (cf. Mt 26:50) and gave Himself willingly to those who crucified Him" (Early Rule XXII1–2). It has been suggested that this chapter of the Early Rule might have been a final testament Francis left his brothers when he journeyed to the Near East in 1219 fully expecting to be martyred for the faith.

4. "The rule and the life of these brothers is this: to live in obedience, in chastity, and without anything of their own, and to follow the teaching and footprints of our Lord Jesus Christ" (Early Rule I:1; p. 109). Francis puts this another way in one of his final writings: "And after the Lord gave me brothers, no one showed me what I should do, but the Most High himself revealed to me that I should live according to the form of the Holy Gospel" (Testament, 14; pp. 154–55). Both expressions make it clear that Francis is not suggesting some abstract pattern of thought as model for the life, but rather, the concrete actions of Jesus Christ as recorded in the Gospels become the "form" that the friars are to follow.

5. Here I have corrected the Armstrong-Brady translation based on the Latin critical edition of Kajetan Esser.

6. "As a matter of fact, blessed Francis had a greater respect for the solemnity of Christmas than for the other feasts of the Lord. Our salvation is

effected in the other feasts but, he said, from the day our Savior was born it became certain that we would be saved! And so on this day he wanted every Christian to exult in the Lord, and, for love of him who gave us the gift of himself, joyfully to give handsome presents not only to the poor but also to the domestic animals and birds" (Legend of Perugia, 110; *Omnibus,* p. 1086).

7. For a synthesis of Scotus's position, and the texts consult, "Allan Wolter, "John Duns Scotus on the Primacy and Personality of Christ," in: *Franciscan Christology,* Damian McElrath, ed. (Franciscan Institute Press, 1980): 139–82. A translation of the text from Scotus's *Ordinatio* on the predestination of Christ can be found on pp. 153–55.

8. This aspect of the Franciscan tradition is developed by Zachary Hayes, "Christ, Word of God and Exemplar of Humanity," *The Cord* 46, 1 (1996): 3–17. Consult also, Ibid., "Christology—Cosmology," in *Franciscan Leadership in Ministry: Foundations in History, Theology, and Spirituality,* (Franciscan Institute Publications, 1997) [*Spirit and Life* 7 (1997)]: 41–58.

9. For a first attempt to think through the implications of the Scotist position for ministry and mission, consult Margaret Eletta Guider, "Foundations for a Theology of Presence: A Consideration of the Scotist Understanding of the Primary Purpose of the Incarnation and its Relevance for Ministry in the Underworld of the World Church," *Cord* 43, 3 (1993): 71–79.

10. For a more developed presentation of the Franciscan theological tradition as the source for the approach to ministry taken in this essay, consult Michael Blastic, "'It Pleases Me That You Should Teach Sacred Theology': Franciscans Doing Theology," *Franciscan Studies* 55 (1998): 1–25.

11. C. H. Lawrence, *The Friars: The Impact of the Early Mendicant Movement on Western Society* (London: Longman, 1994). The book studies all of the mendicant communities established in the thirteenth century, but the primary attention is given to the Franciscans and the Dominicans throughout the book. My comments are reflections focused on what he has to suggest about the Franciscans in the thirteenth century.

12. This dimension of the Franciscan tradition has been developed more fully by me in my article, "Contemplation and Compassion: A Franciscan Ministerial Spirituality," in *Franciscan Leadership in Ministry: Foundations in History, Theology and Spirituality* (Franciscan Institute Publications, 1997) [*Spirit and Life* 7 (1997)]: 149–77.

18. Chaos and Creation

Riveted by the alarm of acute danger, I concentrated on the snake. I desperately repeated to myself the rhyme all country Florida children learn: "Red-on-yellow, kill a fellow; red-on-black, your friend, Jack." The harmless King snake has the same color markings as the deadly coral snake, but the bands alternate in a different order. This snake, five feet away from where my grandson was playing with his toy cars on the front step, was definitely red-on-yellow. I had been told that a toddler would have little chance of surviving the bite of a coral snake.

A shovel was leaning against the side of the house where I could stretch to reach it. Moving more quietly than I ever had in my whole life, trying not to warn the snake, I closed my fingers around the shovel handle. I raised it slowly in the air and brought the edge down on the snake in one breath, chopping it in half. The baby kept playing, making his little car sounds, paying no attention. The contrast of his simple trusting movements and the halves of the deadly snake still coiling under the shovel made me so weak I had to sit on the ground. Chaos had almost broken in.

In recent years I have had a heightened awareness of the presence of chaos in life. I see chaos as an event or energy that comes uninvited, like the snake, and threatens the order of life as it is known and cherished. There are minor incidences that seem chaotic, like locking keys in the car or losing a wallet or waking up with the flu on an important day. I have been using the word *chaos,* however, for experiences with a major impact, disruptions that significantly throw the world out of balance. Chaos brings a shift that jeopardizes something especially valued, that undermines peace. It seems to carry an element of real jeopardy. I have moved through a progression of understandings of the dynamic of chaos. I offer these reflections hoping they confirm your own understanding.

Chaos on the move always frightens me, like the coral snake in the front yard. My instinct is always to try to cut it off before it can do great harm. But gradually I have discovered chaos can strangely sometimes be grace. It can open the door to creation.

Little in my childhood family or education prepared me for how hard life can be. Maybe it was thought that children should be protected, or maybe I just missed the warnings. When I look back I realize there were family sayings that pointed to it, like Mom's saying, "It's a great life, if you don't weaken." Or, "Life is just a bowl of cherries…with pits." I guess there were indications. They just didn't sink in.

It was a long time before I grasped the reality of chaos. I thought that life was meant to be orderly. I believed that events unfolded in a certain expectable way, and that in the lives of people who did what they were supposed to do, there was a kind of peace and stability.

I think one reason I believed this for so long is that we had a very orderly household. Both Mom and Dad were very organized: he as a general and she as an English teacher. I graduated from high school in 1959, so more than half my life had been lived in the famous '50s, the *Leave it to Beaver* and *Father Knows Best* years that are almost a metaphor for a secure and predictable period. This time is sometimes called "the Eisenhower Era." I not only lived in the Eisenhower Era, I even went to Eisenhower's inaugural parade!

There was actually a hint connected with Eisenhower that could have served as a warning about chaos, if I had taken note of it. Mom and Dad had been invited to the White House for a dinner.

Mom had very thin, fine hair, hard to style in any elegant fashion, and she was trying to look her best for the dinner. She had placed a curler in the front of her hair to give it a little lift, and was planning to take it out at the very last minute. Dad's assignment was to remind her. Apparently, when they pulled up at the White House, there was a lot of activity and confusion: doors being opened, Secret Service checks taking place. In any event, when she came home she still had the curler in her hair. *"Oh no!"* we heard her cry out as she glanced in the mirror, "George! You never reminded me!" If I had known the significance, this event could have provided a little notice that things do not always turn out as we have planned.

For the most part, in our home in Washington things were arranged to happen on schedule. Sheets were changed on every bed each Monday. Mattresses were turned once a month. (One month they were turned side to side, the next month up to down.) Meals were eaten at about the same time every day, and dishes were always done right after the final plates were cleared.

There were schedules for when the windows were washed, the shutters repainted, the closets cleaned. A list was hung on a bulletin board in the kitchen to write down any item that was used up, so it could be replaced at the next trip to the store.

That order provided me with a great sense of security in those years. The worldview taken for granted was that if you behave yourself, if you conscientiously do the things you are taught, somehow all will be well.

The same view was reinforced in school. I got a wonderful education from the Religious of the Sacred Heart in their Academy in D.C., and I remember it as the most orderly of all environments. We got marks posted on charts each week in something called "Cooperation" and something else actually called "Order." There were medals, cards, and ribbons given out by Reverend Mother weekly, rewarding and signifying that one was orderly and cooperative. I thrived in this atmosphere and set new records in the history of the school for cooperation. My senior year I was what they called the Head Blue Ribbon.

I can still see our small class of young women at graduation in white organdy dresses for the ceremony on the front lawn. We wore dark green laurel wreaths on our heads, and our faces were filled with innocence and wonder, idealism and eager hope.

I went on to college, then married very young. Soon thereafter things stopped proceeding in an orderly fashion.

My husband was in the Army, and we had the upheaval of moving on an average of once a year. Things were just about unpacked in one place when it was time to think about repacking them again. Babies were born one after the other, all of them born weeks overdue, none of them sleeping through the night until they were at least two *years* old.

Laundry seemed to breed and multiply in the hamper until the only space not filled with clothes to be washed was filled with dishes to be done or toys to be put away.

I loved the children totally, but I was often overwhelmed by the unpredictability of motherhood, by the sudden high fevers, the incredible pranks, the accidents. Boo fell out of a shopping cart and broke his arm. Randy ran through the sliding glass door and had hundreds of stitches. Kadee got the worst case of chicken pox the pediatrician had ever seen, with pox even in the whites of her eyes. All three were up for any adventure, and what one didn't think of, the others did. Baby-sitters sometimes made elaborate excuses not to return.

Little by little I was forced to let go of my notion of an orderly universe. At least in any life I was able to manage, life was not tranquil and schedulable. What you expected often did not happen. What you dreaded often did. Most unimaginable of all, after thirteen years, came a divorce.

If anyone had told me, standing on the long green lawn of the Academy of the Sacred Heart, in my white organdy graduation dress with my blue ribbon and Sodality medal and laurel wreath, that I would be divorced from the father of my children, I would have simply said, "You are totally mistaken."

In the disorder of divorce I came up against chaos. "And where is God in all of this?" I anguished. It was a very big question.

In the years that led up to the divorce and in the years since then, off and on, in some form or another, I have been wrestling with the question of God and chaos.

I realize now that this is a familiar human challenge. In every life there come things we do not understand, unwelcome events like rejections and accidents, injustices and disappointments, the loss of jobs, the death of dreams. We lose people we love and we can't seem to get rid of people who drive us crazy. (My good friend Benni confirmed this last reality a week ago when she was describing to me someone she has to deal with regularly. She said, "Have you heard the expression that a person grows on you?" "Yes," I replied. "Well," she said, "this person is a crop failure.")

Terrible things happen to us, sometimes with little warning. Not long ago I was thoroughly disheartened by a sequence of events that had rolled through our family like a stream of enemy tanks. "Rotten growth opportunities," I have heard them labeled, or what I have come to call chaos.

About that time I discovered something that was both fascinating and somehow deeply comforting for me. I learned that there is a chaos theory in physics and mathematics. The Chaos Theory was arrived at with great struggle by scientists in the second half of the twentieth century. Their struggle reminds me of my own. The stages of evolving their theory are similar to the stages I have gone through trying to make some sense of my life.

The first scientific stage, paralleling my first stage, was the experience of an orderly world. Hidden in what was considered objective experience was the unquestioned assumption that the fact of order is permanent and universal. The world of Newtonian physics and Euclidian geometry, where natural laws governed all, was like the world of our family in the Eisenhower Era, where you always had a clean linen handkerchief and had name tags neatly sewn in all your school clothes. It was the Catholic world of *The Question Box,* a book we studied in college in which was listed all possible questions about the faith and the answers to every one. All the answers were not only knowable, but written out for you. "Where is God in chaos?" was not one of them.

The second stage for the scientists and for me was the stage where the assumption that life is orderly was challenged by the undeniable reality of chaos. In James Gleick's fascinating best-selling book called *Chaos: Making a New Science,* he describes that scientists using modern technology came upon happenings that did not fit the theories and equations of classic science. Amazingly, for centuries, when scientists found discrepancies that did not fit the theories, they discarded the discrepancies as errors and ignored them. The researchers just assumed there had been some mistake, or that the numbers were too small to be taken into consideration.

With the accuracy available through modern computers, however, it was much harder to dismiss what did not fit. Beginning in the 1960s, some pioneering scientists began to focus on these discrepancies where matter or numbers departed from the expected norms, erupting off into what they named "discontinuities," or " bursts of noise," or "Cantor dusts." There were clear instances where events, like turbulence in weather or the spread of epidemics, or shapes, like the edges of a coastline or the configuration of DNA strands, did not conform to predicted patterns.

> These phenomena had no place in the geometries of the past two thousand years. The shapes of classical geometry are lines and planes, circles and spheres, triangles and cones. They represent a powerful abstraction of reality, and they inspired a powerful philosophy of Platonic harmony.
>
> Euclid made of them a geometry that lasted two millennia, the only geometry that most people ever learn. Artists found an ideal beauty in them, Ptolemaic astronomers built a theory of the universe out of them. But for understanding complexity, they turn out to be the wrong kind of abstraction.[1]

Reading Gleick's account was riveting for me. I was excited and grateful for the way it explained what I had experienced in my life. I read the next paragraph out loud to myself three times, savoring it:

> Clouds are not spheres, Mandlebrot (one of the early chaos scientists) is fond of saying. Mountains are not cones. Lightning does not travel in a straight line. The new geometry mirrors a universe that is rough, not rounded, scabrous, not smooth. It is a geometry of the pitted, pocked, and broken up, the twisted, tangled, and intertwined....[2]

Holding the book in my hand I jumped up. "Exactly!" I shouted. "That is the texture of my real life: twisted, tangled, intertwined."

Sitting back down I read on as Gleick described mathematicians and physicists coming upon the reality of chaos. They did not know how to explain it, but there it was. It was so unsettling to the scientific world that attempts to get papers published in professional journals were met with refusal and even contempt. Those who had uncovered chaos were stranded in their discovery, unsure in what direction to proceed.

I reflected that I had been in this stage a long time. I had come upon chaos (or chaos came upon me), and I did not know how to fit it into my understanding of life. It was not that I experienced everything as disorder, but it loomed very large for me that disorder was an indisputable fact of life. Jobs could be terminated with little notice. Wonderful candidates could lose political races to creeps. Family members could have mental breakdowns. Beloved friends could be diagnosed with cancer.

As I came to know chaos better, I knew it often surfaced at the worst times. After a while I almost expected at least someone in the family to be sick at Christmas. I identified with a column in our paper that described the columnist, Steve Otto's, family holiday illness. He asked, "Have you ever tried Robitussin mixed with egg nog?" I laughed, understanding just what he meant. Even at celebrations, chaos shows up.

In the era when I first began to recognize the fact of significant chaos in my life, I was haunted by the sense that somehow this shouldn't be, that there must be something wrong with me, something wrong with life that there was so much turmoil. It should be fixed. Like editors of scientific journals who refused to publish chaos articles, I thought it should be made to go away.

A great breakthrough came for me one day. At the time, I was the associate director of the Center for Continuing Formation in Ministry at the University of Notre Dame. This was a sabbatical program for people in full-time ministry in the church: priests, religious, and lay ministers. One of the great parts of the job is that I sat in on the classes.

On this afternoon passionist scripture scholar Carroll Stuhmueller was teaching a course for us on the psalms. He said that the praise psalms were praising God for creation, and often for creation in the sense of deliverance from some kind of turmoil. He said that the concept of creation for the biblical people was never creation out of nothing, but always creation out of chaos.

He told us that the Hebrew word for chaos was *tohu wa bohu.* "It sounds like what it is," he said. "If you have *tohu wa bohu* you know you've got trouble!" He explained that those ancient people considered chaos always to be lurking on the edge of creation, ready to take it over.

Stuhmueller's class had a profound effect on me. I was sitting in the back row of the classroom for his lecture, exhausted and raw from dealing with significant crises in every generation of our family. When he explained how the Israelites experienced life, I was somehow comforted at a very fundamental level. I felt reassured that there is not necessarily something wrong with me if life seems on the edge of chaos. That is just the way things are and always have been. Hearing that this was the experience of the biblical peoples, that it is the pattern of the scriptures, really consoled me. My story was their story.

I was freed to see the chaos as an objective reality, as a normal part of life. Somehow once I was able to accept the fact of chaos, I had more room to find and savor the reality of creation. I thought less about the terrible things that happen, realizing freshly that wonderful things happen too. I began to collect stories of life breaking through.

A favorite in my collection is this: In the country about five miles from the little town in central Florida where I raised my kids, there is a man named Everett Boney. Mr. Boney has worked with cows all his life long, and is still doing it in his late seventies. When he was eighteen he was kicked in the eye by a horse and from then on was blind in that eye.

Six months before the story was told to me, cataracts had begun to grow over his good eye. He went to an eye doctor, but the doctor said he wouldn't take the chance of operating on it because it was the only good eye. Mr. Boney was really discouraged, thinking he would gradually lose all his sight.

Someone suggested he seek a second opinion, so Mr. Boney drove 100 miles to Tampa to see a specialist. That doctor looked at the cataracts on his eye and said, "I think I can fix that." He operated on it, and was completely successful. Mr. Boney now had 20/20 vision in that eye.

Then the doctor said, "What's the matter with your other eye?" Mr. Boney said, "Oh, it's useless. I was kicked in that eye by a horse when I was eighteen and it's been blind ever since."

The doctor said, "Well, I think I can fix that." He operated on the other eye, and completely restored the sight. 20/20 vision! Mr. Boney, now nearly eighty, sees better than he has since he was eighteen.

In the process of claiming more objectively the truth that although terrible things happen, wonderful things happen too, I moved to a deeper sense that there is a rhythm to things.

I heard with new ears the ancient poetry of Ecclesiastes 3:

There is an appointed time for everything,
and a time for every purpose under heavens,
A time to be born and a time to die;...
A time to mourn, and a time to dance,
A time to scatter stones, and a time to gather them,

on through that listing that has resonated with the experience of every human life for thousands of years. All the different rhythms and seasons, contrasts, currents, patterns, turnings. Everything has a time.

Hearing that passage in a liturgy one day I thought of an exchange I had with Catherine Mason, my neighbor for years when I lived in South Bend. She was ninety-one. She walked a mile each way to Mass every day on the Notre Dame campus, she played bridge every week, she wrote to her children and grandchildren and great-grandchildren.

On this day, I was washing my nine-year-old car getting ready to sell it. I was crying as I washed it because it was the last car that had belonged to Dad and Mom, the last one they both drove. As I emptied the glove compartment I found things I had forgotten were in there, like the bill of sale with Dad's signature and a notebook with notations of gas mileage and oil changes in Mom's writing.

Catherine came by and stopped to talk, and I told her it was hard for me to say good-bye to the old Volkswagen, and she said simply, "There comes a time."

I was very moved by that. She said it with a seasoned poignancy of someone who has said good-bye to many things. To her husband. To the big, old house where they had raised their eight children. To many of her friends. "There comes a time." Planting and uprooting the plant. Building and tearing down. Keeping and casting away. Embracing and being far from embraces.

There are seasons, and there's not something wrong with us that some of those seasons are for difficult, disorderly chaotic events.

After that conversation came the beginning of what I would call stage 4 of my grappling with the issue of chaos and creation.

Stage 1 was the foundational period of stability and order that seemed to define how life should be.

Stage 2 was the frightening discovery of chaos. Life (mine at least) was not orderly, and something was very wrong with that.

Stage 3 was the realization that chaos is part of life. It has seasons that alternate with creation.

The last stage was the slow dawning of a delicate conviction that chaos and creation did not just coexist in reality, but that sometimes chaos is the raw material of creation. The *tohu wa bohu* is not necessarily evil. Perhaps creation is not the result of combat between good and evil, as many primitive myths portray, a very closely contested victory for the forces of good. It may be that chaos is energy, power, untamed and unformed, but not bad. It could be shaped and channeled, tamed and understood in ways that bring new creation to life. Something may need to die before something else can be born.

Something newer, better, fresher may come into being than we ever could have hoped or imagined.

An example that fascinates me is one I just heard last year. I was visiting my son Boo. (He is my youngest. His real name is Robert, but we've always called him Boo.) He is a captain in the Army legal corps, and at that time was stationed at Ft. Rucker, Alabama. He and his wife Caroline lived in the nearby town of Enterprise. It was my first visit, and they were giving me the grand tour of the post and the town, stopping in the middle of the little downtown to show me a famous landmark statue.

"It is the only monument in the world to an insect," Boo said, dryly, waiting for me to comment.

"An insect?"

"Take a look." He drove close to the white statue on a tall pedestal in the middle of a fountain. The statue was of a woman draped in Grecian style holding over her head: a BUG!!

"What in the world is it?"

"A boll weevil, Mom. Here's the story. This area was a one-crop farm area, like most of the South. The crop was cotton. When the boll weevils came up from Mexico in 1915, almost the whole crop was destroyed.

"This all but paralyzed the economy of the county and the surrounding areas. The farmers were unable to pay their bills, merchants were caught in the squeeze and couldn't meet their obligations, bankers were caught with loans that could not be called in.

"H. M. Sessions, a banker who had advanced money on the crop to many farmers, preached diversification of crops. This was a pitch for the wisdom of having more than one potential source of income. In addition to or instead of cotton, to raise corn, or livestock, or maybe try peanuts, a crop that was beginning to be grown and sold for many different purposes.

"Farmers were reluctant to give up farming cotton, because it was all they knew. Generations before them had grown it on this same land. Only a few tried diversifying the first year, but with the continued disaster the weevil wrought the second year, most began to change to different crops, particularly peanuts.

"The farmers of Enterprise not only regained their losses, but they prospered as never before. As it turns out, cotton is a very labor-intensive crop. The money and effort it takes to produce a living in cotton is far greater than for a crop like peanuts. The new crops brought many times the profit that cotton had yielded.

"And so it was decided," Boo concluded in his tour guide voice, "to dedicate a monument on this spot where we are today."

Getting out of the car, I walked over and read the inscription on the base: "In profound appreciation of the boll weevil and what it has done as the herald of prosperity, this monument was erected by the citizens of Enterprise, Coffee County, Alabama, in the year of Our Lord 1919."

Clearly, I said to myself, creation out of chaos. I stood there for a long time looking at the monument, thinking about life.

Over and over, now that my ear is tuned to the music of this dance, I hear these stories. I heard a man say, "When I went bankrupt I discovered that life was about love not money."

My friend Lona said, "When I got hit by a truck riding my bicycle my back was broken. As strange as it sounds, in my terrible recovery I learned to savor joy."

"When my son got in trouble with drugs," one woman told me, "I thought it was the end of the world. But in his recovery process, he discovered God and himself."

There seems to be a pattern here if we look hard enough, if we listen carefully enough.

This is what the chaos scientists discovered as well. If they ran the chaotic numbers long enough through the computers, if they observed the experiments long enough in the laboratories, they found a pattern in the results. There was a consistent configuration in the plotting of the results they called "a strange attractor." There was a pattern in the distribution of the numbers that was a constant. This was true no matter what the content of the chaos observed was: population growths or turbulence in weather or dripping faucets or epidemics. A perplexing pattern emerged deep in the chaos.[3]

There is a pattern like this at the heart of our Judeo-Christian revelation. Like the inexplicable strange attractor or mathematical constant, it is the ever-recurring mystery that is the theme of scripture and the theme of each human life. Theologian Bernard Cooke refers to it as the "master myth" *(Sacraments and Sacramentality)*. It is the pattern of life from death. Liberation from bondage. Resurrection after crucifixion.

My favorite story about this pattern in our family happened five years ago. I offer it hoping it will remind you of a story of your own. Perhaps someday you will pass your story on to me.

My father died just before Christmas, and five months before that my mother had died. Their deaths were hard; both slow, grim, and painful.

I don't know which was worse, Dad with Alzheimer's disease being so confused, so unable to bring his own great mind to bear on his suffering; or Mom, still perfectly alert, knowing everything, her understanding exposing her to the terror of the collapse of her own body around her. The simplest things became so difficult: breathing, turning over, swallowing.

So Mom died first, in the summer, and then, after an agonized fall, Dad. In the last weeks he was very bewildered and agitated. What I remember the most are his hands. He had beautiful hands, strong and well-shaped, with long expressive fingers. Mom, whose hands were small and square, with short, unpoetic fingers, used to point out Dad's hands to us when we were growing up. "Look at your father's hands, girls," she would say to us. "Doesn't he have beautiful hands?" In the end those hands were very restless, those fingers endlessly plucking at his blankets. It was December 21 that his hands came to rest at last.

After the funeral I went back to my job at Notre Dame for the semester with a sense of being bewildered, unmoored, somehow lost without my parents. Orphaned, even at fifty.

In May I left to go home for the summer to Florida to my house in the town where I raised my children. When I got home I discovered that my daughter Kadee was pregnant. She and John had been married for seven years, and she had waited until I got home to tell me in person. That very day she had had a sonogram, which she showed to me. I was absolutely awestruck. Looking at a picture of your first grandchild within the womb of your own firstborn is an extraordinary experience. The baby was a boy, due in October, nine months after my father's death.

When he was born I flew down to see him, and pulled up in their yard just as they drove in from the hospital. Kadee was holding him in her arms in a soft white blanket, and the first thing I saw were his hands. Long hands for a baby. Fine long fingers...that were plucking at his blanket. Tears streamed down my face.

Pain does not have the final say. A pattern emerges in mysterious upheaval, in all the alterations of darkness and light. God brings life from all our forms of death, creating out of chaos once again.

Notes

1. James Gleick, *Chaos: Making a New Science* (New York: Penguin, 1987), 94.
2. Ibid.
3. Ibid., 152.

Elizabeth A. Dreyer

19. A Tradition of Spirit:
Breathing New Life into Ministry

Theologians have been voicing concern about the seeming irrelevance of the Trinity to the average Christian for the last several decades. Karl Rahner has suggested that in their practical life, Christians are "almost mere monotheists" and even imagined that if the church announced the discovery of a fourth person in the Trinity, it would go unremarked in terms of people's everyday faith. He goes on to ask, "How can the contemplation of any reality, even of the loftiest reality, beatify us if intrinsically it is absolutely *unrelated* to us in any way?"[1]

A further issue contributes to a less than lively doctrine of the Trinity at present. For even when one does give proper attention to the threeness of the Trinity as well as to its oneness, one notices that throughout the tradition, in spite of repeated protestations to the contrary, some persons are "more equal" than others. In the drama of the Western Christian tradition, the second person as Logos has been given the lead, the first person has had an equally substantial supporting role, especially in the doctrine of creation, and the Holy Spirit has had to be satisfied with a "walk on" part.

As a result, more and more theologians are turning their attention to theologies of the Trinity, while others attend to the particular role of the spirit.[2] In yet another approach, spirit-Christologies keep son and spirit in creative tension, attesting to their inseparability.[3] Much of this work responds to Rahner's question about the need to relate the Trinity to the Christian life in fresh and dynamic ways. Catherine Mowry Lacugna builds her theology of the Trinity on the premise that the doctrine of the Trinity is ultimately a practical doctrine with radical consequences for the Christian life.[4] And Jurgen Moltmann, who has written extensively on the Holy Spirit reminds us that

> the gift and presence of the Holy Spirit is the greatest and most
> wonderful thing which we can experience—we ourselves, the
> human community, all living things and this earth. For with the
> Holy Spirit is not just one random spirit that is present, among all
> the many good and evil spirits that there are. It is *God himself,* the

276

creative and life-giving, redeeming and saving God. Where the Holy Spirit is present, God is present in a special way, and we experience God through our lives, which become wholly living from within. We experience whole, full, healed and redeemed life, experience it with all our senses. We feel and taste, we touch and see our life in God and God in our life.[5]

Moltmann sees the spirit's presence, not as a distant, abstract theological concept, but rather as bringing life to all of creation—body, soul, mind, spirit, earth, and cosmos.

These words lead us to examine our consciousness of the spirit's presence and to invite the spirit to become a more intimate and lively part of human existence. This essay reflects on the theology and spirituality of the spirit in relation to ministry. In particular, I look to some of our medieval ancestors in the faith to "be on the watch" for images and narratives of the spirit that might shed light on our own efforts at renewal. We will sample texts from a number of figures who called upon the spirit in their own ministries. How did these "holy ones" think about and express their experience of spirit? Even though the Holy Spirit has not held center stage in the tradition, Christians have faithfully turned to the spirit, and spoken of the spirit, using language and imagery that, in spite of the distances of history, reach out to bring new life to Christians in the twenty-first century.

The context for a theology and spirituality of the Holy Spirit is always the Trinity in its fullness. Any talk about the spirit must include awareness of the first and second persons and their interrelationships. In the third century, Irenaeus used a metaphor that serves us well as we strive to keep the Trinity and unity of God in creative tension. Irenaeus referred to the son and the spirit as the "two hands" of God—hands that do God's work in creation.[6] If we keep this image before us, we will remain aware of the spirit's relationship to the other persons. As we undertake the spiritual journey as ministers, attending both to our own life in the spirit and to noticing, calling forth, and nurturing the spirit life in others, we can imagine ourselves and our communities touched, held up, offered, prodded, challenged and embraced by God's two hands.

In this essay, we reflect on that hand of God we call spirit in order to examine some of the major images used to give voice and shape to the spirit's presence in the medieval tradition. We see how their images and narratives functioned in their time and place and ask how they might function now in new and transforming ways in our lives and ministries. Out of many possibilities, I have chosen three themes that point to the role of the spirit and have a distinctive relationship to ministry: staying in touch with God's generous love; maintaining a heart of flesh; and remembering that ministry is a call to service.

Staying in Touch with God's Generous Love

In every age the challenges of ministry are legion. One of these challenges today involves the tendency to narrow our focus to the nitty-gritty problems of church structures and politics. The open and expansive dispositions that initially motivated people to serve gradually give way to diminished preoccupations and sometimes petty concerns. We forget about or get distanced from the wide open spaces of God's endless love.

An antidote to such ministerial constriction is the image of the spirit as the overflowing fullness of God. This image is rooted in neo-Platonism, one of the major strains in the Christian tradition. The term *neo-Platonism* is attached to a way of thinking about the world that has its roots in Hellenism, and that was subsequently taken over and transformed by early Christian writers. One of the enduring values of this worldview is its ability to notice and be in awe of the magnificence of God. Neo-Platonists lure us to stand under the starry sky and be wowed by its immense beauty. Throughout the tradition, God's magnanimity was imagined in a number of ways. One such image is that of the overflowing fountain, the *fons plenitudo,* the primordial source from which love and grace overflow to the son and spirit and thence to creation.

This image captured the imagination of many medieval theologians. It was an appealing way to speak about the generosity of God. Often this emphasis on God's generosity was reflected in treatments of the gifts of the spirit (1 Cor 1:7) that point back to the gifts mentioned in Isaiah 11:2–3:

> There shall come forth a shoot from the stump of Jesse, and a branch shall grow out of his roots. And the spirit of the Lord shall rest upon him, the spirit of wisdom and understanding, the spirit of counsel and fortitude, the spirit of knowledge and the fear of the Lord. And his delight shall be in the fear of the Lord.

Experience of the spirit's gifts provide a concrete touchstone within the context of the Christian life that points to God's disposition as Gift-Giver—the One who wishes for us, and indeed enables us to possess, and behave toward others out of a well-spring of, such holy dispositions.

In the midst of a critical flock, it may be difficult for ministers to experience their own gifts. Some years ago, a seminary student lamented in class that after a service in which she presided and preached, a member of her congregation complained about how she had delivered the announcements! Taking time to recall and celebrate God's gifts is crucial to maintaining one's joy and equilibrium. Awareness of God's generous love is also central to one's ability to notice the ways in which God has gifted others. One of the major functions of ministry is to be able to "notice" the glory of God in the community and call attention to it. One has to know about the giftedness of one's own life in order to see it in the lives of others.

This image of the "overflowing fountain" was given a distinctive pneumatological thrust when linked with Paul's famous phrase in Romans 5:5: "God's love has been poured into our hearts through the Holy Spirit who has been given to us." This imagery gave birth to a certain way of understanding the Trinity and salvation history in which the spirit functions as a kind of culmination in a process that begins with the creator God, becomes embodied in the incarnate Christ, and ends in spirit fullness. In the early church, Basil gave expression to this trinitarian fullness. "Behold in the creation of these beings the Father as the preceding cause, the Son as the One who creates, and the spirit as the Perfecter; so that the ministering spirits have their beginning in the will of the Father, are brought into being through the efficacy of the Son, and are perfected through the aid of the spirit."

Contemporary systematic theology has raised questions about the legitimacy of this image as a way to speak about God. If one pushes this metaphor to its logical conclusion, it can suggest that God's act of creation was not entirely free if the nature of God's goodness results in its automatic outpouring, as when a cup overflows when it is filled past its brim. This metaphor can also subtly introduce a hierarchy among the persons that is seen to jeopardize their radical equality as God. In this view, one could say that part of the spirit's neglected status is due to the spirit's coming out third of three and therefore holding an inferior position to the first and second persons. Of course, the image of God's overflowing generosity ending in a kind of spirit fullness could put the spirit in a superior position as the culmination and highest fulfillment of the expression of God's love. Either way, we lose the tradition's belief in the radical equality of the three persons.

But when one examines the powerful, moving, and poetic language of the tradition that gives voice to God's overflowing love, grace, and mercy, one hesitates to discard the image too precipitously. Of course, theologians need to search for reasonable, coherent, and philosophically convincing statements about God. But there must be a way to do this without disregarding images like the *fons plenitudo*—an image that has been such a staple of the tradition and, I suggest, a rich resource to renew Christian life, the ministry and ultimately, the face of the earth.

Medieval texts, with roots in biblical language and imagery, are replete with images of moving, flowing, rippling, cascading fluids used to communicate a sense of the spirit's presence. Hildegard of Bingen (1098–1179), twelfth-century Benedictine abbess, prophet, and visionary, whose nine-hundredth birthday we celebrated in 1998, combined images of planting, watering, and greening to speak of the presence of the spirit. She linked the flow of water on the crops with the love of God that renews the face of the earth, and the souls of believers.[7]

In her vision on the sacrament of confirmation, Hildegard sees a tower, immense and round and made of a single white stone. In this image, she sees the sweetness of the Holy Spirit, "boundless and swift to encompass all creatures in grace.... Its path is a torrent, and streams of sanctity flow from it in its bright power."[8] For Hildegard, the ineffable Trinity is "manifested in the outpouring of the gifts of the power of the Holy Spirit." The spirit's sweetness is perfected in the flowing gifts of the spirit bestowed with the anointing at confirmation. Building on the grace of baptism, confirmation brings insight and courage in abundance.

In the thirteenth century, Bonaventure of Bagnoreggio (1217–1274), known as the "second founder" of the Franciscan Order, builds on the Neoplatonic tradition of Pseudo-Dionysius that saw God's love as self-diffusive goodness. Bonaventure, too, makes use of images of flowing liquids to communicate an idea that was very important to him—the utter generosity of God. This idea was not a distant, abstract theological principle for Bonaventure. His texts suggest that God's generous love was central to his own experience and to his teaching and preaching. God's liberality is visible above all in the incarnation, in the sending of the spirit, and in the spirit's endless gifts, virtues, fruits, and beatitudes. As a Franciscan, the cross was the symbol *par excellence* of God's generous love.

In a Pentecost sermon delivered in Paris to the Friars Minor in 1253, Bonaventure invited his brothers "to gather in, ruminate on, and embrace with affection the unparalleled event of Pentecost, since it revealed so clearly the divine mysteries."[9] In order to communicate the unimaginable love of God as spirit poured forth into our hearts, Bonaventure creates a sermonic *tour de force* by "piling on" biblical language that refers to moving, flowing liquids— mostly water that is flowing, gushing, bubbling, poured out. Springs become rivers (Est 11:6). Rivers flowing out of Eden water the garden (Gn 2:10). The river of the water of life flows from the throne of God (Apoc 22:1). Streams flowed from Lebanon (Cant 4:15). God will fill the dry stream bed with pools of water (2 Kgs 3:16). A fountain will be opened to cleanse the house of David (Zech 13:1). A spirit of judgment and burning will wash away the filth of Jerusalem (Is 4:4).

These images are enhanced by the alliteration of the Latin words used in this sermon. Take a moment to read these words aloud in order to sense what the friars were hearing. Allow the sounds to wash over you in order to "hear" the abundant flow of God's love: *effundam, effusam, fluvium paradisum irrigantem, per fontem scaturientem, fluvium, procedentem, per puteum viventis et videntis me, per puteum aquarum viventium, per alveum torrentis, per aquas Gedeonis, distributam, opulentam, fructuosam, infusio, diffusionis, abluerit, mirabiliter largiflua, amplificata.* This six-hundred-year-old sermon stands as a powerful testimony to the creative ways in which Christians throughout the ages have tried to communicate a kind of love that surpasses all imagination. Then, as now, we need to recall and speak about our experience of God's utter magnanimity toward creation.

Bonaventure's soaring rhetoric had practical ends with which we can identify. The specific needs of his thirteenth-century community were different from ours, but the distance of time is bridged in our common desire to contribute to the holiness of the community we call church. When Bonaventure was General of the Franciscans, the order was filled with tensions between those who wanted to maintain a close imitation of the ways of Francis and those who wanted to adapt, making changes to accommodate new situations. Many of us have experienced Christian communities that are likewise torn apart by contrasting visions and values. For Bonaventure, it was the spirit who assists in the proper living of the vows, in holding his religious community together in unity, in making good decisions.

His presentation of an utterly generous God was intended to arouse a deep sense of gratitude in his listeners. He further links the spirit of gratitude to the gift of humility, without which leadership flounders. For Bonaventure, humility was the basis of complete spiritual health. As ministers, do we not identify with these goals? We too can call upon the spirit to assist us in living a life of virtue; in our struggles for peace and community among the faithful; in responding with care to the many decisions that must be faced each day. Gratitude and humility are not only at the center of the Christian life, but are also crucial to a life given to ministry as well. An ungrateful, arrogant minister is surely an oxymoron!

Teresa of Avila (1515–1582) also uses the image of water to speak about her experience of God's grace in the soul. Although she does not refer explicitly to the spirit, it is easy for us to see the link in her understanding of God's graces to her. In *The Book of Her Life,* we find her famous description of prayer, known as "the four waters."[10] The soul is "watered" or nourished in four modes that reflect the progress of the soul. First, you may draw the water from the well yourself, using a bucket or some receptacle. This way takes a lot of energy and work. Second, you might have the assistance of a water wheel or aqueduct. These instruments take up some of the burden, making it easier for the person to obtain water. In a third image, one may get water from a river or stream. Here the water flows freely, making it even easier to obtain the waters of grace. At the culmination of this process, grace is experienced like a rain shower that drenches the soul. All the soul has to do is stand outside and with no effort at all, one is inundated with God's endless love. The garden of the soul receives moisture from all four waters, but as one grows intimate with God, human effort recedes, opening the way for an experience of God's magnanimously free and abundant love. Teresa suggests that the soul should rejoice at how good a gardener the Lord is!

Today we return to images of the spirit in order to bring new life and energy to our experience and understanding of the third person of the Trinity. Elizabeth Johnson calls upon the biblical images of wind, fire, and water to speak of the spirit. She describes the image of water as both "elemental,"— essential for life—but also capable of destroying life.[11] She writes, "As a symbol of the spirit, water points to the bottomless wellspring of the source of life and to the refreshment and gladness that result from deep immersion in this mystery."[12] We are invited to play imaginatively with water imagery in the Bible, using these metaphors to infuse our awareness of the spirit as the one who brings life to our timid, dry, and deadened spirits. In Genesis, the spirit creatively hovers over the waters (Gn 1:2). Through Ezekiel, God promises to sprinkle clean water and a new spirit on us (Ez 36:25–26). In Isaiah, the gifts of the spirit are like a cascade of water from a vessel (Is 32:15–18). Joel speaks of the sons and daughters whose flesh is drenched with the spirit of prophecy and vision (Jl 2:28–29). In a gesture to the marginalized, Jesus promises the gift of living water to the woman of Samaria (Jn 4:7–15). And Paul reminds us that we are not only justified in faith, inheritors of peace, recipients of grace, and able to rejoice in the hope of sharing God's glory, but we can also even rejoice in suffering, which can produce endurance and character and hope, because "God's love has been poured into our hearts through the Holy Spirit who has been given to us" (Rom 5:5). In sum, the spirit is the agent whose flowing gifts give us life, all manner of gifts, and make effective Christ's words, "Come to me, all you who are heavy burdened" (Mt 11:28).

This flowing spirit imagery nudges us to reflect on our own experiences of liquids: an ice-cold drink of water when our tongues are parched; a cool shower after days of camping or at the end of a long journey; clean clothing; a leaping splash into the ocean. Images of beer- and wine-making in which huge vats of rich golden or reddish-purple liquid pour forth in abundance become a sacrament of God's spirit endlessly outpouring love into our hearts. We are enjoined—and rightly so—to live simply and to share what we have with others. But this should not preclude the occasional indulgence or gesture of abundance to remind us of the free, joyful, endless love of God for us.

Such splurges will take on as many forms as there are people. It can be as simple as giving oneself permission to do nothing for an hour, to take a walk, or to read a novel or go to a movie in the midst of endless ministerial demands. Some may actually put on a slicker and go walking in a warm spring rain. Instead of carrying an umbrella for protection, one lifts one's face to the torrent, tapping in to the exhilaration of the freedom and abandon of God-with-us. It may take the form of an unexpected, "extravagant" gift to someone we love. When I was growing up, we called them "unbirthday presents."

The heart of the call to ministry is to notice God's endless love in and around us and to witness to this love—to encourage and support those who know a generous God and to draw back the veil that hides this face of God to those who do not see. Openness to the spirit's magnanimous presence takes at least two forms. We must open ourselves, get free of ourselves, in order to experience the genuine abundance of God's love. The ego and the endless demands of work must be invited to step to the rear for a moment in order to create a "space" in which it is possible to feel and acknowledge the infinite ways in which God loves us in the spirit. The second form is perhaps more fundamental. For the primary way human beings find out about God's love is through the love that we receive from other human beings. If we don't let each other know when we feel such abundant love, it will be harder to imagine what God's generous love must be like. We express such love by signs, gestures, behaviors, gifts. There is no pragmatic purpose to such love. It is just there to be felt, acknowledged, expressed, and celebrated. We can express this kind of love to our families, to our friends, and to those we serve in ministry—especially to those whose circumstances are likely to obscure the presence of God's great love in the spirit.

Maintaining a Heart of Flesh

Medieval accounts of the spirit's role in transforming the affections offer insufficiently tapped linguistic, conceptual, metaphorical, and imagistic resources to aid us in our ministries and in our hungers to experience the lure of God's love, the conversion of our desires and fears, and in our prayer to love God, friends, neighbors, and enemies well.

Love

The Holy Spirit has been that person in the Trinity associated particularly with love. One of Augustine's major theological and spiritual contributions was to envision the spirit as the bond of love between Father and Son. Hildegard of Bingen has left us this biblical description of the Trinity that links the spirit with the freshness of creation and the heat of Pentecost fire:

> And so these three Persons are in the unity of inseparable substance; but They are not indistinct among themselves. How? He Who begets is the Father; He Who is born is the Son; and He Who in eager freshness proceeds from the Father and Son, and sanctified the waters by moving over their face in the likeness of an

innocent bird, and streamed with ardent heat over the apostles is the Holy Spirit.[13]

In a metaphor for which she is well known, Hildegard connects the spirit with "greening," which can also serve as a metaphor for transforming human affections. For those of us who don't live in the country, the image of "greening" may not readily come to mind as a way to think about the spirit. And yet, all of us depend upon the fruit the earth produces for food and for many by-products that make our lives comfortable. Hildegard of Bingen lived in the Rhine Valley and looked out on the green hills that spoke to her of God's presence. At the age of eight, Hildegard was sent to live with a holy woman, Jutta von Sponheim. Later she tells us that she was the recipient of visions from her earliest childhood. After becoming abbess in her teens, Hildegard wrote to Bernard of Clairvaux to ask him to help her judge the authenticity of her extraordinary experiences. After receiving his blessing and that of Pope Eugenius III, Hildegard became a well-known religious leader and prophet, preacher to clergy and laity alike. She wrote treatises on theology, the virtues, the healing arts of medicine, the first morality play, a library of choral chant for her community, and an extensive correspondence with bishops, popes, emperors, as well as with religious and laity.

Hildegard combined images of planting, watering, and greening to speak in a special way of the presence of the Holy Spirit. She linked the flow of water on the crops with the love of God that renews the face of the earth, and by extension the souls of believers. The idea of "greenness" or *viriditas* played an important *theological* role in her spirituality. The editors of the English language edition of her letters lament, "This *viriditas,* this despair of translators, this 'greenness' enters into the very fabric of the universe in Hildegard's cosmic scheme of things. In Hildegard's usage it is a profound, immense, dynamically energized term."[14] Hildegard connects *viriditas* with moisture *(humor, humiditas).* Without moisture the earth would lose its greenness and crumble like ashes. In the spiritual realm both *viriditas* and *humiditas* are "manifestations of God's power, qualities of the human soul, for 'the grace of God shines like the sun and sends its gifts in various ways; in wisdom, in greenness, in moisture.'" Without "greening," virtues become dry as dust and the spiritual life is compromised.[15]

"Greenness" was a concept that expressed and connected the bounty of God, the fertility of nature, and especially the presence of the Holy Spirit. Barbara Newman comments about this aspect of Hildegard's thought, "If you are filled with the Holy Spirit then you are filled with *viriditas.* You are spiritually fertile, you are alive."[16] Hildegard understood "greenness" in ways that resonate with aspects of ministerial experience. For example, after many years of labor, ministry can leave us feeling weary and even empty. It is not a 9-to-5 job that makes few demands on the psyche. At times, one has to struggle to maintain a heart of flesh. Hildegard describes a prelate who is filled with weariness *(taedium)* as one who is lacking in "viriditas," and she counsels the neophyte in religious life to strive for "spiritual greenness."[17] Hildegard's admonitions are on the order of "tough love." She does not pamper or empathize with lukewarmness. Rather she chides that part of us that is fickle—as in "on again, off again" with God—as having some greenness, but "not much." And should we be unfortunate enough to close ourselves off from the spirit's admonitions, we will dry up and become completely dead.[18]

Fear

Another affection that stands in need of transformation is fear. Most of the saints were faced with difficult challenges in the church, in their communities, and in their own spiritual journeys. Some had to overcome a sense of inadequacy; others risked official disapproval and censure; and yet others were afraid to make themselves vulnerable by speaking out in order to lead, to preach the gospel, or to bear witness to God's presence. Many of the saints identified with the struggles of the apostles. The challenges of ecclesial leadership are a constant in the tradition up to the present moment. In every age, it is the Holy Spirit who builds up the faith of the church. In response to timidity in the face of challenges our ancestors in the faith called upon the spirit, recalling that same spirit's gift in casting out fear at Pentecost. It is the spirit who transforms fear into courage.

Fear can block us from discerning and choosing to speak an effective word in the many settings of ministry. Ministers are called upon to "speak a word" not only with their voices but also with their actions. Preaching is at the heart of the ministerial task. Preaching can be considered in its more formal, proper sense as reflection on the Word of God in various liturgical settings. But most of the time preaching is informal—speaking the good news to persons to whom we are sent. The account of the first Pentecost in Acts describes the effect of the spirit on the speech of the disciples. When the tongues of fire descended on the disciples, they began to speak in other tongues (Acts 2:1–4). Then Peter prophesied with words from Joel: "I will pour out my spirit upon all flesh, and your sons and daughters shall prophesy.... I will pour out my spirit; and they shall prophesy" (Acts 2:17–18). And Peter's words were effective. When he preached repentance and baptism in the name of Jesus for the forgiveness of sins, the Holy Spirit's gifts were received and those who heard him were baptized (Acts 2:38, 41).

The effects of the spirit's presence on our ability to preach, teach, and prophesy is attested throughout the tradition. Augustine the bishop comments on the effect the spirit had on Peter. Augustine seems to identify with Peter, perhaps wishing that he had Peter's courage and gift to preach and convert. He describes Peter's tongue as transformed from bondage to liberty and from diffidence to confidence.[19]

> And then that spirit, pervading him thus with the fullness of richer grace, kindled his hitherto frigid heart to such a witness-bearing for Christ, and unlocked those lips that in their previous tremor had suppressed the truth, that, when all on whom the Holy Spirit had descended were speaking in the tongues of all nations…he alone broke forth…in the promptitude of his testimony on behalf of Christ…. And if any one would enjoy the pleasure of gazing on a sight so charming in its holiness, let him read the Acts of the Apostles (2.5): and there let him be filled with amazement at the preaching of the blessed Peter…. Let him behold that tongue, itself translated from diffidence to confidence, from bondage to liberty, converting to the confession of Christ the tongues of so many of His enemies….[20]

We know that Augustine experienced trying times in his ministry, and that he turned to the spirit to illumine his intellect and will to convey the Word of God in a compelling way. He opposed the Donatists, who had a vision of a "perfect" church that was quite different from Augustine's idea of a worldwide, inclusive church. He knew that there were sinners in abundance in the church, but he wanted somehow to make room for them. Faith communities today also stand in need of a truthful, effective gospel word. Augustine saw the effect of the spirit on Peter and no doubt wished that he too might be used as an instrument of good in the community. These sentiments are not foreign to today's ministers. Throughout history the church has been in need of the spirit's gifts, visible in those who opened themselves to the spirit's power—preaching and witnessing to the truth of Christ's redeeming love.

None of these feelings is foreign to an active, committed minister. The need to listen to the heart with a discerning spirit is a daily occurrence. The ongoing graces of Pentecost give us confidence to delineate the sources and contours of our fears, and to petition the spirit for release from them. They also lead us to identify destructive forces in church and society and to examine why we do or do not work against them.

One does not set out to speak a prophetic word, but a heart filled with love and courage is moved by suffering and emboldened to speak out against it. Abraham Heschel queries about prophets: "What gave them the strength to 'demythologize' precious certainties, to attack what was holy, to hurl blasphemies at priest and king, to stand up against all in the name of God?"[21] Who are our prophets—those who open themselves to the spirit and witness to God's presence by their words, and above all, by their actions? The sources of the prophet's courage in the tradition are multiple—openness to the spirit; summons from God; a sensitive conscience; the ability to "cross over" imaginatively to the sufferings of others; boldness of feeling that has the potential to engage others in the struggle. Like fourth-century Hippo and twelfth-century Bingen, our own time calls for ministers who speak a prophetic word to real persons in concrete, historical situations of sin and suffering.

We have spoken of the spirit's power to transform our loves and fears. But there are many other affections that need to be held in the spirit's embrace. Today, the affections have come again into the theological spotlight. Themes of *eros,* friendship, passion, and desire are again receiving the attention they deserve. In addition, theological and spiritual traditions are enriched by psychological, physiological, literary, and social scientific perspectives. Feminist theologians are in the midst of a major recovery of wisdom traditions that wed knowing and loving. Ethicists explore the role of the heart in morality. Still others ground the theological task in a mystical falling in love with God. And many Christians in the wider faith community aim at a contemplative existence that has been described as a "loving gaze at the world."

Persons who respond to the call to ministry do not do so out of lukewarm affections. Rather, they hear God's call with a generous heart. But years of service can dull our affections, making them flat and indifferent. The "fire in the belly" that may have launched us on the path of ministry may now be but an ember or even worse, cold ashes. The "saints" in the tradition and the "saints" in our midst invite us to call upon the power of the spirit to bring us back to life, to rekindle our fire, to cast out fear, to renew the face of the earth.

Ministering with Intelligence

Throughout the tradition, love has been the bedrock of Christian faith and theology. If one were to ask about the ultimate meaning of ministry, the answer would have to be love. But in addition, one has to take note of the central role of intellect as well. Ministers are midwives or brokers of an intelligent faith. Words that describe much of what a minister does include reading, thinking, preaching, teaching, theologizing, enlightening, meaning-making. What has the spirit to do with this side of ministry?

As we have seen, Western pneumatology images the spirit as the bond of love between the first and second persons of the Trinity. The second person is the word, the *logos,* the principle of reason and intelligibility. But neither the Bible, nor most of the tradition is interested in strictly logical categories. Especially in the mystical literature, there is a fluidity and a freedom in talk about God. Qualities that are attributed to one person of the Trinity in one text are linked to another in a different setting. For example, in the first epistle of John, we read that the spirit is the witness of Jesus coming, because the spirit is truth

(1 Jn 5:7). And in the gospel of John, we witness a reversal of these standard associations of word and spirit. The spirit is linked with truth: "If you love me you will obey my commands; and I will ask the Father and he will give you another to be your Advocate, who will be with you forever—the spirit of truth" (Jn 14:16–17). The Holy Spirit not only teaches what Jesus taught, but also causes this teaching to enter hearts.

In his commentary on John 16:13—the Holy Spirit leads us into all truth—Augustine compares the knowledge that comes from our own spirit with the knowledge of God that is the Holy Spirit. Because of the spirit, who is God, God is able to know about earthly things. But since there is nothing in us naturally that would allow us to know the things of God, we need the spirit. Only with the spirit's help are we able to know what takes place in God.[22]

This is a rather dramatic statement. Without the spirit, we are cut off, closed off, blocked from entrance into the world of God. *Without the spirit, we cannot know God.* The Holy Spirit is the power, in both God and in us, that makes it possible for us to know one another. Augustine sees the spirit as leading believers to a more mature stage in the experience of faith in which one not only has the gift of faith, but also *knows* it. Augustine distinguishes between possessing the gift of love, which is the Holy Spirit, and the further stage of being conscious that one has the gift. Pentecost is understood by Augustine as a fuller possession of the spirit. One who loves, he says, has the power of the Holy Spirit. This spirit presence makes believers worthy of a fuller possession, that is, a conscious knowledge of what they had.[23]

Faith is not intended to be a mindless, empty "going along," but rather an integral part of one's whole being—heart, mind, speech, and behavior. The spirit empowers us to say, "Jesus is Lord" (1 Cor 12:3). Optimally, one proclaims "Jesus is Lord" not because someone told us to, or because this is what we have always said, or in the interest of some kind of magical results. One confesses faith in Jesus as Lord most fully when one is engaged "with deliberate consent of the will." Those persons say it properly "whose utterance in speech really represents their will and intention."[24]

Augustine acknowledges a range of ways that faith can be intelligent. He speaks of that kind of learning that comes from love and that we call wisdom. He also admits the chasm between the divine and the human by teaching that the spirit infuses us with a "certain learned ignorance" because of our infirmity. But in the heat of daily life in the church, he combated the fundamentalism and anti-intellectualism around him. In a letter he writes, "Far be it from us to think that God would hate in us that which distinguishes us from the beasts.... Love understands wholeheartedly."[25]

Augustine was not only committed to speculative thought, displayed so brilliantly in his *On the Trinity and The City of God,* but he was intent on inviting others to understand the faith, so that they might open themselves to the spirit's power and become intelligent Christians in their own right. In his ministry he was tireless in leading his people to understanding. In a sermon he preaches, "God has made you a rational animal, set you over the cattle, formed you after His Own image.... Don't be like a horse or a mule, which have no understanding" (Ps 32:9).[26] Meditation, he says, can help lead us to understanding. It's as if he says, Don't be just a stupid believer, but rather, live in the spirit, that is, seek understanding, vision, wisdom, and the joy that accompanies ease in being good. Without the spirit's active presence, individuals may hear about the good news of salvation, but they are unable to know the truth about God's life; or that God dwells within (1 Jn 3:24; 4:13). The presence of love and the gifts and fruits are signs of the spirit's presence, but being conscious of that love is a fuller gift. He links the fullness of the spirit's truth with a mature faith.

Augustine reminds ministers of every age that the spirit not only empowers belief, but also enables Christians to come to maturity in faith, that is, to know, to will, and to rejoice in one's faith. Commitment to an intelligent faith is visible when rigorous training is afforded those preparing for ministry. It is visible in ministers' willingness to continue to update their education, taking advantage of lectures and workshops, keeping theology renewed, preaching afresh, insuring that teaching skills are honed. Ministers also need to have confidence in the intelligence of those they serve. Ragged, careless presentations serve no one. Even worse is the stance taken by some in ministry that the laity are unable to handle the truth of theological discussion and insight. Augustine stands before us as a model of intellectual rigor for himself and for his congregation.

Hildegard, too, links the spirit with truth. She writes to ministers in the church, calling them teachers whom the Holy Spirit inspired by "writing true doctrine in their hearts."[27] The Holy Spirit's task is to make the disciples understand internally the words of Jesus, to make them grasp such words in the light of faith, to make them perceive all the possibilities and importance of such words for the church. In this biblical view, the message of Jesus is not far removed from us, because the Holy Spirit helps us to internalize it, to grasp it spiritually, and to discover in it a word of life. The doctrine of the Holy Spirit is not new doctrine but a deeper understanding of the mystery of Jesus.

Hildegard appropriates the spirit's gift of understanding in a very personal way as well. The unlettered but brilliant Hildegard explains her understanding of the scriptures, of theology and doctrine, and of medicine and music through the tutoring of the spirit. In one of her major theological works, the *Scivias,* she turns to the spirit to ensure that her readers will absorb the message God is sending through her. In the first part of this text, God speaks at the end of each account of her six visions with the refrain: "Therefore, whoever has knowledge in the Holy Spirit and wings of faith, let this one not ignore My admonition, but taste it, embrace it and receive it in his soul" (I 6:12). This sentence functions like a mantra, effecting what it says by its very repetition. As one reads the words over and over, they penetrate more deeply into one's existence, effecting the very kind of appropriation and absorption of the truth that the Holy Spirit desires for us. Tasting, embracing, and receiving the word produces not a cursory, superficial understanding, but a deep, thoughtful, intentional appropriation. The method of *lectio divina* is led by the spirit and produces knowledge in the Holy Spirit.

In her descriptions of Pentecost, Hildegard suggests that while Jesus taught the disciples at great length, his words did not have the power he wanted them to have. Jesus even shows frustration with their slowness of understanding. But after the infusion of the spirit at Pentecost, these same slow disciples spoke with deep understanding of the purposes of God and the kingdom. While Jesus supplied the words, the Holy Spirit's coming in tongues of fire effected a change, making it seem as though the disciples had heard them for the first time—with understanding.[28]

A sacred trust of the ministry is to assist people to make their faith intelligible. Faith cannot be exempted from the high level of understanding achieved by so many Christians in other aspects of their lives. Like Augustine and Hildegard, ministers need to lead and prod people away from a faith that is simplistic or superstitious. They need to fight a bifurcated world in which we send astronauts into space and yet are satisfied with the faith we learned in fourth grade. Ministers can invite people to call upon the spirit to enlighten their faith with wisdom and understanding. Faith and reason are not enemies but partners.

This particular meaning of Pentecost might be linked to the "aha" experience of Archimedes when he discovered the principle of water displacement while relaxing in the baths. All of us can recall such "aha" experiences when the "light goes on" within us as insight dawns. We may hear the gospel every Sunday, or engage in formal prayer every day, but then something happens to lead us to a new level of realization of its existential meaning and the message begins to take root in us and bear fruit in a new way. There is a new kind of ownership of the gospel. I am not a Christian simply because my parents were Christian, but because I *know* something of what it means and I embrace it freely and intelligently. Such insight usually comes when the meaning of our faith is broken open by the experiences of life's joys and sorrows. Suffering can bring insight into the cross. Encounters with nature and beauty can reveal the face of God. Growing old and dying brings us face to face with the meaning of surrender to God.

For those who have been on this journey of intelligent faith for some time, the spirit nurtures ongoing conversion in which one allows the power of the spirit to penetrate more and more deeply over a lifetime. In this case, the spirit leads from glory to glory, to an ever-deepening grasp of the things of God and the committed living out of this meaning in our everyday lives. Ministers can call upon the spirit as they invite people to use their minds to reflect on their lives in light of the gospel, to learn about the tradition, and to see themselves as theologians in the broadest, truest sense of that term.

Ministry as Service

The final and perhaps most foundational image of the spirit for ministry is that of the spirit as servant. Catherine of Siena (1347–1380) offers a most unusual metaphor of the spirit as a waiter at table. Catherine was an Italian laywoman, member of the Dominican Third Order called the "mantellate," who spent her life caring for the poor and the sick, leading a loyal band of followers in the ways of the Lord, and struggling to bring peace to a fractious church embroiled in war and schism. Catherine's care and concern for others is characterized by a spirit of energy and indefatigable vitality that causes people to marvel at her.

She is also the author of some four hundred letters, twenty-six prayers, and a major theological work entitled *The Dialogue*. Major hallmarks of her theology include both trinitarian and eucharistic themes. Her writing style is marked by a penchant for images. Catherinian scholar, Mary T. O'Driscoll, comments, "Metaphor trips over metaphor; one image barely formed, gives way to another."[29] Using eucharistic symbols that were very familiar to her, Catherine sees the persons of the Trinity as table, food, and waiter.[30] God says to Catherine, "I am table and I am food." Catherine adds, "The hand of the Holy Spirit was dispensing this food, sweetly serving those who relished it."[31]

Catherine tells us that those who experience the Trinity in this way are at the upper reaches of the spiritual life, a stage characterized by an ability to notice God's gifts and graces. She records what God says to her about the spirit, "This gentle waiter carries to me their tender loving desires, and carries back to them the reward for their labors, the sweetness of my charity for their enjoyment and nourishment. So you see, I am their table, my Son is their food, and the Holy Spirit, who proceeds from me and the Father and from the Son, waits on them."[32] In a variation on this theme of service, Catherine images the spirit as the cellarer—"the fire and the hands that are the Holy Spirit—tapped the cask on the wood of the most holy cross."[33] The spirit serves all kinds of food—for the soul, for the intellect, for the neighbor, and in a startling juxtaposition of opposites, the spirit serves us hunger for God, for others and for the world! In other words, the spirit serves us God and every spiritual and material gift.[34]

As ministers, we are called to invite ourselves and others to enter more fully into awareness of the spirit's presence, to give gifts of service to the spirit who, in turn, offers them to God who reciprocates with further gifts of love.

We go to the table to receive the food of hunger for the community's holiness and to imitate the spirit in faithful acts of service to church and world. This insight that Catherine expressed with the help of a metaphor from daily life continues to inspire across the globe and across the centuries.

> The Holy Spirit is the light that banishes all darkness, the hand that upholds the whole world. In that vein I recall his saying not long ago, "I am the One who upholds and sustains the whole world. It was through me that the divine and human natures were brought together. I am the mighty hand that holds up the standard of the cross; of that cross I made a bed and held the God-Man nailed fast to it." He was so strong that if the bond of charity, the fire of the Holy Spirit, had not held him, the nails could never have held him.[35]

For Catherine, the spirit's strength is a strength of love and service.

This image of the spirit as waiter calls us to reflect on and repent of ministry that has been tainted with arrogance and the trappings of an aristocratic existence. It is not easy to discern the ways in which power can be used for the good without being coopted by negative forms of social and ecclesial wealth and power. What does it mean to call upon the spirit, to invite the spirit to descend on our heads in the form of tongues of fire? Catherine helps us to see that one way to be filled with the spirit is to be a servant to others. We who live in an affluent society need to have a strong desire and a healthy dose of creativity in order to discover ways to be servant in our minds, hearts, attitudes, behaviors, and trappings.

Jesus is the chief model, as the one who washed the feet of his disciples. But there are others among us who can point the way as imitators of this Jesus. It is possible to function as a servant in any walk of life. Those who clean and fix and serve at table do so more obviously. Those who walk in the halls of power have a greater challenge. But there is no social role that prohibits one from understanding what one is doing as service to others and to the world. In a distinctive way, ministry announces itself as diakonia and so bears the responsibility to be faithful to the call to be of service to others. There are those among us who have opened themselves to the spirit of service, who walk among us in a spirit of openness and humility and from whom we can learn. Many of them are poor. All of them are poor in spirit because filled with the spirit.

Conclusion

God calls out to our human frailty as ministers. We are invited to heed Hildegard's words, "Cry out and speak of the origin of pure salvation, until those people are instructed, who, though they see the inmost contents of the Scriptures do not wish to tell them or preach them, because they are lukewarm and sluggish in serving God's justice.... Burst forth into a fountain of abundance and overflow with mystical knowledge, until they who think you contemptible because of Eve's transgression are stirred up by the flood of your irrigation."[36]

As ministers in the church of God, we are invited to call upon the spirit to bring us life, to renew our faith, our lives, our work. Those who walked before us in the faith remind us to invite the spirit into our hearts at this moment in history as we face a new millennium. This spirit who is the sign of God's indefatigable goodness and love, leads us to gratitude, humility, and servanthood. Ministry is a privilege, not something that is owed us. We call upon the spirit to transform our affections, to turn hearts of stone into hearts of flesh, to lead us to wash the feet of our sisters and brothers, to turn our fear into courage and joy. Each day the spirit calls us to be mindful of gifts and to be grateful for a generous God. Each day the spirit reminds us to allow our hearts to be moved by the joys and sufferings of the world and to offer a prophetic word, a loving glance, a gentle touch. And each time we get up to preach or teach, let us prepare well and call upon the spirit to make us intelligent and clear and insightful, thus inviting others to a more mature faith that makes sense in the context of the whole of life. And above all, let the spirit grant us humility that will allow us to serve others in honesty and simplicity of heart and to face the daily failures and frustrations of ministry without bitterness or despair.

We end as we began—with the Trinity. This exploration of the spirit's gifts and powers comes to fullness and completion when the spirit returns to take up her place in the loving communion of Father and Son. God acts in history in creation, incarnation, and sanctification. God-with-us involves the ever-present, ever-loving work of God's two hands—son and spirit. The lives and work of all Christians provide the concrete extension of these two hands. As ministers, we have a distinctive role—called to join hands with son and spirit and with those we serve. The communion of the Trinity—of God, of the church, of the world, and of the cosmos provide the horizons within which we offer the service of ministry. We add our voices to those of the faithful who have prayed this prayer, *Veni Creator* since the ninth century.

> Come Holy Spirit...
> enrich our throats with speech;
> inflame the light of our senses;
> pour love into our hearts...
>
> Through you may we know the Father
> and recognize the Son
> and may we always believe
> in you, spirit of both.[37]

Notes

1. Karl Rahner, *The Trinity,* trans. Joseph Donceel (New York: Herder and Herder, 1970), 9–21.

2. The entire issue of *Theology Today* 54, 3 (October 1997) is dedicated to the theology of the Trinity. See also works by Leonardo Boff, Joseph Bracken, Colin Gunton, Catherine Mowry LaCugna, Thomas Marsh, Anne Hunt, Christoph Schwogel, and Thomas Weinandy.

3. Ralph Del Colle, *Christ and the Spirit: Spirit-Christology in Trinitarian Perspective* (New York: Oxford, 1994); Paul W. Newman, *A Spirit Christology: Recovering the Biblical Paradigm of Christian Faith* (Lanham, Md.: University Press of America, 1987). For works on the spirit, see Yves Congar, David Coffey, Ralph Del Colle, James Dunn, Jose Comblin, Mary Ann Fatula, G. W. H. Lampe, Kilian McDonnell, Jurgen Moltmann, G. Muller-Fahrenholz, and Michael Welker.

4. Catherine Mowry LaCugna, *God for Us: The Trinity and Christian Life* (San Francisco: HarperSanFrancisco, 1991), 17, 377.

5. Jurgen Moltmann, *The Source of Life: The Holy Spirit and the Theology of Life* (Minneapolis: Fortress, 1997), 10.

6. Irenaeus, *adv. Haer.* IV, pref., 4; also V,6,1. Elizabeth A. Johnson criticizes this metaphor for containing a subtle hierarchy that suggests inequality rather than equality of persons in the Trinity. To the extent that the symbol of God functions, this inequality then shows up in the Christian community. However, she also counsels against taking symbols too literally. While the former caution is well taken, I think it possible to look at the metaphor of Trinity as God and God's two hands in a number of ways, not all of which support the idea of a literal hierarchy or lose sight of the unutterable nature of God. "Trinity: To Let the Symbol Sing Again," *Theology Today* 54, 3 (October 1997): 306, 309.

7. Hildegard of Bingen, *Scivias* (New York: Paulist, 1990).

8. Ibid., II.4.2, 190.

9. Bonaventure, Sermon II for Pentecost.

10. Teresa of Avila, *The Book of Her Life,* chs. 11–22.

11. Elizabeth A. Johnson, *Women, Earth and Creator Spirit* (New York: Paulist, 1993), 48.

12. Ibid., 49.

13. *Scivias,* III.7.9, 418.

14. *The Letters of Hildegard of Bingen, Vol. 1,* trans. Joseph L. Baird and Radd K. Ehrman (New York: Oxford, 1994), 7.

15. Letter, 85r/b. Ibid., 195; Letter, 85r/a, 194.

16. Barbara Newman, "Hildegard of Bingen," video (Washington, D.C.: The National Cathedral, 1989).

17. *Letters,* 7.

18. *Scivias* III.10.4, 475; and III.10.7, 478.

19. Augustine, "On the Gospel of John," Tractate XCII.2.

20. Ibid.

21. Abraham Heschel, *The Prophets: An Introduction* (San Francisco: Harper and Row, 1962), 12.

22. "On the Gospel of John" Tractate XXXII.5.

23. Ibid., Tractate LXXIV.2.

24. Augustine, "Our Lord's Sermon on the Mount," II.XXV.83.

25. Augustine, Letter CXX.3 and CXX.13.

26. "Our Lord's Sermon on the Mount," LXXVI.

27. Letters, 61.

28. *Scivias* III.3.7.

29. Mary T. O'Driscoll, "St. Catherine of Siena: Life and Spirituality," *Angelicum* 57 (1980): 311.

30. Catherine of Siena, Letter 62. *The Letters of St. Catherine of Siena, Vol. I,* ed. Suzanne Noffke (Binghamton, N.Y.: Medieval & Renaissance Texts and Studies, no. 52, 1988), 199.

31. Ibid., Letter 47, p. 145.

32. *Dialogue* 78. Catherine of Siena, *The Dialogue,* Classics of Western Spirituality (New York: Paulist, 1980), 146.

33. Letter 37, p. 126.

34. Letter 53, p. 161.

35. Letter 29, p. 103.

36. Ibid., I.1.

37. Cited in Yves Congar, *I Believe in the Holy Spirit* (New York: Seabury, 1983), 109–10.

SECTION IV.
SPIRITUAL DIRECTION AND MENTORING

In "Seasons in Spiritual Direction," Margaret B. Guenther speaks in simple, helpful, encouraging words about the process of spiritual direction. As a good, experienced "spiritual navigator," Guenther urges us to be more sensitive to where both the director and directee are during the predictable and surprising phases of direction. For this to happen, patience is often the key virtue involved—especially during the "painful season."

Complementing Guenther's piece is "Spiritual Direction: Stalking the Boundaries" by Bruce Lescher. It discusses four challenges "postmodernity" presents to spiritual directors in our time. They are the role of the ecclesial community, the understanding of "spirituality," the nature of discipleship, and the vision of what spiritual direction is. He then goes on to suggest several types of responses to each challenge. According to Lescher, to live and guide others in "a structure that the tradition never contemplated" requires us to consider a three-step process: "To listen deeply to the other…to Christian tradition…[and to] foster a conversation between the person and tradition."

Following Guenther's and Lescher's essays is a related piece by David Lonsdale entitled "Spiritual Direction as a Prophetic Ministry." In it Lonsdale discusses the dangers of a spiritual direction that becomes domesticated and privatized. He also contends that "biblical prophecy offers an illuminating and challenging paradigm" for contemporary spiritual directors to hold as a way to keep direction faithful to the liberating mystery and word of God. In recent years technique has often taken center stage in the education of spiritual directors. Lonsdale, aptly recognizing the charismatic nature of a call to guide others in direction, points to the need not to be captured by knowledge, albeit helpful, so as to keep this process of ministry based in the prophecy tradition.

In "Speaking of Prayer," Phyllis Zagano reflects on the nature and needs of the spiritual relationship. She also addresses in three thought-provoking sections the attitude language, form, and content of spiritual direction. Drawing on both classic and contemporary writings, as well as her own sensitivity and experience to the challenges and wonders of spiritual direction, she raises issues that are essential if the lines are not to be blurred between this relation-ship and psychotherapy and counseling.

Edward Sellner's "Celtic Soul Friendship and Contemporary Spiritual Mentoring," the final essay of this section, opens with a simple, moving story of gentle, wise friendship, an *anamchara*. He then deftly shares with us several dimensions of a soul friendship. In doing this he offers us stories that clarify the points and—as good stories will—educate the heart. Following this he presents three "awarenesses" for a soul friend to have in being present to others. When I finished this paper on Celtic soul friendship, I *felt* the reality, poetry, and mystery of this precious relationship. It is a helpful, prayerful essay, which I think you will find quite rewarding.

20. Seasons in Spiritual Direction

For everything there is a season, and a time for every matter under heaven.

For many faithful churchgoers, "spiritual direction" is not a household word. The picture conjured up may be frightening, suggesting an unhealthy relinquishing of responsibility to a Rasputin-like guardian of the soul. Or there may be an aura of the medieval or monastic about the term—attractive, perhaps, but far removed from the complexity and chaos of our lives at the beginning of the twenty-first century. Then, too, we might think of spiritual direction as something desirable for the especially holy among us—clergy, perhaps, or seminarians and members of religious communities—but neither available nor appropriate for "ordinary folk."

Yet the need and hunger for spiritual guidance have always been there, even when we lack the vocabulary or the trust to identify our questions: Who are we in our relationship with God? How do we pray? How can we live out our professed beliefs? What do we do with our inevitable falling short?

These are the questions we bring to spiritual direction. The ministry is ancient and, until recently, much neglected. Now, however, it is being rediscovered. This has happened in part because of the cursillo movement, but even more basic are the failures of mainstream religion, the New Age movement, and psychotherapy to satisfy the profound but unarticulated yearning of the individual Christian for a deeper relationship with God. The tradition is there: it remains for us to build on it, to work out a model of spiritual direction that is alive and meaningful for those in the "mixed life"—for laity and clergy who are psychologically aware, who are seekers, and who have no romantic illusions about recreating the Middle Ages. Because we are speaking of an art, not a science, the ministry defies precise definition. The spiritual director is a midwife of the soul, present and attentive as new life emerges. The spiritual director offers hospitality, in the holy tradition of Abraham entertaining the angels. The spiritual director is a teacher, after the model of Jesus, who was called "Teacher" by those who loved him. But whether we call him teacher, midwife, or host, the spiritual director is always and above all a holy listener.

The holy listener does not engage in friendly chats or problem-solving sessions. Rather, the conversation of spiritual direction occurs in the spirit of the twelfth-century Cistercian Aelred of Rievaulx, who echoed the words of Jesus in Matthew's Gospel when he said, "Here we are, you and I, and I hope a third, Christ Jesus is in our midst." The holy listener knows that the space between himself and the directee is sacred space, God-filled space. And he knows that he does not work alone.

So the holy listener is able to put herself out of the way and thereby to be totally present to the person sitting opposite. Because she is disinterested (which is not at all the same as uninterested!), she is able to listen critically but not judgmentally. She is able to ask hard questions, to sit comfortably with silence, not to be frightened by tears, and to rejoice in God's love. The holy listener is totally open, ready for whatever may come. This is a ministry of detached love and concern, although the holy listener does not *fix* anything. Above all, the spiritual director is humble and reverent, for she knows that she is being entrusted with another's very being.

Who are these holy listeners? Spiritual directors are men and women, lay, ordained, and members of religious communities. They may be highly trained in theology, or they may be "simple" people of prayer who walk closely with God. They are people of tested faith who have survived the peaks and valleys of the spiritual life, to say nothing of the arid plains and swamps.

Director and directee meet regularly, usually for an hour once a month but sometimes at greater intervals. Confidentiality is inviolate: the director never repeats what he has heard. The meeting is implicitly prayerful, and usually there is spoken prayer as well. There is also room for the intimacy of shared silence. Many people want to talk about prayer or to ask for help in finding a place for God in their busy lives. Others want to make sense of their lives, that is, to see their day-to-day struggles through the lens of their Christian commitment. Since there is a "God component" in all our human experience, any matter of deep concern can provide the raw material for the direction session.

Although there are valuable books on the subject and responsible training programs for those possessing the charism for this work, even the experienced director is never a finished product; he continues to learn, grow, and discover the joys and depths of this ministry. Similarly, those receiving direction find themselves moving to ever-deeper levels of prayer and insight. The work of spiritual direction is the undertaking of a lifetime; theoretically, at least, the same director and directee can remain in conversation for decades. Even in our highly mobile society, a fruitful relationship typically lasts for years, long enough to move through many seasons, as numerous and as richly varied as those set forth in the familiar passage from the Book of Ecclesiastes:

For everything there is a season, and a time for every matter under
heaven:
>a time to be born, and a time to die;
>a time to plant, and a time to pluck up what is planted;
>a time to kill, and a time to heal;
>a time to break down, and a time to build up;
>a time to weep, and a time to laugh;
>a time to mourn, and a time to dance;
>a time to cast away stones, and a time to gather stones
>together;
>a time to embrace, and a time to refrain from embracing;
>a time to seek, and a time to lose;
>a time to keep, and a time to cast away;
>a time to rend, and a time to sew;
>a time to keep silence, and a time to speak;
>a time to love, and a time to hate;
>a time for war, and a time for peace.

Here is a broad picture of human life in all its stages, phases, and seasons. It goes without saying that we do not control the seasons. In our lives, there will be easy times and hard times, times of darkness and times of light, times of comfort and times of discomfort, times of richness and times of loss. As spiritual directors, we live through those seasons with the men and women who come to us. We live with them through the times of taking in and working toward the future—sowing, planting, building up, gathering stones together—and we live with them through the times of letting go, discarding, even dying. The seasons provide the raw material for our work together as we try to discern action of the Holy Spirit in the directee's life. To be sure, this may be experienced by the directee as the absence of God. In the old language of the tradition, there are seasons of desolation as well as times of consolation, when the sense of abandonment is most acutely painful to one who has once experienced a sense of God's presence, enfolding love. It is our task to help our directees live through times of waxing and waning and to help them remain open to the action of the Holy Spirit in their lives, especially when "nothing is happening."

There are, of course, seasons in the direction relationship itself. There is the initial period of exploration. Even when the chemistry is good, trust does not develop immediately. As the director learns the directee's story and gains a sense of the person sitting opposite, the seeker too is reaching out and testing the reliability of the man or woman he has sought out as a spiritual guide. This is the time when expectations are examined and projections are gently dealt with. The directee may want to know our qualifications or at least how we came to this ministry. I make it a practice to inquire, "Is there anything you want to ask me? Is there anything you want me to tell you about myself?" A little judicious self-disclosure by the director at the outset can go a long way toward establishing a comfortable and open relationship.

This is the time too when ground rules are established. How often do we meet? And for how long? How much and what sort of contact is acceptable between meetings? (I discourage casual "mini-sessions" and telephone calls unless the directee is experiencing a genuine crisis; then I am happy to make myself available.) The directee may have questions about payment. Because I regard spiritual direction as a ministry rather than a profession, I refuse payment but welcome gifts of gratitude to the outreach programs of my parish. However, a growing number of directors have a regular fee schedule. Whatever the financial arrangement, it needs to be understood clearly from the outset by both partners in the dialogue.

It is good, too, in the early stages of the relationship to make clear that the initial meetings are exploratory. Sometimes it is immediately apparent that the match is a good one, but it often takes time for the directee to feel secure in self-disclosure. To let the conversation find its real depth requires patience on the part of the director. And it requires a fairly strong ego to ask sincerely, after three or four meetings, whether the relationship is "working" for the directee. It is all too easy for the directee to feel trapped when she has made a wrong choice. Then there is no alternative but hanging on doggedly in a fruitless relationship or—more likely—simply disappearing.

As the work progresses, there are seasons of clarity and unclarity—those times when both director and directee seem sure of the path, in the words of the *Book of Common Prayer* are "going from strength to strength" and then those other times of waiting for the pond to clear, when clarity can come only from patient letting be. Then there are seasons of crisis, those catalytic, discernible turning points. Sometimes the work is embraced more eagerly and enthusiastically, but often a season of crisis can be identified by growing resistance in the directee. And of course, if the relationship continues, we encounter the broad plateaus, "when nothing is happening."

Finally, there is the season of closure, when the direction relationship must end. Sometimes it has gradually and almost imperceptibly turned into friendship, precious and spiritual, but the necessary distance has gradually been lost. When this happens, it takes courage to seek a new director while maintaining the friendship that has developed. It takes even more courage for the director to realize what has happened and to help the directee find a new guide. Sometimes one or both partners in the conversation sense that it is time for the directee to move on, to expand her vision or embrace the challenge of working with someone else. Closure comes too if the director becomes seriously ill, retires, or dies. Most frequently, though, the relationship is terminated because of geographical necessity: director or directee moves too far away for regular meetings. Despite the long tradition of direction by letter, there is no substitute for sitting face-to-face and *talking*. Prayers and silence are hard to manage, either in letters or on the telephone.

While we can predict and even, to some extent, control the seasons of the relationship itself, we do not determine the seasons in the directee's life. Some are predictable, determined by the ordinary rhythms of life and the directee's life stages—marriage, the birth of children, career advancements and disappointments, children leaving home, retirement, bereavement, approaching death. Others are more subtle, and the directee may not recognize them without help.

Two implicit questions underlie the work of spiritual direction: "Where am I?" and "Where am I going?" We are not static, but rather, in this life, we are wanderers and sojourners, even if we live all our lives in the house where we were born. Like a navigator, the spiritual director can help us take a sighting and find the coordinates—at least for now!

It can be enormously helpful to the directee just to have a name put on the season—this is a time to keep or a time to cast away, a time to speak or a time to keep silent, a time to plant or maybe a time to root up what has been planted. The director's task is not to diagnose or prescribe, but merely point out the possibilities and raise the questions. (Maybe that is what we are *really* about—asking the right questions!) So with the distanced love that is characteristic of the direction relationship, we can offer interpretations from *our* perspective. *Offer* is the operative word here: as spiritual directors we invite, but do not impose. As midwives of the soul, we can encourage, remembering that the literal meaning of the word is to "give heart." We can remind the directee that seasons are just that—seasons. Delightful or desolate, hope-filled or troubled, they do not last. Following upon one another, they pass and change.

Sometimes we will need to say, "Hang in there, hold on, stick it out" even when prayer seems *very* arid and God seems *very* distant. At other times, we might be called to say, "Let go, move on, embrace the new thing that looms before you even as it threatens to overwhelm you. You're ready for it." This is a delicate business, the great mystery of discernment: to know those times when we must speak boldly and to know those times when we must hold back. As the author of the Book of Ecclesiastes says, there is indeed a time to keep silence and a time to speak. And regardless of all the wise books, creative training programs, and powerful support groups, and regardless of our own broad experience and dazzling theological competence, we still take it case by case, humbly praying for guidance, and hoping that at least we do no harm. If our work is truly Christ-centered, if we remember Jesus' promise that when two or three are gathered in his name, He will be in their midst[1]—then we will be well guided, we won't get into trouble, and God will indeed even use our mistakes!

It can be helpful to remind the directee of movement and progress. When the sense of newness and adventure that marked the beginning of the relationship has diminished, and meetings have become predictable, the directee might feel stuck. Something as simple as, "Do you remember where we were a year ago? Or six months ago? It sounds as if you feel stuck, but I— sitting outside and trying to listen very attentively—can see that you are not. The Holy Spirit is at work, even when it doesn't feel like it."

It is easy to feel stuck because inevitably there are seasons of darkness and fallowness. By darkness here I don't mean necessarily dramatic times of crisis—although these can indeed be dark times—but simply those times when there is no clear light. These are not joyous times. They are tedious at best and must somehow be got through.

I was reminded of the inevitability of these dark times and even their usefulness in God's great economy recently when I was procrastinating by reading the garden column in the *New York Times*. It is not a column that is important in my life, since I have no garden. But that morning I stumbled on a spiritual truth, of which the columnist was probably quite unaware. A reader, who lived in the heart of the city with a tiny terrace garden, had asked, Why don't my morning glories bloom? The expert's answer was simple: They can't bloom in the city because there is not enough darkness. They are coded genetically to respond to alternation of light and dark, and the unnatural light of the city prevents the natural development of the plant. Too much brightness interferes with the sequence of seasons.

The people who come to us for spiritual direction may be unable to hear of the necessity, the inevitability, indeed the goodness of darkness. But as spiritual directors we need to know and accept it. It can keep us centered, compassionate, and hopeful even in dark times.

Similarly, we must remain aware and accepting of the inevitability of seasons of fallowness. In the spiritual life as in our secular careers, we can be seduced by the vision of a spurious kind of progress. Explicitly and—more insidiously—implicitly, our society bombards us with the message: Don't stop, don't stand still, keep moving! So we keep moving, even when we are not quite sure of the *why* or *whither.* I was caught up short when a wise spiritual friend pointed out that busyness, relentless activity for its own sake, is really a form of sloth. There must be times of slowing down, letting the field lie empty, uncultivated and fallow. There must be times of dormancy. The word is of course derived from the Latin *dormir* and from an even more ancient Sanskrit word meaning "to sleep." To be fallow, to be dormant is to be in a state of temporary inactivity. It can be a time of resting and regrouping. It can be a time of quiet before the emergence of some great New Thing. After all, volcanoes are dormant. Sometimes we need to stop, to be still, and to pay attention. "Behold," says God to the exiled people of Israel, "I am doing a new thing; even now it springs forth. Do you not perceive it?" (Is 43:19).

There are such long stretches when seemingly nothing is happening, those times when the directee arrives with the statement: "I needed to see you so badly; I couldn't wait for our appointment, and now it feels as if there is nothing to talk about. I don't know what I want to say." As directors, we often hear words like these; and as directees, we no doubt utter them. I know, at least, that I do! It seems as if nothing is happening—and of course that is not true. These are almost always significant meetings, perhaps because the directee has been compelled to let go of the need to organize and achieve.

As we live through the seasons with our directees, we need to cultivate tolerance, indeed the trusting acceptance of open-endedness in ourselves and in them. This doesn't come easily. This was brought home to me again and again during the years in my work at the Center for Christian Spirituality at the General Theological Seminary. Our participants, a mature group of people, drawn to the ministry of spiritual direction and therefore with at least some understanding of its ambiguity, often became restless and uneasy when they had to live for a time with open-endedness. It was hard to relinquish even an unconscious expectation of results: I have met with this directee x number of times, so by now we should have reached this or that level of spiritual depth or evinced this or that degree of growth.

It was no doubt different with the abbas and ammas of the Egyptian desert or with Aelred's Cistercian brothers in the twelfth century; but we busy, high achievers in the industrialized West want facts, clear timetables, lucid statements of purpose, and precise goals. It is challenging and a little frightening to let go of control, simply to sit and be and wait upon God. But that's what it's about: we wait for the pond to clear. The more vigorously we stir the water, the slower will be the process. Indeed, it will be impossible. The stuff floating in the pond is often good organic stuff, the material of potential spiritual growth and vitality. It can even be beautiful in its own way, but the pond must be allowed to clear. Here the *Tao te Ching* provides guidance:

> The ancient Masters [read: spiritual directors] were profound and
> subtle.
> Their wisdom was unfathomable.
> There is no way to describe it;
> all we can do is describe their appearance.
>
> They were careful
> as someone crossing an iced-over stream.
> Alert as a warrior in enemy territory.
> Courteous as a guest.
> Fluid as melting ice.
> Shapable as a block of wood.
> Receptive as a valley.
> Clear as a glass of water.

Do you have the patience to wait
till your mud settles and the water is clear?
Can you remain unmoving
till the right action arises by itself?

The Master doesn't seek fulfillment.
Not seeking, not expecting,
she is present, and can welcome all things.[2]

As directors, we must be patient. We may be so eager for the relationship to "work" that we become anxious with slow progress or what seems like no progress. But spiritual growth cannot be rushed. I suspect that every director has sat through sessions that resemble reports on "What I did on my summer vacation." I have found that, just when I am about to get impatient and autocratically redirect the conversation or, worse yet, fall into a chat about tourism, the directee gets to the real issues. We work through layers of conversation, some seemingly trivial and unrelated, but still they must be patiently peeled away. Frequently, even when the relationship is "working" well, just when I think we have gone as far as we can go, we glimpse new depths. Then we peel away another layer.

We live in a society that is obsessed with time and with productivity, but almost oblivious of fruitfulness. Perhaps most of us urban and suburban folk have wandered too far from our agricultural roots; certainly we have come to see the provision of food as a matter of production, the output of chicken factories and agribusinesses. We speed up the processes of nature, manipulating the reproduction of animals and forcing the growth of crops. Somewhere the slow work of God has got lost in our collective thinking, at least in the secular world, and all too often in the institutional church. And maybe even in spiritual direction and friendship.

But fruitfulness is something else. Fruitfulness takes time; fruitfulness allows for, even requires periods of fallowness and dormancy. True fruitfulness is really beyond our control; to be sure, we can work against it and try to thwart it, but we cannot compel it. True fruitfulness comes when—in the words of the Letter to the Ephesians[3]—we grow up into Christ, in God's own good time and on God's terms.

Fruitfulness is not a matter of achievement. It might never show up on a résumé. It cannot be reduced to a list of items to be added up: service on committees; various good works however admirable; the number of devout books read, marked, learned, and inwardly digested; the number of prayers said or the hours spent praying. True fruitfulness is a matter of *being* rather than *doing*. It may come upon us so gradually that we aren't aware. It has a way of creeping up on us; indeed, we may be the last to notice. We don't get a report card or a grade point average, and it's impossible to keep score. It calls for trust and letting be.

It calls for willingness to wait. Here the director must set the example. I have noted our time obsession, how uneasy we are with stretches of empty time. And how quickly we label time spent waiting as *wasted* time. To be sure, waiting implies expectation: one waits for *something* or *someone,* in contrast to aimless, hopeless, empty existence. Yet there is a bleakness about waiting, a provisional quality. We are not enjoying the present, nor savoring the memory of the past, but living in expectation of the not-yet.

One can wait with dread, resignation, or with joy. Waiting with joy, possibly with an admixture of fear or at least anxiety, resembles the waiting of pregnancy. We come to spiritual direction because God has got our attention, indeed has favored us with a mini-Annunciation. We are waiting for a new birth, a birth that like all births brings radical change. In spiritual direction, we are waiting—to use the image beloved by Meister Eckhart—for the birth of God in our soul. To put it another way, in the words of the Psalmist, our soul is waiting for God.

To wait is part of the human condition. But instead of being an inevitable and regrettable waste, it is a condition for growth, potentially holy and even Christlike. Whether we like it or not, such waiting often lies at the heart of spiritual direction. In the words of Teilhard de Chardin:

> Above all, trust in the slow work of God,
> We are, quite naturally,
> impatient in everything to reach the end
> without delay.
> We should like to skip
> the intermediate stages.
> We are impatient of being
> on the way to something unknown,
> something new,
> And yet it is the law of all progress
> that it is made by passing through
> some stages of instability—
> And that it may take a very long time.
>
> And so I think it is with you.
> Your ideas mature gradually—
> let them grow,
> let them shape themselves,
> without undue haste.
> Don't try to force them on,

as though you could be today
what time (that is to say, grace and
circumstances acting
on your own good will)
will make you tomorrow.

Only God could say what this new spirit
gradually forming within you will be.
Give our Lord the benefit of believing
that his hand is leading you,
and accept the anxiety of
feeling yourself in suspense and incomplete.

Yet equally important are the active seasons in spiritual direction, those often difficult times when crisis serves as a catalyst to spiritual growth. The ancient words from Ecclesiastes remind us that life is not bland and static, but that change is unavoidable and rarely easy. They remind us that there is no simple recipe to ensure smooth, untroubled progress. They remind us that crisis is inevitable and, while rarely comfortable, by no means always negative. After all, the Greek root of the word means "decision," so crisis per se is a neutral term, denoting a turning point, a dividing line, or a moment of truth. A crisis can be an occasion for destruction or for growth, a movement toward death or toward new life.

I would prefer to live without crises. So would the people who come to see me for spiritual direction. But that is really beside the point. For spiritual directors, it is essential to be aware that these difficult, sometimes painful, at the very least, unsettling seasons can be spiritually fruitful.

We need to resist the determinedly upbeat Christianity that seems to be abroad these days. We know the cliches—God never sends more than we can bear *or* this suffering is somehow a sign of God's special favor. Even more insidious is the idea, implied or explicitly stated, that we are somehow to blame when we find ourselves in difficult times. (Maybe we are! But often we are not.) It is no help to a directee to be left feeling that if her faith were stronger or if she prayed more or somehow more expertly, she would not find herself in distress.

Our tradition, as reflected in both the Hebrew scriptures and the New Testament, makes clear that troubled times—seasons of crisis—are part of the human condition and that, more to the point, we often feel abandoned by God. A cursory reading of the psalms shows that the people of Israel were not strangers to those difficult, threshold times:

My spirit shakes with terror; how long, O LORD, how long? My God, my God, why have you forsaken me? and are so far from my cry and the words of my distress? O my God, I cry in the daytime, but you do not answer; by night as well, but I find no rest. Save me, O God, for the waters have risen up to my neck. I am sinking in deep mire, and there is no firm ground for my feet. (Psalms 6, 22, and 69)

Truly, as the author of Ecclesiastes says, there is nothing new under the sun. These are the prayers of a person in crisis, in spiritual and physical anguish.

Similarly, the gospel accounts of the life of Jesus remind us that we are not promised a rose garden, but rather that other garden of pain and abandonment, when we are compelled to enter a place of darkness and passivity. The English Franciscan W. H. Vanstone has written compellingly of this in a deceptively simple little book called *The Stature of Waiting*.[4] Drawing chiefly on the Gospels of John and Mark, he points out the dramatic division of Jesus' ministry into two distinct parts. The Jesus whom most of us prefer to emulate, certainly the Jesus to whom we are drawn is active: he preaches, teaches, argues, travels, heals, prays, and feasts. Grammatically, he is the subject, not the object, of most sentences. But at the moment of crisis—the turning point—when he is arrested, given over, handed up, he becomes passive. After that, he speaks very little and is *done unto*. He is abandoned by his friends and feels abandoned by God.

Then there is the Dark Night of the Soul, a significant part of our spiritual tradition, most eloquently articulated by Carmelite John of the Cross in the sixteenth century. This is not so much a crisis of physical suffering (although John was no stranger to pain and gratuitously inflicted cruelty), but rather a spiritual crisis characterized by a sense of abandonment. It is a disoriented, arid season when old ways of praying no longer serve. Inevitably it is a state of suffering, as—in the language of the tradition—consolation gives way to desolation. Although it might not feel quite the opposite, the dark night is viewed as a sign of God's favor. Similarly, a crisis can be a turning point toward a season of growth and vitality. But first there must be surrender, a letting go and stripping down.

There are, of course, also "happy" crises, turning points when health and hope begin to replace abuse and despair. The beginning of recovery from addiction leads many people into exploration of their spiritual identity. Similarly, the beginning of recovery from abuse—sexual, emotional, or physical— leaves the directee with a fresh perspective and newfound energy to embrace the big questions of meaning. It is a joy to work with such a seeker, filled with gratitude and on fire with the love of God.

Just as acute suffering and a pervasive malaise can cause people to turn to some form of psychotherapeutic counseling, painful critical seasons can also be an invitation to undertake spiritual direction. Or, for those already comfortably in a direction relationship, such times can signal the need to go deeper, to dig in, to go to work, to let go of niceness, to *grapple*. Chronic or life-threatening illness of one's self or one's spouse or partner inevitably raises questions of deep meaning and the urge to explore them. Pastoral care of those whose death is imminent is an opportunity for ad hoc spiritual direction, even though it may never be labeled as such. It has been my experience that family members, no doubt because of their own grief, are typically unable to talk about the next threshold; and most caregivers simply do not have the time. It is a privilege to listen to the dying and to offer a safe space where they may speak candidly.

The empty nest brings many women to spiritual direction; when they are freed from the obligation of nurturing others, there is time to reflect on their own experience and worth. Loss of meaningful work is another catalyst. Unemployment is a major spiritual crisis of our time, and even planned and welcome retirement is a jolt. Suddenly, there is empty time, time that can be filled with trivial pursuits or time that can be embraced as a gift.

All these are seasons, in one way or another, of apparent loss. Most strikingly, bereavement—which can include the death of a significant relationship—is a time when priorities are clarified, the trivial is swept aside, and the essential questions loom in one's consciousness. All these seasons can be times of despair and emptiness, *or* they can be opportunities to go deeper. Obviously, the director or spiritual friend takes his cue from the person on the threshold. It is enough to be a supportive presence, leaving the directee free to discover grace in apparent darkness and emptiness that characterize the threshold.

There often are elements of depression in these difficult times of crisis. This is natural and predictable, for example, in bereavement or when someone lives with chronic, debilitating physical pain. I would never minimize this. But not the same as extreme, chronic, disabling clinical depression. To acknowledge that it can be an occasion for spiritual growth is by no means the same as saying that suffering should be induced and encouraged. Here spiritual directors and psychotherapists can cooperate, sharing the same raw material but viewing it through a different lens. It has been my experience that they coexist quite comfortably and fruitfully. So while the director may offer a referral to someone who is clinically trained, he does not abandon the directee.

Besides the rather dramatic and easily identifiable seasons of crisis, there is also the season of growing awareness in the mature directee of transience and mortality, which is not the same as a crisis precipitated by illness or bereavement. Rather, the directee realizes gradually or suddenly that something is missing, that there is something more than everyday busyness, and that time is precious. This growing concern with ultimate meaning coincides with recognition and acceptance of one's own mortality. It may come to some in their mid-thirties, to others in their fifties or sixties. (It is, of course, possible to live in denial and avoidance until life's end. Clearly, these are not people who seek out a spiritual director.) This is not so much a morbid preoccupation with impending death as a stirring of vocation. Cognizant of her limitation, the directee begins to live into the question, "Why am I here? What am I supposed to do with my life?" It is possible to play the endgame with passion, embracing the new thing that springs forth.

Common to all of these catalytic crises—the painful ones and the joyful challenge of new beginnings—is the fact that the old ways aren't working. Prayer feels arid and mechanical. God seems remote or indeed not to be. The directee experiences a sense of threshold, dis-ease, and uncertainty. Basic questions arise about identity: Who am I in the sight of God? Do I matter? What is going to happen to me? With Mary Magdalene, the directee may cry out (or whisper), "They have taken the Lord out of the tomb, and we do not know where they have laid him" (Jn 20:2b). Of course this seeming loss is not a loss, but the inevitable next step toward the encounter with the risen Christ. Mary Magdalene, at that point, however, perceived only the very real pain of loss and disorientation. So too the directee experiencing a time of crisis feels that the elusive Christ has escaped, eluded her—just when she thought she had him neatly contained.

This experience is not unique to major times of crisis, though it is observable, even predictable in them. It happens and continues to happen to us in our Christian journey, if we are brave enough to accept the freedom and strength God offers us. Maybe it happens as we continue to exercise our intellectual powers in study and find our scriptural and theological preconceptions challenged. Even more likely, it happens in our *everydayness,* our routine, our faithful "getting the job done." Suddenly or gradually, we are aware that Christ has gotten away from us. It may be too painful to acknowledge our all-too-human wish to contain him—not in a tomb, but in the tastefulness of a well-executed liturgy.

In the gospel story of Mary Magdalene at the tomb, however, there is the ongoing implicit invitation to stand up straight and look around in all directions. For her, as for us and our directees, he's right there. Do we recognize him, or do we suppose him to be the gardener? The message is clear: We can either go on peering into emptiness, lifelessness, and death, or we can stand up and look around. We might see something new—a broader vista, a richer scene.

Crisis is a characteristic of transition, a necessary prelude to growth. I know of few transitions, even when they are necessary or even welcome, that are without pain. In the spiritual life, if we continue to grow, our icons—our windows to God—eventually turn into idols and need at the very least to be placed gently on the shelf. (Smashing such beloved and useful old friends seems unduly violent.) Then we need to wait, sometimes in the darkness and sometimes in loneliness, for new icons to emerge. In spiritual direction, this might mean exploring new imagery for God. Yes, God is king, father, shepherd, and judge. But God is also rock and eagle, to say nothing of the tender mother of Psalm 131. It might also mean exploring new ways of praying,

breaking loose from accustomed molds and stretching boldly. Here the director can encourage and reassure: maybe you need to put the prayer book aside
for a while. You can pray while you do your daily running. Or while you scrub
the kitchen floor. You can pray without words. Or with your own spontaneous,
down-to-earth words that sound nothing like the liturgy. You might check out a
Taize chant service or a centering prayer group. Maybe you need to draw or
paint your prayers. Or write them in your journal—maybe poems or letters to
God. Of course, the wise spiritual director does not suggest trying everything
at once. Rather, this is a time for gently suggesting new possibilities and
encouraging boldness. Directees often have difficulty accepting the freedom
that can accompany a turning point.

Apocalyptic times are never easy, whether they occur on a grand scale
societally or on a small scale in individual lives. It is all too easy to see old
forms passing away, the seemingly immutable changing before our eyes, and
all the loss that accompanies change. What is never clear, when one is living in
the midst of a crisis, are the emerging new forms. In other words, it is often
difficult for the directee to perceive his own spiritual growth. Here the director
can be helpful. Of course, I would never say to someone who turned to me in
the midst of turmoil and pain, "Wow! What an occasion for spiritual growth!"
But I would know in my heart the great law of the conservation of spirit, analogous to the law of conservation of matter: in God's economy, nothing gets
wasted, no matter how it might look at the time and no matter how we might
attempt to thwart, deny, and ignore it.

Writing about friendship, Aelred of Rievaulx might well be speaking of
spiritual direction:

> A man [and presumably a woman] is to be compared to a beast if he
> has no one to rejoice with him in adversity, no one to whom to
> unburden his mind if any annoyance crosses his path or with whom
> to share some unusually sublime or illuminating inspiration.

> But what happiness, what security, what joy to have someone to
> whom you dare speak on terms of equality as to another self; one to
> whom you need have no fear to confess your failings; one to whom
> you can unblushingly make known what progress you have made in
> the spiritual life; one to whom you can entrust all the secrets of your
> heart, and before whom you can place all your plans![5]

Such a friend and empathic listener would offer a safe place to a directee in crisis. Such a director would be a supportive, prayerful presence, a haven of stability in a time of upheaval. Nothing would be too absurd or shameful to be brought
up. How many direction sessions begin with the words, "I know I shouldn't feel

this way, but…"? When one "speaks on terms of equality as to another self," the tyranny of "shoulds" is destroyed and fruitful candor is possible.

Such a director would also offer a safe place for rejoicing, for recognizing and celebrating the "happy" crises. Directees are often reluctant to bring good news, for fear that they will appear boastful. It is easier to denigrate or accuse ourselves. But the wise friend characterized by Aelred is open and non-judgmental, ready to hear about "progress made in the spiritual life." Our spirituality can become so heavy! We suppress our dreams and our urgent longings, convinced somehow that our experience does not matter and, sadly, that God cannot be concerned with *us*. The wise friend, however, is worthy of being entrusted with the secrets of the directee's heart and "all his plans." This means that she can see new life coming from seemingly dead places. She can encourage the directee to trust and value himself and to embrace the newness of the next season.

As we move with our directees through the seasons, we work in awareness of the danger of spiritualizing ordinary experience, that kind of glib compartmentalizing that carefully puts God "up there" somewhere, far from real life. We can encourage our directees to be mindful of the God-component in all human experience, even or especially when it feels like the absence of God. We ourselves remain aware of the insidious little demon of niceness, which makes the directee unwilling to wrestle, as Jacob wrestled with the angel at the ford of the Jabbok. Sometimes both director and directee forget that ours is a God who knows us intimately, who invites us into relationship, and who is ready to wrestle. We can encourage the directee to acknowledge darkness, pain, and anger. The psalms, particularly, are an excellent resource for the directee who fears that God cannot deal with candor or with temper tantrums.

Further, in painful seasons we can hold the directee in prayer when she feels unable to pray herself. We can avoid platitudes and the temptation to fix, teaching ourselves (and our directee) to avoid quick answers but rather to live comfortably with ambiguity. We can discourage self-blame and self-reproach by the directee; this is a time for the least directive of us to be tough and repetitive. The directee may need to hear many times that she is known and loved by God, regardless of the season in which she finds herself. Finally, as already noted, we can encourage boldness in the exploration of new ways of prayer. In short, as our directees move through the seasons, we are midwives of the soul—supportive, encouraging, challenging, and comforting, often willing just to sit and hold a hand as we wait together.

The preacher tells us that along with the time to weep and the time to mourn, there is also a time to laugh and a time to dance. The work of spiritual direction can easily become somber and ponderous. After all, director and directee are dealing with ultimate concerns, seeking to deepen a relationship with the unknowable God. We need to remember that there must also be seasons of *celebration.* We can encourage the cultivation of habit of gratitude, and we can invite the gift of joy and wonder in all God's works. We can let go and loosen up. I was struck not long ago when I recalled that, in the fourteenth-century English of Geoffrey Chaucer, the word *silly* meant "blessed." We can help our directees be open to those seasons of sheer joy, those times of holy uselessness.

If relationship continues long enough, director and directee will move through a number of seasons together. Both will be richer. Both will be blessed.

Notes

1. Matthew 18:20.

2. Stephen Mitchell, *Tao te Ching: A New English Version with Foreword and Notes* (New York: Harper and Row, 1988), 15.

3. Ephesians 4:15.

4. New York: Seabury, 1983.

5. Aelred of Rievaulx, *Spiritual Friendship* (Kalamazoo: Cistercian Publications, 1977).

Bruce H. Lescher

21. Spiritual Direction: Stalking the Boundaries

Some Personal Background

Spiritual direction involves a process of self-revelation to another person.[1] Consequently, I begin this article by telling you something about me. I do this to clarify my social location and to assist you in gauging the relevance of what I say for your own context.

General background: I am a fiftysomething white Roman Catholic layman of predominantly German stock. I was raised in a suburb of Cleveland, Ohio, and the traditional values of my midwestern roots deeply influence the way I see the world. Throughout my adult life I have ministered primarily in educational settings. I love teaching and have taught at the high school, undergraduate, and graduate levels in various cities: Cleveland, South Bend, Seattle, Austin, Chicago, Berkeley. For several years I was a brother in the Congregation of Holy Cross, and the values and spiritual disciplines I interiorized in the congregation still influence my spiritual practice as well as my vision of ministry as a collaborative project. Currently I coordinate a program for men and women who are experienced ministers and are taking some time out for personal renewal and theological updating.

More specifically: this article arises from the death of my friend Richard. Richard was a gay man whose struggle with HIV/AIDS changed my life. Early in our friendship I judged him negatively based on my traditional midwestern values. But Richard was patient with me, and, as his struggle with the virus unfolded, we talked regularly, honestly, and deeply. HIV accelerated his process of spiritual maturation. His compassion and wisdom blossomed for all to see. From his position as an outsider who is condemned by church and society, he came to powerful insights about the inclusiveness of Jesus' good news. He became a mentor and teacher to his friends and coworkers; certainly he was to me. I dedicate this article to him, hoping that I might face the challenges of my topic with half his wisdom, courage, and honesty.

I've been involved in the ministry of spiritual direction since about 1980. As a spiritual director I listen a lot. I listen most intently to the women and men who have graced my life by allowing me to accompany them on their journeys. But I find that this discipline of intentional listening overflows into other areas of my life. I wind up listening to a friend over dinner as we catch up after not seeing each other for a few months, or to a student who in a conversation after class expresses her excitement about some exploding insights, or simply riding the elevator with a neighbor complaining about his old motorcycle.

As I listen I image myself more and more as one who is stalking a boundary, now on this side, now on that, always aware that the boundary is near. What boundary? That is what I hope to explore in the following pages.

The Postmodern Context

The ministry of spiritual direction finds itself in an unprecedented context, one that holds both promise and peril. We live in what scholars across a variety of disciplines call "postmodernity."[2] The great themes that gave rise to the modern world—the advance of science, the objectivity of reason, the forward march of human progress—came crashing down in the late twentieth century. Those of us in the postmodern world are left with the deconstruction of these great themes. *Postmodernity* is an amorphous term that is anything but univocal, but it would include the following characteristics:

Suspicion of meta-narratives. A meta-narrative is a story that claims to encompass all stories and gives a total explanation of reality. In the sixteenth century, for example, European nations subsumed colonial cultures into the myth of the superiority of Western culture. Or, more recently, since the Enlightenment, people have placed faith in the ability of reason to lead to scientific and social progress. Such meta-narratives, contemporary literary criticism has demonstrated, mask the ideology of those who construct them. By ideology I mean ideas and concepts that are presented as objective but which serve the self-interest of those who put them forward. Western culture's claim to superiority, for example, masked the greed and thirst for power that led to the pillaging of colonial peoples. It also denigrated the wisdom and truth to be found in those people's cultures.

Concomitant with this distrust of meta-narrative is distrust of what Sanks calls "totalizing institutions," those institutions which lay claim to a meta-narrative.[3] The foundational institutions of society: familial, educational, political, economic, and religious are no longer trusted, and their totalizing claims are seen as masking self-interest and excluding the voices of the marginalized.

Often enough religious institutions deserve the distrust and suspicion in which they are held. Religious tradition is marked by what Jim and Evelyn Whitehead call "grace and malpractice."[4] Religious institutions have justified racism and sexism as God's will. Religious leaders have been corrupted by power and wealth. Churches have covered over sexual abuse by their clergy. They have served the wealthy and neglected the poor. Finally, some of them have responded to the postmodern context by appealing to fundamentalism. They avoid the pluralism of viewpoints by insisting on the objective certainty of their meta-narrative. At various times in history, and certainly today, believers struggle with the malpractice of their churches. Dorothy Day was quoted as saying that Christ is crucified on the cross of the church.

Otherness. Postmodernity has witnessed the emergence of "the other." Meta-narratives silenced the voices of women, of racial minorities, of those who were different from the mainstream. Our understanding of ourselves, our brothers and sisters, our world, and even our God has been impoverished by the loss of these voices. Postmodern thinkers thus emphasize the importance of allowing "the other" to be other, of not assuming that his or her story is really the same as my story only under different appearances.

The particular and the local. If modernity was marked by the search for universal explanations, postmodernity is marked by the value of the particular. Language and symbol are situated in particular cultures in particular places: in the Lakota people of South Dakota or a base community in a barrio of Lima, Peru. The worldviews arising from such contexts are not reducible to one another. Theology increasingly acknowledges pluralism in theology, speaking of "theologies" rather than "theology."[5]

Eclecticism. This follows from all that has been said. Sanks speaks of "a willingness to assemble and combine elements from various traditions, including modernity...without seeking a synthesis or harmony, as manifested especially in architecture [i.e. the tendency in postmodern architecture to mix in one building styles from different ages]."[6] Truth is not to be found in one, totalizing viewpoint; hence one is left with a plurality of competing viewpoints, and one can weave together elements from various viewpoints to create a sense of meaning.

Implications for Spiritual Direction

Ministry changes as the contexts in which ministry is carried out change. Postmodernity presents spiritual directors with challenges not faced before in the history of Christian spirituality. Here I will single out four such challenges: the role of the ecclesial community, the understanding of "spirituality," the nature of discipleship, and the vision of what spiritual direction is. I will suggest that a spectrum of responses exists for each challenge, and any given spiritual director may locate himself or herself somewhere on these spectra.

First, the role of the ecclesial community. Historically, spiritual direction has been understood as a ministry *of an ecclesial community.* The spiritual director ministered not simply in her or his name, but as a representative of a normative community, whether that community was a small group of nuns or monks, a local parish, or a mainline denomination. The director, in the process of listening to the directee's story, mediated the wisdom and norms of the community. Within Roman Catholicism this role of the spiritual director was most clearly embodied in the post-tridentine practice of receiving spiritual direction within the sacrament of penance. The confessor or director interpreted the penitent's words in light of the church's creedal and moral norms.

Today, the relationship between spiritual direction and ecclesial communities is less clear, and in some cases may be challenged as relevant at all. Ecclesial communities tend to be "totalizing institutions," that is, they offer the Christian story as a meta-narrative which gives meaning to people's lives. Thus churches and denominations are subject to the same suspicion that marks people's attitude toward government, schools, and corporations. Today's spiritual seekers often hold ecclesial communities in distrust. Such suspicion challenges a spiritual director to locate herself or himself on a spectrum, ranging from director as mediator of a communal wisdom to director as one not attached to any ecclesial community.

Postmodernity's second challenge involves the understanding of "spirituality." In the postmodern context, "spirituality" becomes separated from "religion." Spirituality concerns one's personal spiritual quest (even when lived out in relation to others and in commitment to social causes), whereas religion concerns the institutionalization of religious values in dogma, cult, and church polity. Spirituality is in, while religion is out. Sociologist Meredith McGuire, in researching people's spiritual practices, records the response of one interviewee whose answer is typical: "I'm probably not very religious, but I consider myself a deeply spiritual person."[7] This challenges a spiritual director to locate himself or herself on a spectrum of responses, from understanding spirituality as a way to live out (thus be reliant upon) creedal and moral norms to "spirituality" as a layer of human experience deeper than and unrelated to institutional formulations.[8]

This understanding of "spirituality" leads to postmodernity's third challenge to spiritual direction: altering the nature of discipleship. In previous contexts the seeker was a *disciple,* attempting to interiorize and integrate a wisdom being handed on by an ecclesial community. A clear embodiment of this understanding is apparent in Roman Catholic religious orders prior to Vatican II, where a novice changed his or her name, family, and even clothing in taking on a new identity. The novice immersed herself or himself in the charism and practices of the community. In the postmodern context, the seeker is pressured to become a *consumer,* picking and choosing from various spiritual traditions in order to develop a spiritual practice that works for him or her. This is not to say that all seekers become consumers, but contemporary North American culture pushes people in this direction. One need only walk into a bookstore (real or virtual) to find books, videos, and audiotapes on a dizzying array of spiritual disciplines. The relationship between seeker and community is reversed: the seeker does not conform to the wisdom of the community, but rather the wisdom of the community must appeal to the seeker. In her research in San Antonio, McGuire encountered committed spiritual seekers who melded, for example, Roman Catholicism, traditional Aztec rituals, and Buddhist meditative practice.[9] This understanding of "spirituality" suggests a spectrum of responses, from director as disciple who passes on a wisdom tradition to director as one who works with seekers who discern and select among various traditions.

Postmodernity's fourth challenge concerns the vision of what spiritual direction is or the nature of this ministry. Historically, the ministry of spiritual direction has involved two significant dimensions, which for the sake of discussion I will label "charismatic" and "professional."

The "charismatic" dimension means that some people are given gifts (a listening heart, a discerning spirit) that enable them to be good spiritual directors. One sign of possessing such gifts is that others seek out this person as listener and adviser. The monastic roots of spiritual direction clearly demonstrate this dimension. An initiate would attach himself or herself to a wise elder, an abba or amma. Such elders had the gift of discernment, the ability to "give a word" to the one seeking guidance; they did not hold institutional office but rather attracted disciples by the quality of their lives.

The "professional" dimension indicates the need for a director to have some knowledge and skills. In the Christian tradition, a director, for example, ought to know something about scripture, about the teachings of the great mystics, about different styles of prayer. A director ought also to have good listening skills and be able to pick up psychological dynamics such as projection, transference, and countertransference.

Ideally, a spiritual director would integrate the polarities of charismatic gifts and professional background, would integrate the call of the spirit and suitable training. In a postmodern context, however, because of suspicion of ecclesial communities, directors can experience pressure to separate the polarities. They can be pushed toward becoming either *professionals* or *independent experts*. On the one hand, they experience pressure to become a professional. If ecclesial and communal practices and norms are suspect, one can still lay claim to proper education, training, supervision, and adherence to a code of ethics.[10] A guild replaces a church as a validating organization. Spiritual directors are pushed toward imitating professional therapists, a process already well under way in North America. On the other hand, they experience pressure to become a charismatic, independent expert. Modernity, with its emphasis on reason and science, tended to equate the spiritual with the ethereal and unreal. Postmodernity, however, with its distrust of totalizing reason and acknowledgement of indeterminacy in both nature and history, displays an openness to the spiritual dimension of life. Witness, for example, the interest in angels so evident in popular culture, or the openness to the teachings of pre-modern cultures. Print and audiovisual media are populated with spiritual teachers who attract followers but who are not validated by either an ecclesial community or a guild (for example, Deepak Chopra or Jean Houston). Spiritual directors may experience cultural pressure to assume the role of independent teacher. This suggests a spectrum of responses, from director as one who holds the tension of charism and profession, to director as either professional or unattached spiritual teacher.

Getting a Handle on What's Happening

In postmodernity, the spiritual director, I believe, often becomes the person who mediates between a denomination and the contemporary seeker. The seeker might not talk to a minister or official representative of the institution but would talk to a spiritual director precisely because he or she may be seeking guidance in his or her spiritual quest. The director stands at the boundary between the religious institution and people's personal spiritual quests.

How are we to understand the dynamics of this situation? For purposes of illustration I would like to draw an analogy from the writings of Thomas Merton, the Trappist monk and author. In his biography of Merton, William H. Shannon notes that in 1962 Merton wrote a number of articles and letters expressing his alarm over the United States' willingness to use nuclear weapons in a first strike against the Soviet Union.[11] Merton argued instead for Christian nonviolence. He acknowledged the validity of the "just war" theory, a central aspect of Catholic moral theology. But Merton felt that the modern experience of nuclear weapons outstripped the categories of the just war theory. A nuclear missile launched against a Russian city would obliterate the distinction between combatants and noncombatants. Contemporary experience did not disprove the tradition; it rather raised questions with which the tradition was not equipped to deal. Shannon says that Merton "tried to balance his loyalty to accepted Catholic tradition with the demands his conscience made on him in a situation that the tradition had never contemplated."[12]

Many spiritual seekers, I believe, find themselves in an analogous situation. They live in "a situation that the tradition never contemplated." Their experience lies outside the categories of their tradition, and in fact may call those very categories into question.

Two Examples: The Experience of Women,
the Experience of Gay/Lesbian Persons

In recent years perhaps the clearest example of the tension between personal experience and institutional stance involves the experience of many women and of many gay and lesbian persons. Here I will not attempt to give an overview of the important work being done in both women's and gay/lesbian spirituality; rather, I will share some personal impressions.[13]

Jennifer is a Sister of St. Ann in her mid-forties.[14] She has given nearly twenty years of her life to church ministry and is currently director of religious education in a large parish. While working on her M.A. in theology, she read widely in feminist theology. Lately her prayer has blossomed as she images a God with feminine qualities. She finds male-only references to God in the liturgy to be increasingly problematic. She is angered by recent official Catholic statements suggesting that Catholics not even discuss women's ordination. At times she wonders if she is wasting her talents in parochial ministry, where her position could be terminated with a change of pastors.

Jennifer's struggle exemplifies the dilemma faced by many women as they confront the history of Christianity. Feminist scholarship has convincingly demonstrated that women have been pushed to the margins of both theology and church governance. Two marginalizations interlock: the image of God as male, and the exclusion of women (in some denominations, most notably Roman Catholicism) from ordained ministry. Women are *experiencing* the feminine dimensions of God despite the preponderance of male imagery in the tradition. Women are *experiencing* their exclusion from some forms of ministry as arbitrary despite claims that Jesus intended such exclusion and it cannot be changed.

The experience of gay and lesbian persons provides a second example of the tension between experience and the tradition.[15] Chad is in his early thirties. He became aware of his homosexual orientation as he entered puberty. He lived in the closet until a few years ago when his desire for integrity pushed him to come out, first to his coworkers at the accounting firm and then to his family. He and Thomas have been together for five years and, like all couples, work hard to nurture and maintain their relationship. Chad regularly attends Sunday mass and volunteers every Thursday evening at the parish's soup kitchen.

Catholic moral theology distinguishes between sexual orientation and sexual acts. Based on a theory of natural law, the moral tradition sees homosexual acts as inherently disordered and counsels all gay and lesbian persons to live celibately. In several cities and states the church has opposed legislation that would recognize domestic partnerships or legalize homosexual marriage. Understandably, Chad struggles to remain part of the parish in the face of such theological and political opposition. Yet he understands his orientation as one of God's gifts to him, and he feels that this parish is his church too!

How to Respond?

Boundaries abound in postmodernity: story/ideology, spirituality/religion, searching/consuming, community norms/respect for the individual. And perhaps most pertinent here, the boundary between religious institution and personal spiritual quest. Spiritual directors are invited, I believe, to compassionately and creatively stalk these border lines. I suggest a three-step process.

First, *listen deeply to the other.* Encourage, indeed empower, the directee to articulate his or her experience. The very act of telling one's story, of putting one's experience into words, can be liberating. Once my story is out there, I can reflect upon it from a different standpoint.[16] In such listening, the director allows the other to be other. The director especially allows this other to be himself or herself when he or she is that "other" who has been ignored or silenced by a religious tradition or mainline culture. In as much as they are the products of human effort, all traditions and cultures favor some people and disparage others, give voice to some and silence others. The director may even feel discomfort as this "other" challenges the beliefs or categories of her or his own tradition (I certainly have!). Yet traditions ossify when they attempt to tell people what their experience must be; they remain vibrant only when they allow themselves to be changed in the light of new human experiences.

Second, *listen to Christian tradition.* Here I would make a distinction between religious tradition and religious institutions.[17] The Christian spiritual tradition is pluralistic and multivalent; it stretches back into history through more women and men than could ever be mentioned here. It includes shining lights like Thomas Merton, Dorothy Day, Thérèse of Lisieux, Francis de Sales, Teresa of Avila, Martin Luther, Catherine of Siena, Bonaventure, Julian of Norwich, John Climacus, Anthony, Paul of Tarsus, Jesus of Nazareth; and its roots reach into the Hebrew scriptures. It includes countless ordinary and forgotten holy folk who lived gospel lives and left this world a better place for their being here. Different currents of this tradition are now institutionalized in denominations and sects, yet the river of tradition is wider and deeper than any of these institutions.

Listening to the tradition enriches the practice of spiritual direction in at least three ways: it affirms plurality, it provides some basic road maps, and it resists the hegemony of contemporary culture.

The Christian tradition affirms plurality: there is no one way to God. Persons who are just beginning to be serious about the spiritual quest especially need to hear this. Sometimes they are tempted to find the "right way" (and when they find it, they want everyone else to follow it!). The great mystics have traveled many paths; they have lived by trusting in reason and distrusting it, by way of light and by way of darkness; they have been nuns, husbands, bishops, dissenters, hermits, and activists. Thus beginners can be encouraged to try different prayer styles and spiritual practices until they find some that "fit" for them. Beginners might also be anxious because they are not praying the "right way" or following the "proper" spiritual disciplines; they want to "get it right." Tradition responds, "Relax! There are many rooms in God's wide and gracious house."

Second, tradition provides some basic maps of the spiritual journey. The contemporary seeker need not wander in a wilderness with no sense of direction. While spiritual writers use different metaphors and symbols to describe the spiritual journey, they agree that growth occurs in stages and that moving into a new stage often calls forth a change in the way one prays. Such maps and metaphors can serve as helpful guideposts, especially to a seeker who is frustrated that her or his prayer has become dry and seemingly fruitless. The tradition also speaks of the detours that can lead to self-delusion. Teresa of Avila and Ignatius of Loyola, for example, are masters of unmasking human pretension. Knowledge of the teaching of such spiritual masters can help today's searcher avoid mistakes that others have made.

Finally, tradition resists the hegemony of contemporary culture. In a culture that often judges people by wealth or looks or intelligence or productivity, the Christian spiritual tradition affirms that each human being is of infinite worth, created in the divine image. In a culture that pushes people toward isolation and anomie, the tradition affirms the importance of relationship and community. It does not view human beings as isolated invididuals but rather assumes that to be "person" is to already be in relationship with family, friends, and society. In a culture that reduces "person" to "consumer," the tradition judges the authenticity of one's spiritual life by how one lovingly serves God and others.

Third, *foster a conversation between the person and tradition.* As indicated previously, fostering such a conversation is often a delicate task. Seekers who have been hurt by religious institutions will question the relevance of tradition. Yet the dialogue between seeker and tradition can be enormously fruitful to both. Contemporary seekers do have experiences not anticipated by the tradition, and such experiences call the tradition to develop and expand. Contemporary seekers also have biases and blind spots that can be challenged by the accumulated wisdom of tradition.

Contemporary understanding of the patriarchal bias of Christianity and insights into the feminine nature of the divine challenge the tradition to the core. They will, I believe, forever alter both theology and spirituality. Listening to women's experience is critical for the very survival of Christianity. Feminist scholars are posing questions not anticipated by past formulations. Even more significant for spiritual direction, women and men are *experiencing* a God not imagined by the tradition. At the same time tradition can enrich women's experience. Elizabeth Johnson, for example, believes that there are elements of the classical theological tradition that "would further the emancipation of women."[18] The liberation of women is enriched and strengthened by understanding this movement as the unfolding of God's action in the world and not simply as a political force. And Constance FitzGerald suggests that women's contemporary experience of impasse (of coming up against situations which seem to have no solution) can be enriched by John of the Cross's explanation of the Dark Night of the soul.[19]

Homosexual persons, speaking from a position of marginalization imposed by both church and culture, are likewise challenging Christian teaching. Contemporary research on homosexuality questions the traditional assumption that sexual orientation involves moral choice (and is hence "unchosen"). Further, many gay and lesbian people experience their orientation as a blessing, not a curse. James L. Empereur speaks of "homosexuality in a new key" and notes, "Homosexuality is one of God's most significant gifts to humanity. To be gay or lesbian is to have received a special blessing from God."[20] What blessing? For one thing, gay and lesbian spirituality seeks healing of the traditional split between body and spirit, sexuality and spirituality. For another, the gay and lesbian community has been a model of compassion and loving care in dealing with the ravages which HIV/AIDS has wreaked upon the gay community in particular. Spiritual directors have much to learn from listening to the experience of gay and lesbian persons. In so doing directors may be challenged to deal with their own homophobia. At the same time, the tradition can challenge gay believers. Some gay spiritualities, for example, affirm the value of multiple sexual contacts as a way of subverting the oppression of heterosexual society. Christian spirituality would challenge such an interpretation.[21]

Such examples illustrate the potential riches to be found in placing the seeker's experience in dialogue with tradition.

Summary

Today spiritual directors minister in a postmodern context, a context marked by suspicion of meta-narratives, openness to "the other," interest in the particular and the local, and eclecticism. Postmodernity affirms the importance of the spirit in a way that modernity did not, but it also challenges traditional understandings of "spirituality" and of the ministry of spiritual direction. Above all, I believe, this context invites the spiritual director to stalk the boundary between religious institutions and personal spiritual quest. In doing so, she or he can listen to the directee's experience, listen to tradition, and foster conversation between the two. In doing so she or he might listen in a special way to the voices of those others who have been silenced and marginalized. The spirit often speaks through such "others" in a special way, calling the Christian community to ever deeper truth and ever-greater life. Truth that sets us free; life in abundance.

Notes

1. I am opting to use the traditional vocabulary of "director" and "directee." Many persons prefer less hierarchic language such as "spiritual companion" or "spiritual friend." I am keeping the traditional terms because I want to preserve the asymmetrical nature of this relationship; both director and directee are equal as adults, but the time they spend together is focused on the directee, not the director.

2. Paul Lakeland, *Postmodernity: Christian Identity in a Fragmented Age* (Minneapolis: Fortress, 1997). For a shorter treatment see T. Howland Sanks, "Postmodernism and the Church," *New Theology Review* 11 (August 1998): 51–59.

3. Sanks, "Postmodernism," 52.

4. James D. Whitehead and Evelyn Eaton Whitehead, *Method in Ministry: Theological Reflection and Christian Ministry*, rev. ed., (Kansas City: Sheed and Ward, 1995), 8.

5. See, for example, Robert J. Schreiter, *Constructing Local Theologies* (Maryknoll: Orbis, 1985).

6. Sanks, "Postmodernism," 52.

7. Meredith B. McGuire, "Mapping Contemporary American Spirituality: A Sociological Perspective," *Christian Spirituality Bulletin* 5 (Spring 1997): 1–8; quote is on p. 1. See also John A. Coleman, "Exploding Spiritualities: Their Social Causes, Social Location and Social Divide," in the same issue, 9–15.

8. For a rather extreme statement of this latter position, see Diarmuid Ó Murchú, *Reclaiming Spirituality: A New Spiritual Framework for Today's World* (New York: Crossroad, 1998).

9. McGuire, "Contemporary American Spirituality," 3–4.

10. See, for example, Tad Dunne, "The Future of Spiritual Direction," *Review for Religious* 53 (July–August 1994): 584–90. I have explored issues of professionalization in "The Professionalization of Spiritual Direction: Promise and Peril," *Listening* 32 (Spring 1997): 81–90.

11. William H. Shannon, *Silent Lamp: The Thomas Merton Story* (New York: Crossroad, 1993), 209–24.

12. Shannon, *Silent Lamp*, 221.

13. For an introduction to women's spirituality, see Joann Wolski Conn, ed., *Women's Spirituality: Resources for Christian Development* (New

York: Paulist, 1996). For gay spirituality see Richard Hardy, *Loving Men: Gay Partners, Spirituality, and AIDS* (New York: Continuum, 1998), and James L. Empereur, *Spiritual Direction and the Gay Person* (New York: Continuum, 1998). For lesbian spirituality see Bernadette J. Brooten, *Love Between Women: Early Christian Responses to Female Homoeroticism* (Chicago: University of Chicago Press, 1996).

14. The examples used in this section are composite figures and do not represent actual persons.

15. For insights into gay and lesbian issues, I am drawing upon several conversations with Richard Hardy and a meeting with some gay students at my present school.

16. For a helpful study of the dynamics of self-articulation in spiritual direction see Janet Ruffing, *Interpreting Stories of Faith: Spiritual Direction and Narrative* (New York: Paulist, 1989).

17. I am indebted to Sandra Schneiders, IHM, who pointed out and explored this distinction in a conversation.

18. Elizabeth A. Johnson, *She Who Is: The Mystery of God in Feminist Theological Discourse* (New York: Crossroad, 1992), 5.

19. Constance FitzGerald, "Impasse and Dark Night," in Tilden Edwards, ed., *Living with Apocalypse* (San Francisco: Harper and Row, 1984), 93–116.

20. Empereur, *Spiritual Direction*, 1.

21. See, for example, J. Michael Clark, "Gay Spirituality," in Peter H. Van Ness, ed., *Spirituality and the Secular Quest* (New York: Crossroad, 1996), 349–53.

22. Spiritual Direction as Prophetic Ministry

> Spiritual direction is "in" again with a vengeance. There are work-shops, institutes, cassettes, courses, books galore. Everywhere, and in all (Christian) traditions, there is a concern with the inner life and with personal guidance. Many positive and creative developments have occurred. Writers...have produced popular books aimed at a much wider market than mine was. Institutes...and networks have grown up to train people, mainly lay women and men, as spiritual directors. There has been consid-erable attention to the role of women....And of course there has been the remarkable revival of interest in and practice of Ignatian retreats. All this has been exciting, healthy, positive, hopeful....[1]

In the five years since Kenneth Leech wrote those words, these trends have continued and have become even more widespread, both geographically and across different Christian traditions. At the same time reservations, anxieties, questions, warnings, and criticisms about this state of affairs have found a voice, and in fact the introduction from which I have quoted was largely an expression of Leech's own concerns about current trends. Leech is one among several people who have highlighted concerns and anxieties that are especially relevant to the theme of this essay. The movement toward "professionalizing" spiritual direction, for example, which includes establishing accreditation, awarding diplomas and doctorates, and charging fees, is seen as "potentially extremely dangerous."[2] For Leech spiritual direction is a charismatic (in the best sense of the word) activity. Spiritual directors need to be well grounded in the Christian spiritual and theological traditions, but their ministry is not derived from "professional" training; it is rather a by-product of a life of prayer and holiness. When spiritual direction tends to move out of the Chris-tian community into the private consulting room, it is especially necessary to reaffirm that, in the classical Christian tradition, spiritual direction takes place within the life of the Christian community with its "corporate framework of sacrament, discipleship and social action in a context of theological reflection and social struggle. Only within such a context can it make sense and make progress."[3] Moreover, Leech claims, "much spiritual direction presupposes an understanding of spirituality which is not wholesome and only tenuously Christian, and which reflects the individualism and privatisation of religion in the West rather than any embodiment in a corporate tradition."[4] And "much current writing on spiritual direction, as on spirituality as a whole, has lost its roots in scripture and tradition and has colluded with the current culture of contentment and narcissism. Consumer capitalism is only too good at co-opting such approaches to spirituality." Consequently, "I am horrified at the way in which a lowly and humble ministry has been institutionalised and privatised, and, for all the talk of its 'social implications' de-politicised."[5]

Kathleen Fischer, also writing specifically on spiritual direction but from a feminist perspective, affirms her opposition to any approach to spiritual direction which preserves or reinforces dualistic forms of thinking and action which are present in Christian spirituality: for example, the separation of the inner from the outer life, the personal from the sociopolitical; the maintenance and reinforcement of gender, ethnic, and other hierarchical dualisms; the cultivation of a spirituality of the next world which eschews social and political engagement the search for justice in this.[6] Positively, Fischer proposes a new understanding of Christian growth and wholeness which addresses these problems and goes beyond dualistic thinking.

Other criticisms of certain forms of contemporary spirituality also apply to some approaches to spiritual direction. In the context of a study of mysticism, for example, Grace Jantzen raises the question as to whether "involvement in spirituality might actually deflect attention from the real needs of people."[7] Some of the most popular books on prayer and spirituality have a strong emphasis on personal, psychological well-being. Topics such as anxiety, depression, loneliness, suffering, bereavement, and sexuality are discussed as "essentially private issues for an individual to work through in his or her own way." (She cites Henri Nouwen, Gerard Hughes, Matthew Fox, and M. Scott Peck in this context.)[8] Many popular writers advocate silence, prayer, meditation, or other spiritual exercises and disciplines as a means of increasing inner peace, finding calm for coping with life's hard knocks, healing, dealing with guilt, making life-affirming decisions, or attaining personal well-being and growth.

To make these observations is not to minimize or deny the value of personal well-being, peace of mind and spirit, a sense of self-worth, or the ability to cope with personal suffering and make creative decisions. Jantzen's fundamental point, however, is that these approaches to spirituality, which enjoy enormous popularity, fail to address the issue of structures in church and society that create and sustain the oppression, anxiety, and other ills that people experience. "The social and political policies that make for starving children, battered women and the evils of rising fascism are still there unchallenged as people learn through prayer to find the tranquillity to live with corrupt political and social structures instead of channelling their distress and anger and anxiety into energy for constructive change."[9] Consequently there is the danger that spirituality and, by extension, spiritual direction become domesticated for the sake of a privatised spirituality. When this happens,

> the relation between (spirituality) and social justice cannot be addressed. The net result…is the reinforcement of the societal status quo, as intellectual and religious energy is poured into an exploration of private religiosity rather than into social and political action for change. And this in turn has the effect not only of turning the attention of those seeking deepened spirituality away from issues of justice, but also of leaving the efforts for justice to those who have abandoned concern with spirituality, seeing it as having nothing to offer in the work for structural change.[10]

This essay begins by acknowledging the validity and importance of these concerns, criticisms, and questions. I do not intend, however, to try to answer them point by point, much less to defend every aspect of the current state of affairs. My contention is that biblical prophecy offers an illuminating and challenging paradigm for contemporary Christian spiritual direction. In this essay I therefore sketch an understanding of Christian spiritual direction as a prophetic activity, an understanding which, at the same time, might also address, albeit in a more indirect way, some of the issues raised by critics. I begin with an outline of some characteristic features of biblical prophecy and then devote the remainder of the essay to showing ways in which contemporary Christian spiritual direction might be genuinely prophetic.

Prophecy

In his book on prophecy, Walter Brueggemann[11] presents a typology of prophecy by way of a schematic discussion of several different historical contexts in the Jewish scriptures in which prophecy is found. In this he makes use of a fundamental contrast between two paradigms, which represent two very different forms of consciousness and the cultures that spring from them. On the one hand, there is "royal consciousness," or the consciousness and culture of "the empire," which is based on power and control. This stands in contrast and conflict with "prophetic consciousness," which represents a response to "royal consciousness" and is based on radically different values. In Egypt, where the people were in a state of slavery and increasing oppression by the empire and its culture, Moses responded by speaking the prophetic word of Yahweh in opposition to the "empire consciousness" of the ruling regime. In the power of that word he led the people to freedom. The second context for prophecy is that of Solomon's kingship. Here, in conditions of affluence and assimilation to neighboring cultures, the royal consciousness and its practices are no longer those of an alien power but have been adopted and assimilated by the king himself and his regime. Features of Solomon's regime include an oppressive social policy, which exploited the people for the sake of the royal court and its extravagant needs; an assumption by the king of complete authority; ruthless protection of the status quo and of the power of those who wielded power; and consequent resistance to change. Crucially, the adoption of kingship in Israel meant a rethinking of the relationship between Yahweh and the people; Solomon's regime had established "a controlled, static religion," in which God was domesticated, the sovereignty of God became subordinated to the purposes of the king, and all access to God was effectively under royal control.[12] Consequently, the freedom of God to be God and the original relationship between the people and Yahweh had become obscured if not lost. The third biblical context of prophecy is the time of the exile. Here, once more the community is an oppressed and subject people far away from their own land. Their temptation, to which the prophets offer a response, is assimilation to the "false" consciousness and culture of the conquerors. In all these different settings the prophets raise their voices.

Clearly these different contexts have parallels in the contemporary church and world. It is not unknown, for example, for a church as an institution with a strong authority to take on some of the features of the royal consciousness: claiming complete authority over beliefs, behavior, and values; protecting its own version of tradition; defending the status quo and resisting change; domesticating and controlling access to God; protecting the power of those who exercise power in the institution. In such circumstances it is not unusual for members of the church simply to be assimilated to this dominant culture. Others, however, see the dangers of such assimilation and raise prophetic voices. Moreover, as regards the relationship between the Christian community and the surrounding world, Christians in the affluent West tend to be more or less assimilated to the pervasive capitalist, consumer culture in such a way that inertia, defense of the status quo, resistance to change, and the assumption that all is well make a critical, prophetic response difficult. "We also are children of the royal consciousness."[13] In a culture of comfort and contentment, who is ready to welcome disturbing voices, an alternative vision, a transformation of consciousness and values? On the other hand, however, Christians in other parts of the world who do not enjoy such affluence are themselves poor, enslaved, oppressed, and alienated, because of dominant social, economic, and political regimes and structures, which are sometimes supported by the church. Here adopting a prophetic stance holds other dangers: prophets are often killed, even now.

The first element in the prophetic task is criticism. In Brueggemann's account of prophecy, "the royal consciousness leads people to numbness, especially to numbness about death."[14] Prophetic insight, therefore, consists in recognizing what others may not see or may want to deny, the presence and the operations of death in the community. "The most radical criticism of the prophet is grief over death."[15] This criticism arises, not so much out of anger, but out of compassion and mourning in solidarity with those who are afflicted by the activities, forces, and structures that give rise to destruction and death. It is compassion with those who mourn and shared grief at the presence of death that drive prophetic criticism and protest. "The task of prophetic imagination is to cut through the numbness, to penetrate the self-deception,"[16] and the proper idiom for this is the language of grief and lament. For this aspect of prophecy, Jeremiah is the paradigm.[17] His prophetic task is to exhort and encourage the people publicly to recognize the presence of death denied by the dominant (royal) consciousness and to howl in grief. That is because a particular insight of biblical faith is the awareness that "grief, embodied anguish, is the route to newness."[18]

The second main feature of the prophet's task is to see visions and dream dreams. Not only do prophets lament and criticize, they also feel themselves impelled to imagine and to lead others to imagine the radically new: an alternative consciousness and ways of being. "The royal consciousness leads people to despair about the power to new life. It is the task of prophetic imagination and ministry to bring people to engage the promise of newness that is at work in our history with God."[19] It is characteristic of a dominant consciousness to be convinced that radical newness is neither desirable, because it threatens those who benefit from the status quo, nor possible, because it falls outside our conventional rationality and ways of thinking.

This crucial task of prophecy, therefore, the evocation of a vision of the new that both amazes and energizes, is rooted not in temperamental optimism or an evolutionary or deterministic view of history but in faith in a God who is both free and faithful. It rests on hope in a gracious God, which is to be found in the deepest parts of a community's memories and traditions. Moreover, the possibility of making this vision a reality lies not in the exercise of power to control, organize, and manage but rather in surrender in faith to the ever-faithful God who both desires and has the capacity to bring God's own promises to an almost unimaginable fulfillment. Fulfillment lies "in receiving and not grasping, in inheriting and not possessing, in praising and not seizing."[20]

Second Isaiah is Brueggemann's paradigm for this aspect of the prophet's calling: "Behold I am doing a new thing" (43:19). He focuses in particular on the word of forgiveness of Isaiah 40:1–2; on the radical political announcement of Isaiah 40:9–10; on the dethronement of the Babylonian gods and the enthronement formula of Isaiah 52:7; and on three particular images of newness: the new song time of the new reign (Is 42:10); birth to the barren one (Is 54:1); and the images of nourishment (Is 55:1–3) leading to new vitality (Is 40:28–31), as also in Isaiah 58:9–11:

> Yahweh will give strength to your bones
> And you shall be like a watered garden,
> Like a spring of water
> Whose waters never run dry.

Jesus may also be seen as belonging to the line of the prophets, and his career contains all the elements of the prophetic task. Prophetic criticism is present in the infancy narratives (cf. especially Mt 2:16–23 and Lk 1:51–53; 2:17–20). Like the older prophets, Jesus claimed to speak and act in God's name. Moreover, "the ministry of Jesus is, of course, criticism that leads to radical dismantling."[21] This is seen in his readiness to forgive (Mk 2:1–11); in his ability and readiness to heal, even on the sabbath (Mk 3:1–6); his willingness to eat with outcasts (Mk 2:15–17); and his attitude toward the temple (Mk 11:15–19). Like the prophets, Jesus is moved to compassion, especially in his identification with the marginal people and the outcasts, the victims of the present order; it was over them that the forces of death had the greatest power. His is in fact a compassion that extends to all who are harassed and helpless (Mk 6:34; 8:2; Mt 9:35–36; Lk 7:12–13), and it is further exemplified in the parables (Lk 10:33; 15:20). Like the prophets, too, he grieves with those who grieve in the presence of death (Jn 11:33–35; Lk 19:41–42). The crucifixion of Jesus is the decisive criticism of the royal consciousness in that the power of God, embodied in Jesus, takes the form of death. Life takes the shape of death and power the form of suffering. "The cross is the ultimate metaphor of prophetic criticism because it means the end of the old consciousness that brings death on everyone." It represents "the assurance that effective prophetic criticism is done not by an outsider but always by one who must embrace the grief, enter into the death, and know the pain of the criticised one."[22]

As well as criticizing, Jesus also energized and amazed. The announcement of the new causes both wonder and consternation in the birth narratives (Lk 1:46–55; 1:68–79; 2:18–20). And "the ministry of Jesus is of course the energising that leads to radical beginnings precisely when none seemed possible."[23] Where there was sickness, alienation, despair, and death, he brought healing, fellowship, hope, and new life (for example, Lk 7:22), which consistently elicited from those who had eyes to see and ears to hear responses of "amazement" and "astonishment" (cf. Mk 1:27; 4:41; 6:2; 6:51; 7:37; Lk 5:26; 9:43; Mt 7:28; 17:6; 22:33). Moreover, Jesus' teachings cannot be separated from his prophetic actions; they both support his deeds and in turn are confirmed by them. The "beatitudes" in a sense epitomize his teaching. If the "woes" recounted in Luke (6:24–26) represent a criticism of the prevailing consciousness, the "blessings" placed alongside constitute a source of amazement and energy. And "the strangeness of this prophetic energising is that it is addressed precisely to the non-persons consigned to non-history."[24] Jesus posed a threat to the upholders of the dominant consciousness by teaching that the "wicked" and the outcasts are as acceptable to God as the "righteous" and might go ahead of them into the kingdom of God. He amazed people by the possibilities contained in his vision of the kingdom that God could and would bring about.

> ...inside it
> There are quite different things going on:
> Festivals at which the poor man
> Is king and the consumptive
> Is healed; mirrors in which the blind look
> At themselves and love looks at them
> Back; and industry is for mending
> The bent bones and the minds fractured
> By life.[25]

It is consistent with the prophetic tradition that Jesus' teaching, although addressed to the whole community, is rejected by the dominant group and accepted only by a marginal minority. Likewise, the fact that this teaching represents, paradoxically, both continuity and a radical break with the old is also part of the prophetic pattern. The blessings and Jesus' teaching as a whole open those who receive them to a different future in which, as in the old prophets, in continuity with the past, a faithful God is free to offer and to give. Finally, for Brueggemann the resurrection of Jesus represents "the ultimate act of prophetic energising in which a new history is initiated....The resurrection of Jesus made possible a future for the disinherited, the poor, the hungry and the grieving."[26]

At this point I would like to highlight one feature of prophecy which has relevance to spiritual direction. At the present time being prophetic is often identified in a simple and direct way with action for social justice. The understanding of prophecy that I have outlined here, however, sees its primary aim as being both far broader and more profound, namely, a radical transformation of consciousness.[27] A consciousness, in the sense of a particular understanding of the world and of human life, with a corresponding set of beliefs, attitudes, aspirations, and values, clearly also encompasses certain kinds of human choices and activities and a particular social order. On the basis of the word of God, the prophets both criticized the dominant consciousness and the culture it encompassed and also evoked and claimed an alternative vision. The emphasis on social justice in some of the prophets can be seen as one aspect of this desire for a radical transformation which went beyond mere changes in social actions, structures, and institutions. Social and political changes are but one dimension of a change of consciousness. In biblical prophetic thinking a new social order based on justice arises out of such a profound change of consciousness in members of a community.

Spiritual Direction

In this essay I presuppose a particular paradigm of spiritual direction. Jean Daniélou once highlighted a very important distinction between biblical and Greek understandings of *spirit,* and of the meaning of the statement that "God is spirit." According to Greek ways of thinking, inherited from Plato and Aristotle, "God is spirit" means that God is immaterial. In biblical thought and speech, by contrast, the statement means that God is life-giving breath, a wind, a storm, an irresistible force. Hence the ambiguity of the word *spirituality:* either it means immaterial or animated by the Holy Spirit.[28] This essay presupposes a biblical understanding of the spirit of God as breath, a wind, a fire, a force, a source of life, energy, and wisdom, with a capacity to animate and shape the whole of life, both personal and corporate.

Spiritual direction is a charismatic activity, that is to say, it is an activity conducted by people especially gifted for it, in which one person helps another to allow the breath of the spirit to animate and shape every dimension of life. The qualities required for spiritual direction may be enhanced and developed by experience and training. Moreover, although spiritual directors normally work with individuals or small groups of people, nonetheless, the horizon within which they operate has to be far larger than the needs of individual persons or small groups and larger even than the needs of the church. Spiritual direction aims to help a directee to discover what the spirit of God is doing or desires to do in the world and in their own circumstances, and that requires a perspective which is open to the presence of the spirit in the whole of creation and in every dimension of human life.

I also assume that directees desire to live in union with God and are willing to be regularly attentive to the mystery of God wherever, in life as well as in prayer, they encounter that mystery. It is this attentiveness to the mystery of God, rather than any relationship with a director, that is the primary source of understanding, wisdom, and energy for action, growth, and transformation. In spiritual direction conversations directees give an account of their experiences of life and of God, or, perhaps better, of God-in-life, over a particular period of time. The role of a director involves the modest task of helping the directee to understand more fully her experience in faith and, on the basis of that understanding, assisting her to make discerning choices; choices which are shaped, we hope, by the wisdom and energy of the Spirit of God.

Spiritual Direction as Prophetic Activity

From our brief survey of prophecy it is clear that prophetic speech and action spring from a contemplative base, in the sense that they are rooted in the prophet's attentiveness to the mystery and the word of God. This attentiveness to God is a source of insight, energy, and courage, such that the word of God is both the light by which the prophet understands and makes judgments and the fountainhead of power for change. Like prophecy, effective spiritual direction also depends upon constant attention to the same mystery, wherever that mystery is revealed and encountered. Director and directee together search for an understanding of the world in the light of that mystery. Without this contemplative attention, which is a necessary quality for director and directee alike, the possibilities of prophetic insight and courage are greatly reduced, and spiritual direction runs a grave risk of failing to drink from the waters that give it meaning, shape, and vitality.

Like the prophets and Jesus, spiritual directors too are members of a community of faith. This may seem an obvious observation, but with the current trend toward professionalizing spiritual direction and its partial assimilation, in some models, to counseling and psychotherapy, it needs to be stated. As we have seen, biblical prophets were far from being disinterested spectators watching a game from the safety of the grandstand. Membership in a community and solidarity with the people form the often painful place from which they speak and act. This enables and at the same time commits them to share fully in the joys and sorrows, pain and exaltation, hope and despair of the community. In times of oppression and affliction, their compassion draws them into sharing the people's griefs and suffering. And in a culture of affluence and contentment, when the cutting edge of the word of God has been blunted or lost, the prophets are compassionate figures, uncovering the hidden sickness at the heart of their own communities, which believe themselves to be in fine fettle and claim peace where there is in fact no peace. It is out of shared grief and affliction or joy and prosperity that prophetic words are spoken and deeds performed.

Christian spiritual directors are in a privileged position to share in the experiences of their faith communities, for it is precisely the joys and sorrows, hopes and fears that their directees confide in them. Moreover, their readiness to engage in attempting to live a Christian life in a community of faith, worship, theological reflection, and social struggle, with its potential and its limitations, enhances their credibility as directors. And it is exactly that engagement, together with knowledge of their own and other spiritual traditions and discerning reflection, which form the basis for their effectiveness as directors. Furthermore, as we have already noted, not only are prophets engaged and compassionate members of a community but they also speak and act for the sake of the community (and a wider world). Likewise, the work of spiritual direction is undertaken for the sake of the community and the wider world. Doubtless, in a notably pluralist world and church, directees' and directors' perceptions about the exact nature and boundaries of the Christian community (or the multiple communities, groups, or networks to which they belong) vary from person to person and from place to place, as do the ways in which they share in its life. But it is difficult to see how notable disengagement from the life of the community provides a credible and effective place for directors, if their activity is to be Christian, prophetic, and effective.

On the other hand, however, directors, like the prophets, also need to be able to maintain a "critical distance" from the prevailing consciousness and culture on the basis of the word of God, while at the same time sharing profoundly in its joys and griefs. Without this capacity for challenge and criticism there is a real danger that directors will simply reinforce existing attitudes, prejudices, habits, and structures and consequently be unable to discriminate or assist their directees to discriminate between the forces of life and death, light and darkness—which is precisely what they, as directors, are called upon to do.

Spiritual direction involves taking part in a movement of transformation which involves, at different times, rejoicing, grieving, criticizing, imagining the new and finding in it both amazement and energy for change; and all of this on the basis of faith in a faithful and free God who leads us into the future. The directors' privilege is that of being invited to accompany, assist, encourage, and support others in the same movement of transformation. Their main resource is their experience, reflected on in tranquility, of consistently if falteringly trying to collaborate with the spirit in a similar transformation of their own lives and their own world. In accepting this invitation and carrying out their task, directors can also learn from the prophets' example. First, in a situation of crisis, the prophets encouraged the people to name their griefs and to address the causes of those griefs, namely the forces and structures, both overt and hidden, of affliction, destruction, and death in the community. Second, the prophets offered symbols which challenged and subverted the prevailing state of hopelessness in which new life seemed unimaginable. They retrieved and reactivated from the deepest memories of the community the forgotten symbols, the dangerous memories, which had once been creative of new life. Third, they encouraged people to bring to public expression the hopes and yearnings for newness and the visions of how things might be that were lost because they had been denied for so long. This meant rediscovering and reimagining the possibilities of a life with God who promises and is utterly faithful to those promises. And fourth, while the prophets often spoke in poetic metaphors, they also, crucially, linked their vision of the new to specific circumstances, so that the alternative imagined life was not grandiose pie in the sky but had real personal and political content.[29] All these are vital means for directors in response to the invitation offered to them to accompany, assist, encourage, and support others in a movement of transformation animated and shaped by the spirit of God.

If spiritual direction is an agent of transformation, then questions arise as to the scope of its merit. This brings us to some of the issues with which this essay began. Does spiritual direction have to do with helping people to cope on a personal or private level with depression, physical or sexual abuse, violence, racial or sexual discrimination, homophobia, and other conditions without also paying critical attention to the structural and institutional, social and ecclesial causes of these conditions? Is the focus of direction to be change in the person while leaving social or structural factors unchanged? What is the scope of the vision of the new which spiritual direction fosters?

We have seen that the cry of the prophet is for a profound transformation of consciousness; the replacement of a prevailing false consciousness by a new vision and life-giving way of being, animated and shaped by the source of true life, the covenant with God. "Consciousness" in this sense is more than an "inner" state of mind; it also encompasses a way of being in the world of a whole community or people and the ideas, attitudes, aspirations, values, choices, relationships, structures, and institutions that promote and sustain that way of being. Moreover, the separation between personal and social, private and political, which is assumed in much Christian thinking about spirituality was unknown to the prophets. As part of their lament and criticism, the prophets identified the causes of grief, oppression, or stagnation in the community. These causes were both social and personal: in Egypt, the oppressive power of the Pharaohs and the persons and structures which sustained that regime; in Solomon's kingdom, both the culture and systems of governance and the actions of individuals; in the time of exile, both the activities of Israel's enemies and the social structures which betokened forgetfulness of their life with God. Moreover, personal religiosity without social justice was unacceptable to the prophets. In response to the presence and power of the forces of death, the prophets not only called for a return to right relationship with God but also insisted that this must be embodied in every dimension of the life of the community. Moses, for example, did not counsel the people to find peace of mind in bearing as best they could the effects of oppression and slavery, but addressed the oppressive regime itself. In a time of assimilation, affluence, and contentment, the prophetic response was not to advise the "private" practice of religion and righteousness, but to challenge the culture, structures, and institutions of Solomon's kingship. And the future for which the Book of 2 Isaiah cries in eloquent longing envisages not so much an "inner" change in individuals as a radical transformation in every aspect, personal and corporate, of the life of the community, rooted in the graciousness of God. Similarly the kingdom of God proclaimed by Jesus is as much a social as a personal reality, invoking communal and structural as well as personal newness.

It is true that spiritual directors deal mainly with individual persons (or small groups). Unfortunately, for too long, spiritual direction has been too much shaped by a Greek rather than a biblical way of thinking and by a theology of individual salvation, and has consequently been too confined to dealing with the spiritual as "immaterial" and with the purely personal dimensions of life. If, however, the aim of spiritual direction is to foster life in the spirit, so that the spirit of God may animate and shape every area of life, and if it is to be truly prophetic and Christian, it may not limit itself to a consideration only of a selection of those areas. It must find ways of addressing as a unity personal, structural, and institutional factors in church and society; that is to say, both those that sustain life in the spirit and those that tend to kill it. To separate the two is to create and maintain a false dichotomy, because the personal, the ecclesial, and the political are inextricably interwoven; they inevitably interact with and interpenetrate each other. To address personal factors without giving attention to the others is to focus on only part of life, not the whole, and almost always leads to distortion, since the spirit of God is active in the whole. Structures and institutions, both sociopolitical and ecclesial, have the power both to enhance life in the spirit and to diminish or even extinguish it. All areas of life are very much the business of good Christian spiritual direction, which can offer stimulus, assistance, and support both for prophetic criticism and for imagining and creating conditions, personal, sociopolitical, and institutional in church and society, in which all human persons, without exception, may live within creation with the dignity that is due to them as sons and daughters of God and sisters and brothers of Jesus Christ.

An important step in prophecy, as we have seen, is that of finding an alternative vision that offers a different way of being from that of the dominant consciousness. The poet Seamus Heaney believes that this offering of an alternative (subversive) vision of how things might be is also the task of the poet. He bases his remarks on Wallace Stevens's notion of the poet as the creator of "supreme fictions" and on Simone Weil's words, "Obedience to the force of gravity. The greatest sin." He writes,

> And in the activity of poetry, too, there is a tendency to place a counter-reality in the scales—a reality which may only be imagined but which has weight because it is imagined within the gravitational pull of the actual and can therefore hold its own and balance out against the historical situation. This redressing effect of poetry comes from its being a glimpsed alternative, a revelation of potential that is denied or constantly threatened by circumstances.[30]

The invitation to take part in encouraging, creating, and implementing such redressing, alternative visions recalls directors to their fundamental task: to foster life in the spirit, the alternative, transformed life that is the kingdom of God. Moreover, the use of imagination in conjuring up alternative possible ways of being is often a crucial source of energy for growth for directees, especially in situations in which hopelessness reigns. Most spiritual directors, however, are not themselves poets. Nor is it for them, as directors, to impose their own alternative visions on their directees; that would be an abuse of power. It is the directees' own griefs, laments, criticisms, and alternative visions, not those of the director, that provide the resources for transformation. The directors' privilege and skills lie rather in accompanying, helping, encouraging, and supporting directees in this crucial, prophetic use of imagination as they envisage and move into their own visions of the new in relationship with a gracious God.

In the final part of this section I would like to highlight two features of these alternative visions as they occur in the context of spiritual direction. First, these visions look to the past as well as to the future. They represent a retrieval in the present of the memories of women and men of spirit and of life-giving events and symbols from the recesses of the past. Thus we find the prophets invoking, time out of mind, alternative visions by way of remembering the mighty deeds of God and recalling the people to the covenant that a God who liberates graciously made with their ancestors. Thus dangerous memories, insights, beliefs, and symbols embedded in tradition and history guided the shaping of alternative visions and helped to validate them. For a contemporary Christian community, this movement seeks to unite faithfulness to the past, to the subversive memories of Israel, and of Jesus of Nazareth, with openness to a future toward which God is leading us. Second, both for the biblical prophets and for those involved in spiritual direction today, this process of imagination finds its vigor and its validity in the promises and the freedom of God. The "new creation" is grounded in the desire and freedom of God to fulfil God's own promises. Consequently, a spiritual director will constantly help a directee to turn again and again to those places where God is both revealed and concealed: the created universe, human history, the scriptures, the symbols, rituals, traditions, and life of the Christian community. All of these have potential as sources both of a new vision and of the energy to shape that vision into a living reality.

In the world of the prophets and of Jesus, the appeal and power of the vision of the new lies in its capacity to surprise, to evoke wonder, and thus to provide energy for transformation. In the setting of spiritual direction, the same is also true. In turning constantly to the contemplation of the mystery of God, a directee is likely to be surprised, amazed, and awed by the richness of that mystery and the possibilities that it offers. All experienced spiritual directors can recall occasions when directees have come into the room astonished by a new, hope-filled vision that they have received, not from the director herself, but from being provoked, surprised, and captivated by the mystery of God, while the director walks alongside. In this way the scriptures and traditions of the faith community once again become a liberating and energizing word and the histories of men and women of spirit become empowering memories. As the vision of the kingdom of God and the presence of the spirit gave meaning and energy to the first followers of Jesus, so too its possibilities in our present and future become a source of energy for transformation.

Conclusions

This essay has outlined an understanding of spiritual direction as a prophetic, charismatic activity that is exercised in the Christian community at the service both of its members and of those outside who wish to make use of it. In conclusion I simply want to draw attention to some of the implications of this paradigm. It is worth noting that, if this understanding of spiritual direction is true, it may pose a threat to some aspects of the institutional life of the church and those who hold power in it, as is the way of the prophetic in any age. Again, if this understanding is true, the community needs courage if it is to endorse and support those who hold or are drawn to it, since it contains the possibility of radical transformation for individuals, for the community, and beyond in every dimension of life.

This understanding of spiritual direction also implies that those who would be effective Christian spiritual directors are usually marked by certain qualities. In the first place it reaffirms the gifts that consistently appear in spiritual directors in Christian history. These include a demand that directors be, at least in some discernible measure, "possessed by the Spirit" and thus gifted for the task; second, that they be people who have struggled with the realities of both prayer and life, including their own inner conflicts and demons; third, that they be well acquainted with scripture and the different Christian spiritual and theological traditions; and finally that they be persons of discernment in their own lives and thus capable of leading others in discernment. The particular understanding of spiritual direction as prophetic activity, which I have outlined in this essay, also suggests certain further qualities for directors: for example, that they steep themselves in the biblical tradition of prophecy as a primary paradigm to give shape and direction to their activity of spiritual direction; that, over against understandings of "spirit" that owe more to Greek philosophy than to the Bible, they imbibe a Christian theology of creation and incarnation and the spirit that gives proper value to the body and to the structures and institutions of society; that, at the same time, they develop, on the basis of dangerous memories contained in scripture, history, and tradition, a critical understanding of the contemporary world and a capacity to read it both with "generosity" and with "suspicion," both "with" and "against" the grain, to be able to assist their directees in genuine discernment. In current training programs for spiritual directors, counseling and therapeutic theory and skills often hold a prominent place. If equal emphasis were also laid upon a prophetic paradigm of direction, that might go some way towards addressing concerns about the "professionalization" of spiritual direction.

Notes

1. Kenneth Leech, *Soul Friend: Spiritual Direction in the Modern World* (London: Darton, Longman and Todd, 1994), xv–xvi.

2. Ibid., xvi.

3. Ibid., xvii.

4. Ibid., xvii–xviii.

5. Ibid., xviii.

6. Kathleen Fischer, *Women at the Well: Feminist Perspectives on Spiritual Direction* (London: SPCK, 1989), ch. 2.

7. Grace M. Jantzen, *Power, Gender and Christian Mysticism* (Cambridge: Cambridge University Press, 1995), 18.

8. Ibid., 18–19.

9. Ibid., 20.

10. Ibid., 21.

11. Walter Brueggemann, *The Prophetic Imagination* (Fortress, 1978).

12. Cf. Ibid., 34.

13. Ibid., 44.

14. Ibid., 46.

15. Ibid., 62.

16. Ibid., 49.

17. Brueggemann quotes, e.g., Jer 4:19–20; 4:23–26; 8:7; 8:22–9:2; 4:30–31; 30:12–3; 31:15–20.

18. Brueggemann, *Prophetic Imagination,* 90.

19. Ibid., 62–63.

20. Ibid., 79.

21. Ibid., 83.

22. Ibid., 95.

23. Ibid., 99.

24. Ibid., 104.

25. R. S. Thomas, "The Kingdom," *Collected Poems 1945–1990* (London: J. M. Dent, 1993), 233.

26. Brueggemann, *Prophetic Imagination,* 107.

27. Cf. also Bruce Vawter: "The social message was admittedly a major emphasis, but its explanation is to be found in the function of an Israelite

prophet—serving as a conscience for his people in precisely those matters where conscience was needed," (*The New Jerome Biblical Commentary*, London: Geoffrey Chapman, 196).

28. Quoted by Yves Congar in *I Believe in the Holy Spirit, Vol. I: The Holy Spirit in the "Economy": Revelation and Experience of the Spirit* (New York: Seabury, 1983), 4.

29. Cf. Bruggemann, *Prophetic Imagination,* 68–70.

30. Seamus Heaney, *The Redress of Poetry: Oxford Lectures* (London: Faber and Faber, 1995), 3–4.

Selected References and Suggested Reading

Walter Brueggemann, *The Prophetic Imagination.* Fortress Press, 1978.

James M. Keegan, "To Bring All Things Together: Spiritual Direction as Action for Justice." *Presence: The Journal of Spiritual Directors International* 1,1 (1995): 4–19.

Kenneth Leech, *Soul Friend: Spiritual Direction in the Modern World,* new revised edition. London: Darton, Longman and Todd, 1994, ch. 6.

Phyllis Zagano

23. Speaking of Prayer

"Well, speaking of prayer...."

The sentence trailed off, faded, and died, as it often does. An awkward silence entered the room and sat between the two conversants. They looked at each other, and then away, and again at each other. Another topic jumped up to entertain their thoughts and words.

The pattern repeats itself a thousand times in myriad ways in the general course of ministry, and in the particular relationships between novice mistress and novice, confessor and penitent, spiritual director and directee. Prayer is the most intimate of our human relations, and consequently the most difficult part of our lives to communicate to another human. Yet an honest prayer life calls for its examination in the presence of another person, for the lack of a relationship within which prayer can be safely discussed risks solipsism, in thinking about prayer and in prayer itself. No matter how singular and solitary actual prayer is, growth in holiness ordinarily requires assistance.

So speaking of prayer—talking about the who, what, when, where, why, and how of prayer—is a cornerstone of growth in personal holiness, in personal spirituality. Speaking of prayer—that is, engaging in spiritual direction of the soul's relation to God, to self, and to community, with the aim of growth in holiness—has undergone a revival of sorts and come to be more common among Christians.[1] It is a ministry that has spread beyond clerical and denominational boundaries to embrace laics of all denominations, both as directors and directees.

The term "spiritual director" sometimes evokes unnecessary control, and so to describe this ministry the terms "spiritual guide" and "spiritual companion" are often used. For the purposes of this essay, the term "spiritual director" reflects and encompasses the mature accompaniment this ministry demands, and includes the preferred notions of "guide" and "companion," without the controlling implications of "director." To be sure, the spiritual director is a person of many analogies. He or she is gracious host, healer, teacher, and friend who prays for those welcomed into direction, and who above all engages in the holy listening of the heart.[2] The director receives holy speech. The conversation is clearly one speaking of prayer.

In these pages I discuss speaking of prayer, the acts of holy speech and holy listening as interpersonal communication, as ministry dependent on: first, the triangulation of honesty, equality, and trust; second, on a common spiritual-theological language; and, lastly, on a professional recognition of how to conduct a spiritual direction interview. Each of these practical areas further depends on the listening with the heart that cannot be taught, but only experienced, whether as director or directee. It is that lived compassion of Christ that allows the director to help the directee speak about individual experience and encounter with the living God. For this essay I depend deeply on the tradition of spiritual direction as known through John Cassian and Ignatius of Loyola.

Since most ministers are familiar with spiritual direction in theory and in practice, my purpose is to elucidate a few points specific to the establishment and maintenance of interpersonal communication within the spiritual direction relationship and, by extension, within any ministerial relationship. For the most part, however, I refer specifically to the spiritual direction relationship.

Honest and Equal and Trustworthy

Speaking of prayer was a well-known discipline in the early church, where the relationship between director and directee was one of master and disciple. The director was doctor, counselor, intercessor, mediator, and sponsor for the disciple come to learn the interior life.[3] Those who most earnestly sought to learn about the interior life apprenticed themselves to desert fathers (either hermits or monastics), whose maxims and sometimes stern penances pointed the apprentice toward ways of overcoming the triple concupiscences of the world, the flesh, and the devil in the development of the interior life. Usually the problems of possessions, the body, and of pride were self-apparent as initial obstacles; the question was how to battle them interiorly and exteriorly. Early on the notions that developed into the evangelical counsels of poverty, chastity, and obedience began to solidify. The goal was, and remains, union with God, in all that that entails. The singular project, for master and disciple, was to live constantly in God's presence.

In the late fourth century, John Cassian and his friend Germanus set out to learn from the fathers of the desert. We know some of what they learned in Cassian's *Institutes,* which focus on desert monasticism, and in his *Conferences,* which comprise instruction on the anchoritic life.[4] For Cassian the task at hand was clear:

> This, then, is the goal of the solitary, and this must be his whole intention—to deserve to possess the image of future blessedness

in this body and as it were to begin to taste the pledge of that heavenly way of life and glory in this vessel. This, I say, is the end of all perfection—that the mind purged of every carnal desire may daily be elevated to spiritual things, until one's whole way of life and all the yearnings of one's heart become a single and continuous prayer.[5]

This clear goal required guidance, even in its definition, by and for the individual seeker.

The *Conferences,* set as dialogues between master and disciple, hand down the wisdom of those who traveled the geographical, psychological, and spiritual *solitudo vastissima.* No matter the level of interior growth in the spiritual life of the disciple, the disciple trusted the master, and the conversations that took place between them had the characteristics of honesty and, to a certain extent, equality.[6] It was understood that the disciple was being tested as the master had been.[7] Just as Cassian reports in the *Institutes,* where the monastic supplicant is required to stand ten days outside the monastery before being admitted to the care of the elder who served as guest master and "novice director," the notion of equality did not extend to position within the community of believers except insofar as all are equal before God and all are challenged to take their baptisms seriously.

The humble master would acknowledge his own past difficulties, and no doubt gain consolation in recognizing them in the disciple. In the formation process Cassian describes, both the master and the disciple were wholly and transparently honest with each other in this respect. The sense of equality, or "equalness," allowed both master and disciple to recognize that each was a pilgrim seeking union with God, one longer on the road than the other. Hence the disciple grew to trust the master. In the anchoritic instruction of the *Conferences,* the disciple would subject himself in informal obedience to the master; in monastic instruction it was much the same. The formation of the solitary required that the disciple live with or near the master; the formation to monastic life kept the supplicant apart from the community until the master determined he could be taken in for further formation.

What is clear in Cassian is the import of the spiritual guide, and how he understood the task of handing down the wisdom of the desert or the monastery. Both anchoritic and monastic formation call for an elder, one both holy and wise, to accompany the neophytes coming either to the desert or the community. Instruction in the spiritual life required that the disciple trustingly suspend judgment and give over authority to the elder. The objective sought— to conquer self and humbly live a life of discernment in order to reach the goal of union—was examined by both neophyte and elder through the range of activities we call spiritual direction today.

The conversations between master and disciple presented advice gained by experience, not detached authoritarian dictates. Such remains the balance to be struck in contemporary spiritual direction, centered as it must be in open communication between director and directee. The attitudes of honesty and equality before God must be present within the relationship in order to create and sustain the basic attitude of trust between the two.[8]

We are concerned here with the ability and inability of directors and directees to speak freely of prayer, and the limits and parameters of that speech. The seriousness of the relationship requires bilateral freedom and promise: freedom in honesty and equality, and the implicit (or, where necessary, the explicit) promise of trust that neither will willingly change the nature of the relationship. Specifically, unlike the desert hermit or monastic, the contemporary director does not enter into the directee's life, and the directee ought not seek to enter into the director's life, if the equation in holy listening and holy speech is to be maintained. This may seem like an obvious professional obligation, but either circumstance can alter the honesty and equality—or "equalness"—and, consequently, the trust necessary for spiritual direction conversation to be engaged in at all.[9]

Honesty in conversation implies equality and trust, and the director's ability for independent thought. While most contemporary individuals do not have access to a desert father or mother, whether a modern-day anchorite or a monastic guest master, those generous souls who serve as spiritual directors can encourage the necessary trust by presenting themselves as unequal "equals," that is, without unnecessarily attaching themselves to any status other than that of an "elder," a status gained by long prayer and experience. That is, the place of the director is set within the conversation, not by external status on a parish or even retreat house staff, or assignment as seminary or novitiate spiritual director. Any status other than that of simple Christian, despite the understanding that education and training are necessary to the ministry of direction, can carry with it appurtenances of power that disrupt the necessary honesty and equality, and endanger trust. Briefly, authority is never an argument for anything.

While this may seem a rarefied and theoretical approach to the dynamics of interpersonal communication, it is worth examining specifically for the sort of errors that can arise mostly unknowingly in spiritual conversations between two people of good will.

The only way two people can be completely honest with each other is to know that each totally accepts the other and will not harm the other. Such is part of the basic contract between the director and directee. Given the uncommitted world we inhabit, the understanding of the contract might need revisiting every so often, as persons of different backgrounds and training generously come to the ministry of spiritual direction. If one person in the relationship is to be essentially equal to the other, with one a bit farther down the road than the other, their equality must be immediately apparent. The necessary "equalness" is not immediately apparent, for example, to the individual coming for direction to the member of a large parish or retreat house staff, especially in a retreat setting where directors and directees are introduced as a group. The unavoidable "we/they" dynamic established by first-night gatherings of this type, which is solidified by a team approach to ministry,[10] can chip away at the humility necessary for the director to be wholly honest with the directee. The director who heavily identifies with the team has a concomitant lack of freedom in the directing relationship. That is, while a team approach can support the psychological and spiritual needs of the directors and directees, the group dynamic often sets into motion other dynamics and controlling mechanisms that encourage a "we/they" attitude, granting identity to "we/directors" even when the objective is to create communion among "they/directees."[11]

One communication difficulty that can evolve within the team approach to either retreat direction or ongoing direction often evolves from innocent lapses, if not in professionalism at least in consciousness. The director regularly chatting in the hall, rather than waiting in his or her office at the appointed time for a meeting, for example, can put the directee on notice that he or she is an "outsider," and less important than the "insider" relationship taking up the directee's appointed time. Beyond, the directors engaged in the chat may not recognize their need to publicize their belonging to a group, which need can cause other delays and interruptions that disrupt and imperil honest and equal communication: visitors knocking at the door, telephone calls, even the silent click of an answering machine can interrupt the conversation and sometimes irretrievably send off the directee's thought. Each can alter the nature of the discussion from one wholly involved in the transcendent to something else.

Seasoned directors might argue that the transcendent is the least of the content of most spiritual direction. While we are corporeal beings and live in the real world, I submit that the larger portion of the conversation is, or at least should attempt to be, concerned with the same problems the desert fathers were concerned with: prayer, the realities of God, and the dangers of illusion, all as they fit into daily life. Each needs to be humbly considered, and the initial virtue (or grace, in Ignatian terms) to be begged for is simple humility. Once pride begins to be conquered, or at least recognized, the spiritual direction relationship moves forward.

If humility is the first and constant step in the spiritual life, then, in Cassian's words,

> the first proof of this humility will be if not only everything that is to
> be done but also everything that is thought of is offered to the
> inspection of the elders, so that, not trusting in one's own judgment,

one may submit in every respect to their understanding and may know how to judge what is good and bad according to what they have handed down.[12]

The elder-director has traveled and travailed these desert paths before. He or she is open in unconditional—that is specifically nonjudgmental—love for the directee. In fact, for the most part, the necessary conditions of honesty, equality, and trust revolve around the necessary unconditional love the spiritual director must have for the directee, as distinct from but not unrelated to the unconditional positive regard the therapist would have for the client in a therapeutic relationship.[13]

For the purpose of this essay, I posit that the director and directee are not within any formal power relationship. While, as noted earlier, neither should they be, I would further posit that it is nearly impossible for director and directee to be in what we would ordinarily understand as an "equal" relationship, except before the Lord. One is clearly the master, and the other clearly the disciple, yet they walk trustingly side by side. It is an equality born of humility that opens the channels of communication between director and directee, and that maintains the openness necessary to the relationship.

Of course the dual problems of equality and honesty as they impact on trust cannot be resolved definitively here, or elsewhere, because they are essentially not resolvable and because they are the areas most attacked by the disparate spirits that would seek to block the relationship and impede any growth in the Lord. Both director and directee are well advised to recall that spiritual directors are not ethereal beings disconnected from society. Most live "in the world." Most belong to one or another group, yet are still able to function independently. Telephones ring, and people stop in the hall to chat; in either case it is fairly easy to intuit which involves lack of professionalism and which is simple happenstance. Only an imaginary situation is perfect, only an imaginary director or directee lives in absolute and perfect freedom for every spiritual direction conversation. It is enough, as we progress in this topic, to recognize the pitfalls that exist in the search for honest, equal, and trusting conversation in the Lord, and then move on.

Vocabulary for Spiritual Direction

Assuming the director-directee relationship includes a two-sided effort at freedom in equality, with its consequent honesty and trust, there needs to be an agreement as to what precisely comprises the language of spirituality.[14] For the most part, language depends on experience, and the directee who is seeking union with God at the purgative, illuminative, or unitive stages of spiritual development will understand as much as he or she experientially is able.[15] Even so, the director of souls will be careful to aid the individual learning about the life toward union with God by assisting with the language of spirituality in an appropriate manner.

First, a spiritual-theological language must be understood as distinct from the language of psychology. The distinct languages of spirituality and of psychology parallel the distinct traditions of each. While both have as their goal the fully free human, they are not the same. As most specialists agree, "to blur the boundaries until they are indistinguishable is to do ourselves and others a disservice."[16] This does not eliminate the need for psychological training on the part of the spiritual director. However, while any spiritual director needs a basic understanding of human psychology to complement training and education in the other components of spiritual direction, training in spiritual direction (including its psychological components) more often comes after the individual has been sought out for ongoing direction by others, supporting the concept of spiritual directing as more a charism of the church than an office to which one might aspire and be appointed. That is, one does not set out to become a spiritual director, one simply grows into it.

Specifically, the first circumstance necessary for "learning" spiritual direction is that the individual becoming a spiritual director is sought out by others, in addition to being one who "has been engaged on the spiritual journey and receiving spiritual direction for a number of years and is recognized as having qualities of mind and heart which enable people to open up and enter into a relationship of trust as they seek to explore and develop their own relationship with God."[17] Formal training in spiritual direction, and consequently in psychology as it is necessary for spiritual direction, comes as a part of that natural process.

The requisite qualities that comprise the call to spiritual direction are recognized through speech; people seek out others based on what they hear. A tremendous indicator of the "qualities of mind and heart" in the modern age is the language the director uses, and the ways the director uses language. Speech, the conveyor of the soul, is what presents the director's own understandings of prayer, of self, and of connectedness with the world to others. If the director's ordinary speech is encrusted with the terms of psychology, or infected with jargon, the potential directee might be confused at best or even turned away from what seems an insurmountable linguistic barrier. That language barrier is sometimes reinforced by the well-meaning efforts of some training programs which, following the norms of ordinary group psychology, develop jargon—or even cant—of their own. This further reinforces the insider/outsider trap described earlier, and in a real sense disconnects the directors from the exquisitely rich Christian tradition of spirituality and spiritual direction. Hence, directors are well advised to distinguish "growing edges" and "conversion," for the first depends on human resolutions and the latter depends on listening to the Lord. In fact, the simple distinction between the pastoral counseling and spiritual direction often rests on this simple formula.

Psychological counseling and psychotherapy are even further away from the practice of spiritual direction. While many adaptations of psychological method are cognizant of and respectful toward religious experiences, many others are antithetical toward them, and hence their language has in built maladaptations to religious experience. In part this depends on psychology's attempt at objective description of subjective experience, whereas spiritual direction is wholly involved in a subjective relationship objectively known but subjectively understood. Any language necessarily has an objective component to it, even where it is nonscientific. But to replace the language of theology with the language of psychology is to risk replacing spiritual direction with pastoral or psychological counseling, or psychotherapy. Of course, overly "pious" language is not the antidote to pure scientific description, but the ordinary theological language of simple Christians is the preferred modality for the spiritual direction conversation, no matter how much psychological training the spiritual director may have.

Again, this does not in any way detract from the genuine need of spiritual directors to be well formed in human psychology and well aware of current psychological schools. Nor does it deny the excellent psychology present in classic spiritual writings. The separation that is necessary is between the language (and therefore methods) of psychology and the language (and therefore methods) of spiritual theology.

Psychology and theology are distinct complexes of knowledge. The modern science of psychology is further divided by its method, aspect, functions, principles, tasks, and the concept of the human person.[18] Theology, also a complex, is by definition the science of faith, that is, the way in which the "act and 'content' of Christian (and ecclesiastical) faith" is studied.[19] The danger of confusing terminologies is the ease with which they may be transferred in a nonspecific manner. That is, while there is a fluid line of demarcation between the world of psychology and the world of theology, the spiritual direction conversation enters each world, yet must remain a conversation primarily centered on the spiritual. To separate sets of terminologies goes far in separating these two distinct worlds.

To be clear: The spiritual direction conversation will and often must of needs be involved from time to time in matters more specifically psychological. In fact, much of the work of spiritual direction involves assisting in the growing attendance to disparate interior movements of spirit, which in other quarters could be described in psychological terms. But spiritual direction is not the disclosure of self known to psychology, and where the object and goal of the particular conversation is growth in the spirit, maintaining the language of spiritual theology will assist in recalling the reasons for and the expectations of that conversation.

The Spiritual Direction Conversation

Up until this point we have investigated the basic attitude necessary for the director and directee to engage in a spiritual direction conversation, and the essentially theological vocabulary necessary to that conversation. Now we will move to the conversation itself, in form and content.

Clearly, the spiritual director and the directee must recognize that the key relationship within their relationship is with God and, as Kevin Culligan points out,

> the directee's relationship with the human director simply supports, confirms and clarifies through the director's own honesty, caring and understanding the directee's growing relationship with God...[and] implies that the director fulfills his role as an instrument of God's guidance by being a guide in prayer.[20]

It is not immediately necessary here to distinguish between the spiritual direction conversation as it takes place in ongoing direction from the conversation as it takes place in retreat direction, except to recognize the compactness and intensity of both the retreat experience and the direction relationship within the retreat. For either ongoing direction or retreat direction, the conversation which is the "stuff" of spiritual direction depends on the notions, discussed earlier, of honesty, equalness, and trust, and the requisite conditions for that honesty, equalness, and trust. As Abba Serapion taught, and Cassian presented in the *Conferences,* it is disclosure that routes evil from the mind and from the heart:

> Today you have triumphed over your conqueror and adversary, defeating him by your confession more decisively than you yourself had been overthrown by him because of your silence....After he has been disclosed, this most wicked spirit will no longer be able to disturb you, nor shall the filthy serpent ever again seize a place to make his lair in you, now that by salutary confession he has been drawn out from the darkness of your heart into the light.[21]

Compare this advice with that of Ignatius in the Exercises:

> when the enemy of our human nature tempts a just soul with his wiles and seductions, he earnestly desires that they be received secretly and kept secret. But if one manifests them to a confessor, or to some other spiritual person who understands his deceits and malicious designs, the evil one is very much vexed. For he knows

he cannot succeed in his evil undertaking, once his evident deceits
have been revealed.[22]

The varied spontaneous interior movements that the directee notices must in and
of themselves be recognized as temptations that can be eased by their very exposure.[23] Clearly, the voicing of temptation does much to dispel it, and yet the most
serious temptation is not to voice any temptation, that is, the most serious temptation seems to be the "demon of self-sufficiency," as Segundo Galilea calls it,[24]
which creates the sort of spiritual and emotional isolation that makes entering
into a spiritual direction conversation and relationship extremely difficult, either
initially or at any time during retreat or ongoing direction.

So each master here—Cassian and Ignatius—and countless others, supports the open revealing of the matters of the heart trustingly to the director. It
is a given for both masters that the relationship, and the language of the relationship, are spiritual and theological, for each precedes the particular detach-
ments and methods of modern psychology. It is especially important to note
that in no way is the director's conversation to be manipulative, even if the
objective is to bring the directee to a self-recognition that would engender
growth in freedom.[25]

Ignatius further provides for the privacy of the exercitant: under no circumstances should the director "seek to investigate and know the private
thoughts and sins of the exercitant, nevertheless, it will be very helpful if he is
kept faithfully informed about the various disturbances and thoughts caused
by the action of different spirits."[26] The voluntary disclosure of the exercitant's
interior movements of consolation and desolation, as Ignatius describes them,
may be accompanied by the voluntary disclosure of a recollection of sin history, but this latter may not be actively sought by the director. This instruction
is prefaced by Ignatius's clear statement in Annotation 15, that the director
"should permit the Creator to deal directly with the creature, and the creature
directly with his Creator and Lord."[27] This is a crucial point to the understanding of the spiritual direction conversation, for the conversation truly takes
place between two persons in the presence of the Lord. The director's presence, language, and speech are all aimed at this critical reality; the focus is and
must remain on the directee's present relationship with God, not on "old business" except insofar as such is a true present concern.

Hence the ministry of holy listening depends on the openness of the
directee, and equally on the discretion, that is, unwillingness to pry, on the part
of the director. This is an especially important note, since the term "evocative
questioning" has come to the fore in professional discussions about spiritual
direction, and its meaning, on the face of it, is specifically antagonistic to the
sort of discretion Cassian, Ignatius, and other great masters expect of a director. It is one thing to encourage a reticent person to speak more freely about his

or her relationship with God by asking, "Do you wish to say more about that?" or, "Can you describe that for me a little more fully?"; it is quite another thing to dig into a clearly embarrassing memory of sin intuited from the content and context of the conversation with the same questions. The director simply may not ask the sort of leading questions that would manipulate the directee into a discursus on his or her personal sin history, despite its inevitable rising within the mind and heart of a directee who is moving through one or another stage of the spiritual life, or who is moving through the Spiritual Exercises of St. Ignatius either in a Nineteenth Annotation or Thirty Day experience, or who is moving through the pattern of creation, redemption, and sanctification in another type of retreat.

In fact, manipulation in speech is ultimately one of the deepest threats to the spiritual direction experience, for it eventually (when recognized) can set the directee to doubting how much God's grace has brought this or another insight, and how much it was the result of a given psychological manipulation on the part of the director. That is, manipulation endangers trust. Clearly, psychological manipulation is a danger on the part of both the directee and the director, and is almost always a temptation to pride. Hence the well-tested recommendations of many spiritual writers for both parties to the spiritual direction conversation to continually and well recognize their creaturehood before the Lord.

Other matters can initially cause a disagreeable conversation, or one that grows to be so. Directors humbly recognize that sometimes individuals are beyond their help, either psychologically or intellectually. Both circumstances create conversational difficulties, and uncomfortableness on the part of the director or the directee, and incur the professional obligation on the part of the director to guide the directee to closure and to another director, or to professional psychological assistance. Whether the directee simply stops coming, due to his or her own understanding of incompatibility, or the director recognizes that there seems to be no movement and hence ought to initiate a reevaluation of the relationship,[28] the guiding virtue is humility.

It is important to recognize an additional point about the content and form of the spiritual direction conversation: the force and power of nonverbal communication. Generally speaking, nonverbal communication refers to gestures, postures, facial expressions, symbolic clothing, and similar phenomena that exist within a conversation. For our purposes, we must include the location of the spiritual direction interview and its design and decor, and recall the considerations above relative to the comportment of the director in relation to the directee and other staff or team members in a parish or retreat house setting.[29]

Traditional communications research into nonverbal communication divides its considerations into various categories,[30] but for the purposes of this essay the two most important are known as "performance codes" and "artifactual codes," and either one positively or negatively invokes what might otherwise be known as "presence."

In spiritual direction, performance codes include the responses of the director to the directee's constellation of communicative cues, that is, to the directee's communicative language, content, and mannerisms. Performance codes would include facial expressions (smiles, frowns, grimaces), eye movements (winks, blinks, averting of the eyes), gestures, bodily posture, and, as a subcategory of performance codes the various paralinguistic phenomena that are indirect conscious or unconscious responses: voice quality, speech, nonfluencies, sighs, yawns, laughter, grunts. Obviously, since the spiritual direction conversation is nothing if it is not two-way communication, the obverse is also true. There is much the director can discern by and through the nonverbal communication of the directee.

The second major category of nonverbal communication important to the ministry of spiritual direction is artifactual codes. Artifactual codes result from nonverbal communication through manner of dress (both religious dress and dress that reflects a given socioeconomic status), cosmetics (perfumes, makeup, use of hair dye), grooming, office decor and furnishings.

A third category of nonverbal communication—contextual codes— partly relates to the spiritual direction conversation, in that it applies to the use of time and space. Hence, as earlier, the use of the directee's time for hallway chats or various interruptions sends a very powerful and very negative signal to the directee.

Each of these three[31] impacts the spiritual direction conversation in various ways. Contextual codes surround the entire spiritual direction relationship, insofar as all conversations are held within a certain context and every context imparts meaning. Performance codes and artifactual codes impart meaning, very often unconsciously, and can both enhance and interrupt the spiritual direction conversation.

Obviously, the discerning spiritual director is alert to nonverbal cues on the part of the directee. The director should also be aware of his or her own nonverbal cues and communications to the directee, some of which are gender specific. For example, the male director who unconsciously signals agreement by the single wink of an eye might consider the effect of such wink on a young woman directee; similarly, the female director who places a large pink candle between her and a directee ought perhaps consider the possibility that it might be taken for a phallic symbol.[32] Other examples abound, and some are unavoidable. Age and eyeglasses are pretty much a given. Other nonverbal communications (artifactual codes) are up for consideration: whether to wear a religious habit, ring, or Roman collar; whether to use hair coloring, lipstick, nail polish; to brush hair over the bald spot, to tan or not to tan? Directees, who come to be with directors in a space safe for vulnerability are often hypersensitive to the merest hints of narcissism and insecurity on the part of the director, even if only unconsciously. Further, consider the nonverbal communication (performance codes) involved when the director gives an unwelcome and unexpected (not to mention unprofessional) hug to the directee, or yawns in the middle of a conversation.

No director, of course, wishes to willingly signal sexual or emotional predatoriness, anger, hostility, ridicule, or boredom within a spiritual direction conversation. The grace to recognize and manage these and other interior movements during the spiritual direction session is much of the stuff of spiritual direction and the spiritual direction conversation as it rightly focuses on the directee's experience of God. This call to a state of "other directedness" distinguishes the spiritual direction conversation insofar as its content rarely centers on the director, except where the director is rightly using a personal example to aid the directee and not simply to move the conversation along.

Personal qualities and characteristics of the director will ensure the appropriate stance within the spiritual direction conversation, and so the director is well advised to conduct self-evaluation that seeks growth in any of a number of areas, beginning with an understanding of himself or herself as an instrument of God's work with others, who meets them with compassionate respect and recognizes, among other things, the varied ways in which interpersonal communication can be disrupted. These include being able to recognize interior movements and attend to them in oneself, and maintaining an appropriate personal manner.[33]

Being a holy listener engenders holy speech, and it is that sacred ground in sacred trust the director and the directee walk together.

Conclusions

Assuming all other considerations are in place and director and directee are in an harmonious relationship, what then comprises the holy speech and holy listening of the spiritual direction conversation? If the requisites of honesty and equality have engendered trust, and a common vocabulary of spirituality has been discovered, and the parameters of the spiritual direction conversation are agreed to and understood, precisely what comprises the interpersonal communication of spiritual direction?

I submit that the holy speech and holy listening of the spiritual direction conversation are just that: holy speech and holy listening. Where other matters infect the conversation and distract either the director or the directee from the project—the growth of the directee in freedom to holiness—the conversation is no longer one of spiritual direction. Whether these other matters are intense psychological considerations or mere frivolity, either can take over the discussion and, eventually, the relationship.

In addition to the matters under discussion, holy speech and holy listening require the appropriate manner. The clearest understanding of effective interpersonal communication includes the understanding that all communication is two-way and involves more than simply speech. In fact, all communication begins with nonverbal communication of one sort or another: one's dress, attitude, and manner are all broadcast well before the initial hello, which may be followed by a smile, a handshake, and, finally, a greeting. Different situations communicate different things to people coming for direction: signs, extraneous noise, room colors, and furnishings each present the artifactual codes spoken of above that produce meaning.

The task of the director, then, is to be aware of many facets of communication while entering into and continuing the sacred and trusting conversations of spiritual direction. The spiritual direction conversation requires complete presence and availability to the directee, without verbal or nonverbal distractions, as well as concentration on the matter proper to spiritual direction, in order to provide the holy listening that will engender holy speech.

Holy listening, then, means listening with heart and mind, with each sense and eliminating all distractions and personal agenda both interior and exterior. It means to listen in silence without unnecessary interruptions, distractions, or curious questions. Holy listening sometimes does ask for repetition, for understanding or for emphasis, but it restrains us from correcting the directee's reality, for his or her perceptions are in fact a personal reality. Holy listening nonjudgmentally encourages the conversation, with understanding and with open questions that neither corner the directee nor pry into private matters.

Holy listening can be fine-tuned by training and by practice, but it depends upon the gifts of the spirit, on the graced qualities of love, joy, peace, patience, kindness, generosity, faithfulness, gentleness, and self-control,[34] each of which strengthens the charism of the ministry of spiritual direction as one of love, patience, kindness, generosity, faithfulness and gentleness lived with self-control in joy and in peace.

Holy listening, in fact, is holy speech, and in its simplicity it will bring both director and directee closer to God.

Notes

1. Lavinia Byrne, among others, warns against its popularity. Lavinia Byrne, "Test the Spirits," *Tablet* 246 (August 15, 1992): 1011–12.

2. Margaret Guenther describes the qualities of the director as gracious host, good teacher, and participant in the midwifery of the soul. Margaret Guenther, *Holy Listening: The Art of Spiritual Direction* (Cambridge, Mass.: Cowley Publications, 1992).

3. Irenee Hausherr, *Spiritual Direction in the Early Christian East*, trans. Anthony P. Gythiel (Kalamazoo, Mich.: Cistercian Publications, 1990).

4. Cassian, while filled with the sexism of his era, is fairly complete. Desert mothers were around. See Josep M. Soler, "Les Meres du desert et la maternite spirituelle," *Collectanea cisterciensia* 48 (1986): 235–50 (previously published in *Studia Silencia* 12 (1986):45–62 and published in translation in *Theology Digest* 36, 1 (Spring 1989): 31ff and Benedicta Ward, *Harlots of the Desert* (London: Mowbray & Co., 1987).

5. *John Cassian: The Conferences* (10.7.3), trans. by Boniface Ramsey (New York and Mahwah, N.J.: Paulist, 1997), 376.

6. Equality, or "equalness," is possible and necessary in the master-disciple relationship in the sense that and only insofar as each recognizes his or her creaturehood before God.

7. Some of what follows on Cassian depends on Edward Sellner, "Cassian and the Elders: Formation and Spiritual Direction in the Desert," *Studies in Formative Spirituality* 13 (November 1992): 305–22.

8. Other formative processes are unavoidably unequal and distinct from contemporary spiritual direction. The juridically bound positions of novice mistress or master or confessor each have in-built power. While spiritual direction can and does take place within these relationships, because the confessor while bound to secrecy renders judgment, and the novice mistress or master appropriately reveals matter in rendering judgment, for the purpose of this essay they are excluded.

9. Boundary issues, and liability questions, are the stuff of another essay, but for the necessary communication of spiritual direction boundaries must be respected. See Jonathan Foster, "Liability Issues in a Ministry of Spiritual Direction," *Presence* 2, 3 (September 1996): 50–53, and Thomas Hedberg and Betsy Caprio, *A Code of Ethics for Spiritual Directors* (Pecos, N.M.: Dove Publications, 1992).

10. Team ministry in the giving of the Exercises of St. Ignatius of Loyola has evolved and spread since 1969, when a team of Jesuits headed by John English, S.J., first gave the Exercises as a team to a large group of people. This approach has successfully been adapted by other retreat houses, with the cautions I note above. For specific discussion of team direction of the Exercises in varying cultures, see Virginia Varley, "Culture and Current Practice," *Way Supplement* 76 (Spring 1993): 32–43, esp. 40.

11. While this essay focuses on the spiritual direction conversation, it is well to note here the concomitant problem specific to engaging in the Exercises in a group, which is that individuals can feel they are being herded through them, or feel upset at being laggards when they sense that they are not quite in step with the rest of the group. Exercitants can almost always tell

358 Handbook of Spirituality for Ministers

where they are with the "program" by the daily homily, which often matches where the team thinks they should be on a given day.

12. *John Cassian* (2.10.1).

13. Kevin Culligan, "Toward a Contemporary Model of Spiritual Direction: A Comparative Study of St. John of the Cross and Carl Rogers," in *Carmelite Studies: Contemporary Psychology and Carmel*, John Sullivan, ed. (Washington, D.C.: ICS Publications, 1982), 95–166, esp. 134, 140, 146–150.

14. In a somewhat different context, in *InFormation*, the newsletter of the Religious Formation Conference, I argued that the phenomenon of replacing the religious terms of theology with the secular terms of psychology is deleterious to spiritual direction in general and to the vocation/formation process in particular. I continue to hold that view. Phyllis Zagano, "Speaking of God," *InFormation* 6, 4 (July–August 1998): 1–2, 8–9.

15. "Stages of spiritual development" is an awkward concept, because each and all named may be experienced alone or in concert with one or both of the others at various points in life. However, the terms are classic, and so both useful and necessary.

16. Mary Grant and Pamela Hayes, "Spiritual Direction and Counseling Therapy," *Way Supplement* 69 (Autumn 1990): 69.

17. Ibid., 64–65.

18. Edward Zellinger, "Psychology," in *Encyclopedia of Theology: The Concise Sacramentum Mundi*, Karl Rahner, ed. (New York: Seabury, 1975), 1315–17.

19. Karl Rahner, "Theology," in *Encyclopedia of Theology: The Concise Sacramentum Mundi*, Karl Rahner, ed. (New York: Seabury Press, 1975), 1688.

20. Culligan, "Contemporary Model of Spiritual Direction," 105.

21. *John Cassian* (2.11.4), 92.

22. *The Spiritual Exercises of St. Ignatius*, trans. Louis J. Puhl (Chicago: Loyola University Press, 1951), no. 326: 145–46.

23. "It is of just such non-free spontaneous tendencies in himself that the exercitant is asked to inform the director so that with the help of his [the director's] expert guidance, the exercitant may learn to experience and recognize their evil source in the very act of feeling them." Paul J. Bernadicou, S.J., "The Retreat Director in the Spiritual Exercises," *Review for Religious* 26 (1967): 672–84 reprinted in *Notes on the Spiritual Exercises of St. Ignatius of Loyola: The Best of the Review 1*, ed. David L. Fleming, S.J. (St. Louis, Mo.: Review for Religious, 1983), 31.

24. Segundo Galilea, *Temptation and Discernment,* trans. Stephen-Joseph Ross (Washington, D.C.: ICS Publications, 1996), 76.

25. This implies a conundrum as regards the Exercises, which are specifically designed to bring the exercitant to a self-recognition that engenders

growth in freedom. I would therefore distinguish between the pattern of the Exercises and specifically manipulative speech.

26. *Spiritual Exercises,* no. 17, 7.

27. Ibid., no. 17, 6.

28. John J. English, *Spiritual Freedom*, 2d ed. (Chicago: Loyola University Press, 1973, 1995), 7–8.

29. What follows applies as well to supervisor-supervisee communications in the supervision of spiritual directors.

30. Randall P. Harrison, "Nonverbal Communication," in *Handbook of Communication*, Ithiel de Sola Pool, Wilber Schramm *et al.*, eds. (Chicago: Rand McNally and Company, 1973), 93–115.

31. The fourth, mediational codes, is much of the stuff of contemporary communications research into media, which control so much of our view of reality.

32. I wish these examples were a fiction, but they are not.

33. James A. Borbely, S.J., "Developing Competence as a Director in the Ignatian Tradition," (1992), n.p.

34. Galations 5:22–24.

Edward C. Sellner

24. Celtic Soul Friendship
and Contemporary Spiritual Mentoring

Sometime ago, in the autumn of the year, a close friend of mine died unexpectedly. In the ensuing confusion caused by this sudden loss, my wife and I tried to comfort his widow and children, notify other long-distance friends of his death, participate in the wake and funeral, and, then, after the burial, resume our daily lives as if nothing had really changed. In effect, of course, through our many activities, we were attempting—very unconsciously I must say—to deny our feelings of anger, grief, and powerlessness in the face of death. The body and soul, however, have a wisdom of their own. That winter, on Christmas Eve morning to be precise, I had a vivid dream that affected me in many ways.

The dream opened with me in a room filled with old acquaintances from another time in my life, all of whom were suffering (in the dream) from various forms of illness. Suddenly, Jerry, my dead friend, appears and motions me to sit down in a chair across from him. I hesitate, surprised at his presence in the room when I know that he is really dead! Yet, he persists (as was his way in my conscious life). As I seat myself across from him, he begins to communicate with me in the sign language of the deaf, while pointing, quite deliberately, it seems, to first his and then my heart. Never having learned sign language, in the dream I still clearly understand what he is saying to me: "You and I will always be friends." I am dramatically affected by the meaning of his gestures, for immediately the words, "Jerry, I miss you," come to my lips, and I begin to cry.

I awoke with those words on my lips, my eyes filled with tears. As I recalled the dream, I began to cry even more. My wife, JoAnne, awakened by the sounds, listened as I told her of my dream, and then, leaning over to comfort me, said quite simply, "That was a beautiful dream."

In retrospect, I have come to see it in that light. Not only did the dream help me grieve wholeheartedly, it also helped me recognize the importance of my friend's presence in my life, and how, in the reality of love that transcends space and time, that relationship will never die. With its vivid imagery and symbolic language of the soul, the dream also revealed to me why that friendship was so important. Jerry, over the years, had become a mentor to me, and

360

in many ways a spiritual guide—although I did not associate those terms with him as our relationship was developing. An older man, characterized by his humor and his compassionate listening, he was someone to whom I had often gone to pour out difficulties in making decisions and discerning the future direction of my life. I did not expect Jerry to answer my questions for me, and he never did, respecting the painful dimensions of my own freedom. He was, however, always there as a sounding board, and, most of all, someone with whom I could speak openly, honestly, and without fear about anything.

In many ways, Jerry fit St. Augustine's description of a friend: a person with whom we can share the counsels of the heart. As the dream sequence with him pointing to his heart and mine revealed, Jerry was truly someone with whom I could speak the language of the heart, a form of communication that can lead to the greatest communion: the communion of souls. In the midst of my own uncertainties and inability to act, which were making me psychologically and spiritually sick (symbolized in my dream with the images of sick people), he was someone who helped me move toward greater decisiveness, maturity, and health. What came to my mind, as I reflected on the dream were the words of John Henry Newman's personal motto, in Latin, *Cor ad cor loguitur,* meaning "Heart speaks to heart." In that loving form of communication, transformation often happens and wisdom is learned firsthand. It is this language of the heart that I believe to be the foundation of any effective ministry of mentoring or spiritual guidance.

The value of this ministry, especially for and by lay Christians, is being rediscovered today. Despite differing ecclesial and denominational loyalties, many people are finding a great deal of meaning in relationships of spiritual friendship, companioning, or mentoring. Some have been professionally involved in the more formal ministry of spiritual direction for years; others are now wondering whether they should be. A large number are presently participating in theological and spiritual formation programs that will better prepare them to do the many varieties of pastoral care which that type of ministry encompasses. If memory is both our greatest teacher, as St. Augustine believed, and "the mother of creativity," as the American psychiatrist Rollo May posits, then our collective memory as expressed in our spiritual traditions can be a rich source of ongoing guidance for us all.

In this essay, I explore one important tradition of spiritual mentoring that has been the focus of my research and writing over the years: that of the Celtic soul friend. Since I first heard the word in graduate school at the University of Notre Dame, it and the spirituality out of which it came has haunted my dreams and captured my imagination. To better articulate "soul friendship," I briefly trace its historical origins, relate some of the ancient stories that shed light on its meaning, and discuss the implications of that tradition for us today.

The Early Celtic Church and the Soul Friend

Long before theological and political conflicts tragically divided Christianity, one of its most ancient and creative churches grew to prominence, primarily in the lands we now call Ireland, England, Scotland, Wales, the Isle of Man, and Brittany, on the northern coast of France. This early Celtic church existed from the fifth through the twelfth centuries with its own unique ecclesial structures and spirituality. Although never united administratively, these churches experienced a large measure of unity among themselves through their monastic lifestyle, respect for women's leadership, love of nature, and appreciation of friendship and kinship ties. In these churches, a person who acted as a teacher, confessor, or spiritual guide was called by the Irish and Scots an *anamchara* or by the Welsh a *periglour* or *beriglour,* terms that mean "friend of the soul" or "soul friend." Although this type of ministry was eventually associated by the Western church primarily with the ordained male priest in the sacrament of reconciliation, in the earliest days of Celtic Christianity such relationships were open to lay people and ordained, women and men alike. A story, linked with St. Brigit of Kildare and found in the early ninth-century *Martyrology of Oengus the Culdee* attests to the importance of the *anamchara:*

> A young cleric of the community of Ferns, a foster-son of Brigit's, used to come to her with little gifts. He was often with her in the refectory to partake of food. Once after going to communion Brigit struck a bell. "Well, young cleric there," says Brigit, do you have a soul friend?"
>
> "I have," replied the young man.
>
> "Let us sing his requiem," says Brigit.
>
> "Why so?" asks the young cleric.
>
> "For he has died," says Brigit. "When you had finished half your ration of food I saw that he was dead."
>
> "How did you know that?"
>
> "Easy to say," Brigit replies. "From the time that your soul friend was dead, I saw that your food was put directly in the trunk of your body, since you were without any head. Go forth and eat nothing until you get a soul friend, for anyone without a soul friend is like a body without a head; is like the water of a polluted lake, neither good for drinking nor for washing. That is the person without a soul friend."[1]

This story, set in the context of a meal with references to death and water, has symbolic, sacramental connotations that most Christians would recognize. It suggests that Christian Celts believed that soul friends were crucial to human sustenance and spiritual growth, and that such mentoring relationships were ultimately related to friendship with God.

When we consider the rich history of this Celtic church, main sources for an understanding of the *anamchara* are the stories found in certain Celtic hagiographies or biographies of the saints, many of which, though compiled in the Middle Ages, contain earlier, sometimes very primitive materials. For more than six centuries, from the 600s to well beyond 1200 C.E., monastic hagiographers in the Celtic churches composed the Lives of literally hundreds of Celtic saints. These hagiographies provide a wealth of information about soul friendship, and its immersion in the everyday life and spirituality of Celtic Christianity. They reveal how common soul friend relationships were between men and men, women and women, and women and men, and, as the story of Brigit and the young cleric shows, the importance of everyone having a soul friend, including the laity. In these ancient stories, particular dimensions of soul friendship emerge:

First, soul friendship is associated with great affection, intimacy, and depth. As we learn in a passage from the eighth century *Liber Angeli* (Book of the Angel): "Between holy Patrick and Brigit, pillars of the Irish, there existed so great a friendship of charity that they were of one heart and one mind."[2] Soul friends share what the Greeks and Romans as well as early church fathers and mothers equate with true friendship itself: one soul in two bodies, two hearts united as one. In the hagiographies, this intimacy is manifest in very ordinary emotions and simple gestures. St. Brendan, for example, smiles warmly when he thinks of Ita, his foster mother, and Ita, in turn, experiences the slow passage of time when Brendan is away; Finnian calls his student Ciaran "O little heart" and "dear one," and blesses him before Ciaran leaves the monastery of Clonard; Brendan and Ruadan build their cells near one another so that they can hear the ringing of each other's bells.

When it comes to identifying soul friends in our lives, it is well to look to those with whom we feel a great deal of affection and trust. Who are those who make us feel welcome or with whom we sense a kinship of like ideals, goals, spirituality? In what ways, if we are acting as a soul friend to others, can we offer them hospitality: an atmosphere in which they feel accepted, a relationship in which they are not judged for what they have done or failed to do? How might we create a space and an environment where others can discuss freely their conflicts, their need for prayer and quiet, their questions about what life is asking of them next? Soul friendship is where we find that hospitality and space to be honest with ourselves.

Second, soul friend relationships are characterized by mutuality: a profound respect for each other's wisdom, despite any age or gender differences, and the awareness that each person in this relationship is a source of many blessings. This quality of mutuality is, fittingly enough, expressed symbolically in the stories by the exchange of gifts. Brigit gives Finnian a ring, Columcille sends the holy virgin Maugina a little pine box that helps cure her, David of Wales gives Findbarr his horse. Mutuality is perhaps most vividly expressed in a story from the Life of St. Ciaran of Clonmacnoise as he prepares for death:

> When the time of his death at the age of thirty-three drew near to the holy Ciaran he...told the brethren to shut him up in the church until Kevin should come from Glendalough. After three days Kevin arrived....At once Ciaran's spirit returned from heaven and re-entered his body so that he could commune with Kevin and welcome him. The two friends stayed together from the one watch to another, engaged in mutual conversation, and strengthened their friendship. Then Ciaran blessed Kevin, and Kevin blessed water and administered the Eucharist to Ciaran. Ciaran gave his bell to Kevin as a sign of their lasting unity which today is called "Kevin's Bell."[3]

Theirs was obviously a relationship, as the story implies, with eucharistic dimensions, for with the love of each other, they were able to discover throughout their lives and, most especially at the time of death, reasons for gratitude.

This is one of the greatest awarenesses that comes to those who act as soul friends: the recognition of how much we receive from those whom we love and love us, or from those who seek us out. Frequently in our ministries, we find that another person's search for answers clarifies our own questions; that precisely because we have taken time to be present with someone, perhaps a total stranger, we are given an unexpected gift. When and if we lose the sense that others whom we mentor are a source of many blessings, it may be time to make a retreat to a quiet place for a day, weekend, or week—or a retreat from this particular ministry. A definite sign of burnout is when we feel that we have nothing more to give—or to receive.

From what the hagiographies imply, a third characteristic of soul friends is that they share common values, a common vision of reality, and, sometimes, an intuitive sense of the potential leadership of younger protégés. Both vision and intuition are referred to in the story of Ciaran and his spiritual mentor, Enda:

> After that Ciaran went to the island of Aran to commune with Enda. Both of them saw the same vision of a great fruitful tree growing beside a stream in the middle of Ireland. This tree protected the entire island, and its fruit crossed the sea that surrounded Ireland, and the birds of the world came to carry off some of that fruit. Ciaran turned to Enda and told him what he had seen, and Enda, in turn, said to him: "The great tree which you saw is

you, Ciaran, for you are great in the eyes of God and of men. All of
Ireland will be sheltered by the grace that is in you, and many
people will be fed by your fasting and prayers. So, go in the name
of the God to the center of Ireland, and found your church on the
banks of a stream."[4]

In this story, although both friends have the same vision of a mighty tree growing in Ireland, it is the older, more experienced man who is able to interpret it
for the younger in a way that obviously contributed to his self-esteem and,
thus, his ability to turn that vision into reality. Soul friends are like that.

If we look back over our lives, we can begin to name those as soul
friends who gave us encouragement at a time we needed it the most, or helped
us discern certain talents that we didn't know we had. If we are sponsors, mentors, teachers, or spiritual guides today, we may often have a better long-term
view of another's potential for leadership than the other person does. We need
to share that vision with her or him. Depending on the circumstances in which
neither family, society, nor churches may offer this positive view, our soul
friendship may be crucial to that person's psychological growth and his or her
particular expression of creativity—if not to Christian faith itself.

Fourth, the ancient stories of soul friendships tell us that such relationships include not only affirmation, but the ability to challenge each other when
it is necessary to do so. This is sometimes the most difficult aspect of any intimate relationship, for we naturally seek to avoid conflict with those whom we
love or with whom we minister. Without this quality of courageous honesty,
however, our friendships can soon become superficial, stunted, and eventually
lost. The story of the courage of a holy woman, Canair, in confronting Senan,
an elder whom she admired who lived on Scattery Island, provides a good
example of this aspect of soul friendship:

Senan knew that Canair was coming, and he went to the harbor to
meet and welcome her.

"Yes, I have come," Canair told him.

"Go," said Senan, "to your sister who lives on the island to
the east of this one, so that you may be her guest."

"That is not why I came," said Canair, "but that I may find
hospitality with you on this island."

"Women cannot enter on this island," Senan replied.

"How can you say that?" asked Canair. "Christ is no worse
than you. Christ came to redeem women no less than to redeem
men. He suffered for the sake of women as much as for the sake of
men. Women as well as men can enter the heavenly kingdom.
Why, then, should you not allow women to live on this island?"

"You are persistent," said Senan.

"Well then," Canair replied, "will I get what I ask for? Will you give me a place to live on this island and the holy sacrament of Eucharist?

"Yes, Canair, a place of resurrection will be given you here," said Senan. She came on shore then and received the sacrament from Senan.[5]

Evidently, Canair's willingness to openly express her personal *and theological* views in a direct yet loving manner did much to clarify her relationship with Senan and his with her. Judging from this story, the older man was unaware of his exclusivity—a blindness that could only be effectively removed by what he himself acknowledges as her "persistence."

Today, in our churches especially, there should be no room for the exclusion in any form of people from ministry, leadership, or positions of decision making because of race or gender, for in Jesus' own life we find an openness to all. Soul friendships, in particular, if they are to deepen and grow, need the honesty and courage that Canair demonstrated, as well as that which Senan's actions show: the willingness and courage to change.

A fifth pattern that appears in the stories of the Celtic saints is that *anamchara* relationships are centered upon God, *the* soul friend in whom all other friendships are united. True soul friends do not depend upon each other alone, but root their relationship in God. All the stories of the saints refer to this spiritual dimension, but one story in the Life of Findbarr is the most explicit symbolically. In it we find intimations not only of this need for reliance upon God, but also of the qualities identified earlier, those of affirmation, mutuality, and deep love:

After the death of a certain bishop, Findbarr was much concerned at being without a soul friend. So he went to visit Eolang, and God revealed to Eolang that Findbarr was coming to see him. Eolang...immediately knelt before Findbarr, and said the following, "I offer to you my church, my body, and my soul." Findbarr wept openly, and said, "This was not my thought, but that it would be I who would offer mine to you." Eolang said, "Let it be as I have said, for this is the will of God. You are dear to God, and you are greater than myself. One thing only I ask, that our resurrection will be in the same place." Findbarr replied, "Your wish will be fulfilled, but I am still troubled about the— soul friendship." Eolang told him, "You shall receive today a soul friend worthy of yourself." This was done as he said, for Eolang in the presence of the angels and archangels placed Findbarr's hand in the hand of the Lord....[6]

This task of centering our lives on God and helping others do the same is not as easy as it may sound. Too often, without our conscious awareness, we expect others to make decisions for us, or, if we are spiritual directors or even ordinary mentors, to follow unquestioningly what we perceive to be our "helpful advice."

A daily handing over of our lives to the care of God and helping others to do the same, as Eolang did for Findbarr, can give us the strength to be responsible, first of all, for our own decisions and commitments, and not try to take care of everyone else's. A daily centering can also, as Alcoholics Anonymous reminds us, help us to "let go and let God": to let go of any demand, however subtle, for "results" or "changes" in someone else, and "let God" work as God will. Carl Jung had a saying from the ancient Greeks carved above the door of his house in Kusnacht, Switzerland, "Called or not called, God will be there." We have only to recognize that profound reality, and, in our relationship with others, discern when it is necessary to get out of the way so God can act. With a spirituality of "letting go and letting God," we may find that our resentments diminish as we give our friends and loved ones the freedom to be who they are: genuinely human and thus capable, like us, of making right choices as well as of making mistakes—and learning from them. When our spirituality is centered in God, our expectations become more realistic of others *and of ourselves,* and we find—with God's help—the ability to forgive and move on.

According to hagiographies of the Celtic saints, a sixth characteristic of soul friends is that they appreciate, as did the desert Christians, both friendship and solitude as resources for their daily living and, ultimately, for preparing to die. No hagiography expresses this better than Bede's Life of St. Cuthbert, about a seventh-century Anglo-Saxon saint from northern England whom some believed to have been born in Ireland, so immersed was he in Celtic spirituality. Cuthbert's life clearly reflects a spirituality that values both friendship and solitude, being active in ministry and having a cell. For years, he was involved in pastoral ministry and monastic leadership on the tiny island, Lindisfarne, yet consistently made time in his busy schedule to be away. Finally, to prepare to die, Cuthbert was given permission to build a solitary cell on Inner Farne Island nearby, where he "entered," Bede tells us, "with great joy...into the remoter solitude he had so long sought, thirsted after, and prayed for." Even then, despite his attempts at finding solitude, great numbers of people continued to come to him, Bede says,

> not just from Lindisfarne but even from the remote parts of Britain, attracted by his reputation for miracles. They confessed their sins, confided in him about their temptations, and laid open to him the common troubles of humanity they were laboring under—all in the hope of gaining consolation from so holy a man.

> They were not disappointed. No one left unconsoled; no one had
> to carry back the burdens he came with.[7]

As is evident from the stories about him, Cuthbert's life was a constant struggle to both serve others well and to care for his own solitary needs.

It is the same struggle for most contemporary soul friends. Theirs too is
a life torn between care for others and care for self. Like Cuthbert, they
attempt to somehow find some sort of balance of both their needs for community and for solitude. They make time for the people they serve, but they also
set limits to their availability. They make time in their busy schedules for family and intimate friends, but they also build a cell or find a place away where
on a regular basis they can listen to the silence and to the voice of God in
nature—and in their own hearts.

This pattern of integrating friendship and solitude, prayer and work, is
obviously not always easy to maintain. But, as we try to make this pattern of
the Celtic saints our own, we can begin to experience an inner serenity that not
only allows us to deal better with the demands of modern living, but to help
others carry—and sometimes leave behind—the burdens that they bring to us.
All of this is good preparation for our own ultimate life work: dying well.
Thomas Merton, the Trappist monk and spiritual writer, referred in his journal
shortly before he died to his happiness with certain friendships as well as his
joy at being in a hermitage in the Kentucky hills, where he was finally, like
Cuthbert, able "to live in silence...in the shadow of a big cedar cross, to prepare for my death and my exodus to the heavenly country, to love my brothers
and all people, to pray for the whole world...."

A seventh characteristic of soul friendship that emerges in the stories
about the saints is that such a relationship is associated with tremendous bonds
of endurance. These friendship ties can survive geographical separation, as the
story of two soul friends, Molaise and Maedoc, relates:

> Maedoc and Molaise were comrades who loved each other very
> much. One day as they sat praying at the foot of two trees, they
> cried, "Ah, Jesus!, is it your will that we should part, or that we
> should remain together until we die?" Then one of the two trees
> fell to the south, and the other to the north. "By the fall of the
> trees," they said, "it is clear that we must part." Then they told
> each other goodbye, and kissed each other affectionately. Maedoc
> went to the south, and built a noble monastery at Ferns, and
> Molaise went north and built a fair monastery at Devenish.[8]

The two friends evidently never forgot what each meant to the other, and,
despite the geographical distance, prayed often for the well-being of the other
and met again when circumstances allowed.

Other early stories tell how soul friendship endures the passage of time. Columcille moves to Iona in order to bring Christianity to the Scots, but he continues to long for Derry and his friends in Ireland—and they for him. Brendan consistently returns to Ita for advice after his journeys to foreign lands. In another story from the Life of Maedoc of Ferns, we see how, besides the soul friendship he has with Molaise, one he has with Columcille survives death itself:

> Once Maedoc was teaching a student by a high cross at the monastery of Ferns. The student saw him mount a golden ladder reaching from earth to heaven. Maedoc climbed the ladder, and when he returned sometime later, the student could not look in his face because of the brilliance which transfused his countenance...."Columcille has died," Maedoc told him, "and I went to meet him with the family of heaven. He was my own soul friend in this world, so I wanted to pay him my respects." The student told this story only after Maedoc's death, when he had become an adult and a holy man himself.[9]

What is so powerful about this last story is that it draws upon the ladder imagery, a symbol and theme of spiritual progress and intimacy with God frequently found in Judeo-Christian spirituality—from the dream of Jacob in the Old Testament to Jesus' promise to Nathaniel that he would see, if he followed him, "heaven laid open and, above the Son of Man, the angels of God ascending and descending" (Jn 1:51). The same ladder imagery appears in the writings of Plato, Origen, John Climacus, Walter Hilton, Luther, Calvin, and on through to our present age. Thus, not only does this story of Maedoc seem to say that soul friend relationships survive even death, but that soul friends are a way toward union with God.

Soul Friendship Today: Being a Cell and Listening to the Heart

All the early Celtic saints seem to have been changed profoundly by *anamchara* relationships—whether the soul friends themselves were female or male, human or angelic, or whether they offered a compassionate ear or a challenging word. They were keenly aware that God is very close to those who speak as friends do, heart to heart. This ministry of the *anamchara,* with its one-to-one focus, contributed greatly to Western culture's increased emphasis on the integrity and worth of the individual and upon his or her spiritual and psychological development. Our modern therapeutic and counseling professions find their roots in this ministry. Soul friendship also affected the entire history of Christian spirituality, affirming as it did the conviction that a person's relationship with God can take the form of effective dialogue, and that whenever sins or faults, grief or human vulnerability are openly and honestly acknowledged, healing begins and God's presence is experienced, sometimes unforgettably.

To be a soul friend today presupposes certain awarenesses that are derived from this spiritual tradition. According to Nora Chadwick in her classic, *The Age of the Saints in the Early Celtic Church,* the *anamchara* was originally someone who, as a companion, shared another's cell and to whom one confessed, revealing confidential aspects of one's life. She believed that the Celtic tradition of spiritual guidance was strongly influenced by the desert Christians, and that the rise of the *anamchara* in the Celtic churches was a natural development that may be related to the *syncellus,* "the one who shares a cell" in the Greek Orthodox Church.[10] Conscious of this, soul friends today are aware of the importance of sharing a cell: those deeper parts of us, our hearts and souls, where identity, meaning, and passion dwell. This free exchange of soul and heart, based upon a grateful acknowledgment of mutuality, is the greatest gift we can give others or receive from them. In a world of increasing complexity, in a culture where fear, violence, and cynicism flourish, it is no wonder that people long for relationships of genuine intimacy, stability, and depth. Being accepted and loved by another person is to be cherished, and not taken for granted—as is the experience of being heard when one is not even sure what it is one is trying to say. Soul friendship is a relationship that acts as a container, a cell in which we can face the truth of our lives without fear. Soul friendship is a place of sanctuary where the worst part of us can be acknowledged, so that genuine change can begin to occur. Soul friendship is also a relationship, a place where our joys and accomplishments can be celebrated wholeheartedly. Healing and the integration of mind and heart happen where there is mutual honesty and trust.

A second awareness about soul friendship today is the importance of listening to the heart. A number of early Irish writers were fond of the expression "to see with the eyes of the heart," while the opening lines of St. Benedict's Rule, written in the sixth century, implies that the heart has an ear with which any novice or neophyte should learn to listen attentively. St. Patrick and the other Celtic saints evidently both *saw* and *heard* with the heart, paying attention to what their physical eyes saw and their experiences taught them, but also to what their feelings, intuitions, and instincts were telling them to do. They knew that this attentiveness to the inner world gave them the ability to hear the voice of the Holy Spirit in their hearts speaking to them possibly of works yet to be created, of spiritual adventures yet to be undertaken, of contributions to family, kin, and tribe yet to be made.

In many ways, prayer for soul friends today is the discipline of beginning to listen, truly listen with the eyes and ears of God. In the heart, we can discover our identity and vocation. In the heart can also be found God's peace, or *quies,* a Latin word expressing both sanity and serenity. In the heart, we find a window to our souls. By praying daily, by paying attention to the heart, we can begin to acquire a wisdom that transcends intellectual knowledge alone. The early Celtic Christians believed that the best spiritual director, mentor, or soul friend is the person who is "competent to answer for his or her own soul first." We gain that competence by listening to the heart.

A third awareness about soul friendship is that it thrives in a particular kind of spirituality: a spirituality of ongoing conversion and reconciliation, starting with ourselves. Through our willingness to change, and our efforts to bring about unity and reunion with those whom we may feel alienated, hostile, misunderstood, or insecure, we set an example of Christian leadership today. Such leadership incorporates the values of the saints and the wisdom of their stories. Such leadership is grounded in a spirituality that is global in its vision and creation-centered in its scope. It invites the full participation of laity, women, and marginal peoples in church life, its sacraments and decision making. It cherishes the warmth of the hearth, family life, and a circle of friends. It acknowledges the significance of daily life and work, the so-called "ordinary" aspects of our lives, as sacred soil for soul making. Such leadership is willing to work for qualitative changes in our culture and our Christian churches— especially our churches, for if they do not model equality and respect for others, the truth and hope of the Gospels can quickly be lost to this generation and the next, our children's and grandchildren's.

Conclusion

If we look back on Celtic soul friendship as described in early literature as well as Celtic Christian practice through the ages, we can see how much it is an expression of Jesus' own words of encouragement to his disciples: "I call you friends. Love one another, as I have loved you" (Jn 15:12–17). In many ways soul friendship is a paradigm of all ministries, for, like Jesus' own, conversion and reconciliation are *the* work of every Christian no matter who does it, where it happens, or what form it takes. Even if our ministry at times seems insignificant or of no lasting effect, it can have salvific value in the ultimate "scheme of things" when it brings people closer to God through experiences of friendship, acceptance, forgiveness, and love. Certainly, as the stories of the Celtic saints express and as my own dream of my dead mentor, Jerry, pointing to his and my heart, confirm: Soul friendship joins friends together, as the fourth-century desert father, John Cassian, suggests, in "a common dwelling that neither time nor space nor death itself can separate:"[11] the dwelling of the soul and of the heart. A more contemporary source, twentieth-century Breton writer, Angela Duval, expresses this in another way, in her poem, "My Heart:"

My heart is a Cemetery
In it are countless graves
In it always a new grave
Graves of friends and relatives
My heart is a Cemetery!

My heart is a Cemetery
But no!
My heart is a Sanctuary
Wherein live My Dear Departed![12]

Notes

1. Whitley Stokes, ed., *The Martyrology of Oengus the Culdee* (London:1905), 65.

2. The Book of the Angel, in Ludwig Bieler, ed., *The Patrician Texts in the Book of Armagh* (Dublin: Dublin Institute for Advanced Studies, 1979), 191.

3. See Edward Sellner, *Wisdom of the Celtic Saints* (Notre Dame, Ind.: Ave Maria Press, 1993), 86–87.

4. Ibid., 84–85.

5. Ibid., 77–78.

6. Ibid., 131–32.

7. Ibid., 109.

8. Ibid., 169.

9. Ibid., 173.

10. See Nora Chadwick, *The Age of the Saints in the Early Celtic Church* (London: Oxford University Press, 1961), 103 ff. and 149.

11. See Cassian's Conference 16, ch. III, in P. Schaff and H. Wace, eds., *A Select Library of Nicene and Post-Nicene Fathers of the Christian Church*, Vol. XI (Grand Rapids, Mich.: Wm. B. Eerdmans, n.d.), 451.

12. Oliver Davies and Fiona Bowie, *Celtic Christian Spirituality: An Anthology of Medieval and Modern Sources* (New York: Continuum, 1995), 226.

SECTION V.
PRAYER

Richard Hauser echoes the Vatican II and papal ("Lord and Giver of Life") call for us "to rethink our approach to every aspect of Christian life in terms of the Holy Spirit" and then emphasizes the centrality of such a call in ministry. In "The Minister and Personal Prayer," one of the ways he does this is by taking us down the road with him in his own deep appreciation for a nourishing prayer life. His ideas, disciplines, and spontaneity make this a lovely essay to pray with and use as a structure for our own work with others who are ready to enrich their spiritual lives.

In "The Interior Life of Jesus as the Life of the People of God," William Reiser emphasizes the closeness, the solidarity of God with us—not just as individuals but also as communities. His emphasis on the social character of faith is both refreshing and helpful in our ministry. He also recognizes that "many of our religious experiences are at the root corporate." That a marriage, not just an individual, can enter a dark night of the soul is but one point in this creative essay, which you will enjoy pondering over. He cites some of the fine theological thinkers of the day, to make this a work of particular value.

In Janet Ruffing's essay, "Socially Engaged Contemplation: Living Contemplatively in Chaotic Times," we are called back to the balance of living in the world with God in our hearts. Drawing upon the wisdom of Walter Burghardt, Gerald May, Thomas Merton, Martin Buber, Thomas Kelly, and the poet Mary Oliver, as well as her own honest hopeful insights and the experience of others, she encourages us to continually reorient ourselves so we are not pulled in too far to a "speed crazed world." One of the most helpful papers in the book, this is an essay to meditate over and try to put part of what is shared into practice on a daily basis.

Keith Egan and Ernest Larkin have written complementary articles to complete this section. Egan's "Contemplative Meditation: A Challenge from the Tradition" gently calls us to renew ourselves "to that gifted mindfulness of the presence of Jesus Christ that is the goal of Christian prayer." In it he recalls for us several "moments in the tradition" that urged him to be more contemplative, less self-absorbed, more centered in simplicity. Ernest Larkin in "Contemplative Prayer as the Soul of the Apostolate" continues the connection between the interior life and fruitful ministry. In focusing on "the stillpoint of the soul," he reflects on the heart of the matter for him (and for many of us), the need for quiet, centered time with God. As in Keith Egan's article, we get the gentle, well-articulated reminders we need so as not to drift from the source of all life.

Richard J. Hauser

25. The Minister and Personal Prayer: Evoking the Spirit of Jesus

Recently I had a disturbing experience. I had just completed a morning presentation on spirituality to a group of ministers. The presentation had included a discussion on the centrality of a relationship to Christ for ministry. I had used such phrases as "friendship with Christ," "intimacy with Christ," "becoming one with Christ." I explained that the goal of a church minister is to be able to exclaim with Paul, "I live, now not I, Christ lives in me." Questions ensued from the dozen ministers present. We then paused for a break. One of the ministers caught me, took me aside out of view, and confessed, "I have no idea of what you mean when you talk about having a relationship with Christ. Is it like a human friendship? How do you know whether you have one?" Evidently my jaw dropped and he felt the need to assure me his question was real and he was not just "putting me on." He continued, "All my life I've heard this and never knew what it meant. Tell me what if feels like for you. How did you develop this relationship?"

This experience stirred many personal feelings and led ultimately to my reflecting on the nature of ministry itself and on my own self-understanding as a Christian minister. Since my primary personal and professional interests concern contemporary spirituality with a focus on the role of the Holy Spirit, I began exploring my question on ministry in terms of the Holy Spirit. This lead to my reflecting first on Christian spirituality, then on Christian ministry, then on personal prayer, and finally on the role of personal prayer in the life of the minister—and my own life.

The Holy Spirit and Christian Spirituality

The Second Vatican Council (1962–1965) was crucial in reappropriating the Christian tradition on the centrality of the Holy Spirit in all Christian life. Before Vatican II an appreciation of the role of the spirit was virtually absent from our consciousness. Before reflecting on the role of the spirit in ministry, it is helpful to review three shifts in models that flow from the teaching of Vatican II and reawaken our awareness of the centrality of the spirit in all Christian spirituality.

These shifts relate to the church, the self, and spirituality. *The first shift in models concerns the church.* In recent decades we have witnessed two differing, though complementary, models of church. Each model assigns a distinctive role to the Holy Spirit—since I am a Roman Catholic, the primary reference of church is to my own tradition, but I've learned that my insights are applicable to Protestant traditions also. In the first model, the Holy Spirit is indeed present in the church, but the church is seen primarily as an institution governed by hierarchical authority—for Catholics: priests, bishops, pope. The Holy Spirit guided the institution through the hierarchy and the hierarchy, especially the local priest, guided the people. The institution rested secure because an infallible guidance in faith and morals was promised to it. In the second model, the Vatican II model, the Holy Spirit is present in the church, but the church is seen as the people of God—the entire community of believers, head and members united in one body of Christ. While continuing to guide the church corporately, the Holy Spirit also guides the members individually. The following excerpts from chapter 1 of the *Constitution on the Church* highlight this truth elegantly:

> The Spirit dwells in the Church and in the hearts of the faithful as in a temple (cf. 1 Cor 3:16; 6:19). In them he prays and bears witness to the fact that they are adopted sons (cf. Gal 4:6; Ro 8: 15–16 and 26). The Spirit guides the Church into the fullness of truth (cf. Jn 16: 13) and gives her a unity of fellowship and service. He furnishes and directs her with various gifts, both hierarchical and charismatic, and adorns her with the fruits of His grace (cf. Eph 4: 11–12; 1 Cor 12:4; Gal 5: 22).

> In order that we may be unceasingly renewed in Him [Jesus] (cf. Eph 4: 23), He has shared with us His Spirit who, existing as one and the same being in the head and in the members, vivifies, unifies, and moves the whole body. (All quotations from Vatican II are from *Documents of Vatican II,* Walter M. Abbott, ed., New York: Guild Press, 1966.)

The second shift in models relates to the self and flows from the model of the church as the body of Christ. Christians are discovering anew a central element of the New Testament message: the role of the spirit within the self. Again Vatican II was crucial. Before the council an appreciation of this role was virtually absent from our consciousness; after the council it dominates consciousness. Only during the early '70s, when doing my doctoral dissertation in theology, did I myself finally begin grasping this role. The plethora of books on the spirit and spirituality in the '70s is an indication that I wasn't alone.

What is the role of the spirit within the self? Treatment of the role of the spirit must begin with the Last Supper discourse in John's Gospel. Jesus is comforting his disciples, having told them of his imminent departure.

> But now I am going to the one who sent me, and not one of you asks me, "Where are you going?" But because I told you this, grief has filled your hearts. But I tell you the truth, it is better for you that I go, for if I do not go, the Advocate will not come to you. But if I go, I will send him to you. (Jn 16: 5–7) (All scripture quotations are from *The New American Bible,* Nashville: Thomas Nelson, 1971.)

But he assures them it is better for them that he goes; the spirit he sends will take his place, guiding and strengthening them in their mission. Indeed this union with himself through the spirit is the condition for apostolic effectiveness. The Gospel could not be more clear.

> Remain in me, as I remain in you. Just as a branch cannot bear fruit on its own unless it remains on the vine, so neither can you unless you remain in me. I am the vine, you are the branches. Whoever remains in me and I in him will bear much fruit, because without me you can do nothing. (Jn 15: 4–5)

Jesus' prediction is fulfilled at Pentecost when the spirit descends on the community. The Acts of the Apostles gives witness to the working of the spirit in the apostolic church. Note the difference in the disciples before and after the coming of the spirit.

Among New Testament writings the epistles of Paul are a most eloquent witness to this power of the spirit—a power he received only after his conversion to Christ at Damascus. For Paul, belief in Jesus, with the subsequent infusion of the life of the spirit, is the source of all power. It is a new principle of life. Paul contrasts it with the flesh and its tendency to sin.

> But you are not in the flesh; on the contrary, you are in the spirit, if only the Spirit of God dwells in you. Whoever does not have this Spirit of Christ does not belong to him. But if Christ is in you, although the body is dead because of sin, the spirit is alive because of righteousness. If the Spirit of the one who raised Jesus from the dead dwells in you, the one who raised Christ from the dead will give life to your mortal bodies also, through his Spirit that dwells in you. (Rom 8:9–11)

A note on the activity of the spirit in the self is important. The Holy Spirit joins our human spirit; it does not replace it. We humans enjoy three modes of activity flowing from the three dimensions of our being: physical, psychological, and spiritual. It is helpful to imagine three concentric circles: the center is the spirit, the middle is the mind, the outer is the body. Every human activity engages all three levels. Our physical and psychological activities are obvious to all. But what are our spiritual activities? The spiritual level is the level of our freedom, our freedom to *respond* to the spirit or not to respond. The Holy Spirit joins our human spirit, *initiating* within us the desire for goodness—without the spirit's presence we would not even have the desire. Responding to the spirit then transforms the other levels of our being, the physical and the psychological. The spirit is the principle for *all* Christian life and ministry. Traditionally this indwelling of the spirit has been called "sanctifying grace." Ministry and personal prayer—like every Christian activity—is a response to the spirit.

An important corollary flows from this truth: We can trust our inner selves. At our center we have God's spirit to guide us. Previous approaches to spirituality did not adequately acknowledge that presence. Commonly they taught that the self cannot be trusted because of fallen human nature and inherited original sin. This inherited brokenness so dominated our consciousness that we undervalued the power of redemption from sin. Since we could not trust this inner self, it became necessary to look outside ourselves for external guidelines. Contemporary approaches also acknowledge brokenness—hence the emphasis on discernment of good *versus* evil spirits—but they also acknowledge the real effect of Christ's redemption. We have been freed from the slavery of sin; therefore, we can trust our inner selves—grace in us is stronger than sin in us. Frequently we Christians have substituted fidelity to prescribed formal prayers—morning and night prayers, meal prayers, Divine Office, prayerbook formularies—for a more interior response to the spirit.

Unfortunately the Vatican II theological renewal concerning the Holy Spirit still remains contrary to popular beliefs. Many of us live within a different model of the self—I'll call it the Western model of the self. I call it the Western model because it is the model I recognize as dominating the approach to God in myself—and in my brothers and sisters in the Western Hemisphere. In this model God is solely transcendent—in heaven—and so not dwelling within the self through the spirit. Since God is in heaven God cannot be the initiator of good actions. Though the Western model duly acknowledges that we are made to know, love, and serve God in this life and so be happy in the next, it gives God no role in these actions until after they are performed. Then it grants that God rewards us with grace in this life and heaven in the next. But in the Western model we are the initiators of our own good deeds—including ministry and personal prayer. In this model sanctifying grace is often erroneously understood as the treasury of merit stored in heaven earned by good works.

The Western view of self is taken not from the New Testament but rather absorbed from several aspects of our culture. Our culture is secular. Our view of the self tends also to be secular; we do not recognize God's presence within us and its influence on our inner motivation. At best we give intellectual assent that through baptism we receive sanctifying grace and so God is with us, but this presence of God has no implication for understanding daily motivation. Our culture is also capitalistic. We give financial rewards conditioned on performance; we presume God gives spiritual rewards the same way, rewarding the just with grace—and perhaps even material prosperity—and withholding these rewards from the unjust. Our culture is individualistic. We prize independence and eschew any dependence. Yes, we find dependence on God's grace demeaning also. Without giving it much thought, we just presume we earn our salvation like we earn everything in life, by our own hard work. This view has disastrous effects on our understanding of ministry and prayer. Since the spirit is not present within us, ministry and prayer cannot be a response to the spirit.

The third shift in models concerns spirituality itself. Unfortunately we Christians have not drawn out implications of the above models of the church and the self and applied them to our practice of spirituality—or to ministry and personal prayer. Christian ministry and prayer is a response to the spirit. Today the focus of attention has shifted from external performance of spiritual disciplines, such as prayer, to an internal response to the spirit in our hearts. Paul teaches his Jewish communities that they have been freed from subservience to the 613 Mosaic laws and are now called to respond to an inner law: "But now we are discharged from the law, dead to that which held us captive, so that we serve not under the old written code, but in the new life of the Spirit" (Rom 7:6). This truth also highlights the inadequacy of the Western model's understanding of good actions as self-initiated and emphasizes the scriptural teaching that all good deeds are spirit-initiated. Prayer, for instance, is not a matter of observing formal obligations and of performing external acts but of responding internally to the spirit.

In short, Christian spirituality is more concerned with the quality of heart underlying our ministry and prayer than with their external performance. Prayer and ministry not flowing from the heart do not fulfill Jesus' commandment of love. The Gospels present Jesus as having the most difficulty with a group of people who perfectly fulfilled externally all the commandments, the Pharisees. Jesus refers to them as whitened sepulchers. Externally they kept the commandments, internally they violated the very essence of the commandments, love. Luke's parable on the Pharisee and the tax collector going to the temple to pray calls attention to the centrality of our quality of heart in prayer. The Pharisee boasted in his fidelity in keeping all the commandments, emphasizing his superiority to the tax collector.

But the tax collector stood off at a distance and would not even raise his eyes to heaven but beat his breast and prayed, "O God, be merciful to me a sinner." I tell you, the latter went home justified, not the former; for everyone who exalts himself will be humbled, and the one who humbles himself will be exalted." (Lk 18:13–14)

Previous approaches to spirituality often seemed more concerned with the external performance of prayer and ministry than with the quality of heart underlying them. Indeed, we usually examined our consciences in terms of sinful actions performed or omitted. For instance, we focused not on whether we hated our neighbor but on whether we performed hateful actions. Likewise we focused not on whether we praised God at Sunday worship but on whether we fulfilled our obligation by being physically present—our dispositions were irrelevant.

John Paul II's 1986 encyclical on the Holy Spirit *Lord and Giver of Life* is an apt keynote for all our reflections. Referring to the Gospel of John and Christ's promise to send another advocate to take his place, the pope succinctly summarizes the Christian tradition on the Holy Spirit as sanctifier.

The redemption accomplished by the son in the dimensions of the earthly history of humanity—accomplished in the "departure" through the Cross and Resurrection—is at the same time in its entire salvific power, transmitted to the Holy Spirit: the one who "will take what is mine."...(para. 22)

The pope echoes Vatican II's emphasis on the Holy Spirit by insisting we adequately understand the Christian vocation only when we understand the role of the Holy Spirit—the *entire effect* of the redemption is brought about by the Holy Spirit! The pope challenges us to rethink our approach to every aspect of Christian life in terms of the Holy Spirit. What then are the implications for ministry?

The Holy Spirit and Ministry

Much has been written about ministry, and the topic can be divided and subdivided in many different ways. But I believe a consensus exists flowing directly from the model of the church as the body of Christ discussed previously: all ministry in the church is inspired by the spirit and is a continuation of Christ's own ministry. We ministers are Christians who act in the name of our churches to advance the Church's mission of serving God's kingdom. We act as ministers both through formal ordination, commissioning, or appointment, but also as baptized Christians responding to the call of the spirit. In this latter sense all Christians are in some way ministers because we are members of the body and as such called to perform our special roles for the sake of the body. And all ministers as members of the body of Christ receive an empowerment from the Holy Spirit (a charism) to be effective representatives of Christ in serving the kingdom of God. Christian ministry, then, is service to others for the sake of the kingdom in the name of the church *inspired by the Holy Spirit* and *incarnating the presence of Christ.*

This centrality of the Holy Spirit in ministry, the focus of our reflections, is supported both by scripture and by church teaching. It is supported using Christ's address to his disciples at the Last Supper in John's Gospel. Having explained to them that he must depart, he exhorts them not to lose heart, for it is actually better for them that he go "for if I do not go, the Advocate will not come to you." He promises to send the spirit to them to take his place to be their new comforter and advocate. He exhorts them to remain united with him and, using the famous vine and branch image, promises them that if they remain in him they will bear much fruit for the kingdom. Further, Christ assures them that they need not be afraid of his departure because the spirit of truth will guide them in their witnessing to him. Note the centrality of the spirit in uniting the disciples to Christ and establishing the foundation for ministry.

The centrality of the spirit is supported also using Paul's image of the church as the body of Christ. This image highlights both the equality of all in the body as well as the difference of roles in the body. The equality of all members within the body is clear: "There is but one body and one Spirit, just as there is but one hope given all of you by your call. There is one Lord, one faith, one baptism; one God and Father of all, who is over all, and works through all, and is in all" (Eph 4:4–6). Equally clear is the difference of roles (ministries) within the body: "There are different gifts but the same Spirit; there are different ministries but the same Lord; there are different works but the same God who accomplishes all of them in everyone. To each person the manifestation of the Spirit is given for the common good" (1 Cor 12:4–7). Note that Paul's image of the body of Christ highlights the spirit as the source of all life within the body. Membership in the body flows from the spirit received through faith and baptism. Specific roles (charisms) within the body flow from the special gifts given by the spirit to different members of the body for the sake of the entire body. But each member of the body acts on behalf of Christ and becomes Christ's representative in performing service to other members. Note the centrality of the spirit as the principle of both incorporation and empowerment in the body of Christ and as such the foundation for ministry.

This centrality of the spirit is echoed in Vatican II documents on ministry, both in the documents on ministerial priesthood and on lay apostolate. *The Decree on the Ministry and Life of Priests* clearly specifies that the anointing of the ordained confers the Holy Spirit and thereby configures the priests to Christ, enabling them to act in the person of Christ the head of the body.

Therefore, while it indeed presupposes the sacraments of Christian initiation, the sacerdotal office of priests is conferred by that special sacrament through which priests, by the anointing of the Holy Spirit, are marked by a special character and are so configured to Christ the priest that they can act in the person of Christ the head." (para. 2)

This centrality of the power of the spirit in establishing a living union with Christ in ministry is reaffirmed in *The Decree on the Apostolate of the Laity.*

> The laity derive the right and duty with respect to the apostolate from their union with Christ their Head. Incorporated into Christ's Mystical Body through baptism and strengthened by the power of the Holy Spirit through confirmation, they are assigned to the apostolate by the Lord himself. They are consecrated into a royal priesthood and a holy people (cf. 1 Pet 2:4–10) in order that they may offer spiritual sacrifices in everything they do, and may witness to Christ throughout the world.... For the exercise of this apostolate, the Holy Spirit Who sanctifies the People of God through ministry and the sacraments also gives the faithful special gifts (cf. 1 Cor. 12:7), "allotting them to everyone according as He wills." (para. 3)

> Since Christ in his mission from the Father is the fountain and source of the whole apostolate of the Church, the success of the lay apostolate depends upon the laity's living union with Christ. For the Lord has said, "He who abides in me, and I in him, he bears much fruit: for without me you can do nothing" (Jn 15:5). (para. 4)

John Paul II in his 1988 exhortation *The Lay Members of Christ's Faithful People* reminds us again of the centrality of the gifts of the spirit as the foundation for the minister's participation in Christ's own ministry.

> Indeed, the Church is directed and guided by the Holy Spirit, who lavishes diverse hierarchical and charismatic gifts on all the baptized, calling them to be, each in an individual way, active and co-responsible.

> The ministries which exist and are at work at this time in the Church are all—even in their variety of forms—a participation in Jesus Christ's own ministry as the Good Shepherd who lays down his life for the sheep (cf. Jn 10:11), the humble servant who gives himself without reserve for the salvation of all (cf. Mk 10:45). (para. 21)

In short, all aspects of Christian ministry flow from the minister's empowerment by the spirit, which enables the minister to incarnate Christ's presence in the world and continue Christ's own ministry.

I believe that the biggest challenge for ministers is not the external performance of services, no matter how conscientiously performed; our biggest challenge is becoming internally the Christ whose presence we prolong. To a great extent the effectiveness of ministry flows from a heart transformed by the spirit of Christ and then overflowing to others. And so our relationship to Christ is central. And there are many elements in Christian spirituality contributing to this living union with Christ; among these the eucharist and sacraments are primary. But my own experience teaches me that a regular rhythm of personal prayer is also vital. Personal prayer enkindles a oneness with Jesus, which then flows over into ministry. I believe I was stunned by the question cited at the opening of this essay because I could not imagine doing my own ministry without the support and confidence flowing from the presence of Jesus.

The Holy Spirit and Personal Prayer

We ministers have responded to the call of the spirit in accepting our ministries; now we want to continue listening to the spirit to allow the spirit to lead us to continual communion with Jesus. And we know that the spirit who calls us to ministry will also bring us to this communion in order to ensure the fruitfulness of our ministry. Further we know that this same spirit will lead us to Jesus in personal prayer; "No one can say: 'Jesus is Lord,'" except in the Holy Spirit (1 Cor 12:4). And so we want to learn to pray ever more deeply in the spirit.

I remember when I learned to pray in the spirit. I was teaching as a non-ordained Jesuit at a mission in South Dakota. Our life was very difficult. Regular Order included rising at 5:00 A.M. and retiring after the students were asleep around midnight. We were expected to do an hour of meditation before 6:30 mass in the Mission Church. I always had great difficulty praying in these circumstances and as often as not would spend the hour in Church distracted or sleeping. Eventually sheer physical exhaustion drove me to begin sleeping late, getting up only in time for mass. Daily meditation had always been presented to me as essential for living the Jesuit life, so I experienced continual guilt for skipping it. But every evening after the students had quieted down in the dorms I'd walk down the highway under the stars, often for more than an hour. I recall being discouraged and lonely and pouring out my heart to Christ. I also recall returning from these walks peaceful, feeling close to Christ, and wondering how I could survive without these walks. But my conscience continued to bother me for skipping daily meditation. Then one night I had a startling realization: I was not skipping daily meditation, I was doing it at night! I was walking down that highway each night to be with the Lord—not to fulfill a religious obligation. Previously I prayed not primarily because I wanted to but because I was supposed to. I had finally discovered a rhythm of being totally open to God and allowing God's spirit to unite me with Christ. And, unbelievably for me, I actually looked forward to these walks. I had learned to pray.

There are many ways of describing prayer. Prayer for me is simply "the movement of the heart toward God under the influence of the Holy Spirit." Prayer is a "movement of the heart": no heart movement, no prayer. It cannot be identified either with words we say or thoughts we think. If there is no internal movement, there is no prayer. Indeed, prayer need not even be accompanied either by words or by thoughts. In Christian tradition the deepest prayer transcends both. And the movement occurs only when we are "under the influence of the Holy Spirit." Our tradition teaches that spirit abides with us as a permanent indwelling gift of God. Though the spirit, or sanctifying grace, is always present, we are not always in touch with that presence. When we are not in touch with the spirit, we cannot respond to it.

And in prayer the movement of the heart under the influence of the spirit is ultimately "toward God." The spirit moves us toward the Father and toward Jesus. Just as Christian theology sees the spirit as the bond of union between the Father and the Son in the Trinity, so the spirit is our bond of union with the Father and Jesus. Note that we do not really pray *to* Mary or *to* the saints; more accurately we go to them to pray *with* them to the Father and Jesus. In the communion of saints the spirit unites us with Mary and the saints. And we on earth are united with them *as they now* are in heaven. In heaven they exist in continual movement of love and praise to the Father and Jesus; as such they can be privileged intercessors for us. With them we then move toward communion with the Father and Jesus. The deepest yearnings of our hearts in the spirit are always toward the Father and Jesus, so we join Mary and the saints in their procession of praise and love of God. It's impossible to imagine Mary's not wanting to unite us more deeply to her son and to the Father. As ministers—indeed as Christians—we are called to a loving dependence of a child to a caring Father, and in no way do we want to discourage prayer to our Father. But as ministers we are also called to a relationship with Jesus, and so we allow the spirit also to lead us to Jesus in prayer—in no way should the focus of this essay be seen to imply that prayer to the Father is less important than prayer to Jesus.

A note about the purpose of prayer is important. Often we unreflectively assume we begin prayer for the purpose of seeking specific favors from God. However, deeper reflection reveals that what we are really seeking is a confirmation of the love of Jesus and the Father. The purpose behind all our prayers is a deeper communion with the Father and Jesus. Though we may be led to prayer for many different reasons, as we continue praying we eventually realize our deepest need is for God's presence and support: the Spirit has transformed our initial desires. The process is not unlike Jesus' transformation in the Garden of Gethsemane. He begins initially seeking to have the chalice removed but ends yielding to God's will and presence. I believe we experience over and over again the truth of Augustine's exclamation, "Our hearts are restless until they rest in Thee."

And there are many levels of experiencing presence and communion with God in prayer. And each is a sign of the spirit's presence. The very desire for God's help is already a rudimentary experience of communion, even though the desire may be interspersed with preoccupying distractions. At this level the spirit has transformed our desire but not the other dimensions of the self. At a deeper level the movement toward God in prayer may be accompanied by tranquility and peace. The spirit makes us aware that the world is in God's hands, and we rest in the security of our relationship with our loving Lord. This is the usual experience. But at an even deeper level, the spirit so unites us to the Father and Jesus that we lose conscious awareness of this communion. During the momentary experience itself self-awareness recedes, but we are able to reflect upon the experience afterward. The experience leaves a residue of wholeness, joy, contentment.

Reflection on my prayer experiences leads me to a surprising conclusion (one I would not have made ten years ago): I find my heart drawn to God as frequently during spontaneous prayer outside my formal prayer time as during the times I set aside for formal prayer. I've noticed certain conditions foster these spontaneous movements of my heart to God.

The times and places are important. During school days the experiences occur most frequently in evenings after I've completed my day's work. Having put aside preoccupation with projects, I decide either to take a leisurely walk around campus or to sit in one of my favorite places, such as the bench before the piazza fountain fronting the College Church or in a secluded university garden behind the Administration Building. During weekends they can occur anytime, providing I've put aside preoccupations with work. I must give myself enough time for the experiences to occur, minimally fifteen minutes, ideally a half-hour, and I must never feel rushed.

I should note that these experiences of spontaneous prayer, especially as they occur in natural settings, have affected my approach to retreats and vacations. I now choose places for my annual retreats primarily because of their settings. I find my heart moves spontaneously to God through nature in ways that totally refresh me. I consider the formal reflections characteristic of retreats as no more important than simply enjoying the Lord's presence in nature. Against this background God gives me the insights I need for my life. I also choose settings for my annual vacations that facilitate spontaneous prayer. I see vacations as similar to retreats, as times to be recreated by enjoying the presence of God, not simply as times to be distracted from my daily life. I choose places that foster spontaneous prayer because of their settings.

I also find myself breaking into spontaneous prayer at other times during the day. Most commonly these occur after a particularly successful class or presentation or walking down the campus mall on an especially beautiful day. And they occur when I'm faithful to times of formal prayer. I believe we sensitize ourselves to the spirit-dimension of our being during formal prayer and this dimension then breaks forth spontaneously during daily activities.

The Holy Spirit and Methods of Prayer

The question for all prayer methods is how to integrate our human efforts with the role of the spirit. What method of prayer should we use during this time to facilitate responding to the spirit and reaching communion with Jesus and the Father? Remember our role is providing the conditions to maximize our response to the spirit. Each of us has our own rhythms for maintaining union with God. These observations are attempts to share what has been working for myself. They do not imply that this is the way it should be done. Since we humans are multifaceted beings comprised of body, mind, and spirit, it is important that we find guidelines for use of our bodies and our minds to maximize our response to the spirit. The following rhythms work for me; we each must find our own.

An appropriate use of our bodies—that is, the right time, place, and setting—is important for facilitating the spirit. First the time. After rising, showering, and shaving, I light a candle before my prayer wall. I spend sixty to ninety minutes in spiritual disciplines. Having gotten coffee, I begin by journaling; then, putting the coffee aside, I move to the morning office; finally, I move to personal prayer for the last twenty to thirty minutes. I never rush, spending as much time journaling as needed. The journaling clears my head and allows me to process what has built up in my psyche, matter that could emerge as distractions in personal prayer. Often journaling provides the topic for the subsequent prayer. In my experience a regular, even daily rhythm is necessary. There is the story of the Zen novice asking the Zen master whether it is necessary to meditate daily. The master's response: "Only meditate on the days that you eat."

Next the place. I pray in my own room—which doubles as a bedroom—in a chair next to a large window with an eastward exposure, overlooking the secluded garden mentioned earlier; the chair faces my prayer wall. It is upholstered and comfortable, but supports me firmly in an upright position. Alongside the chair on a side table I place all the materials I need: my journal, a Bible, the daily office, a lectionary, meditation books related to the liturgical season. I love this room; it is away from my offices. The window, open in warm weather, gives direct access to the sights and sounds of the garden and to the warmth and light of the rising sun. My prayer wall is hung with favorite icons, prints, and crucifixes gathered over the years; I rearrange the wall for different liturgical seasons and feasts. The physical setting—the time, place, furniture arrangement—is key. The regular rhythm of entering this environment at this time each day not only prepares the conditions for facilitating the spirit but often occasions immediate communion with the Lord. Given the desire for communion with God, praying can be simple: just find the right time and place and go there regularly! For me, when I was at the mission, the right time, place, and posture was walking down the highway late at night.

An appropriate use of our minds—that is, the right prayer method—is also crucial for facilitating the spirit. We will reflect on three most common methods of prayer: *lectio prayer, centering prayer, mantra prayer. Lectio prayer* (shorthand for *lectio-meditatio-oratio-contemplatio* prayer) is a response to God's presence in God's word. This method is based on the truth of God's presence in the word. The "Word of God" has multifold meanings. God is present in the *scriptural word;* traditionally most have found the scriptural word has been the most helpful starting point. God is also present in the *created word;* some find focusing on God's presence in creation—the beauty of nature—a more effective beginning. God is also present in the *existential word;* many find focusing on God's presence in events and people of their lives the most effective beginning. But any aspect of creation or embodiment of creation—images, poetry, music—is a word of God and possible starting point for prayer, since God is present in all aspects of reality sustaining them in existence and using them to bring us into communion: "Creation proclaims the glory of God." In lectio prayer we choose an aspect of God's word to focus our attention, and then we wait, listen, and respond to the word of God—under the influence of the spirit. Our effort is placed in attending to God's word and, as much as possible, avoiding distractions to our attention.

In lectio prayer we are led by the spirit toward a progressively deeper response to God's presence in the word. The internal dynamic frequently moves from thinking *(meditatio)* about God's presence in the word, to praying *(oratio)* to God about our reactions to this presence, to simply resting *(contemplatio)* in God's presence without either thinking about God or even consciously praying to God. Guigo II, a twelfth-century Carthusian abbot, gives the classic expression of the internal dynamic of this prayer:

> You can see…how these degrees are joined to each other. One precedes the other, not only in the order of time but of causality. Reading *(lectio)* comes first, and is, as it were, the foundation; it

provides the subject matter we must use for meditation. Meditation *(meditatio)* considers more carefully what is to be sought after; it digs, as it were, for treasure which it finds and reveals, but since it is not in meditation's power to seize upon the treasure, it directs us to prayer. Prayer *(oratio)* lifts itself up to God with all its strength, and begs for the treasure it longs for, which is the sweetness of contemplation. Contemplation *(contemplatio)* when it comes rewards the labors of the other three; it inebriates the thirsting soul with the dew of heavenly sweetness. Reading is an exercise of the outward senses; meditation is concerned with the inward understanding; prayer is concerned with desire; contemplation outstrips every faculty. (Guigo II, *Ladder of Monks,* Kalamazoo, Mich.: Cistercian Publications, 1978)

The goal of the process is contemplation that "outstrips every faculty" and rests in communion with God unmediated by our own activity. Our activity recedes; God's increases: God holds us to God's self with little or no effort on our part. My prayer at the mission began with my reflections about my day, usually focusing on the challenges of my ministry; this "existential word" became the means through which the spirit worked to lead me to communion with Christ and the Father. Most nights this ended in contemplation, a resting in communion with the Lord out there under the stars. This contemplation empowered my ministry for another day.

An image, adapted from Abbot Thomas Keating, may help us understand the process. The spirit is the river; the word of God the boat; God the ocean. Recall the self-in-God model. We live in the river (the spirit). In prayer we allow the spirit to direct our attention to the boat (the Word of God). Focusing on the boat we move with the boat into the ocean (God). The dynamic of spontaneous prayer is quite similar. Some aspect of God's word catches our attention; through the spirit we respond and are brought into communion with God.

Centering prayer is quite different from lectio prayer. It is based on the truth of God's presence in the *center* of our being, beyond the level of thoughts and desires. It presumes the Scriptural Model of the Self. In centering prayer we respond to God directly, unmediated by reflections on God's word. The method, taken from the fourteenth-century English classic *Cloud of Unknowing* and popularized by Trappist Fathers Keating, Pennington, and Menninger, is simple. We choose a favorite appellation for God, such as, "Father," "Abba, Father," "Jesus," "Lord," "Rabboni." We begin prayer with this "sacred word" and simply sit in faith and love before God. We do not begin with any reflections about God flowing from the word of God; we simply are in faith before God. Our goal is to be totally receptive to the spirit so that the spirit can hold us in communion. Interior silence is the matrix for our receptivity.

Keating's advice for handling thoughts is simple: Resist no thought, react to no thought, retain no thought; simply return to the prayer word. Note we do not return to this word unless a thought arises. Thoughts inevitably arise, and we let them pass, returning to the prayer word. Thoughts even have a positive quality to them, because as we let them pass we are evacuating from our psyches obstacles to the contemplative communion with God; they are actually part of the purification process. Handled well, they move us toward interior silence—the non-attachment to thoughts. Eventually thoughts may recede and we can be before God in faith with little use of the prayer word.

> Once you grasp the fact that thoughts are not only inevitable, but an integral part of the process of healing and growth initiated by God, you are able to take a positive view of them. Instead of looking upon them as painful distractions, you see them in a broader perspective that includes both interior silence and thoughts—thoughts that you do not want but which are just as valuable for the purpose of purification, as moments of profound tranquillity. (Thomas Keating, *Open Mind, Open Heart,* New York: Amity House, 1986, 112)

> When everything in the unconscious is emptied out, the kinds of thoughts that were passing by in the beginning will no longer exist. There is an end to the process of purification. Then the awareness of union with God will be continuous because there will be no obstacle in our conscious or unconscious life to interfere with it. (Keating, 102)

The goal of the process is contemplation that "outstrips every faculty" and rests in a communion with God unmediated by our own activity—the same goal as lectio prayer.

The image of the river (the spirit), the boat (the Word of God), and the ocean (God) is helpful for grasping the process. Remember we live in the river (the spirit); in centering prayer we simply move in the river *directly* into the ocean (God). The sacred word is not a boat; we do not use it to foster thinking *(meditatio)* and loving *(oratio)* as in lectio prayer. The sacred word serves only to symbolize our intention. The spirit brings us directly into communion without reflection on the word of God.

The assumptions and dynamics of *mantra prayer* are similar to those of centering prayer. It enters the Christian tradition formally in the fifth century in the *Conferences* of John Cassian. In mantra prayer we also respond to God directly, unmediated by reflections on God's word. But we come to prayer with a previously chosen mantra, not merely with a sacred word. And in mantra prayer we consciously attend to our mantra; in centering prayer we don't consciously attend to our sacred word but rather use it to resymbolize our intention of being receptive to the Lord only after we have been distracted. We begin prayer slowly, repeating the mantra, coordinating its four phrases (indicated by asterisks) with our inhaling and exhaling (most, though not all, authors suggest coordination with breathing). Cassian notes that the desert fathers preferred "O God * come to my assistance * O Lord * make haste to help me." The most famous mantra in the Christian tradition, however, is the Jesus Prayer that arose with the Greek fathers in the fifth century: "Lord Jesus Christ * Son of God * have mercy on me * a sinner." Any phrase can serve as a mantra. I frequently recast scriptural passages into mantra form. Among my favorites: "The Lord * is my shepherd * there is nothing * I shall want"; "You are my servant * whom I have chosen * my beloved * with whom I am pleased"; "I am the vine * you are the branches * without me * you can do nothing." But any rhythmically repeated vocal prayer, such as the rosary, can serve as a mantra.

The method for handling thoughts is similar to that of centering prayer. When thoughts occur we simply let them pass and return to the rhythmic repetition of the mantra. Repetition of the mantra is the matrix for our receptivity to the spirit. Our effort in this method is to let pass all thoughts that occur and to return to the repetition of the mantra. We do not reflect upon the mantra but simply use it to focus our minds and to symbolize our intention to pray. If we begin reflecting upon the mantra itself, we have switched methods from mantra prayer to lectio prayer. However, as we become still we may want to drop parts of the mantra or even the entire mantra. We may use only the appellation "Lord" to symbolize our intention. If this occurs we have moved from mantra prayer to centering prayer.

Recall again the image of the river, boat, and ocean. In mantra prayer we move in the river (the spirit) directly into the ocean (God). The mantra is not a boat; it serves only to refocus our minds and symbolize our intention. And the goal of mantra prayer is identical to lectio prayer and centering prayer—contemplative communion with God that "outstrips every faculty."

> The holy men of the Orthodox Church see the essential task of the Christian life as being to restore this unity to man with a mind and heart integrated through prayer. The mantra provides the integrating power. It is like a harmonic that we sound in the depths of our spirit, bringing us to an ever-deepening sense of our own wholeness and central harmony. It leads us to the source of this harmony, to our centre, rather as a radar bleep leads an aircraft home through thick fog. (John Main, *Word into Silence,* New York: Paulist, 1980, 15)

The Best Method of Prayer?

Praying is an art, not a science. The goal of all prayer methods is communion with Jesus and the Father. Since only the spirit can bring about this communion, our role is to provide conditions that facilitate the movement of the spirit. Communion remains a gift. I once believed—erroneously—that my conscientious use of a particular method *guaranteed* good results in prayer. There is no "best way" to pray; whatever works is best for us. Through trial and error we discover how best to be open to God. Robert Frost's little poem "Not All There" catches the challenge for praying well:

I turned to speak to God
About the world's despair;
But to make bad matters worse
I found God wasn't there.

God turned to speak to me
(Don't anybody laugh);
God found I wasn't there—
At least not over half.

The following are some additional reflections on what helps me "be there" in prayer; I am not presenting them as ways everyone *should* pray!

Sometimes no method is needed. Frequently after lighting my candle, settling into my prayer chair, sipping my coffee, and journaling, I find myself already held to God by God with no further effort needed on my part, so I stop journaling: I am already centered. If I use my prayer word to sustain my intention, I am doing centering prayer. I have developed a facility for being drawn by the spirit into communion by the regularity of being present to God each morning at this time and in this place. The setting has not only prepared me for praying but has actually as itself occasioned it. Perhaps my journal recordings have brought to mind some blessing, some word of God, from the previous day. The blessing becomes the occasion, the sacrament, for awakening consciousness of God and for resting gratefully in the presence of God. The spirit moves me from gratitude to communion and contemplation. All I know is that I have no desire either to reflect upon or pray over the blessing. Or perhaps the recordings have recalled a need. The need then becomes the occasion, the sacrament, for awakening consciousness of dependence on God and resting in silent acknowledgment of my helplessness without God: "Be still and know that I am God."

Occasionally, in the process of journaling, saying the office, or praying, my attention is caught unexpectedly by some aspect of the garden outside my window: I see the sun rising through the trees, I hear a song of a bird or rustle of leaves, I smell the fragrance of the garden and feel the wind on my face. I have no desire to continue reflecting or praying: I find myself held by God to God—I am centered. Nature has become the sacrament occasioning communion with God and contemplation.

Frequently also my attention is caught by one of the icons or prints on my prayer wall. I rotate works of art according to my needs: a print of the Vatican Museum's fourth-century sculpture of the good shepherd, the Vladimir Madonna icon, Fra Angelico's *Anunciation.* I also rotate favorite works of art relating to the current liturgical season; each season finds me anticipating my favorite seasonal prints and responding to them anew: Hick's *Peaceable Kingdom* for Advent, Gorgione's *Adoration of the Shepherds* for Christmas, Perugino's *Crucifixion* for Lent, Fra Angelico's *Noli Me Tangere* for Easter. I believe the spirit offers seasonal graces to help us savor more deeply the liturgical season. I may find myself held by God to God through these images with no desire to think about them—I am centered. The images have become the sacrament occasioning communion with God and contemplation.

Sometimes a combination of methods is more effective. If I have not experienced the drawing of the spirit toward communion and contemplation during journaling and the morning office, I need to decide how I will spend my prayer time. Most frequently I choose some aspect of the Word of God for reflection, and so begin with lectio prayer. Usually something from the previous day or one of the readings from the office presents itself. During special liturgical seasons I use meditations or scriptural readings related to the season. I often look over a seasonal meditation book. I read the author's reflections and then put the book away and wait to see how the spirit will move in myself. I believe we can stifle the spirit by forcing ourselves to think about someone else's inspirations rather than being sensitive to our own. Meditation books are helpful only as starting points.

The starting point for prayer is usually my life, the existential word of God as I am experiencing it. I have had little luck—and in the past wasted much time—forcing myself to reflect on meditations written by others and unrelated to my daily life. I believe God continually manifests God's self in all creation and history *and in my life*—though the spirit. I choose some aspect of God's word from my previous day—a person or event. I bring the matter to mind and begin focusing my attention upon it. I put distractions aside as they occur and attempt to keep my mind gently on God's word. I *wait* in God's presence, *listen* to God's speaking through the word in my heart, and *respond* in any way the spirit moves. The Benedictine tradition describes the effects of the spirit's transforming the heart: The spirit directs our attention to the word *(lectio)*; the spirit transforms our minds prompting suitable thoughts about the word *(meditatio)*; the spirit transforms our wills prompting suitable desires and affections about the word *(oratio)*; the spirit leads us to rest in God's presence beyond thoughts and desires *(contemplatio)*. I believe that *listening to God* is a better metaphor for the prayer process than the traditional *speaking to God.* We speak only in response to the spirit and only after we have listened!

The goal of prayer is resting in a communion with God that is beyond thoughts and desires. When I reach this peaceful state I find it helpful to switch from lectio prayer to mantra prayer. I use the mantra to keep my mind occupied, to prevent distractions from arising. The gentle repetition of the mantra sustains my intention. At this point I am held to God by God with virtually no effort on my part. This restful state is often referred to as the prayer of quiet. This beginning contemplation is marked by conscious awareness and enjoyment of God's presence. But sometimes this reflective consciousness recedes, and we enter momentarily an even deeper state of contemplation. We become aware of this special grace only when we return to reflective awareness.

I often move from mantra prayer to centering prayer. After a period of mantra prayer, I may find the mantra unnecessary and even bothersome. My faculties are quiet; I am centered. I am able to be in faith and love toward Jesus and the Father using my sacred word. When distractions arise, I let them pass renewing my intention by my sacred word.

All in response to the spirit!

Evoking the Spirit of Jesus in Prayer

We ministers are called to be one with Jesus, "Live on in me as I do in you....Whoever lives in me and I in them will produce fruit abundantly, for apart from me you can do nothing" (Jn 15 4–5). It is through our openness to the spirit sent by Jesus, the spirit of Jesus, that we live on in Jesus. I've learned that a regular rhythm of personal prayer is necessary for living this relationship in my daily ministry and, further, that it is absolutely crucial during periods of stress—as during my time at the mission.

I believe that Jesus himself models the centrality of prayer for ministry, and even the centrality of prayer during periods of stress. Jesus lived in communion with his Father and his ministry flowed from that communion. One cannot read the Gospels, especially the Gospel of Luke, without being struck by the frequency of Jesus' withdrawal from the crowds to be with his most dear Father in prayer, and, in addition, to seek special guidance and strength from his Father during key moments of his ministry and during periods of stress. Among these key moments of withdrawal are the forty days in the desert, after the baptism by John the Baptist before beginning his public ministry, the night in prayer before choosing the apostles, the retreat and transfiguration at Tabor before the journey to Jerusalem, the prayer in Gethsemane before his passion and death.

Our oneness with Jesus in ministry is never more important than during times of stress. An occurrence during what remains today the most stressful period of my own ministry confirms my belief in the necessity of a relationship with Jesus. Six of our university students died in two separate accidents within several weeks. The students, well known, admired, and loved by many on campus, were innocent victims of drunken drivers. Many of our students had never experienced the loss of close friends and were traumatized by the accidents, not able to resume their normal lives for weeks, some for months. I knew most of the deceased well—one even lived in the dorm across the hall from my room. Many came to me for help day and night. All the while I attempted to be faithful to my normal duties. I became aware I was dangerously close to total exhaustion. One Saturday I enrolled at a local church in a day-long Intensive Journal Workshop of Ira Progoff. The Progoff format involves dialogues with key projects, people, events in one's life. The process includes centering, allowing the dialogue to well up from deep within oneself, recording the dialogue in the journal, and finally sharing the experience with the group.

At one point in the day we were asked to dialogue with our primary wisdom figure. I chose Jesus. We (Jesus and I) were dialoguing about my exhaustion and my desire to care for our students as Jesus cared for his people. An image of Jesus the good shepherd emerged along with the words of John's Gospel, "The good shepherd lays down his life for his sheep." This image was that of the fourth-century statue unearthed in the catacomb of St. Callistus in the 1930s. I had seen it in the Vatican Museum in Rome; it had made a great impression on me. It is the first three-dimensional representation of Jesus in Christian history, preceding even the crucifix. During the periods that Christians had to practice their faith in secret because of Roman persecutions, the image was safe because it could be mistaken as a perfectly acceptable Roman image of a man bringing an offering of a lamb to a pagan god. This good shepherd sculpture depicted a strong young man, beardless, wearing a short Roman tunic and carrying a lamb on his shoulders. In the dialogue I spoke a sentence I have never forgotten: "You carry me and I'll carry your people." And I received a response: "You carry my people and I'll carry you." That was all. I was transformed. I returned to school a different person.

During the weeks that followed the workshop, I continually returned to the image of the good shepherd—especially during times of exhaustion. I relived our encounter each time. And I was strengthened to be like Jesus in "laying down my life for my sheep." Each time the spirit of Jesus was truly present, acting and transforming my inner self, and I was truly responding. I count the period of the accidents and their aftermath as a time of intense personal transformation through the power of the spirit sent by Jesus.

The image remains powerful to this day. A print of this image hangs prominently on my prayer wall, often occasioning in prayer a communion with Jesus. From this communion my daily ministry flows.

Each of us ministers has the challenge of discovering how the spirit sent by Jesus is moving within, helping us experience our identity in him, so we can truly be his hands and heart in our world. My advice to any minister asking for help in establishing a relationship with Jesus is simple: Find an image or saying of Jesus from the Gospels that speaks directly to your life, return to it regularly in prayer, and wait, listen, and respond to the spirit of Jesus speaking through it. The relationship will emerge, and at times even be profoundly experienced. And don't be discouraged. No matter how disturbing and preoccupying the external events of our lives may be, we can always pray because we've been given the spirit to help us in our weakness. I think Paul had his own tumultuous life in mind—and perhaps also Jesus' experience in Gethsemane—when he wrote to the community in Rome, a community that experienced persecution and even death for their faith in Christ:

> The Spirit too comes to help us in our weakness. For when we cannot choose words in order to pray properly, the Spirit himself expresses our plea in a way that could never be put into words, and God who knows everything in our hearts knows perfectly well what he means, and that the pleas of the saints expressed by the Spirit are according to the mind of God. (Rom. 8:26–27)

A Note to the Reader

Those wishing fuller treatment of the topics in this essay may wish to consult two of my previous books: *In His Spirit: A Guide to Today's Spirituality* (Mahwah, N.J.: Paulist, 1982), a guide to contemporary spirituality with a focus on personal prayer; and *Finding God in Trouble Times: The Holy Spirit and Suffering* (Mahwah, N.J.: Paulist, 1994), a reflection on the New Testament message on understanding and dealing with suffering focusing on the role of the Holy Spirit and the examples of Jesus and Paul.

William Reiser

26. The Interior Life of Jesus as the Life of the People of God

On Thursday, July 23, 1998, the *New York Times* carried a front-page article on the rapid spread of AIDS in South Africa. Inside there appeared a picture of a sixty-four-year-old grandmother whose daughters had died in this epidemic, leaving her to care for fifteen grandchildren. The following day the *Times* carried another front-page article about a different kind of epidemic, graphically summarized in a picture of a starving child from the Sudan. Between drought and civil war, the human casualties could eventually reach the hundreds of thousands. Two weeks previously, the *Times* had featured a report on declining birth rates in Europe. A thirty-three-year-old woman from Sweden told an interviewer, "There are times when I think perhaps I will be missing something important if I don't have a child....But today women finally have so many chances to have the life they want. To travel and work and learn. It's exciting and demanding. I just find it hard to see where the children would fit in."

Tragic stories like the ones from Africa appear every day in the media: the flooding of the Yangtze, repression in Myanmar, car bombs in Northern Ireland, death in the desert after illegal crossings of the United States–Mexican border. For the attentive Christian reader, listener, or viewer, such reports from all parts of the globe force a reaction. We think, we wonder, we ask questions about how and why such disasters happen, our imaginations fill in the blanks as we try to piece together the stories and destinies of other human lives. We may complain to God, we pray with fresh meaningfulness the psalms of lament. And while we appreciate the many pressing reasons that the roles of women throughout the world have rightly been undergoing a profound change, that third *Times* story alerts us to examine carefully what Western culture esteems and deifies. Will our pursuit of individual fulfillment prove in the long run to have been our spiritual as well as our social undoing?

The Interior Life of Jesus

It is not difficult to imagine that Jesus would have been drawn into the events and circumstances of his time in much the same way that we are pulled into the local crises, daily concerns, and global distress that make up our historical moment. Not only was his preaching and teaching firmly rooted in the everyday scenes, exchanges, and concerns of life in first-century Galilee; but also both the path he took and the fate he suffered were ultimately determined by the political, social, religious, and economic realities into which he had been born. That Jesus was constantly interacting with those realities is something of which every gospel reader needs to be aware in order to grasp who Jesus was and what was the nature of his mission. The message about the kingdom did not fall from the sky in universal, timeless aphorisms; we might have found that sort of message true, but we would hardly have found it interesting and beautiful. Rooted in the history, the faith, and the social and cultural circumstances of Israel, the message about the kingdom took further shape within the everyday world in which Jesus lived. It was a world in which men fished, plowed fields, or survived as day laborers. There were heavy taxes, dishonest judges, and families quarreling over inheritances. Women cooked, cared for the children, and sometimes (like Martha's sister) aspired to be disciples of a great rabbi. The world in which Jesus was raised was in all respects ordinary. One cannot conceive of Jesus *not* entering into conversation with people about all sorts of things, from the scandals and intrigues of Herod's palace, the Roman occupation, burdensome taxes, and the failing religious health of the temple in Jerusalem to the problems of making a living, raising a family, being unemployed, losing an only child, or falling hopelessly into debt.

Although it certainly manifested a transcendent character, the kingdom of God had to do with the present age. The new heaven and the new earth of which scripture speaks (Rev 21:1) was not envisioned to be a life in the clouds, above and away from the world God had created. Rather, that imagery referred to the early church's confident hope that human beings and their communities would be totally liberated and transformed; and this transformation would occur within human history. One day there would indeed be a *new earth.* The apostles would have communicated that sure, joyous message of hope because Jesus had preached it during his lifetime.

Jesus and His People Always Belong Together

To think or theologize about Jesus in isolation from his people drives a wedge into the gospel narrative; it robs Jesus of the real history that comes from being fully inserted within the life of a people. Such separation fractures the gospel narrative into this-worldly and otherworldly components, and with that fracturing of the gospel Christian prayer and spirituality come under severe stress. A debilitating dualism between earth and heaven is introduced into the story, and once Jesus becomes separated from the life of his people one can never figure out what exactly salvation consists of. A major example of that stress can be seen in the valiant attempts many devout men and women have undertaken to maintain a balance between the active and contemplative sides of their lives, as if immersion in the world would tear them away from God. But the persistent, unavoidable and essentially healthy tension in our prayer life should be arising from an altogether different direction, namely, from trying to find God in the world without letting the world and God collapse or fold into one another.

Theological reflection about Jesus would probably be a lot more fruitful if we regularly started with the question, "How is Jesus *like* us in all things?" than with questions such as, "How is Jesus different from us?" or, "What makes Jesus unique among the great religious figures of the world?" These latter questions can push our christology away from us, in the direction of disinterest and irrelevance. By "like us" I do not mean that we should simply stress those details of the gospel stories that underline and confirm his humanity: the fact that he had feelings and emotions, the fact that he prayed and was tempted, the fact that there were things he did not know and that he had to live with limitations, and so on. Rather, emphasizing that Jesus was "like us" should call attention to the way his interior life was shaped by other Israelites, by the way their world broke into his mind and heart, by the way the lives and fortunes of the families of Galilee and beyond drew him out of himself and into them. In short, if we could have looked into Jesus' soul, we would have found there the people of God.[1]

We find striking confirmation for this idea in the fourth Gospel, even though in that gospel Jesus often sounds otherworldly and the word *world* sometimes carries a negative, even dualistic tone. Yet John has expressed for us a profound Christian conviction:

> For God so loved the world that he gave his only Son, so that everyone who believes in him may not perish but may have eternal life. (Jn 3:16)[2]

The phrase *God so loved* confirms everything that has been revealed to us about the nature of the divine mystery, and in pondering those three words a believer might well be moved to tears with contrition, humility, and gratitude. But *world* is presented here as the object of God's love: the world in all its goodness and messiness, with its righteous and its sinners, with all its beauty and its suffering. In pondering this, do we not have to conclude that the love of God is unthinkable apart from the world, and that any approach to God born out of ecstatic love for the divine mystery is sooner or later going to route us back into all the histories with which the Word enters into lasting, loving solidarity? We shall never understand the nature of God's love until we know something about its object. Jesus' words, "For where your treasure is, there your heart will be also" (Lk 12:34), should apply to God as well as to us. God's treasure—God's beloved "son"[3]—are the people of God, particularly the poor and afflicted among them. Sooner or later we are bound to discover in them the heart of God.

The gospel narratives rarely portray Jesus alone, all by himself. He becomes progressively alone during the passion story; that is true. On several occasions he withdraws to pray, while the temptation scene suggests a stark solitude all the more remarkable because, unlike John the Baptist, Jesus moves around the towns and villages of Galilee, makes friends, shares meals, and is endlessly being approached by men and women in need. His teaching, his parables, his interpersonal exchanges, and his actions show us someone engaged by daily life, thoroughly familiar with its demands and possibilities, and in no way urging his followers to escape it by retreating to the wilderness or seeking sanctuary at the temple in Jerusalem. Jesus lived and died for his people. Whatever the nature of his union with God, the one thing we can be reasonably sure of is his solidarity with the men and women of Israel, especially those who were poor or in any way afflicted.

Expanding the Experiential Base of the Word Abba

The point about solidarity is important spiritually; that is, it bears upon the development of our own interior lives. Not infrequently theologians and other religious writers have directed their readers to consider the Abba address as a significant pointer to Jesus' religious experience.[4] In that address and in the intimate prayer that it implies they believe they have detected the experiential manifestation of Jesus' divine nature. The dogmatic counterpart of the Abba prayer becomes the hypostatic union. The one who knows and calls upon God in such intimate terms must surely possess the spirit of God in an exemplary and distinctive way; he is preeminently the Son of God.

Furthermore, the logic continues, what Jesus is by nature we become by grace. Thus Jesus has shared the same spirit with us; we too are thereby God's daughters and sons, called to know and address God with the same confidence and intimacy as Jesus himself.[5] A section of Edward Schillebeeckx's monumental study Jesus, for example, is entitled "Jesus' original Abba experience, source and secret of his being, message and manner of life." Schillebeeckx admits, however, that one has to go about establishing the meaning of that experience indirectly, on the basis of Jesus' overall message and action.[6] James Dunn examines the use of Abba in the gospel traditions and concludes:

We can say with some confidence that *Jesus experienced an intimate relation of sonship in prayer:* he found God characteristically to be "Father"; and this sense of God was so real, so loving, so compelling, that whenever he turned to God it was the cry "Abba" that came most naturally to his lips. We can also say, though with less confidence, that Jesus himself thought or *sensed this relationship with God to be something distinctive*—not unique, but distinctive: he encouraged his disciples to pray in the same way, but even then he seems to have thought of their relationship as somehow *dependent* on his own, as somehow a *consequence* of his own.[7]

Instead of focusing on the word *Abba,* some writers prefer to concentrate on Jesus' possession of the spirit; he could be described as a "spirit person." The way Jesus was filled with the spirit made him different or special. Marcus Borg writes,

Like Jewish Spirit persons, and like Spirit persons in other cultures, Jesus was known for his intimate communion with "the holy," or "the sacred," through such means as meditative prayer and fasting. Because of that communion, he (like them) was able to mediate the power of the sacred into this world in the form of miracles, especially the healings and exorcisms....Experientially in contact with the sacred, Spirit persons frequently have a striking authority and presence: they speak from their experience and radiate a numinous presence.[8]

Nevertheless, Jesus was not celebrated for his asceticism, and we do not really know what sort of prayer he engaged in on those occasions when he went off by himself. Did he *meditate?* Had he been gifted with infused contemplation? We need to be wary of assuming that Jesus enjoyed the highest states or forms of prayer, because the terms "higher" and "lower" are relative terms which in the end do not tell us as much as we might think about a person's relationship with God; and the gospel texts do not delve into the nature of Jesus' prayer. The evangelist Mark's memory about the use of *Abba,* I believe, has been pressed into teasing us into aspiring to the same sort of intimacy with God as Jesus is imagined to have possessed.

There are several difficulties here, however. First, a great deal is made to rest upon a single Aramaic word. Granted that *Abba* might well reflect Jesus' actual usage (a point made stronger by the numerous references to God as Father in the other Gospels), the meaning behind his usage would have to be pieced together from everything else in Jesus' life. As Schillebeeckx noted, we would have to ask what Jesus' teachings, parables, healings, encounters, exorcisms, expressions of faith, and his prophetic passion for the things of God reflect about his interior life. The term *Abba* by itself reveals precious little.[9] Second, speculating about what God was like for Jesus does not benefit us, unless, of course, his experience of God is seen to be the pattern for our own. Jesus' mission was not to disclose a new God, nor was it his mission to reveal a new way of experiencing the traditional God of Jewish belief. The God in whom Jesus placed his trust and to whom he prayed, like a son, was the God of Israel. And Jesus approached that God as a son of Israel, that is, with the faith and obedience that should have typified every daughter or son of Abraham. What counts, then, is not what makes Jesus' experience of God different from that of everybody else, but in what way Jesus exemplified the holiness within his religious tradition at its best. We stand to learn a lot more about Jesus' religious experience from the psalms than from the word *Abba*. For while the Gospels do not depict Jesus regularly quoting or reciting the psalms (Jesus and his disciples did sing several psalms as they concluded the Last Supper), we can be reasonably certain that they formed a considerable part of the fabric of his faith.[10]

The God of Jesus was first and last the God of Israel. To have a relationship with that God, however intimate and intense it may have been, had to be at the same time having a relationship with God's people. After all, the God of Israel was a God *of* and *for* people. To think of that God apart from all the families and genealogies, all the characters and events that made up the history of Israel, would have reduced the mystery of God to a colossal abstraction. According to the biblical narrative, Israel's God even selected the land on which the children of Abraham were to settle! Look into the eyes of God and there one will behold the people of God; look deeply into God's eyes, and there one will behold the landless poor, the exploited, the orphans and widows, the marginalized and heavily burdened, the wayward sinner. If anything, the follower of Jesus beholds in God's eyes not just the sons and daughters of Abraham, but the truly chosen ones: the men and women of every time and place who hunger and thirst for God's justice and redemption.

In studying Jesus, the Christian of today is not likely to discover a dramatically new and more intense experience of the mystery of God than can be found within the Hebrew scriptures. The God of Jesus was above all the God of Israel. The prospect of locating something brand new about God in the Gospels is very tempting theologically, because such a discovery would confirm Christianity's uniqueness and difference.[11] Besides, we live in a God-thirsty age, and many people are hankering for the peace and seclusion of a desert cave, or a monastery, or a retreat house, or a mountaintop where they could discover God in the way they imagine Jesus to have experienced his *Abba*.

To understand Jesus, however, we need to look in a different direction. In him, as in his prophetic forbears, we are more likely to encounter an intensification of the life of the people of God.[12] Jesus experienced intensely the anxieties, the concerns, the hopes, the sinfulness and desperation, the longing for freedom and deliverance and daily bread that the rest of Israel sought after. Perhaps it was in sharing their life that Jesus knew and experienced the life of God. The more deeply one shares the life of the people, the more radical and prophetic one's own thinking and action become. The more deeply one enters into the mystery of God, the more urgently one feels the passionate concerns of the God who walks in and among the people.[13] Abba and world are connected through the mystery of divine love and solidarity. *World* has to be recognized and named as an essential ingredient within the Christian experience of God. Solidarity, not uniqueness, might be the more illuminating category for trying to grasp who Jesus is and what he has done. After all, incarnation announces closeness, not distance. If so, then (at least for Christians) the experience of solidarity might appropriately be described as religious.

The Interior Life of the People of God

Not only do individuals have spiritual lives; so do groups. I think this is detectable in the case of individual religious communities and particularly of religious institutes viewed over a long period of time. Their collective spiritualities grow, branch out, and become seasoned. The same observation can be made with respect to countless Christian marriages and families. Indeed, couples and families occasionally develop remarkable, although almost always uncelebrated, household spiritualities.

The difficulty, however, is that so many people have grown accustomed to relating to God individually, out of their own personal circumstances, that they fail to notice to what extent their interior lives are indelibly communal and corporate. For instance, they may read the Bible privately and pray from it by applying passages to their own situation. Yet the Bible, from its composition to its transmission and preservation, is above all a product of believing communities. To pick up a Bible is to hold a very long history of religious expression in one's hands. The same idea applies to sacramental worship. No matter how private one's encounter with the risen Jesus in the sacraments might feel, the rituals and liturgical prayers are celebrations of an entire people's faith. Indeed, the spirit of Jesus binds us together and makes us increasingly aware of the whole body of Christ. Thus we profess in the creed our belief in the *communion* of saints.[14]

Faith has an evident social character. We observe this (1) in the genesis of faith within families and believing communities; (2) in its ongoing development and continual dependence upon the example of others for confirmation and nourishment; (3) in the unseen voices of the believing tradition that carry us forward; and (4) in its ultimate goal, which is union with God and God's people. Without these elements working together in harmony, none of us would be able to say, "I believe in God"; each "I believe" presupposes a "we believe." The more explicitly we attend to these elements, the more aware do we become of the actual working of God in our lives. The same four elements would also have been operative in Jesus' life, of course. Analyze Jesus' faith as disclosed to us through the Gospels, and there one will find the faith of the Jewish people.

But in addition to the social and communal nature of coming to faith there are three other elements to bear in mind.

First, believers truly experience God in their hearts, minds, and souls; yet the holy mystery that approaches them is a mystery that reveals itself to many: not as one Being who shares grace with countless individuals, but as One whose nature it is to dwell among a people. The life of God in us is common life. Hence Paul writes that *all* have been made to drink of *one* spirit (1 Cor 12:13). This is the same spiritual vision we find behind the Last Supper discourse in the fourth Gospel, in which Jesus speaks of his followers' union with himself and the Father. Inner life is common life.

Second, many of our religious experiences are at root corporate. We lead lives, not only as individuals, but as a people. Thus whole peoples live, struggle, suffer, rejoice, grow, and face death. Whole peoples undergo processes of purgation; an entire community, even a marriage, can enter a dark night of the soul. It is the experience of generations that has sedimented itself in scriptural texts, and when a solitary believer relates to those texts, he or she is stepping into the religious world of the entire people of God and joining voice with them. That, of course, is precisely what the crucified Jesus did when he uttered the opening words of Psalm 22. He was hardly the first to be crucified, and he would not be the last; not the first believer to have felt abandoned by God, nor by any means the last.

The experience of generations leads to the emergence of proverbs and other expressions of popular wisdom. It can also lead to the development and testing of rules for discerning spirits or of discriminating between what gives life and what leads to death. Theologians speak of the *sensus fidelium,* the intuition and sensibilities of ordinary men and women who possess deep faith instincts. And the emergence over centuries of distinctive spiritualities in the church, each one lived, tested, refined, and developed by men and women who were truly "friends of God,"[15] testifies further to the corporate nature of religious experience.

Sin, too, has a corporate history. Evil embeds itself in the fabric of social institutions, in the way economies generate income, in the destructive ways of thinking about others that we know as prejudice. It is transmitted across generations and ratified in the form of tribal and ethnic hatred, bitter memories of oppression, and the thirst for vengeance. But if sin has its corporate history, so does forgiveness. Just as an entire people can fall into idolatry, so also the whole people has to seek forgiveness. The biblical record of divine mercy corresponds to the history of a people's repentance. The sense of being forgiven as a people, in other words, is different from the experience of the individual believer before God repenting and receiving pardon. In fact, this is the sort of forgiveness Jesus was preaching in the gospel: Israel's definitive return from exile and once for all reconciliation with God.[16]

Third, the life of the people can transform and even become the interior life of the individual believer. Increasingly what fills the person's soul are the collective hope and aspirations of others. What sharpens and deepens that hope might be the experience of struggling to make ends meet and provide for a family; anxiety and desperation; a sense that ultimately the world does not make sense, that it is not governed by justice and wisdom; the experience of being humiliated and betrayed by those with the power and resources to redress wrongs; the feeling of being forgotten by God and preyed upon by demons; or the communal equivalent of the soul's dark night when God seems utterly still and powerless. No matter what personal suffering or loss the individual may undergo, the sufferings and losses of the people always feel more acute; and in a paradoxical way, the more one enters into the experience of the people, the more one discovers a consolation that casts his or her own suffering and loss in a less fearsome light, the support of numerous unseen others. One's personal desiring shows itself, transformed and enlarged, to be the desiring of the whole people of God. Such is the grace of a genuinely Christian or evangelical solidarity. The experience of solidarity is nothing less than an experience of salvation.[17]

Just as solidarity means sharing the hard and bitter aspects of a people's life, it can also lead to an immersion in the history of their waywardness. None of us stands above the sinfulness of our society or culture, as if we had been miraculously preserved from any contamination by the moral failure around us. Although we are certainly not responsible for the sins of our ancestors, we have inherited the legacies of their hardness of heart. Moreover, whenever leadership in any area fails—on the part of politicians, educators, investors, employers, executives, newscasters, the military, lawyers, churchpeople—the rest of society pays the price. The individual praying "Lord, have mercy" each week asks not only for personal forgiveness, but for the forgiveness and healing of the wider human family of which we are all a part. In fact, realized solidarity implies that one feels incomplete, not so much on the basis of personal sinfulness, but because so many remain tragically separated from God. One feels and makes one's own, in other words, the waywardness of the people. That is why Jesus was able to stand in the Jordan with all the others who went to hear John and confess their sins. He stood and prayed there in real solidarity. Jesus could sincerely pray, with them, "Have mercy on me, O God, according to your steadfast love" (Ps 51:1). Without pretending he could relate to the

sentiments of the psalmist when the prayers of Israel begged God for pardon
or celebrated God's compassion and forgiveness.

The Gospels show us clearly how much Jesus connected his message
with the daily lives of his listeners. Many of their concerns were quite local
and ordinary, as we gather from the everydayness of the parables. Other concerns, however, touched the lives of all the people together; these had to do
with the renewal and liberation of Israel, the arrival of God as king, and the
subsequent reordering of every aspect of national life, which God's arrival
would necessitate. As we said previously, Jesus' immersion in the life of his
people, sharing their concerns, has to be our starting point both in understanding him *and* in understanding important dynamics within every Christian's
interior life. Jesus' solidarity with his people was not the consequence of his
experience of God but its very condition of possibility.[18] Whatever the import
of Jesus' addressing God as *Abba,* one thing seems reasonably sure: What
gave shape to his sense of that word was not the serenity and order, say, of a
retreat house or the cloistered silence of a convent but his familiarity with
human life in the towns and villages of Galilee.

The Danger of Individualism

Individualistic tendencies and behavior seem to be characteristic of us
both as North Americans and as products of twentieth-century Western culture. We live in a society that exaggerates the values of privacy, individual
achievement, the acquisition of material goods.[19] For a fully Christian understanding of what it means to be a human person, however, whatever we say
about the individual must take into account the fact that we belong to societies
and communities. The individual believer, we realize, never approaches God
in isolation. Because we have been baptized into Christ Jesus, we approach
God only as one of God's children and alongside all our brothers and sisters.
No matter how solitary the prayer we make, the sacramental reality of which
we are a part is the church, the body of Christ. Whenever one Christian prays,
all believers pray. Whenever one pleads for mercy, all are begging God's
mercy and forgiveness. Where one Christian rejoices in God's goodness, the
spirits of each and every one are engaged in thanking and praising God. And
whenever one person of faith cries to God for bread, or for a homeland, or for
liberty, or for justice, all believers are making that prayer with and in her. The
metaphor that each believer is an athlete running a race for his own personal
glory obscures the point that, when it comes to salvation history, the human
race wins or loses together.

There are social and intellectual forces within our culture that militate
against true and lasting solidarity. We certainly know how to organize ourselves into powerful political and civic groups, which then advocate our

respective social and economic interests. Unfortunately, such organizations may do little more than spread individualism farther and wider, for rather than thinking of the well-being of the whole of society or of the whole human family, they create enclaves of special interests. This risks leaving the members of the larger body at war among themselves; or if not at war, then in a permanent state of hostility, suspicion, and fear. Although as believers we are capable of compassion, the modern world has known too many instances in which compassion quickly reached its moral limit and societies burst apart in ethnic or religious violence. The scourge of that violence should be a sober warning to all of us not to take our religious sensibilities for granted by presuming that we are holier, firmer in our faith or in our grasp of the gospel, than others. Whenever violence erupts because of religious differences, or whenever people resort to political or ethnic cleansing while continuing to think of themselves as true believers, humanity is given another bloody demonstration of what happens when God and world are divorced within our religious experience.

Without doubt, our daily effort to live the gospel will eventually bring us face to face with the limitations of our social worlds, and those limits can easily turn deadly. Consider Jesus and the resistance he encountered once he crossed social and religious boundaries by associating with "sinners." We may be tempted to turn back, or even to settle for the status quo. After all, a partial realization of the gospel has to be better than none at all! Yet if we have been correct in suggesting that the life of God and the life of the people are inseparable, then realized solidarity can only be won and maintained through a vigorous Christian asceticism.

Solidarity: A Foundational Christian Experience

By now it should be clear that for a Christian, solidarity can appropriately be described as a religious reality. In the face of unbridled individualism, solidarity is a powerful antidote to moral isolation and preoccupation with oneself. While Christian spirituality obviously holds no copyright on the term *solidarity,* its prominence today even in secular circles suggests that there is more God-seeking going on in the world than meets the eye. The search for deep, lasting solidarity must be taken seriously as one of the major signs of our times.[20]

In responding recently to an interviewer's question as to what sort of society he would like to see in the future, Basil Hume said,

> First, it is a society which places the value of each human life centre stage....I would then add...a deeper recognition of our common human identity. My vision is of a society which will nourish the spiritual [and] also of a society that will look out for the weak and marginalised, promote freedom, and *nurture an inclusive solidarity*

based on the dignity and worth of all its members. I am called to express my concern for the poor throughout the world, to do what I can to combat injustice, *to express my solidarity with other people.*[21]

Such a vision, he is telling us, is universal in its scope, not regional. He speaks of an "inclusive solidarity" that requires concrete expression through action on behalf of justice. Nevertheless, Cardinal Hume's prayerful longing will have to remain unsatisfied so long as any trace of injustice, marginalization, or disregard for human life afflicts the world. The church prays the same way in its liturgy through phrases such as "until you come in glory" or "thy kingdom come." Solidarity, in other words, is an eschatological reality: partially realized, eagerly awaiting fulfillment.

In his book *The One and the Many,* Martin Marty drew upon the work of the Polish philosopher Leszek Kolakowski, who had written,

Flights from the indifference of the world via edifices which enable us to be absorbed in communal life through identification with family, tribal, or national groups is not by any means worthless; but it does seem that in this respect the all-or-nothing rule prevails, that therefore partial or fleeting identifications do not truly exist.[22]

For Kolawkowski (and for Marty) we will not be able to overcome the dehumanizing forces in our world by associating ourselves with only one group that suffers. Solidarity with victims entails solidarity with *all* victims, regardless of who they are. The unfolding of solidarity as an idea and as practice means that the local or the regional never marks the boundary of one's compassion, concern, or prophetic outrage. We may work for justice and peace at the local level, just as Jesus did. But the Christian soul and its prayer, when grounded in the spirit, operate on a world scale.[23] In this light we may better understand the sentiment behind the phrase "for many": "This is my blood of the covenant, which is poured out *for many*" (Mk 14:25), which the eucharistic prayer expresses as "for you and *for all.*" Jesus' imagination eventually came to embrace the whole world, not just one part of it, not just the lost sheep of the house of Israel (Mt 15:24). The moment of the gospel story when he recognized the openness of the gentiles to the message about the kingdom—the great sign of Jonah—would have to be the tip-off.[24]

A World That Makes No Sense

Believing that God exists does not demand much mental energy or conceptual adjustment on the part of those of us who have been raised in a world that already makes sense. Given our economic and domestic security, given the enormous technological strides we have witnessed in fields like telecommunications and medicine, and given the philosophical assumptions about rationality that still linger in the Western thought-world, assenting to the proposition that God exists comes relatively easily, even if that assent tends to remain at the notional rather than the practical level.[25] However, for men and women living in societies where insecurity prevails, where they are constantly threatened with violence, where disease and famine are daily companions, and where governments are both radically unstable and uncommitted to fighting injustice, assenting to the proposition that God exists is likely to be much more difficult, if not downright impossible. On the basis of what evidence is a person going to accept such a claim? How can people believe in God when so much in their experience indicates that there is no God, certainly not a God of justice, wisdom, and power?

The question is ancient, as we know. An interesting feature about the Bible, however, is that we find two distinct strains of thought about this question. The Wisdom literature in particular gives us one attitude toward the world, namely, that it was created through the instrumentality of wisdom itself. The world has been found good in God's eyes, and blessed; and for those with real vision, "the heavens are telling the glory of God; and the firmament proclaims his handiwork" (Ps 19:1). A second, darker strain appears, for instance, in the opening chapters of the Book of Jeremiah. There the prophet has been ridiculed, rejected, and punished for speaking the truth. He chastises the people as a whole for their infidelity and certain individuals for their greed:

> For scoundrels are found among my people;
>> they take over the goods of others....
> They know no limits in deeds of wickedness;
>> they do not judge with justice the cause of the orphan, to make
>>> it prosper,
>> and they do not defend the rights of the needy....
> For from the least to the greatest of them,
>> everyone is greedy for unjust gain;
> and from prophet to priest, everyone deals falsely.
>> (Jer 5:26, 28; 6:13)

On all sides sinister clouds are menacing the nation and chaos appears imminent. Nevertheless, despite the enormous disorder so evident in the human world, the prophet maintains his basic faith in God. God is still the protector of the orphans and widows in the land. On what grounds, however, does the prophet's conviction stand? It cannot be on the basis of evidence, since the sad reality is that injustice and greed *have* prevailed against the defenseless and the innocent; otherwise the prophet would not have said in the gate of the Lord's house, "If you do not oppress the alien, the orphan, and the widow, or shed innocent blood in this place..." (Jer 7:6). In this case, the prophetic conviction about God's justice and judgment stands in sharp contrast to the people's everyday experience, and that is remarkable. A sense of God remains firm in a world where things do not make sense, where divine design is by no means apparent, where the effects of wisdom have been covered over by sinfulness, and where God's law has failed to protect the most vulnerable members of society.

The interior life of the people of God, then, does not necessarily rest upon the experience of a good, secure, and ordered world, or even of a good world gone sour, or a world intended to be good for some but not for others. In fact, the underlying experience is often quite the contrary, which means that belief in God in such a case is empowered more by desperation, hope, and confidence than by evidence of wisdom, justice, and order. This would explain why the Christian story, and the central place of the cross within that story, speaks so powerfully to defenseless, disenfranchised poor people. God in the midst of chaos appears to be their elementary religious experience; an out-of-joint world in which the forces of good hardly seem victorious is a major ingredient of their interior life. The logic of the cross is easy to grasp when one is living on the bottom.

I am not suggesting that poor people never experience beauty or goodness, or that they never have reasons for giving praise and thanks to God. Those occasions might be rare, however, given the severe conditions under which many of them have to live. The daily plight of Palestinians on the West Bank or of refugees from Kosovo, or the devastating social and political instability that affects so many people throughout Africa, understandably becomes the *normal* way in which the world presents itself. Even the hopelessness that marks the lives of many youngsters growing up, say, in Los Angeles or New York City, can make any message about God's goodness and care nearly impossible to hear.[26] Again, the underlying shape of their interior lives has been largely determined by frustration, rejection, and impassable social and economic boundaries. Under such circumstances, the cross speaks loudly and forcefully, not as a call to revolution (although there is certainly a subversive side to the story of Jesus' crucifixion), but as what is most logical and evident. God suffers in and among his people, and the cross is the enduring sign of divine oneness with people who have nothing but hope to sustain them.

It is important for the rest of us, for whom life has been immeasurably more secure and promising, to be alert to where solidarity takes us. The interior life of the people of God necessarily includes the cross. Our point here is not only that the passion and death of Jesus persists in the suffering of his sisters and brothers (in itself an extremely powerful Christian insight). The point, rather, is that there is a great mystery at the heart of the world's darkness, something that speaks of the presence of God. From one point of view, Job's wrestling with God was spiritually simpler. He knew what a life of blessing consisted of. The only thing he had to figure out was how a person who had kept God's law and behaved righteously could ever incur such crippling misery. For Job, what was at stake was the integrity of the divine promise, the logic of blessing and curse as revealed to Moses and recorded in Deuteronomy. In the case of the Bible's poor, however, there is no fall from blessing, no contrived testing of people who were prosperous and righteous. The world routinely shows itself as cruel and capricious. Yet in spite of their suffering, they are not utterly faithless; and that is what points us toward the mystery that pervades their interior life.

The Myth of the Innocent Poor

To prevent our spiritual theology from becoming muddled it is important to have a clear idea of what the word *poor* refers to. Solidarity and the preferential option for the poor are conceptual twins; one always implies the other. Whether we view solidarity as the result of having made an option for the poor or as the living expression of that option, from the point of view of Christian theology solidarity takes us into the world of the poor and into the heart of God. When Paul wrote,

> For you know the generous act of our Lord Jesus Christ, that
> though he was rich, yet for your sakes he became poor, so that by
> his poverty you might become rich. (2 Cor 8:9)

he was articulating a profound truth, not a pious exhortation: a truth that should fix itself permanently in our imagination and our prayer. The poverty of which Paul speaks had to be a real poverty, even if his use of *rich* in the same text is metaphorical.[27] *God's* solidarity with the world in and through Jesus orients us in a specific direction.

Nevertheless, there is a persistent temptation to interpret the words *poor* and *poverty* as metaphors for the human condition. This is regularly done by people who do not want to feel themselves excluded from the mystery of God's loving solidarity with a poor and sinful world, since they know that they cannot in all fairness be considered materially poor.

One helpful way of dealing with this awkwardness might be to distinguish between being poor and being needy, as Peter Henriot does:

> I do not think it is accurate or helpful to call "poor" all those who
> have particular needs, no matter how great. They are "needy,"
> deserving of our immediate care and worthy of our special con-
> cern. We should indeed respond to them with our attention, our

love, our ministry—but not under the rubric of responding to the poor.[28]

Another way might be to create a second category, namely, those who are poor in spirit, as Matthew does: "Blessed are the poor in spirit" (Mt 5:3). The poor in spirit, it could be argued, are those who have acquired the virtue of solidarity; their manner of living, thinking, and acting give concrete expression to the option for the poor.[29] The words *poor* and *poverty,* however, really should apply first and foremost to the materially poor. Otherwise the recurring summons of the prophets to be mindful of the poor loses its punch, and it becomes easy to overlook the fact that Paul's appeal to "the generous act of our Lord Jesus Christ" was made in the context of taking up a collection for the poor of Jerusalem.

Yet however we resolve this concern about not wanting to feel left out of God's preferential love, we must remind ourselves that the poor are not automatically more beautiful, more humane or more religious than those who are materially well off. There is absolutely nothing to romanticize about the physical conditions that create poverty. Simplicity of life is commendable and virtuous; but severe deprivation, exploitation, ignorance, violence, illness, and premature death signal how tragically out of joint the world is. The only motive consistent with the gospel story that explains why religious embrace the vow of poverty is solidarity. For them, following Jesus means an interior life grounded in the experience of solidarity with men and women at the bottom, with victims everywhere and with all of the world's poor.[30]

The human reality is, of course, that among every social class we find both good people and bad ones, men and women whose lives are God-oriented and those whose lives are not. There are people of great means who are truly poor in spirit, and there are materially poor people whose souls have been overtaken by resentment and covetousness. When God speaks of "my poor people" through the voice of Jeremiah, the voice is clearly referring to all the people, rich and poor alike, who have proven adulterous (Jer 8:19, 21; 9:1); here *poor* equivalently means "sinful." The prophet might be hinting that the poor are less culpable than the rich, for he says,

> Then I said, "These are only the poor, they have no sense;
> for they do not know the way of the Lord, the law of their God.
> Let me go to the rich and speak to them;
> surely they know the way of the Lord, the law of their God."
> (Jer 5:4–5a)

Nevertheless, all alike had broken the yoke of the Lord's instruction and thus merited punishment (Jer 5:5b).

Any suggestion, then, that the poor do not need redemption, or that the opening words of Jesus' proclamation, "Repent and believe in the good news" (Mk 1:14) do not apply to them, would be badly mistaken. People may be materially poor, but it does not automatically follow that they have a corner on salvation.

Yet what about those desperately poor men and women who really are God-oriented in the way they think and live from one day to the next? On what basis do they hang on to their hope and faith? In their case, if we discern carefully, we are likely to discover interior lives firmly rooted in an experience of solidarity: solidarity, first, with those others who are like them in being poor, and second, with *all* others because we share the same humanity.

In other words, among the poor who have faith there is an experience of oneness with the rest of God's people that sustains them from day to day and empowers them to hold fast to their belief in God. Sometimes (as in Latino spirituality) that oneness is mediated by an intense devotion to the crucified Jesus, because the horizon behind the cross is nothing less than suffering humanity itself—impoverished, exploited, betrayed, cast out.[31] The cross thereby makes the world of broken lives sacramentally present, raised to the level of the suffering of God. In the end, the life of the people mediates the life of God; the shared experience of suffering confirms the abiding presence of God.[32]

And how do we account for their coming to faith in the first place? Answering from a Christian perspective, I would say that their faith was awakened from having heard the gospel story (probably in fragmentary fashion, just like the rest of us) and grasping intuitively that *that* story is wonderfully and truly their own. Their grasp may be incomplete; it normally requires further instruction, reflection, and appropriation. Yet it seems to me that faith and hope are awakened by hearing, just as Paul said (Rom 10:17). One hears the story of Jesus and recognizes within it the story of God, which is at the same time the story of God's people. One hears—intuits—the reality of divine solidarity and one knows that this reality embraces above all those in the world who are poor. In the mystery of divine–human encounter, the person who hears in this way touches the very One whom Jesus addressed as Abba.

Notes

1. The phrase "People of God" (*Populus Dei*) has a more restricted meaning in the second chapter of Vatican II's *Dogmatic Constitution on the Church* than I am intending here. For our purposes, "people of God" (lower case) embraces all those who belong to God: those with religious faith, men and women of good will, yet above all those who are poor and who for that reason alone are especially loved by God.

2. All scriptural quotations are taken from the *New Revised Standard Version*.

3. The important biblical text in this regard might be the following: "Then you shall say to Pharaoh, 'Thus says the Lord: Israel is my firstborn son. I said to you, "Let my son go that he may worship me." But you refused to let him go; now I will kill your firstborn son'" (Ex 4:22–23). See also Wisdom 18:13.

4. The Aramaic word appears in Mark 14:36 and twice in the earlier writing of Paul (Rom 8:15 and Gal 4:6). The seminal work on the significance of *Abba* is Joachim Jeremias, *The Prayers of Jesus* (Philadelphia: Fortress, 1978). See pp. 11–65.

5. Oscar Cullman, for instance, writes, "The fact that Jesus also teaches the disciples to pray 'Abba' means that despite his extraordinarily intensive awareness of sonship, he also wants to lead them to an intimate conversation, into union with God" [*Prayer in the New Testament* (Minneapolis: Fortress, 1995), 42].

6. Edward Schillebeeckx, *Jesus: An Experiment in Christology* (New York: Seabury, 1979), 256–71. See also Walter Kasper, *The God of Jesus Christ* (New York: Crossroad, 1984), 170–71; and Jacques Dupuis, *Who Do You Say That I Am?: Introduction to Christology* (Maryknoll, N.Y.: Orbis, 1994), 49–50. Bernard Cooke pointed out that Schillebeeckx's treatment of Jesus focused on Jesus' experience of God rather than his own self-identity, an idea that Cooke himself then pursued. What I would add is that Jesus' experience of God cannot be dissociated from his experience of God's people. See Cooke, *God's Beloved: Jesus' Experience of the Transcendent* (Philadelphia: Trinity Press International, 1992), 1–24.

7. James D. G. Dunn, *Jesus and the Spirit* (Philadelphia: Westminster, 1975), 26. See also his *Christology in the Making: A New Testament Inquiry into the Origins of the Doctrine of the Incarnation* (Philadelphia: Westminster, 1980), 22–33.

8. Marcus J. Borg, *Conflict, Holiness and Politics in the Teachings of Jesus* (Harrisburg, Penn.: Trinity Press International, 1998), 88. See also Roger Haight, "The Case for Spirit Christology," *Theological Studies* 53, 2 (1992): 257–87.

9. Joachim Gnilka writes, "To be sure, we become aware of this special relationship with God, illumined for us as if by a flash, in the little word 'Abba' only if we add and bring to bear the entire context of his mission." See *Jesus of Nazareth: Message and History* (Peabody, Mass.: Hendrickson Publishers, 1997), 262–63.

10. In the psalms we find, for instance, familiar expressions of praise, adoration, and thanksgiving, celebrations of divine goodness and the beauty of the natural world, moments of serene confidence, desolation, surrender, love,

and contrition. All of these presumably entered into Jesus' interior life. As Jeremias put it, "Jesus came from a people who knew how to pray" (*Prayers of Jesus*, 66).

11. I am not concerned here with theological questions connected with what is distinctive about Christianity. My point is that whatever is distinctive ought not to be traced to the religious experience of Jesus. Paul, of course, was the first to wrestle with the theological relationship between Israel and Jesus in Romans 9–11. Two works that examine the relevant theological issues are James Dunn, *The Partings of the Ways Between Christianity and Judaism and Their Significance for the Character of Christianity* (Philadelphia: Trinity Press International, 1991); and R. Kendall Soulen, *The God of Israel and Christian Theology* (Minneapolis: Fortress, 1996).

12. I have developed this point further in *To Hear the Word of God, Listen to the World* (New York: Paulist, 1997), 168–74.

13. The famous words in the opening paragraph of Vatican *II's Pastoral Constitution on the Church in the Modern World* might suitably be employed to underline this point: "The joys and hopes, the griefs and the anxieties of the men and women of his age, especially those who were poor or in any way afflicted, these too were the joys and hopes, the griefs and anxieties of Jesus."

14. An excellent elaboration of the rich experiences underlying our communion with others is Elizabeth A. Johnson, *Friends of God and Prophets: A Feminist Theological Reading of the Communion of Saints* (New York: Continuum, 1998).

15. Johnson takes this phrase from Wisdom 7:27: "Although she is but one, she can do all things, and while remaining in herself, she renews all things; in every generation she passes into holy souls and makes them friends of God, and prophets."

16. As N. T. Wright puts it, *"Forgiveness of sins is another way of saying 'return from exile.'"* See his *Jesus and the Victory of God* (Minneapolis: Fortress, 1996), 268. And again, "The point is that *Jesus was offering the return from exile, the renewed covenant, the eschatological 'forgiveness of sins'*—in other words, the kingdom of God" (272).

17. See Joyce Murray, C.S.J., "Liberation for Communion in the Soteriology of Gustavo Gutiérrez," *Theological Studies* 59 (1998): 51–59.

18. Friedrich Schleiermacher's appeal to the category of "God-consciousness" was fundamentally misdirected. It would have made better sense scripturally to speak of Jesus' "people-consciousness" in order to gather some idea of what God might have meant to him. See no. 88 and following paragraphs of *The Christian Faith* (Edinburgh: T. and T. Clark, 1928; 1968).

19. For more extensive discussion of this point see Robert Bellah *et al.*, *Habits of the Heart: Individualism and Commitment in American Life* (Berkeley: University of California Press, 1985); and Martin E. Marty, *The One and*

the Many: America's Struggle for the Common Good (Cambridge, Mass.: Harvard University Press, 1997).

20. An example or two will have to suffice. See Douglas Sturm, *Solidarity and Suffering: Towards a Politics of Relationality* (Albany, N.Y.: SUNY Press, 1998); and Richard Rorty, *Contingency, Irony, and Solidarity* (New York: Cambridge University Press, 1989), 189–98.

21. Cardinal Basil Hume, "Our Restless Society: Finding a Cure," *Tablet*, June 13 1998, 763. Emphasis added. Some of the ecclesiological dimensions of solidarity are discussed by Juan Hernandez Pico, S.J., in *Theology of Christian Solidarity* (Maryknoll, N.Y.: Orbis, 1985; coauthored with Jon Sobrino), 43–98.

22. As cited by Marty, *One and Many*, 162.

23. Gil Bailie writes that "empathy for victims is Christianity's cardinal virtue....By acclaiming the victim as Lord, the Gospels slowly begin to awaken an empathy for victims everywhere" [*Violence Unveiled: Humanity at the Crossroads* (New York: Crossroad, 1995), 27.] The gospel, in other words, invites us into a deep and abiding solidarity with all God's people, particularly with those crushed by injustice.

24. That Jesus understood that God's purposes were ultimately intended for the whole world, again see Wright, *Jesus and Victory of God*, 308–19. The reference to the sign of Jonah in Matthew 16:4 follows after Jesus' encounter with the Canaanite woman of great faith (Mt 15:21–28), the great crowds who came to him for healing and wound up praising the God of Israel (15:29–31), and who then spent three days with him receiving instruction (15:32). The crowds appear to have been gentiles.

25. Hans Küng writes, "Affirmation of God implies an ultimately justified fundamental trust in reality. As radical fundamental trust, belief in God can suggest the condition of the possibility of uncertain reality. If someone affirms God, he knows why he can trust reality" (*Does God Exist?: An Answer for Today* [New York: Doubleday and Co., 1980], 572. See also his *On Being a Christian* [New York: Doubleday and Co., 1976], 62–88); and Heinrich Fries, *Fundamental Theology* (Washington, D.C.: Catholic University of America Press, 1996), 32–33. But why could we not conceive of people believing in God without having found reality to be trustworthy? The idea that reality is basically trustworthy might well be something of a philosophical or cultural luxury, a point which I failed to appreciate in some earlier writing (see *The Potter's Touch: God Calls Us to Life* [New York: Paulist, 1981], 22–30).

26. See, for instance, Luis J. Rodriguez, *Always Running: La Vida Loca: Gang Days in L.A.* (Willimantic, Conn.: Curbstone Press, 1993); or William Finnegan, *Cold New World: Growing Up in a Harder Country* (New York: Random House, 1998). The virtue of this sort of writing (it is abundant) is that it provides vivid accounts of human lives on the underside of history. Furthermore,

such writing can tease out of us a passionate, intense form of prayer as our souls open to the world and start to feel bruised by its sin and its pain. In the same category I would place books such as Iris Chang, *The Rape of Nanking* (New York: Basic Books, 1997); *Children of Cambodia's Killing Fields: Memoirs of Survivors*, edited by Kim DePaul and compiled by Dith Pran (New Haven: Yale University Press, 1997); Ricardo Falla, *Massacres in the Jungle: Ixcán, Guatemala, 1975–1982* (Boulder: Westview Press, 1994); and Philip Gourevitch, *We Wish to Inform You That Tomorrow We Will Be Killed with Our Families: Stories from Rwanda* (New York: Farrar, Straus and Giroux, 1998). Works like these might even be classified as a type of world scripture.

27. See my article "Solidarity and the Reshaping of Spirituality," *Merton Annual*, vol. 11 (Collegeville: Liturgical Press, 1999).

28. Peter Henriot, S.J., *Option for the Poor: A Challenge for North Americans* (Washington, D.C.: Center for Concern, 1990), 25. As cited by Thomas H. Smolich, S.J., in "Testing the Water: Jesuits Accompanying the Poor," *Studies in the Spirituality of Jesuits* 24, 2 (St. Louis: Seminar on Jesuit Spirituality, 1992).

29. It was John Paul II who referred to solidarity as a virtue: "The fact that men and women in various parts of the world feel personally affected by the injustices and violations of human rights committed in distant countries, countries which they perhaps will never visit, is a further sign of a reality transformed into *awareness*, thus acquiring a *moral* connotation,...When interdependence becomes recognized in this way, the correlative response as a moral and social attitude, as a 'virtue,' is *solidarity*." See his 1987 encyclical letter *On Social Concern (Solicitudo Rei Socialis)*, no. 38 (Washington, D.C.: United States Catholic Conference, 1988), 74.

30. I have elaborated the connection between the option for the poor (and thus the realization of solidarity) and religious life in *Religious Life Today: Re-Thinking a Promise* (Los Angeles: Rogate Publications, 1994).

31. In the final chapter of his book *The Faith of the People: Theological Reflections on Popular Catholicism* (Maryknoll, N.Y.: Orbis, 1997), which is entitled "Popular Religion as an Epistemology (of Suffering)," Orlando Espín does not go far enough. He writes that it is important to "notice (first) that God is active in Latino suffering, and *not* solely as responsible for that suffering, and (second) that the people feel themselves capable of changing the will of God" (168). This may be correct, but what needs to be added is the element of solidarity precisely as a way of knowing and understanding the mystery of human suffering. Solidarity is an integral part of Latino spirituality, particularly in South America, although it might not always be easy to detect behind the baroque piety of the people.

32. Did not Paul have something like this in mind when he wrote, "For whenever I am weak, then I am strong" (2 Cor 12:10)? In moments of weakness

and great personal suffering Paul had experienced the power of the risen Jesus. Granted Paul was speaking to the Corinthians out of his commitment to the gospel and deep union with the risen Jesus, nevertheless the fact that God, in the life and death of Jesus, has revealed the depth of the divine solidarity with suffering humanity means that *God has always been present there*, enduring the poverty and oppression of God's people. And if God is really there, then some men and women even in their poverty are bound to discover the mystery.

27. Socially Engaged Contemplation: Living Contemplatively in Chaotic Times

Currently, many people in American society seem to be longing for a slower pace of life, a less frenzied rhythm, a less compulsively busy daily round. Even more important, they want a daily round that fosters in them an openness to the deepest yearnings of their hearts, truly wanting to discover anew how to embrace a contemplative way of living. A recent issue of the *Utne Reader* used these telling phrases: "finding your natural rhythm in a speed-crazed world"[1]; "A balanced life—intervals of creative frenzy giving way to relaxation—is what people crave;"[2] and even more intriguing, a series of descriptions by public personalities, from race car drivers to composers, on ways they "put on the brakes."[3]

Juliet Schor, author of the 1992 best-seller, *The Overworked American,* identifies economics, not technology, as the major reason for the speeding up of American life. Jeremy Rifkin in *The Time Wars,* writes, "We have quickened the pace of life only to become less patient;...we have become more organized but less spontaneous, less joyful. We are better prepared to act on the future but less able to enjoy the present and reflect on the past."[4]

Pastoral ministers are no strangers to this cultural phenomenon of the speeding up of American life. They, too, long to live more contemplatively and often wonder how they can feel so driven and deprived of a contemplative sense of God's presence when their very call to ministry and its relentless demands seem to be their greatest obstacle to experiencing it. Some, of course, long for a relationship with God of real depth, but never really have the opportunity or the formative means to nurture this dimension of their lives. So-called "normal" ministry schedules rarely include quiet time for reflection, silent prayer, or retreats of significant length.

Others, nonetheless, have managed to commit themselves to the spiritual disciplines that fostered a contemplative dimension within lives of active ministry. These ministers are contemplatives in action and have learned to cultivate and maintain a contemplative attitude toward life in both prayer and action. Some among this latter group, in my experience, appear to be experiencing an eclipse of or loss of peaceful immersion in the divine presence and wonder what may have gone wrong. This loss may be a result of "burnout" or overextension in ministry, family responsibility, and ever-lengthening community agendas. These ministers may simply have become unable to set appropriate limits to their caregiving activities and are no longer devoting enough energy or time to contemplative practices. For others, this loss may be the result of dramatic changes within their operative theologies, their painful confrontation with the suffering of people who are poor and marginalized, or their own personal experiences of loss in the midst of ever-increasing institutional and personal stress.

Others continue to pray, but may not entirely recognize the depth of this prayer because their prayer experience differs so markedly from their expectation and prior experience. Others may find times of retreat wonderfully fruitful and nourishing but find daily prayer, or a regular pattern of living in and from this level of depth, nearly impossible once they return to their daily round. They may be helpless to confront their own resistance to the transformation God is trying to work in them. Thus, they delay it by neglecting their contemplative lives outside of solitary time, either frequent focused prayer throughout the week, or periodic times of retreat.

In this essay, I explore this inherited dichotomy and reclaim the essential unity of action and contemplation as core elements of spirituality. In the process, I hope to shed some light on some of the objective difficulties pastoral ministers experience in wanting to be in God so desperately yet often finding themselves farther away than many would like to admit. Finally, I want to describe some characteristic features of contemplative experience that is socially engaged. By "socially engaged contemplation," I mean both the social and cultural context in which contemplation occurs, deeply affecting one's consciousness, and the way the "stuff of life" of pastoral ministers who accompany people who are poor or who struggle with other concrete forms of oppression emerge in their contemplative prayer.

Descriptions of Contemplation and Contemplative Attitude

Just what are contemplation and a contemplative attitude toward life? Contemplation can be understood in three different yet related ways. First, it points "to a practice, something we do, something we set aside discrete periods of time to undertake." To contemplate means "something like: to consider, to look upon, scrutinize, study, mediate on, turn our attention fully and clearly to something, to open our hearts to something we are beholding. It means especially, turning our attention to the actual."[5]

This activity of contemplating is paradoxical. It is doing something but is closer to not doing anything at all. The monastic tradition had a word for it, *otium*—contemplative leisure—something akin to sabbath rest. Or an art the

Italians have mastered called the "sweet art of doing nothing." Monastic life in its most authentic times carefully maintained a culture in which this contemplative leisure was valued and nurtured. This kind of leisure is not "time out" or "time off" but an interior and exterior quality of openness and attentiveness. In this state of mind, one is alert, awake, connected to the divine presence and one's own heart. This contemplative quality of consciousness differs remarkably from the way many people "do nothing" in front of the TV, which may be "time off our feet" but which does not necessarily enliven our hearts and awaken our attentiveness. The passivity of watching TV is more often a distraction, a form of numbing, a constriction of consciousness and a deadening of feeling.

Second, contemplation points to an underlying dimension of human experience, a state of consciousness that is actualized through such practices. "It is characterized by intense attention, intuitive understanding, a depth and fullness of feeling, and experience of union with a larger reality."[6] So it is not simply something we do but a way of experiencing that is awakened in us. Gerald May offers a number of rich descriptions of this kind of consciousness: "Contemplation is most frequently defined as an open, panoramic, and all-embracing *awareness,* brought into fullness of living action, an attitude of the heart and a quality of presence rather than just a state of consciousness."[7] May elaborates further: "Contemplation happens to everyone. It happens in moments when we are open, undefended, and immediately present. People who are called contemplatives are simply those who seek the expansion of the moments, who desire to live in that quality of presence more fully and continually."[8]

Third, contemplation also implies "the reality which is disclosed and made accessible in such an experience. This might be called: the sacred, the divine, the realm of grace, the mystery of God. Thus contemplation is not merely a practice, nor merely a state, but also an *encounter,* a meeting."[9] This definition of contemplation emphasizes the experience of discovering oneself in contact with, in relationship to, in the presence of ultimate reality. It is this deepest level of encounter with the Holy Mystery in which we experience the essential unity of the love of neighbor and the love of God, the essential interrelatedness of all that is. When we dare to relax our "driven egos," we may be graced with unspeakable revelation and a love poured out by the Holy Spirit into our hearts with which we can dare to embrace reality itself. To encourage an increase in this experiential awareness, literally to live contemplatively, requires both resisting the outer voices from the local culture as well as resisting the internalized inner voices from this culture. It requires us to adopt particular practices: taking time for reflection, for prayer, for leisure. Above all, it requires our learning how to shift our consciousness so that we can open our hearts and vision to a fullness of reality precisely when do not have time for solitary contemplation.

Practices Nourish a Contemplative Approach to Action

Here, I believe we can learn from other religious traditions with great fruitfulness. Many meditation traditions teach ways of working with breath: counting breath, breathing fully and consciously, synchronizing breathing and walking, connecting a mantra or prayer phrase with breath. Others—t'ai chi, shibashi, yoga—employ movement patterns, which through specific attentive movements gradually integrate mind, body, spirit so that our hearts open and our consciousness deepens without necessarily trying to "sit still" while our thoughts race on without us. These practices cultivate an open, spacious form of consciousness, which is not as easily captivated by our compulsive inner programs. When we practice becoming fully present in this way, we are more easily able to recognize the emergence of the divine presence in our experience and to enter into the great cycle of the mutuality of care and presence in our ministerial and personal relationships.

Of surprise to many is the fact that many ministers are often engaged in these contemplative practices without necessarily being aware of it. For instance, in spiritual direction, women say they are not praying or are not praying very well, and yet when pressed for what is happening, they describe themselves as almost always "praying" in this brief way—acknowledging that they are not alone, that God is weaving through their days, constantly emerging and disappearing from view as they move through their daily round. Often God is very present, but they are so busy that they do not enjoy the peacefulness, rest, refreshment of such moments because they do not stop to savor them. They are not quite able to assimilate the grace. These moments of presence do not exactly feel like Tabor, gazing on the face of Christ with such awe and joy that one doesn't want to leave. This is a more situated form of contemplation.

Misconceptions and Alternative Interpretations about Contemplation

Too often, the tradition teaches that contemplation is some highly desirable experience in which we recognize and understand almost nothing of what is happening. Or it occurs to the very special and very few—an erroneous position corrected by Vatican II, which taught that contemplative prayer is the normal unfolding of a regular life of prayer for all Christians who so persevere. Or the tradition suggests that if powerful images or experiences in the senses occur this must not be contemplation. Or one must be secluded in some beautiful place.

I claim almost all of these impressions as partly erroneous because I believe contemplation occurs in very many ways. It may emerge in deep imaginative prayer when we release control of the line of imaging and God reveals God's self anew. Or it may be in the context of a simple breathing practice with nothing other than mutual presence. Or it may occur in the practice of centering prayer, as one silently holds a sacred word expressing one's intention toward God. Or it may occur to someone walking down the street, gardening, in the shower, in the midst of a pastoral or personal conversation. What makes it contemplation is not the location but the experience. Any time we touch our truer, deeper selves and some intuitive sense emerges of God's presence to us, this situation is contemplation. It is as much a matter of intention as it is attention.

Practices That Facilitate the Shift from Self-Preoccupation to Awareness

In addition to prayer and mindfulness practices, I read poetry, personal narratives, and mystical writings to foster this contemplative attitude. These uses of language help me feel and perceive beyond the clichéd and superficial conventions of culture. I am also turning to music, to nature, to fully embodied experiences that help me shift from my own anxious inner program of busyness or racing against the clock, to reconnect with more of life concretely in the present moment. Many different kinds of sensory experiences can help. For some, the domestic arts of cooking or sewing, when done with a focused attention rather than split attention, achieve the same end. Practicing an art form can facilitate this shift, as well as can receptive attention given to another's creation. This movement outward to beauty, to sound, to the senses often has a way of breaking through a habitual set of well-worn preoccupations that prevent present moment awareness.

The World's Pain Discloses Itself in Contemplative Awareness

Contemplative consciousness is often characterized, as Walter Burghardt put it, as "taking a long loving look at the real."[10] It doesn't matter what the starting point is. All reality leads us more deeply into God, who sustains all of it, both the sublime and the beautiful, the loving and the gracious, the painful and the conflicted, evil and sinfulness, suffering and healing—all of it. Burghardt's phrase is quite telling because it so totally unites vision— really seeing, a seeing through to the heart of the matter, a seeing beyond the surface and the superficial. This is a loving openness to reality, the reality of the other, the reality of creation, the reality of God.

Barry and Connolly describe this ability to become absorbed in reality as an experience of transcendence and self-forgetfulness. "Thus, one effect of paying attention to something outside of ourselves is that it can make us forget ourselves and our surroundings. Contemplation leads to, or rather is an experience of transcendence—that is, of forgetfulness of self and of everyone and everything else except the contemplated object."[11] Such a contemplative stance is particularly open to the very real forms of suffering in our world. Pastoral ministers as disciples who companion and console others in their suffering are called to contemplate Christ not only on Tabor but on the cross as God's love poured out upon the world. This contemplation of the crucified leads to faithful love—intercession, accompaniment, and service. Pastoral ministry invites contemplation of Jesus' suffering now in all who are disfigured, oppressed, struggling—every time hearts are moved to compassion. Pastoral ministers accompany the suffering, walk with them as Jesus did with the disciples on the road to Emmaus. Compassionate hearts feel the world's pain. When such pain passes through our hearts, we are led to intercession and to action. Our action leads us back to prayer as we are both challenged by the poor and suffering and also gifted by their resilience and hope.

Frequently, some of our contemplative experiences as ministers are more embodied, more immersed in connection and in care than in solitude. A contemplative stance in the midst of action is so often a process similar to that reported in the resurrection narratives when the disciples' eyes suddenly open, like scales falling, while they ponder the mystery. At such times our hearts are so held in God we become unafraid to feel the world's pain as well as our own. We become absorbed in the deep mysteries of life and death, of love and grace, of freedom and joy. Like the women who go weeping to the tomb, our sorrow turns to joy as we find nothing is as it appears on the surface. There is more than death, more than sorrow, more than defeat, more than disappointment. There is a livingness and a lovingness that overwhelms and surprises us.

An example of such compassionate contemplation that issues in intercession, a partnering with God while feeling one's own pain and God's for the world, is this account from a spiritual direction intern:

> I woke up with gratitude in my heart for all the blessings in my life. Today I celebrate the joy of the gift of priesthood. I took my bible and prayed over the whole of John:17. As I prayed, an overwhelming sense of sadness and grief permeated my whole being. There was a sense of loss and anger over the way things are going in the church. As I continued to pray, I was feeling the anguish and confusion of the many people who suffer and continue to suffer. Then I saw myself praying inside a cold, darkened church with all the other people who seemed to be in anguish like myself. Later I noticed someone approaching me and putting her hand on my shoulder saying, "I have told you this so that you will have peace by being united with all the rest. The world will make you suffer. But have courage! I have overcome the world!" It was then that I recognized those last words. They were the very words I used during my ordination as my theme, John 16:33. I ended my prayer

with a sense of assurance and determination to move on in spite of difficulties. I never thought that such a verse would continue to be my strength and reminder after fourteen years of ministry. Here, I realized that I may not be called to take suffering away in the church and in the world but here I am to be one with all who suffer to overcome everything, suffering included. To provide warmth and light to this cold and darkened church that needs to open up so that the light will penetrate the inside and that people may enter to warm each others hearts.[12]

Martin Buber says, "We listen to our inmost selves and do not know which sea we hear murmuring." John Dunne, reflecting on this statement, asks, "Is it a sea of human longing? Is it a sea of divine love?"[13] When we allow ourselves to be affected by God's longing and our own, we open ourselves to this blessed ambiguity when we encounter our own pain and the world's pain. When our hearts are filled with compassion and sorrow over the suffering of ourselves and others and moved to respond, we may not know which sea we hear murmuring—our personal mystery or the mystery of the sea of God's love, which remain inextricably related to one another.

Contemplation as a long, loving look at the real is open to whatever form the mystery chooses to reveal itself to us. It is not restricted to pain, but I think many ministers have more than our share just now. And that grieving or suffering can blind us to a deeper hope, a deeper joy, a deeper peace, and even prevent us from recognizing and responding to dazzling beauty.

Definitions of Contemplation from the Mystical Tradition

Gerald May collected some moving and lovely definitions of such contemplation from the tradition. Which ones evoke something of your own hearts and desires? Gregory of Nyssa: "Divine wakefulness with pure and naked intuition"; Ignatius of Loyola: "Finding God in all things"; Brother Lawrence, "The Pure loving gaze that finds God everywhere"; Marie of the incarnation: "Seeing God in everything and everything in God with completely extraordinary clearness and delicacy"; Elizabeth of the Trinity: "A kind of continual communion through all things by quite simply doing everything in the presence of the Trinity"; or finally, Catherine of Genoa: "Hanging by God's thread of pure love."[14] Each of these descriptions suggests a kind of seeing, a blessed intuition or perception that sees beneath the surface reality to what really is, the world in God and God in the world. Each of them bespeaks an openness of heart, a willingness to be affected by reality at the heart of the world. And each of them suggests a quality of alertness, watchfulness, and a depth of response. If we are numbed to ourselves, to life, stressed out and unconscious, we will not experience the world this way. We need to adopt whatever practices of attention, reflection, meditation, and intention that will help us keep our hearts and eyes open and responsive.

Thomas Merton recorded one such instance of contemplative oneness in *Conjectures of a Guilty Bystander.* It was, ironically, for this silent Cistercian, an urban experience.

> In Louisville, at the corner of Fourth and Walnut, in the center of the shopping district, I was suddenly overwhelmed with the realization that I loved all those people, that they were mine and I theirs, that we could not be alien to one another even though we were total strangers. It was like waking from a dream of separateness, of spurious self-isolation in a special world, the world of renunciation and supposed holiness. The whole illusion of a separate holy existence is a dream....Then it was as if I suddenly saw the secret beauty of their hearts, the depths of their hearts where neither sin nor desire nor self-knowledge can reach, the core of their reality, the person that each one is in God's eyes. If only they could all see themselves as they really are. If only we could see each other that way all the time. There would be no more war, no more hatred, no more cruelty, no more greed....I suppose the big problem would be that we would fall down and worship each other. But this cannot be seen, only believed and "understood" by a peculiar gift.[15]

He develops his insight on this experience by describing the center of the self as the "virgin point of the soul":

> At the center of our being is a point of nothingness which is untouched by sin and by illusion, a point of pure truth, a point or spark which belongs entirely to God, which is never at our disposal, from which God disposes of our lives, which is inaccessible to the fantasies of our own mind or the brutality of our own will. This little point of nothingness and of absolute poverty is the pure glory of God in us. It is so to speak [God's] name written in us....It is like a pure diamond, blazing with the invisible light of heaven. It is in everybody, and if we could see it we would see these billions of points of light coming together in the face and blaze of a sun that would make all the darkness and cruelty of life vanish completely....I have no program for this seeing. It is only given. But the gate of heaven is everywhere.[16]

Impediments to Contemplative Presence

If Merton could experience this seeing on a street corner, what impedes us? Within many modern cultures, a first obstacle is the cultural addiction to "busyness"—our inability to resist a very time-bound sense of reality. We often feel busy and like it. We maintain a mental and emotional program that fills every available moment with activity or thoughts and feelings about the next dozen things on our "To Do" lists. This constant preoccupation with time and its use constricts our feeling states and diminishes our awareness of the depth dimension of reality. Since this state of mind and heart is highly valued in our society, we are continually reinforced in such efficiency by conversation, work rewards, and unreflective agreement to this pattern.[17] Second, I believe that our self-absorption gets in the way. This self-absorption is part of our busyness, but it is also more than that. Essentially, we can not recognize the "gate of heaven" unless we have the developed capacity for presence and for a capacity to become absorbed in the other. *Presence* means being at home in ourselves, fully there. If we are preoccupied with our worries, our griefs, our "To Do" lists, we are separated, cut off from the present moment and the deeper reality of God's presence and of anyone or anything else. To be present means to be consciously experiencing, noticing, responding. It is an experience of mutuality in that we are open to another as well as ourselves, consciously available to being affected by the other. If you can remember a time when you were captivated by beauty, you'll get close. Or if you recall a time in a relationship of such mutual attending, such as the way a nursing mother and child interact, totally absorbed in one another.

Examples of Breakthrough

Let me give you an example. Some time ago, when I was in California for a congregational meeting, a good friend suggested an afternoon at the beach on the Sunday before we returned to our distant ministries. My agenda was doing my personal accounts for nine months! Of course, I wanted to do both. So I went, taking my paperwork with me. We sat on the beach talking, and she spotted something in the water. We attentively watched the horizon. Then we saw the graceful tail of one of three whales as it breached and dove into the water. Eventually, we saw one after another, three separate blow spouts spray into the air. We were, for those few moments, totally absorbed in the unexpected gift of this spectacular display of the whales. I had never seen them so close to the shore, just behind the breaker line, nor seen the wondrous tails fan above the water line. In that instance, I had found a way to honor my need for contemplative presence to the world, to open to the unexpected grace of time with a friend, and also to do a long overdue task. I really did not have to choose between them when I allowed my consciousness to open rather than narrow. Some relaxation of a pattern of relating to time had to occur. I had to loosen up my demands on myself and was rewarded by the refreshment of the sun, water, friendship, whale sighting, and a sense that God was in all of this. So much of this living contemplatively has to do with the attitude and the state of consciousness we inhabit.

Preparing a workshop or a presentation, a common activity for pastoral ministers, also requires a certain disciplined use of time, but the thinking and writing yield a different kind of contemplation—an opportunity to think about a question and one's own experience and that of others. In this process there is often a yielding to intuition, fresh discovery in the process of reflection. There is often for me the sheer joy of writing, once I get started and surprisingly discover what God might want to express through me for the sake of a particular audience. I am affected by the words I think and write. They often emerge in some unexpected way. I discover again that I know something from within my experience, informed by study, which is compelled to expression by the occasion.

I suspect this is a common experience. When we give ourselves wholly over to something without self-consciousness or performance anxiety, we find we know what to write, what to say to someone, how to be in some situation, or even quite concretely what to do. The moments of concentrated leisure—an open attentiveness clearly focused on something particular—opens to deeper levels of meaning and consciousness. From this place, whatever we say or do emerges from the depths. This is what I mean by living and ministering contemplatively. The Quakers call this following the "leading" of God, the opposite of "running ahead of grace." It requires the habit of "continually renewed immediacy" taught by Thomas Kelly.

Practices Support Contemplative Presence

We pray, meditate, center ourselves in solitary prayer so that we might ready ourselves for this ongoing experience. Meditation practices are just that—practices, ways of training attention, ways of quieting or focusing the mind, ways of fostering awareness and attentiveness, unceasingly intending the encounter with divine reality that is always present in the depths of our selves. Sometimes we get through only one or two layers of our conscious concerns. Sometimes we find ourselves deeply resting in the divine embrace. But this quality of awareness and presence is not restricted to solitary time. God is always in our midst and in our own depths; more often than not it is we who are not present. Many times, we simply cannot be—we are confronted with our own poverty, our own limitation, our own inability to take hold of ourselves and go deeper. This is why we belong to faith communities, which might offer us companions on the journey who would support us in our inability and weakness. So much of this is simply part of the human condition. Were it not for my friend, I would have missed the whales! We need others to help us practice less frenetic, less violent, less fragmented, less compulsive ways of living. In this way we counterbalance the socially constructed cultural messages that encourage the opposite by participation in an alternative, intentional social group. To do so we need to make fresh choices to live in the depth dimension of ourselves, to create supportive communities, and to open up to God. To do so we need to cultivate new practices of intention and attention that fit the current shape of our lives right now. We need to learn and practice an almost poetic quality of attentiveness. The poet Mary Oliver claims, "To pay attention, this is our endless and proper work."[18]

This quality of attention enables us to take "a long loving look at the real." It is an acquired habit or practice, perhaps even a virtue. This contemplative attitude is rooted in the very depth of ourselves—the true self that Thomas Merton attempted to describe over and over again—that part of our selves which is always in communion with the divine reality. When we allow ourselves to experience that reality—our true selves already connected to God as the center of our being—initially moments of contemplation that serve to reinforce and help us gain experience of this way of being begin to occur. Contemplative awareness is essentially a way of being and not so much a matter of doing. To experience it requires us to shift away from ego consciousness, control, and willfulness, and move toward openness, vulnerability, and willingness. This spaciousness requires considerable self-discipline to place both our intention and attention in the deep center and to choose to return to it over and over again. Gradually this quality of mystical or contemplative consciousness begins to stabilize and last for longer and longer periods of time.

Development of Contemplative Experience

Characteristically introverted persons usually first discover this sacred ground in solitary prayer, usually of a fairly long duration—thirty minutes or more at a time. Silent retreats of several days' duration help the person become accustomed to this territory; they tend to nourish deeply. When introverts move into action, they often feel somewhat deprived of their connection to this resting in God and the slower, less busy rhythm that directly supports these experiences. In the beginning stages of contemplative prayer, the slightest movement or any interruption from outside, such as a telephone ringing or a knock at the door, can disturb the subtle delicacy of contemplative prayer. As contemplation deepens, the absorption in God becomes so strong that it can be almost impossible to disrupt. From midlife on, introverts established in solitary contemplative prayer may find their most recognizable experiences of God occurring in the midst of activity. They may need more sensual stimulation or a different combination of practices. Experiences of contemplative presence may become more extroverted than they ever imagined.

Characteristically extroverted persons may despair of ever experiencing such tranquil and simple prayer. Their spirits grow restless without some external stimulation. They get bored in the inactivity and find it hard to settle in their center unless supported by a group. Their encounter with the depth of reality may more readily occur in nature, where they can become easily absorbed in some aspect of surrounding beauty. Or they might find their hearts truly burning within while listening to a popular song that feels just like a love letter from God. This form of contemplative presence is rarely described in the classical works on prayer. But it occurs quite commonly. Many whose contemplative moments match these descriptions often find it fruitful to spend some solitary prayer time returning in memory to these moments, reflecting on them further, and re-experiencing them in order to deepen appropriation of this particular touch of God. As extroverts approach the second half of life, the more introverted experience of contemplation becomes available but usually requires shorter amounts of time than introverts need.

Time Required for Contemplative Practice

Although experiences of contemplation have a timeless quality to them, one still must spend enough time in contemplative practice. Many teachers of meditation from different traditions consider twenty-five to thirty minutes of contemplative prayer, Zen sitting, insight meditation, or centering prayer twice per day the minimum to *maintain* the effects of practice that occur in the course of week-long retreats or intensives. Some of these traditions do month-long or three month-long retreats. Most sponsor a day of focused practice once a month. These longer periods of practice help stabilize consciousness in this attentive way of living and being. The removal of all the external events that so easily and exquisitely unsettle us enables the practitioner to recognize how much we ourselves are contributing to our distraction and inability to concentrate. Once we achieve some focus and concentration in the protective environment of the retreat, there is greater possibility that one will gradually integrate this way of being into daily life. Many of these contemporary adaptations of ancient contemplative practices recognize that the process is one of continually beginning over and over again.

While a certain amount of time is required, there are enormous individual differences. Some people do better with less daily time and longer, more intense periods on a day off or on a weekend. The amount of time needed varies with personality, stage of prayer development, and life circumstances. During times of transition or major change or challenge, more time is required.

Contemplative Practices within Ministry

When active contemplatives resume their daily rounds, practice changes. It always does. I am not certain that pastoral ministers have consciously thought about and adopted practices that help maintain this contemplative attitude toward life, but I do suspect that many have made some discoveries. I'm not sure we've dared share them with others. There are countless odd moments during the day, especially when we are changing from one activity to another, that we can claim for a few deep breaths and a return to a more centered consciousness. In those minutes, we can halt the preoccupations and assumptions of our internal taskmaster. Many of us spend a great deal of time traveling, either driving or riding public transit. Such time is often one of those "spaces" we can fill with distraction, or we can reattune ourselves to God's music within or allow ourselves to move from self-absorption to an openness toward encounter and a reality that is always more than us. These internal choices remain ours to make; we often fail to notice we are making a choice at all.

Experience of God in Ministry

The first two kinds of contemplative experiences I described are extremely common for anyone who perseveres in some form of regular practice of prayer. However, I find increasingly that many apostolically motivated men and women are experiencing similar kinds of contemplative awareness in the midst of ministry or in relationships characterized by caring. I also see emerging what I sometimes name "new experiences" of God related to the prophetic utterances or activities of those who promote justice from a religious perspective and a correlative experience in contemplative prayer when situations of injustice or victims of injustice seemingly invade one's prayer.

I suspect that the depth with which ministers have integrated the social justice agenda of the church into our commitments has dramatically increased our experience of pain, compassion, and conflict even within our prayer experience. The appearance of such unsettling forms of awareness may be very disorienting, because we had come to expect contemplative awareness and prayer to be comforting and peaceful, a time of refreshment.

Contemplative Experience While Caregiving

This may be the most common experience of ministers. One under-reported aspect of the important Nygren and Ukeritis study on "The Future of Religious Life" was the "Caring People Study." This part of the research consisted of intensive interviews with religious who were identified by others as being consistently and particularly noted for their ability to care for others. Those who identified them to the researchers experienced their caregiving as nonmanipulative and unselfish. Since the altruistic capacity to care for others is an essential competency for ministry, the findings about caregiving can fruitfully be extended to others. The investigators sought to learn from these outstanding caregivers, as distinguished from codependent, compulsive "do-gooders," how best to describe such altruistic love as an enduring characteristic of apostolic religious life. The researchers were surprised to discover that these extraordinary caregivers rarely suffered "burnout."

> The…study found that, in contrast to typical religious, religious who are perceived as unusually helpful, understanding and caring feel closer to and more trusting of God, who is seen as the source of healing and care….Caring religious connect divine assistance, in contrast to individual effort, with healing experiences. They are less self-controlling and more spontaneously inclined to generosity.[19]

In addition, these caring religious also seek and value the experience of contemplation. They have not been seduced by the "my activity is my prayer" deception. They both treasure their experiences of contemplation in solitary prayer, and they "demonstrate a greater interpersonal involvement in caring experiences." They "describe these relationships as growing and mutual, and as containing a wider meaning or significance beyond the immediate relationship." Their experiences of giving and receiving in their ministry are deeply meaningful beyond each instance. "Finally, these religious experience more joy in caring and zest for living. This contrasts with typical religious, who describe their caring as a response to a need in themselves such as caring out of duty or repayment, or caring in response to special needs such as illness, rejection or trauma of others."

Even more telling, this study found, for these religious,

> there is a third force in the relationship that might…be called…God. The caring religious stays in close touch with God and wants to share [God] with others. When encountering a person in need, the goal of the caring religious is not primarily to relieve his or her suffering, but to create a three-way relationship in which Jesus and the Gospels' values are deeply involved.
>
> Helpers of this type do not see themselves as agents in the process; at most they are partners with…the real source of helping. They do not feel ultimately responsible. For this reason and also because the helping in itself is joyous, caring religious do not as readily "burn out."

This description also explains why caring religious who are so motivated are perceived to be helpful rather than manipulative. Because they so obviously believe they can do nothing of themselves and want to establish a mutually rewarding relationship, caring religious are not perceived as egotistically threatening the self-esteem, interpersonal power or independence of others.... Caring religious live an operative Christology which is simultaneously imminent and transcendent....The immediacy of presence of the caring person to another is possible because of this effort to mediate God, whom they see as benevolent...and the source of their action.

...Those who learn to be authentically caring are inclined spontaneously to generosity, trusting and aware that God acts in and through them. This level of freedom requires viewing God as a benevolent authority in whose name one acts as mediator.

These characteristics, I believe, are richly suggestive of what a "contemplative attitude toward life" looks like to others and what it feels like to the minister within ordinary experiences of caring. It suggests both a program for ministerial formation and a program for renewal. Each of us might well ask, "Do I perceive my apostolic work as an arduous 'To Do' list through which I compulsively rush, or is my ministry so infused with God's activity and presence that I am regularly nourished by God even while I pour out my love upon those who enter my circle of care?" These broad descriptions and observations apply to the entire network of sustaining relationships that enjoy a quality of mutuality: community, family, friendships, colleagues, and those for whom we care in our daily ministerial round.

New Experiences of Socially Engaged Contemplation

There are, I believe, yet other "new" experiences that many pastoral ministers are having. I saw them mirrored in a very helpful way to me in a young peace activist who at the time was still within her original Quaker tradition. Subsequently, I find them frequently in pastoral people whose experience inserts them into situations of oppression or suffering.

Jennifer Haines found herself "led" repeatedly to intercessory prayer at Rocky Flats, a nuclear weapons plant near Denver, Colorado. Her persistence in prayer led to lengthy incarcerations for her nonviolent resistance to the pervasive violence in our culture, most dramatically symbolized by our enchantment with producing ever more deadly weapons of destruction. Haines's autobiographical narrative, *Bread and Water: A Spiritual Journey,* poignantly and powerfully demonstrates some of the dynamics of contemplative consciousness when it is "socially engaged." In her spiritual journey, she carefully describes her constant attentiveness to the consequences of her choices, which she tries to embrace from a stance of peacemaking rather than of contributing to the escalating violence in society, including the prison situation. A common experience of many peace activists, who work carefully with the dynamics of responding nonviolently when themselves attacked for their prophetic speech or actions, is that reflection time is essential prior to and after acts of civil disobedience. The intensity of emotional reactions in oppressive and unjust situations is extremely challenging. It requires the achieved capacity to take hold of one's "passionate thoughts" and impulses, as the desert elders taught, in order not to respond to violence, manipulation, or abusive power simply with anger and opposition. A passage of Jennifer's prepublication version of the manuscript is an exquisite description of the kind of flooding with pain that may occur if we really allow ourselves to care about the poor and to walk in solidarity with them. This moment occurred while she was praying when she lived in an inner-city Denver neighborhood.

> I loved the people a lot. My bed was under a third-floor window that overlooked the street. I would sit sometimes at the window praying. One never-to-be forgotten time, I opened myself to all the pain of everyone on our street—and throughout the neighborhood—and all over the city—and found myself imaging the city as one huge, open, festering wound, raw and bleeding. The pain was almost more than I could bear. I had to pour it out to God—in the most powerful, impassioned, yearning intercessory prayer that I had every experienced. I say then that the heart and well-spring of intercession is pain. To love is to make ourselves vulnerable to pain, and the pain sends us back to God in prayer. Carrying the pain of the world is the work of the intercessor. I felt it and understood it and embraced it."[20]

This is a remarkable testimony. Her distinctive call is to the work of intercessory prayer. But this is no sheltered, socially disengaged contemplative. This is a woman who touches real pain in real people. By feeling it, opening her heart to it, she is able not only to be a compassionate presence in this very poor neighborhood, she herself becomes a spiritual transformer. She pours it back out to God in yearning. The pain enters her, but, and this is vital, moves through her back into God.

Contemplative Intercession and Co-Redemption

I am increasingly convinced that ministers burn out and lose heart in our justice activities because too many begin by carrying so much pain, simply absorbing it numbly without ever turning this pain and their hearts expectantly back to God. Jennifer's experience is not Tabor; it is clearly pure Calvary. Yet unless we really believe in the saving power of Christ's death and resurrection, we dumbly and numbly distance ourselves from God instead of leaning on the heart of Christ and plumbing more deeply the mystery of redemptive love.

Contemplative presence to suffering persons or to situations in the world is a grace. It is one way contemplatives share in the redemptive activity of Christ. Jennifer, at first, is nearly overwhelmed by the intensity of pain she senses just in her neighborhood and city. She instinctively realizes she cannot bear the pain alone. She "pours it out to God." This response requires a certain level of spiritual maturity—a surrender to God. Her glimpse of this socially generated pain and suffering evokes in her a form of intercessory prayer in which she helps transform that pain through her connection with those who suffer and her connection with God. She contributes to transformation on the spiritual level, and she herself is transformed toward compassionate loving if she maintains her connection to God's all-embracing love and compassion. She, of herself, cannot carry this kind of pain, nor does God expect that of us. Yet we are called to embrace those who suffer.

The Shock of Contemplative Suffering

Such moments of insight and contemplative love often take a person by surprise. "Contemplation requires the willingness, honesty, and courageous desire to face into ourselves just as we are and our world just as it is—no distortions, no exclusions, no avoidances, no anesthesia. It means entering our own emptiness, our unrequited longing."[21] The effect of encountering seemingly unresolvable suffering is perilous. We discover our helplessness in the face of such suffering, our fear, our resistance to suffering at all. Some instinctively isolate ourselves even from God. Instead of instinctively giving this pain into the divine embrace, we experience it in a state of separation from God. Suffering that evokes such a strong, almost unconscious level of resistance is also capable of profoundly challenging our view of God and our ability to maintain hope in the face of the enormity of evil that God does not seem to mitigate.

When scenes of suffering and pain invade prayer, prayer itself may be the place of struggle against hopelessness, despair, and negative feelings about others. According to Gerald May, "Contemplation may lead to deep trust and faith, but not to uninterrupted peace of mind. It opens us in love to the suffering and brokenness of the world as much as to its joy and beauty."[22] It is easy to confuse this searing and transformative quality of contemplative experience with "vicarious traumatization," a clinical description emerging in psychotherapy, which notes the traumatizing effects on the therapist or others in a helping relationship of witnessing the psychological and physical effects of trauma on those with whom they work.[23]

I have found it helpful to suggest to directees who discover the world's pain invading their contemplative experience to consciously place their pain and the world's pain in God's heart. In this way, the directees can join their love and active concern for actual people with whom they are connected to God's infinite, supportive love. They can let this kind of suffering pass through their hearts and awareness, giving it back over to God without absorbing it and becoming possessed by it. I learned this approach from Joanna Macy, who describes a process called "breathing through," from the socially engaged Buddhist tradition. She works with breath, imaging the transformation of suffering by breathing it into one's body, directing it to pass through the heart, and out of one's heart into the "world net."[24] It can easily be adapted to embrace healthy heart practices and a theology of co-redemption within Christian practice.

Such moments of exquisite pain, which are both personal and social or structural, are uncomfortable, complex, and confusing. There is clearly a spiritual form of interbeing or intercommunion as well as a physical form. If all life on this planet is a complex interaction among persons and all other forms of life, so too do persons affect one another spiritually in profound ways. If pastoral ministers are integrated into the larger community and engaged with ever-expanding communities, we can expect to be affected by, as well as contribute to, both social grace and social sin.

The shift in our worldview that is emerging from the new cosmology fosters a shift in contemplative experience from the personal and peaceful immersion in divine presence and love to experiencing mystically the interdependence of every aspect of the creation, including that of oppressor and oppressed, the mystery of evil that seeks to be transformed through the ongoing offer of redemptive grace.

Case Study

An experience of a recent retreatant is useful for showing some of the dynamics and characteristics of contemplative experiences. There was in the course of this religious woman's retreat a series of profound mystical experiences related to the mystery of the cross as she was uniquely experiencing it.[25] It was the fourth retreat she had made with me, and she had sensed that, prior to the retreat itself, something very profound was already inviting her. The overall result of this retreat experience was a breakthrough into a sustained mystical union that had been impending for several years, but that was impeded or delayed by a pattern of excessive busyness and avoidance of contemplative prayer during her cycle of demanding apostolic ministry. On retreat, she gave herself over fully to contemplative prayer. Witnessing her experience yielded for me both awe and a deeper understanding of some of the dynamics of these experiences that I had been exploring for some time.

The retreat began with attraction to a sculpture of Jesus in agony, which sister had discovered and photographed in the Garden of Gethsemane on a recent pilgrimage to the Holy Land. She brought it with her in addition to Bonaventure's Tree of Life. She felt drawn to begin her retreat in the mystery of life-giving suffering. This imaged scene of the suffering one in agony eventually became the place of unitive love for her. The cross, although a locus of suffering, was also experienced as life-giving. But the process of the retreat required that she allow the pain to open her to God's love in the world and for her. She began her retreat feeling the burden of empathy that opens her to so much pain in ministry. She actually prayed for this grace: "Give me the grace to desire to be with you (Jesus) in this scene (agony). Help me to surrender, to go with you where you lead. Help me to contemplate my sins and the sins of the world that contribute to this alienation and, then, to find you in the experience of powerlessness, anger, fear, anxiety, loss or whatever else surfaces."

Here was a pastoral counselor and campus minister in touch with the effects of walking with others in pain, aware of her own pain, and a willingness to seek God in and through it intentionally. Later the same day, her prayer began to be answered. The compline service was celebrated on the rooftop that night under the summer sky. A large fire was lit as the central symbol for the service, and poetic lines about God's creative fiery spirit were read from Hildegard of Bingen. This retreatant, however, recalled the television scenes of the embassy bombing in Nairobi, and was flooded with scenes of the surrounding area and the people she had served as a missionary there several years before.

Yet, she stayed with the experience of social sin and the world's pain in the company of Jesus. However, the suffering of the innocent children led her to compose and sing a rather cynical song of lament detailing the effects of terrorists and our indifference. The refrain was a Kyrie...a plea for mercy. As the experience deepened, she was tempted to engage in this presence to suffering *alone*. She was helped by the invitation to seek God in this prayer and take with her the company of any other helpers, saints, angels. And she was invited to be in this prayer in a positive intercessory mode.

Despite predictable resistance to the deepening mystical experience and its painful qualities, sister responded to gentle challenge around the resistance, and amazing transformations occurred. As her unitive prayer shifted to spontaneously imaged scenes with Jesus, even within the thematic archetype of suffering and redemption, many scenes depicted increasing mutuality with Jesus, and the song of lamentation transformed into a song of jubilation. The prior year she had scenes of the radiant, transfigured Christ; this retreat was the crucified one. In one of her meditations, the Christ commissioned her to participate in redemption. These images led her not only to pray for the victims of injustice but to be aware of what she could do personally to alleviate the causes. Her prayer then deepened still further into being crucified with Christ. She was able to stay with this challenging experience, which became increasingly more mutual in the relationship with Christ and which then began to be filled with images of life...nurturance, flowing water, and others. This led to the transformation of the garden of union and to spiritual gifts that would help her not be overwhelmed by the negative suffering in the world. Gradually, the experience of God moved on through a complex set of images that integrated many polarities in her life and brought to completion an entire movement toward transformation, healing, and union.

Features of Socially Engaged Contemplation

There is much we can learn from this sister's experience. Her prayer experience was consoling, but not in a stereotypical way. If she were unable or unwilling to stay with the unfolding depth of her mystical experience, she may not have been able to go through the pain of her images and the resolution of her negative emotions in response to them. Her contemplative experience grew out of her connection with the pain of her world. She experienced her world as Jesus did in and through her. The compassion of Jesus enabled her to contemplatively encounter the brokenness in her world, in her, in the people with whom and to whom she ministers. This type of image does not arise in a person who is not in touch with herself and the griefs, hopes, and joys of her world. This kind of imaged prayer expresses her intuitive connection with Jesus present in her world, in her, in her compassion, in her pain, in her ministerial activity and contemplative prayer. This is a unitive image of Christ the lover and crucified one, with whom she shared a mission of redemption or liberation. She could let the pain and suffering of the world affect her because of her contemplative union with Jesus, which God reveals to her in her prayer. Her abiding union with Jesus became conscious in her prayer because she was moving through her world and her ministry in an ongoing contemplative connection with God. This is truly a moment of transformation, a moment of revelation for her: she was not as alone as she felt, and yet she felt quite helpless. Somehow, the felt connection with Jesus enabled her not to be daunted by the seeming helplessness. Does anything in this experience ring true to your own experience of encountering the pain of the world? Do you not also experience both feelings of helplessness and simultaneously a mysterious empowerment?

Within the retreat experience, this sister was keenly aware of the support she was receiving from the process of the spiritual direction sessions, liturgy, and the natural environment. Although this graced experience was clearly God's action in her, she needed accompaniment, much of it silently empathic.

This was an important form of social support combined with her spiritual companions in the process, the founders of her religious tradition. In addition, some of the emotional intensity was focused and released through the use of expressive arts. She drew a series of pictures expressing key images she received in prayer, composed and sang her lamentation, and she used a variety of gestures and postures in her prayer. She also used movement meditation and other forms of physical activity to help her release the increasing energy of the experiences and to ground herself afterward.

Finally, it seems to me that her experience, as well as Jennifer Haines's, illuminates another key aspect of this contemplative experience of the world's pain. Each person seems to be affected by a local or particular form of social suffering. There is a specific and personal connection to a person or situation. For instance, Jennifer was aware of her neighborhood and city. The retreatant was connected to the city of Nairobi in her personal history. The connection is specific, not universal or global. It is as if the situation or situations to which one has personal connection is sufficient. One does not need to be flooded with everything in all parts of the world at once. Rather, when the heart opens compassionately to one event, person, or situation that enters contemplative awareness, everything else is also present but does not need to become explicitly visualized or worked with. The retreatant was focused quite clearly on particular instances, and that particularity of focus contributed to her personal transformation from helplessness and fear to active compassion, concern, and strength within the contemplative experience.

Conclusion

Immersion in the world just as it is—both its dazzling beauty and its terrifying darkness—opens in us a distinctively different kind of contemplative experience, which is rooted in embracing all of it. It is a result of our relinquishing the protectiveness of ghetto Catholicism prior to Vatican II, which often separated us from the world's pain through the structures of ministry and church. Today we are more involved, more aware, and more vulnerable. We are more deeply affected by our complex social awareness unless we defend against it by assuaging the pain with consumerism or other forms of distraction instead of undergoing the transformation of that pain and of ourselves in a contemplative process. We can avoid both the pain and the transformative process through some other form of "numbing," of restricting our feeling and our care.

We are so bombarded by the enormity of suffering and injustice in our world that it is easy to become immobilized. Unless we learn to plumb this mystery, and not simply be overwhelmed by it, we can easily close off our openness to the very real concerns that urgently require some response from us. But to do so, to learn to be contemplative with our hands as well as our hearts, requires us to allow the pain of the world or at least that of those individuals and situations to which we are called to respond to actually affect us, to touch us deeply, to somehow reveal to us our neediness and helplessness. It is a subtle combination of acting wherever and however we can, and at the same time recognizing, as the religious in the Caring People Study did, that we do all of this with God. It includes the realization that we can be present even when we can't stop the injustice or completely relieve the suffering. At the same time, such a union of contemplation and action requires us to actually live in God. As Jennifer Haines did, we need to learn how to let life's sorrows ripen in us, to let pain pass through our hearts. Too often we stop right with our own hearts and absorb the distress without letting these sorrows pass through us back into God's heart. And finally, it requires active strategies to remain in connection and relationship with others who support in us this contemplative path and active concern for the world.

As pastoral ministers we cannot exercise the prophetic dimensions of ministry unless we are sufficiently present to God to receive any clear word, leading, or invitation to action in response to concrete situations. I believe we can only truly become both contemplative and prophetic as a unity. Prophesy emerges from a deeply contemplative attitude toward life. It is just as concerned with energizing others with hope and promise and possibility as it is with grieving and denunciation. Only experiences of amazement or genuine wonderment empower an authentic word of hope. These experiences are part of the lifeline for socially engaged contemplatives. They are among the means of keeping hope alive. The role of prophets is to envision a future that is better than the present. *Better* in this context means truer, less deceptive, an overcoming of illusions that maintain radical states of bondage and injustice.

I mentioned previously that I find reading narratives and poetry, listening to music, and inviting my body to mediate grace helpful. One of the reasons I am currently attracted to these expressive forms is that they are concrete. I often find my own experience mirrored in the experiences of writers. Contemplative life is always particular. Stories and images of actual experience facilitate a contemplative life that is both real and possible. As pastoral ministers, we can only humbly strive to respond to the concrete invitations of grace that are ours. But I do believe there is persistent grace in our midst. I do believe that our personal and collective journeys are amazing. We can reorient ourselves over and over again to the deep and abiding Godward focus of our living. We can adopt or adapt whatever new disciplines or practices will assist us to do what we most want to do in this new context. When our contemplation is socially engaged, we can help one another discover light through the darkness, peace in our restlessness, concentration in our dispersion. We can dare to speak our hopes and dreams and desires for a spiritual quality of living and for a more just world; we can help one another find our unique apostolic-contemplative rhythms in our speed-crazed world.

Notes

1. Cover, *Utne Reader* (March–April 1997).

2. Jay Walljasper, "The Speed Trap," *Utne Reader* (March–April 1997), 45.

3. "How Do You Put on the Brakes?" *Utne Reader* (March–April 1997), 47.

4. Cited by Walljasper, "Speed Trap," 43.

5. Robert J. Egan, "Contemplation in the Context of Contemporary Culture: Reflections on Spiritual Direction in Dialogue with Cultural Analysis and Criticism," Unpublished Keynote for Spiritual Directors International Conference, February 1990, Burlingame, California, 4.

6. Ibid., 4.

7. Gerald R. May, *The Awakened Heart: Living Beyond Addiction* (San Francisco: HarperCollins, 1991), 192.

8. Ibid., 193.

9. Egan, "Contemplation," 4.

10. Walter J. Burghardt, "Contemplation: A Long Loving Look at the Real," *Church* (Winter 1989), 24–28.

11. William Barry and William Connolly, *The Practice of Spiritual Direction* (New York: Seabury, 1982), 49.

12. Prayer Journal, March 14, 1997, used with permission.

13. John S. Dunne, *Loves Mind* (Notre Dame, Ind.: University of Notre Dame Press, 1993), 113.

14. Gerald May, "The Experience of Contemplation," *Spiritual Book News* (May 1992).

15. Thomas Merton, *Conjectures of a Guilty Bystander* (Garden City, N.Y.: Image Books, 1966), 156–58.

16. Ibid., 158.

17. I develop this theme in greater detail in "On Resisting the Demon of Busyness," *Spiritual Life* (Summer 1995), 79–89.

18. Mary Oliver, "Yes! No!" *White Pine: Poems and Prose Poems* (New York: Harcourt Brace and Company, 1994), 8.

19. David Nygren and Miriam Ukiritis, "Executive Summary, Forus," *Origins* 122 (September 1992): 269, for this and all subsequent citations from the study.

20. Jennifer Haines, *Bread and Water: A Spiritual Journey* (Maryknoll, N.Y.: Orbis, 1997).

21. May, *Awakened Heart*, 193.

22. Ibid., 193.

23. See Laurie Pearlman and Karin Saakvitne, *Trauma and the Therapist* (New York: Norton, 1995), esp. ch. 13: "Vicarious Traumatization: How Trauma Therapy Affects the Therapist." By definition: "Vicarious traumatization is a process through which the therapist's inner experience is negatively transformed through empathic engagement with clients' trauma material" (279). It "results in profound disruptions in the therapists's frame of reference, that is, his basic sense of identity, world view, and spirituality. Multiple aspects of the therapist and his life are affected, including his affect tolerance, fundamental psychological needs, deeply held beliefs about self and others, interpersonal relationships, internal imagery, and experience of his body and physical presence in the world"(280). The same researchers found that the negative effects of vicarious traumatization "are modifiable when addressed actively" (281). Avoiding isolation in the process of dealing with others' trauma are among the ways of actively addressing VT in the helper.

24. Joanna Macy, "Taking Heart: Spiritual Exercises for Social Activists," *The Path of Compassion: Writings on Socially Engaged Buddhism*, ed. Fred Eppsteiner (Berkeley: Parallax Press, 1985).

25. Used with permission.

Keith J. Egan

28. Contemplative Meditation: A Challenge from the Tradition

Ministry without prayer is a body without a heart. But, what kind of prayer keeps ministry pulsing with life, the life of grace? Is it not prayer that, in the imagery of St. Bernard, brings one into that wine cellar where one is anointed by the Holy Spirit? Ministry that flows from this wine cellar is under the guidance of God's spirit, whom John of the Cross calls one's chief agent, mover, and principal guide.[1] Modern Canon Law, that of 1917 and 1983, listed various forms of prayer including "mental prayer" as the responsibility of the then officially recognized ministers and ministers-to-be of the church: clerics, religious, seminarians, and novices.[2] However, in this post–Vatican II era, when ministry is no longer restricted to ordained ministers and to religious, the question must be asked: What kind of prayer is needed for an effective spirit-filled ministry by all who are called to minister in the church, whether they be lay, religious, deacons, or priests?

Of course, the eucharist, which is "the source and summit of the Christian life,"[3] is at the heart of all Christian ministry and is an essential nourishment of all Christian prayer. Moreover, a prayerful hearing of the Word of God, in public and in private, is another necessary component for a life of effective ministry. But, in this essay I shall make a case for contemplative meditation as especially appropriate for those who minister in this post–Vatican II era, the New Pentecost, when it is time for a greater sensitivity to the Holy Spirit in life, prayer, and ministry.

In a day when the language of meditation and contemplation is no longer as precise as it once was and is, in fact, often ambiguous, I will begin with a working definition of Christian *contemplative meditation.* I take contemplative meditation to be that practice of interior prayer that especially prepares one for the transforming power of the presence of Jesus, whether that presence is mystical or not. This claim for the appropriateness of contemplative meditation is a challenge for the ministers in the Christian churches of our day. Is there not more than enough evidence that Christian churches need to become more contemplative, that is, to live more fully under the influence of the Holy Spirit, the architect of Christ's presence, as Christians work to build up the body of Christ?

In a lucid essay about what is to be done in the face of the overwhelming secularization of modern culture, Louis Dupré calls for a turn inward so that there may be a *"personal* conversion of the heart."[4] I believe that contemplative meditation is such a turn inward, a journey into the core of one's being, into the depths of the human heart. This turn inward is a turn to eventual silence and wordless prayer.[5] While careful reflection on the scriptures, especially on the Gospels, is essential to every minister's life, there is a need to go beyond the intellectual reflections that occur in discursive meditation; in fact, the need is to let the Spirit take one beyond rational discourse *about* God into the presence of the living God. Contemplative meditation is a practice that prepares one to hand oneself over to the living and loving God so that one may minister fully aware of one's baptismal configuration to Jesus Christ.

The signs of our times appear everywhere to beckon the Christian churches to become more contemplative. The practice of contemplative meditation heeds a widely recognized call to seek and find God within, as Saint Augustine so memorably did and about which he so eloquently wrote: "you were within me and I was in the external world....You were with me, and I was not with you."[6] Teresa of Avila had the same conviction about where to seek God. She wrote, "Within oneself, very clearly, is the best place to look; and it's not necessary to go to heaven, nor any further than our own selves; for to do so is to tire the spirit and distract the soul, without gaining as much fruit."[7] Teresa admitted that she took a page from Augustine when she recommended the journey within through what she called the prayer of recollection.[8] These two great contemplative voices from the tradition compellingly point to a place within where we can seek and where we can find God whom Augustine found to be "more inward than my most inward part and higher than the highest element within me."[9]

In our day the call for a more contemplative prayer is writ very large on the horizons of those with the desire to lead a deeper spiritual life. One instance is the huge interest in centering prayer of various kinds. William Johnston, that astute student of contemplative prayer has observed

> the number of modern people who are practising meditation and find themselves drawn into the deeper states of consciousness that are ordinarily called mystical. Beginning with the repetition of a mantra, or awareness of the breathing, or the savoring of a phrase from sacred Scripture, they feel drawn beyond thinking and reasoning to a unitive consciousness wherein they rest silently in the presence of the great mystery that envelops the whole universe.[10]

Johnston is taking note of the numerous people of faith who have chosen to practice some form of contemplative meditation. I take it that Father Johnston is here using the word *mystical* to mean what occurs beyond the rational movements of the mind, not necessarily the mystical stages outlined by a Teresa of Avila in the higher dwelling places of her *Interior Castle*. These higher stages of mystical prayer were made even more distinct from one another by theology in the post–Reformation era. The rigid lines between what is ascetical and mystical and between meditation and contemplation were not present in the patristic era nor in the earlier Middle Ages.[11] These divisions have a place in understanding spiritual progress, especially in the hands of wise and seasoned spiritual guides. However, these distinctions when too finely drawn can give a false portrait of God's subtle work within the human spirit, as if God can work in only one way or that the spirit is not active in the human heart throughout one's earthly pilgrimage from baptism to death. Teresa of Jesus discerned the beginnings of God's mystical work as slow, deliberate, and intermittent as is evident in her discovery of the difference between the prayer of quiet and passive recollection.[12] God's work is the work of love drawing the human person toward loving union with God's self. Contemplative meditation is an openness to this loving divine activity however and wherever it may lead one. This prayer is contemplative in the same sense that, throughout the Middle Ages, the monastic life was described as contemplative life, that is, the life of the monk or nun was considered a readiness for God's gift of contemplation.

It is not necessary to consider contemplative meditation in the extraordinary sense in which we have labeled an event as "mystical." Karl Rahner has enriched our understanding of the spiritual journey with his description of mysticism that can be ordinary/everyday mysticism[13] or a mysticism that has encountered God so deeply within the human person that she is fully transformed by Christ's presence. This latter mystical transformation culminates in what Teresa of Avila calls "spiritual marriage." When Rahner wrote that "the devout Christian of the future will either be a 'mystic,' one who has 'experienced' something, or he will cease to be anything at all,"[14] his description is of someone who has experienced *something,* not necessarily the higher reaches of the mystical life. Professor Dupré interprets Rahner in this way:

> I am reminded of Rahner's remark that Christianity in the future will be mystical or it will not be at all. That expression is too strong only if we consider the mystical as the exceptional rather than as the spiritual experience that belongs to the essence of religion, accessible to all believers. The original meaning of *mystical* included the common Christian awareness—at whatever degree—of a divine presence in Scripture, religious doctrine, liturgy, and nature.[15]

Women and men in our age have rediscovered meditation of all kinds, but there seems to be a widespread desire for something more than the mental prayer and discursive meditation that was the spiritual fare of the era that preceded Vatican II. That something more is the transformation that occurs when God takes human consciousness beyond its own powers of rational discourse into the divine presence, all the way from ordinary baptismal grace to the extraordinary union with God in love, and on into what John of the Cross calls "that beatific transformation..., a total transformation in the immense love of God."[16]

In this discussion of contemplative meditation, I am not referring to mystical phenomena but to that gifted mindfulness of the presence of Jesus Christ that is the goal of Christian prayer. It is no mere coincidence that, when so many Christians seek to live more consciously in the presence of Jesus, the foremost English-speaking historian of mysticism, Bernard McGinn, has argued for presence as the principal model for understanding Western mysticism.[17] Is not presence, mutual presence, a requirement of all truly human relationships whether they be with one another or with God? Contemplative meditation is a practice that regularly orients one toward living consciously in the presence of Jesus, so that the spirit of Jesus can accomplish what is God's will for her. I am making a case from the tradition for the practice of that meditation which seeks the transformation from self-absorption to an awareness of the divine presence.

For many years it has been my privilege to teach the Christian theological and spiritual traditions. As I have made my way through these traditions, I have been struck by the persistence of the call to prayer that savors the presence of God. What follows are some moments in the Jewish-Christian tradition that I have chosen to illustrate this call to a more contemplative prayer. These moments are a recurring theme, a melody, that keeps appearing as a reminder of an important facet of our spiritual tradition. This recurring theme culminates in contemporary movements like centering prayer, advocated by Thomas Keating and Basil Pennington, or in John Main's Christian meditation. This essay can hardly be a history of these moments, nor can it be even an exhaustive list of these occurrences in the tradition. Rather I will point out those figures and texts that have left me with a conviction that the present movement of contemplative prayer needs to be taken seriously because the tradition invites us to do so. Though these moments are personal selections made as a result of my study of the tradition, they are, I feel, significant moments in anyone's reading of the tradition.

I begin my walk through the tradition by taking note of the Hebrew root *haga* in the Old Testament. *Haga* connotes oral recitation. But, it is clear from the contexts in which this root appears that *haga* suggests much more than mere recitation. Note the earliest instance of *haga,* which occurs in Joshua 1:8: "This book of the law shall not depart out of your mouth; you shall meditate *(haga)* on it day and night, so that you may be careful to act in accordance with all that is written in it." Meditation identifies one with God's law, which is a manifestation of God's presence. More is intended here by *haga* than repetition. In verse 5 of this chapter the Lord says, "As I was with Moses, so I will be with you; I will not fail you or forsake you." The Lord ends with this promise: "The Lord your God is with you wherever you go"(1:9). Here *haga* and divine presence are associated in what could be considered an external sense rather than an inner presence. But who would limit God's presence to the external in this context or in other Old Testament uses of this root word?

Better known, but in the same vein as the text from Joshua, is Psalm 1:2: "Their delight is in the law of the Lord, and on his law they meditate *(haga)* day and night." This verse became a favorite of patristic and medieval writers. John Cassian quotes one informant from the desert who recommended that meditation "should consume all the days and nights of our life...."[18] At the beginning of his *Sermons on the Song of Songs,* Bernard of Clairvaux reminded his monastic audience that this meditation day and night on God's law was a foundation of their spiritual maturity.[19] Later in the same sermons, Bernard consoles a weary monk with the promise of the presence of "the compassionate Lord." Bernard cites in this context Psalm 119:97 on meditation on the law all day long and then states that "when we meditate on his law day and night, let us be assured that the Bridegroom is present...." Psalm 1:2 had a far-reaching impact on Western spirituality through the Carmelite formula of life (1206–1214), later to be known as the Carmelite Rule. Henceforth, this biblical verse occupied a distinctive place at the heart of the Carmelite contemplative challenge "to live following Jesus Christ," since the Carmelite is to remain in or near the cell "meditating day and night on the law of the Lord."[20] This provision of the Carmelite Rule prescribed the solitude with God that gave birth to the Carmelite contemplative tradition and to its consequent mystical manifestations.

But, I return now to the *haga* tradition of the Old Testament. The inward thrust of *haga* is evident in Psalm 19:14: "Let the words of my mouth and the meditation of my heart be acceptable to you, O Lord, my rock and my redeemer," and in Psalm 49:3: "My mouth shall speak wisdom; the meditation of my heart shall be understanding." One other example from the psalms is, "I commune with my heart in the night; I meditate and search my spirit" (77:7). While *haga* involves recitation, *haga* does not remain merely on the lips, but it includes especially, in context, a descent into the heart, where the human and the divine encounter each other.

In the Greek of the Septuagint Old Testament and in the Christian scriptures the *haga* root becomes the Greek *meléte,* a word that carries the meaning of caring for something, taking to heart, practicing diligently. This notion of practice or exercise is close to the meaning of the Latin *meditatio,* which translated *meléte* when the Christian Bible was turned into Latin.[21] The Christian tradition of meditation is, in fact, a movement into the heart, beyond mere mental inquiry. Thus in Hebrew, Greek, and Latin were laid the seeds of a practice that has a long history that is still developing in our time—interior prayer that takes one deep into the mystery of divine presence within the human heart. This tradition of *haga, meléte,* and *meditatio* is a way of tracing the Christian practice of meditation back into its biblical roots.

The tradition of Christian meditation has constantly been reinforced by the reports of Jesus who went off alone to pray: "In the morning, while it was still very dark, he got up and went out to a deserted place, and there he prayed"(Mk 1:35)[22] The disciples were witnesses of the regular recourse to solitary prayer by their teacher. However, we have few reports of the manner or content of the prayer of Jesus. Yet, there is the opportunity to eavesdrop at Gethsemane and at the Last Supper discourses of John's Gospel and, of course, we have received that paradigm of Christian prayer, the Lord's Prayer. What we know is that Jesus was a man of prayer who intimately experienced God. In that intimacy was revealed through Jesus to Christians the gift of God's fatherhood.

Contemplative meditation is a prayer like that of Jesus that opens one up to intimacy with God. Christians have discovered the gift of that intimacy through the centuries. Ignatius of Loyola led those who made his spiritual exercises to intimacy with God through, for example, a colloquy that can become like the conversation of a friend "who speaks to another."[23] For Teresa of Avila prayer was an intimate sharing between friends.[24] John of the Cross tells us that the Dark Night of the spirit brings "loving friendship with God."[25] John of the Cross, in fact, was bold enough to claim that the contemplative could so grow in intimacy with God that she would experience a certain equality with God, an equality born of profound friendship with God. John wrote, "Souls possess the same goods by participation that the Son possesses by nature. As a result they are truly gods by participation, equals and companions of God," and "Since the soul in this state possesses perfect love, she is called the bride of the Son of God, which signifies equality with him. In this equality of friendship the possessions of both are held in common...."[26] Contemplative meditation is a journey into this intimacy with God. Ignatius, John, and Teresa prayed in such a way that they experienced God as a friend. Such friendship is the stuff of great and creative ministry. No better evidence exists than a ministry to the world initiated by Ignatius and which continues to this day in his Jesuit family and among those touched by Jesuit ideals. Teresa, who would have loved to minister to those separating themselves from the church,[27] ministered rather to a reform of contemplative life in the church. John of the Cross's ministry was as compassionate and far-reaching as his prayer life was intense. Had his health been better he would have been a missionary in Mexico.[28]

These three reformers of the sixteenth century have left us a legacy of contemplative prayer that only in our time is becoming fully the legacy of the whole church and that has been the spring from which the waters of uncommon ministry have flowed.

But, allow me to go back to the early church and the women and men of the desert for whom meditation on the Word of God was the very cornerstone of their life. For them personal meditation on the scriptures was akin to the "recitation of the Scripture at the public or private *synaxis* and should not be too sharply distinguished from it," says Douglas Burton-Christie.[29] The desert's wisdom about meditative prayer serves as a constant reminder that all Christian prayer is rooted in the Word of God. Scripture guarantees that prayer is under the influence of the Holy Spirit while scripture and liturgy keep prayer wholly Christian. We know from John Cassian that the prayer of the desert sometimes issued in a prayer that could only be described with the symbol fire. Abba Isaac spoke of the Lord's prayer as leading one "by a higher stage to that fiery and, indeed, more properly speaking, wordless prayer which is known and experienced by very few."[30] It is entirely God's business who receives the gift of this fiery prayer, but interior prayer that regularly makes one available to God's will is surely oriented to contemplation. The women and men of the desert are the tradition's grand witnesses to the call to search intensely for God within. These Christians of the desert knew well the wisdom of Gregory of Nyssa: "To seek God is to find him; to find God is to seek him."[31] Listening to the sayings of the desert is a powerful incentive to meditate and to let God's wisdom take over in one's life. One need only recall Thomas Merton, who has left a telling testimony to these sayings and their decisive impact on him in his collection of sayings called *The Wisdom of the Desert.*[32]

The wisdom of the desert made its way west with John Cassian, who influenced Benedict's Rule. Benedict in turn has left Western Christianity another powerful reminder of the need to make leisure time for God, which is an essential aspect of the Benedictine life known as *lectio divina.* Moreover, Benedict's Rule preserved from the monastic tradition of the East the habit of memorizing and repeating parts of scripture.[33] *Lectio divina* has been a mainstay of Western monastic life, but in the last three decades *lectio divina* has given birth to a number of adaptations that make available various forms of *lectio divina* to those outside the monastic family. Like the prayer of the desert, *lectio divina* emphasizes the centrality of scripture in Christian prayer,[34] and is a monastic charter for contemplative prayer shared now with the whole church.

The Carthusian monk Guigo II (d. 1188) gave a classic formulation to *lectio divina* in his letter to Brother Gervase in which the steps of monastic prayer are designated as *lectio, meditatio, oratio,* and *contemplatio.* For Guigo monastic prayer is a journey from the biblical text *(lectio),* to inquiry *(meditatio),* to response to God *(oratio),* and finally to the gift of God's presence as contemplation.[35] Guigo's ladder is a reminder of the human ascent to God and the divine descent into the human heart. This mutual movement of the human and the divine is like the angels ascending and descending on Jacob's ladder.[36] Guigo's ladder has also inspired various modern versions of this prayer, which is a journey to contemplation when that is God's will.[37] *Lectio divina* is one more instance in the tradition of the value of contemplative prayer.

In the next century after Guigo's, Thomas Aquinas (d. 1274) wrote that "devotion is an act of the will by which one readily gives oneself to the service of God." In this context Thomas asked whether contemplation or meditation caused devotion. In his discussion of this question, Thomas used the word *contemplation* to speak of "a simple attention of mind to the things of God, rather than a discursive process of reason *about* the same things."[38] Thomas argued that contemplation or meditation was a cause of devotion, but Thomas was not one to make hard and fast definitions for contemplation. But, I find in this article of the *Summa* (2.2.82.3), a recognition by Thomas of the higher orientation of contemplation. Thomas insists that both meditation and contemplation cause that devotion which renders one prompt in the service of God, a service of which Christian ministry is manifestation. As Walter Principe has so plainly demonstrated, one will be God-centered with Thomas Aquinas as a guide in the spiritual life.[39] Contemplative meditation is not theology, but theology, like that of Thomas Aquinas, is solid foundation and a prophetic call to God-centeredness.

Were space permitting, I would have traced here the christological meditations fostered by the Franciscans and especially by St. Bonaventure (d. 1274), but that story has been told elsewhere both recently and very ably.[40] In the late Middle Ages meditation became more systematic and detailed. That development saw a distant culmination in the very discursive meditation books of the first half of the twentieth century. But, one must not denigrate what suited another time. During those centuries when discursive meditation books abounded, there were always those, and their number was not small, who heeded the call to move from human reasoning to divine contemplation. I think here of Francis De Sales and his spiritual legacy. Perhaps we have an opportunity now to integrate approaches that seemed more divergent in former times than they do now by bringing meditation and contemplation into creative tension with each other.

Though I have already mentioned the three great Spanish mystics of the sixteenth century—Ignatius of Loyola, Teresa of Avila, and John of the Cross—I would say that these three Spaniards came along when the church badly needed them. Ignatius has given to the church a model of contemplative prayer that issues in ministry, a ministry that badly stood in need of renewal. Ignatius's colleague, Jerome Nadal, put his founder's integration of contemplative prayer and ministry succinctly when he described Ignatius as a "contemplative in action."[41]

Ignatius had developed the habit of "finding God in all things." He thus extended his prayer into ministry so that his ministry was lived in the mystery of Christ and was shaped by the presence of that mystery.[42]

Teresa of Jesus discovered and promoted what she called the "prayer of recollection," which is very much akin to modern centering prayer but in a less structured form. Teresa's nuns wanted to know how to live and how to pray. Her response was *The Way of Perfection.* In chapters 28 and 29 of this work, Teresa taught this prayer of recollection to which modern authors add the word *active* (recollection) to distinguish it from gifted, more mystical, passive recollection. But, it is clear from Teresa's comments on this prayer of recollection in these chapters of *The Way* that she meant the practice of this prayer to be a preparation for contemplation. Teresa stated that, in this prayer, a soul "enters within oneself to be with God," and it is "centered there within itself." Teresa was convinced that "the Lord taught me" this prayer that makes one available for contemplation: "If then the Lord should desire to raise you to higher things he will discover in you the readiness, finding that you are close to Him."

John of the Cross, ever the attentive spiritual guide, wanted his directees to be led to contemplation. He urged his followers to give up discursive meditation for contemplative prayer when they were made ready for this invitation. Recall how upset John was with one of the three blind guides of the soul, the spiritual director, who stands in the way of one's call to contemplation. While John of the Cross did not teach any method of prayer, it is clear that John wanted his directees to heed the call to contemplative prayer.[43] My conviction is that John would have been happy to promote what we are referring to in this essay as contemplative meditation. Keep in mind that John, the mystical contemplative, was a very busy administrator and much involved in a host of ministries, especially that of spiritual guidance. John's experience of God was the crucible in which his ministry was forged.

Another significant moment in the tradition of contemplative prayer came when a spiritual son of John of the Cross, Brother Lawrence of the Resurrection (d. 1691), practiced and taught a simple method of contemplative prayer. Lawrence's *Practice of the Presence of God* has appealed to spiritual seekers across ecumenical lines. This soldier turned Carmelite cook and sandalmaker has taught countless people to live more fully in the presence of God. Listen to one of his maxims:

> This [practice of the] presence of God, somewhat difficult in the beginning, secretly accomplishes marvelous effects in the soul, draws abundant graces from the Lord, and, when practiced faithfully, imperceptibly leads it to this simple awareness, to this loving view of God present everywhere, which is the holiest, the surest, the easiest, and the most efficacious form of prayer.[44]

Brother Lawrence preached a simple but demanding contemplative meditation that stands ready to serve busy ministers who wish to remain mindful of God as they serve their neighbors.

Now to our own times. There is little doubt that Thomas Merton, Trappist from Gethsemeni, Kentucky, is the most widely read monk produced by Western monasticism. Moreover, no one more than Merton has opened up for the churches at large the possibility of contemplation and for prayer that is oriented to contemplation. I often think that *Seeds of Contemplation* (1949) and *New Seeds of Contemplation* (1961) began in mid-century what is coming to fruition now. These books, as well as other writings by Merton, took his readers by surprise. They extend an invitation to be open to contemplation as a gift that God is more ready to offer than we once imagined. Merton taught us to live and to pray with minds and hearts open to God's presence. In 1949 Merton wrote,

> Since the interior life and contemplation are the things we most of all need—I speak only of contemplation that springs from the love of God—the kind of considerations written in these pages ought to be something for which everybody, and not only monks, would have a great hunger in our time.[45]

Merton would be surprised at how seriously his invitation has been taken. Unknown to himself or anyone else at the time, Merton anticipated Vatican II's grand proclamation of the "Universal Call to Holiness."[46] Merton set that holiness before a diverse reading public, a holiness previously thought to be the property of the cloister but for which there is now "a great hunger" by countless spiritual pilgrims. Those of us who grew up avidly reading Thomas Merton find it difficult, I am sure, to realize that only recently there occurred the thirtieth anniversary of his untimely death.

Nearer in time is another prophetic voice on behalf of contemplative prayer, that of Joseph Cardinal Bernardin (d. 1996). This Chicago archbishop urged on his listeners and readers a commitment to a life of prayer. His recounting of the meal with priest friends that changed his life has become a modern classical moment in our spiritual lore. What a powerful reminder it is from a man whose life became so transparent. For Cardinal Bernardin, prayer had become the necessary foundation of a God-centered life. If one wishes to minister like Joseph Bernardin, one must take seriously the challenge implicit in the story of his "conversion."

> About seven years ago [this was written in 1983], I came to understand that the pace of my life and the direction of my activity were unfocused, uncentered in a significant way. This created a certain unrest. I came to realize that I needed to make some changes in my life, and chief among these was a renewal of personal prayer.

Mention of prayer may evoke an image of "saying" prayers, of reciting formulas. I mean something quite different. When we speak of the renewal of prayer in our lives, we are speaking of reconnecting ourselves with the larger mystery of life and our common existence. This implies becoming disciplined in the use of our time, in the use of Centering Prayer, and in the development of a contemplative stance toward life.

When this happens, we begin to experience healing, integration, wholeness, peacefulness. We begin to hear more clearly the echoes of the Word in our own lives, in our own hearts. And as that Word takes root in the depths of our being, it begins to grow and to transform the way we live. It affects our relationships with people around us and above all our relationship with the Lord. From this rootedness flow our energies, our ministry, our ways of loving. From this core we can proclaim the Lord Jesus and his Gospel not only with faith and conviction but also with love and compassion.[47]

I must now conclude this rapid and selective survey of moments in the tradition that have urged on me a more contemplative approach to prayer. To advocate a more contemplative approach to prayer must imply no pretentiousness. Rather, growth in contemplative pray is growth in simplicity, very much like God's own simpleness. Contemplative meditation is a wellspring of love of God and love of neighbor.

What have I learned from making this pilgrimage through the tradition? First of all, that Christian prayer and especially contemplative prayer must be rooted in the Word of God as proclaimed in the liturgy and as read and studied on our own. Scripture and liturgy are the guardians of our Christian pilgrimage through life and the guarantors of the Christian character of our prayer. To pray contemplatively I must foster a sense of awareness and attention so that I may eventually develop the contemplative prayer that John of the Cross called "the practice of loving attentiveness" to God.[48] To do this I must develop the habit of listening in every aspect of my life so that I may listen more attentively for God's presence. I need also to develop the habit of regular, daily times for prayer; otherwise the clutter of modern life soon makes short work of my good intentions. Such a habit will remind me that contemplative meditation is the "stillpoint" around which one integrates the rest of one's life so that, no matter what anxieties assault me, I know, in faith, that God is at the center of my existence. A God-centered life is the authentic human core from which one then loves both God and neighbor. The tradition soon teaches one that prayer, if it is about anything, is about love. Teresa of Jesus knew that love of neighbor is *the* test of love of God.[49] Love of neighbor is also *the* test of our contemplative prayer. The last letter I received from my dissertation director,

Dom David Knowles, on June 22, 1974, several months before his death, contained this conviction about prayer and love that I am sure he would not now reserve to religious:

> Meanwhile, remember me in your prayers. I am old—but do not feel it, least of all mentally—but I am more sure than ever that prayer (of the heart and soul) is the first work of a religious—prayer that is love.

Ministry is an expression of love or it is lifeless busyness doomed to extinction. My reading of the tradition tells me that ministry becomes a service of love when it arises from the gifted presence of Christ nourished by contemplative prayer. Experience of God's love in prayer and our response to that love engender that simple trust and confidence in God that was the hallmark of the recently named doctor of the church, Thérèse of Lisieux, who wished to be a "*Mother* of souls," as well as a warrior, priest, apostle, doctor, and martyr.[50] Although this young woman who prayed simply and contemplatively died at twenty-four in a secluded Carmelite monastery, she and her simple prayer have become a powerful inspiration for ministry throughout the world.

As I close, I am well aware that I have said next to nothing about the character and actual practice of contemporary contemplative meditation in our time. You will find a clear and perceptive exposition of contemplative meditation in Fr. Ernest Larkin's essay, "Soul of the Apostolate," elsewhere in this volume. With that reassuring thought, I bring this survey to a close.

Notes

1. *The Living Flame of Love,* 3, 46. *The Collected Works of St. John of the Cross*, rev. ed., trans. Kieran Kavanaugh and Otilio Rodriquez (Washington, D.C.: Institute of Carmelite Studies, 1991), 691.

2. *Codex Iuris Canonici* (1917) Canons 125, n.2; 595, n.2; 1367, n.1. *Code of Canon Law, Latin-English Edition* (Washington, D.C.: Canon Law Society of America, 1983), Canons 276, II, n.5; 663, nn. 1 and 3; 246, n.3.

3. *The Dogmatic Constitution on the Church*, n. 11.

4. Louis Dupré, "Spiritual Life and the Survival of Christianity," *Cross Currents* (Fall 1998): 384.

5. Romano Guardini, *Prayer in Practice*; "Image Books" (Garden City, N.Y.: Doubleday, 1963).

6. Augustine, *Confessions;* trans. Henry Chadwick (Oxford: University Press, 1992), 10.xxvii. 38.

7. *The Book of Her Life* 40, 6, *The Collected Works of St. Teresa of Avila*, I; trans. Kieran Kavanaugh and Otilio Rodriquez (Washington, D.C.: Institute of Carmelite Studies, 1976), 279.

8. *The Way of Perfection* 28, 2, *Collected Works of St. Teresa*, II (1980), 140.

9. *Confessions*, 3.vi.11.

10. William Johnston, *Mystical Theology: The Science of Love* (London: HarperCollins, 1995), 1.

11. Bernard McGinn, "Asceticism and Mysticism in Late Antiquity and the Early Middle Ages," in *Asceticism*, eds. Vincent Wimbush and Richard Valantasis (New York: Oxford University Press, 1995), 58–74.

12. *The Interior Castle*, *Collected Works of St. Teresa*, *II* (1980), 489, n. 1 and the whole of the Fourth Dwelling Places.

13. Karl Rahner, *The Practice of Faith*, eds. Karl Lehmann and Albert Raffelt (New York: Crossroad, 1986), 69–77.

14. Karl Rahner, *Theological Investigations* 7, trans. David Bourke (New York: Herder and Herder, 1971), 15.

15. Dupré, "Spiritual Life," 386.

16. *The Spiritual Canticle,* 39, 2, *Collected Works of St. John of the Cross,* 622.

17. Bernard McGinn, *The Foundations of Mysticism, Vol. I: The Presence of God: A History of Christian Mysticism* (New York: Crossroad, 1991), xiii–xx.

18. John Cassian, *The Conferences*, trans. B. Ramsey (New York: Paulist, 1997), 11, XV.

19. Bernard of Clairvaux, *On the Song of Songs I*, trans. Kilian Walsh (Spenser, Mass.: Cistercian Publications, 1971), 1.1.

20. *Albert's Way*, ed. M. Mulhall (Rome and Barrington, Ill.: Institutum Carmelitanum, 1989), 2–3.

21. *Dictionnaire de Spiritualité,* 10, col. 908.

22. See also Luke 5:16; 6:12; 9:18, 28; 11:1.

23. Ignatius of Loyola, *The Spiritual Exercises and Selected Works*, ed. George Ganss (New York: Paulist, 1991), 138.

24. Margaret Dorgan, "Prayer," *HarperCollins Encyclopedia of Catholicism*, ed. Richard McBrien (San Francisco: HarperSanFrancisco, 1995), 1037.

25. *The Dark Night* 2.7.4, *Collected Works of St. John of the Cross*, 408.

26. *The Spiritual Canticle* 39, 6 and 28, 1, *Collected Works of St. John of the Cross*, 624, 584.

27. *Way of Perfection*, 1, 2, *Collected Works of Saint Teresa*, 41.

28. *God Speaks in the Night*, trans. Kieran Kavanaugh (Washington, D.C.: Institute of Carmelite Studies, 1991), 538.

29. Douglas Burton-Christie, *The Word in the Desert* (New York: Oxford University Press, 1993), 122.

30. Cassian, *Conferences*, 9, XXV.1.

31. Quoted by Huston Smith in *How Can I Find God?* ed. James Martin (Ligouri, Mo.: Triumph, 1997), 191.

32. New York: New Directions, 1960.

33. *RB1980: The Rule of St. Benedict in Latin and English with Notes,* ed. Timothy Fry (Collegeville, Minn.: Liturgical Press, 1981), 446.

34. Kevin Irwin, *"Lectio Divina," The New Dictionary of Catholic Spirituality*, ed. Michael Downey (Collegeville, Minn.: Liturgical Press, 1993), 596; *Dictionnaire de Spiritualité*, 9, cols. 470–510.

35. Keith J. Egan, "Guigo II: The Theology of the Contemplative Life," *The Spirituality of Western Christendom*, ed. E. Rozanne Elder (Kalamazoo, Mich.: Cistercian Publications, 1976), 106–15.

36. Genesis 28:12.

37. See William H. Shannon, *Seeking the Face of God* (New York: Crossroad, 1990).

38. *Summa theologiae* (Blackfriars ed.: 1964), Glossary 270.

39. Walter Principe, *Thomas Aquinas' Spirituality* (Toronto: Pontifical Institute of Mediaeval Studies, 1984), 29.

40. Bernard McGinn, *The Flowering of Mysticism; Vol. 3 The Presence of God* (New York: Crossroad, 1998), see index.

41. Ignatius, *Spiritual Exercises*, 231, 459. On Ignatius as a mystic, see index of this work and Harvey D. Egan, *Ignatius Loyola the Mystic* (Wilmington, Del., 1987).

42. Ignatius, *Spiritual Exercises*, 459.

43. *Living Flame of Love,* 3.62.

44. Lawrence of the Resurrection, *Writings and Conversations on the Practice of the Presence of God*, ed. Conrad De Meester; trans. S. Sciurba (Washington, D.C.: Institute of Carmelite Studies, 1994), 41, n. 31.

45. Thomas Merton, *Seeds of Contemplation* (New Directions, 1949), 13.

46. *Dogmatic Constitution*, ch. 5.

47. M.-Basil Pennington and Carl Arico, *Living Our Priesthood Today*, 122–23. See also Joseph Bernardin, *The Gift of Peace* (Chicago: Loyola University Press, 1997), 96–100; and *How Can I Find God,* 97–100.

48. *Living Flame of Love*, 3. 35 and *passim*, 687.

49. *Interior Castle*, 5.3.8, 351.

50. Thérèse of Lisieux, *Story of a Soul*, 3d ed., trans. John Clarke (Washington, D.C.: Institute of Carmelite Studies, 1996), 192.

Ernest E. Larkin

29. Contemplative Prayer
as the Soul of the Apostolate

The "soul of the apostolate," in the unsurpassed classic of Dom Chautard,[1] is the interior life, cultivated by liturgy, mental prayer, and custody of the heart. Chautard shows the organic connection between personal spiritual life and fruitful ministry. This essay specifies this teaching. Expanding on the soul analogy I focus on the stillpoint of the soul, the center that holds together the whole spiritual edifice. This center is the place of contemplation. I argue that the practice of contemplative prayer can be the organizing principle of the interior life and the ultimate root of ministry. This is not the only way, but it is an ideal way to put ministry on a solid spiritual foundation. Commitment to this form of prayer does not cancel out the other exercises of the spiritual life; they remain intact, but with new life coming to them and to ministry from the personal realization of the abiding presence of God. Contemplative prayer is the heart of the matter.

In this age of information glut and hyperactivity, dominated by technology and the demon of busyness, contemplative prayer is countercultural. But scores of people have taken it up, perhaps as a countervailing trend against the superficiality, the mindlessness, and the distractions of postmodern life. New contemplative prayer forms have sprung up to help people back to their centers. William Johnston writes that

> everywhere we see Christians of all ages and cultures sitting quietly in meditation. Some sit before a crucifix or an ikon in one-pointed meditation. Others sit and breathe as they look at the tabernacle. Others practice mindfulness, awareness of God in their surroundings. Others recite a mantra to the rhythm of their breath. Others, influenced by Zen or yoga or *vipassana* open their minds and hearts to God in the universe....[2]

These prayer forms seek contact with God in direct and pure ways; they nourish in a radical way the faith that does justice.

Two examples of these new contemplative methods are centering prayer and Christian meditation. The former is promoted by "Contemplative Outreach" under the leadership of Thomas Keating, O.C.S.O., and the latter, designed by John Main, O.S.B., is taught by the World Community of Christian Meditation, whose director is Lawrence Freeman, O.S.B. Both methods are ways of praying contemplatively. They are not mystical prayer, but self-chosen ways of practicing deep silence before God, in quiet and stillness, remaining in loving awareness of the indwelling God.[3]

These new practices get beyond the imagination or the processing of deep thoughts. They are more than ejaculatory or aspirative prayer. Contemplative prayer in the sense used here is silent prayer, not only beyond words, but beyond images and concepts, beyond discursive reasoning and the outpouring of affections. One stands alone before God, waiting to be touched with the love poured into our hearts by the spirit who is given to us (see Rom 5.5). The waiting is the contemplative prayer, the touch or inbreaking of God is contemplation. There is a distinction between these two: the contemplative prayer is the means, the contemplation the goal, and the contemplation may be an ordinary grace of peaceful presence to God or infused contemplation. The prayer is positioning oneself to welcome the spirit, the contemplation is the spirit praying within.[4] The two ways of contemplative prayer discussed here are examples of the many ways in practice today; they are chosen for examination in this essay because they are typical, popular, and accessible.

Prayer and Action

Prayer in general and action for others are the two prongs of the Christian life. On retreats I often say that we have only two things to do in life: to pray and to do justice. We pray to be loved by God and to love God in return. We do justice to share that love in service to sisters and brothers. Justice includes all right relationships.

Both elements are essential. We are called to be mystics and prophets. Mystics know God by way of love. Prophets speak up for God and do God's work. The Christian vocation is prayer and prophecy, contemplation and action, love of God and love of people. John Paul II expressed this double call beautifully in these words: "We need heralds of the gospel who are experts in humanity, who know the depths of the human heart, who can share the joys and the hopes, the agonies and distress of people today, but who are at the same time contemplatives in love with God."[5]

Activists who do not pray are do-gooders who do their own thing, often in self-serving ways. Thoreau makes the sage comment, "When you see someone coming toward you to do you good, run for your life." Rootedness in God promotes objectivity and selflessness. True love is other-centered, indeed God-centered, and prayer in some form is essential for this focus. People have to break out of their egoistic worlds. Prayer helps them do that. It puts them in touch with truths bigger than themselves, with Truth itself, and so it helps them be self-effacing, less aggressive, and more compassionate. Prayer helps them do God's thing.

By the same token the pray-ers can lock themselves into prayer and close their eyes to Lazarus at the gate. Such people practice a religion of comfort, as easement for the burdens of life. This is a lopsided spirituality, one that is too self-regarding, too unworldly, too removed from human suffering. In this perspective, spirituality helps one find some meaning and acceptance of suffering, perhaps by "offering up" the pain of life even in experiencing social evils; little thought may be given to the unjust conditions that caused the problem in the first place. There is merit in accepting unavoidable suffering, but a balanced spirituality addresses systemic injustice too. The justice piece is essential in contemporary spirituality. The whole gospel is both faith and justice; this calls us to change not only ourselves, but the world.

We need to be activists who pray and pray-ers who do justice. This essay addresses the first half of the equation. I write as a Carmelite, and Carmelite theory starts with prayer and moves to action. But while Carmel emphasizes the inner life, it is wholly committed to peace and justice too. "The work of justice," the superior general of the Carmelites wrote in a recent circular letter, "must be an integral part of our preaching of the gospel and inform everything we do." Prayer and justice are a both/and dyad, never either/or.

Our basic assumption, then, is that ministry in general and social action in particular need prayer as a foundation and support. Christians who want to change the world according to the principles of the kingdom of God need to be guided by the gospel. They are collaborators with God, ministers of Christ, promoters of the social mission of the church. They must act out the mind of Christ. To get on track and to stay there, to be faithful over the long haul is the work of faith and love; an Enlightenment mentality that considers social equality, freedom, and human progress as the supreme good is not enough. Earthly goods are values, but they need to be inserted into the broader picture of the redemption of the whole person. Otherwise the commitment to human progress easily falters or becomes violent.

Contemplative Prayer

The real question is what kind of prayer best supports a commitment to justice. The comprehensive answer is a balanced prayer life, a combination of liturgy, vocal prayer, and private meditation. It would smack of magic to reduce a prayer life to a single formula, even a contemplative practice like centering prayer or Christian meditation. But within the context of a healthy spiritual practice one of these two prayer forms can be the new ingredient to revitalize an entire prayer life. Contemplative prayer puts the emphasis on the essential, the contemplative dimension. Either one of the two forms can be chosen as a daily staple. Once chosen, it becomes a consistent practice, faithfully pursued twice each day, a discipline that has high priority in one's daily schedule, because it is the centerpiece of one's prayer life. Centering prayer or Christian meditation are not new fads, but are the contemplative tradition in contemporary dress. They are new wine in new wineskins, but they represent an old way of life that has been proven in the cloister and is being transported into secular life.[6] The new way of life is anchored in the two concentrated periods of twenty or more minutes of prayer each morning and evening, a practice that brings the contemplative dynamic into the whole day.

One reason for the popularity of these prayers is their practicality. They open up the possibility of a contemplative life for the average person of faith by teaching a clearly defined method of prayer. They represent the Western contemplative tradition in a "how-to" fashion. The West has been long on philosophical treatises on contemplation, on stages and passages, even on ladders of perfection. But there has been little instruction on how to get on the ladder. One was supposed to grow into this prayer style. One would pray contemplatively when one was ready for it, that is, when one had negotiated the earlier stages and now loved God enough to dispense with words and feelings and just be there with the Lord. In this view relationship with God was like any other love relationship. It would begin with long conversations, pass through periods of high sentiments and affections, and end up in a restful, person-to-person presence. When two parties came to know and love each other in a deep way, like Grandma and Grandpa on the front porch, they would sit together in silence and enjoy each other's company. For one who knows God deeply, silent and solitary prayer becomes a need, and noise of any kind is an intrusion.

The new contemplative prayer forms anticipate this development. They go immediately and directly to the projected end result of all mental prayer, bypassing personal input except for loving attention; they move immediately into a stance of watching and waiting. Many who have taken up this practice have testified to a longstanding hunger for a deeper prayer life; they have wanted to experience God (not just thoughts about him), to know God, to know God as a friend and not just an impersonal taskmaster. How to achieve this? How to get closer to God? The answer of the contemplative tradition is to enter into the depths of one's own being, where God is present and active in trinitarian life. Enter there with your whole being—body, soul and spirit—and you will find God.

These prayer forms are basically Western; they come out of the mystical tradition of the Christian world. They are biblical and christological, and they emphasize love as the way to the knowledge of God.[7] They appropriate and update the teaching of Western classics like John Cassian's *Conferences* (fourth century) or the anonymous *Cloud of Unknowing* (fourteenth century).

The Far Eastern contribution has to do with the body: posture, breathing, and relaxation, elements that the East has developed into fine arts. As the combination of both Western and Eastern elements, these forms are truly something new in contemporary practice.[8]

West and East

The monastic *lectio divina* is the context of centering prayer and Christian meditation. *Lectio divina* is a spiritual reading and reflection on the scriptures, leading to prayer and contemplation. The objective is the contemplation, so the movement is from discursive activity to silent presence. The contemplative outcome has been overshadowed in the recent past; discursive prayer has dominated Catholic piety since the anti-mystical prejudices of the seventeenth and eighteenth centuries. The new methods of contemplative prayer were designed to reverse these trends and put contemplation back into mainstream Christian spirituality. The prayer methods are like transfusions for the process of *lectio divina*. They do not replace *lectio;* they pump new life into all the phases of mental prayer by highlighting its contemplative orientation.

This relation to *lectio divina,* mentioned frequently by Thomas Keating, indicates the biblical character of centering prayer. John Main's method too is a praying of the scripture. His repetition of the mantra or holy word is the echo of John Cassian's advice to repeat a pregnant phrase from the psalms as a prayer formula.[9] Both methods are embedded in the Christian tradition and work out of a biblical worldview. They recognize Christ as the way to the Father after the manner of Teresa of Avila, who learned from experience that one never gets beyond the Sacred Humanity, even in the highest mystical experience. Their approach is the "introversion" of the Western tradition, exemplified in Augustine and in the apophatic mystics. This way consists in entering into oneself. One moves within as best one can, beyond the superficial layers of the psyche, of ego, of thoughts and feelings about God, to the stillpoint of the soul, the dwelling place of God. Beginners move in that direction; mystics touch the stillpoint.

Social activists or busy ministers need not fear that the movement within remove them from the world and its concerns. The journey within is the journey into reality, the reality of the whole person, of humanity, and of the universe. The center holds everything, because it is my deepest self and the dwelling place of God. My center mirrors God. The more we are in touch with ourselves, the more we are in touch with God, with others, and with the whole social fabric. This deep union makes us concerned about people, ecology, and the environment.

These insights help us understand why contemplation is at the ultimate source of ministry. Each human being is like a cone turned upside down. The point holds the whole edifice. That stillpoint is our center, where God touches us. The top half of the cone is our outer selves, the region of the sensibility, connecting us with the visible world. The bottom half is our spiritual selves, where we are receptive to God. We begin our journey to God on the upper level of the cone, circling around and spiraling downward to the center. The journey is the longest we will ever take, because it involves the transformation of our whole being in God. The deeper we go, the more integrated we will have become. Our knowledge and love of God grows apace with this development.

None of us is alone in the universe. We are many cones, and all of us are united together in the same one center, that is, the spirit of Christ. We form the huge circle of humanity and the universe like so many pieces of a pie. We all have the same one center, the cosmic Christ, the spirit of God that holds and animates everything. The deeper our life—that is, the closer we are to the center—the more in touch we are with everyone and everything. In our spiral down to the center, the love of God and the love of neighbor work in consonance. They are the one same love with two expressions existing in the same degree of perfection. The more we love God, the more we love the world made in the image of God, and the more we are committed to making the world conform to that image.

How do we make the journey to the center? By letting go and letting God. On the ego level we are in charge; we control the operation. But analysis shows that the spirit is leading us even here. Our task is conversion. The level of ego is also the level of the false self, which tends to construct reality according to its own image and to seek its own glory. This is the level of addictions and compulsions, hang-ups and attachments. We must let go of whatever imprisons us. This happens as we come to know and love the God of the Gospels by our human efforts under grace, and eventually by mystical gifts, when we move beyond our "trifling good works," as Teresa of Avila says,[10] and enter the region of the spirit. Here God intervenes more directly, and we are simply receivers of knowledge and love. We enter this realm of freedom by our own work of knowing and owning the truth about ourselves and dealing with the chains or the threads that imprison us. But full freedom will happen only on the spirit level, through the gift of the Holy Spirit. Full freedom, which is perfect poverty of spirit, is the underside of the gift of contemplation. It comes with contemplation. Both poverty of spirit and contemplation, therefore, are the work of the Holy Spirit; in their full realization they are wholly unmerited and passively received.

In active prayer we cooperate with the spirit, using our graced human potential to grow in knowledge and love of God and to deal with our conversion. In centering prayer and Christian meditation we are engaged in simplified active prayer but moving toward the region of the spirit, where God is the agent and we are receivers. These prayers are a paradoxical mixture: they are active forms of contemplative prayer. They are antecedent to the time when infused contemplation is the only option, though they continue after that time as well. These prayers anticipate the onset of fully infused contemplation. They knock at the door of the spirit level by reversing the ordinary way of pursuing a goal, which is to take charge and control the outcome. Instead these forms reject busyness, chattering, and the expression of personal desires and feelings; their goal is relaxation before the Lord, though with gentle concentration and attention, waiting on the Lord. This active-contemplative prayer leads one to the threshold of the divine presence, where one hopes to be invited within; the experience of God's presence is gift, the work of faith, hope, and love.

The experience has many levels and it is always by invitation only. Over time, and we hope very soon, one will be invited into the mystical dwelling places of Teresa of Avila's "interior castle." But the immediate invitation is to love, not to some particular experience, according to the dictum of Teresa, that "the important thing in prayer is, not to think much, but to love much."[11] This loving is the response to being loved by God, because "the love of God consists in this, not that we have loved God, but that God has loved us" (1 Jn 4:10). These new contemplative prayer forms are human attempts to tune in directly to the experience of being beloved of God.

How can we nervous, distracted, anxious people silence the "chattering monkeys" of our minds and simply *be* with our God? We need some technique, some method to quiet our minds and dwell peacefully with the God who is present within us. The wisdom of the East helps us here. It is the wisdom of the body.

The West has tended to treat the body as the enemy; at best it paid little attention to Brother Ass. The East says the body is our friend at prayer. The body is the royal road to the spirit. Sit up straight in imitation of the lotus position, breathe deeply and rhythmically, and a calmness begins to invade your being. The correct position at prayer, a straight spine, is practically a guarantee of real prayer; it is enlightenment itself, according to the Buddhists. In this relaxed and alert position we take up a practice that is found in both John Cassian and *The Cloud of Unknowing* but has long been associated with the East. This is the mantra or holy word, which we use in no way as a magic formula, but as an expression to focus and keep attention on the God within and to express consent to the divine presence. We let go of all other thoughts and feelings, just noting them and letting them pass like ships on the surface of the river; we observe the ships from below in the calmness of the depths. Centering prayer uses the holy word as needed and as a sign of consent to God's presence and action; Christian meditation repeats the mantra from beginning to end, because the mantra *is* the prayer of silent attention. For Christian meditation the mantra is "selfless attention" that empties the mind in order to welcome the fullness of the divine presence.

Why Contemplative Prayer Is the Soul of the Apostolate

I am proposing centering prayer or Christian meditation, one or the other, as the cornerstone of the spirituality for any demanding ministry, especially social action. The reasons for this position have been suggested throughout this paper. I will now sum up the argument in three considerations.

The first is that contemplative prayer is the very heart and soul of all prayer. C. S. Lewis says that prayer is either contact with God or sheer illusion. Prayer is dialogue, conversation, encounter, and these qualities are part of all mental prayer, especially contemplative prayer. The ultimate success of *lectio divina* is the fourth act, which is contemplation; centering prayer and Christian meditation set their sights immediately and directly on this experience by quieting the soul and waiting in simplicity for the God who will surely come. The assumption is that all reflection and prayer in *lectio* and in liturgical and vocal prayer will have a greater measure of contact with God because of this practice.

A story appearing in the *London Tablet* some years ago helps locate the essence of prayer. The Archbishop of Canterbury at the time was being interviewed on television, and he was asked about his prayer. "Do you pray?" was the question. "Yes," he answered, "I pray each day." "And how much do you pray?" He answered, "About a minute." There was surprise on the interviewer's face, so the archbishop added, "Of course, it takes me about twenty-nine minutes to get to that one minute." The new forms of contemplative prayer hope for better results than the one minute through faithfulness to a discipline that raises the level of the person's whole prayer life.

This contemplative experience is difficult to describe. It is no one particular experience. Sometimes it is consoling, warm, euphoric; more often it is a "nothing experience," dry and empty. The essential is neither one nor other of these feelings, but loving faith, open and receptive to God's love. There is usually no perceptible awareness of the action of the spirit.

Thérèse of Lisieux may help us here. The contemplative prayer of her years in the convent was seldom self-validating. It was presence to Jesus in pure faith, without any sensible overflow of consolation. Whatever delight there was in the prayer was spiritual and based on the faith conviction that she was pleasing God. The prayer itself was dry and empty, but she knew she was loving the Beloved and drawing strength from the encounter. It was a discipline and love offering.

Most of that time she sensed that God was hidden behind a cloud, asleep in the boat as with his disciples (Lk 8:22–25). This was a presence in absence, which is the typical experience of the "Dark Night" in St. John of the Cross. But even this silent presence disappeared in the last year and a half of her life, when Thérèse had no sense whatever of a world beyond the senses. The pious thoughts of the past now seemed like illusions. She experienced total absence of God without alloy. There was no sense of God, no feeling for heaven or the once familiar world of grace. Thérèse offered her own explanation of this horrible suffering:

> [Your child] is resigned to eat the bread of sorrow as long as You desire it; she does not wish to rise up from the table filled with bitterness at which poor sinners are eating until the day set by You. Can she not say in her name and in the name of her brothers, *"Have pity on us, O Lord, for we are poor sinners!" [Luke 18.13]* Oh! Lord, send us away justified. May all those who were not enlightened by the bright flame of faith one day see it shine.[12]

She experienced the plight of sinners and atheists, their "night of nothingness"[13] and despair. They may not feel the pain; they may live in denial and avoidance through medicating themselves and substituting ersatz gods. But Thérèse experienced the full force of their nihilistic state; she took on their pain in redemptive suffering. Here as in all her prayer life Thérèse correctly assessed the value of poverty of spirit. She wrote the following words to her sister Marie: "Let us love our littleness, let us love to feel nothing; then we shall be poor in spirit, then Jesus shall come to look for us and transform us into flames of love."[14]

Poverty of spirit is the chief condition for the level of the contemplation that is the outcome of contemplative prayer. God comes to the poor, the *anawim* like Mary in the Magnificat (Lk 1:46–55). He touches them from his dwelling place in the stillpoint of their souls. God is always there in the center, but the contemplative must journey to that center through layers of obstruction and following the lead of the spirit. The end of the journey is full presence in the stillpoint; it is called "transforming union" and it consists in being totally and continuously present with the Lord. There are intermittent and partial mystical experiences of the stillpoint along the way, described by Teresa of Avila in the fourth to the sixth dwelling places of the *Interior Castle*. The seventh and last mansion is the transforming union. The earlier dwelling places do not have this direct and immediate touching of God, a phrase that is a classic metaphor for the mystical experience. The contemplative experiences of the earlier mansions are something less; they represent a peaceful resting in God, but from a distance, with a presence to God rather than in God. These experiences are the original projected outcomes of centering prayer and Christian meditation; with growth they will be exchanged for the mystical experiences. Only at the end of the journey is there full possession of the stillpoint. Then the "spark," as the stillpoint is also called, will burst into the living flame of love.

Contemplative prayer pursues the Beloved on this journey. Its strategy is to make oneself as vulnerable as possible to the divine inbreaking. Contemplative prayer lives in the hope that God will come, indeed is coming, whatever the emotional tone of the time at prayer. Those who practice this prayer are convinced that there are breakthroughs all along the way. They know that God is always ready to give himself to those disposed.

A second reason for promoting contemplative prayer is discernment. This prayer is a direct way to the truth of things. In this prayer one is reduced to silence, beyond our self-serving thoughts and feelings. Silence is the way to truthfulness. Our true self comes to life. This is the self that is rooted in God; it comes from God and leads back to God. This is our real self, not the one we have fashioned according to our own image and likeness. This self is the bearer of truth. Whatever the level of the contemplation enjoyed in the practice of the contemplative prayer, it will be an experience in some fashion of this true self.

Centering prayer and Christian meditation contribute to the growth of the true self. The false self is sidelined; it withers from being neglected and overshadowed. But it is also shown up and revealed as the enemy of one's deeper truth. We are easily victimized by the sin in our lives and in the world. The capital sins, for example, spawn disordered desires of pride, lust, avarice, and the rest. Our own efforts to deal with these things are only partially successful, according to St. John of the Cross,[15] because the capital sins continue their disruptive action from the underground of the unconscious; they are part of the person's shadow. They come out in disguised forms such as spiritual pride or gluttony. Contemplation uncovers this pathology and challenges the persons to own their sins and to deal with them, not necessarily in the formal prayer time, but in a proper forum such as a twelve-step program. This healing process is the purification described by John of the Cross as "the Dark Night of the Senses." Only contemplation can heal the roots of sin. It does this by revealing them in their true colors and by mustering the strength to deal with them effectively. This process of purification—Keating calls it the "dismantling of the false self"—is happening in the lives of practitioners of contemplative prayer.

As purification takes place, a new consciousness emerges, which Meister Eckhart calls *Gelassenheit*. This term means "letting things be," seeing things as they are, reading the situation accurately without projection. *Gelassenheit* happens when the person is connected with the living God and lets other gods die. It is the outcome of detachment; it is the reward of seeing the world with the eyes of faith. This frame of mind helps one choose the right course of action. Social analysis and the study of each situation are still necessary, but *Gelassenheit* assures greater objectivity and truth.

Contemplative prayer is also the handmaid of spiritual discernment in another way. Spiritual discernment proceeds less by way of rational analysis than by affective consonance or dissonance. One interprets the affective resonances of a given experience. The discerner "senses" what is in accord with or in opposition to God's will. The judgment is by a "feel" for the truth. It is judging by connaturality or affinity, much as a chaste person, for example, knows intuitively what is or is not chaste in a given case. Spiritual discernment is possible only for a spiritual person, one who cultivates a deep and faithful prayer life. Contemplative prayer fosters that kind of relationship. It puts one in contact with the spirit and brings forth the harvest of virtuous attitudes described by St. Paul as fruits of the spirit: "love, peace, patient endurance, kindness, generosity, faith" (Gal 5:22). These are qualities of true Christian ministers who are driven, not by anger, hurt, or violence, nor even by ideology, but by the spirit of God, who is working in them for the building up of the kingdom of God.

The third and final reason for recommending this prayer as the keystone of one's prayer life and the ideal preparation for ministry is its personal quality. Contemplative prayer brings about a truly personal relationship with Jesus Christ. Jesus walks at one's side as friend and support, reminding us that he is in charge, that it is his church, and that we are not the final court of responsibility. One's mantra becomes like a nickname that comes to mind in moments of quiet or crisis and calls up the Lord's presence. There is a sense of intimacy between God and the person.

With contemplative prayer as a regular practice there is less danger that the "first and greatest" commandment might fall in abeyance. Today the possibility of a personal relationship with God is often cast into doubt. Love for God is flattened out into a variety of horizontal expressions, all of them reduced to loving people.[16] To love another person is indeed to love God himself, but this is the secondary expression of the love of God; the first way is to love God in God's very self. Loving God himself, who is Abba, our mother and father, is our birthright as Christians. We are called to a Person-to-person relationship with each member of the Trinity: this is the ultimate purpose of life and the measure of its fulfillment. We are called to be friends, not mere servants (Jn 15:15), to dwell like branches on a vine. Jesus says, "I am the vine, you are the branches. Those who live in me and I in them will produce abundantly, for apart from me you can do nothing" (Jn 15:5). Contemplative prayer explicitly cultivates this personal relationship.

One especially important role for this personal friendship with Christ is in the area of suffering. Jesus is no stranger to suffering. In his earthly life he sought out and befriended the downtrodden and the hurting. Their needs are still his preferential option. We should not be surprised to find suffering in our ministry, since we act in imitation of him. The cross is the validation of all Christian life and ministry. It is part of the human condition and the Paschal Mystery of dying and rising with Christ. So there will be the cross in ministerial life, suffered in failures and opposition, in boredom and discouragement, in sheer weariness and disappointment, in persecution and even martyrdom. How shall ministers manage this fearsome challenge? With Paul we ask, "Who can rescue me from this body of death?" The answer too is Paul's: "Thanks be to God through Jesus Christ" (Rom 7:24–25) .

One especially efficacious form of the grace of Christ in ministry is experience of his personal presence in our lives. The faithful practice of contemplative prayer builds that sense of abiding presence, that knowing Christ by name, that intimacy of walking with him. There are no doubt other ways of growing in the knowledge and love of the Lord, but the way of contemplative prayer is the pearl of great price for many ministers today. It is a special gift for our time and the guarantee of a solid spiritual foundation for ministry. For those who take up its practice, it will be the soul of their apostolate.

Notes

1. Dom Jean-Baptiste Chautard, O.C.S.O., *The Soul of the Apostolate*, trans. with introduction by Thomas Merton (New York: Doubleday Image, 1961).

2. *Mystical Theology* (London: HarperCollins, 1995), 134.

3. In a popular flyer entitled "The Method of Centering Prayer" by Thomas Keating and distributed by "Contemplative Outreach," the following guidelines are set down for this prayer:

1. Choose a sacred word as the symbol of your intention to consent to God's presence and action within.
2. Sitting comfortably and with eyes closed, settle briefly and silently introduce the sacred word as the symbol of your consent to God's presence and action within.
3. When you become aware of thoughts, return ever-so-gently to the sacred word.
4. At the end of the prayer, remain in silence with eyes closed for a couple of minutes.

The following description of "How to Meditate" appears in the introduction to John Main's *The Inner Christ* (London: Darton, Longman and Todd, 1995):

Sit down. Sit still and upright. Close your eyes lightly. Sit relaxed but alert. Silently, interiorly begin to say a single word. We recommend the prayer-phrase 'maranatha.' Recite it as four syllables of equal length. Listen to it as you say it, gently but continuously. Do not think or imagine anything—spiritual or otherwise. If thoughts and images come, these are distractions at the time of meditation, so keep returning to simply saying the word. Meditate each morning and evening for between twenty and thirty minutes. (p. v)

4. These distinctions are elaborated in a recent article by Ernest Larkin, "Contemporary Contemplative Prayer Forms—Are They Contemplation?" *Review for Religious* 57 (January–February, 1998): 77–87.

5. Address to Sixth Symposium of European Bishops, 1985.

6. Thomas Keating, *Intimacy with God* (New York: Crossroads, 1997), 15–21.

7. A videotape program by Ernest Larkin, entitled "Contemplative Prayer Retreat," addresses the theological building blocks of the two forms of contemplative prayer under discussion. The program is published in three cassettes by the Carmelite Institute, 1600 Webster St. N. E., Washington, D.C., 20017.

8. William Johnston, S.J., in *Mystical Theology,* 134, calls them neither Western nor Eastern, but "a third way, a *tertium quid.* It is the Gospel of Jesus Christ in a new world."

9. *Conferences of John Cassian*, trans. Colm Luibheid: Classics of Western Spirituality (New York: Paulist, 1985), Tenth Conference, 131–32; 138; 139–40.

10. *Interior Castle, III Mansions,* ch. 1, in E. Allison Peers' translation, *Complete Works of Saint Teresa of Avila* (New York: Sheed and Ward, 1946) II, 222.

11. *Interior Castle, IV Dwelling Places,* 1.7 in Kieran Kavanaugh/Otilio Rodrigez translation, (Washington, D.C.: Institute of Carmelite Studies, 1980), 319.

12. *Story of a Soul,* trans. John Clarke, O.C.D. (Washington, D.C.: Institute of Carmelite Studies, 1975), 212.

13. Ibid., 213.

14. *Letters of St. Thérèse of Lisieux*, II, LT 197, September 17, 1896, trans. John Clarke, O.C.D.: Washington, D.C.: Institute of Carmelite Studies, 1988), 999.

15. *Dark Night*, I, 2–8.

16. Edward Vacek, S.J., "Religious Life and the Eclipse of Love for God," *Review for Religious* 57 (March–April, 1998): 118–37; also "The Eclipse of Love of God," *America* 174 (1996): 15–16.

SECTION VI.
GROUP, COMMUNITY, AND MARITAL WORK

"Spiritual Conversation Groups: Con-Spiring with the Spirit" by Kevin Gillespie offers a wealth of information that is essential for parish and other spiritual communities for at least two reasons: (1) We often don't realize how central group process is to people's spiritual formation, and (2) even when we do, we fail to employ basic knowledge of the characteristics, functions, principles, standards, methods, stages, and possible paradigms for group spiritual formation that are already at our disposal. This essay begins to address these two points.

Robert A. Jonas, in "The Empty Bell: A Contemplative Community," shares with us a vision of a sanctuary for the study and practice of Christian meditation and prayer, which became a reality in a town just outside Boston. In this practical essay he provides principles, practices, and schedules. He also presents theological and christological assumptions that are held by his community. These reflect the deep thought and theological reflection that were and are involved in forming the philosophy that gives life to what is done and envisioned at the Empty Bell. Their ministry offers creative hope and a good model for others in this new millennium.

"Gender Issues in Ministry with Couples," by Kathleen Fischer and Thomas Hart, addresses the concern persons in ministry should have for just and healthy female-male relationships. It brings us into "some of the darker corners of sexism in marriage." A tremendous amount of material on biblical foundations and resources for a new paradigm on gender relations is condensed in this essay, including a new vision of marriage and a discussion of the implications that such revisioning has on preparing couples for marriage (and providing very practical suggestions in this regard). Although the authors hope that this information will deepen the health of all marriages, they also pay attention to the often hidden reality of domestic violence. This concluding essay of this section is an important one for all those involved in ministry and pastoral care.

C. Kevin Gillespie

30. Spiritual Conversation Groups: Con-Spiring with the Spirit

Ever since Jesus proclaimed, "Where two or three are gathered together in my name, there I am in the midst of them" (Mt 18:2), Christians have met in groups in order to con-spire with the spirit of Christ. Such a group con-spiracy has happened because Jesus himself liked to be in groups. In Mark's Gospel alone there are sixty-four occasions on which we find Jesus within the context of a small group (Icenogle, 1994, 195–96) Despite this frequency, there is a tendency to forget that much of what we know about Jesus comes out of his conversations with others in groups. It is no accident that the Christian faith emerged from spiritual conversation groups formed around the inspirations of Jesus.

This survey of spiritual conversation groups will use as a hermeneutic tool the notion of con-spiracy with God. A variety of group spiritual modalities will be presented in an effort to demonstrate how spiritual conversation within a group may enhance a person's life of prayer. Taken from Haughey's *The Conspiracy of God* (1976), the notion is meant to suggest that small groups through their conversations are collaborating with the Holy Spirit. Such a notion comes from an understanding of the Holy Trinity as relational to the human being by way of "Spiration." As Haughey notes,

> The eternal procession of the spirit within the Godhead is by way of Spiration, the theologians tell us. When the gift is given to men (sic) in time It proceeds from the Father and the Son. When It is received the spirit becomes a *Conspirer* in man (sic), with the recipient and the spirit breathing as one. Because the spirit is the spirit of love, the two become as one, as if in a communion. (my emphasis) (Haughey, 1976, 63)

What Haughey describes as the "spiration" between the individual and the Holy spirit may be said also about the relationship between the Holy Spirit and a group of individuals who are gathered to share conversation in matters of the spirit. The language expressed within a group and between its members often involves how one's prayer has been or has not been inspirational.

471

Through the listening presence of a group and their supportive responses what tran-spires is meant to in-spire the one who may be dis-spirited. This process can only be done through the Holy Spirit, that is, in con-spiracy with God. They are in effect, con-spirators with the Holy Spirit.

Recent History of Con-Spiracies

While there has developed a rather extensive literature on the signifi-cance of one-to-one spiritual direction, there has, relatively speaking, been lit-tle literature on group spiritual direction. Perhaps the earliest article on the topic was written by Halenworth (1968). He saw the value of applying group methods for spiritual direction when he stated,

> In the group method every member of the group is seen as a poten-tial source of growth for everyone else in the group....The basic challenge in such an approach is to release the potential for growth that exists in the very relationships of the members to one another in the group. Ordinarily the relationship of a subject to an authori-tative figure does not release this group potential. (Halenworth, 1968, 71, 72)

It should be noted that Halenworth's work was written primarily for those engaged in the religious formation of seminarians and religious. A decade later, Sullivan and Horstman (1977) described the experience of a group of lay people who engaged in a group retreat based upon the 19th Anno-tation of the Spiritual Exercises of St. Ignatius.[1] Their article highlighted how lay women trained in spiritual direction were able to use and adapt individual direction strategies for a group.

Lord (1987) describes her experiences of group spiritual direction by applying Gerald May's distinction among spiritual formation, spiritual guid-ance, and spiritual direction. For May (1979), "spiritual formation" is a more general term denoting the deepening of faith and spiritual growth and includ-ing educational endeavors. Spiritual guidance, on the other hand, suggests not only a deepening of one's relations with God but also a living of the effects of the relationship in daily life. Third, spiritual direction is a formal one-to-one relationship between a director and a directee who distinguish various move-ments of spirits. Lord uses May's distinctions to characterize how in a group of eight women she offered two hours of spiritual formation that included an hour of spiritual guidance and an hour of spiritual direction.

More recently, McKnight (1995) presents three distinct models of group spiritual direction. One that she labels "a circle of support" involves the gath-ering, including the sharing of a meal, of five congregational leaders who for several years have come together once a month for three to four hours. After their meal together, they each present a "critical incident" from their ministries. Such incidents often reflect their roles as leaders in their respective religious communities. Group members, in listening to a "critical incident," understand that they are not to engage in problem solving, but are to allow for a forum for shared searching.

Group sharing through physical meditative practices is another form of group direction that McKnight considers. Such a model invites participants, during a six- or twelve-week series, to express spiritual movements of their lives, in a manner that takes into account their physical presence with one another expressed through body language. Centered on certain yoga exercises, the group pays attention to the subtle movements of the spirit keenly noticed through their shared silence and in their breathing exercises.

A third model of group direction described by McKnight involves coming together around a "sacred garden." Such a community gathers for prayer in a seven-month process to focus upon significant themes of nature. Special emphasis is placed upon the sacredness of the earth, a shared awareness of natural foods and herbs, and a rhythmic sensitivity to ritual and to women's "herstory."

In summarizing her survey of these three forms of group direction, McKnight finds six characteristics in common. They are

- *Intentionality:* The individual and collective purpose of the gathering is for the growth in holiness.

- *Trained Leadership:* The leaders of each group had been professionally trained in the arts of discernment and guidance.

- *Literal Acknowledgment of the Presence of God:* That is to say, prayer is the central means by which the group names and images God.

- *Accountability through Supervision:* By means of individual or group supervision, the group leaders were professionally accountable and were thereby able to maintain the integrity of the group process.

- *Active Participation by All Members in the Process:* Instead of concern addressed directly to the leader as the sole authority, there was a sense of a common empowerment. In this respect, group spiritual direction differs from individual spiritual direction. In the former there is a drawing from the wisdom of "all of us," whereas in the latter there is "the one" (higher) and "the many" (lower).

- *Commitment and Stability:* A common expectation of confidentiality and fidelity to the gatherings. (McKnight, 1995, 42–44)

McKnight's presentation of these three quite distinct spiritual gatherings suggests how differentiated group spiritual direction has become. Such differentiation contrasts with the more formal structure developed in recent years by the Shalem Institute, which may be viewed as a school of spirituality.

The Shalem School of Spirituality

Since 1973 the Shalem Institute for Spiritual Formation has provided spiritual formation to hundreds of Christian believers. The Institute defines itself as an "ecumenical Christian organization calling the people of God to deeper spiritual life for the world" (Shalem, 1998, 2). Under the leadership of Tilden Edwards, Shalem has emerged as one of the leading institutes of spirituality in the world and the largest training program for group spiritual direction. Its approach to spiritual formation may be viewed through the writings of four authors who have been associated with Shalem: Tilden Edwards, Gerald May, Shawn McCarty, and Rose Mary Dougherty. A review of their works will provide a comprehensive understanding of what group spiritual direction is and how far it has progressed since its original inception.

The work of Rev. Tilden Edwards, an Episcopalian priest, has been at the heart of the Shalem Institute's prominent influence in the area of spirituality in general and in group spiritual formation in particular. Edwards's first book, *Spiritual Friend* (1980), devoted an entire chapter to the then-emerging group model. Based primarily on the experiences that he and his colleagues at Shalem had with groups, his reflections provide a fine summary of their work up to that time. Among his observations, Edwards (1980, 18–82) considers formation groups as having four primary functions:

- *Sanctuary:* A quiet and open environment that enhances relaxation, coping, and a sense of presence;

- *Teaching:* The introduction of particular spiritual disciplines and practices;

- *Reflection:* Creating opportunities for the expression and interpretation of one's spiritual journey;

- *Accountability:* Personal attention to personal prayer disciplines.

These four functions give spiritual formation groups a distinct quality that may complement individual spiritual direction. Such a contrast is taken up by Edwards when in an earlier essay by one of his colleagues at Shalem, Shawn McCarty, McCarty (1976, 864, 865) lists some of the advantages and disadvantages of spiritual group counseling. Some of the advantages that McCarty cites:

1. Availability for more people;

2. Opportunity for a variety of clarifying comments, questions from more people;

3. More appropriate for the development of a sense that true Christian holiness has a corporate dimension;

4. Additional benefits and support for group members from hearing about others' faith journeys, even when one's own is not in focus;

5. The possibility of enrichment from and deepened appreciation of spiritualities and prayer styles other than one's own.

Five of the difficulties of group spiritual counseling that McCarty lists are:

1. Individual faith journeys vary in the direction they take, the intensity with which they are experienced, and the pace at which they proceed;

2. In a group, depending on the size and frequency of the meeting, the individual gets less attention;

3. It is more difficult for some people, especially the more introverted, to be open and self-revelatory in a group where trust levels vary;

4. Negative dynamics like domination and competition in a group can block openness to the spirit;

5. There is a greater possibility of confusion caused by conflicting comments from different members.

Edwards (1980, 182–84) also speaks of five factors that are crucial for a spiritual formation group's healthy development. They are environment, size, time, standards, and rhythm. Edwards suggests that the environment for directing groups should "reflect an inviting sanctuary" that would contain a quiet setting with low lights and a carpeted floor. He also recommends the use of a candle to lend a sacred tone to the meeting.

Edwards says that to be effective a group's size should range from eight to twenty members. Fewer than eight members he sees as reducing the diversity of input, whereas more than twenty diminishes the dialogue. There are two factors associated with time: the length of a meeting and the length of an individual's commitment to the group. Edwards believes that group sessions should last at least an hour and a half but no longer than three hours. Between six weeks and ten months should be the length of one's commitment to a group. Opportunities for recommitment should be offered, without pressure.

Edwards describes two categories of standards: "within the group" and "outside the group." The standards within are:

1. Giving priority to group sessions;

2. Beginning and ending on time;

3. Silence in room (except during group reflection and after sessions);

4. No smoking, drinking, eating in room;

5. Attentive patience: with doubts, frustrations, boredom, judgments, restlessness, and elation.

"Outside the group" standards include:

1. Daily discipline of open attentiveness in solitude and in daily activity;

2. Reading is secondary to firsthand experience, but taking on at least one relevant book during the group's life might aid motivation, confirmation, and clarity;

3. Discrimination in sharing personal experience with others outside the group;

4. Remembering that the fruits of the spirit, a trusting mind, and an open heart are important, and not experiential "highs" and "lows";

5. Teach others what you learn only and if you feel confident about it in your own experience;

6. Prayer for those in group.

In a more recent work, Edwards (1995) sees the group as helping the person in the formation of "the spiritual eye that can notice the Divine Spirit at work" (Edwards, 1995, 127). He cautions against deceptions and diversions that may lead a group away from its original purpose. He finds, for instance, that too great an emphasis upon socializing, "feeling good," or cognitive insights may detract from the group's main intent of spiritual conversation.

Over the years in its work with formation groups, Shalem has developed a distinct method whereby group spiritual direction takes place. This method was developed by Rose Mary Dougherty (1995), who has served as Shalem's director for group spiritual guidance. The method elaborated in her book is as follows:

1. Silent gathering (20 minutes): A means for gathering of hearts into a common desire for God.

2. Sharing by one person (10–15 minutes): The group listens without interruption.

3. Silence (3–4 minutes): Enables participants to find God in what has been shared and to be more able to respond from a place of freedom;

4. Response (10 minutes): During this time the facilitator needs to make sure that members do not move into a "fix it" mode or offer too many ideas or images;

5. Silence (5 minutes): A time to pray for the one who had just presented. The presenter may take this time to write some notes;

6. Repetition of steps 2 through 5 for the next member. (Dougherty, 1995 50, 51)

Dougherty's book, *Group Spiritual Direction,* was later complemented by a video that provides a closer examination of the process. The video highlights the creative and innovative work performed at the Shalem Institute, which now includes training for people beginning programs in group spiritual direction.

Common Factors in Group Therapy and Group Spiritual Direction

For the past several decades the most important introductory text in the field of group work has been Irving Yalom's *The Theory and Practice of Group Psychotherapy.* First published in 1970, Yalom's work has gone through four editions and has been the standard textbook for the growing number of group therapists.

At the heart of Yalom's treatise is his consideration of the curative effects of group therapy. In the most recent edition (1985), he lists eleven such effects: instillation of hope, universality, imparting information, altruism, the corrective recapitulation of the primary family group, development of socializing techniques, imitative behavior, catharsis, existential factors, group cohesiveness, and interpersonal learning. Not all of these curative factors are pertinent to the dynamics of group spiritual direction. Several are, however, and they include the instillation of hope, universality, altruism, and interpersonal behavior and group cohesiveness. It would be well then to consider briefly such factors within the context of group spiritual direction.

Like those in many gatherings, participants in group psychotherapy can *instill hope* through one another. As Yalom notes, observing the improvement in another member of the group fosters a sense that the same is possible for oneself. Consequently, *hope* is engendered.

Within the context of group spiritual direction the same may apply. To listen to the developments in another's prayer life may serve as a support for one's development in prayer. Issues of personal darkness and discouragement may be overcome by simply listening to the ways in which the spirit has worked in the prayer life of a peer.

Universality contrasts with isolation. Yalom speaks of the relief that members of a therapy group experience when they realize that others may share similar difficult circumstances and feelings. The principle of *universality* has been one of the central tenets of support groups, helping individuals to cope with behaviors and circumstances that may have led them to feel alone, especially experiences that have remained secretive rather than shared. Anonymity groups such as Alcohol Anonymous, Gamblers Anonymous, and Narcotics Anonymous have proven universality to be of vital importance.

Using *universality* as a principle, participants in group spiritual direction, while not meant to be therapeutic in focus, may be a source for one's secrets to be shared. Relying on trust, not only can one's darkness be turned into light, but also what one hears in the dark may come to be seen in the light (Mt 10:27).

For Yalom, *imparting information,* while helpful, requires caution. Unlike many self-help practices, where information about addictive behaviors, diseases, or stages of loss is needed, the giving of advice or didactic instruction in therapy groups often proves counterproductive. This is especially true for psychodynamically oriented groups. Direct suggestions, according to Yalom, have proven to be least helpful.

For participants in a spiritual direction group, *imparting information* or giving advice has benefits as well as liabilities. At times a group member's suggestions may serve to guide another's prayer life. On the other hand, consistent advice giving will throw off the group's balance. A sense of mutuality may be lost, and the one who gives advice may be seen as a director rather than a peer-participant. Some groups seek to counteract these tendencies by asking participants to make suggestions sparingly and only with the preface, "If this were my prayer...."

By *altruism* Yalom means the sense group members have of assisting each other. Through the process of one speaking and the other listening within an atmosphere of mutuality, a spirit develops that helps members to transcend themselves. For Yalom such a spirit of *altruism* is made evident in the encouragement and reassurance members may share with one another. *Altruism* demonstrates the principle that the best way to help others is to let them help you.

Altruism is clearly manifested in group spiritual direction as engendered by the active prayer life of the participants. Indeed, the spirit of altruism tends to be an essential characteristic of many members' lives. There is a gracious generosity of spirit. The converse is the aversion that members may have to allowing themselves to be helped. As at the washing of Peter's feet (Jn 13:1–13), there may be a reluctance to be served characterized by a strong defensiveness.

Yalom sees *existential factors* as expressing a person's life struggle. Such issues as death, freedom, isolation, and meaninglessness often emerge and are expressed within the group therapy process. One of the unique attributes of group therapy is that it can create and foster a context wherein participants may share the vulnerabilities of their existence.

Group spiritual direction easily lends itself to existential discussions. A person's prayer often touches upon loss, loneliness, or meaninglessness. On such occasions one may wonder where God may be found in difficult and tragic circumstances. Group spiritual conversation, like group psychotherapy, offers a "holding environment" in which such concerns may be voiced. Unlike group therapy, however, group spiritual conversation provides a distinct environment where participants are intentionally open to the spirit of God and seek to name the spirit's movements for one another. In this respect, group spiritual direction may be seen as developing an ecology for the spirit. That is to say, the intentional con-spiracy of group members creates ways whereby movements of the spirit may be readily named and facilitated in and through participants' interactions with one another.

Con-Spirators in Action

To provide a glimpse of several of the dynamics of group spirituality, I present examples of typical issues and responses. Parts of three conversations are presented; each is followed by a brief commentary. A group contains six members including the facilitator. Their names are Steve, Anna, Judith, Barry, Charles, and Maureen (facilitator).

Presentation 1, Barry's Issue: Spiritual Direction versus Counseling

Maureen begins the session with a brief prayer. Then allows for a five-minute silence, after which Barry shares what has been happening in his prayer.

Barry: "This week my prayer has taken me to some new places in my life, but I am not sure what to share. Some of it involves not only my relationship with

God, but concerns another relationship. It concerns some anxieties I have had about a friendship with a woman at work, and I am not sure how much to share about it here."

Maureen: "Would you share with us how you have brought the relationship to God? And what has happened when you have done so."

Barry: "I see, that's helpful. Without going through all the details, let me say that I have found myself being both comforted and challenged. I have been comforted when I discussed with the Lord my affection for this woman. On the other hand, I felt challenged when I heard the Lord asking me the question where I am going with the relationship...."

Comment

Notice how important it is that a person's sharing include some real issues in that person's life, but that it be focused on prayer. This is one of the differences between group spiritual direction and group psychotherapy. In the latter Barry would be allowed a fair amount of time to express and elaborate his feelings for the purpose of developing emotional insights and self-understanding. Maureen's comment helped Barry to consider the relationship within the context of his friendship with God. While realizing that much more could be said, Maureen did not try to solve Barry's problem.

Presentation 2, Judith's Issue: Dryness, Desolation, Doubts

Judith: "Since our last meeting I have been having some difficulties in sensing God's presence, both in prayer and in my daily life. It's not that I am avoiding prayer. I just don't feel as enthused about it." (She continues for several more minutes in a similar vein.)

Charles (after some silence): "As I heard you, Judith, I was reminded of situations in my life when praying was difficult. On such occasions I traced the dryness to when I last felt God's presence. Then I noticed that an emotional event had occurred that I had not yet processed adequately. Another time a series of work-related projects had really been exhausting me, and I found prayer becoming just another project to get done. And so I wonder if the same might be true for you."

Comment

Charles's response has within it components of empathy and identification. The value of such a response depends on Judith's sense that Charles has heard her. It is important to mention that Charles does not seek to "fix" Judith's dryness in prayer. He must, however, be careful not to overidentify so much that the focus shifts to him rather than Judith. For instance, Charles might have said, "I once had the same problem and this is what I did.... Maybe if you do the same thing as I did your problems in feeling God's presence would be solved." If Charles were to have made such a response, it would be the facilitator's responsibility to move the focus back to Judith and to the "mystery" she was presenting, not to the problem.

Presentation 3, Anna's Issue: The Use of Metaphors

Anna: "This past month I have been praying over the story of the potter in Jeremiah. I felt drawn to it, since I have started pottery class and have really found it relaxing and recreative, not to mention challenging. Learning to do pottery has helped me to have a new understanding of the passage: 'like clay in the hand of the potter, so you are in my hand.' The image of being in the hand of God has helped me get through some difficult moments the past few weeks." (She continues on in a similar vein.)

Steve (after a period of silence): "Anna, the image of a potter that you present seems quite powerful, especially since you are now learning pottery. It is almost as if the spirit led you to learn the craft of pottery and to listen through the vehicle of pottery. A number of years ago this same image was helpful for me, and I sense that it will continue to influence your life for a long time. I am happy for you."

Comment

Steve's affirmation of Anna's metaphor was an effective way for him to connect with her and to give her a sense that she was listened to. Metaphors have a way of doing that. Indeed, one might say that it is through metaphor that the thoughts of the head are connected to the emotions of the heart. Much of our explicit and implicit understandings are accomplished by means of metaphor. Since the time of Jeremiah, the metaphor of the potter has brought human hearts to the heart of God.

Class Con-Spirators

For the past two years I have been conducting a two-semester course on group spirituality. The first semester course, entitled "Group Spiritual Formation," offers students an opportunity to understand developmental factors and spiritual influences that shape their images of God. During the second semester, in a course entitled "Group Spiritual Guidance," students are exposed to the major writers on spirituality. In both courses students participate in spiritual conversation groups. Throughout the two semesters students are divided into groups of four or five and asked to share their prayer life, using in an abbreviated form the Shalem guidelines as presented by Dougherty and discussed earlier. Unlike the Shalem model, however, the groups meet for only thirty minutes and the role of the facilitator is rotated among the members of each small group. Each week, after they meet in small groups, the students return as an entire class and we process the group dynamics. To ensure confidentiality, each facilitator is asked only about the process and not about the content of the group dynamics. In addition, each student was asked to keep a journal and to comment, within the boundaries of confidentiality, on how they found their respective group evolving for them.

In processing with the facilitators each week, I have noticed that the several curative factors described by Yalom occur also in group spiritual direction. For instance, during the first several weeks of a semester, as the group became formed, I would hear comments dealing with *universality* when facilitators mentioned how group members found some common ground in struggles they shared with one another. There were also comments of how some participants listened and responded to a member's sharing *(altruism)*. On the other hand, there were occasional reports of participants attempting to solve or fix another member's problem.

Over time, as the members slowly became comfortable with both the sharing process and others' styles, a sense of trust gradually emerged. Toward the end of the first semester, several but not all group facilitators would remark that there was a sense of bonding indicative of group cohesiveness, one of Yalom's curative factors. Moreover, in the students' journals I would read how much they looked forward to the group direction time. For some, it became the most important period of their week. Perhaps the real impact of the group spiritual conversations could be seen in the fact that the next year some of the students decided to form a spiritual group of their own. They chose to continue their con-spiracy with God.

Parish Con-Spirators

Parishes are perhaps the most likely setting for the formation of spiritual conversation groups. Such groups may take many forms. One successful approach recently developed was an Ignatian retreat group based on Annotation 19 of the Spiritual Exercises of St. Ignatius of Loyola. Some fifty parishioners participated in the retreat, which was an adaptation from the Ignatian "thirty-day" or "four-week" model. The ages of the participants ranged from the mid-thirties to the early seventies. They were divided into three groups and met every other week, beginning in October and continuing until May.

Throughout that time only one meeting was missed and that was during Christmas vacation.

Every week, participants were given several passages from scripture based upon the specific "weeks" or phases of the Spiritual Exercises. They were asked to pray each week for either five periods of thirty minutes of prayer or four periods of forty-five minutes. The meeting opened with the lighting of a candle, followed by some silence to recall graces received during the two weeks since the last meeting. Participants were given two to three minutes to present some movements in their prayer. These presentations lasted about forty-five minutes. Following these presentations there was a period in which participants could ask other group members to elaborate on their prayers. A parish priest served as the facilitator and would invite the group to focus on three simple questions: How may your light shed light on another's light or darkness? Where are you in the assigned scripture passages? Where is God?

The experience was quite profound for all those involved. After the experience some members continued to meet. When interviewed several years later, one of the participants remarked, "Before the retreat I felt empty. Through the group I found a place where I belong. I needed to have that outlet in order for my prayer to come alive by my speaking and sharing it."

Another participant remarked, "The group makes you believe in your lights. You can't experience them with just one person." The priest-facilitator himself believed, having had years of directing and being directed one-to-one, that group spiritual experience "is no longer second best."

Con-Spirators of the Future

Through a variety of examples this brief survey has examined several methods and modes of group spiritual conversations. One might wonder whether spiritual groups will become more commonplace in the future. There are no hard statistics on the number of such groups. There have, however, been studies that suggest an increasing number of groups formed around people's search for spirituality. In Wuthnow's (1994) edited volume there exist a number of case studies that suggest the existence of a movement toward small groups collecting around communal and spiritual topics. The studies describe how many such groups are forming outside the traditional structures of "mainline" religions. Perhaps such a movement is in reaction to the American penchant for individualism that Bellah and others (1985) aptly described. If the movement toward small groups does take hold in American culture, one might speculate that spiritual conversation groups, whether informally gathered or formally structured such as those using the Ignatian or Shalem models, will become vitally more important. Indeed, they may well represent a significant response for fostering the spiritual lives of individuals who have become dis-satisfied with traditional forms of religious gatherings.

At the same time, as McCarty points out, group spiritual gatherings, in contrast to individual spiritual direction, allow for the greater availability for sharing one's spiritual life. Individual spiritual direction, while it may facili-tate an individual's spiritual growth, may be seen as less accessible and more of a luxury. For these two reasons, then, group spiritual conversations may become a new paradigm for spirituality. As a consequence, there may well be the need for future spiritual ministers to be trained in both individual and group spiritual direction. Spiritual guides may need to know how to become con-spirators with the spirit.

Note

1. In his *Spiritual Exercises*, St. Ignatius of Loyola suggested ways for those "engaged in public affairs or necessary business" to make the Exercises. One contemporary adaptation is for a retreatant to pray one hour a day instead of four or five over thirty weeks instead of thirty days. The retreatant would also see a director once a week instead of once a day.

Selected References and Suggested Reading

"About Shalem." *Shalem News,* September 1998, p. 2.
Bellah, R., et al. *Habits of the Heart.* San Francisco: Harper and Row.
Dougherty, R. (1995) *Group Spiritual Direction: Community for Discernment.* New York: Paulist.
Edwards, T. (1995) *Living in the Presence: Spiritual Exercises to Open Our Lives to the Awareness of God.* San Francisco: Harper.
———. (1980) *Spiritual Friend.* New York: Paulist.
Halenworth, Q. (1968) "Group Methods in Spiritual Direction." *Review for Religious:* 71–75.
Haughey, J. (1973) *The Conspiracy of God: The Holy Spirit in Us.* Garden City: Image Books.
Iconogle, G. W. (1994) *Biblical Foundations for Small Group Ministry: An Integrational Approach.* Downers Grove, Ill.: InterVarsity Press.
Lord, D. (1987) "An Experience of Group Spiritual Direction." *Review for Religious* 36, 2: 279–94.
May, G. G. (1979) *Pilgrimage Home: The Conduct of Contemplative Practice in Groups.* New York: Paulist.
McCarty, S. (1976) "On Entering Spiritual Direction." *Review for Religious* 35, 6: 854–57.

McKnight, F. (1995) "Group Spiritual Direction: Intentionality and Diversity." *Presence* 1, 3: 29–44.

Muto, S. and van Kaam, A. (1998) *Epiphany Manual on the Art and Discipline of Formation-in-Common: A Fresh Approach to the Ancient Practice of Spiritual Direction*. Pittsburgh: Epiphany Books.

Sullivan, M. and Horstman, D. (1977) "The Nineteenth Annotation Retreat: The Retreat of the Future." *Review for Religious* 46, 2: 277–85.

Van Kaam, A. (1976) *Dynamics of Spiritual Self-Direction*. Denville, N.J.: Dimension Books.

Wuthnow, R. (1994) *"I Come Away Stronger": How Small Groups Are Shaping American Religion*. Grand Rapids, Mich.: Eerdmans.

Yalom, I. (1985) *The Theory and Practice of Group Psychotherapy*. New York: Basic Books.

Yalom, B. (ed.) (1998) *The Yalom Reader: Selections from the Work of a Master Therapist and Storyteller*. New York: Basic Books.

Robert A. Jonas

31. The Empty Bell:
A Contemplative Community

The Empty Bell is a small contemplative sanctuary in Watertown, Massachusetts, just outside Boston. About twenty people think of the Empty Bell as their
spiritual home. Another twenty drop by occasionally, and our mailing list goes
out to more than five hundred people, some of whom come to special events.
In addition to our weekly gatherings, we offer periodic (nonresidential)
retreats focused on Christian topics or on the Christian-Buddhist dialogue. As
a nonprofit, tax-exempt corporation, our mission statement declares

> The Empty Bell is a sanctuary for the study and practice of Chris-
> tian meditation and prayer. Our purpose is to learn the history and
> practice of the Christian contemplative path as rooted in the
> Gospels, and to explore its common ground with other ancient
> Wisdom teachings. We give special attention to the Christian-
> Buddhist dialogue, and to artistic expression of spiritual insight.

Most Empty Bell activities take place in a renovated carriage house
behind our home. During the 1993 renovation project, I felt inwardly guided by
images of simple Catholic monasteries and Japanese zendos. We took out one
bay of a two-bay garage on the first floor, and in its place created a gathering
space that includes a bathroom, waiting area with couch, kitchenette, and new
stairwell to the second floor. The entry door and the door at the bottom of the
stairs transmit soft light through full-length, soji-screened windows criss-
crossed with cherry latticework. On the walls hang an icon of the Trinity, a
framed copy of the Buddhist Heart Sutra (in Japanese), and a long, narrow painting that depicts a Chinese mountain scene. A simple Southeast Asian bust of
Buddha rests on a cherry shelf beside the door to the second floor. In the stairwell hang a colorful painting and a brightly colored Tibetan Buddhist tapestry.

The second floor is one large room with a new maple floor. The door
jambs, window frames, exposed beams, and the frames for the baseboard heat
are all fashioned in cherry wood. In the center of the room, twelve meditation

cushions (zafus and zabutons) form an oblong circle around a white wool rug. With additional meditation benches and chairs the space accommodates up to twenty-five people. In the center of the rug a flat, woven basket holds a candle in red glass, a delicate statue of Kwan Yin (the Buddhist boddhisatva of compassion), and a small cross made from the wood that was used to construct the coffin of Henri Nouwen, a Roman Catholic priest and our dear spiritual friend who died of a heart attack in September 1996. On the walls hang several Christian icons: Elijah being fed by ravens in the desert, Mary holding the baby Jesus, the shepherd Jesus holding a lost lamb.

Weekly Community Gatherings

Empty Bell participants tend to be white professional men and woman who were raised Christian—both Protestant and Roman Catholic—and then "went East" to learn meditation in Buddhist, Hindu, or New Age contexts. We are primarily service providers: teachers, ministers, lawyers, nurses and doctors, writers, editors, administrators, psychologists, social workers, and artists. Personal meditation, retreats, travel to Asian countries, and extensive reading have led many of us to reexamine our childhood faiths, and to seek an integration of these distinctive spiritualities. Some of us, never having had experience in formal meditation, have simply become spontaneously interested in the deeper dimensions of contemplative prayer or in the Christian mystical tradition. Some of us have returned to our churches, seeing the Empty Bell not as a substitute for traditional liturgies, but rather as a special place to explore the contemplative dimension of the gospel and our lives. Our gatherings reflect these interests.

The Empty Bell offers three weekly meditation and prayer times on Thursday and Sunday mornings. At first I led all meetings, but over the past two years a group of about ten leaders has emerged. Several times a year I meet with these leaders to meditate and pray, and to discuss our vision and common concerns.

Structure of Empty Bell Gatherings

8:30–9:00 A.M	*Silent meditation*
9:00	*Greetings and Christian scripture reading*
9:10	*Contemplative reflection on scripture (by leader)*
9:15	*Sharing (whole group, response to silence and/or the readings)*
9:40	*Silent meditation and spoken prayers*
9:45	*Announcements and end*

Over time a consensus has emerged about the structure of our worship together. Thursdays and Sundays are almost identical in organization.

We begin with a half-hour to forty-five minutes of silence. Those who come early sit in silence or chant together until 8:30 A.M. At that time the leader taps a large Japanese temple bell three times to signal the start of the meditation. We leave plenty of space between each tap so that we can savor the gradually diminishing sound of each ring. The leader's attentiveness to this task expresses a sensitivity and quality of care that reminds us all to slow down, and to breathe more deeply, from the belly. Some of us have trained in zazen, some in insight mindfulness meditation, some in centering prayer, some in various forms of mantra or breath practice. We do not require that everyone be "doing" the same thing in the silence. Rather, we expect that the spirit of God leads each person in his or her own way. Sometimes, into the silence, the leader might (with closed eyes) say softly, "Gently returning to this moment," or "Gently returning to the breath," or "Christ tells us that we are the Beloved. Breathing in God's love." Offering occasional, gentle guidance in the silence lends support to those whose minds are running wild with self-talk. Most often, there is no speech in the silence.

If the leader speaks, he or she usually includes him or herself in the suggested focus by using the pronouns "we" or "us" rather than "you" or "your." Instead of saying, "Bring awareness to your breathing," the leader might say simply, "Bringing awareness to the breathing." Instead of saying, "Visualize God's love coming to you with each in-breath," we might suggest, "Knowing that God calls us each the Beloved, can we breathe in that assurance with each breath?" As leaders, we avoid setting ourselves up as experts. We assume that the One who teaches is both within us and among us, and that the center of the action is not within the leader, but everywhere. Leaders bear some special responsibilities in practical matters such as lighting candles, arranging the cushions and chairs, ringing the bell, introducing readings, offering reflections, leading prayers and announcements, and generally being "where the buck stops" in terms of the comfort and safety of participants. But leaders are not trying to be objective "professionals" in terms of theology, liturgy, or psychological well-being. During a gathering, leaders can expect to receive the spiritual support of others, and to listen to the guidance of the Holy Spirit along with everyone else.

At the end of the silence the leader rings the temple bell again three times. And again the resonance of each ring is allowed to dissipate gradually and completely before the next ring. The leader then welcomes everyone, thus initiating a general exchange of greetings (usually nonverbal) in the whole group. Sometimes, when there are new members, we do a "go-round" with each person saying his or her name. The leader then introduces the readings for the day from the Hebrew scripture, the Epistles and the Gospels. We read from a small, monthly pamphlet published by Novalis, a Roman Catholic publishing house in Canada. The Empty Bell receives copies of *Living with Christ* each month, and many core members of the community subscribe. Thus, most participants will have a copy of *Living with Christ* sitting next to their meditation cushion during our gatherings. The booklet contains all the Hebrew and Christian readings that are being used in Roman Catholic churches on that particular day. It is important for us to know that often these readings are the same in Episcopal and other Protestant churches around the world.

On Sunday mornings we usually read the Hebrew scripture, the psalm responsorial (as an antiphonal response), and the epistle. Before the gospel we share a Taizé or other Christian chant led by our cantor for the day. So that everyone's voice can be heard, each person reads at some point from the *Living with Christ* booklet. We adjust how much each person reads (one line to a whole text) based on how many people are present. After the gospel there is a moment of silence. Then the leader begins a sharing time by offering a brief contemplative reflection on the readings.

The sharing time that follows is meant to be quite personal, focusing on how the Holy Spirit is (or doesn't seem to be) moving in that person's life. We have an agreement to avoid merely giving information to others or trying to convince others of something. We also agree not to seek advice from or give advice to individual members. Rather, we intend to speak from that dark wordless territory where God is working in our lives, right now, at this moment. We suggest that everyone use the personal pronoun "I." Sometimes the spirit of these sharings is lively and funny—there is often much laughter. And sometimes the spirit is quiet or even sorrowful. We are looking for the "frontier" where something new is happening in our lives, especially in our relationship with God. Sometimes we fall into long periods of silence together. The sharing time is like a Quaker meeting, though it may be a bit more personal than some Quaker gatherings.

This 20–30 minutes of sharing is a highly valued part of our time together. Indeed, God comes alive for many of us in silence. But God also works through speech and listening. This is not a time for theological discussion, ideological argument, literary or historical-critical Bible study, or the emotional insight work of psychotherapy. We are simply here to listen to God together. But this simple goal is sometimes very difficult for smart professionals with postgraduate degrees. As children and young adults, none of us received training in how to listen well.

After a few experiences in which newcomers seemed to disrupt the deep listening of this sharing time, I drafted a document called our "Principles of Sharing," which outlines what we think is happening in both the silence and sharing at the Empty Bell. This document then circulated in the community and was edited by several members. Now, we ask that all new participants read this document before coming to a Thursday or Sunday gathering. Thus, new-comers can discern if this kind of meeting and worship is really what they want. Here are the precepts we intend to follow, not as dogma, but rather as laying out a direction, like true north on our spiritual compass:

Empty Bell Principles of Sharing

Almost all gatherings at the Empty Bell include silence, and individual sharing in the group. In this society, such opportunities are rare, precious, and fragile. Over time, we have found that this kind of "holy conversation" is most fruitful when certain principles of understanding and behavior are followed.

Principles of Understanding

1) *Silence is often the dwelling place of God.* Silence is at the heart of authentic listening and speech. In silence, we are listening inwardly for the presence of the Holy Spirit. Sometimes we call this deep listening "practicing the Presence."

2) Our minds are often involved in judgment and comparison (of ourselves and others). But practicing the Presence is a disciplined, *inward listening that is non-judgmental.* In this type of listening, we cultivate a tone of mercy, compassion and unconditional love toward ourselves and others. We are not looking for what is wrong or right about ourselves or others, but simply for "what is" in the context of God's love. Deep listening requires an attitude of neutral, compassionate inquiry.

3) Authentic contact with God and others is always made in some present moment. But, too often, we are not truly present. Too often, we are distracted, thinking about the past or the future, or analyzing our experience. Our mind is sometimes a tree full of monkeys! One aim of our spiritual practice is *to be truly present* with our whole selves in each moment.

4) When we do speak, we are not merely trading information, or even telling interesting stories. *Holy speech* comes from a deeper place, and *creates something new* as it is spoken. A new space, and new possibilities are opened up in the speaker's and the listener's heart.

5) *Good listening happens in the whole body,* not only in the ears and brain. When I listen to someone speak, I try to listen with my heart, belly, and skin.

6) Authentic speech emerges out of a deep, interior place where the old and new circulate, where what we *already* knew before we sat down, and what we don't yet know somehow come together. In true speech there is something new for the speaker, some discovery, and a sense of aliveness that accompanies this new frontier. This inner frontier of new speech is the Holy Spirit, a dynamic, safe, and sacred place. The Holy Spirit is always new. *God is the newest thing there is!* These statements are not merely interesting ideas, but rather, *experiences.*

7) The most powerful dimension of being with others is not in the trading of words, but in the felt-sense of simply being together. In this dimension, less is more. Without saying a word, *simply being-with* can be relaxing, blessed and fruitful.

8) It is best when every person in the group feels at home, safe, and invited to share. In fruitful groups, each individual intends *to listen the other members into speech.* In such groups, each individual inwardly invites his or her neighbor to speak first. There is no competition for clever ideas.

Principles of Behavior

Sitting

1) *Sit up straight* on your cushion, bench or chair. Please do not extend your legs into the center area. While keeping the spine straight, relax the body. Relax, but stay awake. We are on holy ground. If there is pain in the joints or the back, take a moment to bring awareness to the pain, and relax into it before shifting the body. Soften into the pain. Know that working with emotional and physical pain is an important part of the contemplative path.

2) Occasionally, during the sharing time, *bring awareness to your body,* especially to any areas of tension. Ask yourself what that tension is about, and then relax into the tension, to see what happens. At other times, bring awareness to breathing, letting it be. Sometimes, that is where the real action is—not in the verbal conversation.

Speaking and Listening

1) *For new participants, it is better to listen more,* and to speak less or not at all in the first meeting, or until you feel a strong prompting from the spirit. In this way, you can more easily catch the subtle, deep flow of dialogue that is practiced here.

2) *Listen for feelings* within yourself and within the other, as much as for content. In fact, consider emotions that arise, pleasant or unpleasant, as an important part of your spiritual practice. For example, I might ask myself, "What feelings are stirring within me as I listen to this person?" When I speak, I might ask myself, "Where in my body are these words coming from?" Consider such questions as koans that take us deeper without necessarily providing a final answer.

3) *Do not give or ask for advice.* We are here to plumb our own depths, from within our own bodies, not to tell others what to do, even necessarily to help them. If someone says, "I don't know what to do about such-and-such," we simply listen with our inner ear and with our heart. Assume that people's not-knowing is a good thing, and that our job is simply to be with them lovingly in their not-knowing. This practice invites God into our not-knowing.

4) *Pay close attention to pronouns.* When speaking, try to use the personal pronoun, "I." This pronoun often carries more emotional and spiritual depth, and invites more intimacy. Occasionally, the pronouns "we" and "you" (when used to mean "anyone") are appropriate, especially when we speak about universal truths. But too often we leap to the universal level of things before we are truly grounded within our "I."

5) *A felt-sense of silence* must be maintained, *even in the midst of conversation.* "Billiard ball" or "ping-pong" conversation—where each individual's words ricochet off another's—tends to be unfruitful. If things move too fast, we tend to verbalize old opinions and depth is lost. Thus, before speaking, breathe into your belly and into your motives for speaking. Asking yourself a question, such as "Why am I saying this *now?*" will deepen your self-knowledge and your subsequent speech. Give space to those speakers who may need to pause and then go on.

6) Before speaking, *be aware of those members who have not spoken yet.* Assume that they might need a little more silence in which to find their words. If you have already spoken, wait a bit longer before you speak again. Practice discernment. Stay awake!

7) You may notice *the lightness or playfulness of the atmosphere* here. This lightness arises from the sense of safety that people feel to be simply who they are. It is not unusual for both tears and laughter to arise together, or in close proximity. Since the sharing is often deep and exploratory, we do not expect people to be smooth and elegant in their speech. We are simply sharing our experience with trusted friends.

Being in Community

1) *Consider everything that is shared as confidential.* That is, in all personal sharings, we do not tell others outside the group what a specific person said or did, unless we have that person's permission. Sharing our own personal experience of being in this community can be a gift to ourselves and to others when we do it with respect for individual confidentiality.

2) One of the most fruitful dimensions of being in a group is *working with judgments about others,* and with the mind's tendency to compare oneself with others. Judgments and comparisons are not bad in themselves. Rather, they are simply how the mind works. Bring awareness to these inner activities, relax into them, and then explore them with an attitude of compassionate inquiry. Those who leave a group because they are uncomfortable with another member miss a golden opportunity for knowing themselves and God more deeply. Stay with it! If problems persist, speak to the leader.

3) We encourage each member of our community to *create a period of silent meditation, contemplation or prayer, each day.*

4) *We support each other to live lives* of creativity and service in our work, families, and communities.

Our Theological and Christological Assumptions

At the Empty Bell, we assume that the Holy Spirit is a real presence now in the same way that he or she was present to Jesus two thousand years ago. God's presence is not only "out there" in the world, separate from us in space and time, but also within us, within this temple we call our bodies and in our own awareness and consciousness (1 Cor 2:16; 1 Cor 6:19; Phil 1:20f). The holy is not merely "up there" in another heavenly location, but neither is God merely identical with us and the physical world. God is somehow, subtly, both *within* our personal awareness and also *within* the world "out there." Jesus' life is our model and inspiration. His life as recorded in scripture provides us with clues about where, in our own experience, to look for the holy.

Many of Jesus' followers sought, and even now seek, to idealize him, to make him a kind of spiritual celebrity with magical powers. But he resists these efforts. Jesus always points to God, not himself, as the source of spiritual authority and goodness (Jn 7:16ff; Jn 8:28ff; Lk 18:18–19). When people are healed in his presence he doesn't take personal credit, but rather empowers them to consider their own faith in God as the source of the healing (Mt 17:18ff; Mk 5:25ff).

When Jesus' followers want to disown their own spiritual authority by projecting it onto him, he tells them, "I do not call you servants any longer, because the servant does not know what the master is doing; but I have called you friends, because I have made known to you *everything* [my emphasis] that I have heard from my Father" (Jn 15:15). In fact, Jesus says, "The one who believes in me will also do the works that I do and, in fact, will do greater works than these, because I am going to the Father" (Jn 14:12).

When Jesus' followers fear that in losing him they will also lose God, he tells them, "And if I go and prepare a place for you, I will come again and will take you to myself, so that where I am, there you may be also" (Jn 14: 3). He doesn't say that we will be in a place that is merely *like* his place, but rather that we will be exactly where he is. That is Jesus' radical promise. When his followers become afraid that Jesus will gather up his own blessings, go into God, and forget them, Jesus replies, "I will not leave you orphaned; I am coming to you. In a little while the world will no longer see me, but you will see me; because I live, you also will live. On that day you will know that I am in my Father, and you in me, and I in you" (Jn 14:18–20). He doesn't say, "I *will* be in my Father and you in me," but rather, "I *am* in my Father and you in me." As Christians we are called into a future, but somehow this future is already here, now.

In my Christian upbringing, the full resonance of Jesus' empowering message was overshadowed by the teaching of original sin and by images of God as a severe male personality behind the clouds. I had heard the message that Jesus wanted me to completely share his direct experience of God's unconditional love. But most often I idealized Jesus as perfect while I was doomed to be forever guilty, adrift in the melancholy hope that he would come to save me from my life. Forgiveness and the unconditional love of God were meant to come "someday," but certainly not today. They were gifts to a future self, not this very self.

Without knowing it, the religious guides of my childhood taught that I must become someone different, someone "better," in order for God to love me. This apparently benign moral teaching set me off on a wild goose chase to escape the moment-to-moment suffering of my daily life. I didn't know that Christian salvation was not about God coming down to yank me out of my suffering, everyday life, but rather a transfiguration of my own experience right now, no matter how "negative." This is what faith in transfiguration means, that somewhere in the depths of my own fear, anger, envy, guilt, irritation, sorrow, and joy, God is working a transformation. I didn't know, because no teacher ever mentioned it, that we who follow Christ are heading to the place of awareness where we too can say with St. Paul, "Now not I, but Christ in me" (Gal 2:20). In Christ, self-consciousness drops away into the depths of God, and a new larger consciousness is born in us.

I've come to appreciate that the achievement of Paul's "not I" requires clear intention and great effort. Each of us must decide if we want to undergo this radical transformation. But even then, we cannot do it alone. We are too frail, too prone to temptation, and our egos are not enthused about this project. We need the continuous stirring of God's grace and a supportive community (with good teaching!).

Transformation in Christ is extremely difficult because our everyday centers of awareness have become cramped and gnarled with pain and fear. Our ego or "I" does not want to give up or die. It thinks that it can control the situation, manage things to avoid pain and increase pleasure. It will even use religion to stay in control. Our deepest self knows that we come from and will return to God. But the "I" of our personalities hates this idea. "I" wants to be everything and wants everything to revolve around its ideas, pleasures, and desires. Contemplative practice is not designed to jettison, unload, or suppress this self-centered "I" so much as to investigate it, to see through it with God's help. When we meditate we do not set aside our egos and personalities, but rather, with God's grace, throw open their doors and windows so that God can stream through us, opening, healing, and enlightening all that we are.

Jesus shared God's love by listening from deep within his own human personality, by listening into God who was not only within him, but his own true self. As he heard, he spoke and lived. Gospel accounts tell us that he did not speak on his own, but only what he "heard" from his Abba, his Father (Jn 12:49–50). St. Paul tells us that Jesus emptied his "I" (Phil 2:5–8) so that God's love could come through. But how does one become "empty"? And if "I" is becoming empty, who is doing the emptying? At the Empty Bell this question has become a koan, an open-ended question that one must *live* rather than merely answer. How did Jesus live his boundless awareness in God?

It is interesting to contrast our common depictions of Jesus and Buddha. Jesus is never depicted as sitting in one place for long. He prays in solitude and then walks with compassion among the common people. He gravitates to those who suffer and to those of great faith. If we reflect on his human awareness or consciousness, we assume that his actions were grounded in a certain kind of awareness or consciousness. At the Empty Bell we assume that, in part, Jesus' self-emptying *(kenosis)* was a spiritual practice—something that he *did* inwardly. We cannot know exactly what mental and physical methods or techniques he used. He left us no audiocassettes of retreat addresses! Perhaps Jesus trusted us to discover our own methods by simply listening deeply to his parables and the gospel stories about him. His parables express a heartfelt, spacious awareness that transcends the apparent opposites of first/last, richer/poorer, now/later, ambition/humility, judgment/no-judgment, hope/hopelessness, God's presence/absence.

In the practice of self-emptying, St. Paul says that we too can have the same mind that was in Christ Jesus (Phil 2:5). But what is the nature of this mind and this awareness? How can we cultivate it? Self-emptying is not self-rejection.

Rather, it is a gradual letting go or detachment from superficial aspects of ourselves. Self-emptying is the act of reaching toward our deeper, truer self. We do not need to *become* the one who is loved unconditionally because that is something we already *are,* in God's eyes. Therefore, we are *not* practicing Christian self-emptying if we habitually reject our own thoughts, feelings, desires, concerns, or history. Rather, self-emptying is a way of relating both to what we like in ourselves and what we don't like, seeing ourselves in the larger context, from Christ's perspective.

Here is a fundamental teaching of Jesus that has been insufficiently appreciated by many Christians: Christ's mind and perspective is not something "out there" but something *within* each of us. It is something that we *are.* It does not judge, but simply invites us into God (Jn 12:47). When we reflect on our inner life from this perspective, we find that even in our inner life, God's grace falls upon both the just and the unjust, the things we like about ourselves and the things we don't. The Jesuit mystic St. Ignatius (1491–1556) named this practice, in his Spanish tongue, *indiferencia.*

When we cultivate contemplative awareness, we are not seeking to become indifferent in the sense of a lazy, careless attitude. We are not seeking to become nihilists who believe in nothing concrete. We are not seeking to become immoral like those whom St. Paul cautioned us against—those who would use their freedom in Christ for selfish purposes. Rather, we are actively longing for God's presence, and completely indifferent to how God will show up for us in this moment. The spirit may be moving right there in my shame, jealousy, envy, anger, greed, fear, or my irritation at a certain person. In contemplative Christian practice, it is not good enough for us to simply reject these "negative" thoughts and emotions as bad. We notice their effect on our lives and then we make a more difficult demand on ourselves, that is to investigate these things, to see what deeper impulses, needs, and fears are motivating them. Most often we find that all roads—even the obscure, cluttered forest and desert trails—lead to God.

Perhaps *indiferencia* was the ambient quality of Jesus' consciousness. To perceive with *indiferencia* means to simply accept what is true: that I cannot control God. This very difficult spiritual practice cultivates a calm availability to God in everything, so that eventually we come to the unself-conscious virtue of "finding God in all things."

Like a precious stone, Jesus found that his every experience, pleasant or unpleasant, refracted God's light into many beautiful colors. Jesus' story is our story. But the design of Jesus' life is not meant to be a cookie cutter pressed onto the dough and everyday details of our individual lives. We are not all supposed to be single, male, Jewish carpenters! Rather, we are meant to be unique incarnations of the divine, each in our own way. We might ask ourselves, "How is God shining through this moment as I sit on this cushion, as I play with my children, as I drive to work, as I shop, as I plant these bulbs, as I ponder this decision, as I type on this computer, as I give this lecture, as I plan this meeting—how is the spirit working in what I now see, feel, touch, know?" The theology of incarnation is not merely religious dogma, but a moment-to-moment *practice* that leads to transformation.

If we take a quiet moment to reflect on the actual quality of our inner life, we notice a continuous stream of thinking, feeling, remembering, worrying, analyzing, and planning. We trust that God is moving in all this mental and emotional activity. But where? At the Empty Bell we bring awareness to our experience, much like the shepherd who goes in search of the lost lamb. We are seeking the "still, small voice" of God, looking for God's footprints, hoping to find God's will right there within the cacophony of our everyday lives. Whether we are sitting in total silence or speaking and listening to someone else speak, we are simultaneously listening inwardly for the spirit's movements within and among our thoughts and feelings. We assume a natural human inclination to deny and escape from the intensity and reality of our lived existence, an inclination to conceive reality the way we want it, not the way it actually is, an inclination to prefer pleasure to pain. But in the contemplative tradition we intend always to follow this principle of listening for God, "not somewhere else, not another time, not another person, but here, now, and me, just as I am."

In this effort we follow the inspiration of Roman Catholic mystics and theologians such as Karl Rahner, one of the few Christian thinkers so bold as to speculate on Jesus' actual mental and emotional processes, his consciousness. In his "The Ignatian Process for Discovering the Will of God in an Existential Situation," and his "Dogmatic Reflections on the Knowledge and Self-Consciousness of Christ," Rahner agrees with St. Ignatius that we can have actual experiences of God's will that move us to make choices different from the ones that we might make on our own.[1] In my childhood it seemed to me that Jesus was perfect and I was not, that Jesus always saw, heard, and did the right thing, without all the blood, sweat, and tears that often accompanied my choices. I assumed an infinite difference between God's will and mine, that God's will was all good and mine all bad. But Rahner is saying something different. He does not mean merely that we ourselves want, see, hear, and know one thing while God wants, sees, hears, and knows another. The choices we make as a result of listening to God are not "different" in that sense. All of our choices are "our own," but only some of them have been opened up to the enlightening spirit of God.

Rahner holds up the possibility that somehow, God's awareness and will are right here, within our own human awareness and will. To be sure, God may appear in *what* we know and see, but more fundamentally, God is in the *how* of our knowing and seeing, as *a way of* seeing all objects, not as a particular "what" but as *a way of* experiencing all "whats." In scripture we read that "since we are God's offspring, we ought not to think that the deity is like gold, or silver, or stone, an image formed by the art and imagination of mortals" (Acts 17:29).

Neither God nor Jesus Christ is limited to any particular object of awareness, any portrait, memory, vision, or dogmatic formulation. "No one has ever seen God" (Jn 1:18). And yet, our faith offers the possibility that many of us, especially Jesus, have heard as God hears, have seen as God sees, have known joy and compassion as God knows. For Jesus and for us, God does not necessarily appear as any particular object of our awareness "out there," but rather as the pervasive, invisible backdrop to all our experiences "of" anything. God's awareness is the very source of our own awareness and is moving there as the implicit ambiance of our knowing, seeing, and sensing in each moment.

That God does not appear objectively within our conceptual or interpersonal life does not, of course, mean that God is somehow precluded from appearing through objects of our awareness, such as in nature, memories, mantras, stories, liturgies, or even in a person such as Jesus. A particular piece of music or a conversation may be revelatory. But in the very next moment, it may no longer convey God's presence to us. We must be careful to allow God the freedom that God *is,* careful to allow ourselves the freedom that we *are.* For Rahner, God's awareness—and will—is like "a horizon within which all traffic with the things and notions of daily life takes place." In Christ, we share this infinite horizon, a

> direct and conscious presence to God,...an unsystematic attunement and an unreflected horizon which determines everything else and within which the whole spiritual life of this spirit is lived....[It] is the permanent basis for all other spiritual activities....This presence belongs to the nature of a spiritual person as the tacit factor in self-awareness which orders and explains everything but cannot be explained itself....This doctrine of the spiritual, unformed and non-conceptual and non-objectified basic condition of a spirit...is also precisely the way in which we must conceive the direct and personal presence of the Logos to the human soul of Jesus.[2]

Sitting in silence, with our backs straight and our eyes closed or gazing down at the floor in front of us, we feel that we are right there at the horizon, where God sits down and listens as the traffic of our memories, future-thinking, worries, and joys goes by. God may appear in a particular object or "what" of my awareness, in a memory, in the eucharist, in the midst of a hymn, in a vision of the future, but we know that somehow this "what" is God's way of giving me nourishment on the way to a fuller realization of God as the source and destination of *all* that I see, hear, touch, and know. Somewhere there, in the midst of my knowing anything at all, is the Lord.

Contemplation at the Cross of Time and Eternity

At the Empty Bell we understand God to be the source of both time and eternity—transcending, and yet present to, our everyday understandings of time. The contemplative tradition offers the possibility of experiencing these two dimensions of time simultaneously. When is the time when God will appear in God's fullness? In the Gospel of Luke (17:20–21), we read,

> Once Jesus was asked by the Pharisees when the kingdom of God was coming, and he answered, "The kingdom of God is not coming with things that can be observed [again, not as an object of awareness]; nor will they say, 'Look, here it is!' or 'There it is!' For, in fact, the kingdom of God is [already] among you."

One Sabbath in Nazareth, Jesus goes to the synagogue (Lk 4: 16–24). Standing before the scroll of the prophet Isaiah, he begins to read the words,

> The Spirit of the Lord is upon me,
> because he has anointed me
> to bring good news to the poor.
> He has sent me to proclaim release to the captives
> and recovery of sight to the blind,
> to let the oppressed go free,
> to proclaim the year of the Lord's favor.

Jesus reads with unprecedented power, as if these words are no longer merely information about another time, but rather as if they are expressing something that is happening *right now*. Ordinary time is broken open. When Jesus rolls up the scroll and sits down, everyone falls silent. Wondering what that moment of silence must have been like, I remember a trip that our family took to the Grand Canyon last year. I had gone on retreat there many years before, but my wife Margaret had never seen it. Margaret is a woman who senses God's presence in nature, so I had been looking forward to her seeing the canyon for the first time. We arrived on a clear day, just as the sun set. Coming to the first lookout at the South Rim, I hurried ahead and looked back as she descended the stairs to the edge. As she walked slowly, one step at a time, lifting her eyes to the vast reaches of time and space in the canyon, she smiled incredulously, tears forming in her eyes. She did not want to speak. She wanted to be silent as if only silence could do honor in that moment to the soundless, infinite beauty at her feet.

I imagine it was like that for some of the Jews who had come to synagogue that day. The doors of their customary assumptions had fallen off the hinges. Most of them were so unnerved by the extraordinary grace of Jesus' presence that they became confused and angry. They even wanted to kill him for what they felt was a mortal presumption into divine territory. But perhaps a few understood that God was as present to them in that moment as God was to Abraham, Ruth, Elijah, and Miriam. As they sat in awe, Jesus spoke simply, into the silence: "Today this scripture has been fulfilled in your hearing" (Lk 4:16–22). Such breakthrough moments are happening still, but many well-meaning Christians have lost touch with the radical call of Jesus' Now! They fail to see that Christ's Now is exactly the same as this present Now.

Jesus opens up his listeners' minds to the grand canyon of infinite time that yawns within us and among us. At the Empty Bell we assume that when we sit in God's presence, we are sitting both in our time and in God's time. One Catholic mystic who knew well this truth was the medieval Dominican friar, Meister Eckhart, who once wrote that in God,

> All that happened a thousand years ago, the day of a thousand years ago, is no more remote in eternity than the moment in which I stand right now; again, the day which will come a thousand years from now, or in as many years as you can count, is no more distant in eternity than this very moment in which I stand presently.[3]

We sit and move in eternity with Christ through whom all things, here and there, now and then, are born. Matthew describes one paradigmatic moment of time and eternity in Christ when, on a mountaintop, Jesus is transfigured before his friends. His face and clothes are suddenly "shining like the sun," as Jesus seems to be conversing with Moses and Elijah (Mt 17:1–3). In Christ, the fulfillment of our past is available in each present moment.

Some contemplative Christians and Buddhists, having had a glimpse of God's eternity, reject their personal history and the significance of passing events. But Jesus does not do away with historical time and how it seems to move from past to present to future. If infinite time is the vertical dimension and historical time is the horizontal dimension, then Jesus Christ is the one who stands at the crossing of the two. His life testifies to our faith that the God who transcends all time freely chooses to enter into time, motivated purely by love and compassion. This is what we Christians mean by the incarnation—not only that God became flesh in the Nazarene Jesus, but that in pure freedom and compassion, God chooses to infuse everything, including each ordinary moment, with God's eternity. Now, and forever, God's time and our time are interwoven. God has put eternity in our hearts as a place from which to see our lives and the lives of others (Eccl 3:11). This is true not only for Jesus, but through him, for each of us.

The weaving of time and eternity often reveals itself in stories. Hebrew and Christian scriptures set before us a core story about how the holy interacts with us. Thus, even though God transcends all concepts and stories, we choose to hold this paradox, that the unknown God becomes understandable, sense-able in Jesus and in us. We humans love stories. They thrill us, scare us, inspire us, and call us into new ways of being. Through stories we find meaning and discover our identities. Jesus' story is an archetype of all our stories, helping us to interpret all other stories. Jesus was blessed as the beloved of God. He lived in accordance with this deep identity. He prayed alone, gathered friends, and lived out his belovedness with compassion and love toward others. Along the way he experienced much joy, but also suffering and death. Through these "negative" experiences he remained rooted in God's love, a love that brought him and his followers through death into an experience he called eternal life. In our Christian faith, this archetypal story also becomes our own.

The German theologian Hans Urs Von Balthasar has described Christ and his story as a kind of inward "form" *(Gestalt or Gebilde)* that we use intuitively to guide us in the shaping of our own lives. The Christ-form is not meant to overshadow the form of our unique historical lives, but rather to fulfill what is naturally there. In this he follows the ancient Latin saying that God's grace is meant to perfect the natural world, not to destroy it and replace it with something else *(Gratia perficit naturam, non supplet)*[4] We believe it really is possible to have the same mind or Christ-form that was in Jesus (Phil 2:5ff). It is a potential form that we live into, one that fully integrates past, present, future, and eternity. Even though we live in eternity as Christ does, we simultaneously live as the person Jesus did, in our everyday stories that have a beginning, middle, and end. Each of us has a past, a present, and a future. And yet God is fully present in each of these dimensions all at once. In Christ we embody this spiritual paradox. The past is over, but God is healing, forgiving, and blessing us there, and the future has not yet come but God is already accomplishing things there.

Of course, when we search our memories we may find times when it seemed that God was absent. And when we look into the future we worry and are afraid that we will give up on God or that God will abandon us. Jesus experienced time in this very human way too. He too cried out in fear. But our faith tells us that even in the flow of his remembering and anticipating, he stood firmly rooted in God's present Now, the exact same Now that is available to us in each moment. Our faith tells us that gradually, in this life and hereafter, we are moving into this Now when God's love and joy make all things new. We are all moving into this holy moment when our time and God's time are perfectly integrated in one life. Therefore, Jesus and we too live both in the full presence of God, and simultaneously in the promise that the fullness is coming. This is one of the essential paradoxes of our spiritual lives, expressed in Christian theology as "already and not-yet." We always live from within our developing stories, but always in eternity, in God.

Empty Bell History and Leadership

In the spring of 2000 we celebrate six years as a contemplative community. Originally, the inspiration for the Empty Bell came to me in prayer. I "saw" a circle of good friends sitting on cushions. All were from different spiritual traditions and yet were the most intimate of friends. They wanted to simply sit in silence with each other and also to support each other to go back into their own communities to serve, to bless, and to heal. After the initial inspiration it would be another three years before we found the right location for the vision. When we finally renovated a small carriage house in the style of a Japanese zendo, I wasn't sure how to invite people. I wasn't sure what to call this new place. Even though the initial vision came from prayer, the only model that came to mind was a professional one.

With a doctorate in education and psychology from Harvard, I had been a workshop leader and psychotherapist for many years. A subsequent master's degree in theological studies at the Jesuit Weston School of Theology prepared me to teach foundational courses in theology and christology. Then, after several years of receiving spiritual direction, both in the Zen Buddhist and Christian traditions, and convinced of its value, I began to integrate spiritual and psychological work with my clients. Initially, I thought of this new space as an office with a spiritual ambiance. I would offer workshops and retreats and I would invite other teachers from the psychotherapeutic, Buddhist, and Christian communities to do the same.

In the Empty Bell's first three years I also offered many half-day retreats on particular themes often associated with the Christian liturgical year—Advent, Christmas, Epiphany, Lent, Easter, and Pentecost. Sometimes I invited coleaders from non-Christian traditions, often Zen masters or Tibetan lamas. Themes included "Emptiness: Buddhist and Christian," "The Birth of Christ in John's Gospel," "Evagrius of Ponticus on Christian Meditation," "Early Christian Classics," "Exploring St. Paul's 'Mind of Christ,'" "Psychotherapeutic Healing: A Buddhist/Christian Dialogue," and "Christ and the Healing Tao."

These special educational retreats were often well attended. Soon, a core group of people emerged who wanted to go into more depth on some topics. We developed a Tuesday evening course on the Christian mystics, meeting for eight weeks in the fall and spring. During the three years of this course we drew on the Paulist Press series, "Classics of Western Spirituality." Prior to each meeting, individuals in the group of ten would read the same chapter from spiritual masters such as Evagrius (345–399 C.E.), Cassian (360–435), Symeon the New Theologian (949–1022), the author of the *Cloud of Unknowing* (1349–1395 C.E.), St. Hildegard of Bingen (1098–1179), Julian of Norwich (1342–1413), St. Teresa of Avila (1515–1582), and others. During the week we would each pray with the readings, looking for those places where we felt most deeply touched by a story, metaphor, poem, or spiritual insight. In the subsequent meeting we would begin with twenty minutes of silence, and then share with the group our prayerful response to the reading. Those of us with some theological training found this thoughtful but personal process to be a refreshing alternative to the intellectual approach that is taken in seminaries. But in terms of the course content, I still thought of myself as a teacher.

In another weekly forum, I led a small group that focused on the Gospel of John as a text of transformation. Over the weeks and months of our evening gatherings, we read John together prayerfully, chapter by chapter. Believing that our Christian tradition has overemphasized morality, social action, and belief while essentially ignoring Christ's astounding teachings on consciousness, awareness, and transformation, I presented John's Gospel as a text for transformation. What does it mean, in our experience, to be transformed in Christ? What habits, thoughts, emotions, and behaviors seem to block us from this transformation? I asked each participant, including myself, to pray these questions throughout the eight-week semester. We learned that some of the most common barriers to transformation are the self-limiting beliefs we have about ourselves, beliefs that make us smaller, less creative, less free, less clear, less visionary, less strong, and less joyful than we really are. And we discovered the nascent potential and skill of a small Christian community to empower its membership by believing that the good news is something real for each person, news that makes a difference. Standing in the midst of St. John's vision, we simply listened to one another in love, expecting that each person could step even further into the reality of being God's beloved and then sharing that joy with others. By the end of our series, most participants had taken practical steps to change their relationships and even their jobs.

In all these workshops and retreats I felt that my leadership style was changing. Perhaps because several participants returned for many workshops, I began to trust the wisdom of the groups more and more. As we meditated, prayed together, and as we shared our stories of divine encounter (or abandonment), I began to see that while I might have some valuable theological knowledge and some psychological insights, the real teacher was the Holy Spirit in our midst. Gradually, it seemed clear that I needed these gatherings as much as the participants did.

As I prepared the Empty Bell mailing list each fall and winter I watched the list grow to more than five hundred people in three years. But I also noticed that most participants in our programs came from a pool of about twenty people. A sense of community was developing among us, the reality of which was nourished most dramatically in the fall of 1995 when my friend Fr. Henri Nouwen lived with our family for the first three months of his sabbatical year. I had known Henri since 1982, when, as a Harvard graduate student, I went to a lecture that he gave at the Harvard Divinity School. Henri left Harvard in the mid-'80s to pursue a life in the international community of handicapped people called L'Arche. In the early '90s he had asked me to accompany him and other L'Arche members as they gave retreats. I had contributed occasional talks on contemplative topics and played the shakuhachi (a bamboo flute practiced as meditation in the Japanese Zen tradition). Now in 1995, Henri lived as our guest, settling in to hide from his admiring fans and to write. During his three-month visit he framed out three books—*The Inner Voice of Love, Can You Drink the Cup?,* and *Bread for the Journey.* Each morning he said the eucharist in his room or in the Empty Bell. On Sundays the Empty Bell community shared the eucharist with him.

In his Eucharistic gatherings as pastor for the L'Arche Daybreak community in Richmond Hill, Ontario, Henri had always used the small, monthly booklet of daily readings called *Living with Christ.* Over the months of Henri's presence with us we liked and grew accustomed to reading this booklet. After Henri left we incorporated *Living with Christ* in our ongoing Thursday gatherings and continued to meet on Sundays. Through his homilies, our community absorbed Henri's primary spiritual emphasis: that each of us, like Jesus, is the beloved son and daughter of God. Eternally beloved, even before we are born. We discovered that when belovedness is our ground of being, we are less likely to be motivated by fear, shame, greed, crude ambition, or what others think about us.

At first, I led all Empty Bell gatherings. But after a couple of years, when other commitments took me away, others stepped forward. For over a year, Susan Brown, who had come to Empty Bell offerings from the beginning, led every other Thursday. As our sense of community and mutual trust deepened, I felt comfortable handing over Sunday leadership to a few others—Caitlin, Kevin, Jody, Donna, Ruth, David, Richard, Sam, Jeannie, Lisa, and Joe. Now Thursday leadership at the Empty Bell is rotated among a group of four, and Sunday leadership among a group of eight. Often I will come as a participant when others lead.

To support this evolution in leadership we created a leaders' group meeting of eight to fourteen people. Fortunately, by chance, this group has included equal numbers of men and women. At first, we met quarterly to discuss questions and issues such as difficult dynamics in group participation, when and how to respond to members in great distress, how to handle intense feelings that arise while leading, how to interpret difficult scripture passages, how much contact to make with other group members outside our official gatherings, what to do when the sharing time becomes too "heady," whether or not to say something in the silence, and so on. Now, in our fifth year, this leaders' group meets monthly and has taken on other leadership responsibilities, including coordinating volunteers for special interfaith events that we sponsor, and offering quarterly retreats for the Empty Bell community.

At first, I continued seeing clients for psychotherapy at the Empty Bell. But gradually, I and those who came to me for one-on-one accompaniment seemed more motivated to explore spiritual issues than psychological ones.

So, in 1995 I stopped taking clients in psychotherapy and devoted one-half of each workday to offering spiritual direction. At the end of 1999, the Empty Bell hosted three other spiritual directors who meet one-on-one with people to focus on their prayer lives.

I think that this evolution of leadership from one person, myself, to the leaders' groups has benefited everyone. For me, by the spring of 1998 I was feeling "burned out." I realized that I needed a sabbatical, some time to rest, reflect, and write. It was wonderful for me to realize that I could come to the Empty Bell gatherings, to meditate and pray with others without being in the role of leader. Especially in this past year, 1999, I have realized that this community has resources of knowledge, wisdom, and healing presence that transcend me and my personal vision and resources. I have realized that I need this community and that we are now co-creators of a very special contemplative experiment in community.

In 1997 one of our members, a lawyer, offered to help us achieve nonprofit, tax-exempt status for the Empty Bell. With Jim's astute lawyering and friendship, that goal was achieved. Four people in the community volunteered to be on our first official board. Now we are looking for a few good people outside our community to sit on the board and to share their wisdom. At this time we do not have a vision of great expansion for the Empty Bell. We are a small, intimate community of Christian contemplatives who seek to deepen our own lives in the spirit together and to bring that spiritual rootedness to our work as teachers, lawyers, psychologists, pastors, editors, social workers, administrators, and artists. We will also continue to create two or three interfaith events each year, especially for those interested in Buddhist-Christian dialogue.

As spiritual directors and therapists, many of us on the Empty Bell board and in the leaders group see many people who experience intense suffering. Their pain has many sources, with psychological, social, economic, and political roots. Some of this pain is simply given as part of anyone's life and approaching death, and some is from the speed and fragmentation of urban life. We feel that a regular contemplative practice such as ours has helped us to be more centered, calmer in the midst of turmoil and pain, and more inclined to acts of compassion. In our meetings we often talk about whether or not we should have a more aggressive outreach effort. Now that we are officially a nonprofit, we could seek larger donations to finance outreach projects.

Twelve years ago I began leading contemplative groups in Episcopal, Roman Catholic, and Unitarian parishes in New England. Under the auspices of the Empty Bell I have continued this ministry. In addition, many leadership groups from parishes come here for short retreats. In this outreach ministry, I have found a hunger for silence among Christians. Many parishioners tell me that they have never had more than a few seconds of silence in their liturgical experience, and they want more. But when I offer extended visitations to parishes I find that while silence is initially appealing to just about everybody, long-term contemplative groups attract few members. Many people with families don't see how they can create time to just *be* when so much needs to be done. Others find silence disconcerting. When unconscious memories and emotions begin to rise through the surface of their busy minds, some become afraid and stop the practice.

Quite often, the personal support that beginning meditators need to go deeper is absent. I wonder if more Christians with a contemplative interest would take up the practice if they found leadership and support in their parishes. In the Roman Catholic tradition we have been pleased to see two international contemplative organizations do just that. Contemplative Outreach (led by Trappist Fr. Thomas Keating), and the John Main Institute for Christian Meditation (led by Fr. Laurence Freeman), provide rich networks of education, leadership, and support for lay Christians, primarily in the United States and England. Also, Shalem Institute in Bethesda, Maryland, is an outstanding model of a Christian contemplative study and practice center that has, in my mind, successfully integrated the apparent contradictions of Protestantism and Catholicism, contemplation and action, professionalism and community, and ordained and lay leadership.

At Empty Bell board meetings and in our leadership group we often wonder if more of us should be going out to parishes. There are practical difficulties. Everyone is a professional with a very full life. Do we have the time to do this, or should we let go of some of our professional work in order to do this ministry? We also wonder if we should set up a training program for others who want to start groups like ours. Should we organize more group spiritual direction gatherings here? We feel that we are a very young, small community of Christians who are listening in the spirit together, opening our hearts to each other, and helping each other to live more fully and courageously in our relationships and work. We hope that we are open to whatever vision the spirit brings to us.

Notes

1. Karl Rahner, *Theological Investigations,* 283; "Dogmatic Reflections on the Knowledge and Self-Consciousness of Christ," in *Theological Investigations V* (Baltimore: Helicon, 1966), 193–215.

2. Rahner, "Dogmatic Reflections," 208–10.

3. Meister Eckhart, in Reiner Schurmann, trans. and comm., *Meister Eckhart: Mystic and Philosopher* (Bloomington and London: Indiana University Press, 1978), 55.

4. *The Glory of the Lord: A Theological Aesthetics, Vol. I, Seeing the Form,* trans. Erasmo Leiva-Merikakis, ed. Joseph Fessio, S.J., and John Riches (San Francisco: Ignatius Press, 1982).

Kathleen Fischer and Thomas Hart

32. Gender Issues in Ministry with Couples

A former student of ours, now in charge of education programs at her church, shared how shocked she was by a parishioner's recent disclosure. A woman in one of her programs confided to her that her bruises were not from a fall, as she had previously said, but were the result of a beating by her husband. How could this be?, Sally found herself wondering for days. The husband seemed like such a good person. He was a regular churchgoer, a leader in church activities, a man much respected by all who knew him. Sally was shaken. Her ministry was ushering her into some of the darker corners of sexism in marriage.

Amidst the daily demands of ministry, an issue like sexism can seem remote or purely theoretical. Yet sexism is always operative, and always has a negative impact on people's lives. A clear awareness of it opens one's eyes to the many opportunities one has in ministry either to reinforce patterns of gender inequality or to help create just and healthy relationships between women and men. In this essay, we focus on the new context that feminist thought creates for ministry with couples. Confining ourselves to the Judeo-Christian tradition, we briefly describe the patriarchal vision and its biblical roots, shed a different light on the texts on which it chiefly relies, and point to other passages in scripture that ground a fresh vision of equality and mutuality between the sexes. In the second part of the essay, we offer concrete suggestions for working with couples in various pastoral situations today.

Biblical Foundations for Just and Healthy Gender Relationships

Patriarchy and Gender Relations

Patriarchy is the term commonly used for sexist social structures. It derives from the Greek *pater/patros* (father) and *arche* (origin, ruling power, or authority). A patriarchal system is one in which power belongs to the dominant man, and all others are ranked below him in a series of graded subordinations ending with the least powerful. In religious societies, this order is held to be divinely established.[1]

In the patriarchal family, men rule over the women, children, and slaves in their households. But there is this distinction. Minor sons and male slaves can eventually attain to full majority and rule their own households. But women, who can never be fathers of families, are considered minors by nature. The sexism here could hardly be clearer. Males are inherently superior to females; it is simply the natural or divine ordering of things. And so the dynamics of ownership or possession permeate the relations of the sexes.

One of the most influential expressions of this pattern for Christians is the set of rules for the ordering of the household set forth in Ephesians 5:22–33. Often read at weddings, this "household code" is an exhortation to wives and husbands to dedicate themselves to its vision for Christian marriage. Like similar codes found in Colossians 3:18–4:1 and in 1 Peter 3:1–7, the passage presents the ideal Christian household as a hierarchically ordered unit.[2]

The codes treat relationships between three pairs—wives and husbands, children and parents, slaves and masters—as relationships of subordinates to superiors. They exhort the lesser member of each pairing to behave appropriately, showing obedience and submission to those in authority. The exhortation to the greater member is that he be loving and fair. But there is no question about his divinely established authority. There is often a clause that includes a specific christological reference to motivate or theologically justify the prescribed behavior. Thus we read in Ephesians:

> Wives should regard their husbands as they regard the Lord, since as Christ is head of the Church and saves the whole body, so is a husband the head of his wife; and as the Church submits to Christ, so should wives to their husbands, in everything. Husbands should love their wives just as Christ loved the Church and sacrificed himself for her to make her holy. (5:22–26)

The codes do not call either the prevailing practice of slavery nor the prevailing sexism into question. They simply seek to make these social systems more livable by pressing the master to be humane, even generous. Throughout history these household codes have played a key role in silencing or marginalizing women.

Ephesians has a forebear that is at least equally influential: the second account of creation and the story of the fall in the second and third chapters of Genesis. In the creation story, Adam is on the scene first. Then God decides to create woman as a "helper" for him. God creates the woman from the man's rib, at which the man exclaims, "This at last is flesh of my flesh and bone of my bone; she shall be called woman because she was taken out of man." Because she is taken "out of man" she is derived from him. What is worse, the account of the fall, which follows immediately, seems to present the woman as temptress, as she eats the apple first and then gives it to the man. Scholars point out that many New Testament passages that enjoin the subordination of women appeal to these stories in Genesis.

Ephesians and Genesis are the biblical texts usually invoked to give religious legitimation to patriarchal arrangements. Translated into role relationships in marriage, the patriarchal scheme has generated two prevalent models that overlap in many ways: hierarchy and complementarity. Hierarchy says that the husband is superior to the wife, and that she should be subject to him. Complementarity assigns certain characteristic qualities to men and to women: men are active, aggressive, rational, and material providers; women are passive, emotional, nurturing, and altruistic. The model holds that the male qualities are humanly superior, entitling him to natural leadership. Since women and men are incomplete in themselves, they come together in heterosexual marriage to find their completion by complementing one another.

The complementarity model simultaneously idealizes and devalues the roles of wife and mother. It often romanticizes marriage, teaching women that their fulfillment comes from finding a male partner. It leaves single women feeling inferior and incomplete. The subordination of women to men's authority and control contains the seeds of domestic violence. As more than one man has said, "If a woman doesn't know her place, what's a man to do?" Hierarchical arrangements and the assumptions behind them constitute the oppression that causes so much needless suffering to women and makes it so difficult for them to reach their full potential.

Biblical Resources for a New Paradigm

How can we envision gender relations in a way that respects the dignity and promotes the full development of both women and men? And is there any biblical warrant for a vision of equality and mutuality? Yes, there *is* solid foundation for reform of the dominant sexist pattern in three areas of scripture: (1) the prophetic/messianic justice themes that suffuse both Hebrew and Christian scriptures, critiquing *all* systems of oppression, and coming to full embodiment in the ministry of Jesus; (2) the baptismal formula in Galatians, which calls the later household code of Ephesians into question; and (3) the Genesis texts read with a keener eye. Let us examine all three.

The prophetic/messianic strain in both testaments consistently tells truth to power, often at the cost of the prophet's life. Confronting kings, princes, high priests, and people of wealth—in short, all those profiting from the status quo—it calls attention tirelessly to the poverty and oppression of those ground down by the system. In place of the skewed social order, it calls for relationships of justice, shared power and wealth, and communities that hold diversity together in respectful tension.[3] Jesus, the culmination of this tradition, tirelessly preaches and enacts these same themes. His personal signature is table fellowship with "sinners," the lowest among the people of his time. His out-reach is to all, especially to those suffering the most. And he is notably respect-ful of women, treating them as equals. Throughout his ministry Jesus presents a vision of liberating relationships that is the antithesis of patriarchy. His gospel calls us to move from patterns of dominance and submission toward mutually enhancing relationships. The movement he initiates establishes the pattern for all communities as a discipleship of equals. Divisions based on sex, wealth, nationality, or position are all to be dissolved. This vision of God's purpose is summed up in an early baptismal formula that Paul quotes in Gala-tians; this brings us to our next section.

The baptismal formula of Galatians is radical in its social implications. The text is this:

> There does not exist among you Jew or Greek, slave or freeperson,
> male or female, for all are one in Christ Jesus. (Gal 3:28)

To grasp the force of this simple proclamation, one must have some sense of how old and deeply entrenched the distinctions were between Jews and non-Jews, between slaves and freepersons, and between men and women. All of them are here simply set aside in one sweeping gesture, making way for a new social order in the spirit of Jesus. All persons have equal dignity now. The con-cept is thoroughly revolutionary. Touching our present concern, it grounds a commitment to the full equality of women and men in family, church, and society at large.

How did we get from this passage in Galatians to the patriarchal household code of Ephesians? Galatians is an authentic letter of Paul, and it was written in the early 50s. Ephesians was not written by Paul, though it reprises many of his themes. It was written sometime during the 70s or 80s. What it shows is that an accommodation was made in these intervening years to the surrounding Greco-Roman and Jewish cultures in which Chris-tianity was trying to take root. These still held fast to the old household rules, and so Christians compromised, accepting the entrenched structures. But these are clearly a departure from Jesus' program of a discipleship of equals. And, unfortunately, it has been used subsequently to keep the old patriarchal program alive. Ephesians, in its first three chapters, does insist on the total equality through Christ of Jew and Gentile, a breaking down of the dividing wall. It goes on to exhort and teach how one is to live so as to put this into practice in the church. But it capitulates on the household code, where it does not break down dividing walls but actually sanctions both sexism and slavery, teaching only how to live in as Christian a spirit as pos-sible within the system. What we must do today is resurrect the original resplendent vision.

Finally, what about the accounts of creation and fall in Genesis? Here Hebrew scripture scholar Phyllis Trible comes to our aid, with a careful reexamination of these texts. Her translation and reinterpretation of Genesis 2–3 turns the usual reading of the Adam and Eve story upside down, replacing patterns of dominance and subordination with models of mutuality.[4]

In her exegesis Trible shows that the intention of the account is to show woman and man as equals. The poet of Genesis 2 uses earthy language to depict God as shaping woman from man's rib, just as God earlier formed man from the dust of the earth. But woman is not derived from man any more than man, the earth creature, is derived from the earth. Life, for both, originates from God. The dust of the earth and the rib of man are in each case simply the raw materials for God's creative action. Superiority, strength, aggressiveness, dominance, and power do not characterize the man in Genesis 2. On the contrary, he is formed from dirt; his life hangs on the breath breathed into him by God; and he remains silent and passive while the Deity plans and interprets his existence.

Trible goes on to show that the Hebrew word that has been traditionally translated as "helpmate," suggesting an assistant, subordinate, or inferior, carries no such connotations. The term means a companion corresponding to oneself. In the passage, what God wants for the man is a companion who is neither subordinate nor superior, but one who alleviates loneliness. The contrast is between wholeness and isolation. The words "bone of my bone and flesh of my flesh" indicate unity, solidarity, mutuality, and equality. Being different does not mean being subordinate.

As for the fact that Eve was created after Adam, if the point of the story were to establish superiority, this would be the perfect way to underscore her importance as the culmination of creation. In Genesis 1, human beings are created last to show that they are the climax of God's creative activity; it is on the sixth and final day that God makes humankind. So also does the Genesis 2 account move to its climax, not its decline, in the creation of Eve.

Nor does the biblical narrative sustain a view of woman as weaker or lacking in judgment. In no way does it disparage her. It depicts Eve as curious and perceptive, a seeker of knowledge. It is Adam who is utterly passive. In seizing the apple, woman is fully aware and acts with decisiveness and initiative. She is clearly spokesperson for the human couple. But the story does not say that she tempted Adam. Nor is he described as reluctant or hesitant. He simply follows her lead, without question or comment. His transgression, "and he ate," completes the deed for "the two who are one." The sexes are interrelated and interdependent, mutually responsible for their actions.

This revisioning of Eve affirms the intelligence and powers of women. And it does so in a story that places patriarchal culture under judgment. By telling us that we are creatures made for equality and mutuality, it opens for us the possibility of a return to that kind of relating. We understand the message of Genesis when, rather than asking what the story is about, we let the myth challenge what we are about.

A New Vision of Marriage

This kind of liberating theology points the way to a new vision of marriage. In this model we no longer have two incomplete persons, each presumed to possess only half of the human traits, but two whole persons each of whom has the capacity to develop a wide range of human strengths. Role relationships are based on the actual gifts and inclinations of the two individuals rather than on conventional ideas of what a wife or husband is supposed to be. Mutuality is a basis for empowerment; it fosters the release of new resources in both persons and in their pattern of relating. Each partner simultaneously affects and is affected by the other, the result being a fuller humanity for both. They give to and receive from each other in a rich variety of ways.

But even the enlightened and motivated individual couple cannot solve the problems of sexism alone. There is a reciprocal relationship between the home and society at large. The dilemmas married couples face are generated by the social and religious systems in which we live, and change must happen at those levels as well. If sexism in marriage is to be healed, there must be an end to the subordinate position of women in the church generally. Only as the church encourages and manifests a discipleship of equals will it be able to credibly enliven and reinforce efforts of married couples to find just and healthy forms of relating.

The project of transformation is, in fact, global in scope. Patterns of patriarchy and exploitation are deeply engrained in economic, political, and social fabrics across the world. As theologian Anne Carr points out in her analysis of women, work, and poverty, it is taken for granted by women and men alike in the patriarchal model that work in and for the household—cleaning, washing, ironing, cooking, shopping, caring for the children, the sick, the elderly, and men—is the responsibility of women. It is also taken for granted that this labor is inferior to that done in the marketplace. It is uncompensated and goes largely unrecognized. This same discounting of women's work occurs even when she is employed outside the home, where in the workplace she enjoys less status and receives less pay. It is, Carr believes, the patriarchal structures embedded in home and society that are the source of the denigration of women's labor, and account for the fact that women and children throughout the globe are among the poorest of the poor. Far from embodying prophetic and messianic leadership in this regard, the churches often lag behind many societies in their attention to these issues. Although women do much of the work in the churches too, it is often on a volunteer or unpaid basis, and in limited roles that do not begin to engage their full talents.[5]

Implications for Ministry

How can we promote this new vision of gender relations in our ministries? Several ideas come immediately to mind.

Preparing Couples for Marriage

A recent counseling experience underscored for us the necessity of addressing gender relations early in marriage. The couple were in crisis at midlife. The wife had gotten in touch with a deep unhappiness. She had not been able to develop much of a sense of self in the marriage; she had focused too much on her husband, adapting to his needs, concerns, values, and program. The rest of her energy had gone into the raising of the children. She had very little life of her own. Also, she realized, she hardly knew her husband as a friend. He did not share his inner life with her, nor did he listen with much interest to her sharing of herself. When she finally spoke of all her dissatisfactions, her husband admitted that he was not very happy either. He had almost entirely missed the growth and development of his children into young adults, and they were already preparing to leave home. He had been totally taken up with providing for them. Now it was too late to develop the kind of personal relationship he wished he had with each of them. He also recognized that he had very little inner life, not much in the way of emotional or spiritual substance to share. Looking across the table at one another, husband and wife realized that they had both lost out. Neither had developed the way they wanted to personally or relationally, and they had even lost touch with each other as they had dutifully gone about their assigned tasks.

This bleak scenario can be avoided by the way a couple makes their original plans and arrangements, and this is where ministry comes in. They can be encouraged to share the household chores from the outset, and plan how they are going to share parenting as well. They can pay attention from the beginning to how each will develop the life she or he wishes, and how those lives will be joined. The man can be shown the importance of dedicating himself to the development of his emotional and spiritual life, and sharing his inner, not just his outer, self with his mate. He can give full encouragement and support to his wife's finding of her own self and life as his equal, and she can claim it as her perfect right. The marital relationship would promote that growth into the fullness of individual personhood and life-in-communion that is the Christian vision of marriage.

The occasion of preparing couples for marriage is a fine one for calling attention to unrecognized sexist assumptions and engendering a different vision of marriage. Some questions that prompt the desired reflection are these:

- What will the family name be?
- Who will take care of the children?
- How will careers be worked out? Whose career has priority?
- Who will be responsible for what household chores?
- What will the financial arrangements be?
- What about outside relationships—families, friends of both genders?
- How will decisions be made? What if there is disagreement?
- How fully is each able to take responsibility for her or his own feelings and actions, separately from those of the other?
- Does the relationship feel large enough for two fully developed human beings? What adjustments might need to be made?
- How does each claim and exercise power, and deal with the other's power? How does each regard the issues of manipulation, anger, and violence?
- What outside supports will they draw on to help their marriage and family thrive?

This is also the time for introducing a Christian spirituality of marriage—for framing the daily interaction of married life as a spiritual vocation, a call and opportunity to keep growing in the Christian life, most particularly in our capacity to love. If we are faithful to the dialogue at the center of married life, always trying to tell each other the truth with love, and listening for the voice of God within our human voices, married life will fulfill its function, deepening and gradually transforming us as persons.[6]

Part of the preparation for marriage is the planning of the wedding ceremony. This is a great opportunity for the pastoral minister to assist the couple in fashioning several of the ceremony's principal components: the procession, the readings, the homily, the prayers and blessings, and their proper role in the entire liturgy.[7]

Regarding *the procession* in, the historical root of the long-established custom by which the father of the bride brings her down the aisle and gives her to the groom should be exposed as a sexist practice of ancient Greco-Roman culture. The bride was regarded as her father's property, and he handed her over to the groom to be *his* property in exchange for a price. It seems a poor practice to perpetuate, and there are simple alternatives. The bride can process in accompanied by both parents or by close friends, who present her to the groom. Or the entire wedding party can process in as couples, the bride and groom entering last.

Scripture readings should be carefully chosen. Unless there is going to be considerable clarifying commentary in the homily, which could be turned into a wonderful teaching moment by a well-informed homilist, the readings from Genesis 2 and Ephesians 3 should probably be avoided, since, as commonly understood, they simply reinforce sexist assumptions. Any number of other readings that set forth the contours of Christian love in a fully mutual way are available:

Genesis 1:26–28, 31a	The other story of creation
Ruth 1:16–17	Committed love
Ephesians 3:14–21	Rooted and grounded in love
1 John 4:7–12	God is love
Matthew 5:13–16	Light of world, salt of earth
Matthew 22:35–40	Great commandment
John 2:1–11	Wedding at Cana
John 15:3–11	Vine and branches
John 15:12–17	Love one another
Matthew 5:1–10	The beatitudes
Song of Songs 8:6–7	Love as strong as death
1 Corinthians 13:1–13	Greatest is love

Where sexist language appears in any of these texts, or, for that matter, in any of the prayers or hymns that are chosen, it can easily be changed to inclusive language.

The homily offers a wonderful opportunity for fostering a model of married equality and mutuality as the Christian ideal. Whether it takes its rise from the Genesis 2 or Ephesians 3 texts and puts them in better perspective, or flows from other scripture readings, the homily should present marriage as a vocation rich and challenging, designed for the full development, in an ambience of committed Christian love, of wife and husband and any children who may be given to them. It is also sacrament to the world.

The vows, prayers, and *blessings* that are used in the service can flesh out and reinforce such a vision of marriage. Wife and husband, with some assistance, might be encouraged to compose their own texts. A few examples follow, which can be variously adapted.

Opening prayer:
Gracious God, we gather in your presence today to celebrate the love and marriage of _____ and _____. Bless them as they embark on this mysterious journey of life together. As they support and challenge one another in love through the years, may they help each other grow into the fullness of their personhood. May they bring out the best in each other, and be fruitful in their love, not only in their own family but in the larger communities to which they belong. We ask this in Jesus' name.

Wedding Vow:
_____, I take you for my husband (wife).
I promise to love you faithfully

all the days of my life.
I want my love to mirror Christ's love for you—
faithful, challenging, deep, forgiving,
in good times and in bad,
a creative and renewing force in your life.
With your help, (and the help of our children),
I want to grow into
the fullness of God's vision for me,
and I want to help you do the same.

A Blessing over the Couple:
God of love, you created humankind in your image as woman and man.
Bless this union of _____ and _____, as husband and wife. By the manifestation of their love for one another, they reveal the mystery of Christ present in his body, made of many members, bearing different gifts, joined as one in love. Support them with your own love, that they may live in faithful friendship with one another forever. Let them gently break each other open, that the beauty of each of them might be more fully revealed. Open their hearts to all in need, so that others too may find in their love a visible sign of your love for every person. We ask this in Jesus' name.

Finally, *the role of the couple in the liturgy* can and should communicate much more than it usually does. What we are accustomed to seeing, usually from behind, is an elegantly dressed man and woman upon whose passivity something is being done by an official in the sanctuary. What we would be much more moved to see is a mature and articulate woman and man, in festive but more ordinary attire, joyfully yet with open eyes assuming the responsibilities of Christian marriage. They should be hostess and host, not princess and prince for a day. This is their gathering, and they are the principal actors. The minister's role is not to confer a sacrament on them, but only to witness in the name of the church their conferring a sacrament on one another. For they themselves are the holy thing, and their gift of self to each other in committed love is the sacred covenant that becomes sacrament to us all. So it is fitting that they greet and welcome their guests, and share what this day means to them. In other ways too, they should be encouraged to assume active roles in the unfolding liturgy. They can give us right in this service a glimpse of the kind of marriage we have been speaking of—a manifestation of mutuality, collaboration, equality, a use of the gifts of each. It would give the whole community a much richer experience of what Christian marriage really means.

Converting the Christian Imagination

One way to focus our task as ministers is to think of it as the conversion of the imagination, for it is in the imagination that human deeds begin.[8] In all our words and actions we offer couples images of what relationships can be. The stories we tell, the metaphors we choose, the examples we invoke—all either reinforce a sexist vision or open couples to another way of seeing. Over time, these images are like those gospel seeds that bear new fruit.

This is especially true of the images we use for the divine. We are by now aware how our images of God determine the way we relate to God.[9] We need to emphasize that a couple's images of the divine are very influential in their relating, and form the backdrop to problems of domestic violence. If God is male, patriarchy has a warrant at the highest level. And in the churches, the maleness of God is often simply taken for granted. All talk is of "his" creation and "his" providence and "his" will. The prevailing metaphor for God is "Father," and, of course, Jesus, his son, is also male. The Holy Spirit is then simply presented as another "he." With the constant subtle reinforcement of this linguistic usage, images are planted deep in the mind: God is male, and maleness is normative.

It matters little to daily life that Christian dogma from the earliest times has held that God is spirit and has no gender at all. What is operative is what lives in the imagination, for it is chiefly from image and feeling, not concept, that we live. The image is "Father," and the language is "he." *This* is what has to change if we are ever to loosen the grip of sexism on human affairs. In our time, the battle has finally been engaged. And the struggle is intense, for power is at stake.

The pastoral work of reeducation begins by reminding people of the Bible's own use of multiple images for God—some male, some female, some impersonal. Why do the biblical authors marshal such a variety of images? Because the reality of God is far too rich to compass in any single image. It transcends them all. An image can only highlight a facet or two of the divine. That is why we need many, and the use of multiple images is our best defense against idolatry. Idolatry is the identification of an image with the reality. Where the divine is concerned, the reality transcends all the images put together.

A second pastoral approach is to remind people of that foundational Christian teaching of the longest standing: that God is spirit, invisible, beyond gender, no more male than female. This is another way clearly and simply to underline the distinction between image and reality.

When the foundation of these two truths has been laid, we do well to speak of God sometimes as "her," for God is as validly imaged female as male. It is at first shocking to the system to hear God spoken of this way, precisely because immediately we can *feel* the difference. That is exactly what must happen. Now our imagination and emotions are being addressed, and we are profoundly affected. This seemingly small linguistic change effectively shatters the foundation of patriarchy. And now, we have to remember that the choice is not simply between father and mother: God has many names. God is also, for instance, the mystery, the presence, the friend, the breath of life, and so forth.

Another powerful force in this conversion of the imagination is the person of the minister. Women and men in pastoral work have somewhat different issues to attend to. If you are a man, you might take a look at items such as these:

- Are you careful to avoid sexist language in speaking of God and human beings?
- Are you more comfortable with dependent, nonthreatening women than with those who are self-defined and self-determined?
- Do you sexualize your relationships with women who are attractive to you? Are you flirtatious?
- When you greet or work with couples, do you offer as much respect and recognition to the woman as to the man?
- When you talk with children, do you avoid the stereotypical behavior of praising the beauty of the girl and the abilities of the boy?
- When you delegate tasks, do you look for the most competent person you can find, regardless of gender?
- When you have to make a difficult decision, do you consult as many women as men? How are your advisory boards constituted?
- Are you willing to take a stand on this issue, tirelessly teaching and modeling equal respect and full mutuality, working to end oppression in church and society?

If you are a woman in ministry, your task is harder. You are living in a sexist institution, and, if you are aware, are constantly suffering the prevalent sexism in large and small ways. It is manifest in the manner in which many in authority regard and treat you, as well as in structures and customs long established and taken for granted. It is in the language of scripture, lectionary, and prayer, and often enough in the preaching too. It surrounds you. Even those to whom you minister display sexist attitudes. It is draining, irritating, at times infuriating, and hard to endure. You need the support of women and men who share your dream and convictions. You need a life of prayer.

But the good you can do if you are able to persevere can hardly be overestimated. As women become increasingly visible in ministry, moving into all positions open to them and transforming those ministries, claiming their voices and authority, all women and men have the opportunity to see before them concrete images for a whole new way of living in community.[10]

Naming the Systemic Roots of Marital Dilemmas

It often helps couples when they are brought to see that their gender issues stem from larger societal and religious beliefs. They then realize that many of their negative experiences are due to oppression rather than simply personal failure.

A good example of this is the matter of work and love. The family has been structured in such as way as to leave the primary parenting and domestic work to women—even when women also work outside the home. Work and love have been separated, and assigned respectively to men and women. This has prevented the ethic of love from influencing the workplace very much, and has led to the devaluing of the kind of service family members render one another. It has assigned women the realms of care and self-sacrifice, often to the exclusion of self-care and self-assertion. At the same time it has removed men from caregiving, whether in parenting or in the tending of sick and elderly friends and relatives. Women and men who want to combine fulfilling work and generous love meet many obstacles: inflexible work schedules, inadequate child care, inequities in salary scales, and other resistance from business and professional communities highly invested in the traditional family/work pattern. Action for social change is necessary if the gospel vision of new relationships is to become a reality.[11]

The analysis of oppression in root and manifestation often takes place in women's and men's groups (or mixed gender groups). It is an especially important agenda in men's groups and retreats, since most women's groups already include consciousness raising and the naming of sexism. Men's groups sometimes reinforce a patriarchal understanding of the man's role in marriage and family, even while promoting other positive values such as faithfulness and commitment to the well-being of spouse and family. They need to be directed toward building a society of mutual respect and safety for everyone, with true partnership and shared power. Much depends on accurately pinpointing the sources of distress for both women and men, and recognizing the impact oppression has on all of creation. This means naming the evils of patriarchy and its distortion of all social relations.

Ending Domestic Violence

One of the most serious consequences of the patriarchal marriage pattern is domestic violence, that is, abusive behavior that is psychological, physical, or sexual. Domestic violence is nearly always directed at women. In fact, abusive men are the main source of injury to adult women in the United States. Contrary to common belief, domestic violence is not limited to any age, race, religion, education, occupation, economic or social status. It has complex causes and roots, but professionals who work with men who batter report that assaultive men believe the stereotypes about male-female roles and overiden-tify with the stereotypical male role. They feel they have the right to control anyone with less power or status. Battering is an effective way to establish control and dominance.[12]

Whatever our ministry, we must help end such violence against women. There are a number of helpful resources that give direction to ministers for dealing with it. One of these is Carol J. Adams's *Woman-Battering*.[13] Based on years of work with abused women, Adams's book provides a brief but compre-hensive guide to intervening on behalf of families in violence. She directs her ideas specifically to those in various kinds of Christian ministry.

While we cannot treat all of the complex questions related to the issue of domestic violence, it is important to note some generally recommended approaches to the problem. In our various ministerial settings, we can:

1. *Break the silence surrounding the issue of domestic violence.* Spousal violence is a serious problem, and whether we acknowledge it or not, it is happening in the contexts in which we minister. It is a difficult topic, one which we might prefer to avoid. But once we have become informed and edu-cated ourselves, we can use any number of approaches to educating others with whom we minister: sermons, newsletters, prayers, adult forums, books, and pamphlets.[14] Resources need to be provided for teenagers as well, for they tend to romanticize jealousy and control, and may fail to recognize dating vio-lence for what it is. Abuse of every kind thrives on secrecy. Naming the evil of violence and the need for change is an initial step toward breaking the power of this secret. It also allows battered women to seek help, trusting that they will be heard and believed.

2. *Make safety and referral our primary concerns.* We begin by listen-ing to and believing the victims of violence. In addition, we ensure any bat-tered woman who comes to us complete confidentiality, and make her safety our first priority throughout the process.

Domestic violence is a complex and potentially dangerous situation; it should be handled by those with the experience and skill to respond safely. Referral is best for both the battered woman and the batterer, because each needs specialized help that most ministers are not trained to give. Further, ordi-nary models of couple counseling do not work with such couples, since these models presuppose a context of equal power. In fact, such counseling can endanger the woman; what she says may be used against her and increase the violence. Therefore, the most helpful thing we can do as ministers is become acquainted with sources of help in our area, for example, domestic violence hotlines, emergency shelters for battered women, and treatment programs for men who batter. These resources can provide guidance for us, safety and wisdom for the battered woman, and accountability and sanctions for an assaultive spouse. Domestic violence requires a coordinated community response.

3. *Avoid theology that reinforces spousal battering.* Christian beliefs are often very powerful for a battered woman.[15] If her faith tells her that the good wife is subordinate to her husband; that patience, obedience, and gentleness are womanly virtues; that suffering is to be endured; and that nothing justifies leaving a marriage, then she will stay and endure the violence. Too often women who seek help from ministers receive admonitions to forgive, return to their husbands, and make it work. Emphasis on keeping a family together at all costs ignores the fact that over time, without intervention and counseling, abusive behavior tends to increase in frequency and severity.

What can we say theologically that is helpful? In *The Cry of Tamar: Violence Against Women and the Church's Response,* Pamela Cooper-White summarizes the positive messages the church can uniquely give.[16] We can let battered women know that they are loved by God and do not deserve to be abused. That they are not alone. That this is not their "cross" to bear, but that God wants wholeness and abundance of life for all persons. God does not desire that we suffer, but suffers with us, and works with us toward liberation and joy.

Domestic violence reveals most dramatically how important our ministry with couples around gender issues is. But, as we have seen, concern for just and healthy female-male relationships is a much broader ministry, and it takes many forms. It also has implications beyond itself. Conversion from patterns of dominance and submission is central to solving some of our most pressing global concerns: care for an endangered planet, a viable ethic of love and work, solutions to the widespread poverty of women and children. In all these areas, we find ourselves in the midst of a situation fundamentally skewed and seriously damaging in its effects. The call is to a change of heart, and then to a transformation of prevailing systems. It is a large order, profoundly challenging, worthy of our total commitment.

Notes

1. For a helpful treatment of patriarchy, see Elizabeth A. Johnson, *She Who Is: The Mystery of God in Feminist Theological Discourse* (New York: Crossroad, 1992), 23–27.

2. On the household codes, see Elisabeth Schussler Fiorenza, *In Memory of Her: A Feminist Theologcal Construction of Christian Origins* (New York: Crossroad, 1983), 251–84; E. Elizabeth Johnson, "Ephesians," in *The Women's Bible Commentary,* ed. Carol A. Newsom and Sharon H. Ringe (Louisville, Ky.: Westminster John Knox Press), 338–42; and Sarah J. Tanzer,

"Ephesians," in *Searching the Scriptures, Vol. II: A Feminist Commentary*, ed. Elisabeth Fiorenza (New York: Crossroad, 1994), 325–48.

3. Rosemary Ruether develops these liberation themes in many of her writings. See, for example, *Gaia and God: An Ecofeminist Theology of Earth Healing* (San Francisco: HarperCollins, 1992). Maria Pila Aquino presents a Latin American perspective on liberation themes in *Our Cry for Life: Feminist Theology from Latin America,* trans. Dinah Livingstone (Maryknoll: N.Y.: Orbis, 1993).

4. Phyllis Trible, *God and the Rhetoric of Sexuality* (Philadelphia: Fortress, 1978), 72–143.

5. Ann Carr, "Women, Work, and Poverty," in *The Power of Naming: A Concilium Reader in Feminist Liberation Theology,* ed. Elisabeth Schussler Fiorenza (Maryknoll, N.Y.: Orbis, 1996), 83–88.

6. We develop the spirituality of marriage more fully and show its relationship to each of the usual issues of marriage in *The First Two Years of Marriage: Foundations for a Life Together* (Mahwah, N.J.: Paulist, 1983) and *Promises to Keep: Developing the Skills of Marriage* (Mahwah, N.J.: Paulist, 1991).

7. Helpful suggestions regarding the wedding liturgy can be found in *Alternative Futures for Worship, Vol. V: Christian Marriage,* ed. Bernard Cooke (Collegeville, Minn.: Liturgical Press, 1987); and Gertrud Miller Nelson and Christopher Witt, *Sacred Threshold: Rites and Readings for a Wedding with Spirit* (New York: Doubleday, 1998).

8. This is developed further in Kathleen Fischer, *The Inner Rainbow: The Imagination in Christian Life* (Mahwah, N.J.: Paulist, 1983).

9. There are now many resources addressing this issue. See, for example, Johnson, *She Who Is;* and Sandra M. Schneiders, *Women and the Word: The Gender of God in the New Testament and the Spirituality of Woman* (Mahwah, N.J.: Paulist, 1986).

10. New models of ministry and their implications for Christian community are described in Letty M. Russell, *Household of Freedom: Authority in Feminist Theology* (Philadelphia: Westminster, 1987); and James D. and Evelyn Eaton Whitehead, *The Promise of Partnership: A Model for Collaborative Ministry* (San Francisco: HarperCollins, 1993).

11. The changes needed in family and workplace so that love and work can be integrated in a new way are ably analyzed in Rosemary Curran Barciauskas and Debra Beery Hull, *Loving and Working: Reweaving Women's Public and Private Lives* (Bloomington, Ind.: Meyer, Stone, and Company, 1989).

12. For an analysis of the problem, see *Violence and the Family: Report of the American Psychological Association Presidential Task Force on Violence and the Family* (Washington, D.C.: American Psychological Association, 1996); and Neil Jacobson and John Gottman, *When Men Batter Women:*

New Insights into Ending Abusive Relationships (New York: Simon and Schuster, 1998).

13. (Minneapolis: Augsburg Fortress Press, 1994). See also Marie M. Fortune, *Violence in the Family: A Workshop Curriculum for Clergy and Other Helpers* (Cleveland: Pilgrim Press, 1991); and Rebecca Voelkel-Hauger, *Sexual Abuse Prevention: A Study for Teenagers*, rev. ed. (Cleveland: Pilgrim Press, 1995).

14. For example, a concise and helpful book that addresses the theological and moral concerns of battered women is Marie M. Fortune, *Keeping the Faith: Questions and Answers for the Abused Woman* (San Francisco: Harper and Row, 1987). Fortune is a pioneer in the field and is director of the Center for the Prevention of Sexual and Domestic Violence in Seattle. Do not assume, however, that it is safe for a battered woman to take such a book home.

15. Several fine essays addressing these theological themes can be found in *Violence against Women and Children: A Christian Theological Sourcebook*, ed. Carol J. Adams and Marie M. Fortune (New York: Continuum, 1995). See also Susan Brooks Thistlethwhaite, "Every Two Minutes: Battered Women and Feminist Interpretation," in *Feminist Interpretation of the Bible*, ed. Letty M. Russell (Philadelphia: Westminster, 1985), 96–110; and *Women Resisting Violence: Spirituality for Life*, ed. Mary John Mananzan, Mercy Amba Oduyoye, Elsa Tamez, J. Shannon Clarkson, Mary C. Gray, and Letty M. Russell (Maryknoll, N.Y.: Orbis, 1996).

16. (Minneapolis: Augsburg Fortress Press, 1995), 124.

SECTION VII.
HOMILETICS, SOCIAL THOUGHT, AND LITURGY

Walter Burghardt, the dean of American Catholic homilists, offers insight into his recent work and its relevancy for pastoral ministry in "A Spirituality for Justice." In his essay he does not offer general ideas on preaching but proclaims "the faith that does justice" and points out that spirituality must penetrate justice if it is to come alive for persons in the pews. This essay is both helpful and engaging. I see it as offering a framework for the many opportunities ministers have to preach the Word in settings both inside and outside of liturgy.

In "Reform, Resist, Resign: Catholic and American in the Third Millennium," Lyle Weiss voices concern about the tendency of some people to define spirituality narrowly and to make the good news concerning Jesus "a private possession." In line with Burghardt's essay, Weiss encourages us to recognize that "to be a Christian is to engage in every aspect of human life . . . to promote the realization of God's community…and to shape the values of the larger society." A succinct yet comprehensive section on the development of the church's social thought in American history as well as one on "shaping parish vision" makes this essay especially informative.

In "Women's Liturgical Spirituality," Susan Roll shares with us a movement that flourishes but does so in relative obscurity. In this fascinating essay she offers us a look at some of the reasons for the growth of the movement as well as some of its characteristics and implications—including potential contributions to spiritual depth and authenticity in a church that needs to be aware of "a prophetic sign indicating possible direction for ongoing liturgical reform in the churches." Her essay stirs the creative imagination as well as provides background on a movement that is filled both with energy and future hope. At the very least, it should prompt good discussion; I found it rich and inspiring.

33. A Spirituality for Justice

Almost a decade ago, I had a dream. Nothing quite as revolutionary as the vision of Martin Luther King, Jr., but still, not insignificant for the future of our church, our country, our way of life, our spirituality.

It was springtime 1989. I was in my twelfth year as Georgetown University's theologian in residence, my twenty-third year as editor of the scholarly journal *Theological Studies,* my forty-fourth year on its editorial staff. I sensed it was time to resign both positions. I was touching seventy-five, increasingly aware of the psalmist's warning, "The days of our life are 70 years, perhaps 80 if we are strong" (Ps 90:10). And yet, my mind was still active and insatiably curious, my imagination free and flowing, my emotions spirited. On what should I focus for however many years God might have in store for me? An apostolic area that would engage my background, talents, and interests? Background? Theology, specifically the so-called Fathers of the Church. Talents? Communication: preaching, lecturing, writing, editing. Interests? People, especially and increasingly Jesus' "little ones," the poor and the powerless, the distressed and the downtrodden.

I was then a senior fellow of the Woodstock Theological Center, had in fact been a fellow since its inauguration in 1974. A research organization located at Georgetown University in the District of Columbia, the center was founded by the New York and Maryland Provinces of the Society of Jesus, to put theology to work on social, economic, and political issues. It proved to be the seedplot for my dream. The center had been, and still is, doing impressive work in touching theology to the neuralgic problems of our time, through research and writing, conferences and workshops. An admirable approach indeed. And yet, I worried, this approach reaches only a relatively small number of our people. How might we expand the center's influence, stimulate American Catholics *as a whole* to live and spread our social gospel?

It was then that the dream took on flesh and blood. The heart of the matter? Preaching. Where do American Catholics gather regularly in largest array, even more than for pro football? At weekend liturgies. True, actual head counts show regular weekend mass attendance ranging from only 27 to 36 percent; still,

527

an audience of millions a TV network might profitably barter its soul to win. Not preaching in general, but proclaiming "the faith that does justice." What the president of Catholic Charities, Inc., Jesuit Fred Kammer, integrated as the title of his book *Doing Faithjustice.*[1] It is the inseparable unity our 32nd General Congregation (1974-1975) called "the mission of the Society of Jesus today."[2] It is the mission the then-Superior General of the Jesuits, Pedro Arrupe, confessed was the concept most difficult of all to put across to his society.[3]

The dream, however, had a nightmarish aura. Granted that effective Catholic preachers are not absent from our pulpits, preaching is by common consent not our pride and glory, is all too often dull as dishwater. I cannot forget a pertinent phrase from Dennis O'Brien, a former president of the University of Rochester in New York. In a book engagingly entitled *God and the New Haven Railway and Why Neither One Is Doing Very Well,* he observed that on Monday morning most people on the train station are not likely to see church service as "one of the livelier, more salvational times of week"; their appraisal is more likely to be "Saturday Night Live, Sunday Morning Deadly."[4]

If our proclamation of God's word is to instill new life into the relationship between faith and justice, (1) the minds and imaginations of our preachers must be captivated by a fresh vision, and (2) their hearts must be set afire with a fresh flame. As we shall see, the first demand has to do with a well-preserved Catholic secret: biblical justice. The second demand was strongly urged by Fr. Philip Murnion, director of the National Pastoral Center in New York City. He insisted that our project Preaching the Just Word would fail of its purpose if its exclusive or overriding priority were information, data, skills, or strategies, important as these are. Undergirding all these must be a spirituality, a conversion process that turns the preacher inside out, shapes a new person, puts "fire in the belly." Not two separate, disparate segments; rather a unique wedding of head and heart, of thinking and loving, that would shape a unique retreat or workshop.

But is it only the preacher the project has in mind? Hardly. A homily simply begins the justice project. Once captured by the homily, by biblical justice, each community of Christians must gather to ask three questions: (1) What are the justice issues in our area? (2) What resources do we command to confront these issues? (3) Since we cannot do everything, what concretely shall we do?

Hence the two main structural features of this essay: (1) the justice that should dominate not only our proclamation of the gospel but our individual and communal living; (2) the spirituality that must penetrate the justice if justice is to come alive.

Justice

When I say *justice,* the philosopher in me, the ethicist, has in mind a virtue that impels me to give every man, woman, and child what each deserves, what each can claim as a right. Not because they are Jews or Christians, brilliant or beautiful, prosperous or productive. Only because they are human beings, all shaped of the same dust and spirit. Simply as humans, they can, for example, lay claim to food, a job, a living wage, decent housing, can demand to be treated with respect.

When I say *justice,* the lawyer, the jurist, the judge thinks of Lady Justice, the woman with scales and a sword, her eyes blindfolded or closed in token of impartiality, swayed neither by love nor by prejudice, moved only by what is laid down in law. Legal justice sees to it that just laws foster the common good, that human rights written into law are protected, that the scales of Lady Justice are not weighted in favor of the rich and powerful, that the indicted remain innocent until proven guilty, that the punishment fits the proven crime.

The Hebrews of old knew all that, tried with varying success to live by it. Such justice, they knew, is indispensable for civilized living. They sensed, as we do, that unless we give people what they deserve and what has been written into law, life becomes a jungle, the survival of the fittest, the rule of the swift, the shrewd, the savage. Even so, they lived by something more important still. It is a justice that Yahweh wanted to "roll down like waters" (Am 5:24). It is actually a justice too rich, too opulent, to be easily imprisoned in a definition. Still, back in 1977 biblical scholar John R. Donahue shaped a working definition with admirable succinctness:

> In general terms the biblical idea of justice can be described as *fidelity to the demands of a relationship.* In contrast to modern individualism the Israelite is in a world where "to live" is to be united with others in a social context either by bonds of family or by covenant relationships. This web of relationships—king with people, judge with complainants, family with tribe and kinfolk, the community with the resident alien and suffering in their midst and all with the covenant God—constitutes the world in which life is played out.[5]

It is in this context that we must read what the prophet Micah trumpeted to judges who accepted bribes, to princes and merchants who cheated and robbed the poor, to priests and prophets who adapted their words to please their hearers.[6]

> With what shall I come before the Lord,
>   and bow myself before God on high?
> Shall I come before Him with burnt offerings,
>   with calves a year old?
> Will the Lord be pleased with thousands of rams,
>   with ten thousands of rivers of oil?

Shall I give my first-born for my transgression,
   the fruit of my body for the sin of my soul?
He has told you, O mortal, what is good;
   and what does the Lord require of you
but to do justice, and to love kindness.
   and to walk humbly before your God? (Mi 6:6–8)

"Do justice." Like Isaiah and Jeremiah, like Amos and Hosea, Micah proclaims to Israel that the Lord rejects precisely those things the Israelites think will make God happy. Not because such offerings are unacceptable in themselves; rather because two essential ingredients are missing: steadfast love and justice. And the justice is not simply or primarily what people deserve. The prophets trumpeted fidelity. To what? To the demands of relationships that stemmed from their covenant with God. What relationships? Primarily three: to God, to people, to the earth.

1. *Love God above all else.* This command did not originate with Jesus. It was God's primary demand on Israel: "Hear, O Israel: The Lord is our God, the Lord alone. You shall love the Lord your God with all your heart, all your soul, all your might. Keep these words in your heart. Recite them to your children and talk about them when you are at home and when you are away, when you lie down and when you rise" (Dt 4–7). This, Jesus declared, is "the greatest and first commandment" (Mt 22:38).

Negatively, the first commandment forbade other gods: "You shall have no other gods before [or: besides] me. You shall not make for yourself an idol, whether in the form of anything that is in heaven above, or that is on the earth beneath, or that is in the water under the earth. You shall not bow down to them or worship them; for I the Lord your God am a jealous God" (Ex 20:3–5). The command did not lie long in abstraction; for when Moses delayed coming down from Mt. Sinai with the two tablets of the covenant, the people cast an image of a calf from gold and said, "These are your gods, O Israel, who brought you up out of the land of Egypt!" (Ex 32:4).

2. *Love your neighbor as yourself.* Again, not a command that originated with Jesus. It occurs first not in Matthew but in Leviticus (19:18). And the neighbor was not just the Jew next door. The Lord had commanded, "You shall not oppress a resident alien; you know the heart of an alien [you know how an alien feels], for you were aliens in the land of Egypt" (Ex 23:9; see 22:21). More than not oppressing, "you shall also love the stranger, for you were strangers in the land of Egypt" (Dt 10:19; see 24:17–18). More basically, behind the law lies the covenant, "the great God, mighty and awesome, who is not partial and takes no bribe, who executes justice for the orphan and the widow, and who loves the strangers, providing them food and clothing" (Dt 10:17–18).

Not an easy command. Not only difficult to obey, but difficult to interpret. I cannot believe God meant some sort of psychological balancing act: As much or as little as you love yourself, so much love or so little love shall you lavish or trickle on your neighbor. I cannot disregard the conviction of a solid scripture scholar: With the words "as yourself," Jesus is speaking of "a right form of self-love."[7] Still, I resonate to other biblical experts who suggest that each of us must love every other image of God, however flawed, like another "I," another self, as if I were standing in his or her shoes, especially the paper-thin shoes of the downtrodden and disadvantaged. Here Isaiah is blunt and to the point:

> Is not this the fast that I choose:
>   to loose the bonds of injustice,
>   to undo the thongs of the yoke,
> to let the oppressed go free,
>   and to break every yoke?
> Is it not to share your bread with the hungry,
>   and bring the homeless poor into your house;
> when you see the naked, to cover them,
>   and not to hide yourself from your own flesh? (Is 58:6–7)

Not to hide yourself from *your own flesh.*

It brings us back to the kings of the Old Testament. As God's vicegerents, they had a special obligation to the poor, to those in need, to the helpless. Psalm 72 is instructive:

> Give the king your justice, O God,
>   and your righteousness to a king's son.
> May he judge your people with righteousness,
>   and your poor with justice. . . .
> May he defend the cause of the poor of the people,
>   give deliverance to the needy. . . .
> For he delivers the needy when they call,
>   the poor and those who have no helper.
> He has pity on the weak and the needy,
>   and saves the lives of the needy.
> From oppression and violence he redeems their life,
>   and precious is their blood in his sight. (Ps 72:1–4, 12–14)

What did Jesus add to Leviticus? "This is my commandment: Love one another as I have loved you" (Jn 15:12). This is New Testament justice: Love as Jesus loved. I mean the God-man who not only urged us to love our enemies and pray for those who persecute us (Mt 5:44), but lived what he urged unto crucifixion.

The point I emphasize here is the social focus of scripture. Those who read in the sacred text a sheerly personal, individualistic morality have not understood the Torah, have not sung the psalms, have not been burned by the prophets, have not perceived the implications and the very burden of Jesus' message, and must inevitably play fast and loose with St. Paul.

That social focus of God's book is evident on its opening pages. On the sixth day of creation our incredibly imaginative God did not have in mind isolated units, autonomous entities, scattered disparately around a globe, independent each of every other—entities that might one day decide through a social contract to join together for self-aggrandizement, huddle together for self-protection. God had in mind a people, a human family, a community of persons, a body genuinely one. The Exodus itself was not simply a liberation from slavery. "While liberation from oppression is a fundamental aspect of the Exodus narrative, it is not simply *freedom from* which is important, but *freedom for* the formation of a community which lives under the covenant."[8] John Donahue has summed it up with powerful simplicity: "Men and women are God's representatives and conversation partners in the world, with a fundamental dignity that must be respected and fostered. They are to exist in interdependence and mutual support...."[9]

It is this divine dream for human living that the Second Vatican Council stated unambiguously: "God...has willed that all men and women should constitute one family." Again, "God did not create man and woman for life in isolation, but for the formation of social unity." And "this solidarity must be constantly increased until that day on which it will be brought to perfection. Then, saved by grace, men and women will offer flawless glory to God as a family beloved of God and of Christ their brother."[10]

3. *Our earth: all that is not God or the human person.* Here we encounter a serious challenge to justice. I mean God's directive to the humankind just shaped in the image and likeness of the divine: "Fill the earth and subdue it; and have dominion over the fish of the sea and over the birds of the air and over every living thing that moves upon the earth" (Gn 1:28). Here the Hebrew Testament calls for careful discernment. What is it that Genesis says, and what does it mean?

> The creation stories in Genesis 1–2 literally ground humans in the dust and dirt of creation itself. "The Lord God formed man from the dust of the ground" (Gn 2:7). "You are dust, and to dust you shall return" (Gn 3:19). At the same time, God gives these dirt creatures called humans authority to shape and direct nature. The human tills and keeps the garden of Eden (Gn 2:15). The human

names and defines the animals (Gn 2:20). The human is commanded to have "dominion" over the creatures God has made (Gn 1:28; cf. Ps 8:6).[11]

"Have dominion"? Little wonder that some critics have taken this biblical command as the origin of the Western world's exploitation of nature. In a classic 1967 article, Lynn White, Jr., argued that from Genesis 1 "Christianity...not only established a dualism of humans and nature, but also insisted that it is God's will that humans exploit nature for their proper ends."[12] Granted that Genesis 1:28 has been thus interpreted over the centuries, the text and its context do not in fact justify exploiting nature for human convenience. In Psalm 72, for example, quoted in part previously, the Hebrew term for "have dominion" is used (v. 8; see also Ps 110:2) in a context that describes not only the care that should characterize a king as God's vicegerent, with especial concern for the most vulnerable and fragile, for the widow, the orphan, and the alien. The broader context includes "abundance of grain in the land," grain waving "on the tops of the mountains" (v. 16), fertility in the land associated with prayer for the king (v. 15).

The mandate given humanity in Eden is not exploitation but reverential care for God's creation.[13] The very context "suggests that this human dominion is to be carried out 'in the image of God,' an image that suggests nurture, blessing, and care rather than exploitation, abuse, and subjugation."[14]

Almost a decade ago, Douglas John Hall expressed our relation to material creation with an insight that still attracts me mightily.[15] He rejected a model that struck him as excessively idealistic: Humans are *in* nature. Rejected it because it denies humans any role in shaping the natural environment. He rejected a model that seemed to him excessively imperialistic: Humans are *above* nature. Rejected it because here nature is exploited for human purposes with little or no concern for its injurious impact and no sense of responsibility to a higher authority. Hall opted for the biblical model: Humans are *with* nature. Opted for it because here humans stand to nature in a relationship of steward or caretaker. A steward is one who manages what is someone else's. A steward cares, is concerned, agonizes. Stewards may not plunder or waste; they are responsible, can be called to account for their stewardship. As the psalmist phrased it, "The earth is the Lord's, and all that is in it" (Ps 24:1).

Spirituality

Now to the heart of the matter as it touches this volume: What has biblical justice to do with spirituality, specifically a spirituality for ministers? No response will be intelligible unless we understand what we mean by spirituality.

Not a simple matter, for spirituality has a history; more accurately, has histories.[16] For my purposes, some basics will be sufficient.[17]

What do I mean by a spirituality? St. Paul sparks a useful beginning:
The spiritual person is one whose whole being, whose whole life, is influenced, guided, directed by "the Spirit that is from God" (1 Cor 2:12). Not
some ghostly apparition in outer space, but the third person of the Trinity, the
divine person given us by the Father and the Son, alive within us, shaping us
into images of Christ, shaping us increasingly as sisters and brothers in Christ,
as children of the Father.

How does the Holy Spirit effect this? By infusing into us incredible gifts
we could not possibly produce by our naked human nature. I mean a faith that
at its best is a total self-giving to God, a hope that is a confident trust in God's
promises, a love that enables us to love our sisters and brothers as Jesus has
loved us (1 Cor 13:13). I mean what Paul called "spiritual wisdom and understanding, so that you may lead lives worthy of the Lord, fully pleasing to him,
as you bear fruit in every good work and as you grow in the knowledge of God"
(Col 1:9–10). I mean what Paul termed "the fruit of the Spirit: love, joy, peace,
patience, kindness, generosity, faithfulness, gentleness, and self-control" (Gal
5:22–23). I mean charisms that build up the Christian community, different
gifts to different persons, but "all activated by one and the same Spirit, who
allots to each one individually just as the Spirit chooses" (1 Cor 12:11).[18]

Now, within Catholicism there are spiritualities and spiritualities. Basically, each spirituality lives up to the description I have attempted. Each is a
living-out of the Christian life under the inspiration of the Holy Spirit, through
the gifts the indwelling spirit produces in us for our personal sanctification and
our contribution to the life of the community.

But different social situations, different cultures, different religious
communities, different personalities lay special stress on different facets of the
richness, the breadth and depth, that Catholic spirituality encompasses. And so
we have a cursillo spirituality, a charismatic spirituality, a lay spirituality, a liberation spirituality, a feminist spirituality. We find Franciscans stressing Lady
Poverty, Benedictines emphasizing the common life (community), Jesuits laying particular stress on service. We have individuals imitating the lady mystic
Julian of Norwich, Teresa of Avila or Thérèse of Lisle, Dorothy Day or
Thomas Merton, Swiss theologian Hans Urs von Balthasar or Jesuit paleontol-
ogist Teilhard de Chardin. Special emphases within the one basic spirituality,
to suit different needs, desires, tasks, persons.[19]

Of high significance for my approach here is another recent emphasis.
For all too long and for all too many, spirituality has been identified with our
interior life, what goes on inside of us. A holistic spirituality includes both the
inner experience of God and its outward expression in relationships.[20] That is
why I was delighted to discover, not long ago, a definition that attracts me

mightily: Spirituality is a "process of being conformed to the image of God for the sake of others."[21] For the sake of others.

Biblical Justice

In the light of this, I can only conclude that biblical justice is itself a spirituality. How could it fail to be? Take a man or woman who loves God above all else, to the exclusion of all earth's idols, pleasure and power, wealth and wisdom; who sees in every other, in friend and foe, in Saddam Hussein as well as John Paul II, a reflection of God, a link with God that even sin cannot totally undo; whose life is a ceaseless effort to help the less fortunate, to "send the downtrodden away relieved" (Lk 4:18); who touches each "thing," each product of God's imaginative creation, earth and sea and sky, with respect and reverence. That man or woman is a "spiritual" person in St. Paul's sense. For such an approach to life is impossible unless the Holy Spirit is directing it. Know it or not, this man or woman is "being conformed to the image of God for the sake of others."

What, then, is there to add? A specifically *Catholic* dimension and a systematic method for achieving spiritual growth that centers on the process of *conversion*.

Ecclesial Spirituality

A Catholic spirituality of justice for ministry must be ecclesial. I mean, it takes place within a distinctive community, within the church Jesus founded to continue his work of salvation. That mission was intimately concerned with justice, with the program Luke has Jesus express in the synagogue of his home town: "The Spirit of the Lord is upon me, for [the Lord] has anointed me, has sent me to preach good news to the poor, to proclaim release for prisoners and sight for the blind, to send the downtrodden away relieved, and to proclaim the Lord's year of favor" (Lk 4:18–19; cf. Is 61:1–2).

That mission, the mission Jesus laid on his disciples after his resurrection (Jn 20:21), is the commission conveyed to every person baptized into Christ. We are sent not as rugged individualists, but as part and parcel of a people, members of a body where, as St. Paul insisted, no one can say to any other, "I have no need of you" (1 Cor 12:21). A body wherein the gifts vary (wisdom, knowledge, healing, miracles, administration) but the giver is the same (the same Holy Spirit living within us and ceaselessly shaping the one body).

Negatively, this means that a Catholic spirituality of justice is not a process developed in a sheer me-and-Jesus relationship. That relationship is indeed vital, indispensable; for unless we branches abide in the vine that is Christ, we "can do nothing" (Jn 15:5). Still, ever since the Holy Spirit descended upon the infant church at the first Pentecost, St. Paul's declaration to the Christians of Corinth is basic for Christian living: "In the one Spirit we were all baptized into one body—Jews or Greeks, slaves or free— and we were all made to drink of one Spirit" (1 Cor 12:13). Of that body Jesus is indeed the head, but he is head of a body; and it is within this body that God's grace circulates like a bloodstream. Not only are the sacraments—from the waters of baptism to a final oiling—communal experiences, experiences that bring the church together, encounters with Christ in the context of the community. By God's gracious giving, we are commissioned to be channels of grace to one another.

Over the years I have been thrilled by an insight of a gifted Presbyterian novelist and preacher, Frederick Buechner. Three decades ago he compared humanity to a gigantic spider web:

> If you touch it anywhere, you set the whole thing trembling....As we move around this world and as we act with kindness, perhaps, or with indifference or with hostility toward the people we meet, we too are setting the great spider web atremble. The life that I touch for good or ill will touch another life, and that in turn another, until who knows where the trembling stops or in what far place and time my touch will be felt. Our lives are linked. No man [no woman] is an island.[22]

It would be unfortunate, however, if we were to see justice as a one-way street, where the haves affect the have-nots—the rich are generous to the poor, the learned teach the ignorant, the powerful bend down to the powerless, the more gifted evangelize the less endowed. No. Crucial for a justice spirituality is an expression heard repeatedly in Latin America: "The poor evangelize us."[23] Not only the economically poor but so many of the AIDS-afflicted and recovering alcoholics, refugees and the displaced, women and blacks, Hispanics and Native Americans, political prisoners like Africa's Mandela and enslaved electricians like Poland's Walesa have helped the churches discover what a 1979 conference of Latin American bishops called "the evangelizing potential of the poor."[24]

How do "the poor" actualize that potential? They challenge the churches. By their sheer numbers, by their Christlike endurance under domination and persecution, by their underlying gospel goodness, by their openness to God and what God permits, they have compelled us to look within ourselves, have at times stimulated profound conversion. Theologian Jon Sobrino expressed it clearly and succinctly:

> When the Church has taken the poor seriously, it is then that it has
> become truly apostolic. The poor initiate the process of evangeliza-
> tion. When the Church goes out to them in mission, the paradoxical
> result is that they, the poor, evangelize the Church.[25]

The poor are not simply recipients of apostolic ministry; they are our teachers
and educators. Not only recipients of our spirituality; they help shape it.

Still, a Catholic spirituality of justice is not ecclesial if it is not eucharistic. Simply because, in the words of Vatican II,

> The liturgy is the summit to which the Church's activity is
> directed; at the same time it is the source from which all her power
> proceeds....From the liturgy, therefore, and especially from the
> Eucharist,...that sanctification of men and women in Christ and
> the glorification of God, to which all other activities of the Church
> stretch and strain as toward their goal, are most effectively
> achieved.[26]

Paradoxically, it is not primarily by inserting an ideology that the liturgy
becomes a force for justice. I am not downplaying the power of the homily,
which, as Vatican II asserts, is "part of the liturgical action," is "part of the
liturgy itself."[27] In season and out, I have insisted that an effective justice homily, even though it cannot solve complex social issues, can and must raise a
congregation's consciousness, its awareness. Still, the liturgical action effects
change above all by its own inner dynamic. For the temporal order can be
changed only by conversion, only if men and women turn from sin and selfishness. And for Catholics the primary source of conversion is the mass, which
extends through time and space the cross through which the world is transfigured. I have stated this forcefully elsewhere:

> The Mass should be the liberating adventure of the whole Church,
> the sacrament which frees men and women from their inherited
> damnable concentration on themselves, looses us from our ice-
> cold isolation, fashions us into brothers and sisters agonizing not
> only for a church of charity but for a world of justice as well.[28]

Many years ago Jesuit John C. Haughey recaptured for me a remarkable
insight expressed by government people engaged in a Woodstock Theological
Center project on government decision making. As they saw it, good liturgy
facilitates public responsibility not because it provides principles of solution,
not because it tells the worshipers precisely what to think about specific conflicts, but rather because an effective celebration of the transcendent puts them
in touch with that which transcends all their burning concerns, their particular

perplexities. Good liturgy frees us to sort out the issues we have to decide, because it makes us aware of our addictions and our illusions, casts a pitiless light on myopic self-interest, detaches us from a narrow selfishness, facilitates Christian discernment. It can be, in short, a powerful force for conversion. Good liturgy is not so much didactic as evocative; it lets *God* come to light, allows *God* to be heard.

Very simply, the primary way in which the liturgy becomes a social force is through its own inner dynamism, by its incomparable power to turn the human heart inside out, free it from its focus on self, fling it out unfettered to the service of sisters and brothers enslaved.

In a related way, I have often emphasized that the eucharist's purpose is not only to link us more intimately with Christ—the traditional "You are what you have received"—but to transform us into eucharists. For what is the eucharist? A presence; a presence of Christ; a real presence; a presence of the whole Christ, body and blood, soul and divinity; a presence that stems from love, from the love of a God-man, and leads to love, a crucified love for every man and woman born into our world. This eucharist can make of us, demands that we become, genuine eucharists. I mean that we are present to our sisters and brothers; really present; a presence of the whole person, not only mind and money but flesh and spirit, emotions and passions; a presence that springs from love and leads to love: "Love one another as I have loved you" (Jn 15:12).

An unexpected contribution to an ecclesial spirituality for justice has reached me from Fordham University's Elizabeth Johnson. Ever on the alert for fresh interpretations of expressions most of us take for granted, she has discovered an intriguing ambiguity in the age-old *communio sanctorum*. The latter word could mean either "holy persons" or "holy things," participation in sacred realities, especially the eucharistic bread and the cup of salvation, the meaning when the phrase was first used in the Eastern Church. Medieval theologians, she notes, "played with both meanings." Actually, "there is no need to choose between the two for they reinforce one another." And then Johnson's insight into a profound application today:

> In the light of the contemporary moral imperative to treat the ever-more damaged earth as a sacred creation with its own intrinsic rather than instrumental value, the elusive quality of the phrase's original meaning is a happy circumstance. At its best, sacramental theology has always drawn on the connection between the natural world and the signs of bread, wine, water, oil, and sexual intercourse which, when taken into the narrative of Jesus' life, death, and resurrection, become avenues of God's healing grace. Now, in the time of earth's agony, the sancta can be pushed to its widest meaning to include the gifts of air, water, land, and the myriad

creatures that share the planet with human beings in interwoven ecosystems—the brothers and sisters of Francis of Assisi's vision. For the universe itself is the primordial sacrament through which we participate in and communicate with divine mystery. Since the same divine Spirit who lights the fire of the saint also fuels the vitality of all creation, then "communion in the holy" includes holy people and a holy world in interrelationship. By this line of thinking, a door opens from within the symbol of the communion of saints itself to include all beings, sacred bread and wine certainly, but also the primordial sacrament, the earth itself. Once again, this symbol reveals its prophetic edge as its cosmic dimension calls forth an ecological ethic of restraint of human greed and promotion of care for the earth.[29]

Conversion

Integral to a comprehensive spirituality for justice, for anyone who proclaims justice or simply lives justly, is a conversion. Conversion, like spirituality, is not easy to define.[30] I am not directly concerned here with the sudden, swift, almost instantaneous turnabout, for example, from Saul to Paul, from strict Pharisee to Christian believer. For my purposes, I recommend a more complex approach. I suggest the approach of Jesuit Bernard Lonergan (1904–1984). Lonergan has left us a systematic method for understanding spiritual growth that centers on the process of conversion. But we shall not grasp that process unless we recall several background realities.

The work of justice has for its purpose to fashion community. For community is "the ideal basis of society. Without a large measure of community, human society and sovereign states cannot function. Without a constant renewal of community, the measure of community already enjoyed easily is squandered."[31] For Christians, the profound call to shape community stems from Jesus' prayer to his Father on the eve of his crucifixion that those who believe in him may be "completely one," one as he and his Father are one (Jn 17:20–23). From a Christian perspective, the ideal community is God's kingdom, a social reality: as the liturgy of Christ the king has it, "a kingdom of truth and life, a kingdom of holiness and grace, a kingdom of justice, love, and peace." Injustice—in the biblical sense, lack of love—is what tears community apart, sunders relationships, and divides society into rival sectors.

It is precisely this call to community that gives sin its most significant characteristic. In scripture, sin involves not only our traditional "offense against God," but also the sundering of community. The whole of scripture from Genesis to Revelation is the story of struggle for community, of lapses into division, disintegration, enmity. If biblical justice is fidelity to the demands of a relationship, then sin is a refusal of responsibility; sin creates division, alienation, dissension, marginalization, rejection; sin dis-members the body.

In a sinful world our mission is reconciliation. I suggest that all Christians may apply to themselves what Paul says of himself:

> If anyone is in Christ, there is a new creation: everything old has passed away; see, everything has become new! All this is from God, who reconciled us to Himself through Christ, and has given us the ministry of reconciliation; that is, in Christ God was reconciling the world to Himself...and entrusting the message of reconciliation to us. So we are ambassadors for Christ. (2 Cor 5:17–20) As believers, as faith-filled Christians, our task is to help people to recognize, understand, value, and live accurately the various relationships they have to one another so that they might heal the ruptures that alienate, that destroy relationships. In short, to promote justice.

Healing these ruptures is the function of conversion. What succinctly is the conversion? For Lonergan, a conversion to exact fidelity to four transcendental precepts. What precepts? (1) Be attentive: Focus on the full range of experience. (2) Be intelligent: Inquire, probe, question. (3) Be reasonable: Marshal evidence, examine opinions, judge wisely. (4) Be responsible: Act on the basis of prudent judgments and genuine values. This last, for Lonergan, includes being in love: wholehearted commitment to God as revealed in Jesus Christ. Why are these precepts called transcendental? Because they are not limited to any particular genus or category of inquiry, for example, science or theology; they are simply a normative expression of the innate, God-given, spontaneous, and invariably unfolding operations of human intentional consciousness.

The transcendental method does not permit easy explanation; one has to absorb Lonergan's *Method in Theology,* a challenging invitation to self-awareness, self-understanding, self-appropriation. For our purposes, two aspects are especially significant. First, "in a sense everyone knows and observes transcendental method. Everyone does so, precisely in the measure that he is attentive, intelligent, reasonable, responsible."[32] Second, "in another sense it is quite difficult to be at home in transcendental method, for that is not to be achieved by reading books or listening to lectures or analyzing language. It is a matter of heightening one's consciousness by objectifying it," that is, "applying the operations as intentional to the operations as conscious."[33] Concretely, how does one do that with the four precepts? It is a matter of

> (1) *experiencing* one's experiencing, understanding, judging, and deciding, (2) *understanding* the unity and relations of one's experienced experiencing, understanding, judging, deciding, (3) *affirming* the reality of one's experienced and understood experiencing,

understanding, judging, deciding, and (4) *deciding* to operate in accord with the norms immanent in the spontaneous relatedness of one's experienced, understood, affirmed experiencing, understanding, judging, and deciding.[34]

In connection with those four precepts Lonergan identifies three conversions: intellectual, moral, and religious.

Intellectual conversion is "a radical clarification" of experience. It eliminates a misleading myth about human knowing: that to know is to see, hear, touch, taste, smell, feel. On the contrary, "the world mediated by meaning is a world known not by the sense experience of an individual but by the external and internal experience of a cultural community, and by the continuously checked and rechecked judgments of the community. Knowing, accordingly, is not just seeing; it is experiencing, understanding, judging, and believing." Liberation from the myth, discovering the self-transcendence proper to the human process of coming to know, is to break through ingrained habits of thinking and speaking. "It is a conversion, a new beginning, a fresh start. It opens the way to ever further clarifications and developments."[35]

Moral conversion involves shifting our criteria for decisions and choices from satisfactions to values. It "consists in opting for the truly good, even for value against satisfaction" when they conflict. But "deciding is one thing, doing is another." What remains? To root out biases in the self, in culture, in history; to keep scrutinizing our responses to values; to listen to criticism; to learn from others.[36]

> So moral conversion goes beyond the value, truth, to values generally. It promotes the subject from cognitional to moral self-transcendence....He still needs truth...the truth attained in accord with the exigencies of rational consciousness. But now his pursuit of it is all the more secure because he has been armed against bias, and it is all the more meaningful and significant because it occurs within, and plays an essential role in, the far richer context of the pursuit of all values.[37]

Similarly, religious conversion goes beyond the moral. It occurs when we are "grasped by ultimate concern." It is a falling in love, unqualified self-surrender; it means loving "with all one's heart and all one's soul and all one's mind and all one's strength." It means accepting a vocation to holiness. "For Christians it is God's love flooding our hearts through the Holy Spirit given to us. It is the gift of grace." It involves replacing the heart of stone with a heart of flesh, and then moving gradually to a complete transformation of all my living and feeling, my thoughts and words, my deeds and omissions.[38]

Not a rigid order of conversions—first intellectual, then moral, then religious. Normally, religious conversion is prior to moral, which in turn is prior to intellectual. The experience and acceptance of God's love, the Holy Spirit poured into our hearts, is the beginning of genuine apprehension of what is good, accurate understanding of what is true.

Now Lonergan's approach to conversion is not ivory-tower philosophical theology. As far as justice is concerned, it keeps the underlying spirituality I commend so strongly from being reduced to more and more prayer, fidelity to daily meditation, resistance to temptations, and avoidance of the near occasions of sin—the psalmist's "clean heart" (Ps 51:10). It has to do with truth, with values, with love, with "the eros of the human spirit,"[39] with suffering, with a transformation not only of my innermost self but of my relationship to people and the earth, to culture and history.

Awesome? Yes indeed. But only through such transformation can God's creative dream for community, for the kingdom, be realized. Lonergan saw so clearly that what makes for community, its "formal constituent," is common meaning. Conversely,

> as common meaning constitutes community, so divergent meaning divides it. Such division may amount to no more than a diversity of culture and the stratification of individuals into classes of higher and lower competence. The serious division is the one that arises from *the presence and absence of intellectual, moral, or religious conversion.* For man is his true self inasmuch as he is self-transcending. Conversion is the way to self-transcendence. Inversely, man is alienated from his true self as he refuses self-transcendence, and the basic form of ideology is the self-justification of alienated man.[40]

Here, for me, is a type of conversion (not the only one) that is crucial for a profound spirituality of biblical justice. For its high point, religious conversion is conversion "to a total being-in-love as the efficacious ground of all self-transcendence, whether in the pursuit of truth, or in the realization of human values, or in the orientation man adopts to the universe, its ground, and its goal."[41] It is a conversion not defined by a definite date but enduring and developing through a lifetime. It involves my relationship not only to God and people but to the earth that sustains me; not only a spiritual soul but my mind and heart, my emotions and passions. It is critical not only for individual holiness but for the building of community, for the church's mission to promote the human family, the church's "redemptive role in human society inasmuch as [self-sacrificing] love can undo the mischief of decline and restore the cumulative process of progress."[42]

To sum up: Take biblical justice, that is, fidelity to relationships that stem from our covenant with God: loving God above all idols, seeing in each flawed human an image of Christ, touching every facet of earth and sea and sky with reverence. Link that to life within the *ecclesia,* life within the body of Christ, a life of faith and hope and love, life in ever-widening communities (parish, diocese, universal church) for the building of the human family, life nourished by the body and blood of the risen Christ. Introduce into that complex a ceaseless, never-ending conversion to a communal search for an intellectual value called truth, a communal opting for what is truly good against self-satisfaction, a communal self-surrender to Love incarnate.

With such a spirituality we might begin edging back to storied Eden, to that brief shining moment when humanity was at peace with God, humans at peace with one another, humans at peace with the rest of God's creation. It is still a dream divine. And if the kingdom is not yet—not yet what God had in mind when the Lord looked on everything created and "indeed it was very good" (Gn 1:31)—it just might stimulate our search together for a spirituality that makes us more attentive, more intelligent, more reasonable, and more responsible. In a word, more Christlike.

Notes

1. New York/Mahwah, N.J.: Paulist, 1991.

2. See "Decrees of the 32nd General Congregation," no. 48, in *Documents of the 31st and 32nd General Congregations of the Society of Jesus* (St. Louis: Institute of Jesuit Sources, 1977), 411. The exact sentence reads, "The mission of the Society of Jesus today is the service of faith, of which the promotion of justice is an absolute requirement."

3. See Arrupe's homily at the Ateneo de Manila, Quezon City, Philippines, on the feast of St. Ignatius Loyola, July 31, 1983, commemorating the fourth centenary of the arrival of the Jesuits in the Philippines (*Recollections and Reflections of Pedro Arrupe, S.J.,* trans. Yolanda T. De Mola, S.C. [Wilmington, Del.: Michael Glazier, 1986], 128).

4. Boston: Beacon, 1986, 121.

5. John R. Donahue, S.J., "Biblical Perspectives on Justice," in *The Faith That Does Justice: Examining the Christian Sources for Social Change,* ed. John C. Haughey, S.J., Woodstock Studies 2 (New York: Paulist, 1977), 69. More recently, Donahue has stated that his "earlier reflections should be supplemented by the reflections of J. M. P. Walsh" in the latter's *The Mighty from Their Thrones* (Philadelphia: Fortress, 1987). Specifically, see Donahue's *What Does the Lord Require? A Bibliographical Essay on the Bible and Social Justice,* (Studies in the Spirituality of Jesuits 25, 2: March 1993; St. Louis: Seminar on Jesuit Spirituality, 1993), 20–21.

6. See Léo Laberge, O.M.I., "Micah," *The New Jerome Biblical Commentary*, ed. Raymond E. Brown, S.S., Joseph A. Fitzmyer, S.J., and Roland E. Murphy, O.Carm. (Englewood Cliffs, N.J.: Prentice-Hall, 1990), 16:2 and 5, p. 249.

7. So Benedict T. Viviano, O.P., "The Gospel according to Matthew," *New Jerome Biblical Commentary*, 42:133, p. 666.

8. Donahue, *What Does the Lord Require?*, 14.

9. Ibid., 12.

10. *Constitution on the Church in the Modern World*, nos. 24, 32.

11. Dennis Olson, "God the Creator: Bible, Creation, Vocation," *Dialog: A Journal of Theology* 36, 3 (Summer 1997): 173.

12. Lynn White Jr., "The Historical Roots of Our Ecological Crisis," *Science* 155 (1967): 1205.

13. See Olson, "God the Creator," 173; Donahue, *What Does the Lord Require?*, 8; also James Limburg, "The Responsibility of Royalty: Genesis 1–11 and the Care of the Earth," *Word & World* 11 (1991): 124–30; James Tubbs, "Humble Dominion," *Theology Today* 51 (1994): 543–56, linking dominion with the NT image of Christ and the humble character of his dominion.

14. Olson, "God the Creator," 173–74.

15. See Douglas John Hall, *The Steward: A Biblical Symbol Come of Age* (Grand Rapids, Mich.: Eerdmans, 1990). My summary reflects that given by Olson, "God the Creator," 174.

16. Useful here are two summaries: Walter H. Principe, C.S.B., "Spirituality, Christian," *The New Dictionary of Catholic Spirituality*, ed. Michael Downey (Collegeville, Minn.: Liturgical, 1993), 931–38; and Richard Woods, O.P., "Spirituality, Christian (Catholic), History of," ibid., 938–46.

17. Here I am borrowing from my "Characteristics of Social Justice Spirituality," *Origins* 24, 9 (July 21, 1994): 159.

18. See also 1 Corinthians 12:4–11, 28–30; Romans 12:6–8; Ephesians 4:11–13.

19. Worth reading in this connection is James J. Basik, "Contemporary Spirituality," *Dictionary of Catholic Spirituality*, 214–30.

20. See Michael H. Crosby, O.F.M.Cap., "Spirituality," *The New Dictionary of Catholic Social Thought*, ed. Judith A. Dwyer (Collegeville, Minn.: Liturgical, 1994), 918.

21. See M. Robert Mulholland, Jr., *Invitation to a Journey: A Road Map to Spiritual Formation* (Downers Grove, Ill.: InterVarsity, 1994), quoted by Lawrence S. Cunningham in a brief review, *Commonweal* 121, 1 (January 14, 1994): 41.

22. Frederick Buechner, *The Hungering Dark* (New York: Seabury, 1969), 45–46.

23. See the article, primarily concerned with Latin America, by John F. Talbot, S.J., "Who Evangelizes Whom? The Poor Evangelizers," *Review for Religious* (November–December 1993): 893–97.

24. From the Puebla conference's "Preferential Option for the Poor" (no. 1147), quoted by Talbot, ibid., 894.

25. Quoted by Talbot, ibid., 896, from Sobrino's *Resurrección de la Verdadera Iglesia,* 137–38.

26. *Constitution on the Sacred Liturgy*, no. 10.

27. Ibid., nos. 35 and 52.

28. Walter J. Burghardt, S.J., *Preaching: The Art and the Craft* (New York/Mahwah, N.J.: Paulist, 1987), 129.

29. Elizabeth A. Johnson, "Community on Earth as in Heaven: A Holy People and a Sacred Earth Together" (Santa Clara Lectures 5, no. 1; Santa Clara, Calif.: Santa Clara University, 1998), 13.

30. See Richard N. Fragomeni, "Conversion," *Dictionary of Catholic Spirituality,* 230–35, stressing four categories helpful for understanding the process: autobiographical, biblical, liturgical, and theological (Lonergan's approach is summarized under the last category).

31. Bernard J. F. Lonergan, S.J., *Method in Theology* (New York: Herder and Herder, 1972), 363.

32. Ibid., 14.

33. Ibid.

34. Ibid., 14–15; emphasis mine.

35. Ibid., 238–40.

36. Ibid., 240.

37. Ibid., 241–42.

38. Ibid., 240–41.

39. Ibid., 242.

40. Ibid., 357; emphasis mine.

41. Ibid., 241.

42. Ibid., 55.

Lyle K. Weiss

34. Reform, Resist, Resign: Catholic and American in the Third Millennium

Spirituality and the Minister

Expanding Spirituality

When spirituality is too narrowly defined as concerning only personal prayer or explicit religious experience, such as sacramental celebrations, an essential element of spirituality is ignored and the mission of the church is left undone. *Gaudium et Spes,* the Second Vatican Council's *Pastoral Constitution on the Church in the Modern World,* makes explicit the gospel call to enable the light of the gospel to shine on the structures, practices, and decisions of social, economic, and political life.[1] "The social order requires constant improvement. It must be founded on truth, built on justice, and animated by love....God's Spirit, who with a marvelous providence directs the unfolding of time and renews the face of the earth, is not absent from this development."[2] To live the spiritual life is to promote the values of the gospel in all facets of human life. We are called to work on behalf of the gospel to influence and shape the customs, practices, and structures of social, economic, and political life. When spirituality focuses only on the interior life, it risks making of faith and religion a private matter, separate and distinct from the trials and struggles, the victories and defeats, the hopes and joys of the human community. An important component of spirituality is lost when it is removed from the relational essence of human existence. To appreciate the depths of the spiritual life is to broaden our notion of it to include every aspect of human living. Through this expanded sense we recognize our call to allow the light of the gospel to shine on all things human, be they personal or social. Spirituality is concerned with how we spend our money and how the government spends its money, the values that guide our personal lives and the values that shape American social life, the goals and hopes of our own political involvement, and the goals and hopes of our political processes and decisions. Spirituality is concerned not

546

only with calling us deeper into ourselves; rather, through our relationship with God we are called to greater involvement in the affairs of the world, helping to shape it into a society of justice, love, and peace. To foster growth in our relationship with God and our commitment to mission is the task of the minister of spirituality.

A Minister of Spirituality

To be a minister is to support the mission of the church in its efforts to continue the work of Jesus. Those of us who serve in leadership roles in the church are called to articulate the vision of the church's mission and to enable others to participate in that mission. For most believers, that leadership comes from the local church community and professional ministers of the gospel, for example, spiritual directors, clergy and religious, lay pastoral ministers, counselors. To be a minister is to fulfill a role of leadership in developing the spirituality of the believing community and of the individuals that comprise the community. As leaders in ministry we are challenged to promote the development of all aspects of the spiritual life for ourselves and for all those whom we serve. No matter our individual context or role, our ministry must engage those we serve in such a way that the full vision of the spiritual life is articulated and they are enabled and empowered to make that vision a reality. We must also be open to the witness of the lives of those with whom and for whom we serve, calling us to move beyond our own "comfort zones"[3] to engage the full panorama of the spiritual life.

In many communities, however, political engagement, an essential aspect of the spiritual life, tends not to be emphasized, if it receives any attention at all. For many parishes and for many believers, political involvement as it is expressed in the local community is limited to right-to-life activities such as the March on Washington. Undoubtedly, the church calls us as a people to become active in those issues that are critical to our support for life in all its forms. But such issues constitute only a part of the church's political initiatives. The church's voice can and must be heard on a broad range of issues, especially those concerning the poor and the most vulnerable in our society, as well as in debates regarding economic security, affordable housing, health care, education, capital punishment, euthanasia, abuse, violence, and peace. Popes from Leo XIII to John Paul II have consistently promoted the need for Catholics to become active in the social, economic, and political arenas. The National Conference of Catholic Bishops has written a number of outstanding pastoral letters and reflections—for example, *The Challenge of Peace: Economic Justice for All* and *Everyday Christianity*—affirming our call to shed the light of faith on the political, economic, and social actions and decisions of our day. Despite our rich teaching tradition, far too many Catholics are aware of the church's teaching on sexual morality but are not as well informed concerning our teaching on peace, social justice, and political action. The language of our social teaching often suggests a connection between the life of faith and daily living. Many situations, however, too often reflect an emphasis on interiority rather than social and political responsibility. Our homilies too often promote the development of personal piety and offer kernels of wisdom intended to help the members of the believing community survive the coming week rather than engage them in the mission of the church. The language of our music too often reflects a community that worships its God in a vacuum, untouched by the conditions of everyday life. It has been claimed of parish life that it must focus on the interior lives of believers because we must get our own house in order before we can engage the larger society.[4] The problem with such logic is that the process of getting our own house in order is a lifelong one. As a result the mission of life ceases to be the work of Christ and becomes focused on personal growth and development. Christian life is lived in isolation from the context in which it is intended to grow and develop. As ministers of the gospel, we must, in imaginative and creative ways, articulate the vision of an expanded spirituality that calls believers from all walks of life to participate in the church's mission to transform society in light of the values of the kingdom of God. That reign (or presence) of God encompasses not only specifically religious matters but secular matters as well.

The Development of the Church's Social Thought in American History

Catholic and American

We seek to articulate this vision and participate in this mission in a very specific time and place in history. As Christians we are called to participate in the work of Christ as citizens of the United States of America standing at the beginning of the third Christian millennium. Any vision of an expanded spirituality we might express must also speak to the concrete historical setting in which we find ourselves. Our spirituality calls us to proclaim the gospel in word and deed in the midst of a particular society confronting particular issues, possessing particular strengths and weaknesses, and needing to hear the gospel proclaimed in a particular way. That the spiritual life is not lived in a vacuum requires that we reflect upon the question of how we can best live and proclaim our faith in the United States as we enter the third millennium. In what ways does our society support the values of the gospel? In what ways does our society support values counter to those of the gospel? As a member of both the church and the larger society, what is my responsibility to both communities? Given our political, economic, and social systems, in what ways can I as an individual and we as a church community participate in shaping the larger society based upon the values of the gospel? How should the church relate to the larger society? In other words, how can we bridge Sunday mass to the boardroom, the farm, the voting booth, the factory, or the shopping mall? As we have said, spirituality is not simply a Sunday phenomenon or an issue for quiet, reflective moments. Spirituality is the way in which we live the totality of our lives in God's presence. Recognizing our responsibility to engage the world of economic, social, and political decisions and systems, our spiritual life must lead us to reflect on the ways in which we can bring the gospel to bear on the economic, social, and political issues of our age.

To aid us in responding to these questions, I reflect on the ways in which Catholic Americans have answered these questions throughout our history. My intention is to provide a brief description that will enable us to appreciate, at a foundational level, the origin and development of each style of public Catholicism.[5] There have been three dominant responses to the question of how we can be faithful as Christians living in American society. The first style is often referred to as "republican Catholicism." Locating its origins with John Carroll, who would become the first bishop in the "New World," the republican style recognized the same values operative within the American system of government as were operative in the natural law as understood and proclaimed by the Catholic Church. The second style is often referred to as "immigrant Catholicism." Immigrant Catholicism originated with the immigrant explosion early in the nineteenth century, responding to the needs of these newest Americans who brought with them their Old World customs, traditions, and worldviews. Finally, the third style, "evangelical Catholicism," defined itself in opposition to the values it saw operative in American society. The history of Catholic life in the United States has been defined, in large part, by its understanding of the relationship between Christian discipleship and American citizenship. This question grows more pertinent with each generation, as we struggle as a community with both our identity as a people of faith and our responsibility and mission to the larger society and world.

Republican Catholicism

The vision of church formulated by Carroll and some of his contemporaries was influenced by the spirit of republicanism so powerfully expressed in the founding documents of the new nation and some of the intellectual propositions of the Catholic Enlightenment. First, the church was to free itself of all foreign domination. In the spirit of the country Catholics had helped to establish, self-rule was a fundamental principle upon which the church in the United States was to be built. Carroll's appointment as superior of a Mission Church left many dissatisfied, because it left the church in the United States under the direct authority of the Vatican Congregation of Propaganda that had authority over missions. This created the impression that Catholics were ruled by a foreign power, when they believed what was needed was a bishop who alone would be dependent on Rome. Catholics believed they were connected to the pope through spiritual matters only, understood as including moral and cultic matters but not including behavior in the public arena. They had fought to gain independence from foreign political domination and sought such independence in religious affairs as well.[6] This desire for freedom from foreign influence was united to the sense of being a national church. Having won freedom for the fledgling nation, they wanted their church to reflect the values for which they had fought, rather than the "ethos of a foreign country."[7] Corresponding to this desire to be free from the influence of Rome and the potentially dangerous appearance of foreign domination, Carroll supported the use of the vernacular in the liturgy and for the Bible. Although no official change was ever made, English was common in church services, and Philadelphia publisher Matthew Carey translated the Bible into English. It was important that Catholics not only supported the nation in their quest for freedom but also that they could speak the language of faith in the common language of the nation.

Carroll's republican vision of the church also insisted on the separation of church and state. Such support was influenced by the thought of the Catholic Enlightenment, a movement that attempted to bridge the gap between the social and intellectual revolution of the Enlightenment with the beliefs and practices of the Catholic Church. Religious toleration had originally been supported to protect the Catholic minority in Protestant-dominated colonies. Now it had been accepted as a fundamental right, a right endorsed by the philosophy of the revolution. Separation of church and state violated the traditional Catholic view that envisioned the church and state as being synonymous. In such a view toleration was not acceptable. Carroll saw religious toleration in a positive light and believed that America would light the way with the wisdom of preserving civil and religious liberty.

Another Catholic Enlightenment influence was Carroll's recognition of the need for an apologetic based on reasonable discourse. Aware of the American sensibilities regarding freedom, civil and religious, Carroll understood that conversion could not be coerced. However, he could not expect conversion to occur in a pluralistic setting through the language of Roman Catholicism. Rather, conversion was invited through persuasion based upon arguments grounded in reason and intelligence. Coercion was unacceptable in political dealings between England and her colonies. Coercion was also an unacceptable method for winning converts to the Catholic faith. Conversion needed to be based upon the soundness and reasonableness of the Catholic apologetic.

One final component of Carroll's vision of the church, also influenced by the Catholic Enlightenment, was the full and active participation of the laity. In the United States, this participation was expressed in the development of a more democratic structure in the management of church affairs. This participation grounded the development of the trustee system, lay people elected by parishioners, who would manage the temporal affairs of the parish. Although this form of church governance was opposed to the traditional view that placed all authority in the hands of the clergy, it was very much in keeping with the spirit of the new republic.

Influenced by the two parents of American republicanism and the European Catholic Enlightenment, republican Catholicism was born. "This republican blueprint envisioned a national, American church which would be independent of all foreign jurisdiction and would endorse pluralism and toleration in religion; a church in which religion was grounded in intelligibility and where a vernacular liturgy was normative; and finally a church in which the spirit of democracy permeated the government of local communities."[8]

Republican Catholicism recognized a fundamental compatibility between the American spirit and Catholic belief and practice. It saw many positive characteristics in the government Catholics had helped to establish and the dominant philosophy that ordered the new nation's constitution. The vision endorsed by Carroll and his colleagues was the hinge on an opening door. Carroll was able to establish a version of Catholicism that limited the suspicion of his Protestant neighbors and garnered limited support from Rome. In so doing, it began a process through which Catholics in America would become legitimate participants in American life. The republican aspect of the church's tradition in the United States would continue to see common ground in the spirit of the nation and the tradition of the church, especially in the natural law emphasis in church teaching. Carroll's vision was well suited to the pluralistic context of the United States, adopting a spirit of toleration that bred respect for various religious traditions living under the same constitution. His efforts to promote a view of Catholics as friends and fellow citizens to be trusted rather than as puppets of a foreign power helped to create the possibility, realized later, of the Catholic voice being a viable one in the growth and development of the nation.

Certainly, the republican vision had its drawbacks. As a result of its hope to secure a place of freedom for American Catholics by cultivating a spirit of good citizenship, republican Catholicism risked the compartmentalization of one's faith life. Faith became a private affair, distinct from one's civic participation. Such compartmentalization raises now, as it raised then, the question of our fundamental allegiance. Do Catholics perceive themselves as Catholics first and as Americans second, or vice versa? Republican Catholicism, through its acceptance of the fundamental spirit of the new nation, risked being coopted by the spirit of the dominant culture within which it lived and moved, losing the prophetic role central to the church's vision. Also, the participation and freedom of the American constitutional system promoted similar lay participation and freedom in the life of the church. Like the republican political system, democracy in the life and governance of the church required an informed, involved, and committed laity to flourish. Without such a committed church membership or an informed and active electorate, democratic institutions will fail to realize their potential for the liberation of the human spirit and the development of a society dedicated to justice and peace among all of its people.

Carroll's vision helped to create an atmosphere of acceptance of Catholics in the new culture by establishing the church as a trustworthy voice faithful to the fundamental principles and values of the new nation. It embraced the spirit of religious toleration and respect and secured the potential for a more fruitful and effective proclamation of the gospel by creating a native clergy and a more democratic church. However, it was a vision influenced by fear, which privatized religious faith and risked being coopted by the dominant culture. The influx of immigrants in the nineteenth century would greatly influence the church's self-understanding and would result in an immigrant version of Catholicism. But, the republican tradition did not simply disappear. The republican tradition would continue to be a powerful voice on the American religious and political scenes. It found representatives in such powerful figures as Bishop John Ireland, the eminent theologian John Ryan, and arguably reached its apex in the sophisticated thought of the Jesuit John Courtney Murray. The republican tradition, born in the period of the English colonies and the American Revolution and its aftermath, offered a vision of the church that shared many values with the spirit of American life, values such as freedom, individual dignity, and tolerance. It sought to spread the good news of the reign of God by building on those shared values in the hope of shaping the new nation into the image and likeness of the values of God's reign.

Immigrant Catholicism

Immigration transformed the nation, and it transformed the church. In the hundred-year period between 1820 and 1920, more than 33.6 million immigrants came to the United States.[9] In 1820, the Catholic Church in the United States had the fewest number of churches and the smallest population. By 1850, it was the largest church in the country, numbering 1,606,000 members, a figure that jumped to 3,103,000 by 1860.[10] By the turn of the twentieth century, the Catholic population totaled 12,041,000 members, aided by the nearly 5,000,000 immigrants that had journeyed to America's shores during that period.[11] More than numbers were involved in the increase of Catholicism. Catholics in the United States were no longer a minority of "English-speaking families who had preserved their faith over long centuries of persecution."[12] Immigration had changed the makeup of the American church. By the middle of the nineteenth century, the Catholic population was largely poor, uneducated, and unchurched.

For the most part, they were found in urban centers, were working class, and for-eign born.[13] The emphasis of the church's role changed along with these demo-graphic changes. Instead of a church established in an always potentially dangerous atmosphere, the church was now presented with the task of preserv-ing the faith of the immigrants, a faith often tied to the ethnic and cultural tradi-tions they left behind. Just as the United States was learning how to make one nation of diverse peoples, so too was the church struggling to make one church from among the many different traditions and peoples represented and the her-itage they brought with them to America.

The immigrant style of Catholicism arose from the strong immigrant sense of group consciousness. In the hostile environment of the United States, communion with the group became vital. It also bred a certain defensiveness that placed the needs of the group above the good of the larger society. A prime example of the danger of such a defensive group consciousness was the immi-grant support of the Democratic Party. The Democratic Party, what A. James Reichley calls "the party of equality,"[14] operated on the political philosophy that government was to remain morally neutral so as to preserve the freedom of individuals and groups to pursue their own freely chosen values. This was in opposition to the political philosophy that claimed the role of government was to articulate the moral vision of society and enact laws and statutes designed to promote that vision and develop a citizenry capable of living that vision. His-torically, these differing political philosophies found rhetorical expression in the Lincoln-Douglas debates, with the Democrat Stephen Douglas supporting the former and Lincoln the latter philosophical view.[15] The immigrants largely supported the Democratic Party because of its support for the freedom of groups to pursue their own values, a vision very attractive to minority groups new to the country. It was also a vision that expressed support for the South's pursuit of its own values and way of life, including the institution of slavery. Thus, immigrant Catholics, in pursuing their own self-interest, allied them-selves with a party supportive of the South's freedom to pursue the values of their choice. (The debate between these two political philosophies continues to rage in our country. It is a difficult debate because both sides have clear virtues and vices.) Immigrant Catholicism was willing to use the power at its disposal, therefore, to achieve results that were, at times, in opposition to the republican spirit of reasonable discourse and concern for the larger public good.

The problem facing the immigrant church was one of reconciliation. How was immigrant Catholicism to reconcile its admitted primary loyalty to the church with its obligation as citizens of the nation to participate in the pro-motion of the common good in a pluralistic setting? The immigrants took seri-ously the concept of freedom expressed in the nation's founding documents. In so doing they supported a philosophy that protected their right to pursue the life of an Irish Catholic, German Catholic, or Mexican Catholic, without fear of oppression or the forfeiture of rights guaranteed them by the constitution. The primary danger presented by the philosophy they supported was that the concern for the rights of the individual could become so central that the ties that bind could grow increasingly weak. As a result, the American system would be in danger of being unable to produce citizens with a strong enough sense of civic virtue to maintain the lofty vision of the nation's founding documents. The belief of the immigrant church in dealing with this question was that Catholics could confine their group-conscious, communal loyalties to the arena of church and school, creating something of an alternate universe in the midst of the dangerous world they inhabited. They could also avoid radical movements and power politics by convincing the Protestant majority that Catholics differed from them only in the sphere of religion.[16]

The current status of Roman Catholics in America attests to the success of the immigrant church at one level. The church was able to maintain the faith and loyalty of the immigrants, supporting notions of immigrant identity as they struggled to build a life for themselves in their new homeland. However, the ethos of the immigrant church, at another level, represented a resignation from the common affairs of the larger society. Involvement in the political life of the larger society was the means through which the self-interest of the group was perpetuated. The church succeeded in creating a safe environment for those journeying to the United States. But, self-interest made integration difficult and caused internal division in the church due to the perception that the church was divided. Though stabilizing immigrant identity and developing a sense of the local church community as a school for religion, culture, and the development of the skills required to succeed in their new situation, the vision of immigrant Catholicism was too self-absorbed and isolated from the world in which it lived. As a result it became too occupied with its own needs, often failing to actively participate in and promote the development of the common good, and failing to transform society for the good of all, enabling the nation to embody the gospel values of justice and peace.

Evangelical Catholicism

In the years following World War I a new vision of Catholicism had begun to develop. Nativism, a negative response to immigration and immigrants, had reasserted itself, leading the American hierarchy to intensify its campaigns aimed at the Americanization of its membership. Calls for increasing the numbers of national churches and accommodating demands for national bishops and priests were rejected in the name of developing one American church. The task for the American hierarchy was to make an American church that was still a Catholic church. They sought to build the church community while establishing the parameters of "how American its membership could become."[17] But, with the intellectual contention of a fundamental division between church and culture, a vision of integral Catholicism developed that understood being a Catholic as participating in an alternative way of living that touched upon all aspects of human life.[18] The political and economic upheavals of the age revealed the divisiveness and corruption of modern culture. Social reform had to have a distinctively Christian quality, requiring spiritual means to overcome social ills.[19]

This integral Catholicism found concrete expression initially in the 1920s, when the Catholic "organization" flourished. The Catholic Education Association, the National Conference of Catholic Charities, the Knights of Columbus, and other organizations developed and grew, as did Catholic associations for lawyers, doctors, nurses, artists, librarians, and other professionals. This organizational Catholicism was not a public-spirited involvement in public debates concerning the common good. Such an engagement on behalf of the common good was represented by the thought of Fr. John Ryan. Ryan was a theological bridge builder who sought to engage the wider American population in a dialogue regarding social reform. His was not a utopian vision of a new society. Rather, Ryan attempted to develop criteria by which the justice of the American political and economic system could be measured. For Ryan, the challenge of reform was to establish a method within the system to ensure that democratic capitalism would actually function as a just and equitable system.

This was not the intention of integral Catholicism. Integral Catholicism was an organic community set off against the world.[20] It was a vision of Catholicism that stood in opposition to the sinful ethos of modern American culture. Integral Catholicism had its most important expression in the Catholic Worker Movement cofounded by Peter Maurin and Dorothy Day. Maurin, an intellectual French peasant, and Day, an anarchist devoted to the Catholic Church (a combination Day herself struggled to reconcile), founded a movement intended to meet the needs of people as they encountered them and to confront, through their witness, the injustice of modern life. Catholic Workers lived a life of voluntary poverty, free of the attachments that prevent us from responding completely to the call of Jesus. The Worker embodied Maurin's threefold program for building a new social order: roundtable discussions, usually concentrating on issues written about in the *Catholic Worker* paper; houses of hospitality providing direct service to all; and farming communes that would serve as the economic basis for the new world order. The new society would arise not only through the implementation of the threefold program but also through the spirit with which it was enacted. Salvation could never be forced or mandated; it could only be the fulfillment of a relationship marked by radical freedom. For that reason, the Worker eschewed direct political and legislative action, seeing in it a strategy intended to coerce that which must always be free. The new social order would arise only through the implementation of the Worker's noncoercive, utopian vision of Catholicism and society.

The continuing attractiveness of the Catholic Worker vision is its engagement in direct service, without judgment, to those in need. We live in a time when many requests for assistance fall on deaf ears because of the existence of a smaller number of con artists who supply an, at times, all-too-willing public with a reason not to give to those who need. The Worker believed God calls us to give to the other freely and to not judge the motivations or intentions of the other. Some who work in the political arena are much too quick to denigrate this direct service to those in need, claiming it only serves as a short term bandage. In reality, when one is bleeding a short-term bandage can stop the flow of blood until long-term treatment can be made available. The Worker reached out to those so often forgotten in a society inebriated with the pursuit of greater personal gain. It was comprised of a group of lay people willing to take their baptismal call seriously and who sought to find ways of living that call faithfully and authentically in a complex world. Living in a society they felt suffered from a terrible religious and spiritual deficiency, they attempted to translate the radical call of Jesus into a spirit and style of living that sought to foster a fundamental change in the larger society. It was not a coercive change but a community of love in action that would act as leaven in the world, changing it from within through the free response of others.

The Worker Movement sought to embody the ministry of Jesus. It was an effort, however, primarily determined to reproduce Jesus' ministry in the present rather than engaging the witness of the New Testament in a dialogue with the very different panorama of the modern world. To live the gospel in the present age is to acknowledge the distance that exists between the world of the New Testament and the concrete historical situation of the United States in the twenty-first century. To live the gospel in the modern world requires an ongoing conversation between the texts of the New Testament and the present context. As a result of their gospel vision, they vastly underestimated the significance of direct political action on behalf of justice. In addition, regarding their vision of gospel love, an underappreciated aspect of love is its resistance to that which leads to "the decline in value of the beloved."[21] Love is not unconditional in the sense that it is open to and accepting of the caprice of the other. Such acceptance is a rejection of authentic loving. Love cannot coerce the other to live in faithfulness to their self-transcending value, but neither can it refuse to engage those aspects of life that call forth the other's deeper value. This is true when seeking to embody justice within individual relationships and within societal, structural, political, economic, and legislative relationships. "God's love promotes those structures that promote human flourishing, and it works against those structures that denigrate it."[22] To love in American society as Jesus calls us to love requires that we engage that society on a scale larger than interpersonal relations. To love requires promoting structures that promote human flourishing. In the United States, that includes political and legislative action on behalf of justice.

The Worker became more of a movement for internal church reform than an organization devoted to the transformation of the larger society. It failed to acknowledge the exigencies of proclaiming the reign of God in a constitutional system and to engage the broader possibilities of the common good in a pluralistic society. In that sense, the Worker shares the same distortion of the gospel proclaimed by the immigrant church. The primary concern of the movement was the integrity of the group rather than its responsibility to participate in the shaping of the larger society within the mechanisms and systems by which that society operates. Stanley Hauerwas rightly observed that "to withdraw from the political in order to remain pure is unfaithful and is an irresponsible act of despair."[23] The gospel commissions us to involve ourselves in the messiness of history, to engage in dialogue with the wider community for the purpose of pursuing and living the truth.

John Courtney Murray and the Path of Dialogue

It was such a dialogue that the Jesuit John Courtney Murray, among others, sought to promote. Murray, writing primarily in the 1940s, '50s, and '60s, was arguably the best spokesperson republican Catholicism had produced, laying the theoretical foundation upon which to build a responsible public theology. The immigrant church engaged in political action primarily to advance its own self-interests, interests that were not always in the best interest of the larger community of humanity. The evangelical church, represented by the Catholic Worker, chose not to engage in direct political or legislative action, seeking instead to focus on its own purity and hopeful of creating a new social order one heart at a time. Utopianism was, for Murray, a heresy because, like all pagan heresies of antiquity, it looked backward rather than forward to the Golden Age.[24] Murray suggested a middle way that supported both the community's striving for faithful discipleship and its call to participate in the dialogue concerning the common good.

Murray argued that the truths held by the founding fathers of the nation required ongoing dialogue if they were to continue to be held as true and appropriated as true by future generations.[25] This unfolding appreciation of the value and context of truth could only occur through participation in civil dialogue. The church is called to be a partner in that dialogue, including its voice in the shaping of the values of the country. Although it is true that the wider society does not share or speak the language of Catholicism, he believed the values of Catholicism, open to all through natural law, could create a common universe of discourse. Murray recognized the twofold mission of the church; the mission within the church and the mission to the larger society. Through dialogue, the Truth the church seeks to know and embody in its own life is made available to the larger society through the common language of justice, rights, freedom, dignity, and peace. We should be cautious regarding our reliance on the natural law ethic. Although it could make Christian insights available to the larger society, Christians need to examine social issues theologically and "reflect on social reality in the light of explicitly Christian concerns, sources, and understanding."[26] Our participation in the dialogue should not require jettisoning the grounding of our conversation in the good news of what God has done in Jesus through the spirit.

The way of dialogue therefore respects the freedom of others regarding religious faith and moral truth, a freedom based upon the dignity given humanity by a loving Creator. Yet, through dialogue the church fulfills its mission to proclaim the gospel and engage the wider world in the discussion about truth and justice, about values, principles, and fundamental rights by including its own voice in the conversation regarding the ongoing formation of society and world. The dialogue, and the spirit in which it is undertaken, abhors the moral terrorism perpetrated, for instance, by aberrations of the Respect Life Movement who seek the truth in violence and harassment. Or the self-serving involvement of those who view an arrest as an expression of status that looks nice on their justice résumé. Murray offers us the theoretical foundation upon which to build a vision of a church striving to be faithful to the revelation of God, in Jesus, through the spirit. At the same time, it can and must invite society to ponder the truth of that revelation through dialogue that respects the freedom of the other and lays the foundation for peace. It is a church involved in mission, but a church that lives out that mission in the light of the Paschal Mystery, the life, death, and resurrection of Jesus.

Similar to evangelical Catholicism, Murray's vision of the church rejects coercion as a suitable means to achieve unity. Rather, his approach acknowledges the possibility that the truth of the gospel can be rejected by the larger society. If so, the church must be the community of the long haul, dedicated to proclaiming the message of the gospel in language accessible to the larger society even in the face of rejection and the passage of time. It is a church that must daily take up its cross in the living rooms, courtrooms, factories, shops, offices, roads, and assemblies of the country. It must carry its cross in interpersonal relationships and in political, economic, cultural, and legislative relationships. It is also a church that encounters the spirit of the risen Jesus in all spheres of human life and organization. We must respect the freedom of the other to say no or to hold another view and to recognize and accept that the fulfillment of God's promises will come only at the end of time. But, the experience of the cross and the resurrection are necessarily intertwined, and the reality of the resurrection already touches upon every facet of human existence, even if only in a partial way. Personal and public relationships live in both the shadow of the cross and the light of the resurrection.

The 1960s and the Emergence of the Catholic Left

The tumultuous decade of the 1960s produced the emergence of the Catholic Left. The Catholic Left came to the fore to engage the church and nation regarding the most significant issues of the decade, the injustices of racism, violence, and war.[27] Within the Catholic Left there existed a diversity of responses and approaches to the fundamental questions concerning the relationship between the community of faith and the state.[28] On the one hand, the reformers, more in the tradition of republican Catholicism, recognized a certain compatibility between Catholic values and the fundamental truths of American constitutional democracy. On the other hand, the resisters, more in the tradition of evangelical Catholicism, recognized that there existed a fundamental difference between Catholic truth and the values of American society. For both groups, the issue was what type of civilization was compatible with the Christian vision of human life. For the reformers, the answer was that America, especially regarding the issues of race, abortion, and the Vietnam War, had lost its moorings and was violating its own fundamental principles and values. What was needed was not a new social order but the reformation of the current actualization of the system. The mission of the reformers was to call the country back to its own best self, informed by the values of the gospel. For the resisters, the answer was that America's principles and values were fundamentally opposed to the Christian vision. The state was a body that supported its own best interests and would use force to gain them. It bred a society of rampant individualism and promoted an economic system fundamentally opposed to the gospel vision. To remain faithful to the gospel required a rupture between the church and the state.

Both approaches faced certain dangers. The reformers needed to acknowledge the ongoing danger of being coopted by the larger society, of the values of the gospel being reshaped by the values of American life, and not vice versa. Certainly, the American spirit had taught the church some valuable lessons regarding human freedom and religious liberty. However, despite similarities, the gospel was not identical with the constitution, and the church needs always to maintain the distinction lest it lose touch with its fundamental vision and mission. Also, given the nature of politics and political action, the reformers were always in danger of losing the eschatological thrust of the gospel message. Proclaiming the gospel is not merely winning this or that political reform or passing this or that piece of legislation or establishing this or that political system, as if it were synonymous with the reign of God. The reign of God will not be completely fulfilled until the end of time. Proclaiming

the gospel is to live within the context of God's view of history and the fulfillment of that history toward which we move. Until that time, we are called to
make the reign of God more present in our lives and world.

The resisters, on the other hand, replaced the importance of structural
change with personal authenticity. For the resisters, purity was more important
than the compromise involved in shaping the ethos of a country it believed
was thoroughly corrupt. Second, the resisters typically operated from an apocalyptic eschatology that called for radical action because of our current participation in the end time. An apocalyptic eschatology calls for radical
commitment to the call of Jesus and his example of suffering love. However,
this eschatological vision fails to appreciate the already-but-not-yet dimension
of the reign of God. We know that the fullness of God's reign will come only at
the end of time. In the interim, however, we are called to make that future fullness more present in our world. As such, Christians are called to embody a
spirit of ongoing conversion rather than a radical end time ethic. "The kingdom has already begun, but its fullness will only come at the end of
time…Continual conversion rather than radical transformation fits in better
with this eschatological understanding."[29] In addition, the eschatological view
of the resisters failed to account for the already aspect of the reign of God. Too
often, the resisters seem to believe that little or nothing of the reign of God is
currently realized, failing to acknowledge and accept that the kingdom is in
some form already present.

This eschatological inadequacy had a corresponding christological inadequacy. The reality of Christ's cross fit in well with the resistance approach,
but, based on an apocalyptic eschatology, failed to recognize that the cross
could not stand as the lone symbol for the life and work of Jesus. The cross can
never be completely understood and appropriated in the absence of the resurrection, or vice versa. The emphasis on the cross of Christ as the symbol of
Christian discipleship articulates a vision of paradoxical discipleship. To be a
Christian means that we receive only by giving, we experience joy only in sorrow, we live only by dying. But, as Charles Curran rightly points out, "Sometimes God's love is known and manifested in human love, God's beauty in
human beauty, God's power in human power. Sometimes there is the paradoxical element, but it is not the only element."[30] The resistance approach to social
reform recognized that it would continue to serve as leaven in the world, offering its witness to suffering love. This is much too confined a view of the nature
and mission of the church. "The gospel which the church proclaims calls for
Christians and the church to try to transform and improve the world in which
we live. The role of the church vis-à-vis the world is not always or only that of
resistance and suffering love."[31] Rather, we are a people participating in the
present process of that future fulfillment, a process advanced through faith-
filled personal relationships, through fruitful dialogue, and through direct

political engagement. The kingdom calls us not to withdrawal from the ambi-guities of historical discipleship but to incarnate the values of the kingdom in our historical context.

Assessment

In the long run, the various responses to the issue of the relationship between the church and culture are important and necessary. The evangelical church rightly stressed the importance of the conversion of hearts, but "failed to give enough importance to the need to change institutional structures to bring about greater justice in society as a whole."[32] Immigrant Catholicism rightly recognized the special needs of immigrant groups, though it failed to adequately acknowledge and promote the good of the larger society. Republi-can Catholicism rightly emphasized the need to change and transform institu-tional structures. However, it failed to recognize and appreciate the importance of personal and ongoing conversion, especially for those who ben-efit from the status quo. Even with its inherent dangers and need for continu-ing development, the path of dialogue developed within republican Catholicism and given theoretical support by John Courtney Murray seems to me to be the vision that should inform the fundamental stance of the church and the Christian in a pluralist, constitutional society. The relationship between the church and the world, between the already and the not-yet of the reign of God, between the individual and the corporate is a complex reality that challenges us to recognize that our faith calls us to participate in the shap-ing of our world. That call leads us to engage "the many different economic, social, legislative, administrative, and cultural areas, which are intended to promote organically and institutionally the common good."[33] Our participation in the shaping of that larger society is always Christian participation, informed by the life and message of Jesus of Nazareth and the theological and ethical tradition that flows from the community's openness to the inspiration of the spirit present in our midst.

The immigrant focus on faith identity reminds us of the need to examine issues in our world through the lens of Christian belief and practice. The evan-gelical church reminds us that there are times when the values of the larger society are in direct conflict with the values of the reign of God. In the midst of such conflict the church takes on the prophetic role, calling the world to a higher vision of human life and dignity. The republican church reminds us of our responsibilities regarding the common good and our call to participate in making the kingdom more present in our world through cooperation between the church and societal institutions. The path of dialogue recognizes the strengths and weaknesses of each vision of church, engaging each in a discus-sion regarding the values of the kingdom and the appropriate methods by which the church can shed the light of the gospel on the modern world. This spirit of dialogue applies not only to the relationship between the church and the larger society; it also applies to the relationships that exist within the church. In a time of intense debate within the church community, the importance of the path of dialogue seems essential. We need to engage in an ongoing dialogue concerning who we are as a people and what it means to be a Christian, a disciple of Jesus Christ. We need to engage in an ongoing discussion regarding our mission in the world and how we can faithfully and effectively fulfill that mission. We need to engage in an ongoing dialogue regarding how we can best cooperate with God's plan for the accomplishment of salvation, enabling all people to live in justice and peace. The church must continue to grow as individuals and as a community dedicated to ongoing conversion to Jesus and sharing in his faith. The church must also continue to grow as individuals and as a community deeply engaged in the shaping of the political, economic, and social life of the larger world, that it might increasingly be shaped by the light of God's love and truth.

Implications for Ministry

Shaping a Parish Vision

The fallacy of Christian living is that, to be a good Christian, one needs only to be a nice person.[34] This fallacy is the foundation of much that is offered to the community of faith and by the community of faith, especially in the setting of the local parish. It is a fallacy not because it is wrong but because it is an inadequate and narrow understanding presented as if it were the complete picture. To be a Christian is more than being a nice person, although that can certainly be part of the faith-filled life. To be a Christian is to actively participate in the mission of Christ that includes, but goes far beyond, any congenial notions of goodness and niceness. The parish community must be a school of Christian discipleship, a school that shapes and forms us in every facet of Christian living. It is a school that enables us to develop a spirituality that views all of life in the light of what God has done in Jesus. To be a Christian in the United States and throughout the modern world requires active engagement in the interpersonal, social, political, economic, and religious ramifications of the good news of God's presence and love. Christian spirituality is a life of prayer but also of politics. It is a life of worship and devotion but also of economics. It is a life of intrapersonal and interpersonal relationships but also of societal and cultural relationships. It is a life of ongoing conversion but also ongoing dialogue with the broader world.

Karl Rahner once wrote, "In the past, St. Francis de Sales could write a book of direction, a book of advice, for the cultured ladies and gentlemen of his society to live by. That is to say, he wrote for Christian conduct in the situation of his time. Today we have to have instructions for changing our situation itself. You might say we need books of direction for Christians as human subjects with social obligations that include the obligation to bring about changes in society."[35] We live in an age where the battles for equality inside and outside of the church are still engaged. Ours is an age of ecological irresponsibility, of armed conflict of the highest percentage proportions, of rampant individualism, of the growing gap not only between the rich and the poor but between the rich and the disappearing middle class. We are members of the global village confronting an increasing sense of isolation within our homes and communities. Transnational corporations and advances in technology outdistance advances in ethical thought and reflection. We increasingly feel as if we are manipulated by our environment rather than being stewards of creation. Election after election, candidates are voted into office by a minority of voters. There is great discontent with institutions in general, be they religious, political, or social. Journalists are forced to compete for our viewing time, trying to entertain more than inform. As Andy Rooney once said in an interview, "News nowadays tells us what we want to hear and not what we need to know."[36] More citizens are aware of the box scores and the sale prices than social issues and concerns. *The Jerry Springer Show* is one of the highest rated shows in television syndication. We are daily confronted by a broad range of issues both as Catholics and as Americans. The question so often asked by those confronted with the good news of Jesus in the New Testament—"What must I do?"[37]—is a question to which we need to respond in our own day. It is a question to which we must respond in the particular context of our age and situation.

Given the historical exigencies of life in America today, and the system under which we operate both as citizens and as Roman Catholics, the paradigm of church structure and action should heed the call of the bishops to develop the parish church as a community of moral discourse.[38] The church needs to engage in the dialogue regarding social issues both within itself and with the larger society. "We must learn together how to make correct and responsible moral judgments. We reject, therefore, criticism of the church's concern with these issues on the ground that it should not become involved in politics. We are called to move from discussion to witness and action."[39] "The Jubilee Pledge for Charity, Justice, and Peace," promoted by the U.S. Bishops as a practical response to Pope John Paul II's designation of 1999 as the "The Year of Charity," calls for our commitment to pray for justice and peace, to learn more about Catholic social teaching and the social issues confronting our age. It calls us to serve the poor and vulnerable, to give more generously, and to advocate policies that "protect human life, promote human dignity, preserve God's creation, and build justice."[40] Spirituality clearly calls us into an ever-deepening personal relationship with God. It also calls us to pray, learn, serve, give, and advocate for peace and justice. "In the Catholic tradition, citizenship is a virtue; participation in the political process is an obligation. We are not a sect fleeing the world, but a community of faith called to renew the earth."[41]

The reality however, is that the spiritual resource for most Catholics is not found in bishops' documents, papal encyclicals, or theology texts. For most believers, spirituality is expressed in and through the local parish church. It is within the confines of the parish church that the seeds of spirituality are watered and nourished. The public theology I have broadly sketched is not new to most of the ministers who will read the essays in this volume. The challenge for ministers is to proclaim this more engaged vision of spirituality in the local setting. As leaders in the community responsible for articulating the vision of Christian spirituality and enabling the participation of those whom we serve, we are called to express the consoling and challenging message of the gospel with its personal, communal, and public ramifications. Homilies too often reflect an emphasis on the interior life or on interpersonal relationships. At times they will expand to include the call to service, but rarely do they call us to political involvement. To preach a vision of spirituality that includes active and direct political engagement requires more than a one-time exhortation to vote that is given in or near the month of November. Such an exhortation has no context within the content of the homilies throughout the church year. Homilies should reflect on the implications of the gospel for our development as Christians, our personal prayer, and our personal relationships. Homilies should also reflect on the implications of the gospel on our communal relationships and our responsibility, through service *and* political action, for the common good and the shaping of American values in a context of respect for the freedom, rights, and insights of others.

Hymns sung at weekend mass reflect a praise of God that all too often neglects the context within which we praise God. The Second Vatican Council's *Constitution on the Sacred Liturgy (Sacrosanctum Concilium)* states that the norms and precepts of the liturgy should have regard for "the purpose of sacred music, which is the glory of God and the sanctification of the faithful."[42] To give glory to God and build up the faithful, we should select and write music that respects the ambiguities and realities of life as well as incorporating our broader view of spirituality that goes beyond prayer and service to include political activity. The intercessions, popularly referred to as the prayer of the faithful, usually include an invitation to pray for those in government or civil authority that they might make decisions that promote justice and peace. The implied responsibility rests with those in office to make the right decisions. Our intercessions need to invite us to live up to our responsibility to participate in the process whereby decisions regarding peace, justice, and the common good are made.

Too often, spirituality is compartmentalized in parish life. Social justice ministry is the work of the social justice committee, while the liturgy committee focuses on liturgy, and so on. All parish organizations need to share in the complete ministry of the parish. The social justice committee should serve as a resource for the entire parish, enabling the efforts of everyone in the parish to participate in the social mission of the church. The liturgy committee needs to explore ways the liturgy might raise the consciousness of everyone in the parish, calling them through the sacred rites and symbols of the mass to share in the full mission of the church. Political action should not be the only emphasis in the parish and among its various committees and organizations, but the entire parish is called to become involved in the political action of the church within the arena of their particular ministry.

In a time of increased adult education and a resurgence of interest in Catholic education at all levels, through parochial schools and religious education programs, our educational emphasis must gear itself to proclaiming the broader vision of spirituality. The social teaching of the church continues to be our best-kept secret. Many parishioners will not have the opportunity, or perhaps the inclination, to read bishops' letters and papal encyclicals. But, through homilies, classroom instruction, and adult education programs the message of the church's social mission can become a part of the consciousness of the believing community. Related to parish educational initiatives could be the incorporation of the social mission of the church into Bible study programs. We live in a time of immense and intense interest in the scriptures. Through more careful study and reading of the Bible, the social implications of salvation history can be emphasized along with its significance for our personal relationships with God and others. To be leaders in the church requires creativity and imagination. Specific programs can be initiated for the promotion of the political and economic aspects of our call to follow Jesus. Bulletin inserts, guest speakers, and legislative alerts can all serve as viable means to the end of calling ourselves and the communities we serve to engage in the grand work of the growth of the reign of God in the specific context within which we live. The local parish church is the spiritual home for most believers, and it must be within the confines of that home that the broader vision of the spiritual life must be articulated and empowered.

Conclusion

In the infancy narrative according to Luke, the angel Gabriel is sent to a town in Galilee called Nazareth. Gabriel greets a virgin named Mary, to whom he reveals the essence of the good news of the gospel. "Behold, you will conceive in your womb and bear a son, and you shall name him Jesus. He will be great and will be called the Son of the Most High, and the Lord God will give him the throne of David his father, and he will rule over the house of Jacob forever, and of his kingdom there will be no end."[43] In

Luke's Gospel, the good news concerning Jesus is never given as a private possession. It is given always with the intention of being shared. The two disciples on the road to Emmaus immediately return to Jerusalem to share the good news of their encounter with the risen Jesus with the rest of his disciples.[44] Mary, the one in Luke who is the first to hear and accept the proclamation of the good news, goes with haste into the hill country to visit her kinswoman Elizabeth, who is also with child. In the presence of Elizabeth, Mary praises God in the words of the Magnificat. In so doing, "Luke has made a statement about discipleship and gospel."[45] Mary had the good news proclaimed to her, but during her visit to Elizabeth she does not simply repeat the good news of the sending of God's Son. Rather, her Magnificat is an interpretation of the significance of the sending of God's Son. At the beginning of Jesus' public ministry in Luke, a voice from heaven proclaims Jesus to be God's Son at his baptism. When Jesus appears preaching and teaching, he does not simply repeat what God had spoken. Again, the good news of the sending of God's Son is not repeated. Rather, it is the significance of that sending that is shared. For Luke, discipleship requires that we hear the Word of God, that we do the Word of God, and that we share the Word of God. But, our sharing is not repetition. To share the good news requires that we interpret the significance of the sending of God's Son in such a way that others may hear the word proclaimed as truly good news.

The mission of the disciple of Jesus is the same for us as it was for Luke and the community to whom he wrote. To participate in the mission of the church to share the good news of what God has done in Jesus requires that we do more than repeat the news. We are called to interpret the significance of the good news proclaimed and share it with others. The social mission of the church, a mission in which we all share, is more than proclaiming the mystery of faith that Christ has died, Christ is risen, Christ will come again. The mission of the disciple is to proclaim to the larger world the ramifications of God's sending of Jesus into the world, the significance of Christ's dying, rising, and return. The ramifications of what God has done in Jesus reverberate throughout the world regardless of our explicit recognition of them. As a result of Jesus, the world is on the path to becoming a community of justice, peace, dignity, freedom, and love. To be a Christian is to engage in every aspect of human life, be it religious, political, economic, cultural, personal, or societal, to promote the realization of God's community. To be a Christian is to participate in the dialogue within every aspect of human life and there to allow the light of the gospel message to shine and to shape the values of the larger society. This is not a luxury or a preference. It is a responsibility for all Christians living in fidelity to the gospel. As leaders, we must shape our own communities to be people actively engaged in the full mission of the church. Striving always for greater fidelity to the life and message of Jesus, we will, as individual believers and as a community united in faith, interpret the significance of the good news revealed in Jesus so that the larger society may truly hear it as good news.

Notes

1. *Gaudium et Spes, The Documents of Vatican II* (New Jersey: America Press, 1966), especially part I, ch. IV and part II, chs. II, III, IV, and V.

2. Ibid., 26, 225–26.

3. I was first introduced to this term by Sister Thea Bowman.

4. The spirit of this statement, and sometimes its wording, has been expressed to me through various experiences in parish ministry originating with both clergy and laity.

5. For a more comprehensive treatment of the history of the church in the United States, the work of David J. O'Brien, Jay P. Dolan, and, to a lesser extent, John Tracy Ellis will serve as reliable and insightful guides. I will follow their general flow, attempting to avoid debates that swirl around particular details or personalities that will step onto the stage. Though valuable, these debates are beyond the scope of this essay.

6. Jay P. Dolan, *The American Catholic Experience* (New York: Doubleday Image, 1985), 105–7.

7. Ibid., 107.

8. Ibid., 111.

9. Ibid., 127.

10. Ibid., 160–61.

11. John Tracy Ellis, *American Catholicism* (Chicago: University of Chicago Press, 1956), 85–86.

12. David J. O'Brien, *Public Catholicism* (New York: Orbis, 1996), 35.

13. Ibid.

14. A. James Reichley, *Religion in American Public Life* (Washington, D.C., 1985), 142.

15. Michael J. Sandel, *Democracy's Discontent: America in Search of a Public Philosophy* (Cambridge, 1996), 3–24.

16. O'Brien, 61.

17. Ibid., 161.

18. Ibid.

19. Ibid., 162.

20. Ibid.

21. Edward Collins Vacek, S. J., *Love, Human and Divine* (Washington, D.C.: Georgetown University Press, 1994), 58.

22. Ibid., 59.

23. Stanley Hauerwas, *A Community of Character: Toward a Constructive Christian Social Ethic* (Notre Dame, Ind., 1981), 73.

24. John Courtney Murray, *We Hold These Truths: Catholic Reflections on the American Proposition* (Kansas City, 1988), 23.

25. Murray's thought is very intricate. My summary does not do justice to the genius of his insight, even acknowledging its weaknesses. For a clear statement of Murray's thought, see *We Hold These Truths*.

26. Charles E. Curran, *American Catholic Social Ethics: Twentieth-Century Approaches* (Washington, D.C.: Georgetown University Press, 1979), 287.

27. O'Brien, 236.

28. The source for this schemata is unknown.

29. Curran, 275–76.

30. Ibid., 277.

31. Ibid., 278.

32. Ibid., 287.

33. Pope John Paul II, *The Vocation and the Mission of the Lay Faithful in the Church and in the World (Christifideles Laici)* (Rome, 1988), 121.

34. Moral theology leads us beyond this fallacy by making a distinction between goodness and rightness. Goodness is primarily concerned with our motivations. Rightness is primarily concerned with our actions. Both are necessary in any view of the moral life.

35. Karl Rahner, *The Practice of Faith: A Handbook of Contemporary Spirituality* (New York, 1984), 274.

36. Andy Rooney, source unknown.

37. Matthew 19:16–22, Mark 10:17–21, Luke 10:25–28 and 18:18–23, John 6:28ff, Acts 2:14–38, and 16:25–31.

38. The U.S. Bishops reflect on the parish as a community of moral discourse in chapter IV of their pastoral letter on war and peace. See particularly the National Conference of Catholic Bishops, *The Challenge of Peace: God's Promise and Our Response* (Washington, D.C., 1983), 115–18.

39. NCCB, *Challenge of Peace,* 118.

40. The National Conference of Catholic Bishops/The United States Catholic Conference, *Everyday Christianity: To Hunger and Thirst for Justice* (Washington, D.C., 1995).

41. The National Conference of Catholic Bishops/The United States Catholic Conference, *Political Responsibility: Proclaiming the Gospel of Life, Protecting the Least Among Us, and Pursuing the Common Good* (Washington D.C., 1995), 7.

42. Vatican II, "Sacrosanctum Concilium," 112.

43. Luke 1:31–33.

44. Luke 24:13–35.

45. Raymond Brown, S.S., *A Coming Christ in Advent* (Collegeville, 1988), 69–70.

Susan K. Roll

35. Women's Liturgical Spirituality

One of the most remarkable testimonies to the emerging shape of liturgy and creative ritual as a dynamic part of healthy spirituality is what has been called the "Women's Liturgical Movement." In small local prayer or study groups, intentional faith communities, retreat settings, faithsharing or social action groups, as well as conferences on a national or international level, women of faith are discovering their capacities as active agents planning and carrying out new forms of liturgy, many for the first time as do-ers of liturgy and not merely followers. The documented results over the past twenty-five years have included striking and eloquent symbolic imagery, fresh thought-provoking interpretations of familiar scriptural passages, expanded possibilities for spiritual healing in a supportive setting, and a profoundly relational, not merely mechanical understanding of ritual.

Unlike the Liturgical Movement of the late nineteenth and twentieth centuries, which led to massive reform of antiquated and obscure liturgical structures in the Roman Catholic Church and spurred other denominations to a reexamination of the relevance and authenticity of their worship, the Women's Liturgical Movement flourishes in relative obscurity. Few women belong to communities that can support them during extended scholarly training or full-time research, as did the monastics who laid the academic foundations for liturgical reform. Despite the increasing availability of planning resources and models, most of the new experimental ritual structures and forms developed there never reach a wider audience through publication, and there is no attempt to produce a normative liturgical standard. Yet the silent explosion in creativity with texts, symbols, and ritual actions testifies not only to the brilliance, insight, and hopefulness of women in spite of continuing discrimination in the churches, but to a continuing human need for ritual even in contemporary, highly commercialized Western societies. Liturgical creativity in groups of women contradicts the conventional assumption on the part of many liturgists that modern "man" has lost the capacity to understand or to enter into liturgy.

In this essay we take a look at some background concepts that help to explain and support the growth of liturgical celebrations in groups of women.

569

We examine some specific characteristics of these liturgies and their implications. Finally, we name some potential contributions made by new women's liturgies to growth in spiritual depth and authenticity, both on the part of participants themselves and as a prophetic sign indicating possible directions for ongoing liturgical reform in the churches.

Some Starting Points

The Use of the Terms Liturgy, Worship, and Ritual

Liturgy, whose origins are in two Greek terms meaning "the people" and "work," can be read either as "a work on behalf of the people, a public work" or as "the work of the people, by the people." The first reflects the official sacrifices and honor paid to state gods in the ancient world to secure prosperity and victory for the nation. This term was taken over in the Septuagint translation of the Hebrew Bible into Greek to refer to sacrifices offered in the temple according to Levitical prescriptions, and from there was applied to the Christian worship of the early church. The second notion, "a work by the people," more accurately reflects the way the term is applied to the public worship of the churches in contemporary religiously pluralistic societies. The term *worship,* in its old English roots, means "to attribute value or worth to another," literally "worth-ship." *Ritual,* by contrast, calls up a number of both formal and informal meanings: ritual practices documented by cultural anthropologists or critiqued by ritual theorists, the Roman *Ritual* (a book of official liturgical forms), or in ideas such as "empty ritual" or children's "bedtime rituals," for example.

Liturgy thus suggests a public, official act with some sort of recognized juridical status.[1] To many women engaged in creative ritual, *liturgy* connotes a male-controlled public symbol system that promotes the domination of males over females as a universal norm. The word may refer to an institutionally constructed event that holds little meaning for them or may actively deny their equality or denigrate their dignity. For others, however, to speak of "liturgy" represents a claim to legitimacy. It suggests precisely that the type of experimentation taking place lies well within the broader scope of the gospel and the most authentic Christian tradition of securing justice for the poor, healing those who suffer, and reaching out to all persons with the love of Christ.

For some, *worship* connotes self-abnegation before an all-powerful father God, yet particularly for many Protestants, *worship* would be a more familiar word than *liturgy.* For some people, *ritual* rings hollow as a description of what they do, while for many others *ritual* carries the least baggage of exclusion and pain from the past, since it is associated least with the institutional churches. For those struggling with justice issues at the margins of the church, *ritual* may represent a more inviting prospect.[2]

Women as Theological Thinkers

Up until the mid-twentieth century, women had no recognized input into the formation of the classical theological tradition, and virtually no possibility to undertake theological study. In just a few decades, theological thinking in areas such as scripture, systematic theology, christology, ethics, and sacraments has undergone the beginnings of marked shifts in perspective due to the research and vision of professional women theologians.

Similarly, until the implementation of liturgical reform after the Second Vatican Council, no words written by women were used in any formal rites of the church.[3] Music written from a woman-identified perspective has been virtually unknown in hymnals and choral music, and women's involvement in liturgical space consisted of arranging flowers and washing altar linens. For the first time in recorded Christian history a sizeable, broadly distributed number of women do not merely attend official liturgy and serve in circumscribed roles for which they have been granted permission, but actually design the order of worship. Because of the new self-awareness of women as active subjects, not passive receptive objects in worship, the potential future development of authentic and pastorally appropriate liturgy must confront all the ways in which a patriarchal perspective has been presumed to be normative and universal.

Does this mean that incorporating a woman-identified approach to liturgy will involve the introduction of classically defined "feminine virtues" as a complement to the dominant "masculinity" of the liturgy? This would presume that the male represents the norm and the female the "complement" against which the norm is defined. We need to account for the fact that in the past a thoroughgoing philosophical *dualism,* which set up body and spirit in total opposition to each other, and which underlies much of theological discourse and liturgical practice, has been identified in contemporary thought and progressively deconstructed. Dualism is a tool for abstract thinking, a method of setting up two bipolar absolute, mutually exclusive categories such as black/white, good/evil, light/darkness, rational/emotional, sacred/profane, nature/culture, male/female. Dualism presents itself falsely as an evenly balanced split. In fact, an inherent valuational bias is built into every pair—in each case one can readily identify which of the two components is good or strong, and which is bad or weak. The value bias is determined by whoever holds cognitive hegemony—the power to define the categories—and by which vested interests play a role, with or without conscious intent. Any conceptual split that involves "complementary" characteristics involves the construction of categories using one of these categories as both starting point and center. Women, as well as racial minorities and all those defined by the norm as divergent from that norm, have found themselves consistently on the downside of any supposedly evenly split distinction.

What this means for women's liturgies is that a pivotal role is played simply as women themselves in these settings explore and express their identity, affirm their experiences, speak their truth in their own words, and stand in their own light. Because women are subjects actively involved in doing liturgy, not objects of liturgical pastoral care, the ability to identify with one's own, often long-denied or suppressed perceptions is crucial to authentic ritual celebration. Active agency provides a means to move beyond what has been called "colonized consciousness," the ability only to think, feel, and see what one has been taught to think, feel, and see, disconnected from one's own honest perception.

However, women themselves would often replicate the injustices done to them by presuming a sort of "universality" of women's experience and perspective, particularly if it has been defined from a Northern or Western Hemisphere, white, economically comfortable social position. For this reason a heightened awareness and full acceptance of the rich diversity of experiences and cultures among women contributes to the uniqueness of each ritual or worship event. While some liturgists have spoken of an "inculturation" of the liturgy among women, paralleling inculturation in various ethnic or national cultures, the fact remains that women's relative secondary position takes place across the spectrum of global and historical cultures, assuming a different character in each.[4]

The Perspective of Ecofeminism

One classic example of dualism has been the identification of women with nature. Particularly in the literature of the early modern period, marked by the rise of science and technology, both women and nature have been considered primitive, chaotic, and dangerous unless tamed and made to serve useful functions by "man," the exemplar of culture over nature and rationality over emotion. Just as ecological theology provides shifts in understanding and perception concerning the relation of human persons with their natural environment, ecofeminism analyzes the domination-submission paradigm that underlies both patriarchal male/female and human/nature relations. Whereas scripture texts such as the second creation account in Genesis (in which the man names all the creatures including the woman), and Psalm 8 exalt the domination of "man" over all of nature, a more contemporary interpretation suggests instead that "man" bears the responsibility of stewardship over creation. Yet because the stewardship model leaves intact the preeminence of "man" in taking care of nature (and implicitly by extension, of women), a third interpretation emphasizes the innate organic connections among all of creation in a balance of mutuality and just relations. This third approach serves to relativize the pretensions of any one species, or any gender within that species, to innate superiority over the rest.[5]

For women's ritual, the result of this new thinking means not only a wide scope of creativity in the discovery and use of natural symbols,[6] but a heightened awareness of the underlying unity among all of creation, since all are loved into being by God. In the literature this is expressed as the "metaphor of connectedness." This does not mean an uncritical acceptance of the alignment of women with nature and men with culture, but it does entail that worship of any sort should express embodied connectedness and mutuality with other persons and other created elements. In this perspective worship would no longer present as the norm an attitude of penitential self-abnegation before a God trumpeted as dominator, victor, or glorious almighty Father, but rather an attitude of trust in an incarnate God, a God whose transcendence does not legitimate oppressive power nor provide a rationale for human persons to arrogate dominating power to themselves.[7]

Characteristics of New Women's Liturgies

1. The distinctiveness that marks each celebration indicates that the primary characteristic of these liturgies is their *contextual* nature. Each ritual takes place among a certain group of women in a certain space and time, and even if the structure and texts were to be reused, the context of each gathering would remain unique. On a theoretical level one might argue that any liturgical event takes place in an unrepeatable time and space, but what distinguishes new women's liturgies is their conscious willingness to affirm the legitimacy of difference rather than promulgating a universal standard or drawing ritual boundaries that exclude and demean others.

2. Women's rituals may express symbolically a variety of passages and life events for which no Christian ritual exists in the sacramentary: a rite of sending for a young person leaving home or an older person entering a care facility, the blessing of a house (or its re-blessing following, for example, damage or robbery), the "croning" or recognition of elder status in a wise older woman, or a blessing for someone departing on a mission or to welcome someone returning after a long journey. Certain categories of ritual pertain to realities physically unique to women: menarche, childbearing, menopause, even a rereading of the Jewish traditional "mikvah," the bath of purification following one's monthly period as a way for women to reclaim the goodness of their own bodies.[8] Women's liturgies may show a stronger awareness of their placement in time and space on a cosmic level: solstice and equinox, lunar phases and the solar cycle, and the seasons and their impact on human persons are reflected in the choice of texts and symbols to strengthen the organic link of persons with their natural environment. Finally, rites may

embody spiritual healing from trauma, whether symbolizing a healing process already accomplished or as a therapeutic occasion for a person or persons to open themselves to the possibility of healing, and to invite others to focus their support and energy in prayer for those in need of healing.

3. The process by which women in small local groups, sometimes called "sacred circles," go about enacting liturgy testifies to the shift in approach to planning and presiding. Instead of a sole presider who monopolizes the significant texts and ritual actions, one finds more often a deliberate diversity of roles, or even two or three "presiders" acting together. Planning is generally undertaken by a small group delegated by the larger group or even a constellation of smaller groups in dialogue with each other to plan different parts of the projected liturgy, though there may be exceptions if a group has never met before or participants do not know each other. Mutuality, interchangeable responsibility, and circular direction-giving take the place of monarchical, hierarchical, or controlling leadership as a working model. Opportunities for dialogue, contributions of insights, recalling and naming special persons to be remembered, or sharing prayers for those in need open the circle to an even-handed interchange among participants particularly in small groups.

4. The actual setting for such celebrations may vary from one woman's basement rec room to a major congress hall seating thousands. When possible the preferred configuration of such space is in a circle or concentric circles with moveable seating, not rows of pews with poor sight lines facing one wall, a flexible arrangement that spatially mirrors the shift in leadership style from pyramidal to circular. The space needs to be unencumbered enough to permit body movement on the part of all participants, which may range from arm or hand gestures to circle dances or other rhythmic coordinated movement. Processions, always a part of Christian paraliturgical practice and even common in Roman pre-Christian religious custom, move participants through space together involving the whole body in worship. Outdoor celebrations, when possible, can be particularly conducive not only to movement by a number of participants over a field or other large space, but to a ritual use of spatial orientation in the four directions, or of greater attention to cosmic entities such as sun, moon, and stars.

5. In this connection the concept of liturgical time has been expanded when interwoven with new women's liturgy. The existing liturgical year, with its inbuilt seasonal rhythms,[9] may be coordinated with a succession of facets of the life of Christ and of Christian celebration through the ages, but part of the distinctive character of women's liturgy lies in its willingness to draw on deeper roots for a sense of religious time. This includes the earth rhythms of solstice and equinox, phases of the moon, the turning of the seasons in whatever way they may be manifested in the particular locality, and the multilevel symbolic linkage of time with human phenomena (for example, in the Northern

Hemisphere the "dying" of nature in November, corresponding to the feasts of All Saints or All Souls as a time to remember those who have died). Although some commentators have tried to argue that women are closer in their felt bodily rhythms to the phases of the moon, a monthly rhythm resembling the menstrual cycle, while solar time corresponds to the patriarchal time of church and state, a more flexible, less dualistic metaphor of ritual time might be that of a journey. Individually or as a community, the experience of time as a journey allows for a sense of progression without linear sequence, of growth and decline as well as the reaching of plateaus, and of a sense of directionality without a rigidly predetermined structure of expectations. The journey allows the person, and the worshiping community, to respond to a sense of God's guiding presence in a spontaneous and open-ended way.[10]

6. It goes without saying that the language used is not only nonsexist, nor just inclusive, but emancipatory in the sense that language usage names the evils inhibiting and oppressing women while providing wings to transcend the evils of the past and move toward a future vision of justice and hope.[11] The choice of texts for reading, meditation, and common response may be taken from a vast range of sources, both prose and poetry, from throughout history. The use of text at women's liturgies may involve scripture texts read through women's eyes, particularly those most neglected in the readings selected for the lectionary: accounts of respected women prophets, accounts of miraculous healing of women by Jesus, or the historical and theologically significant fact that Jesus entrusted the news of his resurrection to Mary Magdalene, the "apostle to the apostles." Texts may also draw from early church sources pertaining to women, particularly women apostles and martyrs (Thecla, Perpetua, and Felicity) or women ministers (Phoebe, Lydia, among others) in such a way as to reclaim lost traditions of women and situate them as proclamations of God's living presence within a contemporary worshiping community of women. Other sources may include contemporary poetry, first-person accounts, biography, or fiction.

One notable restoration of a classical ritual genre has been the use of litany. Whether used to name and denounce structural and personal evils that afflict women—as in a rite of exorcism—or to name valiant women and muster courage to live according to their model, or to pile up petitions of praise and thanksgiving, litanies embody both rhythm and progression, which catches up the participants into a dramatic crescendo.[12]

7. The often brilliantly creative use of natural, visual, and tactile symbols, symbolic movement and gesture testifies amply to the heretofore undervalued giftedness of women as originators and agents of liturgy. Classic primordial elements receive new overlayers of symbolic signficance—the placement and use of rocks, twigs, flowers, and such do not merely decorate the worship space but express deeper layers of meaning in the context of the

ritual itself. Fire, for example, traditionally taken as a symbol of light, heat, or destructive power, can be reclaimed in the context of women as hearth fire, the central orientation point of the home, the source of cozy warmth, welcome, security, and well-cooked food.

Water represents a number of paradoxical symbolic connotations—the source of all life and the main element constituting the human body, water can also mean dissolution, destruction, chaos, and death. In baptism Christians enter into the death and resurrection of Christ by being reborn to new life. From a woman-identified perspective, the life-giving quality of water may recall amniotic fluid, the balance of ecosystems, and the fundamental necessity of clean water, women's roles in traditional societies as those who carry heavy jars of water over great distances or who wash clothing at the riverside. Water may be used in ritual in pools or basins, washing, blessing, affirming a common physical basis for the existence of all living beings. Water may also signify cleaning and self-purification for women, though this raises the question of whether nature here becomes the dumping ground for human dirt and decay, shattering the potential sense of organic unity of all creation characteristic of women's worship in an ecofeminist perspective.[13]

8. New music composed by women from lived experience is abundantly available for use in ritual. In particular, songs of solidarity end up serving as anthems for a particular group, such as "Keep On Moving Forward" at the rituals of the more than one thousand participants at the first European Women's Synod held in Gmunden, Austria, in 1996.

9. Basic foodstuffs such as bread, fruit, water, milk, or wine are given imaginative use, sometimes with very ancient roots, such as the use of milk and honey recalling both the promise to the Hebrew people of a land "flowing with milk and honey," and their use as part of the early church's rites of initiation. Because of the negative connotations of the apple, which recall the Garden of Eden story (Genesis 3) and the way in which women have historically been blamed for the "sin of Eve," the blessing and sharing of apples reclaims this fruit and the dignity of women at the same time, affirming and blessing women's search for knowledge and wisdom.[14] Pioneering interfaith seders employ the structure of the Jewish Passover seder to commemorate women's suffering, truncated possibilities, and thwarted gifts, even slavery, through the ages in a shared meal that symbolizes both memorial and shared hope for a future of justice.[15] Bread may be used as a symbol of diversity and inclusivity by highlighting the many ethnic varieties of bread, the sharing of bread as a token of trust and solidarity, or bread itself as a symbol of strength and the power to denounce evil and effect justice.

New Perspectives on Formal Rites and Sacraments

Baptism, the foundational sacrament of initiation, carries as we have said the dual significance of death (dying with Christ) and rebirth to new life, both meanings paradoxically held in tension in the multivalent symbolism of water. The restoration of the catechumenal process for older children and adults preparing for baptism in the RCIA has meant the introduction on the level of official ecclesial rite of many of the newer currents of thought regarding ritual that also underlie women's celebrations. Among these are a person-centered flexibility in terms of time and spiritual growth, the emphasis on discerning the voice of the spirit in one's own life, the accompaniment of a supportive community, and the proliferation of small rites to sustain the catechumen along the way—blessings, exorcisms, scrutinies, perhaps the formal presentation of the creed or a cross. Because the catechumenate does not entail only the cognitive mastery of doctrines and practices, but of hearing the stories of people of faith both in the scriptures and through Christian history, and learning to set one's own life story alongside these models of faith, the ongoing retrieval of women's stories from the edges of memory and neglected documentation fits comfortably into this multilevel model of growth in commitment. It is precisely from this type of model that building new forms of communities of justice derives.[16]

Questions have been raised, however, regarding the development of a theology of baptism that does adequate justice to the dignity and holiness of women's bodies. One aspect concerns baptism as rebirth and the often highly dualistic expressions that surround it—the idea that the spiritual birth ("of water and the spirit") is far superior to mere fleshly birth. The rebirth of baptism is accomplished at the hands of the clergy, as compared to birthing in the flesh, which is the domain of women. In an odd sort of parallel, the old rite of the churching of women after childbirth involved the priest meeting the woman outside the door of the church. After a psalm was recited, the woman was given the end of the priest's stole to hold, and he literally led her back into the church, in a symbolic gesture not dissimilar to a birth process, umbilical cord and all. If rebirth can easily be taken as a symbol of transformation from the contamination of the earthly birth associated with women to a superior spiritual birth effected by men, does the theology of baptism as dying and rising with Christ mirror a similar pejorative approach to embodiment?

Reconciliation in one or another form also represents a prominent theme expressed in women's celebrations. On one level this might entail undertaking (or accomplishing) a journey of healing from an injury done in the past, confronting long-suppressed anger and rage, and coming to a wholeness such that one may make a sort of peace with the past and let go of a desire for revenge. One woman expressed her sense of healing from the trauma of childhood incest by inviting several friends to a ritual in which a number of white hand-kerchiefs that had belonged to her late father, the perpetrator, had been knotted together and strung around the room. At a certain moment, all those present were invited to take hold of the handkerchiefs and untie them, letting them wave and flutter freely.

On a larger scale, the naming of abuses and injustices perpetuated against women as structural sins, and the commitment to refusal of complicity in sin, are forms of penitential rites that shift the focus from individual to social sin, and from individual self-abnegation to the summoning of the energy that can overcome evil and transform sinful structures into justice-bearing ones. Another approach to reconciliation, which parallels the idea of continual conversion characteristic of healthy spiritual growth, is that of learning to listen to one's own conscience, a voice too often suppressed, ignored, or rationalized away in the process of accommodating oneself to fit a relatively subservient role. All of these refer to bringing healing to injury and forgiveness to broken-ness without imitating the sacramental rite of reconciliation as such.

The most striking and potentially controversial phenomenon is that of *eucharist.* According to recent documentation, numerous small groups of women, in the course of ritual prayer, bless bread, wine, or other foodstuffs, share them together, and speak of it unambiguously as eucharist.[17] There is, however, no trace of a sacrificial theology, and these celebrations bear no resemblance to the "Holy Sacrifice of the Mass" in its classic dogmatic formulation. In the field of systematic christology, one prominent question has been, What does it mean to speak to women of the virtue of self-sacrifice, when it is precisely women who, due to the fundamental heteronomy of their lives under patriarchy, can hardly be said to have a self, or to be a self, and therefore have little to sacrifice? When the salvific value of Christ's death on the cross rests upon the presumption of his willing acceptance of victimization, it becomes far too easy to slide into exhorting those with little voice or control over their own lives to imitate Christ as submissive victims of abuse or even violence. So one cannot rightly speak of the phenomenon of womeneucharist as in any way imitating or paralleling the eucharistic sacrifice as formulated in Catholic teaching. The phenomenon is significant, however, because of the growing number and geographical spread of groups that gather and bless bread, much as in an *agape* meal,[18] and it provides an important indicator of growing rest-lessness with considerable consequences for the future of the church.

Toward a New Liturgical Spirituality

What does the proliferation of creative ritual indicate for new directions in women's spirituality? First, if a healthy spirituality is indeed an openness to self-transcendence and an awareness of the reality of the living God in one's life, then one must quite simply be able to trust this God. A god who enforces abject humiliation, requires acceptance of victimization, or threatens worshipers with the terrors of hell as the consequence of ill-considered actions can hardly be addressed with full openness in prayer. One only dares to accept the vulnerability involved in worship within a relationship of trust among members of the worshiping community, and ultimately a sense of safety in the presence of God.

Linked with trust in a God who is not an enforcer or a dominator is the growth in the ability to trust one's own intuition, inner wisdom, or conscience as a personal aspect of the wisdom of God. This capacity to discern clearly one's own inner proddings, one's instinctive awareness of whether a person or situation is trustworthy, whether one's life is moving in an appropriate direction, or whether one is making worthy choices is itself a gift from God. This does not exclude learning to discern the voice of God in other persons or in the course of events in one's life. In a way we are speaking here of the classic virtue of obedience—not construed as passive dependency or conformity to the will of another person, but simply the faculty of listening and responding, *ob-audire* in Latin. A genuine and profound sense of how God's wisdom speaks to one in the depths of one's own heart provides a strong reference point for resisting manipulation.

Rooted in growing self-confidence in one's ability to discern wisely comes a discovery or a clarification of one's own identity, an identity often quite different from the identity one has embraced up to now. For women who have grown up with a "colonized consciousness" that has told them that they are by nature weaker than men, emotional and high strung, incapable of achievements in mathematics or science, and should consider themselves fortunate to be able to serve the needs of others with no sense of who they themselves are, this awareness of one's own identity itself provides a source of strength with which to refuse false or exploitative projected identities.

Women's celebrations, in their extensive creative latitude precisely as prayer and rite, serve to increase a community's flexibility in liturgical prayer. By extension they may increase one's own personal flexibility in private prayer and response to God. The presence of God becomes discernible across a broad span of events in one's life, natural phenomena, small details, odd coincidences, and all sorts of personal encounters. Rather like limbering up and stretching muscles for exercise, one's awareness of God's presence expands and deepens through the delighted discovery of ways in which groups of women can pray and celebrate together.

Women's ritual illustrates that there is no necessary dualistic conflict between liturgy and social justice, or between private prayer and common prayer, but a dynamic mutual flow among them. When justice shapes prayer, the whole person as well as the whole community is strengthened in both the capacity for prayer and a passion for justice.

By awakening women to their own giftedness and providing outlets for that creativity, women's celebrations can strengthen women's positive identity of themselves as loved and gifted by God. For many this can be one way to help deal with specific past gender-linked traumas (rape, incest, abuse, or perhaps social or educational disadvantages because they were women), as well as to confront the personal and collective consequences of the myth of women's inherent inferiority to men in creation. The practice of ritual expresses a deeper sense of what incarnation means: God present in human flesh, embracing our world on our terms, so to speak. For women that can mean a hallowing of women's bodies and beings in a way many never thought possible within the Christian tradition.

It is not unthinkable that the evolution of worship and ritual within women's groups can serve as a potent source for liturgical renewal on the level of formal rites affecting the evolution of worship in the larger church. As occurred in the Liturgical Movement, contemporary women's celebrations show clear parallels with experiments in pastoral liturgy carried out at the grassroots that accompanied scholarly research into the origins of Christian worship. The Liturgical Movement shifted over time away from a focus on liturgical education for clergy and the production of tools such as bilingual missals to help people follow the mass. Eventually this developed into an impetus for thoroughgoing reform of the rites in a more authentic, accessible form. In the same way women's liturgy might well shape the evolving direction of future liturgy in a way that honors more fully the personhood of all those created in the image of God and marked with the sign of Christ in baptism.

Notes

1. In fact, canon 834 §2 of the 1983 Code of Canon Law defines liturgy as "this worship...offered in the name of the Church, by persons lawfully deputed and through actions approved by ecclesiastical authority."

2. For further reflections on these terms as applied to new women's ritual, see Mary Collins, "Principles of Feminist Liturgy," in Marjorie Procter-Smith and Janet Walton, eds., *Women at Worship: Interpretations of North American Diversity* (Louisville: Westminster/John Knox, 1993): 9–26.

3. Martha Ann Kirk, in her introduction to *Liberating Liturgies* (Fairfax, Va.: Women's Ordination Conference, 1989), 10, writes,

In the reform of the Liturgy of the Hours following Vatican II, on some of the feasts of women saints, selections of their writings have been given for the readings. I have raised the question, "Before this reform have the words of women ever been a part of the formal liturgy of the Catholic Church, whether for Eucharist, other sacraments, or Liturgy of the Hours?" I have consulted a number of liturgical scholars who balk at the question. They have not been able to give any instances of a woman's words and of prayer being used in the formal written rituals before Vatican II.

4. Teresa Berger, "The Women's Movement as a Liturgical Movement: A Form of Inculturation?," *Studia Liturgica* 19 (1989): 55–63.

5. See Elizabeth A. Johnson, *Woman, Earth and Creator Spirit* (New York/Mahwah, N.J.: Paulist, 1993): 29–31.

6. Even the use of nature symbols in ritual can embody unexamined attitudes of exploitation, or of expecting nature to purify human contamination or rectify human sin. See L. Teal Willoughby, "Ecofeminist Consciousness and the Transforming Power of Symbols," in Carol J. Adams, ed., *Ecofeminism and the Sacred* (New York: Continuum, 1993), 133–48.

7. Johnson, *Woman, Earth and Creator Spirit*, 23–28.

8. Rosemary Radford Ruether, *Womenchurch: Theology and Practice* (San Francisco: Harper and Row, 1985), 218–22. Ruether cites Rachel Adler as the source.

9. These seasonal rhythms of course are keyed to the climate of the Northern Hemisphere in relatively temperate climates, or alternatively in more northerly regions where the contrast between the hours of daylight shifts dramatically between summer and winter solstice.

10. See Susan K. Roll, "A Feminist Approach to Liturgical Time," *Proceedings of the North American Academy of Liturgy* (1997): 95–107.

11. These three distinctions can be found in Marjorie Procter-Smith, *In Her Own Rite: Constructing Feminist Liturgical Tradition* (Nashville: Abingdon, 1990), 60–67. "Non-sexist language seeks to avoid gender-specific terms. Inclusive language seeks to balance gender references. Emancipatory language seeks to transform language use and to challenge stereotypical gender references" (63).

12. For more examples of the use of litanies, see Susan K. Roll, "Traditional Elements in New Women's Liturgies," *Questions Liturgiques* 72 (1991): 55–56.

13. See Willoughby, "Ecofeminist Consciousness," 134–35.

14. See Susan K. Roll, "Liturgy in the Company of Women: the ESWTR Conference," *Questions Liturgiques* 74 (1993): 231–34, for a fuller description of a celebration by women theological scholars of blessing the apple.

15. Diann Neu, "Celebrative Meal: Celebrating Miriam's Sisters," in Diann Neu, *Women and the Gospel Traditions* (Silver Spring, Md.: WATER, 1989): 16–22, and several booklets subsequently published by WATER outlining various forms of the Passover seder.

16. Marjorie Procter-Smith has worked out a model for women's empowerment based on the structure of the RCIA in *In Her Own Rite*, 154–57.

17. Sheila Durkin Dierks, *WomenEucharist* (Boulder, Co.: Woven Word Press, 1997).

18. An argument can be made from canon law that the participants are not violating the intention of CIC 83 c. 1378 par. 2, "the following incur a latae sententiae interdict...: no 1: a person who, not being an ordained priest, attempts to celebrate Mass" *(qui ad ordinem sacerdotalem non promotus liturgicam eucharistici Sacrificii actionem attentat)*. The intention here is not to mislead others as would be the case if the person presiding claimed to be an ordained male priest, used the sacramentary and lectionary, used vestments and so forth. Survey results in Dierks, *WomenEucharist* among others indicate that participants in womeneucharist are quite clear about the intention of the celebration.

SECTION VIII.

MINISTRY

"Ministry to the Millions in the Middle" by Joseph A. Tetlow describes a group that might be referred to as "the Catholic silent majority." These are the ordinary Catholics who choose to "remain in the church within a culture that values individual choice and has a jealous regard for personal freedom." Tetlow expresses a number of concerns about these individuals, including that they "are made to feel that they have no spirituality at all unless they join a movement like cursillo or the Neocatechumenate, or unless they take up the practice of Carmelite centering or Ignatian discernment." He also addresses how ministers can reach out to this large faith-filled group to help them develop a new spiritual theology and give further shape to a Catholic form of life. This is a stimulating essay that parish staffs would find a wonderful reflection piece for further discussion.

In Lawrence S. Cunningham's essay on "Discipleship," he reminds us that following Jesus was "not a matter of simple pedagogy." Instead "this 'Way' (a key word in Mark) was, after all, the way of the cross (8:34). Those who took up this way had to be people of prayer and fasting (9:23) who were to accept a low status (9:33–36), who must be ready to experience a loss of wealth (10:23–31) and live without the consolation of seeking both that wealth or higher social status (10:35–37; 42–44)." Cunningham then adds that "The true follower of the Way—the disciple—must be ready to accept those who are not of the same background (9:42–45)...[and] the acceptance and love of children (10:17–20)." In this brief, fascinating essay the discussion of discipleship will spur personal reflection and, as in other essays in this book, be ideal for staff discussion and faith sharing around the points made by Cunningham on our key "pilgrimage of the way" in pastoral ministry.

"Reading and Ministry: Applying *Lectio Divina* Principles in a Ministerial Context" by Raymond Studzinski focuses on the question: Could the very practice of pastoral ministry be a source of spiritual input that nourishes the minister, similar to reading the scriptures? Is there a way of "reading" pastoral experiences that brings us into contact with the sacred as much as the reading of scripture does? In responding to these questions in his creative and strong essay, Studzinski addresses the essence of spiritual illiteracy in our times; various approaches to reading: digital text, the printed book, and the scholastic book; the monastic book and *lectio divina;* appropriating *lectio divina* today and *lectio* as a larger process; and finally, applying *lectio* principles in ministry. This essay is a wonderful piece of work.

Wilkie Au's "A Perceptual Approach to Effective Ministry" encourages us to reflect on "the insights of Arthur Combs regarding perceptual organization of effective helpers who know how to use the 'self as instrument.'" He also recommends some of the insights of Ignatius of Loyola, so we can be "wielded dexterously by the provident hand of God" in ministry. In this essay, the attitude and philosophy of appreciation are contrasted with the (temptation) to plunge only into responsible action for (rather than with) others. Often in an effort to *do* good, we fail to note how our perceptions frame our approach. In this helpful, sensitive piece, we are asked to look again so we connect the immediate to the divine in ways that will change us so we can see new possibilities in our service to others.

In "Ministers as Midwives and Mothers of Grace," E. Glenn Hinson reminds us with simple elegance that "grace flows endlessly from the ocean of love. Our task is to assist others in giving birth to and in growing up in grace." In approaching this theme he relies on Augustine, John Bunyan, and Thomas Merton. With Hinson we learn much about being "midwives and mothers of grace" from these three eminent teachers.

Benedict Ashley's "Spirituality and Counseling" focuses on seeking to provide a precise meaning to "spiritual counseling" as distinct from other forms of counseling. Included in the essay are the topics: aims and objectives of spiritual counseling; spiritual counseling and the structure of the human person; Christian spiritual counseling; and counseling risks and gains. As is the case with all of Ashley's work, it is a thought-provoking piece.

In "Spiritual Ministry with Men in Prison," the closing essay of the section and the book, Robert Wieber offers guiding principles that arose from his work as a chaplain. In this short, practical chapter, the author offers us some of the fruits of his own learning on how to reach out to men in prison as well as the keys he believes are part of a pattern that will set the stage for a new lifestyle for inmates. Easy and helpful reading, this topic certainly belongs in a collection such as this.

Joseph A. Tetlow

36. Ministering to the Millions in the Middle

Cardinal Joseph Bernardin once expressed pastoral concern for "the millions in the middle." With his phrase, he created an excellent image of the church in America and simultaneously elicited a grave concern. But who was he talking about? What made him feel concern for them?

In these paragraphs, I try to answer those two questions. I suggest that Cardinal Bernardin was talking about those Catholics who experience God in and through their religion, rather than through what we now call spirituality. He was concerned for them, at least in part, because of the way they had been hurt by the changes following the Second Vatican Council. For the middle millions, those changes were far more than cosmetic: the changes seriously hampered their experience of God. The concern was not that people's feelings had been badly hurt; the concern was that their experience of God had been seriously impaired.

The experience of the middle millions—even their distinct existence—is difficult to get at, so I consider this a tentative exploration. And since the argument seems to keep folding back on itself, I might usefully suggest how this discussion will proceed.

To begin at the beginning, I try to make this enormous population visible, first by excluding some other cohorts and groups and then by describing the middle millions themselves. I believe understanding them depends on seeing the differences between religion and spirituality, so I explore those differences. That done, I point out how, during the past four decades, spirituality has influenced the religion of the middle millions. The influence has been singularly important because their religion is the middle million's lifelong experience of God. I have to contend, then, that the middle millions have been severely tested in the past half-century, as the church made an epochally swift deconstruction of creed, code, and cult. But I believe that the middle millions have been passing the test, and that they are now contributing to the American church's reconstruction of religion as the locus of a vibrant, meaning-filled experience of God in everyday life. I suggest that this reconstruction grows visibly in an emerging form of American Catholic life, which it is underpinning with a new spiritual theology. Finally, I point to some ways in which the needs of Cardinal Bernardin's "millions in the middle" continue to challenge those who minister to them.

Who Are These People?

Anyone who hears Cardinal Bernardin's phrase knows right away whom he was talking about. But the middle millions are difficult to describe in sociological terms. They are not a cohort in any strict sense, like Baby Boomers or the graduates of Catholic colleges. The term *middle millions* might almost be said to describe rather a spiritual condition than a cohort. I could say that I am talking about the *majority* of Catholics, who go to mass at least once a month. I am talking about those four in ten Catholics who worship pretty much weekly. I include in the millions the Catholic Grey Panthers who have ridden out the tsunami of change following Vatican II and the middle-aged who grew up awash in it. I would even include those thirty- and fortysomething Catholics who tend to emphasize Christ active in the sacraments, the real presence, and focus a lot on authority, as well those in difficult marriage situations or single life who are doing what they can to hang on to the church.

In a way, the "millions in the middle" that Cardinal Joseph Bernardin felt concern about are the invisible Catholics, or what might be called the Catholic silent majority or—they really do still exist—the ordinary Catholic. They may be studied for political purposes or for sociological surveys, but they are rarely treated as serious religious beings. Yet they are sticking with the church.

They do not join the roughly 11 percent of every birth cohort during the past generation who have dropped out of the church. Nor do they move into some more visible cohorts who do not drop out but would never think of themselves as being "in the bosom of the church." These are Catholics living on the edges of the church—leading edge or trailing edge. Some on either end live *a prophetic life,* in the sense that they focus on some ill or ills in church and world, castigate the church's responses, and call for changes that they think must be made. They want to reform the church, and tend to rely more on their gift of prophecy than on the great gift of the church as it actually is. Those on one end may demand the Latin mass and those on the other may demand women's ordination. Those who live this prophetic life might noisily leave the church; most continue to be visible members, noisy or not, and work for the changes they believe must come promptly.

Again, some on the edges *live for holiness.* They often enough feel that the church has lost its thirst for cultivating true holiness, and they want to renew the church. Certainly some of them quietly leave the hierarchical church and turn to holiness sects or evangelical communions. But many stay within the church and join some kind of illuminative movement within it such as the neocatecumenate or Opus Dei. Many of these seekers drift from movement to movement, and they seem to hanker for a kind of parallel church for the sake of holiness. I believe these seekers are being served by the many forms of "spirituality" today.

The Middle Millions

These eager or aggressive Catholics——whether they want to reform the structures or renew the spirit, whether they are conservative or liberal—are out on the frontiers of change in the church. Well within these frontiers stand the great majority of the church, who earnestly want to belong in the church.

The middle millions are not a statistical cohort, but they share some common characteristics. For instance, they are not typically readers of Catholic weeklies left or right. They see evils in church and society, but they tend to hold their gaze rather on the good than on the evil. They want to go along with the hierarchical church's decisions and teachings, partly because in the past that has defended their identity in a Protestant nation and partly because of a deeply traditional Catholic attitude toward religious authority. Yet the middle millions are entirely enculturated; they are as individualistic, pragmatic, and nationalistic as the rest of Americans. By and large, though they seem to feel they do not know their faith all that well, they are well educated. Consequently, their failure to accept one or other church teaching or discipline (for instance, the definition of *artificial* in birth control) cannot be explained very easily or comfortably.

The middle millions have to embrace their religion in the current atmosphere of individualism and consumerism. They evidently make a free human decision to remain faithful; the middle millions are not driven into religion by unconscious psychic conditioning from childhood. They cannot correctly be numbered among the emotionally dependent on religion. The middle millions are choosing to remain in the church within a culture that values individual choice and has a jealous regard for personal freedom.

As church members, the middle millions do not demand that the church be other than it is. They do not want to be alienated from the church nor do they want the church to move away from them. On the contrary, they are invested in remaining Catholic and having Catholicism continue distinctive.

For all that, the middle millions are experiencing some distancing within the church. They are puzzled about why priests leave and why vocations dwindle. They are revolted to hear about priest pedophiles among the clergy. They are somewhat bewildered by changes among women religious. They are, commonly enough, put off by divisions among the bishops and offended by strident rhetoric against priests and religious. They feel a bit jerked around by prophets and the aggressively holy. They have the sense that the church in which their lives have been immersed is draining away from them, feeling themselves like baskers on a seaside porch watching an evening tide slip out.

Distinguishing Religion and Spirituality

The distancing they feel is not merely subjective emotion or illusion. The distancing between the middle millions and their church is real, and it is on two flanks: religion and spirituality.

First, *religion* is taking a drubbing in the media and among intellectuals. When the couple sitting in the sixth row, who have for years quietly split their vote between political parties, hear in news reports that religion has become a major political force, they may wonder if what they have is religion, since it has not been a political force in their lives. Or they may come to the crowded pew having just read in the Sunday paper that religion is a private affair, which makes them wonder why they are all gathered in church. They may go home to news stories that blame the gruesome suicides of cults on the insanity of religion, yet the middle millions have been content all their lives with their religion's reasonableness. And it must be said that, when their religious leaders raise the definition of *artificial* in birth control to a major doctrinal matter, they feel the ground shift under their experience of God in the church.

They feel a distancing from the church on a second flank: *spirituality.* In recent generations, the search for the direct experience of God, for an ongoing intimate relationship with the Holy One, has been called *spirituality.* Spirituality is not merely one or other experience; rather, it is a way of living the search for the direct experience of God. "You, yourself, not some idea of You," as Karl Rahner prayed. It is true that not everything Americans call *spirituality* would qualify as such in the church: an esprit de corps ("the spirituality of IBM") or simply a human interiority ("focusing" or "centering") or perhaps some kind of nature mysticism ("New Age spirituality").

But many American Catholics have begun practicing a fully genuine Christian spirituality. They may adapt one of the great traditions but they do not characteristically feel bound to a tradition, and indeed select from any tradition what seems to them serviceable. They pray daily. They have made a serious retreat or spiritual exercises in silence, and many do this annually. They do not make much use of formulaic prayer; they pray mentally. In astonishing numbers, American Catholics (along with other Christians) practice the *lectio divina* of the Benedictine tradition, contemplation in the Ignatian tradition, or meditation in the Salesian tradition. Beyond following the dictates of conscience, they currently tend to "discern" any important decision, or indeed any decision at all. They read spiritual books on prayer and the knowledge of God, and they have produced numerous fine spiritual writers. They have at hand in even the smallest Catholic bookstore (for that matter, even in huge bookstore chains) editions of spiritual masters from Clement of Rome through Edith Stein. And the Catholic who has taken to spirituality reads them.

For perhaps two decades now, this spirituality segment of the Catholic population has been attending workshops and weekends on discernment, prayer, and the connection between spiritual growth and human maturity. Currently, many of those who are living a spiritual life are eager to be trained to give spiritual direction or to guide retreats. It is true that they tend to touch only lightly on certain human experiences that have been at the core of the spiritual life in past ages, including sin and corporal penances. At the same time, they tend to be active in handing on the spiritual experiences they are enjoying. In fact, those who are living an active spiritual life are generally conspicuous among church leaders.

Relocating the Experience of God

Once the differences between religion and spirituality become clear, we can note that spirituality has been enjoying a certain ascendancy in the American church. Unhappily, this ascendancy has fostered some oppositions within the body of the church. To begin with, it has furthered opposition between the individual believer in the church and the community of the church. For spirituality begins with an interior personal experience that (under the weight of postmodern individualism) has become effectively a thoroughly *individual* experience. Religion, on the other hand, begins with a communal experience and cannot be understood at all except in terms of a community. Feeling the ascendancy of spirituality, believers feel solicited to get into this individual experience; yet, prodded by the postmodern search for community, they are bound to keep working at the communitarian experience of religion. Many charismatics keep going to their prayer evenings but continue trying to renew their parishes, not really satisfied with either.

Then again, even in the egalitarian context of the people of God, the ascendancy of spirituality has appeared to be shaping an elite or some elites. Within the church, they are given a special assignment to know God directly and intimately. Everyone else is left to experience "just religion," an all-too-common and extraordinarily dismissive phrase. For what has been going on during the past decades is an implicit redefinition of the experience of God, a redefinition that has placed that experience outside what we generally mean by the word *religion.* The abandonment of Benediction of the Blessed Sacrament is not merely a shift in pieties within the holy place; it marks a shift of the locus for experiencing God from the middle out to the frontiers.

So those who seek God in religion are under pressure to do something else. They feel the general sense that "just religion" isn't enough if they want to experience God. In parish after parish, they are called to spirituality. But, I think it can be argued, most people who live in the middle are not called to the interior personal experience that is spirituality; they are called to the interior communal experience that is religion. It is not that spirituality is too much for them, or beyond their abilities or their grasp. It is simply that they are not called to spirituality. A generation ago, Catholics famously introduced themselves by saying that they were from St. Mary's or Corpus Christi parish. No longer. If Catholics identify themselves as Catholics, they now tend to say they are members of Christian Life Community or cursillistas or communion ministers. So what has happened to those who are just members of St. Mary's or Corpus Christi?

The pressure on the middle millions to turn to spirituality has not happened only in the Catholic Church: Unitarians practice Zen, Episcopalians move into the *Cloud of Unknowing,* and all of the churches have developed what commentators are referring to as a "spirituality marketplace" in which all kinds of interior ware from the church's immensely rich storehouse, and some imported goods, are on offer to all comers.

Put bluntly: The millions are made to feel that they have no spirituality at all unless they join a movement like cursillo or the Neocatecumenate, or unless they take up the practice of Carmelite centering or Ignatian discernment. They share in the general feeling that it is no longer enough to worship, receive the sacraments devoutly, and keep the commandments while living fully in the church. In the current climate—to put the case very strongly—the middle millions seem to have to meditate, and meditate systematically and well, before they can know how to act justly, love tenderly, and walk humbly before their God. This represents a great change; the early church considered *spiritual* those who lived Christian revelation fully and wholeheartedly in everyday life.

The Reappraisal of Religion

Could this be understood as the true call to spirituality of the middle millions? It would seem so. If they are called to spirituality, it must be to spirituality in the church's oldest use of the word: the full and wholehearted living of the Christian religion.

This call will not be readily understood in our day as *spirituality.* For it requires recognizing that religion in its fullest sense includes the experience of God. That is far beyond what Americans now think of religion. We tend to conceive of religion from the point of view of cultural anthropologists. Applying the methodology of experimental science, they have approached religion objectively. That is to say, they make religion an object; they systematically view religion from outside its actual experience. They describe it as a series of beliefs and rituals, taboos and norms, and the creative expression of all these in temples and statues and poetry and song. This means restricting religion to what can be observed from outside of the horizon within which religious *experiences* occur. As scientists, they do not *experience* religion; they *study* religion. The journalist and media maven does not typically experience religion, either; he or she just reports the facts. Looked at in this "objective" way, no one can very easily see how religion might demand and sustain a personal experience of God in everyday life. Since American Catholics have borrowed some of this scientific attitude, we also find it hard to understand how religion is the spirituality of the middle millions.

Yet, religion can be, has been, and in some measure at least continues to be the locus of the experience of God. This is what religion as a human experience means: *Religion is the learned and lived experience of God mediated by the experiences of creed, code, cult,* and, in many peoples' histories, *by the whole culture.* Religion modifies and defines human life from within through all its stages. Each religion realizes a concrete way of living humanly, a way that is absorbed early in life from elders and teachers. Each individual takes into the structure of his or her personality the religion of the family culture, grows into maturity in it, and then gives back to the culture what he or she has taken from it.

Religion in Current American Culture

Genuine religion is the experience of God both working in the real world and transcending the known world. In today's *spirituality,* one is free to join a group or movement and free to leave it, for the community is an adjunct only. But in *religion,* one is under some kind of faith burden, some freight of transcendental obligation. Spiritualities seem fairly able to leap cultural boundaries, and leaders seem willing to make disciples wherever people are willing. Religion, on the other hand, seems rooted in the soil of the people, and if it comes from elsewhere, it must absolutely be *enculturated,* cultured in the soil of this people. Religion belongs to this time and this place. Many American Catholics can recount rather hilarious stories of grandparents who in their youth, having "gone to mass" at the Irish parish, were sent to the German parish because the authorities in their family would not countenance the first mass as valid. Religion grows in the soil of everyday life, however acid or base it may be. Yet the experience of religion simultaneously transcends time and place.

As modernity comes to its epochal end, people fear that the burden of religious belief passed on in and through community (family, parish, church) takes away a person's freedom. Here is another challenge to religion, for many do not instruct their children into the faith, but "leave them free to choose." Under this misapprehension about religion is another about human freedom, and ministers need to be careful of it. It is the identification of *individual* with *personal.* When Americans say, "I personally believe…," we really mean that as an *individual,* we believe something different from what everyone else believes. This identification of personal with individual makes moderns very open to all the experiences we now call spirituality, but it gives moderns serious problems with real religion. For in opposing the *person* and the community, we have tried to deny what is communal in each person. So we come to the *individual* and to individualism.

Following on this, we have to think of each one's *experience* as totally individual, unique, and over against the communal experience. But any reflection at all on what content we put in the word *experience* suggests that an experience is not a single solitary reality, but is a dense construct. In any account an experience presents a complex interaction among several interdependent elements: context, perspective, perception, value, desire, decision, and habit. These elements "construct" each experience, and each and every one of them is shared with others. Context means family and race and historical time. Who would claim that his or her perspective on Bach shares nothing with others' perspectives? Wouldn't we all value a cure for AIDS? Furthermore, all of the elements are ineradicably rooted in the words and phrases each of us learns from others. No word can ever be *my word;* except for the mad Humpty Dumpty, the meanings of words are among us. Even those who think they are "doing their own thing" are almost without fail comically doing what everyone else in their crowd or cohort is doing.

Every human experience comes about in a reciprocal relationship with other human experiences. Every experience is by, for, to, from, about someone or something. Even the rejection of another person is a reciprocal relation, and may well be among the most lasting of relations. A fine metaphor for the way human experience is shared shines out of our genetic code: Each genetic code is unique and individual; each came about in the relationship of other codes; all are reciprocally related to many other individual codes; and all genetic codes are constructed and derived, perhaps ultimately, geneticists speculate, from a single womb.

What Religion Used to Be

These notions about experience influence how we think about religion. For the experience of religion is just such a construct. It happens only in dialectical relationship with others, emphatically including God. It is derived from the historical and current experiences of the entire church. The religious person has introjected many religious perspectives, perceptions, values, and so on while being reared to maturity. And the religious adult is continually invited in freedom to experience creed, code, and cult. Thought about this way, religion appears much richer than any "objective" assessment could report.

Many of us in the West may find it easy to see what religion is and does by becoming aware of our perception of Islam. This religion offers some experience of God and encodes this experience in creed, code, and cult, and in point of historical fact in entire cultures. In the United States, Muslims hold faith in the One Holy God through Mohammed the Prophet, follow a strong moral code, observe prayer rites during each day and a ritual fast for a month each year, and create culture-like behaviors and attitudes in their daily lives. Muslims experience directly what Muslims have created; mediated in that religion, they experience the Most Holy One.

The middle millions have experienced God in their religion. When they attend mass on Sunday, they hear the Word of God and receive the holy bread. In these created things, they experience the divine presence, the incomprehensible, loving, attentive Other. Well, perhaps it might be truer to say that they have the right and the desire to experience the divine presence. The disappointment of that right and desire is the deepest source of their regrets about inadequate liturgy. It is important that those who minister to the middle millions be clear about this. A generation ago, when the young knelt together readying themselves to receive communion, they sang, "Oh, Lord, I am not worthy / that Thou shouldst come to me," and they were singing a personal statement to the Holy One. They would have been puzzled to be asked to do anything else in order to be in touch with the divine. They *were* in touch with the divine, in communion and also through the hymn that was at once their own song from the heart and at the same time the song of the entire church.

The same picture can be filled in for adults. On Sunday evenings in the 1940s, hundreds filed into their parish churches and knelt in silent adoration of the blessed sacrament. They were affirming in action the doctrine handed down to them: Jesus Christ is in some real and true sense present in the sacrament. The fragrance of incense distinguished the holy occasion. Their song, *"Tantum ergo Sacramentum, veneremur..."* resonated with the rich harmony of centuries of faith, but the men and women kneeling there were singing a song that was as much their song as anyone else's. They were experiencing the Holy One, the presence, and this experience marked their lives rhythmically through the years.

Catholic funeral customs have differed considerably in different regions and among different ethnic groups. But one experience has been common: the rites expressed and elicited hope in God. That is to say, Catholics grieving over a death were also and at the same time experiencing hope beyond all human sources, and in feeling that ritualized hope *they were knowing God.* Their behavior at funerals has shown that very plainly. Their hope has not been based on biology or philosophy, nor has it been the exercise of astounding human qualities. The middle millions almost by definition are not marked by astounding human qualities. Neither are they biologically determined to worship or philosophically stoic in loss. Their hope has risen from their espoused shared belief that they live in the hands of God. In that belief, they have experienced God doing the divine will in their lives.

"God's will." Many spouses have remained faithful to marriages that their culture would have chucked over because they had said "For better or for worse" in the experience of "what God hath joined." Many men have remained in union with spouses who were neurasthenic or even psychotic, and many women have remained faithful to spouses who were alcoholics or bundles of character disorders. They have felt their fidelity work in the depths of their personhood, changing and defining them. They have embraced genuine suffering freely, letting it shape them, because their religion gave them to know that God wanted those changes in them and intended that new shape. It was God's will. It will not do to claim that Catholic marital fidelity was due to social custom or human inanition. Married Catholics have experienced the sacrament of matrimony as a living medium for knowing what God wants in them, and in many ordinary cases, for *knowing God wanting in them.* Their assurance that they are doing what the Holy One wishes does not seem any more optimistic than the confidence of those who follow cultural norms for human growth or psychodynamic dictates about human happiness, or any more sanguine than the security of those who discern. While the middle millions are as deeply shaped as any Americans by modern and postmodern individualism, they nonetheless have been clinging to the belief that, since Catholic marriage has two millennia of Christian living to certify it, it may well be a realistic way of knowing what God wants. Whatever interpretation anyone else may put on it, the fidelity of many of the middle millions in difficult marriages rides, in their expressed conviction, on their knowing what God wants of them.

I am not arguing that the millions do not experience God except in their practice of religion. They surely do, and we have good empirical evidence that ordinary people have an experience of God directly in some extraordinary event or moment. For instance, the author of a recent autobiography described himself sitting on top of a mountain, the rising sun lighting his face and tears running down his cheeks, as for the first time in his life he prayed on his own, stunned by God creating and holding him. These "mystical moments" seem eventually to come to almost all who believe and hope in God, and many can recount such an experience. But they are *moments.* Religion and spirituality are understood adequately only as *ways of living.*

Dismantling and Reconstructing Religion

This understanding of religion as the lifelong experience of God throws a new light on what the middle millions went through in the church during the past thirty-five years. External changes have been entirely visible: altar turned around, language familiar now, ministers rising from the pews, traditional pieties become rare, and religious discipline trifling. But the root change in Catholicism was not so visible and has proven very deep. Taken together, the changes on the surface have meant the shattering of American Catholicism as the solid ground of the experience of God. The middle millions can no longer look to the proclamation of the word, to the sacraments, to the rhythm of the liturgical year, to honored traditional symbols, in the expectation that they will experience God in them. They do not even hear that possibility proclaimed. Rather, they hear proclaimed the experience of the community of the people of God—a good and holy experience, but perhaps not so impressive as a substitute for the experience of God.

The view is entirely understandable that postconciliar changes were overdue and almost unavoidable, that they abolished outmoded practices which were not reaching the young, that the practices themselves too often bordered on superstition, and so on. None of that can really be disputed. But when postconciliar changes began affecting churchgoing Catholics' practice of religion, too many North American ministers accepted as true of American experience Rudolph Otto's prophetic pronouncement about European experience: People were losing the sense of the holy, of the *mysterium tremendum et fascinans.*

He seems to have been correct about a sizeable portion of Europe, in which people have suffered a substantial loss of religious reverence and desiring. But in the United States, the substantive loss was neither of a holy feeling nor of an interior yearning; it cannot appropriately be named the loss of the *idea* of the holy. I believe it can be argued that the substantive loss by the end of the century has been brought about by the dismantling of the created means of the experience of God. To put it this way, the loss was of the *practice* of the holy. So the middle millions, as their entire *religion* (not just their rites or just their code) was dismantled, were left without the created resources for experiencing God. From this loss came the vehemence of the feelings about external change.

It should be no surprise, therefore, that the middle millions who stay within the church are tempted to feel with other Americans that creed, code, and cult are too fragile and culturally unrooted to bear the burden of a lifelong, exciting, joyful experience of God. They may be right. After all, the church has set aside centuries of religious culture along with the Gregorian chant. But the church in the United States has been laboring intelligently and intently to reconstruct what was lost—in liturgical rhythms, in parish structures, in catechism and kerygma. And the church has been going well beyond the structures of preconciliar Catholicism, recognizing lay charisms and inviting many more to ministry.

Plainly, the church has made some significant gains. After all, the majority of those who profess to be Catholics attend worship at least once a month and baptize, confirm, and marry their family members according to the church's rites. But what is the coherence of this reconstruction? What core meaning do the external innovations and changes carry?

If Catholicism is once again to be the place where the middle millions experience God, it will have to have grown once again into a coherent religion. That is what the middle millions are looking for in the Church: a creed, code, and cult that cohere in a way of life that gives meaning to all other experiences. That would again allow and enable them to experience God not only on Sundays but all week long, and not only at baptisms and weddings, but all during their lives.

What is this majority of Catholics finding that allows them and invites them to remain faithful and keeps so many of them worshiping regularly? What are those who minister to the millions doing now to charge creed, code, and cult with the Holy Presence? What can the ministers do more of, or do better, or add or subtract?

The Renewal of a Form of Life: Laity

The case can be made, I think, that the church's ministers are now doing two things for the middle millions: they are offering them a new spiritual theology, and they are beginning to give shape to a Catholic form of life.

One development in this form of life is clear just a generation after the council. It is this: What we now casually refer to as *lay ministry* is the engine of an epochal reshaping of Roman Catholic life. Powered by it, the church is making extraordinary efforts in family life, catechetics, liturgy, social programs, parish retreats, parochial outreach into the community at large, and so on and on. And all of these are beginning to cohere into a Catholic form of life.

The form is at present unsurprisingly inchoate, given the sweeping changes that this new form has to incorporate in family, parish, civil, and global life. The ready identification with a parish has disappeared with the territorial parish. Even where territory still functions, the parish today is an *intentional community,* a community made up of people who wish to create and sustain community. Not surprisingly, it is taking a long time to replace the feel of "being one together," which community meant in a the land of anti-Catholicism, with the feel of "mutually strengthening one another," which is what community means in the desert of individualism and consumerism.

But a clear form has begun appearing out of the creative chaos of ecumenism, the global culture, the worldwide church. It is marked first of all by new forms of outreach. Our grandparents reached out through parochial, diocesan, and church-wide structures to the orphaned, the sick, and the poor. Those structures (the Children of Mary, the Knights of Columbus, Charity Hospital, Catholic Girls' Home) replicated European structures, which were their source. Today, Catholics tend to reach out from the church by moving into the voluntary structures of the country (Hospice, Prolife, Greenpeace). Our grandparents did not reach out much inside the church except in formal parochial structures, which were emphatically "Catholic." Today, we reach inside of the church in the communion of adult formation. This is, arguably, the real meaning of scripture study groups, at-home retreats, prayer groups, parish renewal programs, and the many other modes of grouping.

The adult church in America is prepared to help itself in the reconstruction of parish life. Having been as well educated as any Catholic population in history, and arguably better than almost any other, the faithful are prepared to *let their own experience of God instruct others* as each explores what his or her own experience in Christ can mean. An almost quintessential religious ritual in our day is the gathering of adults not only to listen to someone talk but to listen to one another talk. Adults are handing this on to their young, so that while in high school, very many attend "retreats" in programs like Kairos or Emmaus, during which the teenagers witness to one another.

The New Spiritual Theology

In every one of the activities that Catholics now engage in as they reconstruct the parish and form intentional communities, some *meaning* is declared. That meaning is crucial. For the church proclaims itself both supernaturally and naturally an organism; and as developmentalists know, all organisms organize, and the human organism organizes meaning.

The best known example of organizing meaning would be the Roman Catholic mass celebrated according to all of the norms of the church. Those norms make the celebrant responsible for guiding a coherent experience of worship. With narrators and music ministers, he is to bind together the separate and distinct actions of the liturgy—penance rite, scripture reading, homily, prayer of the faithful, offertory, canon, communion, and dismissal—into a whole. The norms are quite explicit on his freedom to do this, for they indicate nine places in the liturgy where the celebrant (or the lay commentator) should replace formulas with introductions or invitations that give meaning to this liturgy at this time for this gathering of the faithful: the opening remark, the introduction to the act of penance, the preparation to hear the readings, the invitation to the prayer of the faithful, the call to the Orate Fratres, the introduction to the Our Father, the invitations to share the sign of peace and to come receive communion, and the final remark before the blessing and sending.

The celebrant ought *not* begin mass with a simple "The Lord be with you" on Thanksgiving Day, or "Before we begin this holy action" when performing a wedding. Starting with his opening remark (or with the remark made by a commentator), he must weave together the reason that this group of faithful are celebrating this particular liturgy, and how the readings speak to the concrete situation of the place and time. This weaving must continue throughout the liturgy. He or the lay commentator should focus the people's attention so that they hear these precise readings and relate them to what is going on that day in the liturgy or in the world at large. Thus, to give an instance, the four alternative sentences given to introduce the Orate Fratres and the Our Father are not *ne varietur,* invariable texts; they are *models.* And as priests and commentators learn how to weave the new spiritual theology into these remarks and invitations, they are giving coherent meaning to the liturgical action.

The mass is hardly the only event where this must happen, and it is not. Ministers are weaving meaning into all the church's religious actions by drawing on the new spiritual theology. A deacon performing a wedding announces that the community has gathered to celebrate the marriages of two couples, faithful through the years, and to witness the wedding of their children, who learned love and marriage from their parents. But ministers are doing the same even in actions that are fundamentally civil. A group of therapists who meet to discuss their work begin with prayer. An organization of ecologists choose the dove as their symbol, consciously invoking the Holy Spirit as source of their efforts to save the planet. A therapist calls her office "Trinity Center." In this way, current ministry is called on to give Christian *meaning* to the significant passages, events, and even the everyday happenings of disciples' lives. The meaning cannot be only tags from scripture; instruction in scripture may prepare Christians for life in some Protestant communions, but it will not be adequate for life in the Catholic Church, where the experience of God hums in every sacramental and paraliturgical action.

In fact, the meaning that ministry is now organizing in the Catholic form of life functions at a fairly sophisticated level—no surprise in an extraordinarily well-educated church. The level can reasonably be called a new spiritual theology, as I have said. A generation ago, those who ministered were finding meaning in European writing, particularly writing deeply colored by neoscholasticism. The church possessed a viable *old* spiritual theology. By the beginning of the twentieth century, that spirituality was basically a complete self-donation to the Truth, and the theology that came with it consisted in doctrine, particularly dogmata. It was made available and usable by authors like Dom Verner More, Josef Pieper, Edward Leen.

Ministers, who were then parish and religious priests and the religious women who created the Catholic school system, proclaimed the real presence, the power *ex opere operato* of the sacraments, the urgency of God's will, the incessant activity of divine providence, the compassionate love of the Sacred Heart. They promoted purity of conscience by censuring bad behaviors that were current in culture and also relatively innocent behaviors that were nonetheless contrary to Catholic identity. Adolescents tended to get stuck in sexual contrariety, it is true; but we take the prejudiced opinion of the church's enemies if we imagine that the nuns and priests were not effective proclaimers of a theology of married and family life, ambitious human development, and the tender care of orphans and the sick. They were effectively handing on learning and culture and simultaneously inculturating Catholicism into American culture.

For about a generation now, not only priests and religious, but also lay American Catholics have been helping a North American Catholic spiritual theology emerge. They have needed it in order to find meaning in the American experience. They deal in this theology with revelation as a whole, but (as in every other age) they have been emphasizing certain parts of it. The new spiritual theology, for instance, does not say a great deal about the processions of the Persons, or about sanctifying grace as such, or about Jesus' death as condign restitution for sin.

What does the new theology address? Overall, it addresses *experience* of God in Christ. The turn to experience as an acknowledged source of theology is a peculiar American contribution. So this new spiritual theology addresses all of the major Christian life experiences, particularly creation, sinfulness, church (including ministry), and knowing Christ. In fact, one of its characteristics is the direct address to real-life experiences, making them the starting point for theological reflection. Shelves are full of reflective books on the experience of conversion and of each sacrament, on the experience of growth in grace, and so on. And—what could be more American?—these same shelves groan under handbooks, guidebooks, and exercise books, the best of which offer extraordinary amounts of scriptural exegesis and hermeneutics, doctrinal explanation, and guides into prayer.

And what about the substance of this theology? It has begun to redress the church's lack of an adequate theology of creation, to begin with. It has become ordinary by now—just a century after the Roman condemnation of the first book (American) reconciling revelation and evolution—to find a theology of ongoing creation informing every kind of theology: Christian anthropology, ecclesiology, ecological theology, spiritual theology. Studies on the stages of human growth and maturation and on gender differences include the asymmetrical relationship between the infinite Creator and the self-realizing creature. At the same time, essays on Christian marriage and on consecrated celibacy have begun to take full account of sin: the sin we do, sin in us, and the structures of sin in the world. Notably, authors are now ordinarily recognizing that *the structures of sin* inhere in human relations, both intimate and distant. The new spiritual theology was challenged by the Fatherhood of God, and has had to grow through an appropriate relationship with the God who chose not to be the Force or the Great Watchmaker, but Father and Mother as well.

Emerging more recently is the profound meaning of living in and through Jesus Christ. This began with the somewhat astonished recognition that Jesus of Nazareth rose again with his wounds still visible. The Holy One had chosen to come into broken human life, to embrace all that it means of growth and error and failure. Christ's inbreaking has transmuted the meaning of "being accepted by God." And the truth that the church lives both Good Friday and Easter Sunday has allowed new spiritual theologians to begin to see the enormous significance of the Holy One's coming into human flesh in order to fail. The new spiritual theology has a good deal to say about human failure and its redemption through the sinless human failure of Christ.

The Challenge to Ministers of the Middle Millions

These few descriptive points from the emerging new spiritual theology may sound like the substance only of homilies. But in the current American Church the theology reaches far beyond that. It is being folded into the instruction of parents preparing infants for baptism. It is seriously presented in booklets for marriage preparation. It is urged as important to marriage counseling. It makes the substrate of ministry to the sick and, particularly, the dying. It is (often tenderly) woven into the counseling of homosexuals. It is the burden of the sharing by religious and lay men and women who guide others through at-home retreats or conduct groups of "scripture sharing." This spiritual theology appears in texts prepared for every kind of paraliturgical act (for example, burials, blessing of homes).

The recreation of a form of Catholic life and the emergence of a new spiritual theology poses a double challenge to those who minister to the middle millions. As must be clear, it poses the challenge of recognizing religion as spirituality, and of revitalizing religion as the locus for the lifelong experience of God. Hence, it summons to *metanoia,* to conversion. That is, each minister must take responsibility for herself or himself in this realm of human experience, the religious. Probably many ministers will have to let go of a commitment to spreading spirituality, to inviting all whom they serve to the prolonged direct experience of God in spiritual exercises. Many will have to decide to find out what religion has been in their lives, and what it is currently; they will have to feel the power of the elucidations of sacraments, of the experience of conversion, of works of piety that enjoy the confirmation of centuries of use (the rosary, for instance).

In brief, those who minister to the middle millions will need to examine their culture-bound attitudes toward religion, toward creed, code, and cult as the lifelong experience of God. Then they will have to let themselves recognize the thirst—a needy desiring—for religion felt by the middle millions, and help to quench it.

A final word about those who profess ministry, who accept a call in the church to minister. Professional ministers are not adequately equipped to help the middle millions who do not have a conscious relationship with God their Creator and Lord. They can give only scanty help unless they enjoy and honor the asymmetrical relationship with the One who is at every moment Creator. More, those who minister to the middle millions need to acknowledge their personal experience of sin in all three of its aspects—the sin I do, sin in me, and the structures of sin—perhaps particularly of the second, which nourishes the roots of Christian humility. For in the world today, the problem about moral guilt is a problem with hope. We have to hope that the sin we suffer from—compulsions and addictions as sin in me—has been and is being redeemed.

Above all else, however, those who minister to the middle millions serve them well if all they do is radiate a hope-filled knowledge of the story of Jesus the Lord. For his penetration into human nature is very far from skin deep. He knows our hearts, which have in their turn been deeply touched by the *mysterium iniquitatis* due to the failure of human parenting, civil arrangements, friendships, and marriage. New theologians are reaching into the gospel for the *story* of Jesus of Nazareth. For about half a century, it has lain buried in its hermeneutical setting, like the face of an icon sunk into its encrustment of gold and jewels. Many writers of the new spirituality are leading the church back to that inspired story of Jesus of Nazareth. The millions in the middle follow that lead when it relates the experience of Jesus and their own experiences. Today, many new spiritual theologians are insisting, meaning comes with story, both each one's and the Savior's. For in the end, the new spiritual theology claims, ministry begins with the story of the minister's life in Christ.

37. Discipleship

New Testament Discipleship

We use the word *disciple* in our common everyday speech to refer to someone who apprentices himself or herself directly to either a master teacher or to that teacher's "doctrine" in order to learn a body of knowledge and acquire certain skills so that the disciple may develop a particular way of living with that knowledge and a certain way of doing things. Thus, we speak of someone who is a disciple of Freud or Jung or a disciple of the Chicago School of Economics and so on. In these instances we imply that the disciples have not only mastered a corpus of learning but have also accepted a certain way of handling that learning, putting it into practice, and using the various master skills learned to teach or analyze or research according to the "school" founded or inspired by the master.

That way of understanding the disciple has an ancient lineage. Greek philosophers had disciples (which developed into "schools" of philosophy), as did the learned rabbis who accepted students to study Torah and to live according to rabbinical traditions. In fact, both the Hebrew and the Greek word that translates into *disciple* means a "learner." Thus, when the New Testament writers used the term *disciple* or *disciples* (and they used a variation of the word about 250 times), there was a history behind the usage that derived both from profane Greek and the Jewish tradition. In both the Hebrew and Greek philosophical traditions, to become a disciple involved, beyond intellectual competency, entering into what Pierre Hadot has called "a way of life."

In the New Testament, the word *disciple* is used to describe not only the followers of Jesus but also the followers of the pharisees, the followers of John the Baptist, and in the Acts of the Apostles, it becomes a term that now seems to be a synonym for Christians. It was from the body of the disciples (carefully distinguished from the Twelve) that the first deacons were chosen (see Acts 6:17).

We should also note in passing that the terms *apostles* and *the Twelve* had quite precise meanings in the New Testament. While the apostles and the Twelve were surely disciples of Jesus, it is not correct to think that the term *disciple* is restricted to either group exclusively or even the seventy (a symbolic number used by the evangelist?) followers of Jesus alluded to in the New Testament. There were surely gradations of discipleship in the New Testament, but we will use the term broadly to mean a follower of Jesus and his teachings. We do not know, for example, how many of those in the crowd actually followed Jesus or identified with him after they heard his enunciation of the beatitudes, just as we do not know who the women were who followed him on his preaching journeys or wept as he passed by on his way to Calvary.

Disciples were expected to identify closely with their master teacher. Discipleship involves a good deal more than simply "taking a class" or "being an apprentice." Even a cursory reading of the Gospels (and especially the Gospel of Mark which is the preeminent Gospel of discipleship) gives us a picture of how close the discipleship culture was. The disciples of Jesus, both men and women, learned not only from his words and parables, but by journeying with him across Galilee and Judea, watching him debate, giving witness to his power to heal and cure, being at table with him in a variety of settings and with a spectrum of peoples, following his ascetic demands of living poorly, watching both his moments of triumph and his terrible final days in Jerusalem. It is not surprising, then, that the noun *disciple* (Greek: *mathetes*) occurs about seventy times in tandem with some variation of the verb "to follow."

Mark's Gospel, written most likely for a community of believers who knew the cost of discipleship during a time of persecution, makes it abundantly clear that being a disciple of Jesus was not to be reduced to simply learning from a master teacher. Mark is not writing about discipleship as something that happened in the past; the construction of his Gospel was for the benefit of the actual conditions under which his community was living. Mark, in short, told the story of Jesus as an aid or a model for those who had to live as disciples at a time of persecution.

Discipleship was a way of life and not a matter of simple pedagogy. This "Way" (a key word in Mark) was, after all, the way of the cross (8:34). Those who took up this Way had to be people of prayer and fasting (9:23) who were to accept a low status (9:33–36), who must be ready to experience a loss of wealth (10:23–31) and live without the consolation of seeking back that wealth or higher social status (10:35–37; 42–44). The true follower of the Way—the true disciple—must be ready to accept those who are not of the same background (9:42–45). This discipleship requires the acceptance and love of children (10:17–20).

When one reads Mark and the other gospel writers we see subtle differences in their approach to matters (in Mark, for instance, Jesus is a teacher, but in Matthew Jesus does not use the term *teacher* or *rabbi* easily of himself) but certain things become very clear about discipleship. First of all, one does not "enroll" in the school of Jesus; one is called: Discipleship is a grace to which people must respond. This discipleship demands a radical conversion of life by which disciples, for example, in John, drop their nets at the demand to "come." Furthermore, disciples do not only learn, they share in the ministry as they are sent out in the name of Jesus to heal, exorcise the demoniacs, preach the good news, and succor the poor. This "extension" of the ministry of Jesus calls for a spirit of sacrificial love by which people give up goods, leave families, compromise reputations, follow Jesus to the death, and so on. In short, discipleship demands that one take seriously the "hard" sayings of Jesus.

This discipleship goes by various names. As we have seen, it is often called "the Way," which was one of the earliest names given to the Jesus movement already attested to in the Acts of the Apostles. Hence, disciples are followers of the Way. It is interesting that in Mark's Gospel the section on discipleship is framed by two miracle stories involving the restoration of sight. The section begins as Jesus leaves Galilee when, in the town of Bethsaida, he heals a blind man (8:22–26) and ends in Jericho where Jesus heals Bartimaeus (10:46–52). Notice in that latter story that in the beginning Bartimaeus sits by the road (the Greek says, literally, "by the way"). At the end of the story after he cries out, "Master, that I may see!" Jesus heals him, and Mark concludes "and immediately he received his sight and followed him on the way."

The way, of course, was the road from Jericho to Jerusalem where the great events of the passion would take place. It is not accidental that he first receives his sight and then follows on the way. He has experienced an enlightenment (the early church referred to baptism as *photismos*—the gaining of light), which permitted him to follow Jesus to his death and resurrection. What Mark alludes to here is very much like Paul's repeated insistence that those who believe in Jesus (Paul does not use the word *disciple* as such; he has his own elaborate vocabulary to describe those who believe in Jesus) enter into his "Paschal Mystery"—that is, his passion, death, and resurrection to new life.

Now, it is legitimate to note that between the time, say, of Mark's Gospel and our lives today there is a vast historical chasm. Mark wrote to a persecuted community; most of us do not live in such parlous circumstances even though in the twentieth century many fellow Christians did live, in fact, under the veil of persecution. Thus, the question arises: To what degree and in what fashion do we participate in the discipleship of Jesus Christ? The response to that question demands a number of observations.

In the first place, it is clear that the New Testament does not point to the sayings or deeds of Jesus as the primary focus of discipleship. Jesus said, "I am the way…" and "Come, follow me." The disciple of Jesus follows the person, and in following the person the teachings and deeds make sense. In that sense, at least, we must somehow learn the secret of modeling Jesus. Paul's letters are filled with these motifs of modeling, such as his insistence that the mystery of Christ can be replicated, by which believers "die" with Christ and then "rise" with him as well as in the affirmation that we should know nothing but Christ and him crucified. For Paul it was what Jesus did (that is, died for our sins) and how he serves as the "firstborn" of many who will be reborn into a new life that gives us the possibility of crying out to God "Abba!" (Gal 4:4–6). It is also worthwhile noting that in that passage in Galatians one already sees a language of trinity. Through the spirit one can cry out "Abba!" because of Jesus. Spirituality, after all, is living in the spirit, as the word *spirituality* itself implies.

Second, those who are disciples learn to act, after the fashion of Jesus, in ways that seem contrary to the logic of common experience but which, paradoxically, give us a new and fuller life. Thus, the disciple is commanded to turn the other cheek, to give the clothes off her back for the poor, to give all possessions up for the sake of the gospel, to return good for evil, to forgive even "seventy times seven," to avoid making himself a stumbling block (Greek *skandalon*—a scandal) for the weak, and so on. These "hard" sayings may not be literally imitable (although some have tried), but they do serve as a measure against which we test whether or not we approximate the demands of the gospel. These demands recorded in the gospel invite us, in other words, to reach toward a greater configuration with the example Jesus set.

It is worthwhile remembering that the reason the gospel can make these demands is that they have first been acted out by Jesus himself. Jesus calls for some kind of simplicity of life because he is the one who has, in his words, no place to lay his head. He can demand forgiveness because he forgave those who did not stand by him and who betrayed him. He can ask us to shoulder a cross because he first carried it to Golgotha. In other words, there is a symmetry between what is demanded and what has been actually done.

How, in fact, do we learn of this Jesus and what he teaches? The New Testament says that we can experience the saving life and message through two means, which are closely tied together. First, we encounter Jesus in the community that has invoked his words and has told his story since his own day. In other words, when we gather in the community that we call "the church" we are there to re-hear the same message that has been preached from the beginning. This is the most authentic meaning of the word *tradition*—the handing down, within the community, of the message of Jesus and the presence of Jesus, who is with us until the end of time.

Second, we experience Jesus through what the New Testament calls "the breaking of the bread"—that sacrificial meal by which we reenact, re-present, and renew (all of these words are crucial) the presence of Jesus among us. In the words of Luke speaking of the disciples on the road to Emmaus: "They recognized him in the breaking of the bread."

The Ways of Discipleship

What we have said in the first part of this discussion sounds rather ideal-ized and perhaps even a little abstract. Most of us do not consciously spend our time explicitly pondering how we can be configured to Christ and perhaps only, under the impulse of God's spirit, do we experience the reality of Christ in word and sacrament. About this we should not fret. After all, as the Second Vatican Council points out, using an old image in the church, we are pilgrims on the way. We are not there yet. We walk a path that is rocky at times and tir-ing. In fact, most people who enter the way of discipleship exercise that way in small incremental ways. We learn in our families and in our communities to forgive, not to discriminate, to pray, to be thankful, to succor the needs of others. We may do that with greater or lesser generosity and discipline. The important point, however, is that every act of this sort is an incremental moment leading us in the way of discipleship. This way of discipleship is a call for both the individual and for the church.

Many people come to a point in their lives when they receive the impulse of the spirit to make a radical choice to be more of a disciple. Under such an inspiration they begin to "perform" as disciples by incarnating the gospel message in concrete ways. In the history of the Christian tradition, people have learned different ways of doing this. When they teach "their" way to others, either by example or formal teaching, they provide a gift to the Christian community that then becomes available for others.

These "gifts" are often called "schools of spirituality," since each had its own emphasis, pedagogy of prayer and action, and so on. The Franciscan "gift" emphasizes poverty, while the Carmelite emphasis is on contemplation and the Ignatian gift is characterized by turning contemplation into action. These various "gifts" and graces of discipleship offer models and hints by which people develop more deeply their vocations as disciples.

Since no single school defines everything about discipleship nor can any school claim that it is the only way, it follows that every period in the life of the church can look for or propose a new way of living the gospel and a new way of discipleship. It is crucial to keep in mind that the church is not a museum enshrining in amber certain forms of discipleship, but a living tradi-tion in which new forms arise to meet the exigencies of the day.

Discipleship and the Kingdom

It is very clear that the most fundamental thing Jesus did in his public life was to preach the "kingdom of God." This kingdom, already present but not fully realized, was behind his words, his prayer, his struggles against evil, and his miracles. It is also crucial to understand that in the formation of his followers he expected them also to build up the kingdom until he would return.

Any close reading of the gospels (especially the synoptic gospels) makes it clear that Jesus's idea of the kingdom was not some airy abstraction. He envisioned a future that would be both a critique of the present structures of the world and a community where the presence of God would render justice, amity, and love among peoples. That kingdom did not arrive in the time of Jesus, and it certainly is not realized now, but it is a kingdom, already announced as coming, toward which every disciple labors.

What are the characteristics of that kingdom? Recent writers have listed, in varying formulations, contrasts between the values of the world and the values of the kingdom. We can slightly amend those contrasts, spelled out in New Testament scholarship in many places, in order for us to get some sense of the radical character of the kingdom as it is understood and preached by Jesus. Human kingdoms emphasize power from on high, domination, the subjugation of social classes based on a rigid hierarchy. Power rests only in a sacred palace or temple accessible only to an elite. By contrast, the kingdom that Jesus preached validates itself not by power but by service. The king gives his life for his people and relationships are based on equity and love. Everyone is called to this kingdom, and those who are judged by the world to be at the margins of society will have a prominent place in the kingdom of God. In other words, the coming kingdom or reign of God stands as a countercultural critique of the historical and political realities as we actually find them in culture.

Obviously, such a kingdom does not exist in fact. It is a kingdom to be realized. If it is to be realized it will be so only if those who profess to be disciples of the One proclaim it. In other words, the disciple commits himself not only to the person and teaching of Jesus but to his vision of what will be yet to come. The Catholic emphasis on social justice, the alleviation of poverty, the rights of the poor and marginalized, then, derives not from some sentimental "social gospel" but from a deep insight into the kind of discipleship demanded by the Jesus who preached the kingdom of God, promised by the prophets, and begun through the public ministry of Jesus himself.

Discipleship, when seen in the light of Jesus's preaching of the kingdom, signifies learning from the person and teaching of Jesus a number of things about life in society. These "things" can be expressed either negatively or positively. To be a disciple of the preacher of the kingdom means not to abuse power, not to exploit others, to look for justice and the ways of justice, to love rather than hate. In positive terms it means to forget the self, to embrace the cross, to work for the kingdom, and so on.

These negative and positive duties are not meant to be abstract and generalized acts of piety. One must be a disciple in the concrete, according to one's position in life and given one's obligations. The disciple of Jesus begins where he or she is. The parent builds the kingdom first in his or her family. The citizen does the same for the community. Everyone has a role in the building up of the life of the church. If that church is truly *catholic* it further obligates us to think of the whole of the world and not just our little corner of it.

The Disciple's Profile

In a recent book on discipleship, moral theologian Timothy O'Connell lists five terms that are essential for the disciple of Jesus.

First, discipleship, of its very nature, demands a relationship. For the Christian, this relationship involves the trinitarian life by which we are related to God through the following of Jesus in the spirit. All relationship, understood in Christian terms, must have reference to the relational character of the triune God professed in the creeds and invoked in the liturgy of the church.

Second, this relationship involves understanding, since, as O'Connell says, nobody lives in a relationship involving the unknown. This understanding is not merely a theoretical assent to teaching but a grasp of who it is we follow in relationship and why. In concrete terms, this means that when we follow Jesus Christ the next step is to understand who he is and for what he stands.

Third, following on relationship is a commitment to be faithful, loving, and personal. Discipleship is not an on-and-off again exercise but a steady way of being and acting.

Fourth, this commitment in relationship means a certain fidelity, so that my behavior is consistent with what I affirm.

Finally, since we are by nature social beings, we affirm our discipleship in the community of like-minded individuals who are not only our companions but who sustain us in our commitments. Thus, discipleship is not only the following of Jesus but the following of Jesus in community.

In sum, the five key terms that profile the disciple, according to O'Connell, are relationship, understanding, commitment, behavior, and affiliation. Their sum is not simply the discrete aspects of a person but the holistic description of who and what a disciple is. Being a disciple is a habitual way of being in the world. The person who is the true disciple will relate to others, the self and God, understand, be committed, behave, and exist in communion in tandem with the mind of Jesus and his person. Obviously, not everyone does that to a level of perfection, but the true disciple is the one whose instincts are those of Christ.

Discipleship and Community

In this profile we put some emphasis on "affiliation." We need to expand that notion a bit by asking this simple question: How does discipleship relate to being a member of the church? One way of answering that is to say that it is the committed community of disciples who make up the church, for, after all, what is the church but that organic body of believers who to varying degrees gather together to affirm their faith and celebrate it in liturgy and service?

We can specify that point further. When one is "in the church," it is there that one hears the story of Jesus and celebrates that story by performing what the Word of God instructs us. This hearing does not happen only in the moment of our own life when we are "in church" at, say, the Sunday liturgy. The church celebrates in present time, to be sure, but it is also the church of memory, which remembers those who have gone before us in the faith. As the Epistle of the Hebrews has it, we form a part of the "cloud of witnesses." The Christian community remembers that tradition of witness by remembering its saints, gatherings its writings, art works, music, and stories to celebrate them. More important, this act of memory allows us, in the present age, to recall, remember, and reenact those who found ways of discipleship in the past.

From the handing down of tradition we have the opportunity to study and emulate the ways people have been disciples in the past while learning, through their imperfections, what is to be deemphasized or to be discarded. The organic growth of forms of piety, spiritualities, sacred gestures, works of art, theologies, and so on provide us with resources for growth. A warning about errors, and the hope that we can advance in our own path of Christian growth, are all aspects of describing the ways in which disciples remain faithful to their commitment.

There is a lamentable temptation to think of the term *Catholic Church* as if it were a vast and complicated institution with general headquarters in Rome and our churches as the branch offices. That is to misunderstand what *Catholicism* means. *The Catechism of the Catholic Church* notes three characteristics of catholicity. In a Christian community where the full gospel is preached, the full range of the sacramental life is celebrated, and the head of that community (the bishop) is in communion with all other bishops and the bishop of Rome (the pope), that community is fully Catholic.

What that description in the *Catechism* means concretely is this: The Catholic Church is both local and universal. The Catholic Church is local when the three criteria are present (hence Chicago, Paris, London, Nairobi are fully Catholic churches) and that locality is somehow linked in an organic fashion to the whole church, whose center is the See of Rome. That tension between local and universal has implications for the exercise and pursuit of Christian discipleship. In practice it means something like this: A disciple lives and exercises her Christian life in a specific place, time, and circumstance, but that disciple lacks something if she does not keep the whole church in mind. Stated another way: The true disciple of Jesus lives and works in a specific place and time but his life cannot be fully that of a disciple if he is not conscious of belonging to a larger community that is both contemporaneous and going back into time. The phrase "Communion of the Saints" could easily be changed into the "Communion of the Christian Disciples." Such a translation is nothing more than an enlargement of Luke's phrase "community of disciples" described in Acts 6:2.

When we reflect on the relationship of discipleship and community, it might be well to remember the position of the distinguished ecclesiologist Avery Dulles, S.J., who has argued over the past few decades that the best "model" for the church itself is the model of the church of discipleship. Hence, Dulles not only views the individual follower of Jesus as simply belonging to the church but sees the church itself, in all of its strata, as ideally being one of discipleship. If that discipleship model of the church were taken seriously it would provide a prophetic edge to the self-questioning of the church. Does the papal office see itself reflecting a model of discipleship? Are the various ministries within the church community (teachers, chaplains, parish priests, religious) judging their ministries according to the concept of Christian discipleship?

Discipleship and the Lived Life

The tradition of the church teaches that people have attempted to live a life of discipleship in quite different ways. Those forms of discipleship, which became conspicuous in Christian history, frequently became so because they were a response to some moment in the culture that called forth a response. What was true in the past is certainly true in our own time. In its pastoral *Constitution on the Church in the Modern World (Gaudium et Spes)*, the assembled bishops spoke directly of the relationship of the Christian life in terms of the exigent demands of the present:

> The People of God labors to decipher authentic signs of God's presence and purpose in the happenings, needs, and desires in which this people has a part along with others in our age. For faith throws a new light on everything, manifests God's design, for the total vocation of people, and thus directs the mind to solutions which are fully human. (*Gaudium et Spes,* no. 11)

A primary thrust of contemporary church teaching has been to orient Christians, in their various states of life and diverse occupations, to take on the task of understanding the moment in which they live and to react to that specific condition as true Christian believers. The spiritual roots that make it possible to detect the "signs of the times" and react to them in a Christian manner, of course, depends on the core experience of being faithful to the Word of God, receiving Christ into oneself, especially in the eucharist, and becoming identified with and a participant of the believing community. Again, it is a dialectical experience of being nourished by the community in order to go out from that community to be a presence in and a participant of that larger human family.

The late Karl Rahner once remarked, famously, that the Christian of the future would be a mystic or would not be Christian at all. Rahner, viewing the rapid secularization of European culture, most likely meant that Christians in the future would be scattered pockets of believers (which he once called the "church of the diaspora") who had deep experiences of God, or they simply would not survive the pressures of an indifferent society. It is true that in some areas of the world, believers at great personal cost remained as true disciples of Christ even when the society in which they lived was actively hostile to them and what they stood for. That is the situation of some Christians today in various parts of the world.

In more tolerant societies, like those of North America and Western Europe, it is not the hostility that a disciple experiences but indifference or polite dismissal. Discipleship is not attacked in such societies by hostile authorities, but it is threatened by the need to conform, by the allure of a materialistic culture, or by the distractions of an affluent society. True discipleship in such societies demands the grace to discern and resist the subtle traps of complacency or passive acquiescence to majority opinion or fashion. To live in such a manner is to avoid what the late Dietrich Bonhoeffer (the author of the classic work *The Cost of Discipleship)* called "cheap grace." Such discipleship need not be dramatic or even conspicuously explicit. Discipleship is, at its most basic, a centered conviction that it is crucial to love self, family, neighborhood, and the larger world by resisting violence, hatred, exploitation, and so on while simultaneously developing a greater awareness of the presence of God in the world, among people, in our own heart. This growth in Christian life and resistance to evil (the classical conversion and aversion of the theological tradition) works itself out in the specific place and time in which we find ourselves, so that we never fall prey to a kind of spiritual abstractionism which makes us self-absorbed and, as a consequence, indifferent to the world in which we live.

Pastoral ministry, of course, is discipleship almost by definition. To be a disciple, then, involves making explicit what is implicit in the term. In the concrete, this discipleship would involve the link between prayer and ministry such that our work never becomes detached from the deep life of faith. Such discipleship further means to work with fidelity and constancy at the tasks at hand, because, as the Christian spiritual tradition teaches so eloquently, sanctity arises from doing the ordinary in an extraordinary fashion. Finally, one will be a true disciple only to the degree that one rests in the conviction that what is done has purpose and meaning in building up the reign of God. Everything that is done to advance the reign of God according to gospel values, no matter who does it, John Paul said in *Redemptoris Missio,* is doing work under the impetus of the Holy Spirit. It is that simple conviction that brings together into a whole discipleship, ministry, and spirituality itself.

Selected References and Suggested Reading

Bonhoeffer, Dietrich. *The Cost of Discipleship*. New York: MacMillan, 1959.

Cunningham, Lawrence (with Keith Egan). *Christian Spirituality: Themes from the Tradition*. Mahwah, N.J.: Paulist, 1996.

Hadot, Pierre. *Philosophy as a Way of Life*. Chicago: University of Chicago Press, 1995.

O'Connell, Timothy. *Making Disciples*. New York: Crossroad, 1998.

Segovia, Fernando. *Discipleship in the New Testament*. Philadelphia: Fortress, 1985.

Raymond Studzinski

38. Reading and Ministry: Applying *Lectio Divina* Principles in a Ministerial Context

Ministry demands time, even the personal time those in ministry should spend on important things like reading. Church ministers know, of course, that they should read the scriptures and theological and pastoral works to enhance and fuel their work and nurture their spiritual lives. But often they are lucky to skim the newspaper and take a quick look at the scriptural readings of the day. There is just no time, or not enough time, for those heavily involved in the service of God's people to read. So reading, spiritual reading, serious reading, gets sacrificed for the sake of the ministry.

But perhaps the very notion of what reading is and how to approach it is something that needs to be reconsidered in our digital age. Maybe the solution to a common dilemma in ministry is not just creating more space and time for reading but re-educating ourselves about what reading is and what we need to read. Could ministry itself be a form of reading? Interestingly, the 1983 Code of Canon Law (Can. 276.2) suggests that the priest's primary means of achieving holiness is the pastoral ministry itself; it mentions spiritual exercises like reading only afterward. Could the very practice of pastoral ministry be a source of spiritual input that nourishes the minister in a way similar to that of reading the scriptures? Is there a way of "reading" pastoral experience that bring us into contact with the sacred much as the reading of the scriptures does? Such questions are the focus of this essay. However, in a period when computer literacy is more and more the mark of the educated, maybe we also need to ask if have we lost the ancient ability to "read" to nourish the soul. Have we lost the ability to read the scriptures, let alone anything else, in such a way that we gain spiritual meaning and direction for our lives? If we have, how can we learn to read again in the fuller, more classical sense?

The Problem of Spiritual Illiteracy

Indeed, what impedes some on the road to spiritual growth, even some of those engaged in church ministries, is precisely their inability to read spiritually, that is, to read in such a way that they are spiritually challenged and not just given information. Despite great strides in reducing illiteracy on many levels, early twenty-first-century society faces the problem of spiritual illiteracy. The ability to read in such a way as to draw out spiritual meaning is strangely wanting. This illiteracy problem is compounded by the emergence of new types of reading (computer literacy) precisely as old ways of reading seem to be slipping away. Are there "schools" where such reading can be mastered? Commentators who worry about the loss of classic reading skills in an age dominated by the screen rather than the book repeatedly ask this question. The apparent threat to established culture by the seemingly continuous revolutions in technology underscores the need for such schools.

George Steiner has lamented the end of the "age of the book" and has dreamed of "houses of reading" where the venerable art of reading could be learned again in an atmosphere of silence and with appropriate guidance and companionship similar to what monasteries have provided for centuries.[1] As the screen has eclipsed the book, people have become spectators, passive observers of what the entertainment culture brings before them. Their sense of themselves and what they need is shaped by the media. Some, breaking out of such stifling passivity, have turned to self-help movements and literature, but with negligible results. What about the classic approaches to spiritual development such as reading?

Steiner has argued that the classic way of reading put people in touch with what he calls "real presence," the very energy of life, that which gives fullness to life and banishes emptiness.[2] That way of reading has been threatened not only by technological advances but also by literary theories such as deconstruction and post-structuralism and by psychoanalysis, which question the relationship between words and meaning, between words and world. As Steiner indicates, the covenant once established between word and world has been broken; the word is in crisis.[3] People are skeptical of what words mean, and of what the world means. To read in the ancient way is not only to decipher the meaning signified by the alphabetic characters but also to read the world as pregnant with meaning. It is to read in such a way that one connects with a presence that is the ultimate source of meaning and an unspoken answer to human questions.

Testimony to the ability to read in this way comes from unexpected sources. The teen David Kern in John Updike's short story, "Pigeon Feathers," learns to read in this fuller way in struggling with a question that plagues him, the reality of the afterlife. He wonders what, if anything, awaits him after death.

Brought up as a Christian, he turns to his minister at a Sunday school class. However, the minister's vapid answer—comparing the afterlife to Abraham Lincoln's goodness living on after him—angers David and even seems to betray Christianity. He looks to his parents for an answer, but there confronts a passionless view of life and ineffectual witness to faith. He hungers and aches for more. One day, though, he finds the answer in the feathers of some dead pigeons he is burying. He, in effect, "reads" pigeon feathers and gets his answer.

> He lost himself in the geometrical tides as the feathers now broadened and stiffened to make an edge for flight, now softened and constricted to cup warmth around the mute flesh. And across the surface of the infinitely adjusted yet somehow effortless mechanics of the feathers played idle designs of color, no two alike, designs executed, it seemed, in a controlled rapture, with a joy that hung level in the air above and behind him.[4]

In "reading" these pigeon feathers David encounters the transcendent, the "real presence" that gives his life meaning and answers his longing.

In order to highlight the shifting attitudes toward what is read and how it is received by the reader, in this essay I describe different approaches to reading that have been developed in the course of history. If Steiner and others are correct, the retrieval of an ancient method of reading may contribute vitally to contemporary ministerial practice. In itself, awareness that there is more than one way to read may open eyes to new possibilities. With so much current emphasis put on reading for information, society may have lost sight of the *formation* that reading can provide. After the sketch of various approaches to reading, I map out more fully the approach to reading developed within the monastic context and called *lectio divina.* Finally I suggest how we can learn to "read" the situations encountered in ministry and life in a similar way.

Various Approaches to Reading

Most of us take reading for granted and seldom reflect on the activity and what it entails. Alberto Manguel in *A History of Reading* has observed, "Reading, almost as much as breathing, is our essential function."[5] It is by reading that we orient ourselves, make sense of ourselves and of our world. Reading, of course, has to do with more than deciphering letters on a page. Concerned parents read the faces of their children; farmers read the sky; and musicians read a musical score—to mention only a few of the many different acts of reading. Yet books are what people most often associate with the activity of reading, beginning very often with children's books still remembered decades later.

When people read, they are not functioning like a Xerox copier; they are doing more than capturing an image of a page in their minds. In fact, reading is an immensely complicated activity—the mechanics and process by which we read are still not completely understood. A number of pieces of the reader's past—for instance, personal experience, what has been read before—converge in a given act of reading. Thus, Manguel notes that reading is "a bewildering, labyrinthine, common and yet personal process of reconstruction."[6]

The practice of silent reading, which is the usual manner of reading today, did not become commonplace until the tenth century. Augustine (354–430) acknowledged Ambrose's (c. 339–397) ability to read silently while also admitting that he himself never did so.[7] Developments such as the increasing use of punctuation and spaces separating words promoted and facilitated the process of silent reading. With the ability to read silently came a new relationship between the reader and what was read. Words could be read more quickly, could be played with in the mind's eye in creative ways. This evolving relationship between reader and book, between reader and text is a crucial dimension of the unfolding history of reading and bears directly on the concern here with a way of reading spiritually. Changes in the mechanics of reading, for instance, whether one reads out loud or silently or reads from a book or a screen, are not without significance for this relationship.[8]

Ivan Illich has noted that the modern-day reader is more like a tourist or commuter who wants to get to a destination as quickly as possible rather than a pedestrian or pilgrim who more leisurely takes in everything along the way.[9] Readers of the past were not in such a hurry and stayed with what they were reading. Furthermore, we live in an age of rapid communication when hypertext and virtual reality are becoming common terminology and the whole notion of book and text are changing. Across the centuries people have had changing attitudes toward the book and the text.

Digital Text

In this digital age the person seated at the computer screen never reads the text itself but only a "virtual version" of the original that is stored in the computer's memory. Consequently, the text is more sharply differentiated from the object on which it appears, whether that be the pages of a book or the computer screen. In fact, for the computer devotee the book may come to be recognized itself as simply a machine for handling text, a piece of technology. As George P. Landow has observed, "We have already moved far enough beyond the book that we find ourselves, for the first time in centuries, able to see the book as unnatural, as a near-miraculous technological innovation and not as something intrinsically and inevitably human."[10] The cursor that appears on the computer screen represents in a way the user who now moves about in the midst of the text.[11] The qualities of the computer are now associated with text, so text is thought of in terms of flexibility, fluidity, and interactivity rather than the stability and authority associated with printed books.[12]

What is further forcing a reconsideration of the notions of text and reading is the existence today of *hypertext.* The term refers to electronic text linked to other texts, images, sounds, and so forth. Readers can move through the text and pursue whatever connections they care to explore. In some ways this diminishes the power of the author while increasing that of the reader, who is now free to follow his or her own interests. The reader can enter hypertext anywhere, can edit, delete, rearrange. Children are introduced to hypertext fairly early in their education via the World Wide Web, a simple hypertext system. The full implications of this form of text and reading for our understanding of self and our culture have yet to be determined.

The book may be increasingly seen as a very primitive piece of technology. And yet, precisely as computers are introducing a new type of literacy, these same digital wonders stimulate needs in the computer literate that these machines cannot satisfy. This plight has led Umberto Eco to remark, "In my periods of optimism I dream of a computer generation which, compelled to read a computer screen, gets acquainted with reading from a screen, but at a certain moment feels unsatisfied and looks for a different, more relaxed, and differently-committing form of reading."[13]

The Printed Book

With the arrival of the printed book, the text had become a stamp that could be imprinted on many pages and distributed broadly. The introduction of typography meant that the accuracy of texts was more assured and that texts could be indexed. Because of movable type and the relative ease of producing reliable copies, texts could be read by many more people. With the simultaneous emergence of a middle class in Western Europe, there were now the possibilities for what George Steiner has called "classical reading."[14] Such reading, in which the reader felt addressed by the text and answerable to it, required not only books but also space, time, and silence for reading, which only a class with some means would have.[15] To read in this way was to engage in an activity we might associate with the concentrated reading done in an academic context. This manner of reading has roots in both the scholastic age and the monastic period. With printing, books became more common possessions, and personal libraries appeared in the homes of the more advantaged.

If Ivan Illich's thesis articulated in his *In the Vineyard of the Text* is correct, the printed book represented a later phase in a larger epoch in which the text, whether on a scribal manuscript or on a printed page, had already acquired an importance in its own right.[16] The text as a record of thought could be considered independently of where it was recorded. This is taken so much for granted by us that we find it hard to imagine that there was a time when text did not have such independence, when it was inextricably linked to the book or the page. The emergence of certain writing techniques and their general adoption, which allowed for the autonomy of the text, marks the first phase of this "textual" epoch, which has the production of printed books as its second phase.

Scholastic Text

Ivan Illich places the emergence of the text from the page at around 1150, some three hundred years before moveable type was invented.[17] Manual techniques of scribes allowed for the text to be seen as an externalization of a logical thinking process where words were mirrors for concepts. Rather than words running together and text undivided into lines, paragraphs, and sections as had been the case in preceding centuries, the page was now optically arranged so the structure of the argument, the thinking, could be clearly seen. All this is so commonplace to us who have grown up in a textual age that we are largely unaware of how revolutionary some of these techniques were when first introduced. But with these twelfth-century innovations, the text could rise off the physical page and be visualized in the mind without the page. The text had acquired autonomy and did not need the page as it once did. In fact, what was written on the page could now be seen as simply a shadow of the text whose existence transcended the concrete page. The text became an object in its own right, in which thought is captured and presented.[18] The book was now a storehouse, a mine, a treasury where text was stored. Indeed, a couple of centuries before printing made it possible to refer to a page number for a particular passage, devices were developed so that the book could be used as a reference tool.[19] The book on which the text had been dependent now became itself a symbol for the text. In philosophical and theological books one found a thought process externalized, an ordered set of reasons carefully arranged on the page. The visual arrangement of the page made it easier to remember the text.

Parallel to and perhaps stimulating this liberation of the text from the page was a focus on the nature of universals in philosophy. The intellectual climate witnessed a movement away from preoccupation with the particular such as the concrete page to concern with the abstract, with universal ideas. Reading itself could be seen as an act of abstraction; the text represented a materialization of abstraction. Exegesis and hermeneutics were performed on the text that described the world and not on the world of concrete particulars to which the text referred. The text, the book, were pointers to the mind where ideas were lodged. In this way the text assumed hegemony and, according to Illich, reading, writing, speaking, and thinking—all became text-molded.[20] Even the mind was thought of as analogous to a text. And with the notion of the text established, the notion of a self that could be similarly scrutinized became possible.[21]

The dominance of text began roughly in the middle of the twelfth century. Text freed from the page of the handwritten book became in the middle of this long epoch the text reprinted in numerous books produced by the printing press. We are witnessing, it seems, the end of that era, as the screen replaces for many the book as a vehicle for the text. We see even more cogently how much our minds have been molded by text; it is difficult for us to conceive what pretextual reading and writing would have been like.

The Monastic Book and *Lectio Divina*

A time when texts did not hold the upper hand is the time when the page was, as Illich describes it, "a score for pious mumblers."[22] Monks read texts aloud when monasticism began in the West; they lived a life centered on such reading. They called it *lectio divina*, sacred reading. St. Benedict (c. 480–550) legislated for such reading in his Rule, the document that shaped monasticism in the West. For monks, the book did not serve as a storehouse for text but as a window on the world and God. The book was a vineyard or a garden where one could go to gather wisdom. Reading, because it was done aloud, had a social and physical dimension. Since a person mouthed the words, part of their impact came from hearing them. One, as it were, chewed and digested them so that they became part of oneself. A reader responded to how they felt to the mouth, to the ears, to the eyes. Reading involved the physical; it engaged the body. Illich informs us that monasteries are sometimes described as "dwelling places of mumblers and munchers,"[23] a sort of commentary on the biblical verse: "How sweet are your words to my taste, sweeter than honey to my mouth" (Ps 119:103).

Reading as a way of life in monasticism has its roots in the Judaic tradition. The books that the monk cherished above all were the canonical scriptures, the revealed word of God. Monks were exposed to that book of books in daily gatherings in choir to sing psalms and hear readings, as well as in times alone reading and meditating on the sacred scriptures. Through those scriptures, monks came to understand themselves and the world around them. The scriptural stories became *their* stories, *their* biographies.

Lectio soon took on the dimensions of a liturgical activity done in the presence of God and others. Because words on the page were first of all triggers for sounds rather than mirrors for concepts, reading created an auditory ambiance. Reading was not a mere individualistic activity; it had clear societal dimensions. To read was to engage in a public act. Before the word read aloud, all were equals. Whereas scholastic reading was in effect restricted to clerics, monastic *lectio* was open to all, an egalitarian activity. Furthermore, monastic reading was pursued for its own sake and not for utilitarian purposes, as reading often seemed to be with the later clerics in the scholastic period.[24] The scriptures provided the monastic reader not with logical arguments (which the scholastic reader would look for in texts) but with a sacred narrative that would lead the reader to wisdom.[25] Indeed, for monks reading was engaging in an act of incarnation, not an act of abstraction. Reading gave birth to the sense waiting to emerge from the page.[26] In this monastic approach to reading we find what George Steiner sees as reading in the classical mold. As he comments, "Where we read truly, where the experience is to be that of meaning, we do so as if the text (the piece of music, the work of art) *incarnates* (the notion is grounded in the sacramental) *a real presence of significant being.*"[27]

In this monastic age the book was a metaphor for reading, for discerning the divine meaning to be found in all things. For the monk saw nature itself as the primordial book waiting to be read. Augustine had drawn attention to the two books God had written—creation and redemption.[28] To read meant not only to comprehend written books but most especially the world, God's primal book. The symbolic, pointing by means of visible things to invisible things, dominated all their reality. Symbols were in the medieval mind not arbitrary, but rather, according to Gerhart Ladner, "were believed to represent objectively and to express faithfully various aspects of a universe that was perceived as widely and deeply meaningful."[29] The monastic reader acquired wisdom through appropriating the symbols. Through *lectio* the monastic reader found a place within the symbolic order much as computer literate readers find themselves with the cursor in the midst of the text. The sacred history chronicled in the sacred books became the reader's history, for the sacred narrative encompassed and gave meaning and coherence to the reader's life.

The practice of *lectio divina*, developed through the monastic centuries, could bring healing to those who had been blinded by sin. Reading would illuminate them, and they would come to see with the eyes of faith. Most especially, readers would come to see themselves as they really are before God. The sacred book would serve as a mirror in which they could see themselves truly.[30] As the scholastic period began to emerge, *lectio divina* distinguished itself more sharply from scholastic reading, which focused on intellectual questions and disputations. *Lectio* was from the outset a *studium,* a study of God's word and immersion in that word, which would transform the reader. Later centuries would reserve the notion of study for intellectual pursuits and separate such study from "spiritual reading," the term that gradually replaced the much fuller notion of *lectio divina.* Monastic reading was the first (and necessary) step in a process of transformation that would lead through meditation to contemplation. Through *lectio,* readers acquired a sense of the order of the world and their place within it. The words read spoke to monastic readers and gave meaning to their lives. Such reading was more formative than informative. This approach, developed centuries ago, could be the type of reading to heal some of our ills.

Appropriating *Lectio Divina* Today

Lectio divina is a tool that can be put at the service of fashioning a spirituality for contemporary ministers in the midst of their busy lives. How then do we appropriate this ancient method for ourselves? Fortunately a number of commentaries on the practice have appeared recently.[31] All would insist that *lectio* begins with the firm belief that God is speaking in many different ways and places and certainly in the sacred text that one reads. St. Benedict legislated that the night office is to begin with Psalm 94 (95), which has the verse, "If today you hear God's voice, harden not your hearts." If God is speaking, then one must read with an ear attuned to the message God is delivering. To read as the ancients did is to read with the sense that God is pointing our way to life in what you read. Christian life is a life of listening and requires that ears be attuned, but also that noise, both interior and exterior, be silenced. Quieting the inner noises, the inner voices of our preoccupations, desires, and feelings, is often the more challenging task. To engage in *lectio* is to concentrate, to focus oneself—one's understanding, will, heart, and imagination—in order to hear and recognize God's voice.

Garcia Colombás has written about *lectio* as "reading God."[32] Such a phrase suggests that reading has as its goal connecting with God. In contrast to so much contemporary reading, *lectio* is not done to gain useful information but rather to bring about a life-giving connection with a real presence. Of course, certain reading materials, such as the scriptures, are especially suited for making this connection. For Colombás, the Bible is *the* book for God-seekers. To really read it, one cannot read it passively but rather must read it as a musician reads a musical score, for the Bible is something to be performed, to be lived out.

Again, in contrast to modern reading practices, the point in *lectio* is not to finish whole books. *The Rule of Taizé* puts it simply: "Read little, but ponder over it."[33] *Lectio* is best pursued in the manner of reading poetry. One needs to savor the words, to read them slowly, to make associations. Like the ancients, we may find it helpful to read the words aloud. The vibrant realization that these words have to do with us and the love relationship that God has with us aids us in slowing us down to take in every nuance, much as we might linger over a recently rediscovered love letter. As with so many things in life, quality and not quantity are important in *lectio*.

Lectio should bring about a conversation. We should find ourselves engaged by what we read so that we are moved to respond in some way. The word that comes to us can be a demanding word. It can ask us to free ourselves from attachments. It addresses us often where we are most vulnerable. It is a "two-edged sword," but a sword that wounds in order to set us free. And it speaks to our own situation and invites our response. In the ancient desert tradition, disciples came to their spiritual elders seeking a life-giving word. The words of the elders and the words of the scriptures had such power in the disciples' lives that they are best spoken of as "word events." They truly were revelation and transformed the lives of eager disciples.[34] To read fully today is to enter into a conversation with life-giving texts that likewise can transform our way of looking at God, the world, and ourselves.

Humility is a prerequisite for reading that is spiritually transformative. Such humility means that one is always aware that what one reads has a plentitude of meaning within it. There is more to be gleaned from even the most familiar texts. Origen, Cassian, Augustine, and other early writers spoke of the spiritual senses of the scripture in addition to the literal sense. While the literal sense set forth fact and event, the spiritual senses dealt with the deeper meaning of the passage. Simply put, the text, beyond its literal message, also has something to say about the mystery of Christ realized among us, about the goal of life in our own union with God, and about an appropriate moral response to the God who speaks.[35] The scriptures have a wealth of meaning that is not exhausted. As we enter into conversation with the text, new meanings continue to unfold. One story from the desert tradition that beautifully underscores the importance of humility and openness before the Word of God tells of Abba Anthony testing some old men who had come to him by presenting them with a scriptural text and asking each one what it meant. "Each gave his opinion as he was able. But to each one [Abba Anthony] said, 'You have not understood it.' Last of all he said to Abba Joseph, 'How would you explain this saying?' and he replied, 'I do not know.' Then Abba Anthony said, 'Indeed, Abba Joseph has found the way, for he has said: I do not know.'"[36]

To appropriate *lectio divina* means to believe that God does indeed speak to us and to read slowly so that we connect with God who speaks. To do *lectio* implies that we allow God's word to address us in our unique situations and transform us as we open ourselves to its full meaning.

Lectio as a Larger Process

In the tradition, *lectio* was typically understood as part of a larger process that would bring the reader into a contemplative experience of God. When the practice of *lectio* was threatened by growing interest in scholastic reading, two works appeared that extolled the value of *lectio* and spoke of it as the initial part of a well-established spiritual program. The better known of these works is *The Ladder of Monks* by Guigo II (d. 1188).[37] But also of importance is the *Didascalicon* of Hugh of St. Victor (d. 1142).[38] Both works relate *lectio* to other practices that build on it: meditation, prayer, and contemplation

(Hugh adds *performance* as another phase, coming prior to contemplation). In Guigo's language these are the rungs of the ladder that leads to God. Both Hugh's and Guigo's works represent an attempt to unpack the fullness of the reading experience by expounding on the steps that for centuries have been seen as following upon it. Meditation originally was simply the repetition, the chewing over, the digesting of what had been read. Through the repetition of the words in the course of the day, people committed them to memory but also continued to savor them and draw nourishment from them. Through this sort of exercise the Bible became second nature to people; they had within themselves, in memory, a reservoir of scriptural passages. The frequently repeated word worked on people, opening them up and transforming them.

Prayer, following upon meditation, is simply the heartfelt response to the word received in *lectio*. Having heard the Lord's voice, the reader now responds in turn, freely, spontaneously. Often the response is nothing other than handing back the words already received but now recognized as the gift they are. An excellent biblical example is the Magnificat, Mary's response to the word spoken to her. Contemplation, the final part, is the apex of the *lectio* process. It is ultimately an experience of God, which may come as gift to the faithful reader. Contemplation as gift is the result of God's free activity. But there is a contemplation that comes as a more normal culmination of *lectio* experience. To contemplate in this sense is to perceive the presence of God in the surrounding world. It is an attending to reality, a seeing of the world, that poets achieve when the transcendent is manifest before them in the drop of dew on a tiny violet. The Bible read faithfully and the liturgy celebrated regularly schools people in this way of seeing.

Lectio in the life of ministers and other Christians begins and ends with the Word of God. That word is enshrined in a special way in the scriptures. It is a word to be read, digested, prayed, and contemplated. If not requiring a large quantity of time, *lectio* does require spending quality time with the word. But from that quality time one learns "reading" as a way of life, not just something to do for some minutes each day. Much as a newly mastered language opens us to communicate with a larger world, so reading the scriptures opens us to reading the larger world around us.

Applying *Lectio* Principles in Ministry

The scriptures most often provide us with texts for *lectio,* but at the same time reading them trains us to read the other texts that life itself provides. The God who speaks in the scriptures speaks in human experience as well. The Rule of Benedict, which legislated for periods of *lectio* in the daily lives of monks, also called attention to the "revelations" that can come from the young in the community or from visiting monks. Christ was to be recognized in the guests and in the sick. In other words, the Rule prescribed a way of reading human experience in the light of the scriptures. *Lectio,* which begins with the scriptures and is sustained by them, amplifies to include life's various experiences. Events, feelings, even conflicts can all have revelatory power. They, too, need to be read and digested.[39]

A striking and apt illustration of the revelatory power of events is found in Flannery O'Connor's well-known short story "Revelation."[40] In the story, Ruby Turpin and her husband Claud, who has injured his leg on their farm, go to a doctor's office to have the wound treated. While waiting to see the doctor, Ruby looks around the waiting room and makes an assessment of the people there. She thanks God she is the way she is and not like the "white trash" and "niggers" who are present. Her self-complacency is ruptured by a young girl who had been staring at her, then suddenly hurls a book and lunges at her. As the girl is bring restrained on the waiting room floor by the nurse and others, she whispers to Ruby, "Go back to hell where you came from, you old wart hog."[41] The event truly disturbed Ruby. She cannot imagine why God would let that happen to her when there were others in the room more deserving of such an attack. She goes home with Claud still shaken by the experience. Later, at the farm, she is outside and notices what appears to be a streak in the sky. It looks like a road going up from earth into heaven. As she looks more closely, she sees there are people on the road. At the front of the line, marching into heaven, are the "white trash" and the "niggers" joyfully singing hallelujahs. At the very end of the line she sees people like herself, who are marching along, shocked as they have their virtues burned away.

O'Connor's story is fittingly titled "Revelation." Ruby tries to read the event of the girl's attack and digest it. She doesn't dismiss it. Eventually a vision comes of the word, not as Ruby would have it, but as it is according to God's design. The story presents us with a paradigm for "reading" the experiences that life presents. The principle undergirding *lectio,* namely that God is speaking, is operative as the event is taken seriously. It is digested, meditated upon, in order to open up to its full meaning. The revelation then comes. Life is different than first imagined. A radical change of outlook is called for. The event, like the scriptures, has layers of meaning and can bring about conversion.

Ministry may not present such dramatic occurrences as O'Connor's story, but it does have its revelatory moments, which need to be read and digested. Conflict, powerful feelings, successes, and failures—all can be read for the deeper message they may contain. Situations and people are like texts that have layers of meaning. To read them properly requires that we take our time and ponder them. To read them too quickly is to stay simply on the surface and to miss the deeper meanings. Humility is important here as well as in reading the scriptures. We need at times to be aware of the categories in which we lock into people and events and prevent new meanings from emerging. The holy poses itself to us in diverse ways, in ways we least expect. The goal in a *lectio* of experience is ultimately to connect with the holy as it comes to us, to respond to it, to let it change and transform us.

Recently, under the tutelage of contemporary science, we have begun to look at nature as encoded and intriguing information. Once again, the natural world around us is seen as it was by medieval monks, as something to be read. By reading it not as a cold scientific equation but as a symbolic reality pointing toward the invisible and infinite, we can come to a new experience of awe and wonder. Awe and wonder, Rudolf Otto has reminded us, are the peculiarly human responses to the holy.[42] Reading that occasions awe and wonder is reading that recognizes the real presence that gives meaning to life. To read that way is truly to live.

Notes

1. "The End of Bookishness?" *Times Literary Supplement*, July 8–16, 1988, 754.

2. See George Steiner, "The Uncommon Reader" and "Real Presences" in *No Passion Spent: Essays 1978–1995* (New Haven: Yale University Press, 1996), 1–19; 20–39; and *Real Presences* (Chicago: University of Chicago Press, 1989), esp. 137–232.

3. Steiner, *Real Presences*, 90–96.

4. In *Pigeon Feathers and Other Stories* (New York: Fawcett Crest, 1962), 105.

5. (New York: Viking, 1996), 7.

6. Manguel, Alberto, *A History of Reading* (New York: Penguin, 1987), 39.

7, Ibid., 43. Augustine, *Confessions,* trans. Henry Chadwick (Oxford: Oxford University Press, 1991), iv, 3, p. 93.

8. Ibid., 49–51.

9. Ivan Illich, *In the Vineyard of the Text: A Commentary to Hugh's "Didascalicon"* (Chicago and London: University of Chicago Press, 1993), 110.

10. "Twenty Minutes into the Future, or How Are We Moving Beyond the Book?" in *The Future of the Book*, ed. Geoffrey Nunberg (Berkeley and Los Angeles: University of California Press, 1996), 214.

11. Landow, George P., 232.

12. Jay David Bolter, "Ekphrasis, Virtual Reality, and the Future of Writing," in *Future of the Book*, 256.

13. Umberto Eco, "Afterword," in *Future of the Book,* 300–301.

14. Steiner, "End of Bookishness," 754.

15. Steiner, "Uncommon Reader," 6–9.

16. Illich, *Vineyard*, 116.

17. Ibid., 3-4. Illich's persuasive presentation of the historical evolution of the text and reading is guiding the discussion throughout this chapter.

18. Ibid., 116–19.

19. Ivan Illich and Barry Sanders, *ABC: The Alphabetization of the Popular Mind* (New York: Vintage Books, 1988), 49.

20. Illich, *Vineyard*, 116–21.

21. Illich and Sanders, *ABC*, 71–72. See also Caroline Walker Bynum, *Jesus as Mother: Studies in the Spirituality of the High Middle Ages* (Berkeley and Los Angeles: University of California Press, 1982), esp. ch. 3, "Did the Twelfth Century Discover the Individual?" 82–109.

22. Illich, *Vineyard*, 2.

23. Ibid., 54, but see also 51–58.

24. Ibid., 82.

25. Ibid., 105–6.

26. Ibid., 123.

27. Steiner, "Real Presences," *No Passion Spent*, 35.

28. *De Genesi ad Litteram, PL* 34, 245; cited in Illich, *Vineyard*, 123.

29. "Medieval and Modern Understanding of Symbolism: A Comparison," in *Images and Ideas in the Middle Ages: Selected Studies in History and Art, Vol. 1* (Rome: Edizio di Storia e Litteratura, 1983), 245.

30. Illich, *Vineyard*, 11–22.

31. Among the more recent are the following: Michael Casey, *Sacred Reading: The Ancient Art of Lectio Divina* (Ligouri, Mo.: Triumph Books, 1995); Mariano Magrassi, *Praying the Bible: An Introduction to Lectio Divina*, trans. Edward Hagman (Collegeville, Minn.: Liturgical Press, 1998); and M. Basil Pennington, *Lectio Divina: Renewing the Ancient Practice of Praying the Scriptures* (New York, Crossroad, 1998).

32. *Reading God*, trans. Gregory Roettger (Schuyler, Ne.: BMH Publications, 1993).

33. (New York: Seabury, 1968), 49.

34. See Douglas Burton-Christie, *The Word in the Desert: Scripture and the Quest for Holiness in Early Christian Monasticism* (New York: Oxford University Press, 1993).

35. See Henri de Lubac, *Medieval Exegesis, Vol. 1: The Four Senses of Scripture*, trans. Mark Sebanc (Grand Rapids: Eerdmans, 1998).

36. *The Sayings of the Desert Fathers: The Alphabetical Collection*, trans. Benedicta Ward (London: A. R. Mowbray, 1975), 4.

37. *The Ladder of Monks and Twelve Meditations*, trans. Edmund Colledge and James Walsh (New York: Doubleday, 1978).

38. *The Didascalicon of Hugh of St. Victor: A Medieval Guide to the Arts*, trans. Jerome Taylor (New York: Columbia University Press, 1991).

39. See Norvene Vest, *No Moment Too Small: Rhythms of Silence, Prayer, and Holy Reading* (Boston: Cowley Publications, 1994), 78–86.

40. In *The Complete Stories* (New York: Farrar, Straus, and Giroux, 1971), 488–508.

41. Ibid., 500.

42. *The Idea of the Holy: An Inquiry into the Non-Rational Factor in the Idea of the Divine and Its Relation to the Rational,* trans. John W. Harvey (Oxford; Oxford University Press, 1950), 12–40.

39. A Perceptual Approach
to Effective Ministry

When a Maryknoll priest who had spent more than thirty-five years working in the foreign missions returned home, he was assigned to the order's development office and given the task of fund-raising. Besides cultivating wealthy potential benefactors and handling the usual mailings asking for donations, his new ministry entailed fostering a better understanding and support of the church's, and especially his congregation's, missionary efforts. One day, after he had given a talk at a parish that was part of the "speakers' circuit" for former missionaries, he was asked, "Father, after your many years of work in the missions, what was the most important thing that you learned?" Having reflected on this very question himself for many hours since his return, he had a ready reply.

> The most important insight I gained, unfortunately only after
> some years of pain and struggle, was that I went over to the mis-
> sions with too much of a sense of responsibility and too little of a
> sense of appreciation. My excessive sense of responsibility led me
> dangerously to the brink of burnout, a state of exhaustion, demor-
> alization, and distaste for ministry. And my lack of appreciation of
> the gifts, talents, and strengths of the people to whom I ministered
> prevented me from helping them recognize and mobilize their
> own resources in facing life's challenges and problems.

This story reveals the significant impact that personal perception—how we see and feel about ourselves, others, and the processes we engage in—can have on our behavior as ministers. "Modern perceptual psychology," states psychologist Arthur Combs, "tells us that a person's behavior is the direct result of his [her] perceptions, how things seem to him [her] at the moment of his [her] behaving."[1] The central thesis of perceptual psychology is that behavior is a function of perception. In other words, our "take on things," more than the forces exerted on us from without, shapes our behavior. Clearly, *perception* as used here means more than "seeing." It refers to "meaning," the

628

peculiar significance of an event for the person experiencing it. According to perceptual psychologists, effective and efficient behavior in any given situation depends upon how people are perceiving at the time. In order to change their behavior, they must first change their perception of themselves and the world.

Influenced by these central tenets of perceptual psychology, Dr. Combs, starting more than two decades ago, was a leading advocate of reforming the way teachers are trained. Rather than focus on the acquisition of educational theories and specific skills, both of which admittedly are important for good teaching, he stressed the importance of developing the *person of the teacher.* In order to produce healthy, responsible, effective helping professionals, Combs contends, teacher training programs "must deal not only with student behavior but also with the inner life of students, especially with student self-concepts, values, and feelings."[2]

The Self as Instrument

The concept of "self as instrument," as applied in such diverse helping professions as medicine, social work, clinical psychology, guidance, and nursing, views effective professional workers not as technicians applying methods in a more or less mechanical fashion according to their training, but as intelligent human beings using themselves, their knowledge, and the resources at hand to resolve concerns and problems confronting them. When applied to the teaching profession, this "self as instrument" concept "makes teacher education a problem in personal becoming, of helping a student discover how best to use himself/herself as a professional educator."[3] Based on a series of research studies conducted at several universities, Combs maintains that "what makes good teachers is not their knowledge or methods, but the beliefs teachers hold about students, themselves, their goals, purposes, and the teaching task."[4] This essay suggests that Combs's contentions about good teachers are equally true about good ministers.

According to Combs, effective teaching is the product of teacher perception or beliefs in the following five major areas:[5]

1. *Empathic Qualities:* Good teachers are phenomenologically oriented. They are keenly aware of the perceptions of other people and use this understanding as the primary frame of reference for guiding their own behavior.

2. *Positive Self-Concept:* Good teachers see themselves in essentially positive ways.

3. *Beliefs About Other People:* Good teachers characteristically see other people in positive ways, as able, trustworthy, friendly, and so on.

4. *Open, Facilitating Purposes:* The purposes of good teachers are primarily broad, facilitating, and process-oriented.

5. *Authenticity:* Good teachers are essentially self-revealing and genuine.

Application to Pastoral Ministry

Are Combs's conclusions regarding effective teachers applicable to other forms of pastoral ministry besides teaching? His findings are presented here to suggest that possibility. Challenging the dominance of behavioral psychology as the theoretical base for the professional training of teachers, Combs's theory about the pivotal importance of perception in good teaching stirred up a good deal of controversy.[6] His critics, operating from a behavioral science framework, required empirical verification of his claims. Some of his hypotheses have been subjected to experimental designs, and their truth claims have been objectively verified. Others, however, remain as hypotheses awaiting empirical verification. His insights are presented here so that those concerned with ministry training might "test" his insights against the data of their own experience of effective ministry. Pastoral studies, not being a behavioral science, happily has the freedom to recognize truths even when they have not been verified by a scientific study! Following a more detailed description of the hypotheses regarding the perceptual organization of good teachers in the five areas cited,[7] this essay shows how the example of Jesus and the attitude of contemporary pastoral ministers lend credibility to Combs's findings about the perceptual organization of effective teachers.

The Effective Helper's Frame of Reference

According to Combs, good teachers are deeply sensitive to the private worlds of their students and colleagues and consider people's attitudes, feelings, beliefs, and understandings as important data in their interaction with them.

- *Internal-External Frame of Reference:* The frame of reference of good teachers can be described as internal rather than external. They possess a keen awareness of how things seem from the point of view of those with whom they interact and base their behavior on this awareness.
- *People-Thing Orientation:* Good teachers perceive the concerns of people and their reactions to be more important than things and events.
- *Meanings-Facts Orientation:* Good teachers are more concerned with the perceptual experience of people (how things seem to people) rather than being exclusively concerned with concrete events.

- *Immediate-Historical Causation:* Effective teachers look for the causes of people's behavior more in their current thinking, feeling, beliefs, and understandings than in objective descriptions of the forces exerted upon them in the past.

Perceptions About What People Are Like and How They Behave

Combs argues that what teachers believe about the nature of their students has an important effect on how they behave toward them. Teachers who believe in their students' capacity to learn, for example, will behave quite differently from teachers who seriously doubt the ability of their students. Teachers with a positive attitude about their students begin their task with hope and assurance of success; they place confidence and trust in their students. Teachers who doubt their students' capacities feel that it is not safe to trust them and may choose inappropriate ways of dealing with them. The following are Combs's hypotheses regarding how good teachers perceive others:

- *Able-Unable:* Good teachers perceive others as having the capacities to deal with their problems and to find adequate solutions to events as opposed to doubting the capacity of people to manage for themselves.
- *Friendly-Unfriendly:* Not regarding others as personally threatening but rather as essentially well-intentioned, good teachers perceive people generally as friendly and enhancing, not evil-intentioned.
- *Worthy-Unworthy:* Good teachers respect and foster other people's dignity and integrity rather than viewing people as unimportant. They are sensitive not to violate the integrity of others or to treat people as of little account.
- *Internally-Externally Motivated:* Good teachers perceive others to be more inner-directed than outer-directed. They see other people and their behavior as essentially developing from within rather than as a product of external events to be molded or directed. They believe people to be creative and dynamic, not passive or inert.
- *Dependable-Undependable:* The perception of good teachers is that people are essentially trustworthy and reliable in the sense of behaving in lawful ways; people's behavior is understandable rather than unpredictable, capricious, or negative.
- *Helpful-Hindering:* Good teachers perceive others as being potentially enhancing and fulfilling of self rather than as impeding or frustrating. They regard others as important sources of personal satisfaction rather than sources of trouble.

Good Teachers' Perception of Self

Perceptual psychology indicates that the behavior of individuals at any moment is a function of how they see their situations and themselves. As with the case of everyone else, the behavior of teachers and other professional helpers is a function of their self-concepts, which vastly influence what people believe about themselves. While teachers who see themselves as able are motivated to try, those who do not think they are able will avoid responsibilities. Teachers who perceive that they are liked by students will behave quite differently from those who feel they are not liked. Teachers who have a high regard for the dignity and importance of their profession will act quite differently than those who doubt the importance and value of their work as teachers. The following hypotheses are postulated by Combs regarding the self-perception of good teachers:

- *Identified with-Apart from:* Good teachers tend to see themselves as part of all humankind; they view themselves as identified with people rather than as withdrawn, apart, or alienated from others.
- *Adequate-Inadequate:* Good teachers generally perceive themselves as good enough, possessing what they need to deal with their problems and challenges.
- *Worthy-Unworthy:* Effective teachers perceive themselves as persons of consequence, dignity, integrity, and worthy of respect. Ineffective teachers view themselves as inconsequential, easily overlooked, and discounted; their dignity and worth are unimportant.
- *Accepted-Not Accepted:* Good teachers sense that they are accepted by students and colleagues alike.

The Perception of Good Teachers About the Purpose and Process of Learning

How teachers view the goals and process of learning definitely shapes their understanding of their role and how best to contribute to the process. The following are Combs's hypotheses regarding the perceptual organization of good teachers in this area:

- *Freeing-Controlling:* The purpose of the helping task is perceived by good teachers as one of freeing, assisting, releasing, facilitating rather than one of controlling, manipulating, coercing, blocking, and inhibiting. Good teachers believe the importance of being helpful rather than dominating, understanding rather than condemning, and accepting rather than rejecting.

- *Larger-Smaller Perceptions:* Tending to view events from a broad rather than narrow perspective, good teachers are concerned with the larger ramifications and meaning of events rather than with the immediate and specific.
- *Self-Revealing-Self-Concealing:* Believing that it is appropriate to be themselves in their professional roles, good teachers are willing to disclose themselves and regard their feelings and shortcomings as important and significant rather than as aspects of the self that should be hidden or covered up.
- *Furthering Process-Achieving Goals:* Good teachers perceive their appropriate role as one of encouraging and facilitating the ongoing process of search and discovery rather than one of promoting or working for preconceived solutions.
- *Open-Closed to Experience:* Good teachers appreciate the importance of experience and remain continually open to new experiences.
- *Tolerant of Ambiguity-Intolerant:* Good teachers can tolerate living with "gray areas" and are not compelled to see everything in dichotomous, black and white terms.

A Look at Jesus as a Teacher

An examination of Jesus' dialogue with the Samaritan woman at the well (Jn 4:1–42) illustrates how Jesus embodied many of the perceptual traits identified by Combs as those of effective teachers. When the woman enters the scene, she is both without faith and without community. Scripture scholar Raymond Brown *(Anchor Bible Commentary)* hints at her alienation from others in the community when he points out the unusual time of her coming to the well. Such a chore was usually done in the morning and evening, not at noon. The woman's choice of a time for coming to the well might well suggest that she structured her lifestyle to avoid encounter with others. Living in an ambiguous moral situation, she might have feared the reproach of her fellow villagers and the kind of moral probing that could easily expose and embarrass her. Thus she schedules her daily routine in a way that avoids confrontation. Yet, in her meeting with Jesus at the well, God shatters the isolating and constricting structures that she imposes on her life. It is through his respectful, patient, and nonjudgmental manner of dialogue that Jesus finally manages to break through the Samaritan woman's resistance to the encounter.

Compassion and empathy make Jesus a very effective teacher. Right away, Jesus perceives the woman's awkwardness in dealing with him, because as a foreigner and a woman, she was used to being discriminated against. So, he approaches her gently with a request: "May I have a drink?" He is attuned to the lingering pain from her five unsuccessful marriages and intuits the poor self-esteem and shame behind her abrupt and unfriendly manner. He notices the tired woman's desire for relief from the daily drudgery of coming to the well for water and teaches her about "living water" that would allow her never to thirst again. Jesus' compassionate love enabled him to listen sensitively to her underlying concerns and feelings and to prepare the woman to receive the revelation of God.

The encounter of Jesus with the Samaritan woman is a remarkable lesson in catechesis, because his dialogue with her truly brings faith and relationship into being. If the purpose of catechesis, is to enable divine revelation to break into a person's life and to help that person respond with living faith, the encounter between Jesus and the woman was certainly a clear instance of successful catechesis. Through the patient understanding and acceptance of Jesus, the Samaritan woman experienced the compassionate and forgiving love of God and was not only brought to believe, but also made a minister through whose words others also came to believe.

The Perceptual Organization of Jesus in Ministry

According to Combs, good teachers are more concerned with the perceptual experience of people—that is, how things seem to them—than with concrete events in themselves. Jesus' sensitive manner of dealing with the Samaritan woman indicates that this perceptual stance was true of Jesus. Another notable illustration of his desire to perceive events from the point of view of others involves his interaction with the woman who suffered from a hemorrhage (Mk 5:25–34). An objective account of the event would chronicle that Jesus noticed that someone had touched his cloak as he was rushing to the house of a synagogue official, whose daughter was desperately ill. Aware that power had gone forth from him, Jesus turned round in the crowd and inquired about who had touched his clothes. Bewildered by his question, the disciples replied that the pressing throng that surrounded them made it impossible to say who touched him. But Jesus persisted in looking around, trying to see who had done it. Only then did the woman, frightened and trembling because she knew what had happened to her, step forward to confess. She "fell at his feet and told him the whole truth" (5:34). What the woman recounted was the personal significance of what had just transpired in such a public arena. No external witness could supply what she went on to disclose to Jesus: how she had suffered from a hemorrhage for twelve years and had spent all her money for long and painful treatments under various doctors without getting better—in fact, she was getting worse. Then moments ago, when she saw him passing through, the thought came to her that if she could touch even his clothes, she would be healed. True to her intuition, once she touched his clock, "the source of the bleeding dried up instantly, and she felt in herself that she was cured of her complaint" (vv. 29–30). Jesus' persistence in finding out what had occurred obviously went beyond getting the facts to hearing firsthand how the people involved perceived the event and were impacted by what transpired. Only after understanding the meaning that the event had for the woman in the context of her history of illness and her long and futile search for a cure did Jesus send her off. "'My daughter,' he said, 'your faith has restored you to health; go in peace and be free from your complaint'" (v. 34).

The attitudes and responses of Jesus to the woman caught in adultery (Jn 8:3–11) further portray the perceptual capacity of Jesus that made him so effective in helping others. "He says no word to the woman until the end. He listens to the Pharisees, to their words, and to their anger with him. But he also listens to the silence of the woman: her guilt, her fears, her need to be accepted for what she is without being judged and condemned. Behind the many different attitudes of those who approach him, Jesus hears their need for forgiveness."[8] By telling her to go away and sin no more, Jesus gave her a new chance and affirmed her ability to reform and rebuild her life. Once again, like Combs's effective teachers, Jesus see others as able to deal with their problems, unlike teachers who doubt the capacity of others to manage for themselves.

Mark's Gospel, in its two different accounts of the miracles of the multiplication of the loaves and fishes, depicts how Jesus' sensitive perception made him aware of the needs not only of individuals, but of groups as well. The second of Mark's two accounts in chapter 8 (vv. 1–10) makes clear that Jesus is moved to action by his perception of the crowd's hunger. Realizing that the great crowd that had gathered to hear his words was without food, Jesus expressed his concern: "I feel sorry for all these people; they have been with me for three days now and have nothing to eat. If I send them off home hungry they will collapse on the way; some have come a great distance" (vv. 2–4).

In contrast, the first account of the miracle in chapter 6 states that Jesus perceived a different need, which, nonetheless, elicited the same compassionate response to the crowd. Here, Jesus is said to have acted because he perceived not the physical hunger of the crowd for food but the crowd's hunger for guidance and meaning. Jesus "took pity on them because they were like sheep without a shepherd, and he set himself to teach them at some length" (Mk 6:34–35). While the two Markan accounts attribute a different reason for Jesus' compassionate response to the crowd, they point unambiguously to the same sensitive quality of Jesus' perception of others and events. In both accounts, Jesus' ministerial outreach begins with a perception of others that is sufficiently sensitive to arouse feelings of compassionate concern. His penetrating perception of the crowd alerted him to people's physical need for nourishment, as well as to their spiritual need for knowledge and guidance.

As with the perceptual organization of Combs's effective teachers, the perception of Jesus is characterized by an empathic orientation to others and a broad understanding of their needs as human beings. The miracles of the multiplication of the loaves and fishes dramatize the reality of the incarnation. Christ's divinity is alluded to by his miraculous powers, and his humanity is attested to by his grasp of human needs. The mystery of the incarnation celebrates the fact that God was not content to love humankind from a distance, but drew near to love humanity close by. This divine love flows from an empathic understanding of people, because the incarnation allowed God to perceive people and human events not only from a distant divine vantage point, but from the internal frame of reference of a fellow human being. Like the effective teachers of Combs's study, Jesus' perception and behavior reveal someone who saw himself as part of all humankind and who possessed a keen perception of people's needs.

"Perceiving" or "seeing" can be said to be the beginning of all compassionate action. Clearly, this was the case with Jesus. To imitate Jesus as ministers is to perceive people and events in a way that issues forth in compassion. The plight of others always stirred Jesus' heart and moved him to reach out in healing and forgiving ways. For example, once a leper approached Jesus, begging to be cured (Mk 1:40–45). Jesus takes in the reality of this afflicted suppliant, paying close attention to his words and actions. Then, moved with compassion, he reaches out to touch the diseased person. Jesus' therapeutic touch issued forth from a compassionate heart. This episode exemplifies a threefold dynamic that characterizes many of Jesus' healing encounters:

1. Jesus is keenly aware of his interpersonal environment, sensitive to the needs of the people around him *(contemplative perception);*
2. He lets what he perceives stir him to compassion *(affective arousal);*
3. Moved by compassion, he reaches out to help *(altruistic action).*

His response to this leper, ostracized from society because of his ailment, was typical of Jesus. Other outcasts of his day—women, foreigners, tax collectors, and prostitutes—also received compassion from Jesus, even as their religious leaders denied them access to the official channels of healing and reconciliation.

Contemporary Pastoral Examples

On July 27, 1998, the *Los Angeles Times* carried a story about "a miracle," the sudden influx of new life to St. Agatha Catholic Church, a seventy-five-year-old church located on a grimy stretch of Adams Boulevard in Mid-City, Los Angeles. Only seven years ago, there was talk of merging St. Agatha Catholic Church with a nearby church because of the dramatic decline of attendance, made obvious by dusty, empty pews. Not only was the largely African American congregation that held the once-thriving church together aging, there was also friction and resentment as a growing number of Latino immigrants moved to the area. The article goes on to recount how this once-fading church is presently being reinvigorated by a new priest and a multiracial infusion of newcomers from all parts of the metropolitan area, attracted by the warmth and liveliness they discover at St. Agatha.

The article indicates that one of the "miracle workers" involved in this resurrection of St. Agatha is its new pastor, Fr. Ken Deasy. "People are coming out to this area and discovering it's a holy land," commented Deasy.[9] His perception of St. Agatha as "holy land," however, was not his first impression upon receiving his assignment to St. Agatha. His initial perception was quite the contrary: "I said, 'Are you kidding? Are you out of your mind?'" he recalled. "I thought it was war-torn, violent, ugly—a place that no one wanted to be."[10] But his perceptions gradually changed. And this shift in perception, the articles hints, is what has helped to usher in the new energies bringing surprising rebirth to this parish.

> On his first day, the church was robbed and all the audio equipment taken. The first words he was greeted with when he walked in were: *"Lo siento, Padre.* I'm sorry, Father. Please don't leave."
>
> But soon, Deasy said, he was moved by the faith and warmth of the community, a place where many struggled against enormous odds.
>
> "I discovered family out here," he said. "I didn't see poverty, I saw huge wealth. I didn't see despair, I saw future. A lot of times you're dealing with people so glad to be getting through the week. There is more willingness to work through struggles than avoid them."[11]

According to Combs's findings, positive perceptions of people's abilities and good intentions promote greater possibilities. This certainly seems to have been the case with the new pastor and the renewal of St. Agatha Church.

Another contemporary expression of the power of perception to influence feelings and behavior comes from the self-description of Bishop Gerald Robert Barnes, who heads the diocese of San Bernardino, California. In an address to the National Council for Catholic Evangelization, Bishop Barnes gave a brief account of his background. Having spent part of his childhood in the projects of East Los Angeles, he and his family were familiar with poverty. After many years of struggle, his father bought a mom-and-pop grocery story above which the family made its home. He went on to recall an incident that occurred when he was a seminarian, riding in the back of his parent's car through skid row in Los Angeles. As the automobile made its way through skid row, Barnes's father had to slam on the brake, just before a traffic light, to avoid hitting a man who was running across the street.

> I said, "Look at that bum. What a waste." My mother turned around and looked right at me in the back seat and said, "He has a mother. He's someone's son." "I saw a bum. She saw someone's son," he told the audience in his keynote speech.
>
> Barnes contrasted his own haughty attitude with his mother's grace: "I was a seminarian. I was studying scripture. Attending daily Mass. I saw a nobody. She was living the Scriptures. She saw with her faith. I was the righteous, arrogant kid. She was compassionate. She saw kinship. A different view. I looked at him with disdain. She looked at him with acceptance. He was somebody."[12]

The few hundred participants at the meeting stood and applauded the bishop's cogent comments about the vital connection between how one perceives reality and the kind of compassionate response expected in those purporting to minister in Christ's name. Bishop Barnes's message seems to corroborate the central thesis of Dr. Combs and other perceptual psychologists who believe that perception directly influences behavior. More important, the examples of the pastor of St. Agatha and the bishop of San Bernardino converge on a common truth: Ministering like Jesus requires modern disciples to imitate Jesus' capacity to perceive people's needs and to respond compassionately to those needs; yet, at the same time, to perceive them not as helpless and unreliable but as trustworthy, capable, worthy of respect, and well-intentioned—all perceptual traits delineated by Combs as characteristics of effective helpers who have learned how to use their very "self as instruments."

Ministers as Instruments United to God

In the *Constitutions* of the Jesuit order he founded, St. Ignatius of Loyola presents an insight regarding effectiveness in ministry that parallels Combs's notion of a good teacher as one who uses one's "self as instrument," but adds to it a vitally important dimension based on Christian faith. To achieve the goals of ministry, Ignatius advises his Jesuits that "the means which unite the human instrument with God and so dispose it that it may be wielded dexterously by His divine hand are more effective than those which equip it in relation to men."[13] Ignatius's advice is based on a perception of God as being present and active at all levels of created reality. God's ongoing labor in the world on behalf of humankind constitutes the essence of ministry. Human beings who engage in ministry do so because they have been invited by Christ to be coworkers in bringing about the reign of God on earth. Thus, ministry is primarily God's redemptive action in the world, and all human ministers are collaborators with God.

> The Ignatian world view offers a call and a vision to join Christ on Mission in an apostolically-based, world-engaging spirituality, working together *in unitative action with God* for the renewal and transformation of church and society.[14] (emphasis added)

Hence, effectiveness in ministry depends on how attuned and united the human instrument is with God's presence and action. To be attuned to the presence and action of God in the world is what Ignatius means by being a "contemplative." Thus, according to Ignatian spirituality, ministers should strive to be "instruments united with God" or "contemplatives in action."

In modern times, this ideal of being a "contemplative in action" challenges ministers to integrate the capacity to wonder, to marvel, to perceive in depth with the capacity to be inspired and moved to altruistic action. In the *Spiritual Exercises,* Ignatius illustrates the threefold dynamic or movement that characterizes the contemplative in action[15]—a pattern that parallels the dynamic of Jesus' ministerial encounters described above.

The first movement is a perceptual one, a way of viewing reality with a wonder that leads to worship, with a recognition that, in the words of the poet Gerard Manley Hopkins, "the world is charged with the grandeur of God...shining forth like shook foil." This kind of perception naturally leads to awe, which for Abraham Heschel is "a sense for the transcendence, for the reference everywhere to Him who is beyond all things."[16] In his classic work, *God in Search of Man,* Heschel writes,

> Awe enables us to perceive in the world intimations of the divine, to sense in small things the beginning of infinite significance, to sense the ultimate in the common and the simple; to feel in the rush of the passing the stillness of the eternal.[17]

The second movement is an affective one, feelings stirred up by one's perceptions. Feelings of indebtedness, gratitude, and love are aroused when one recognizes the loving gratuity of God made manifest in all the gifts of creation: one's very life-breath, family, friends, and all the material requirements needed for survival and growth. The last movement is one of altruistic action. Love, stirred up by gratitude, spills out into service.

In light of this threefold dynamic, ministry training programs intent on producing modern day contemplatives in action must form people who are:

- Capable of perceiving with sensitivity and depth;
- Capable of being moved deeply by their perceptions;
- Capable of gratuitous and committed action on behalf of others.

This essay suggests that formation for effective ministry today would benefit greatly by incorporating both the insights of Arthur Combs regarding the perceptual organization of effective helpers who know how to use the "self as instrument," and those of Ignatius of Loyola regarding the need for ministers who are contemplatively aware of God's presence in the world and are united with God in such a way that they are disposed to "be wielded dexterously" by the provident hand of God.

Notes

1. Arthur W. Combs, "The Personal Approach to Good Teaching," *Humanistic Education Resource Handbook,* 254.

2. Arthur W. Combs, "Humanistic Education: Too Tender for a Tough World?" *Phi Delta Kappan* 62, 6 (February 1981): 447.

3. Arthur W. Combs, "Teacher Education: The Person in the Process," *Educational Leadership* 35, 7 (April 1978): 558.

4. Arthur W. Combs, "New Assumptions for Educational Reform," *Educational Leadership* 45, 5 (February 1988): 39. See also A. W. Combs, *A Personal Approach to Teaching* (Boston: Allyn and Bacon, 1982); A. W. Combs, *Florida Studies in the Helping Professions,* Social Science Monograph No. 39 (Gainesville, Fla: University of Florida Press, 1969); C. V. Dedrick, "The Relationship Between Perceptual Characteristics and Effective Teaching at the Junior College Level" (doctoral diss., University of Florida, 1972); and R. G. Koffman, "A Comparison of the Perceptual Organization of Outstanding and Randomly Selected Teachers in Open and Traditional Classrooms" (doctoral diss., University of Massachusetts, 1975).

5. Combs, "Teacher Education," 558.

6. A critic, Doyle Watts, states, "Combs does not propose to provide our students with teachers competent in knowledge, skills, and abilities. Instead, he would place in the classrooms persons who have been taught by trial and error, who have developed unspecified beliefs and unknown perceptions, and who have arrived at some undefinable state that he refers to as 'become.'" "The Humanistic Approach to Teacher Education: A Giant Step Backwards?" in *Educational Leadership* 36, 2 (November 1978): 90. For a response to Watts's criticism, see Donald C. Medeiros, I. David Welch, and George A. Tate, "Humanistic Teacher Education: Another View," *Educational Leadership* (March 1979): 434–38. See also David N. Aspy and Flora N. Roebuck, "Teacher

Education: A Response to Watts's Response to Combs," *Educational Leadership* 37, 6 (March 1980): 507–10.

7. These hypotheses are summarized in Combs's "Personal Approach to Good Teaching," 256–61.

8. Jacques Pasquier, "Healing Relationships," *The Way* 16 (July 1976): 213.

9. "Miracle Workers," *Los Angeles Times,* July 27, 1998, p. B1.

10. Ibid., B3.

11. Ibid.

12. Arthur Jones, "Bishop's Life Story as a Quest for Grace," *The National Catholic Reporter,* July 12, 1996.

13. Ignatius of Loyola, *Constitutions of the Society of Jesus,* trans. with an Introduction and a Commentary, by George E. Ganss, S.J. (St. Louis, Mo.: The Institute of Jesuit Sources, 1970), part X, no. 813.

14. Michael W. Cooper, S.J., "Ignatian Spirituality: Unitative Action with Christ on Mission," *Presence: An International Journal of Spiritual Direction* 2, 3 (September 1996): 36–37.

15. *Spiritual Exercises of St. Ignatius,* "Contemplation for Obtaining Divine Love," nos. 230–37.

16. Abraham Joshua Heschel, *God in Search of Man: A Philosophy of Judaism* (New York: Harper and Row Publishers, 1955), 75.

17. Ibid.

E. Glenn Hinson

40. Ministers as Midwives and Mothers of Grace

Teaching at Wake Forest University from 1982 to 1984 confirmed in me a growing perception of the importance of grace in human life. Some of the most able and productive students shared with me their need for unconditional affirmation, approval without any reference to achievement. All their lives they had received approval based on performance. Parents smiled when they behaved or received good marks in school and frowned when they didn't. Teachers rewarded them with high grades for good performance on tests or papers and chastened them for poor. No one loved them for themselves alone, with no strings attached. The better their performance, the more that seemed to happen.

Students are not the only persons who need grace. Ours is a highly work- and works-oriented culture in which salvation by works comes naturally. Performance is everything! The more the assembly line worker does, the bigger her bonus; the less she does, the smaller. The faster the truck driver speeds his load to its destination, the higher his pay; the slower, the lower. Many persons moving from a lower to a middle or from a middle to a higher socioeconomic level, as Wayne Oates has pointed out in *Confessions of a Workaholic,*[1] become driven persons, obsessed with achievement. Not just activity but quantity of activity determines how they feel about themselves. Mere doing, however, leaves an emptiness with self. It does not satisfy a deeper inner need and desire for approval completely independent of whether one has done enough to measure up. All of us are Luthers crying out for a God who will love us just as we are, who will forgive us though we have sinned and done what is evil in God's sight, and who will not only forgive but put a seal of approval on us, certifying that we are one of God's own.

In this lies a clue to Christian ministry, not just for those who are professionals but for all Christians. The longer I have tried to minister, the more I have become convinced that the key role of all Christians, the Christian "calling," is to be midwives and mothers of grace for one another. If you will reflect a moment on the imagery, I think you will discern its appropriateness. Midwives assist in the birthing. Mothers nurse and nurture.

642

God alone is the source of grace. God is grace itself. God alone can generate grace and cause it to increase in human lives. "I planted, Apollos watered, but God gave the growth," admitted the Apostle Paul, speaking of the planting of the church at Corinth (1 Cor 3:6). Grace flows endlessly from the ocean of love. Our task is to assist others in giving birth to and in growing up in grace.

To explain how we do this midwifing and mothering, we need to look at the means through which people experience grace. For this I rely heavily on three persons who have borne witness to the centrality of grace in human life at widely separated periods of Christian history: Augustine, John Bunyan, and Thomas Merton. In each of these we may discern four media that turn up repeatedly: experience, especially experience in the "depths"; scriptures and other writings, which we should probably expand today to include other media; the church, broadly conceived to range from a small cell group to the grand churches of Rome, which touched Thomas Merton deeply in a critical moment in life; and other persons. In conclusion, I draw together some insights that might help to improve our own midwifery and mothering. Some persons have a "gift" for this. Others may have no gift, but they can learn. All of us can improve in it.

Experiences

One of the soul-shaking experiences that broke through Augustine's studied indifference to God's knocking was the death of a dear friend in Tagaste, Augustine's home town. After completing his study of rhetoric at Carthage, Augustine had returned to Tagaste to teach. There he developed a deep friendship with a youth his own age, with whom he had grown up and who shared many of his interests. He persuaded his friend to become a Manichaean. Scarcely a year after they established this intimate relationship, however, the unnamed youth, "sweet to me above every sweetness of that life of mine," Augustine lamented, fell ill. Near death, he received baptism as a Catholic and momentarily revived and regained his strength. Encouraged by his recovery, Augustine tried to persuade him to return to the Manichaean fold, but his friend refused. A few days later, while Augustine was away, the young man died. Augustine drowned in grief.

> My heart was made dark by sorrow, he wrote years later, and whatever I looked upon was death. My native place was a torment to me, and my father's house was a strange unhappiness. Whatsoever I had done together with him was, apart from him, turned into a cruel torture.... To myself I became a great riddle, and I questioned my soul as to why it was sad and why it afflicted me so grievously, and it could answer me nothing.[2]

At the time Augustine could find no salve for his sorrow. He could not place the burden aside. In the end he took the geographical route and fled.

> For to me then you were not what you are, but an empty phantom, and my error was my god. If I attempted to put my burden there, so that it might rest, it hurtled back upon me through the void, and I myself remained an unhappy place where I could not abide and from which I could not depart. For where could my heart fly to, away from my heart? Where could I fly to, apart from my own self? Where would I not pursue myself? But still I fled from my native town.[3]

He went back to Carthage.

Even Carthage, however, could not cover up the gaping wound in Augustine's heart. His unassuagable grief stirred up that restlessness that made him question his Manichaean beliefs so deeply he was soon on his way out of that sect. Though often glossed over by Augustine's readers, the painful incident probably did more than any other experience Augustine had to arouse him to the operation of grace in his life.

John Bunyan awakened to the "merciful working of God" on his life as a consequence of a tempestuous inner struggle. Brought up in the heyday of Puritanism, he learned early on to seek to determine whether or not he was among the "elect." The Puritans gave people a method for answering that question. The faithful were to memorize as much of scripture as they could and wait for it to dart into their minds and hearts to convince them one way or another. Sometimes Bunyan received a reassuring word: "Whoever comes to me I will in no wise cast out." And he would feel lifted up. At other times, however, he heard discouraging words, especially those about Esau selling his birthright in Hebrews 12. He became convinced that he was a modern Esau who had sold not his *natural* but, far worse, his *Christian* birthright. He was convinced he had committed the unpardonable sin. He reached a point where he wanted to commit suicide. He found it hard to pray, so swallowed up was he by grief. "Wherefore still my life hung in doubt before me," he wrote, "not knowing which way I should go: only this I found my soul desire, even to cast itself at the foot of grace, by prayer and supplication."[4] After a year or more of living on the verge of insanity, Bunyan began to hear the words, "My grace is sufficient for thee" (2 Cor 12:9). Sitting in the little congregation at Bedford, of which he later became pastor, these words darted three times into his mind: "And oh! me thought that every word was a mighty word unto me;" he said, "as 'my,' and 'grace,' and 'sufficient,' and 'for thee'; they were then, and sometimes are still, far bigger than others be."[5] Still the Esau passage kept coming back until finally he prayed that these two passages—about Esau and about grace—would come into his mind at the same time and do battle. As he described the incident, about two or three days later, they did; "they bolted both upon me at a time, and did work and struggle strongly in me awhile; at last that about Esau's birthright began to wax weak, and withdraw, and vanish; and this, about the sufficiency of grace, prevailed with peace and joy."[6] In *The Pilgrim's Progress* Bunyan depicts this as Christian's battle with the Giant Despair at Doubting Castle. Bunyan entitled his spiritual autobiography *Grace Abounding to the Chief of Sinners.*

Thomas Merton awakened to the operation of grace through experience of loneliness. His mother died when he was six, his father when he was fifteen. Following his mother's death, his father, Owen, dragged him to France and then to England. While Owen traveled around painting landscapes, he put Tom in boarding schools. If you have read stories or seen movies about children in boarding schools, you know how terribly lonely it could be. When his father died, he came under guardianship of his grandparents, but did not live with them. After being "sent down" from Cambridge and coming to Columbia University, he assembled a kind of proxy family among the students and faculty. Reading *The Seven Storey Mountain,* however, leaves one with the impression that Merton found no real family until he arrived at Our Lady of Gethsemani, where he was to spend twenty-seven years of his life. Loneliness was the crucible of grace here, not as a single and short-term experience, but as a lifelong experience.

Scriptures, Other Writings, and Media

A second means of grace frequently cited by the three figures we are relying on is typographic: the Bible and other writings. In our day, however, it is wise to extend the circle to include other media such as movies, for Western culture is going through a transition from a predominantly typographic to a more iconic and tactual character as a result of a vast cybernetic revolution.[7] In addition, we must take care not to narrow the circle too much. Grace may come through unexpected sources, outside the Christian orbit.

That is where grace came from for Augustine. Cicero's *Hortensius,* a work now lost, affected Augustine markedly at age eighteen. Some scholars would say that it led to his "first conversion."[8] Coming into his hands two years after his father died, it did more than sharpen his rhetorical skills.

> This book changed my affections, he wrote. It turned my prayers to you, Lord, and caused me to have different purposes and desires. All my vain hopes forthwith became worthless to me, and with incredible ardor of heart I desired undying wisdom. I began to rise up, so that I might return to you.[9]

At this point, "wisdom" did not come from the Bible. Augustine did not find it really helpful until after his conversion at age thirty-two. One thing that drew him to the Manichaeans was their repudiation of the Old Testament. Not until he heard the allegorical preaching of Ambrose, Bishop of Milan, did he overcome his revulsion at some of the "absurdities" he found there. After conversion, however, he nurtured his faith on the psalms and other scriptures in a monastic setting.

Growing up in a Puritan era, John Bunyan depended far more heavily on the scriptures for his experience of grace than did Augustine or Merton. The Puritans, like all the followers of Luther and Calvin, were people of one book, and they were not prepared to believe anything that did not come from the scriptures or accord fully with them. That is why they remonstrated with the Quakers and the Ranters so vigorously; the Quakers and the Ranters claimed direct inspiration and revelation. Shaken by reading some Ranter writings and realizing he could not decide what was true or false, Bunyan pored over the Bible. "And indeed then I was never out of the Bible, either by reading or meditation;" he wrote, "still crying out to God that I might know the truth, and way to heaven and glory."[10] The meditation he referred to was the type developed by Puritans. Although they may not have admitted it, their method had remarkable similarities to that used by medieval monks and Ignatius Loyola. This approach, as we have seen, put Bunyan on a roller coaster vis-à-vis his security as a believer, for different scriptures told him opposite things. In the end, however, scriptures had to resolve his doubts.

Significant as scriptures, the scroll was absolutely essential to the Christian's journey to the celestial city. However, other writings also acted as media of grace. Two devotional writings his wife inherited from her father, Arthur Dent's *The Plain Man's Pathway to Heaven* and Lewis Bayly's *The Practice of Piety,* started Bunyan on his religious quest. Along the way, Luther's *Commentary on Galatians* made a profound impression. Reading only a little ways, Bunyan related, "I found my condition in his experience, so largely and profoundly handled, as if his book had been written out of my heart." Significant of his high esteem, he went on to add, "I do prefer this book of Martin Luther upon the Galatians (excepting the Holy Bible) before all the books that ever I have seen, as most fit for a wounded conscience."[11]

Thomas Merton, himself a literary figure as well as a monk, discovered the operation of grace through many and varied writings, though most were written by Catholic Christians. Early on, he encountered William Blake and fell captive to him. In *The Seven Storey Mountain* he said of this romance, "I think my love for William Blake had something in it of God's grace. It is a love that has never died, and which has entered very deeply into the development of my life."[12] At Cambridge he discovered Dante, whom he described as "the one great benefit I got out of Cambridge...."[13] At Columbia, under the tutelage of Mark van Doren, he enlarged his contacts with Catholic literature many times over. In Etienne Gilson's *The Spirit of Medieval Philosophy,* he encountered a concept, aseity (God's self-existence), "that was to revolutionize my whole life."[14] The Hindu Bramachari guided him to Augustine's *Confessions* and *The Imitation of Christ,* two other writings that made a profound impression on him. From this point on, Merton read more and more Catholic writings until the 1960s, when he shifted his focus toward oriental wisdom. His own writings show a deep imprint from Zen Buddhist literature, but he ranged far and wide in modern literature—Sartre, Camus, Hemingway, James Baldwin, Flannery O'Conner, and dozens more—drawing grace from all.

From Merton himself we get encouragement to look for grace in media other than typographic. "Books and ideas and poems and stories, pictures and music, buildings, cities, places, philosophies were to be the materials on which grace would work."[15] To these many would add movies such as *Poseidon Adventure, A River Runs Through It, Nell, Schindler's List,* and some other recent offerings to Merton's list.

The Church

Church should be construed broadly enough here to cover both the sacramental concept of Roman Catholics and the Quaker meeting. Sacraments have been acknowledged through the centuries as specific means of grace in all branches of Christianity, and there is no compelling reason to dispute their significance. However, the church itself is what Karl Rahner has called the *Ursakrament,* the original and basic sacrament from which other sacraments draw their meaning. There is good reason, therefore, to focus on the church as a key means of grace.

Although Augustine strayed far from the Catholic Church of Africa during his years as a student in Carthage, from ages nineteen through twenty-eight, he retained some ties even then. His mother had him salted as an infant, that is, enrolled as a catechumen, but she refused to allow him to be baptized even during a serious illness lest he recover and return to his youthful sins. Even in his Manichaean years he continued to attend church on occasion. Yet no matter how far he tried to get away, he could not escape the net altogether because of his ever-vigilant and prayerful mother. She even entreated a bishop who had had some success in rescuing youth from the Manichaean sect to confront her son, but he wisely refused on the grounds that Augustine's arrogance would prevent success. Seeing tears streaming down her cheeks, however, he assured her that "it is impossible that the son of such tears should perish."[16]

Providentially, Augustine came eventually to Milan and to Ambrose. At first he listened to Ambrose only "to try out his eloquence, as it were, and to see whether it came up to its reputation, or whether it flowed forth with greater or less power than was asserted of it."[17] In time, however, he was compelled to go beyond the words to hear the message. Little by little, Augustine became convinced he should "continue as a catechumen in the Catholic Church, commended to me by my parents, until something certain would enlighten me, by which I might direct my course."[18]

More important still than the busy Ambrose and the cathedral church in Milan was a circle of friends from Africa who surrounded Augustine during the years he searched. These included his mother Monica; Alypius, a younger friend from Tagaste who had studied under Augustine at Carthage; Nebridius, who had left home and family in Carthage for no other reason than to live with Augustine "in a most ardent search for truth and wisdom";[19] his unnamed common-law wife, who returned to Carthage when Monica arranged a marriage for Augustine; Adeodatus, Augustine's son by this woman. This little cell group worked diligently to bring Augustine forth from the womb in which he had threshed about for so long. Augustine could write about these friends, "In truth, I loved these friends for their own sakes, and I know that they in turn loved me for my own sake."[20] They confronted him; yet they also gave him freedom to be and to inquire.

John Bunyan would not have accorded sacraments or the church so exalted a place in his experience of the operation of grace as Augustine did in the *City of God,* but *Grace Abounding* and *The Pilgrim's Progress* show he was not incognizant of their place. In Bedford three or four "poor women" intrigued him with conversation about "a new birth, the work of God in their hearts,…"[21] Fascinated by their sincerity, he began to attend the meetings of the Bedford church regularly. Little by little, he became sufficiently comfortable in their presence to talk about his condition. Here the pastor, John Gifford, took Bunyan under wing and encouraged him. For a time all efforts of this group to put props under him fell short as Bunyan's mercurial faith shot up and down. Gifford's teaching, Bunyan observed, "by God's grace, was much for my stability," and helped to deliver him from hard and unsound tests.[22] In the end, it is not surprising that Bunyan finally arrived at the critical stage in the context of this church.

In *The Pilgrim's Progress* Bunyan has almost certainly depicted the Bedford congregation under the rubric of Interpreter's House. Interpreter himself may well be John Gifford. At the conclusion of this section Christian recites a poem reflective of the Bedford church's place in his pilgrimage.

Here I have seen things rare and profitable;
Things pleasant, dreadful, things to make me stable;
In what I have begun to take in hand;
Then let me think on them and understand
Wherefore they showed me were; and let me be
Thankful, O good Interpreter, to thee.[23]

Individualistic as early Baptists were in their understanding of salvation, they knew experientially the church as *Ursakrament*. They differed from Anglicans and Roman Catholics chiefly in their conviction that church is not so much a hierarchy and priests administering grace through sacraments as it is people who receive grace through the reading of scriptures and the preaching of the Word.

Thomas Merton had both negative and positive experiences of the church. In *The Seven Storey Mountain* he dismissed almost flippantly Quaker meetings he had attended as a child with his mother and Anglican or Episcopal services he visited with his father or grandparents. He liked the silence of Quaker services, he admitted, but he did not care for the speeches. "They are like all the rest," he concluded after attending one meeting. "In other churches it is the minister who hands out the common places, and here it is liable to be just anybody."[24] He characterized the Church of England as "a class religion, the cult of a special society and group, not even of a whole nation, but of the ruling minority in a nation." What held it together was "certainly not much doctrinal unity, much less a mystical bond between people many of whom have even ceased to believe in grace or Sacraments."[25]

Merton was drawn toward the Roman Catholic Church precisely because of its mystical and sacramental appeal. Long before he decided to become a Catholic, he visited churches in France and in Rome. In Byzantine mosaics of Rome, he recorded, he found "an art that was tremendously serious and alive and eloquent and urgent in all that it had to say."[26] For the first time in his life, he said, he "began to find out something of Who this Person was that [people] called Christ." Though he could not decode all he saw, "the realest and most immediate source of this grace was Christ Himself, present in those churches, in all His power, and in His Humanity, in His Human Flesh and His material, physical, corporeal Presence."[27] Merton's visit to these churches set him up for an experience of the presence of his father that "overwhelmed [him] with a sudden and profound insight into the misery and corruption of [his] own soul," which caused him really to pray for the first time, "not with my lips and with my intellect and my imagination, but praying out of the very roots of my life and of my being, and praying to the God I had never known, to reach down towards me out of [God's] darkness and to help me to get free of the thousand terrible things that held my will in their slavery."[28]

Merton let all of these feelings lapse during his early years at Columbia. In time, however, he found himself drawn almost inexplicably to attend a Catholic mass. "What a revelation it was," he commented, "to discover so many ordinary people in a place together, more conscious of God than of one another, not there to show off their hats or their clothes, but to pray, or at least to fulfill a religious obligation, not a human one."[29] From the pulpit he heard a sermon that had "the full force not only of scripture but of centuries of a unified and continuous and consistent tradition."[30] The rest of the story is familiar:

how Merton increasingly felt impelled to become a Catholic and finally a Trappist monk. If the church itself represented grace, still more did the monastery, where the City of God had for him its best modeling.

Persons

Many other means or media of grace could be enumerated, but I will conclude with persons. In the stories of all three of our "Doctors of Grace," persons figured prominently. Some have been mentioned already. We can now look more closely at several others.

The person who stands out above all others in Augustine's story as an instrument of grace is obviously Monica, his mother. It is fairly evident, however, that she played both a negative and a positive role. Both she and Augustine's father burdened him with high expectations. In addition, Monica loaded him down with guilt regarding his sexuality. In the early part of the story, prior to conversion, one can hear Augustine screaming between the lines, "Mom, get off my back!" Not surprisingly, when he went to Rome to teach, he slipped away secretly at night lest she call him back to Carthage or go with him.[31] Later, she did follow, persuading him in Milan to send his common-law wife back to Africa in order to take a legitimate one, so young that Augustine had to wait two years for her to reach marriageable age.

Nevertheless, the positive dominates Augustine's interpretation of her involvement in his conversion story. Whereas he hardly mentioned his father Patricius, and then negatively, he wove Monica, always saintly if not always wise, into virtually every segment of the story. His natural mother and his mother the church were virtually one in bringing him to birth as a believer. Her prayers and entreaties kept him in touch with the church even in his prodigal years. Indeed, she conveyed God's word directly.

> Do I dare to say that you, my God, remained silent when I departed still farther from you? Did you in truth remain silent to me at that time? Whose words but yours were those that you sang in my ears by means of my mother, your faithful servant?[32]

When Augustine stole away without her and went to Rome, she continued to pray. And, according to Augustine, God could not help but respond to the pleas of a widow so devout.

> But would you, O God of mercies, have despised the contrite and humbled heart of so chaste and sober a widow, generous in alms-giving, faithful and helpful to your holy ones, letting no day pass without an offering at your altar, going without fail to church

twice a day, in the morning and at evening, not for empty stories and old wives' tales, but that she might hear you in your instructions and that you might hear her in her prayers? Could you, by whose gift she was such, despise and reject from your help those tears, by which she sought from you not gold and silver or any changing, fleeting good but the salvation of her son's soul? By no means, O Lord! Yes, you were present to help her, and you graciously heard her,...[33]

She stayed with him as he despaired of finding the truth. Though no match intellectually, she let her heart speak for her. In Milan she continued her motherly entreaties and prayers, and she was present when Augustine took the leap of faith in the garden at Cassiaciacum. Although she lived only a short while after his baptism on Easter of 387, she had left her indelible mark.

John Bunyan got in touch with God's grace working in his life through many persons. I've mentioned three or four women of Bedford and John Gifford, pastor of the church in Bedford, which Bunyan himself later served. Bunyan's first wife, whose name he did not give, encouraged him in his search and set before him the example of her godly father. His second wife, Elizabeth, stood by him during his twelve-year imprisonment, from 1660 to 1672, for refusal to stop unlicensed preaching. Only eighteen when she married him and saw him hauled off to jail, she cared for his four small children, one of whom was blind. Bunyan could help financially only by making boot laces. She did everything she could to secure his release. Small wonder that Bunyan depicted her story in much happier imagery than he used for his own when he added it to *The Pilgrim's Progress.*

Many persons played significant roles in Thomas Merton's awakening to the operation of grace in his life. From his parents he inherited the sensitivities of an artist, though neither had anything to do with his decision to join the Roman Catholic Church. As a lonely and unsettled student at Columbia University, he acquired a circle of friends, chief of whom was a young Jew named Bob Lax, whom Merton described as possessing "a kind of natural, instinctive spirituality, a kind of inborn direction to the living God."[34] Elsewhere, he characterized him as "steeped in holiness, in charity, in disinterestedness."[35] Lax later received baptism as a Catholic and was ordained a priest. The two persons who had the most to do with steering Merton toward the Roman Catholic Church, however, were Mark van Doren and Daniel Walsh. Van Doren, Professor of English Literature at Columbia, was possessed of "supernatural simplicity" or "a kind of heroic humility," Merton judged.[36] "Mark, I know, is no stranger to the order of grace," he said, "but considering his work as a teacher merely as a mission on the natural level—I can see that Providence was using him as an instrument more directly than I realized."[37] Van Doren steered Merton toward a scholastic approach and away from the dialecticism of Marxism. It was he who, though not a Catholic, posed for Merton the question of his vocation to the priesthood. Van Doren also helped Merton with his early publications. Daniel Walsh was a Thomist and a Professor of Philosophy at Sacred Heart College at Manhattanville who was lecturing at Columbia. Though a Catholic layman, it was he whom Merton first consulted seriously about becoming a priest. He "turned out to be another one of those destined in a providential way to shape and direct my vocation," Merton wrote later. "For it was he who pointed out my way to the place where I am now."[38] Walsh quickly sized Merton up as an "Augustinian," which Merton took as a great compliment, for it put him in the lineage of Anselm, Bernard, Hugo and Richard of St. Victor, and Duns Scotus. He also fingered Merton's vocation to the priesthood. "We sat down in one of the far corners [of a hotel], and it was there, two being gathered together in His Name and in His charity, that Christ impressed the first definite form and direction upon my vocation," explained Merton.[39] Discussing Catholic religious orders that he might join, Walsh spoke with the greatest enthusiasm about the Cistercians and shared his impression from a retreat he had taken the summer before at Gethsemani. Though Merton rejected this suggestion in favor of the Franciscans, Gethsemani turned out to be the place he would spend his entire career as a monk. Dan Walsh later came to live at Gethsemani himself and was ordained there.

Numerous others served as Merton's midwives and mothers of grace in the Abbey of Gethsemani. One of the basic assumptions of monastic formation is the necessity of a spiritual director. Merton served in that capacity for many both inside and outside the monastery. He had a knack for beaming in on the wavelength of another person.

On Being Midwives and Mothers of Grace

What can we learn from these examples about being midwives and mothers of grace? One thing that we should recognize from the start is that grace cannot be manipulated like a puppet on a string, for experience, especially experience in the depths, is one of its most effective aides. There is also no limit to the number of ways people may awaken, in Bunyan's phrase, to "the merciful working of God" in their lives.

Second, awareness of this should encourage patience on our part. We are often too eager to drag people away from their crises like firemen rescuing people from a burning building, and we fail to see that God's grace needs time to shape and mold in the crucible of life. Experience is itself full of grace, and if we give it time, it may do a far better job than we can. Sometimes we can assist more by keeping hands off than we can by trying to strong-arm a struggler. The strong arm approach, which Monica used on Augustine, for instance, probably impeded and delayed his breakthrough. We can empathize with her concern, but a midwife had best wait for the end of the term before she tries to pull the child through the birth canal.

Third, all the means of grace should teach us not to circumscribe too narrowly, thinking grace can operate only through scriptures or through sacraments or through this or that kind of person. Central as scriptures are to the life of Christians and the church, they will not supply the only channel through which God directs gracious love toward people. Indeed, they can create as well as resolve problems of faith, and, as we have seen in Bunyan's case, many will need some guidance in interpreting and applying them to their lives. In the case of Augustine, Bunyan, and Merton, moreover, other writings played critical roles. In *Thoughts in Solitude* Merton has reminded how significant other writings may be:

> Books can speak to us like God, like men [or women] or like the noise of the city we live in. They speak to us like God when they bring us light and peace and fill us with silence. They speak to us like God when we desire never to leave them. They speak to us like men [or women] when we desire to hear them again. They speak to us like the noise of the city when they hold us captive by a weariness that tells us nothing, give us no peace, and no support, nothing to remember, and yet will not let us escape.[40]

In this cybernetic age, as we are moving from a typographic to a more iconic and tactual culture, we must recognize, as Merton did, how many different things may supply "the materials on which grace would work."

Fourth, this cultural transition would seem to encourage Protestants to seek to recover more of the basic sense of awe and wonder Catholics, Anglicans, and Orthodox associate with sacraments or mysteries. Excess of zeal in the reform movements of the sixteenth and seventeenth centuries diminished the sacramental sensitivities. Our Protestant forebears stripped the churches bare and minimized the sacraments. Yet it is almost certainly true, as Abraham Joshua Heschel has noted in *Man Is Not Alone,* that "when mind and soul agree, belief is born. But first our hearts must know the shudder of adoration."[41] The reason many Baby Boomers and GenXers have turned to Eastern cults or experiential ones may be because we have done away with the media that serve awe.

Fifth, mention of Baby Boomers and GenXers underscores the importance of recognizing corporate channels, another point that bears on being midwives and mothers of grace. Both Boomers and Busters have intense interest in spirituality and in community. Many have suffered religious abuse from institutions, but they are drawn toward open and affirming groups such as

Augustine experienced at Cassiaciacum, in which he felt loved for himself and that gave him freedom to seek, or Bunyan found at Bedford, which gave him both encouragement and stability as he pitched around like a small ship on a stormy sea.

Sixth, vis-à-vis persons, we should be conscious of the wide range and manner in which people serve as media of grace. I have heard a friend say that his parents were incapable of being grace to him, but I doubt whether any person is "incapable" of being grace to another. My father was a bright and capable man whose alcoholism cost him his business and his family and prevented him from realizing his potential in life, but he was grace to me. For one thing, the memory of his battle with alcohol has sharpened my own sensitivities to a low tolerance to it. Sometimes others are grace in what we learn from negative experiences, as Augustine learned from the wrong sort of youthful companions. They awaken us to our capacity for wrong. Almost all are mixed instruments, like Monica. Being more positive than negative requires a work of God in our lives.

Notes

1. Wayne E. Oates, *Confessions of a Workaholic* (New York: World Publishing Co., 1971), 47–48.

2. Augustine, *Confessions* 4.4.9; *The Confessions of St. Augustine,* trans. John K. Ryan (Garden City, N.Y.: Doubleday Image Books, 1960), 98.

3. Ibid., 4.7.12, 100–101.

4. John Bunyan, *Grace Abounding* 175; Everyman's Library (London: Dent; New York: Dutton, 1928, 1963), 54.

5. Ibid., 206; Everyman's Library, 65.

6. Ibid., 213. Everyman's Library, 66–67.

7. For a more extended discussion of this, see my address as president of the National Association of Baptist Professors of Religion, "The Educational Task of Baptist Professors of Religion on the Edge of a New Millennium," *Perspectives in Religious Studies* 22 (Fall 1995): 227–37. A paper that I asked students to write on "How I Learn" indicates that students continue to rely on the printed word, but today they count much more on seeing and touching.

8. See Peter Brown, *Augustine of Hippo: A Biography* (London: Faber and Faber, 1967), 40–45.

9. Augustine, *Confessions* 3.4.7, 81.

10. Bunyan, *Grace Abounding* 46; Everyman's Library, 19.

11. Ibid., 129, 130; Everyman's Library, 42–42.

12. Merton, *The Seven Storey Mountain* (New York: Harcourt Brace Jovanovich, Publishers, 1948), 85.

13. Ibid., 122.

14. Ibid., 172.

15. Ibid., 178.

16. Augustine, *Confessions* 3.12.21, 92.

17. Ibid., 5.13.23, 130.

18. Ibid., 5.14.25, 132.

19. Ibid., 6.10.17, 148.

20. Ibid., 6.16.26, 155.

21. Bunyan, *Grace Abounding* 37; Everyman's Library, 16.

22. Ibid., 117; Everyman's Library, 37.

23. John Bunyan, *The Pilgrim's Progress*. Everyman's Library (Rev. ed.; London: J. M. Dent & Sons Ltd; New York: E. P. Dutton & Co Inc, 1954, 1961), 39.

24. Merton, *Seven Storey Mountain,* 116.

25. Ibid., 65.

26. Ibid., 108.

27. Ibid., 109.

28. Ibid., 111.

29. Ibid., 208.

30. Ibid., 209.

31. Augustine, *Confessions* 5.8.15.

32. Ibid., 2.3.7, 68.

33. Ibid., 5.9.17, 125.

34. Merton, *Seven Storey Mountain,* 181.

35. Ibid., 236.

36. Ibid., 138.

37. Ibid., 140.

38. Ibid., 219.

39. Ibid., 261.

40. Thomas Merton, *Thoughts in Solitude* (Garden City, N.Y.: Doubleday Image Books, 1958), 61–62.

41. Abraham Joshua Heschel, *Man Is Not Alone: A Philosophy of Religion* (New York: Farrar, Straus, and Giroux, Inc., 1951), 74.

Benedict M. Ashley

41. Spirituality and Counseling

Physical, Psychological, and Ethical Counseling

The ultimate aim of all counseling is to assist a client to make realistic decisions.[1] These decisions must also be ethical, because unethical decisions ignore the real requirements of human well-being. Unethical decisions would probably lead to consequences that are harmful to the decision maker as well as to others. Counseling help is needed for many types of decisions, only one of which is specifically and directly the client's *spiritual* welfare. What does "spiritual" welfare mean? Today that term and its related nouns *spirit* and *spirituality* are used so loosely as to be almost meaningless.[2] Therefore, I begin this essay by trying to give a precise meaning to "spiritual counseling" as distinct from other forms of counseling.

Four types of counseling can be distinguished, although they are so closely interrelated that they are often confused. First, there is a range of kinds of counseling that we can group as *physical* because they deal directly with clients' bodily well-being. A kind of physical counseling, *economic* counseling helps clients make realistic decisions about how to obtain the material goods necessary or at least useful for a good life. *Medical* counseling helps them make realistic decisions about health. *Security* counseling helps in making realistic decisions about how to protect themselves from injury by external physical forces.

Second, *psychological* counseling (including all types of psychotherapy except those that are purely medical) aims to free clients from those emotional and cognitive factors that limit their ability to make free and objective decisions. Obviously the ranges of these first two kinds of counseling, the physical and the psychological, overlap somewhat, because mental problems can arise from economic, medical, and security conditions that must be corrected or ameliorated before successful psychotherapy is feasible. Conversely, clients who lack the clarity of mind and freedom needed to make realistic decisions cannot deal successfully with physical problems.

Ethical counseling is often confused with psychological counseling, but it actually deals with decisions that are fully conscious and fully free and that require us to choose among alternative ways of acting to reach the realistic goals of human living. Such ethical counseling extends both to the management of clients' own private behavior and to their social relations to other persons. Sometimes the counselor and client agree on a worldview and value system—for example, when both are Catholics who accept the church's faith and moral guidance. In that case the counselor helps the client form a prudent conscience based on the moral norms accepted by both and on a careful examination of the circumstances and possible consequences of alternative decisions. When, on the other hand, the counselor and client have different worldviews and value systems, moral counseling can only take the form of "value clarification."[3] In such cases the counselor can help clients clarify their personal values so as to recognize inconsistencies in their thinking or behaving, but counselors are seldom in any position to attempt to change the priorities of their clients. Hence a client's worldview and value system must be taken as a given, unless it is obviously unacceptable in the society in which the client has to live or becomes seriously dangerous to others. Hence an ethical counselor, for example a lawyer, cannot counsel a criminal to act consistently with his commitment to a life of crime. But the counselor would exceed professional limits if he or she were to attempt to make a Protestant a Catholic, a Jew or Muslim or secular humanist a Christian by changing their religious commitment from one set of moral values to another. Thus, when moral counseling is limited to value-clarification it tends to overlap with psychological counseling, because psychotherapists also generally make no attempt to alter the value systems of their clients unless those systems are obviously dangerous or socially unacceptable.

When, however, the counselor and client have value systems that are the same or largely overlap, the ethical counselor ought not to confine his services simply to helping the client solve particular moral dilemmas. In moral matters it is not enough to make good decisions, it is also necessary to help clients develop moral integrity or good *character*. Character is formed by certain decisional skills or "virtues" that make it easier for a person to act in a consistently moral manner. In helping clients develop such moral skills, counselors can profit from classical "virtue theory" that provides a psychologically based classification known as the *four cardinal virtues*.[4]

In this classification *temperance* (moderation) enables persons to achieve a realistic control of their drives for pleasure, *fortitude* (courage) a realistic control of their drives for aggression.[5] These two sets of drives are essentially biological, and the virtues that control them resemble such bodily skills as are developed by athletes and dancers. In contrast to these two cardinal virtues are two others that perfect the more spiritual aspect of the human person. In the spiritual will, the virtue of *justice* prompts concern for the rights of others. In the spiritual intelligence, *prudence* facilitates moral reasoning for making realistic decisions. Hence, the scope of temperance and fortitude largely overlaps with the field of the drives and emotions with which psychological counseling is concerned, but the field of justice and prudence is especially that of moral counseling.

In our culture various aspects of ethical counseling are performed by various kinds of experts. For example, decisions that affect human rights and hence have an ethical aspect often require the lawyer's advice. Most often, however, people make ethical decisions with the help of the informal counseling of friends or family and the clergy. Yet in my opinion, although the clergy or others with a religious ministry are often called upon for ethical counseling, this is not the type of counseling that more properly characterizes their role. The special role of the clergy is, I would argue, spiritual counseling,[6] although I by no means intend to imply that it is exclusively theirs. Other nonordained persons with adequate theological and pastoral training can perform this task successfully.

Aims and Objectives of Spiritual Counseling

For many people in today's culture, *spirituality* is a term that connotes a certain distaste for "organized religion." Frederick M. Denny, in an essay titled, "To Serve Allah in a Foreign Land: Muslim Spirituality in the North American Diaspora"[7] describes the situation well:

> It might be that "spirituality" is not the best term for characterizing Muslims' religious lives in North America in general. The word has become a euphemism for religion in an age when many people do not choose to affiliate with traditional Christian or Jewish denominational religion, for example, but instead want to enrich their lives by means of a spiritual quest at a personal-individual rather than a tradition-institutional level. In other words, for many people, spiritually is "in" and "religion" is "out." There are various forms of contemporary spirituality, ranging from engagement with Asian religions, New Age movements and Neo-Paganism to non-denominational, usually strongly evangelical Christian churches including the growing "mega-churches" around North America.

Thus even the religious right tends to emphasize private religious experience at the expense of a visible church that has the authority to guide the individual conscience. Yet if one considers that we human persons are intensely social in nature it is difficult to see how an effective spirituality can be achieved except in a community of a common faith. Why would anyone need a spiritual counselor, or how can such a counselor be certified as trustworthy, if individuals can find their own spiritual path without social support? The concept of spirituality, therefore, cannot be separated from the concept of "religion" that implies some kind of human community that shares essentially the same convictions about life.

In my book *Theologies of the Body: Humanist and Christian,*[8] I emphasized that it is a mistake to restrict, as is so often done, the term religion to faith in God or even some transcendent Absolute. Scholars of comparative religion point out that if we are to make meaningful comparisons between the great world religions, we must abstract from the *content* of their beliefs and simply define them by their *function* as "world-views and value systems."[9] This becomes obvious when we note that though everyone considers Buddhism as one of the great world religions, Buddhists do not believe in God or in the human person but in an ineffable Void.[10] If, therefore, we define *religion* as a worldview and value system shared by a community, we should also admit that the secular humanism so widespread in the world today is a genuine religion. Though secular humanists reject the term *religion* as a name for their worldview and value system, it functions for them in much the same way that Christianity, Judaism, Islam, or Buddhism do for their own adherents. Although one of its chief values is "freedom of thought," secular humanism is a unified and coherent worldview in which the supreme value is the autonomy of the individual. Obviously there is a paradox in such an individualistic religion, but that it is the *shared* conviction and way of life of very many Americans can be easily demonstrated by watching TV or reading many of our "self-help" books. In secular humanism the autonomy of the individual is an article of faith, and dissent from that faith entails an excommunication or exclusion from an in-group not very different from the excommunications enforced in the more "organized" world religions. Thus the most workable definition of *spirituality* is a personal commitment to a worldview and value system shared with a committed community the members of which strive to actuate in life in an honest and consistent manner.

Thus, even if the worldview of and value system shared by secular humanists denies the existence of a spiritual realm transcending our sensible experience, it is not an oxymoron to speak of a secular humanist spirituality. It is important to make this point because it means that there will be as many types of spiritual counseling as there are religions, including the spirituality of persons who think they have no religion.

Since there are different kinds of worldviews and value systems each with its own type of spirituality, unless we surrender all personal autonomy and simply conform to the community in which we find ourselves, we are each faced with the inescapable necessity of deciding which is the truest and best. Thus we must compare the range of what Paul Tillich called "ultimate concerns," that is, what a given person values most in life. Karl Rahner spoke of this decision and commitment as the "fundamental option"[11] that involves the "fundamental freedom" of any person at the root of our "categorial freedom" to make particular concrete practical decisions. In the classical moral theology of the Roman Catholic tradition, this was called "the choice of one's ultimate end." St. Thomas Aquinas argued that in every "human act," that is, every conscious and free choice no matter how trivial it might be, the prime motivator of every choice was the ultimate end to which the chooser was already committed. If this commitment was realistically in conformity with the needs of the human person, either those that are innate or those elevated by divine grace, then choices that further that commitment are respectively natural or graced good acts. Choices contradictory to such a realistic commitment are sins, and if they are knowingly, freely, and deliberately made concerning serious matters they are *mortal sins* that convert this commitment to some other ultimate value that is not true happiness. For example, the deliberate choice to do serious harm to another person is a mortal sin that changes one's ultimate end from love of God and neighbor to a destructive self-interest. Sins are said to be *venial* if they do not involve informed, free, and deliberate choices or do not concern serious matters. As such they do not change a person's commitment to true happiness but gradually weaken that commitment at the risk of eventual mortal sin. Thus spiritual counseling, since it concerns commitment to the authentic goal of human life, must help the client become free of mortal sin by conversion to this true goal, and must support a consistent effort by the client also to eliminate venial sin. It is odd that so much writing about spirituality today says so much about love and so little about sin. Granted that the positive aim of spiritual counseling is to deepen the client's commitment to the true goal of life, namely, love of God and neighbor, helping clients free themselves from the bondage of sin, especially mortal sin, is a necessary objective. What physician would talk only about good diet and exercise, and never warn about the effects of bad eating habits and lack of exercise or fail to point out that surgery or chemotherapy for a cancer ought not be refused? Spiritual growth is not possible without a struggle against its negation, namely sin.

Thus "spiritual counseling" in an analogical sense that abstracts from the differences between these religions can be defined as *that form of counseling that aims to help clients discover their fundamental option (ultimate concern, ultimate end) or commitment to a worldview and value system.* It also helps them to consider whether they ought to change that worldview and value system and to live consistently and honestly in conformity to that life goal. Clearly this presupposes that the client is making good physical, psychological, and ethical decisions in relation to this ultimate goal. Yet too often these other types of counseling founder on the failure of a person to recognize who they really are by reason of their fundamental option. Until one faces this issue realistically, life can only be a succession of contradictions that gets nowhere. Hence the specific counseling task for the clergy and others in explicitly religious ministry is *spiritual* counseling, not simply ethical counseling, since it involves what a Christian would call "the salvation of one's soul," that is, one's ultimate concern.

The spiritual counselor, therefore, must help clients explicitly recognize the worldview and value system to which they are in fact committed and which is dominating their lives. They must then be helped to ask and answer for themselves whether without proper reflection they have committed themselves to the wrong goal and need to change it to a more realistic goal. In the process of spiritual counseling, it may become clear to the client that her priorities are inconsistent, confused, or lacking in a dynamic motivation that will make her fully effective in practical life. Hence spiritual counselors or "directors" aim to help clients not only to choose a worldview and value system for their lives, but also to recognize the implications of this commitment and the need to make it more consistent, profound, and dynamic.

Spiritual Counseling and the Structure of the Human Person

In our present culture, however, the evaluation of these different types of human commitment often lacks any criteria. A principle source of this confusion is a faulty anthropology and psychology. Many psychologists today identify human thought and free choice with the activity of the brain. Certainly the marvelous human brain is a necessary instrument for the human activities of abstract thought and free choice. Nevertheless, these specifically human activities transcend the spatial-temporal capacities of a material brain and distinguish human life from animal life and constitute us *persons* whose souls are truly *spiritual,* that is, not of the material order and thus destined to immortality.[12] This distinction from animal life by the capacity for abstract thought and freedom of choice is empirically evidenced by human creativity in language, diversity of culture, and technical control over nature that is grounded in our capacity to explore its laws.

Secular humanists are generally materialists, yet by using the term *spirituality* they admit the possibility that we humans can somehow transcend purely material concerns. For example, they often speak of the "spiritual values" of the fine arts or of other forms of human creativity. Yet they also generally assume that science has established that these "spiritual" activities are purely emotional and subjective and can be accounted for by the identity of our minds with brain activities. Why then call them "spiritual"? On the other hand, it is equally unconvincing to identify the human self with the human spirit alone, as does Platonism and many Eastern religions. Such a claim that the true self is purely spiritual results in the doctrine that the spirit is reincarnated in successive bodies in contrast to the doctrine shared by Judaism, Christianity, and Islam that there will be a bodily resurrection of the total person in eternal life. Such a dualistic anthropology tends to support the notion that the human spirit is only a part of the divine spirit into which after many reincarnations it will be absorbed.

Christian Spiritual Counseling

Christian anthropology shares with Judaism and Islam this conviction that the human person has been created with a material body given intelligent life by an immaterial soul; the two are so intrinsically related that God will restore their union after death in the resurrection. Thus each of us will exist in eternal life as the unique persons the Creator created us to be; not absorbed into some impersonal Absolute. The three monotheistic religions agree that the true destiny of every created person is an eternal life in God's presence. Christians further believe that this communion with a personal God has been made possible by free choice of the Son of God to became incarnate in order to free us by the power of the Holy Spirit from our sinful alienation from the Father.

If this Christian anthropology is accepted, then the counseling relationship itself becomes a paradigm of the interpersonal relationships in which our relation to God is destined to culminate. The biblical God is our supremely wise and patient Counselor as well as our Creator, who bestows on us our individual freedom and guides us on the way to our ultimate fulfillment in the community of all persons, divine and created, who have freely chosen each other in love. Thus Christian spiritual counseling is conceived as a participation in the activity of the divine counselor who is the Holy Spirit, of the Son who has chosen to share our human condition, and of the Father who created us. This participation always has the character of a communion in meditative prayer in which the counselor and the client together seek to respond to the Holy Spirit.

Thus Christian spiritual counseling aims at cooperating with the Holy Spirit in forming human persons in the image of Jesus Christ by the gift of the three theological virtues of Christian faith, hope, and love bestowed in baptism. Faith transforms the human spiritual intellect; hope and love transform the spiritual will. Together they transform the human person into the likeness of Jesus, the God-Man. Eastern Christian spirituality even dares to speak of this as a "deification" *(theosis).* [13] While the cardinal moral virtues free the human person from undue attachment to temporal values, they also facilitate the work of the theological virtues by which the human person attains direct contact with the living triune God.

For modern psychology under the influence of Sigmund Freud, our creative, specifically human activities, even their highest realization in mysticism, are attributed to the unconscious or subconscious psyche. It is supposed that a psychological function that Freud called the "censor" ordinarily prevents these creative processes from entering into the ego of self-conscious life.

Carl G. Jung, though he had greater respect for religious phenomena than did Freud, attempted to explain these processes as the product of a primitive "collective unconscious." I have argued elsewhere,[14] however, that it is utterly paradoxical to assign the highest, most human, most personal, most creative and free activities of the human person to the *animal pole* of the psyche since it is deterministically instinctive and unfree. The great mystics and theoreticians of mysticism, such as Meister Eckhart and Teresa of Avila, locate these activities at the *spiritual pole* of the psyche in a "superconsciousness," an *apex mentis,* or *ratio superior.* (Note that this superconsciousness should not be confused with the Freudian superego that pertains to subconscious life.)

Besides Freud's materialism, two valid clinical observations seem to have misled him. First, we are usually most clearly aware of the contents of the ego, because this is the area of the practical, verbalizable consciousness of everyday life. The superconscious level of the psyche, however, is the level of insights so profound that they are difficult or impossible to verbalize. Thus Jacques Maritain in his *Creative Intuition*[15] showed that when beginning a new work an artist usually has only a formative idea that cannot be verbalized and can only be expressed in the work of art itself. Again, true human love or commitment to a life vocation cannot be adequately verbalized yet they animate the very depths and center of the human spirit. This is why for many, their commitment to matters of ultimate concern or their life goals are very difficult to put into words and can only gradually and with difficulty be formulated. Hence the need for the help of the spiritual counselor to make them explicit.

The second clinical observation that has led to confusing the spiritual superconscious pole of the psyche with its unconscious animal pole is that our creative moments often also involve a release of suppressed images and emotions. In psychoanalytic free association, "a regression in the service of the Ego"[16] takes place in the presence of a nonjudgmental and supporting analyst. Similarly in the process of "brainstorming," people find it easier to formulate creative ideas because the facilitator assures them that no one will criticize unconventional thinking. Nevertheless, there is a vast difference between the suppressed contents of the animal subconscious and the suppressed content of spiritual creativity. What they have in common is simply the lowering of the inhibitions (the censor) necessary for us to carry on the routine of practical everyday life. Perhaps when Jesus said, "Unless you become like little children you cannot enter the kingdom of heaven," he meant that the realm of the spirit can be shut off by the practicalities of adult life and must be again opened to spiritual realities by a childlike transparency.

Thus spiritual counseling and psychoanalysis are similar in that the ego, with its practical, routine concerns, must be quieted in order that suppressed activities of the psyche can emerge and be recognized by the client. They differ in that psychoanalysis seeks to remove the censorship so that the unconscious

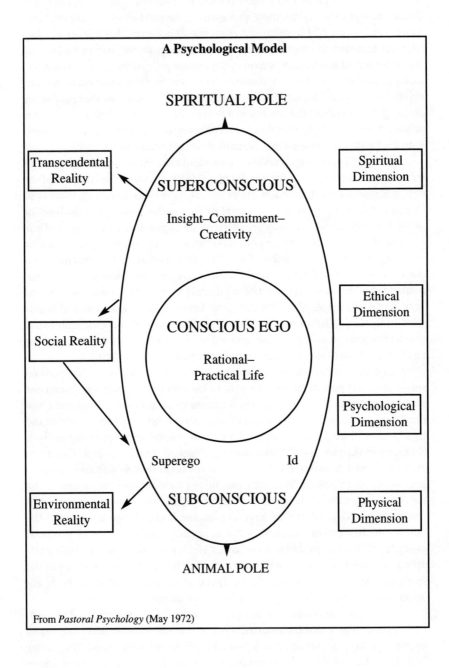

A Psychological Model

SPIRITUAL POLE

Transcendental Reality

Spiritual Dimension

SUPERCONSCIOUS

Insight–Commitment–
Creativity

Ethical Dimension

Social Reality

CONSCIOUS EGO

Rational–
Practical Life

Psychological Dimension

Superego   Id

Environmental Reality

SUBCONSCIOUS

Physical Dimension

ANIMAL POLE

From *Pastoral Psychology* (May 1972)

processes that are reducing the freedom of conscious life may emerge into consciousness, while spiritual counseling seeks to remove the censorship that prevents the emergence of the creative superconscious processes.

St. Catherine of Siena, in her classic *Dialogue*[17] with God the Father, received from him three rules of spiritual counseling.[18] These rules are characteristic of the whole Christian tradition of spiritual counseling from the time of the desert fathers.[19] The first rule is an application of Jesus' warning in the Sermon on the Mount, "Do not judge if you would not be judged." The counselor seeks to understand the working of the Holy Spirit in the client, knowing that the Holy Spirit alone can know the depths of any human person. Unless counselors take this attitude of humility before the client, they will be blinded by their own spiritual deficiencies and tempted to dominate rather than to help the client to spiritual freedom. This rule resembles the "unconditional acceptance" demanded of psychological counselors, yet it goes much further, since it is an awareness of the *sacred* character of the work of the Holy Spirit in the depths of the human person.

The second rule received by Catherine follows from the first. Since the activity of the Holy Spirit in the client (as well as in the counselor) is mysterious, neither must be fooled by superficial religious "experiences." This rule is especially important in our culture, in which "experience" is so highly valued and often too much trusted. Too many seek out spiritual direction in the hope of such novel experiences. While there is indeed an experiential aspect of spiritual life, spiritual progress is not to be evaluated by emotional, imaginative, or even intellectually insightful "experiences." St. John of the Cross urges us not to pay much attention even to genuine visions and revelations. He says that not only are most such experiences liable to illusion, but even when they are genuinely from God their purpose is accomplished for spiritual advancement by the very fact of God's gift. Hence they should be received simply with thanksgiving, not with attachment or with a demand for more.[20] Catherine and John and all the great Christian spiritual writers emphasize that growth in holiness is growth in love of God and neighbor, a love that is founded in faith in God's guidance and of God's love of the neighbor and fostered by hope of union with God and neighbor. Consequently the counselor should be concerned only with whether the client is advancing in the theological virtues of faith, hope, and charity, since Christian holiness consists essentially in these virtues. All good counseling has moments of encouragement and of confrontation with reality. Good spiritual counseling, therefore, encourages every indication of growth in faith, hope, and love and confronts the client with every indication of any other motivation or of any other reliance in the client's spiritual striving except reliance on God in faith, hope, and love.

The third rule transmitted by Catherine is that the spiritual counselor should accept the uniqueness of every client. St. Thomas Aquinas says that God created each human person as a unique image of himself, reflecting something of his own perfection.[21] Every person reflects God in a unique way and thus makes an irreplaceable contribution to God's creation. Consequently the Holy Spirit, as the supreme counselor, leads each person in a unique way to the triune community that is the One God.

Counseling Risks and Gains

In addition to these fundamental principles stated by St. Catherine, counseling experience suggests a number of other cautions and suggestions. The first of these, common to all types of counseling, is the risk of codependence. Temporary dependence of the client on the counselor, of course, cannot be avoided since it is intrinsic to the relationship. This dependence can also legitimately become permanent in cases where the client is a *disciple* of the counselor. Thus in the monastic tradition, monks were often dependent on the guidance of the same abbot throughout a lifetime. It is noteworthy, however, that Jesus said to his disciples, "For if I do not go, the Paraclete will not come to you. But if I go I will send him to you" (Jn 18:7b). He was saying that the kind of dependence they had on him in his earthly life had to yield to a reliance on the interior guidance of the Holy Spirit if they were to fully mature in Jesus' image. A failure on the part of counselors to work to make their guidance *dispensable* by the client can lead to disaster. They are then no longer working primarily for the welfare of the client but to meet their own needs. I know of a well-meaning and spiritually gifted priest who was of help to many as a spiritual director. One nun became increasingly dependent on him for guidance. To have an easier access to his direction than was possible in her cloistered situation, she finally left her community and religious life. The priest counselor in turn came to feel so responsible for her that he finally reluctantly left the priesthood and married her, thus deserting the other clients whom he had helped or might in the future have helped by his gifts as a spiritual director. Evidently, under the guise of a "responsibility" to one client, he had become dependent on her to satisfy his own emotional needs. On the other hand, there are classic examples among the saints where counseling relationships developed into genuine friendships that were of mutual spiritual benefit. Examples are the friendship of the Dominicans Bl. Raymond of Capua and St. Catherine of Siena, that of the Carmelites John of the Cross and St. Teresa of Avila, and that between two founders of religious congregations St. Francis de Sales and St. Jane de Chantal. The letters recording these friendships, however, show great sensitivity to the need to avoid codependency.

Again, spiritual counselors have a double task. On the one hand they must encourage the client and reinforce every indication of genuine spiritual progress. John of the Cross says that most Christians striving for holiness are like the Hebrews in the desert who came again and again to the edge of the

Promised Land. Each time when they were about to enter it, they grew fearful and turned back to wander about for a long time in the wilderness before again approaching the border. "No pain, no gain," say physical trainers, and so in the spiritual life real progress is possible only by plunging into what John of the Cross called "the dark nights of the soul and of the spirit."[22] The first dark night is necessary to free the person from "consolations" (that is, "religious experiences"), the second and more profound to free the spirit from depending on any thing but God possessed by faith, hope, and love. St. Catherine in her second rule speaks of these same periods of spiritual "dryness." It is at these times of darkness that the support of the spiritual counselor is necessary, just as is that of a psychological counselor in emotional crises. On the other hand, the director must not be afraid to confront clients with the hard facts of their defects to which they may be blind or expose their illusions that arise from dubious experiences that can even have a demonic origin.

One of the very important contributions of St. Ignatius Loyola and the Jesuit tradition of spiritual direction is a special emphasis on the ancient concept of "the discernment of spirits."[23] This means enabling the client to become more and more sensitive to the experiential difference between genuine spiritual insights given by the Holy Spirit and bogus insights arising from tainted sources interior or exterior to the person. The classic sign of the authentic guidance of the Holy Spirit explained by St. Catherine and elaborated by St. Ignatius is whether such experiences lead to an increase of effective love of God and neighbor. To this sign St. Ignatius added from his own experience that the genuine guidance of the Holy Spirit is known by the deep interior peace it brings, while illusory "insights" produce spiritual unrest and confusion. He also emphasized the importance of "thinking with the church," of considering whether one's insights are really in conformity with orthodox faith. Yet beginners cannot consistently make this distinction by themselves; they require a director's guidance to become sensitive to it.

The spiritual counselor must never forget that though the essence of spiritual growth is in the deepening of the theological virtues facilitated by the increasing operation of the gifts of the Holy Spirit,[24] these cannot be authentically exercised unless supported by a corresponding growth of the cardinal moral virtues. Various types of currently popular spirituality, often labeled "New Age," that claim to open the way to transcendence without strict moral discipline are false and dangerous. In the Sermon on the Mount, Jesus prefaced his call to his disciples to "be perfect as your heavenly Father is perfect" (Mt 5:48) with the emphatic statement, "Do not think that I have come to abolish the law or the prophets. I have come not to abolish, but to fulfill.... Whoever breaks one of the least of these commandments and teaches others to do so will be called least in the kingdom of heaven" (Mt 5:17, 19a). This warning follows from the supreme commandment of love of God and neighbor, since the theological virtue of love of neighbor requires that we respect the neighbor's rights that the moral law protects.

Thus, as Catherine says, the work of the spiritual director is not to impose his or her own spirituality on their clients. Instead it is to strive to discern in their lives the guidance of the Holy Spirit that is leading them to an ever deeper commitment to love God through loving their neighbor with a love that is rooted in faith and supported by hope. This journey cannot but be a way of the cross, because Jesus said, "Take up your cross and follow me."

Notes

1. For fuller discussion of the types and ethics of counseling, see B. M. Ashley and Kevin D. O'Rourke, *Health Care Ethics: A Theological Analysis,* 4th ed. (Washington, D.C.: Georgetown University Press, 1997), 89–106.

2. For an introduction to the field, see Richard Woods, O.P., *Christian Spirituality: God's Presence Through the Ages* (Allen, Tex.: Christian Classics, 1989); Cheslyn Jones, G. Wainwright, and E. Yarnold, S.J., eds., *The Study of Spirituality* (New York: Oxford University Press, 1986); John Garvey, ed., *Modern Spirituality: An Anthology* (Springfield, Ill.: Templegate Publishers, 1985); Benedict Ashley, *Spiritual Direction in the Dominican Tradition* (New York: Paulist Press, 1995).

3. See Brian P. Hall with consultant editors Maury Smith, Gerald Conway, Michael J. Kenney, and Joseph Owens, *Value Clarification as Learning Process: A Handbook for Religious Educators* (New York: Paulist, 1973) and Brian P. Hall, *The Personal Discernment Inventory: An Instrument for Spiritual Guides* (New York: Paulist Press, 1980).

4. See Josef Pieper, *The Four Cardinal Virtues* (Notre Dame, Ind.: University of Notre Dame Press, 1966) and Benedict Ashley, *Living the Truth in Love: A Biblical Introduction to Moral Theology* (Staten Island, N.J.: Alba House, 1998), 34–40.

5. The Two Drive psychology of Freud was anticipated in the psychology of Aristotle and St. Thomas Aquinas as the *appetitus concupiscibiles et irascibiles* if one understands Freud's death wish as the aggressive drive, as did Karl Menninger, *Man Against Himself* (New York: Harcourt Brace, 1938) and Erich Fromm, *The Anatomy of Human Destructiveness* (Greenwich, Conn.: Fawcett Publications, 1973).

6. As psychoanalysts themselves need analysts, so clergy who give spiritual counseling themselves need spiritual direction. See Louis Camelli, "Spiritual Direction for Priests in the USA: The Rediscovery of a Resource," in Kevin G. Culligan, O.C.D., ed., *Spiritual Direction: Contemporary Readings* (Locust Valley, N.Y.: Living Flame Press, 1983), 188–95. This also applies to nonordained spiritual counselors.

7. In *Listening*, 33, 3 (Fall 1998): 194. Denny teaches Islamic Studies at the University of Colorado, Boulder.

8. Second edition with new introduction (Braintree, Mass.: Pope John Center, 1997, now Boston: National Catholic Center for Bioethics), ch. 3, 51–100.

9. On the functional definition of "religion," see Keith A. Roberts, *Religion in Sociological Perspective* (Belmont, Calif.: Wadsworth, 3rd ed., 1994), 3–26.

10. See William Herbrechtsmeier, "Buddhism and the Definition of Religion: One More Time," *Journal for the Scientific Study of Religion 8* 32, 1 (1982): 1–18, who argues that "the belief and reverence for superhuman beings cannot be understood as the chief distinguishing characteristic of religious phenomena."

11. See Felix M. Poddimattam, O.F.M Cap, *Fundamental Option and Mortal Sin* (Bangalore: Asian Trading Corp., 1986).

12. Of course many suppose this distinction has proved mind-brain identity, but see the questions raised by such prominent scientists as Sir John Eccles, *The Human Mystery,* The Gifford Lectures, University of Edinburgh, 1977–1978 (New York: Springer International, 1979) and Roger Penrose, *The Emperor's New Mind: Concerning Computers, Minds, and the Laws of Physics* (New York: Oxford University Press, 1989).

13. See Tomas Spidlik, *The Spirituality of the Christian East* (Kalamazoo, Mich.: Cistercian Publications, 1986), 332–34 and references in Topical Index, p. 446.

14. "A Psychological Model with a Spiritual Dimension," *Pastoral Psychology* (May, 1972): 31–40

15. Jacques Maritain, *Creative Intuition in Art and Poetry* (New York: Harper, 1954). For fuller discussion, see Benedict Ashley, *Theologies of the Body*, 312–19.

16. On this, see Silvano Arieti, *Creativity: The Magic Synthesis* (New York: Basic Books, 1976).

17. *Catherine of Siena: The Dialogue*, The Classics of Western Spirituality, trans. Suzanne Noffke, O.P. (New York: Paulist, 1980) with commentary by Suzanne Noffke, O.P., *Catherine of Siena: Vision Through a Distant Eye* (Collegeville, Mich., Michael Glazier/Liturgical Press, 1996). For a modern manual that is up to date in its psychology, see Carolyn Gratton, *Guidelines for Spiritual Direction,* (Danville, N.J., Dimension Books, 1980), Vol 3 of *Studies in Formative Spirituality*, ed. Adrian van Kamm CSSp and Susan A. Muto.

18. See Benedict Ashley, "Catherine of Siena's Principles of Spiritual Direction," *Spirituality Today* 33 (March 1981): 43–52. Reprinted in Culligan, *Spiritual Direction,* 188–95.

19. On the Eastern tradition stemming from the desert fathers, see Kallistos Ware, "The Spiritual Father in Orthodox Christianity," in Culligan, *Spiritual Direction,* 20–40.

20. *The Ascent of Mount Carmel,* bk II, ch. 11. For a discussion of such extraordinary phenomena, see Jordan Aumann, O.P., *The Theology of Christian Perfection* (Dubuque: Priory Press, 1962), 654–75.

21. *Summa Theologiae,* I , q. 47, a.-2. False modern notions of "democracy" and "equality" because they fail to see that distinction and uniqueness, though they involve "hierarchy," this hierarchy, according to Aquinas, is *generic.* Though each member of the cosmic hierarchy is generically inferior to beings higher than itself, in some unique specific perfection it is superior to every other creature in the universe. Only God contains all perfections. Thus while brute animals are all inferior to man who is the supreme member of the genus animal, a bird can fly, a fish swim, in ways man cannot. Furthermore every species of bird has substantially unique properties and each individual in a species unique individual characteristics. God is no Xerox machine.

22. *Dark Night of the Soul,* trans. E. Allison Peers, 3rd rev. ed. (Garden City, N.Y.: Doubleday/Image Book, 1959), cf. II, c.1, p.91 for the distinction between the two spiritual nights.

23. See Piet Penning de Vries, S.J., *Discernment of Spirits According to the Life and Teachings of St. Ignatius Loyola* (New York: Exposition Press, 1973).

24. On these gifts, see Ashley, *Spiritual Direction,* ch. 7, pp. 133 ff. and *Thomas Aquinas: Selected Spiritual Writings: The Gifts of the Holy Spirit,* co-authored with Matthew Rzeczowski, O.P. (Hyde Park, N.Y.: New City Press, 1994), and Ashley, *Living the Truth in Love,* 75–78, and Subject Index p. 552.

Robert Wieber

42. Spiritual Ministry with Men in Prison

Every man is brought into prison in shackles. Chains and padlocks are common symbols for men who are kept under lock and key. The goal of this essay is to assist ministers help men who are in prison to find the keys that will unlock their physical (external) and psychological (internal) chains. To connect these two worlds, internal and external, is the goal of spiritual ministry. This means being open to the journey of God's healing and reconciliation.

I have found some guiding principles to be helpful in ministering to men in prison:

- Have respect for men in prison as people;
- Realize the present moment is the most valuable moment;
- Accept where the inmate is presently spiritually and mentally;
- Have self-respect;
- Have faith that all people are able to grow and change;
- Recognize the need for safety, privacy, security, belonging, and trust;
- Establish healthy boundaries;
- Be fair, firm, and consistent;
- Use clear and honest communications;
- Be a good listener.

The first key in my ministry with men in prison is summarized in the following quote: "Listen, my son, to your master's percepts, and incline the ear of your heart."[1] Some components to listening are providing an inviting atmosphere, positive silence, privacy, and "unconditional positive regard."[2] Before I can listen to the men, I need to provide the same components of listening to myself as a minister. I need to listen to God in my life and put my faith in the guidance I receive. Then my listening, whether the person is sitting in my office or I'm meeting him on campus, can be more authentic.

When listening to myself I need to become aware of the preconceived notions that I bring to this prison setting. These notions can sometimes be padlocks that impede the healing ministry. However, if I listen, I am able to discern which links are healing and which are blocking my ministry with these men. In listening I need to find keys that open the gate to growth. In my experience I have found the most basic keys in ministry are *trusting* and *giving trust.*

Some Preconceived Blocking Notions

When trust is given to the men, they receive the first key to a spirituality that is foreign to many of them. There are any number of reasons that they will resist taking this key of trust. "Why should I trust this person?" is a common question. But the real key is hard to recognize, and that is their own lack of self-trust. When we do not trust ourselves, our defense is to blame someone else or something outside ourselves. The misconception of *controlling others* rather than controlling ourselves feeds "all or nothing," "black or white," "either/or" thinking. These distortions are padlocks in the spiritual journey. The question of who to trust becomes a key as one listens without receiving judgment to the person who is raising questions. The first steps of a child require trust in the adults in their presence. Now, a similar trust must be employed, because of the inmate's past negative experiences. These negative experiences are padlocks that can be unlocked with the proper keys.

The proper key is making the appropriate choices to unlock the bondage. A place to share one's bondages is essential to the healing ministry of the men in prison. The inmate's perception about incarceration may be "forced incarceration, or a forced amount of time for something I did not do." He does not view the sentence as a consequence for the wrong he has done. As a result, he is set up for difficulty in making choices for himself in the present moment. Some prisoners view this time as simply doing time, with little thought about changes in themselves; they continue to blame others. Other inmates come to view this time as a chance to learn from their mistakes. This latter view is fertile ground for growth in trusting themselves and allowing someone else to walk with them.

How does one create an atmosphere in which the men can allow someone to walk with them? From the first days of my ministry with men in prison, I tried to exhibit the underlying spiritual principle of self-value by valuing *them.* Being present to them, whether in greeting them while walking through the campus or recognizing them at their programming site, carried a positive message. Whether you like it or not, inmates size you up in the first few days that you are among them. They make judgments on whether you are someone they want to trust. The individual inmate's belief system is tested from the first day you meet. Some have had positive experiences in the past, but most have had negative experiences. However my faith is that the "key" to life and success lies within the individual person, whether inside or outside the prison walls.

How This Belief System Works

Weekly, the new men coming into our prison receive an orientation about how we view them during the time they spend within our institution. This orientation sets the tone, demonstrates the values we live, and shows them how we view them as human beings. This starts by clearly communicating boundaries and emphasizing their freedom to practice or not to practice their spirituality. This openness allows them the opportunity to raise questions—the beginning of trust.

How This Becomes Exemplified

When greeting them with dignity, I experience that dignity is returned. Respecting their questions often results in them sending a "kite" (a letter from an inmate to a staff person) asking for an appointment. In responding to the kite, we sent out a message about who we are. This communication is one of the first steps in creating trust.

In responding to the inmate's kite, one sends a message of respect. When I call the inmate for an appointment, my prayer is that I be a good listener, and that I not need to have all the answers. Trust in the inmate's journey is validated by "unconditional positive regard." Many inmates' experiences have been conditional. True, the physiological needs of food, shelter, and clothing from Maslow's hierarchy of needs are provided by the system. However, for incarcerated men the next levels of safety, love and belongingness, self-esteem, and self-actualization[3] seem to be hidden, even lost. How does an incarcerated man go about reaching these higher levels? According to Maslow, "Self-actualization is possible only after the other needs in the hierarchy are met."[4] Ministry brings a human face with feelings and care to the system.

The first time the inmates arrive in the office, they quickly scan their surroundings. They are moving up to the next level of their hierarchy of needs: safety. Both their verbal and nonverbal communication indicate how safe they feel. In ministering to inmates, listening to them, and allowing silent time for them to reflect is a gift not readily available elsewhere in prison. They verbally acknowledge this frequently. After experiencing safety, when they are accepted as they are, some begin to allow themselves to experience God's love and belongingness. This acceptance becomes catalytic. Being accepted by someone encourages them to address their own self-acceptance.

How This Takes Place

They are experiencing something new: someone is listening without a hidden agenda. Outside, when someone listened to them, it cost them money.

In the prison listening is free. So how does one make it cost something for the inmate, so that he will put forth effort and energy? How can one get them to make a commitment to themselves? From my experience, the inmate who wishes to work on his journey needs not just to verbally say so and then place the burden on me to remember to call him. He needs to write a kite requesting an appointment each time—a different form of writing a check in payment. This exerted energy is indicative of his willingness to begin valuing himself.

The energy of listening requires the cooperation of both the inmate and the minister so that the voice of God can provide direction to his life. Many inmates come into prison with anger and disillusionment about the religious training they received in early childhood. In the 1960s it was called a "crisis of faith" when a person began to understand and claim his own personal faith journey. In "all or nothing" thinking, there is a tendency to dump everything from one's past, rather than taking what is valuable from the early years and assimilating the new information and experiences. However, this demands that one begins to stand on one's own two feet. It can be a lonely place for the individual. This healthy process takes trust in God and in self, and the level of trust of those in religious authority is shaky for a good number of the men. At the same time, finding out about their individual spirituality is a powerful opportunity. This search takes different paths for different men. Our challenge now is to allow the men to follow their own paths, rather than to conform only to our comfort level. This latter position returns us to controlling another person rather than controlling ourselves.

Some respond by reading the Bible from cover to cover and are turned on with fire. Fr. Godfrey Diekmann, O.S.B.,[5] once said that people who have had a tremendous spiritual awakening initially do more damage with their enthusiasm than good. This can be the experience of inmates who are told by such neophytes how to live the Christian life. Inmates receiving these dogmatic proclamations need to be allowed to journey in their own time and way.

Other men reaffirm their spiritual roots by reading, prayer, discussion, and listening to people they believe have credibility. Still others find new meaning in new faith expressions. Many men do well searching in their hearts and are hungry to find out what God wants from them. Inmates request spiritual direction: help finding out what God is directing one to do in one's life. "I am not seeking my own will but the will of him who sent me."[6] It is not attempting to have God direct what I want in my life. So what else is new! Inmates are no different than the rest of us. For the inmate to follow God's way seems difficult, especially when they want control. On the wall behind the desk in my office hangs a wooden carving done by an inmate. It depicts a sailboat moving over rough ocean waters; underneath the image is the saying, "I cannot control the winds, but I can adjust the sails." This has helped men come to an understanding of God working in their lives and how they can adjust without being swallowed by the rough waters.

Assisting Them in This Struggle

As I listen to their stories, this struggle comes up in various ways during their time in prison, living with other men and with themselves. They are beginning to experience feelings that are uncomfortable. However, allowing themselves to experience the uncomfortable feelings gives them the opportunity to build trust in themselves. This is another of the keys to unlocking the padlocks to spiritual growth. In prison culture, life wears the mask of a man needing to be tough; showing feelings is a sign of weakness. However, once an inmate experiences with a trusted person that paradox that experiencing one's feelings brings strength, the links of the chain have a positive connotation for the inmate.

Spiritual ministry creates numerous paradoxes in our lives. The things we fear will help us if we allow ourselves to find the core truth in our thought or situation. How many people would prefer to have you see only their good side, believing you would not accept them if you knew their dark side or negative side or truthful side? Both sides make up our personalities. God does not have difficulty with us. However, we with our misconceptions have this struggle, and at times it leads to denial. If denial becomes our way of life, we will experience tremendous pain. Once we recognize or name the pain, we can get assistance. Physical pain is less difficult for us to identify; it does not carry a stigma. However, because it carries some societal or cultural stigma, emotional or spiritual pain seems more difficult to acknowledge. This is another of the padlocks to growth. Such pains are stepping stones to healing or keys to unlocking the binding chains around us.

We all experience the pain of loss. Men in prison experience loss in a number of ways. For some, it is the time spent in prison. For others, it is the loss of a spouse through separation or divorce; for others it is the loss of children; and for others it is the loss of a family member in death. In ministering to men in prison, it is very important to provide space and privacy so that the person can express his loss. Providing the opportunity for the inmate to express loss is essential to his mental and spiritual health. To be with them in their feelings of anger at themselves for not supporting their families on the outside, or their anger with God, is part of the process that is healthy. Feelings of denial, bargaining, blaming, and acceptance are part of the human condition. This time can also be a catalyst for dealing with relations with self.

Many of these men are experiencing this pain without the physical and emotional support of family presence. Often the men are realizing how close or distant they are with their families. For many inmates, this is the first time they have addressed unresolved issues with family members. To listen to their pain is part of the healing process provided by spiritual ministry. We can become that family that is not available.

A further loss is the loneliness one faces, alone in the midst of other men, with little privacy. We on the outside take for granted such privileges.

A psychological element that can drastically influence this loss process is whether the men are accustomed to receiving support for feeling good about themselves from outside of themselves. This is called "external locus of control." To believe one's value and goodness internally is called "internal locus of control." The intertwining of the psychological and spiritual understanding is another key in ministering to these men. The result of the intertwining, the progression to higher levels of the hierarchy of needs and the embracing of the dark side in us, is shown in compassionate spirituality.

Loving and accepting who we are is compassionate spirituality. This spirituality challenges our negative thinking patterns and assists in changing chosen behavior. To change these choices involves a commitment to one's self-esteem, building positive patterns. Because it is a positive change one is more willing to acknowledge the pain and find methods of walking through it. This positive motivation begins to replace the previous negative attitude. An excellent motivational speaker, Jan Turner,[7] listed three results of a spiritual journey: character, courage, and the ability to be more compassionate. In my ministry with the men, believing in their potential and giving them tools to assist with goal-setting now, at this present time, and not waiting until they get out, starts building these results.

Getting This Accomplished

When we achieve small goals, our attitude beings to be more positive. These small accomplished goals become our chain links to freedom. As Jan Turner stated,

> Our attitude determines performance and attitude to life.
> Our attitude determines our quality of our relationships, our communications and how we get along with others.
> Our attitude, more than any other, determines the outcome of any task.[8]

She gave a great challenge to those of us in spiritual ministry. She pleaded with us to display an "*I care* about you" attitude.

The care attitude is prevalent when listening to inmates completing their Alcohol and Other Drugs Treatment programs. This area requires much attention and ministry. Seeing how connected chemical and other forms of addiction are to crimes with which men in prison are charged, is it any wonder that spirituality initially is not viewed as significant? However, the Alcoholics Anonymous (AA) philosophy states that, on the journey to recovery, the first to go is spirituality and the last to return is spirituality. Realizing that, our work becomes a great challenge rather than a problem.

My goal in ministering spiritually to men in prison is to use the various available keys, while the men are still in prison, to break the shackles of psychological and emotional self-imprisonment. By using these keys now, a new lifestyle pattern is formed; it allows the men

- To start walking with self-confidence;
- To feel good about who they are;
- To know that they need not walk alone, but can ask for assistance during the lonely times;
- To have faith in themselves and in their God;
- To never stop learning.

With such growth, these men will help break their communities' shackles of negative perceptions about ex-convicts.

Notes

1. Prologue to the Rule of St. Benedict.
2. Carl Rogers' theoretical principle.
3. Abraham Maslow's theory.
4. Santrok, John W. (1983) *Life Span Development*. Dubuque, Iowa: Wm. C. Brown.
5. A monk and author of St. John's Abbey, Collegeville, Minnesota.
6. John 5:30, *The New American Bible*. (1970). New York: P. J. Kennedy and Sons.
7. "Attitude: Key to Success." Address given on October 13, 1998, to Faribault Correctional Staff Retreat.
8. Ibid.

Contributors

About the Editor

Robert J. Wicks is chairperson of the Graduate Programs in Pastoral Counseling at Loyola College in Maryland. In addition to being editor of the first volume of the *Handbook of Spirituality for Ministers* and senior coeditor of the two volume *Clinical Handbook of Pastoral Counseling,* his latest authored work is *Living a Gentle, Passionate Life.* His areas of expertise are integrating psychology and spirituality, prevention of secondary stress, and the appreciating process of mentoring.

About the Contributors

Gerald A. Arbuckle, S.M., relates the insights of cultural anthropology to the church, religious life, and evangelization. His most recent books are *Reforming the Church* and *From Chaos to Mission.*

George Aschenbrenner, S.J., is currently director of the Jesuit Center for Spiritual Growth in Wernersville, Pennsylvania, and cofounder of the Institute for Priestly Formation based at Creighton University in Omaha, Nebraska.

Benedict M. Ashley, O.P., is professor of theology emeritus, Aquinas Institute of Theology in St. Louis and adjunct professor at the Center for Health Care Ethics, St. Louis University. He is the author of *Living the Truth in Love* (1997).

Wilkie Au is director of Spiritual Development Services in Los Angeles and adjunct professor of theological studies at Loyola Marymount University. He is a former associate editor of *Human Development,* author of *By Way of the Heart* and coauthor of *Urgings of the Heart.*

William A. Barry, S.J., who is the author of a number of books in spirituality, was formerly associate professor of pastoral theology, Weston Jesuit School of Theology, Cambridge, Massachusetts. Presently, he is codirector of tertianship and a staff member at Campion Renewal Center.

678

Michael W. Blastic, O.F.M. Conv., is a native of Chicago. He has been involved in formation and education for more than twenty-five years. Presently, he serves as dean, School of Franciscan Studies, St. Bonaventure University in New York.

Walter J. Burghardt, S.J., is senior fellow, Woodstock Theological Center; founder and codirector, Preaching the Just Word; coeditor of *Ancient Christian Writers;* coeditor, *The Living Pulpit;* and author of eighteen books and 280 articles.

Annice Callahan, R.S.C.J., who teaches in the Institute for Christian Ministries and the Theology Department of the University of San Diego, has lectured in Australia, Canada, England, New Zealand, and in the United States. She is the author of *Spiritual Guides for Today* and *Evelyn Underhill: Spirituality for Daily Living.*

Lawrence S. Cunningham is professor of theology at the University of Notre Dame and editor of *Thomas Merton: Spiritual Master* as well as author of a number of popular spirituality and theology books.

Elizabeth A. Dreyer is a well-known author and lecturer. She has taught at both The Catholic University of America and Washington Theological Union. Her books include *Passionate Women, Manifestation of Grace, Earth Crammed with Heaven,* and *A Retreat with Catherine of Siena.*

Keith J. Egan holds the Joyce McMahon Hank Aquinas chair in Catholic theology at Saint Mary's College (Indiana) and is adjunct professor of theology at the University of Notre Dame.

Kathleen Fischer and **Thomas Hart,** a married couple, are theologians and therapists in Seattle, Washington. Individually and together they have written numerous books, including *The First Two Years of Marriage* and *Promises to Keep: Developing the Skills of Marriage.*

C. Kevin Gillespie, S.J., is assistant professor in the Department of Pastoral Counseling at Loyola College and the director of the Department's M.A. Program in Spiritual and Pastoral Care. Fr. Gillespie is a fellow in the American Association of Pastoral Counseling and a member of Spiritual Directors International. His area of research and writing has been the relationship between psychology and spirituality.

Marie D. Gipprich, I.H.M., after teaching for many years at the secondary school level, is now a pastoral associate at St. Joan of Arc Parish in Philadelphia where she coordinates liturgical ministries, facilitates adult catechesis, and is involved in a broad range of spiritual formation work.

Margaret B. Guenther is professor emerita, the General Theological Seminary; former director, the Center for Christian Spirituality, and the author of *Holy Listening, Toward Holy Ground,* and *The Practice of Prayer.*

Wilfrid J. Harrington, O.P., is an Irish Dominican and author of more than forty books, including *The Path of Biblical Theology, Mark, Jesus, and*

Paul, The Jesus Story, and *Revelation.* He teaches scripture at the Dominican House of Studies in Dublin and at the Milltown Institute of Theology and Philosophy (Dublin).

Richard J. Hauser, S.J., is professor of theology and director of the graduate programs in theology, ministry, and Christian spirituality, Creighton University in Omaha, Nebraska, and author of three books: *In His Spirit, Moving in the Spirit,* and *Finding God in Troubled Times.*

E. Glenn Hinson is professor of spirituality and John Loftis Professor of Church History at Baptist Theological Seminary in Richmond. His most recent book is *Love at the Heart of Things: A Bibliography of Douglas V. Steere.*

Leslie J. Hoppe, O.F.M., is professor of Old Testament studies at Catholic Theological Union in Chicago, past general editor and on the editorial board of *The Bible Today.* He has published six books, including *Joshua Judges, What Are They Saying About Biblical Archeology, Deuteronomy, The Synagogues and Churches of Ancient Palestine,* and *The Lands of the Bibles.*

Maribeth Howell, O.P., received her Ph.D. and S.T.D. from the Catholic University of Leuven, Belgium. She is associate professor of scripture at St. Mary's Seminary in Cleveland, Ohio. In addition to having taught biblical studies at a variety of levels, she has been a guest speaker for various diocesan and religious groups throughout the United States.

Robert A. Jonas is the founder and director of the Empty Bell, a contemplative sanctuary. He is an author, spiritual companion, and retreat leader. His books include *Rebecca: A Father's Journey from Grief to Gratitude* and *Henri Nouwen: Writings Selected with an Introduction by Robert A. Jonas.*

Dermot A. Lane is president of Mater Dei Institute of Education and pastor of Balally Parish in Dublin. His most recent book is *Keeping Hope Alive: Stirrings in Christian Theology.* He teaches frequently in summer session in the United States.

Ernest E. Larkin, O. Carm., has spent practically all his fifty-two years as a Carmelite priest in educational work, first in his own major seminary, then at The Catholic University of America, and finally at the Kino Institute in Phoenix, Arizona.

Bruce H. Lescher is director of the Institute for Spirituality and Worship at the Jesuit School of Theology at Berkeley, California, where he also teaches courses in spirituality.

Patricia Livingston is a counselor, speaker, and author of the book *Lessons of the Heart.* For seven years the associate director of the Center for Continuing Formation in Ministry at the University of Notre Dame, she was given the 1990 U.S. Catholic Award for significantly furthering the cause of women in the church.

David Lonsdale teaches spirituality and spiritual direction at Heythrop College, University of London. He has been engaged regularly in spiritual directors' training programs and workshops. He was coeditor of *The Way* and *The Way Supplement* for more than ten years and is the author of *Eyes to See, Ears to Hear* and *Listening to the Music of the Spirit.*

Suzanne Mayer, I.H.M., currently directs the I.H.M. Spirituality Center, where she also gives retreats and ministers as a pastoral counselor. She teaches as an adjunct professor at Immaculata and Neumann Colleges' graduate programs. Working with religious and laity groups, she also works as a consultant and facilitator.

Robert F. Morneau is auxiliary bishop and vicar general of the Diocese of Green Bay, Wisconsin. He is a popular speaker, retreat master, and author of eleven books, including *Paths to Prayer* and *A Retreat with Jessica Powers.*

John P. Mossi, S.J., is an associate professor in the Religious Studies Department at Gonzaga University. He received his doctorate from The Catholic University of America and presently facilitates courses in pastoral counseling, spiritual direction, and Catholicism.

William Reiser, S.J., teaches theology at Holy Cross College in Worcester, Massachusetts and is an associate staff member at the Center for Religious Development in Cambridge.

Lucien Richard, O.M.I., is fellow of the University Professors and professor of theology at Boston University. He is the author of several books. His most recent work is *Christ: The Self-Emptying God.*

Susan K. Roll is assistant professor of liturgy and systematic theology at Christ the King Seminary in Buffalo, New York. She received a Ph.D. from the Faculty of Theology, Catholic University of Louvain (Leuven, Belgium) in 1993.

Janet Ruffing, R.S.M., chairs the concentration in spirituality and spiritual direction at Fordham University. She is the author of numerous articles on spirituality, spiritual direction, religious life, and mysticism, as well as the book, *Uncovering Stories of Faith.*

Edward C. Sellner is a professor of pastoral theology and spirituality at the College of St. Catherine and director of *Immram:* Resources for Celtic Spirituality. He is the author of numerous articles and books, including *Mentoring, Soul Making,* and *Father and Son.* He has also given workshops, retreats, and lectures at local, national, and international conferences and settings.

William J. Sneck, S.J., is a Jesuit priest and a licensed psychologist. Having earned his doctorate in clinical psychology at the University of Michigan, he taught at Georgetown University and then served as associate director of novices and assistant director of the Jesuit Center for Spiritual Growth, Wernersville, Pennsylvania. Since 1985 he has taught at Loyola College in

Maryland, where he is now associate professor of pastoral counseling. Professional interests focus on the work of Carl Jung and emotional healing.

Raymond Studzinski, O.S.B., a monk of St. Meinrad Archabbey in Indiana, is an associate professor in the Department of Religion and Religious Education at The Catholic Univeristy of America, Washington, D.C., where he teaches courses in the areas of religious development and spirituality.

Joseph A. Tetlow, S.J., is secretary for Ignatian spirituality in the Jesuit General Curia in Rome and editor of *Review of Ignatian Spirituality.* He has been president of the Jesuit School of Theology at Berkeley and associate editor of *America.* His most recent books are *Choosing Christ in the World* and *Ignatius Loyola: Spiritual Exercises.*

Lyle K. Weiss is a pastoral associate at Sacred Heart Church in Glyndon, Maryland, directing its Lay Institute for Theological Study. He is currently pursuing a doctorate in systematic theology at St. Mary's Seminary in Baltimore. He is author of *God Lives Next Door* and is a recipient of the American Bible Society's Scripture Student of the Year Award. He and his wife, Terry, live in Ellicott City, Maryland.

John Welch, O. Carm., is professor at Washington Theological Union, specializing in Carmelite spirituality and human development. He is the author of *The Carmelite Way* and other studies.

Michaele Barry Wicks received a Master of Theological Studies degree from the Washington Theological Union. She has taught as adjunct faculty in the Theology Department of Loyola College and in the Continuing Education Department of the Washington Theological Union. Currently she offers retreats and workshops on biblical spirituality, scripture, Teresa of Avila, and spiritual formation.

Robert Wieber, O.S.B., Ph.D., is a Benedictine Monk of St. John's Abbey, Collegeville, Minnesota. Currently, he is chaplain at Minnesota Correctional Facility, Faribault, Minnesota.

Jude Winkler, O.F.M. Conv., is a Conventional Franciscan friar-priest of St. Anthony Province. He received his S.S.L. degree from the Pontifical Biblical Institute. He is currently a member of the Companions of St. Anthony, an evangelization apostolate. He also teaches at the Ecumenical Institute of Baltimore, Education for Parish Service in Washington, and other schools.

Phyllis Zagano is cochair of the Roman Catholic Studies Group of the American Academy of Religion. Her recent books include *On Prayer, Ita Ford: Missionary Martyr,* and *Twentieth Century Apostles: Contemporary Christianity in Action.*

Subject Index

Abba, 399–402
Aelred of Rievaulx, 300, 305, 312, 313
Affliction, 73; *see also* Suffering
Age of the Saints in the Early Celtic Church, The (Chadwick), 370
Altruism, 478–79
Ambrose, St., 616, 646, 647–48
Amos, 26–27
Anamchara, 362, 369–70
Anselm, St., 258
Aquinas, Thomas. *See* Thomas Aquinas
Arche, 504
Arrupe, Pedro, 528
Art of Loving, The (Fromm), 163–64
Asceticism, 74
Augustine of Hippo: A Biography (Brown), 165–66
Augustine, St., 163, 196, 262, 283, 286, 385, 643–44, 645–46, 647–48, 650–51, 652–53, 654; contemplation, 443, 460; intelligent faith, 288–89; memory, 96–97, 361; reading, 616, 620; scriptures, 161
Autonomy, 227–34

Baptism, 577
Barnes, Gerald Robert, Bishop, 637–38
Benedict, St., 621
Benedict's Rule, 448, 623–24
Bereavement, 310; *see also* Grief
Bernard of Clairvaux, St., 442, 446
Bernardin, Joseph, Cardinal, 451–52
Bible, 5–6, 408, 645–46; meditation

on, 448; *see also* New Testament, and specific books, e.g.: Genesis
Blind man (Gospel of John), 57–58, 126
Bonaventure, St., 280–81, 436, 449
Boney, Everett, 270–71
Book of Her Life, The (Teresa of Avila), 281–82
Book of Revelation, 6
Books. *See* Reading
Bread and Water: A Spiritual Journal (Haines), 432–33
Brendan, St., 363
Brief on the Liturgical Psalter, 39
Brigit of Kildare, St., 362
Bunyan, John, 644–45, 646, 648, 651, 653

Calvary. *See* Passion
Camara, Halder, 16
Canticle of Brother Son (Francis of Assisi), 257–58
Carey, Matthew, 550
Carmelite Rule, 446
Carmelites, 446, 458
Carroll, John, 549–52
Cassian, John, 344–45, 459, 460, 462; humility, 347–48; mantra prayer, 389, 462; meditation, 446, 448, 459, 460; spiritual direction conversation, 351, 352
Catherine of Siena, St., 291–92, 665, 666–67
Catholic Worker Movement, 555–57
Catholicism, 548–62; Catholic left,

Author Index